CONTENTS AT A GLANCE

SPECIAL EDITION

USING
Microsoft®
Office
Home and Student 2007

Ed Bott

Woody Leonhard

800 East 96th Street
Indianapolis, Indiana 46240

SPECIAL EDITION USING MICROSOFT® OFFICE HOME AND STUDENT 2007

ISBN-13: 978-0-7897-3518-8

ISBN-10: 0-7897-3518-0

Library of Congress Cataloging-in-Publication data is on file.

Printed in the United States of America

First Printing: September 2007

Trademarks

All terms mentioned in this book that are known to be trademarks or service marks have been appropriately capitalized. Que Publishing cannot attest to the accuracy of this information. Use of a term in this book should not be regarded as affecting the validity of any trademark or service mark.

Warning and Disclaimer

Every effort has been made to make this book as complete and as accurate as possible, but no warranty or fitness is implied. The information provided is on an "as is" basis.

Bulk Sales

Que Publishing offers excellent discounts on this book when ordered in quantity for bulk purchases or special sales. For more information, please contact

U.S. Corporate and Government Sales
1-800-382-3419
corpsales@pearsontechgroup.com

For sales outside of the U.S., please contact

International Sales
international@pearsoned.com

This Book Is Safari Enabled

 The Safari® Enabled icon on the cover of your favorite technology book means the book is available through Safari Bookshelf. When you buy this book, you get free access to the online edition for 45 days.

Safari Bookshelf is an electronic reference library that lets you easily search thousands of technical books, find code samples, download chapters, and access technical information whenever and wherever you need it.

To gain 45-day Safari Enabled access to this book:

- Go to http://www.quepublishing.com/safarienabled.
- Complete the brief registration form.
- Enter the coupon code H1CK-L3QE-PEU6-K4E5-NUH5.

If you have difficulty registering on Safari Bookshelf or accessing the online edition, please email customer-service@safaribooksonline.com.

Associate Publisher
Greg Wiegand

Acquisitions Editors
Loretta Yates
Rick Kughen

Development Editor
Rick Kughen

Technical Editor
Todd Meister

Managing Editor
Gina Kanouse

Project Editor
George E. Nedeff

Copy Editors
Heather Wilkins
Mike Henry

Indexer
Lisa Stumpf

Proofreader
Suzanne Thomas

Publishing Coordinator
Cindy Teeters

Book Designer
Anne Jones

Compositor
Bronkella Publishing

CONTENTS

III Using Excel

V   Using OneNote

About the Authors

Ed Bott is a best-selling author and award-winning technology journalist who has been covering the personal computer industry since the days when an 8MHz 80286 was a smokin' machine. Ed's feature stories and columns about Microsoft and its products have appeared regularly in print and on the web for more than 15 years, and he has written books on nearly every version of Microsoft Windows and Microsoft Office—so many, in fact, that he's lost count of the exact number. He is a three-time winner of the Computer Press Award and earned the Award of Merit from the Society for Technical Communication in 2003. Ed and Woody Leonhard won the prestigious Jesse H. Neal Award, sometimes referred to as "the Pulitzer Prize of the business press," in back-to-back years for their work on *PC Computing*'s "Windows SuperGuide." He lives in an extremely civilized corner of the American Southwest with his wife, Judy, and a growing menagerie of affectionate pets who are sometimes smarter than he is. You can read Ed's latest writings at Ed Bott's Windows Expertise (http://www.edbott.com/weblog) and Ed Bott's Microsoft Report (http://blogs.zdnet.com/bott).

Woody Leonhard describes himself as a "Certified Office Victim." With more than 40 computer books under his belt, he's seen parts of Office that would curl your hair. Woody's best known for his fiercely independent website, AskWoody.com, which mercilessly holds Microsoft's feet to the fire, and specializes in keeping consumers informed about problems with Microsoft patches. He's also a Contributing Editor with *Windows Secrets Newsletter*, windowssecrets.com. Woody has won eight Computer Press Awards and, with Ed, two American Business Press Association awards. He moved to Phuket, Thailand, seven years ago, where he now basks in the sun with his wife, Duangkhae, 82-year-old father, George, and all-American beagle, Chronos.

Dedication

To my brother Don, an award-winning teacher who has inspired countless kids to become great journalists.—Ed

To Add, for filling my life with happiness. And to Justin, for keeping me on my toes.—Woody

ACKNOWLEDGMENTS

Thanks to all the folks at Que, who made sure that all the pieces of this book came together on time and in the right order. And we owe a big, big shout-out to the corps of fellow beta testers and Microsoft techies who helped us decode, decipher, unravel, and ultimately explain the mysteries of Office 2007.

WE WANT TO HEAR FROM YOU!

As the reader of this book, *you* are our most important critic and commentator. We value your opinion and want to know what we're doing right, what we could do better, what areas you'd like to see us publish in, and any other words of wisdom you're willing to pass our way.

As an associate publisher for Que Publishing, I welcome your comments. You can email or write me directly to let me know what you did or didn't like about this book—as well as what we can do to make our books better.

Please note that I cannot help you with technical problems related to the topic of this book. We do have a User Services group, however, where I will forward specific technical questions related to the book.

When you write, please be sure to include this book's title and author as well as your name, email address, and phone number. I will carefully review your comments and share them with the author and editors who worked on the book.

Email: feedback@quepublishing.com

Mail: Greg Wiegand
        Associate Publisher
        Que Publishing
        800 East 96th Street
        Indianapolis, IN 46240 USA

READER SERVICES

Visit our website and register this book at www.informit.com/title/9780789735188 for convenient access to any updates, downloads, or errata that might be available for this book.

INTRODUCTION

In this introduction

Once upon a time, Microsoft Office was strictly for the office. Today, its general-purpose tools have been softened and refined, and the capabilities of the programs in the Office family have expanded. Despite the name, Office isn't just for the office anymore.

Microsoft Office Home and Student 2007 is packaged and sold for people who plan to use it at home. Although its individual parts are identical to those found in the Office version used in corporate settings, the day-to-day tasks you're likely to tackle are a little different. That's why, in this book, we've shifted the focus to explain how you can use Word, Excel, PowerPoint, and OneNote to produce school reports, family newsletters, and projects for civic and social organizations. Of course, if you want to use the same technique to sneak in a little work on the weekend, we won't tell.

The audience may be different, but the depth of our coverage hasn't changed. We still assume you're smart, curious, and able to figure out the truly basic stuff on your own. We show you how to use and customize the common parts of Office 2007—the Quick Access toolbar, task panes, and other interface elements—and how to get along with the new, potentially confusing Ribbon interface.

Like its predecessors, Office 2007 still has odd inconsistencies, as well as bugs, features that don't work as expected, and basic interface elements guaranteed to drive expert users crazy. But as we worked with this latest member of the Office family we grew to like it, a lot. Office 2007 still isn't perfect—not by a long shot—but it is more usable than any Office version ever.

Some of what you see in *Special Edition Using Microsoft Office Home and Student 2007* will be familiar to you if you've worked with an earlier edition of this book. We've gone through every chapter, sentence by sentence, testing, verifying, updating, revising, and adding a wealth of new information to ensure that this book is accurate and absolutely up to date.

WHO SHOULD BUY THIS BOOK

If you need an Office 2007 reference book you can rely on—one that won't bore you with the obvious, pull punches when Office comes up short, or turn mealy-mouthed when you hit the really hard parts—you have the right book in your hands.

As with other titles in Que's best-selling *Special Edition Using* series, this book focuses on the unique needs of students and families using Office 2007 at home. We assume you're experienced with Windows, the web, and, for the most part, previous versions of Microsoft Office. If you're like most people, you've probably only scratched the surface of the capabilities in Office and you'd like to learn a lot more without taking a graduate course on the software. We're also certain you've experienced your fair share of Office bugs and annoyances first-hand. Because we're confident you've already figured out the basics, we've spent our time figuring out how these programs *really* work. Trust us—Office still has bugs and poorly designed features, and Microsoft doesn't always make it easy to see how you can combine features or customize applications to increase productivity.

We figure you're smart enough to experiment with basic features and to read the online help when you want to know how an Office program is *supposed* to work. That's why you won't find beginner-level instructions in this book. Instead, you'll find what isn't in the official documentation—key details, insight, and real-world advice you can't find anywhere else. And it's all arranged so you can get in, find the answer you need, apply it to your work at hand, and get out. This book may weigh a ton, but if you need the straight scoop on anything related to Office, this is where you should look first.

How This Book Is Organized

Special Edition Using Microsoft Office Home and Student 2007 is organized into six parts. Naturally, each of the major applications in the Office suite gets its own section. Before diving into specific features of Word, Excel, and the rest, however, we recommend you read through the sections that cover the techniques common to all applications.

Part I, "Common Tasks and Features," covers the essentials of Office, including techniques you can use to transform the Office interface into your own personal productivity center. We show you how to use the Search tools built into Windows Vista so you can find your Office files fast. This section also covers the new SmartArt graphics tools, which you can use to create stunning figures and illustrations with almost no effort.

Part II, "Using Word," covers the oldest and most polished productivity application in Office. We walk you through every customization option (including a few you probably never even knew you needed). We also show you how to supercharge your text-editing and formatting skills, how to manage long documents, and how to automate everyday documents so they practically write themselves.

Part III, "Using Excel," shows you tricks you never realized you could perform with this incredibly versatile tool. Check out the examples in our formatting chapters to see how you can turn drab rows and columns into eye-catching charts. We explain how to master any of Excel's 300+ functions, as well as which ones are worth memorizing. We'll show you how to use PivotTables (and their graphic cousins, PivotCharts) to give you a completely different view of data. Do you have a list of names, addresses, or other information? We also show you how to use the new, improved table-editing tools to sort, filter, and organize lists like an expert.

Of all the Office applications, PowerPoint is probably the least appreciated. In Part IV, "Using PowerPoint," we explain how this program really works, and we help you create compelling presentations you can deliver in front of a large audience or a small one—or completely unattended over the web.

Part V, "Using OneNote," covers the newest member of the Office family. This freeform note-taking program is perfect for use in the classroom, but it does much more. We explain how to use it to gather facts and figures from the web, how to share notebooks between multiple computers, and even how to record lectures or meetings in perfect sync with your notes.

In Part VI, "Advanced Tasks and Features," we focus on ways to extend the capabilities of Office. We explain how to automate Office with macros written in Visual Basic for Applications (VBA). We also explain how you can supercharge Office with downloadable templates and add-ins from companies besides Microsoft. And in this final section, we introduce a few features that you'll need to know if you use Office on a Tablet PC.

CONVENTIONS USED IN THIS BOOK

Special conventions are used to help you get the most from this book and from Office 2007.

TEXT CONVENTIONS

Various typefaces in this book identify terms and other special objects. These special typefaces include the following:

Type	Meaning
Italic	New terms or phrases when initially defined.
`Monospace`	Information that you type or onscreen messages.
UPPERCASE	Typically used to indicate Excel objects, such as functions and cell references.
Initial Caps	Menus, dialog box names, dialog box elements, and commands are capitalized.

Key combinations are represented with a plus sign. For example, if the text calls for you to enter Ctrl+S, you would press the Ctrl key and the S key at the same time.

EXTRA CREDIT

While using Office, you'll find many features that work well together or others that simply don't work well at all without some poking and prodding. We've used a chapter-ending element named Extra Credit to point out key areas in which you can combine features or find startlingly productive new uses for everyday features. The Extra Credit sections boost your skills further by showing you new ways to get things done.

SPECIAL ELEMENTS

Throughout this book, you'll find Tips, Notes, Cautions, Sidebars, Cross References, and Troubleshooting Tips. These elements provide a variety of information, ranging from warnings you shouldn't miss to ancillary information that will enrich your Office experience, but isn't required reading.

TIPS

TIP

> Tips are designed to point out features, annoyances, and tricks of the trade that you might otherwise miss. These aren't wimpy, run-of-the-mill tips that you learned the first week you used Office and don't need us to tell you.

NOTES

NOTE

> Notes point out items that you should be aware of, although you can skip these if you're in a hurry. Generally, we've added notes as a way to give you some extra information on a topic without weighing you down.

CAUTIONS

CAUTION

> Pay attention to Cautions! These could save you precious hours in lost work. Don't say we didn't warn you.

TROUBLESHOOTING NOTES

 We designed these elements to call attention to common pitfalls that you're likely to encounter. When you see a Troubleshooting note, you can flip to the "Troubleshooting" section at the end of the chapter to learn how to solve or avoid a problem.

CROSS REFERENCES

Cross references are designed to point you to other locations in this book (or other books in the Que family) that will provide supplemental or supporting information. Cross references appear as follows:

→ For full details on Word's Quick Parts Gallery and Building Blocks Organizer, **see** "Choosing the Right Document View," **p. 162.**

COMMON TASKS AND FEATURES

CHAPTER 1

GETTING STARTED WITH OFFICE 2007

In this chapter

WHAT IS OFFICE HOME AND STUDENT 2007?

Since its debut more than a decade ago, Microsoft's most popular software package has been aimed at businesses. With a name like Office, that's only natural. And sure enough, most of the new features Microsoft has introduced to Office in recent years are aimed at helping people in corporations work more closely.

So, what's the deal with Microsoft Office Home and Student 2007? A few years back, Microsoft discovered that people use computers outside the office, and that people who spend their days in classrooms and their evenings in home offices do many of the same things their workday counterparts do: They write reports, perform mathematical calculations, give presentations, and do research, among other things. Those are exactly the tasks that the individual programs in Microsoft Office are designed to accomplish.

So, despite the slightly confusing name, Microsoft decided to package some of the Office programs for people who don't normally work in offices. In its first incarnation, this product was called Office 2003 Student and Teacher Edition. That formulation, which required that a student or teacher live in the house before you could legally install up to three copies of Office, evoked howls of protest from people who wanted an affordable alternative to the pricey business-class Office packages.

And thus, for 2007, this particular Office package got a mild reworking, with a new name—Office Home and Student 2007—plus a new license agreement and a new mix of ingredients.

In the Student and Teacher edition of Microsoft Office 2003, the license agreement specified that to legally install and use the software, you had to have a "qualified educational user"—a full- or part-time student or teacher—in the household. That restriction is completely removed in Office Home and Student 2007.

By purchasing the Home and Student edition, you get a significant price break on the cost of the Office software. You also get the right to install Office on up to three computers in your household. (Those stuffy business-focused editions of Office typically allow installation on only one primary computer and one portable computer that is not used at the same time as the primary copy.)

So what's the catch? There are at least two:

The license agreement you get with Office Home and Student 2007 is for "noncommercial use by households." Under the terms of the agreement, you're not allowed to use the software for any commercial or business purpose. But that's a legal requirement, not a technical one. You don't have to show any ID or sign an affidavit to buy the software or to install it, and the software police won't kick down your door if you use your copy of Office to produce a business plan or catch up on some paperwork that you've brought home from the office.

In addition, the Home and Student edition doesn't qualify for upgrade pricing.

In this book, we assume that you're primarily using the software for educational purposes, which is why most of our examples relate to activities you'll encounter in a classroom or a home. But if you notice that we occasionally mention a feature that just might help you be more productive at work…well, we won't tell if you won't tell.

OFFICE HOME AND STUDENT 2007, PIECE BY PIECE

Four programs form the core of Office Home and Student 2007—Word, Excel, PowerPoint, and OneNote. The most significant departure from the previous edition (and indeed from all other editions of Office 2007) is the absence of Outlook 2007, the all-in-one email and personal information manager. Every other edition of Office, without exception, includes Outlook. OneNote, by contrast, is found only in the Home and Student 2007 edition and in the top-of-the-line, premium-priced Office Ultimate 2007 and Office Enterprise 2007 packages. Go figure. In addition, the Home and Student 2007 package includes a handful of smaller programs common to other Office 2007 editions, such as the Picture Manager utility.

NOTE

This book covers the four programs found in Office Home and Student 2007. If you've purchased a different Office edition, the code for Word, Excel, PowerPoint, and OneNote included in your edition is exactly the same, and our advice for working with those programs applies just as well. The same is true if you install a standalone copy of any one of those programs. We do not include coverage of programs that are included only with other Office editions, such as Outlook, Publisher, and Access, nor do we include the more distant members of the Office family, such as Microsoft Expression Web, SharePoint Designer, Project, and Visio.

The most obvious change in Office 2007 is the new user interface, which replaces the old menus and toolbars from earlier editions of Word, Excel, and PowerPoint with a single Ribbon that runs across the top of each program window. (OneNote sticks with the old-style interface and isn't Ribbon-ized.) As you can see in Figure 1.1, the Ribbon mixes icons, menus, and galleries of commands on tabs that roughly correspond to the old top-level menus. Helping you figure out how to accomplish once-familiar tasks with the new interface is a major focus throughout this book.

Figure 1.1
The tabs on the Office Ribbon are the most noteworthy changes in Office 2007, eliminating menus and toolbars.

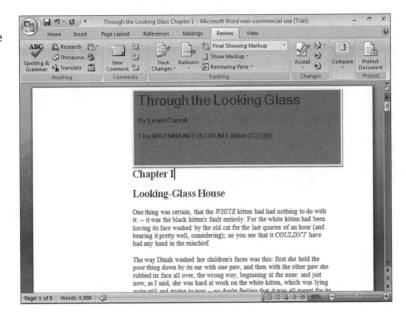

→ For a detailed discussion of all the elements in the new Office interface, **see** "How the Office Interface Works," **p. 28.**

So, what will you find in each program?

WORD 2007

The oldest and most mature of the Office programs, Word is also the most widely used. It's an extremely versatile tool—ideal for creating short documents, such as letters and reports, with enough layout and graphics-handling capabilities to also make it suitable for sophisticated publishing chores.

At its core, Word 2007 is easy enough to use. The basic tools for formatting text, viewing documents, and putting pages on paper have been part of Word for years. Learning the Ribbon-style way to handle those familiar tasks might take some getting used to, though. If you regularly reuse words, phrases, and even whole blocks of text, you'll want to study carefully the new Quick Parts Gallery, which brings together features from older versions of Word (including AutoText, fields, headers, footers, and templates for tables) in a single Building Blocks Organizer (see Figure 1.2).

Figure 1.2
Use the Building
Blocks Organizer to
assemble a Word
document one piece
at a time, using
canned elements or
your own personal
favorites.

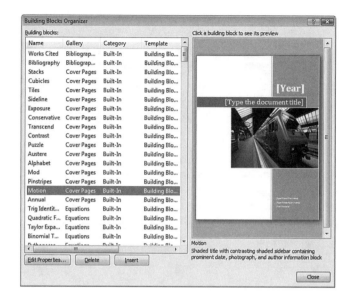

→ For full details on Word's Quick Parts Gallery and Building Blocks Organizer, **see** "Choosing the Right
Document View," **p. 162.**

Among the many hidden (and brand-new) gems in Word 2007 is its capability to morph into
a simple blog post editor. It's an excellent starting point when you want to create a new post
(with or without pictures) and publish it to a weblog.

EXCEL 2007

Excel is an incredibly useful all-purpose number-crunching tool, suitable for tasks as simple
as balancing a checkbook or as complex as creating a doctoral dissertation in macroeconomic
analysis. Excel is also a fabulous tool for keeping track of tables, which were formerly known
as lists. When you designate a range as a list—er, table—you can automatically add totals to
it, easily insert new columns and rows, and change the table's formatting by choosing from a
gallery of ready-made formats like the ones shown in Figure 1.3.

If you were a fan of Excel's chart-making capabilities before, prepare to be blown over by
the improvements in Excel 2007. The process of turning numbers into charts is much simpler, and the charts you end up with are better looking thanks to the new graphic engine
that all Office programs share. (If you're new to Excel, you can get up to speed in a hurry by
reading Chapter 12, "Getting Started with Excel.")

Figure 1.3
This gallery of Quick Styles makes it easy to quickly change the format of a table in Excel.

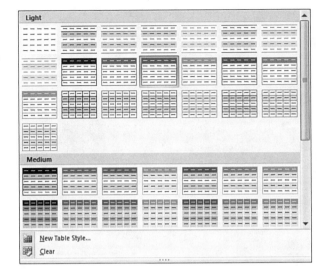

POWERPOINT 2007

PowerPoint has always been an effective way to create PC-based slideshows for presentations in front of a large audience. Recent versions add the capability to create effective web-based presentations as well. You can't truly appreciate the effectiveness of web-based presentations until you create one. PowerPoint can turn slide titles into a table of contents in the left pane of a frame and then display each slide on the right, with the viewer pointing and clicking to drive the show.

An increasing number of schools are using PowerPoint presentations in the classroom as well. They've discovered that it's an excellent way for kids to learn how to organize their thoughts, and it adds a whole new dimension to the classic "show and tell" day.

→ For step-by-step instructions that will help you get a PowerPoint presentation into web format in record time, **see** "Creating Presentations for the Web," **p. 619.**

For novices and experts alike, PowerPoint has earned a reputation as the most user-friendly program in the Office family. That's good news, because many PowerPoint users dust off the program only every few months, unlike Word and Excel. If you can't remember how to create a specific type of slide, look at the Slide Design task pane, which lets you see and preview design templates, color schemes, and animation effects while the slide is visible. The new Ribbon-based interface is especially effective for using the extensive library of professionally designed themes (see Figure 1.4).

You can add annotations to the slides in your presentations and save those comments for later. You can also embed multimedia clips into your presentation and show them using the full screen. You can even create slide shows, with or without captions, from a folder full of photos.

Figure 1.4
Picking a new theme for a presentation changes colors, fonts, and background images with a single click. Themes are shared by all Office programs.

Unlike the documentation—or other Office books—we also show you exactly how to use each of PowerPoint's many file formats.

ONENOTE 2007

The newest member of the Office family, OneNote, is also the most interesting. OneNote's basic organization is the notebook, which in turn contains tabbed sections, which in turn contain pages like the one shown in Figure 1.5. (In this example, we've pasted a snippet from a web page into a OneNote page, saving it and the associated link for future reference.) The whole thing is searchable, sortable, synchronizable, and exportable in a thoroughly elegant way.

OneNote is an ideal program for taking notes in the classroom, but it's also useful for anyone who prefers to keep random thoughts, lists, snippets from web pages, meeting notes, screen clippings, and just about anything else that can be typed or pasted into a loosely structured digital notebook. We devote three chapters to this innovative program. You can learn enough to become productive immediately by reading Chapter 21, "OneNote Essentials."

OTHER OFFICE PROGRAMS

In addition to the major programs, Office 2007 includes an assortment of utilities and add-ins. In Office 2003, some ancient utilities survived; in Office 2007, these have all been replaced. One good example is the Organization Chart tool, which is nicely integrated into the SmartArt feature available on the Insert tab in Word, Excel, and PowerPoint (see Figure 1.6).

Figure 1.5
OneNote's metaphor of a notebook organized into sections and pages is instantly understandable.

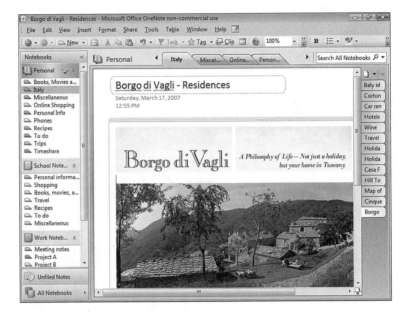

Figure 1.6
Use SmartArt to create and customize informational graphics like this sharp-looking organizational chart.

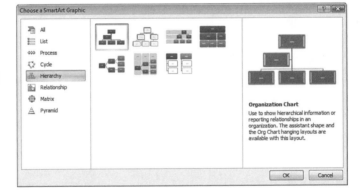

Overall, Office includes an impressive selection of new and useful tools to help you add photos to documents. The ClipArt Organizer feels a bit dated, but it serves its purpose well in helping you punch up documents and presentations with small drawings and pictures.

One utility that was introduced in Office 2003 and survived the upgrade is Microsoft Office Picture Manager (found in the Microsoft Office Tools group on the All Programs menu). It enables you to organize collections of image files that you've taken with a digital camera, scanned from original photos, or saved from websites. You can compress and resize images and perform basic image-editing tasks, such as removing "red eye" from portraits (see Figure 1.7). You can also convert images to alternative formats (from the space-hogging Bitmap format to the more efficient JPEG or GIF format, for instance), a trick that is especially handy when creating web pages.

Figure 1.7
Use Picture Manager to perform basic image-editing chores. The Send Pictures to Microsoft Office link creates an instant document, presentation, or worksheet from your selection.

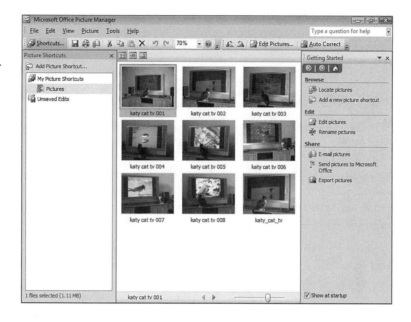

SETUP ESSENTIALS

For most people, installing Office 2007 is ridiculously simple. If you purchase a new PC that includes a preinstalled version of Office, you don't have to do a thing; just find the shortcuts on the Start menu and get to work. To install a retail copy, pop the CD in the drive, enter the 25-character product key from the yellow sticker inside the software case, accept the license agreement, and click Install Now. It isn't quite one click, but it's close. The Setup program goes about its business using the default installation options. No rebooting is required.

The Office program files themselves are included in a large collection of files stored in several formats, including Microsoft Installer files, XML files, and compressed files in the Cabinet File format (using the extension .cab). During the installation process, the Setup program automatically copies these files to the Local Install Source. This is a hidden folder named Msocache, which is stored in the root folder of your system drive.

NOTE

> The purpose of the Local Install Source is to eliminate the need to insert the Office CD whenever you install an optional feature, add a patch or service pack, or modify the existing installation in any way.

Three aspects of setup deserve special mention here. One is Office Product Activation, a controversial anti-piracy technology designed to prevent casual copying; a second is Office Genuine Advantage, a supplemental anti-piracy program that periodically checks your installed copy of Office to verify that you didn't somehow slip a bootleg copy past the activation process; finally, you should know about Microsoft's online services that automatically keep Office up to date.

ACTIVATING AND VALIDATING YOUR COPY OF OFFICE

After you complete the Office 2007 Setup process, you can begin using Office programs immediately. However, you will be required to complete one final step before you can continue using Office past an initial trial period: You must *activate* the product by contacting Microsoft over the Internet or by phone. This measure is intended to stop piracy; as we noted earlier, you can install and activate Office Home and Student 2007 on up to three computers. If you try to activate the program on a fourth computer using the same product key, however, you'll be refused.

For most users with an Internet connection, product activation happens automatically and takes only a few seconds. The activation process generates a "fingerprint" based on the hardware in your system and then associates that ID code with your 25-character product ID. If you reinstall the software on the same computer (after reformatting the hard drive, for instance), reactivation should be automatic. In fact, you can reinstall Office 2007 an unlimited number of times on the same computer. The activation server is intelligent enough to recognize from the hardware fingerprint that your computer hasn't changed.

If you've used all three of your permitted activations and you try to install the software on a new computer or on an old computer that you have upgraded with substantially different hardware, you might have to call Microsoft to get a new activation code. Simply changing a video card or adding a new hard drive won't trigger a request to reactivate Office, but a major upgrade, such as swapping the motherboard *and* switching hard drives *and* replacing the network card, might.

NOTE

> Retail versions of Windows also require activation. However, the rules and regulations for the two products are slightly different. Windows XP allows you to continue using the operating system for up to 30 days before shutting down, as does Windows Vista. Office allows 50 uses before forcing you to activate. Windows Product Activation is also more generous about hardware changes than Office. For more details about Office Product Activation, visit http://office.microsoft.com/en-us/help/HA012334341033.aspx.

A product activation reminder pops up each time you start a new Office program. If you don't have ready access to the Internet, you can delay activation, but don't wait too long. Without activating the product, you can use individual Office programs a maximum of 50 times (each time you start up a different program counts as a single use, even if you are forced to restart after a crash); after you use your 50 free starts, a process that can take less than a week, Office switches into a "reduced functionality" mode, in which you are allowed to open and print files but not edit or save them.

So, after you've jumped through all those hoops, you're in the clear, right? Sorry, no. A separate anti-piracy program called Office Genuine Advantage (a spinoff from the Windows Genuine Advantage program) kicks in periodically to *validate* your copy of Office. The idea is to identify pirated copies of Office that snuck through the activation process using stolen product IDs or hacked program files. At the time we wrote this, the Office Genuine Advantage program was still in a pilot stage and was voluntary, required only if you want to download updates or add-on features for Office.

INSTALLING UPDATES AND SERVICE PACKS

Microsoft occasionally releases software *updates*. Available for download from Microsoft's website and via the Microsoft Update site, these are executable programs, usually small in size, intended to fix specific bugs or to plug security holes in Office programs. Microsoft typically releases security updates on the second Tuesday of each month, a day that Microsoft watchers affectionately call "Patch Tuesday." Less frequently, Microsoft releases comprehensive updates to Office called *service packs*. Because they're typically quite large, service packs are usually made available both via download and on CD.

> **NOTE**
>
> Service packs and updates can be installed on any version of Microsoft Office, including Home and Student 2007. The update program installs all files that are required for your version.

Because updates often fix issues that affect the reliability and security of your computer, it's crucial that you install all available updates. You can take your pick of two tools to help you tackle this task:

- Microsoft Update—This service, introduced in 2005 as an upgrade to the Windows Update service, automatically checks for updates to Windows, Office, and other Microsoft products; to install it, visit http://update.microsoft.com/microsoftupdate. (Note that you must be logged on as a member of the Administrators group to enable this service.)

- Office Update—This web-based service scans your system and identifies any updates you need, based on the Office version you have installed. Unlike Windows Update and Microsoft Update, this service is not automatic. You have to visit the site, install an ActiveX control, and manually scan for updates. The easiest way to reach Office Update is to open OneNote and choose Help, Check for Updates.

We don't recommend that you rely on manual checks for updates. Because updates often plug security holes that can place your computer and your network at risk, it's better to automate the process. That way, you can be assured that updates will be delivered and installed as soon as they're available. When you first install Office, the setup program asks if you want to replace the Windows Update tool with Microsoft Update. If you say yes, you're done. If you turn down the initial offer, you can change your mind later by visiting http://update.microsoft.com.

NOTE

> Don't assume that you should immediately install every update you find on the Office Update site. We strongly recommend installing anything identified as a critical update, but for optional updates, read the documentation carefully and decide whether the update applies to you before installing it.

CUSTOMIZING YOUR OFFICE INSTALLATION

When you select the Install Now option at the initial Office 2007 installation screen, Setup uses the following default options:

- Program files normally go in the Microsoft Office subfolder in the folder to which the %programfiles% variable points. (On most systems, this is C:\Program Files.) In Office 2007, you can specify a different location, although we strongly recommend using the default location.

- Setup removes your previous Office installation (if any) and replaces all installed programs. In the process, it migrates your personal settings and preferences to Office 2007.

- Setup installs a standard set of programs and features. In the case of an upgrade, it automatically replaces all previously installed components with new versions, even if they're not normally part of the Typical Install.

TIP

> If you're not sure whether to use the Custom Install option, choose it anyway. When you do, Setup lets you review all options, and if you accept the default settings at every opportunity, the effect is the same as if you had chosen a Typical Install.

To change any of these options, you need to click Customize instead. This option allows you to use a three-tabbed dialog box to change which pieces of Office are installed. In the Installation Options dialog box shown in Figure 1.8, the icon to the left of each feature shows how it will be installed. A white box with a drive icon means all options will be installed using the method you've specified; a gray box with a drive icon means that some of the options available in that feature will not be installed. Click the plus sign to the left of each feature to see a list of options and adjust each one as needed.

In Office 2007, as in earlier versions, you can configure each Office program and feature separately. On today's large hard disks, it's not worth it to turn off minor features trying to save disk space. Given that Office Home and Student 2007 includes only four major programs, it's unlikely that you'll want to skip any of them; if you do decide that one program isn't for you, clear the check mark to the left of the program name.

Figure 1.8
By using a custom installation, you can select installation options for each Office application.

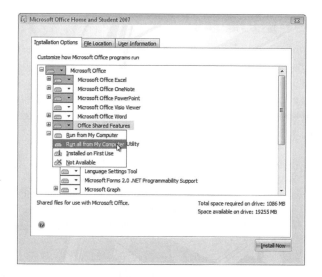

> **NOTE**
>
> As you select each item in the list, text at the bottom of the dialog box offers a capsule description of the feature or program.

The most important reason to learn about this capability is so that you can install interesting capabilities in Office that are not added as part of a default setup.

Normally, three settings are available for each feature and option. Click the drop-down arrow to the left of any feature to see a list of the available options, as shown earlier in Figure 1.8.

- When you choose Run from My Computer, Setup copies all associated program files to the specified location on the user's hard disk, and the application runs the feature locally. This option results in the best performance. The Run All from My Computer option is available only for programs and for features that offer additional options; it automatically installs all options under the selected feature.

- When you specify Installed on First Use for a feature, Setup creates a menu item or shortcut for the specified feature, but does not install the files associated with the feature. In the Typical Install, a number of little-used features are installed using this option. When you first use that menu choice or shortcut, the Windows Installer copies the necessary files to the local hard disk just as if you had chosen the Run from My Computer option. You might be prompted to insert the Office CD to complete the installation.

- Choose Not Available when you do not want to install a feature or create shortcuts that refer to it. In some cases, built-in menus include options that refer to features you've chosen not to install; if you select one of these menus, you'll see an error message that instructs you to rerun Setup.

FIXING SETUP PROBLEMS

Thanks to the Windows Installer, Office 2007 Setup is extremely robust. As the Setup program does its work, it keeps track of each action it takes. If you click the Cancel button in the middle of the process, Setup uses this feature to "roll back" all the changes—undoing any Registry changes and deleting any files you've copied so far. If Setup is interrupted for any other reason—by a system crash or power failure, for example—you should be able to restart Setup and resume at the place where it stopped previously.

TIP

> The Windows Installer creates a hidden folder called Config.msi to store files it removes during the Setup process so you can roll back to the previous installation if necessary. If you find this folder on your computer after successfully installing Office 2007, you can safely eliminate it and recover the disk space without any dire consequences.

Unless you specify otherwise, Setup also creates and saves log files that contain information on all Setup actions—changes to the Registry, files copied, and so on. You can locate these files in your system's Temp directory; each one begins with the name of the Office version, followed by the word Setup and a number. You can open each file by using any text editor.

USING SETUP TO CHANGE YOUR INSTALLATION

When you run Setup on a computer that has Office installed already, you'll see the dialog box shown in Figure 1.9. Use this dialog box when you want to add or remove features, when you need to repair an Office installation that is not functioning properly, or when you want to completely uninstall Office 2007.

You can start Setup in this mode by running Setup from the CD, or by using the appropriate option in Control Panel (Add or Remove Programs in Windows XP, Uninstall or Change a Program in Windows Vista). This is also where you can enter a product key if you're using a trial version of Office Home and Student 2007 and you want to convert it to a paid, licensed version.

ADDING AND REMOVING OFFICE FEATURES

To change the list of installed Office features after running Setup for the first time, run Setup again and click the Add or Remove Features button. The resulting dialog box is nearly identical to the list of features available when you perform a custom installation, as described previously. You can also use this dialog box to change the configuration of a feature—for example, to change a feature that is not currently installed so that it's installed on first use—using one of these techniques:

Figure 1.9
After you install Office 2007, running Setup again allows you to change features or repair the installation.

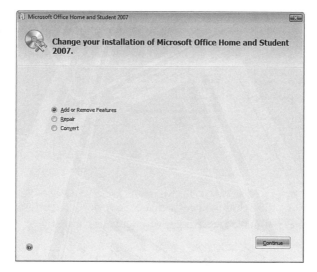

- To add a feature so that it is available at all times, select the Run from My Computer or Run All from Computer check box.

- To configure a feature so that it is available for installation when needed, select the Installed on First Use option.

- To remove a feature, select Not Available.

REPAIRING AN OFFICE INSTALLATION

The Windows Installer maintains a complete record of all Office components you've installed. If you accidentally delete a file or a Registry entry becomes corrupted after installation, the Windows Installer can automatically reinstall the component the next time you try to use it. In most cases, these repairs are automatic: If one of the essential system files for PowerPoint is missing when you attempt to launch the program, for example, the Installer starts automatically and reinstalls the missing file from the original installation source.

If you're experiencing problems with one or more Office programs, including crashes or unexplained hangs, run the Microsoft Office Diagnostics utility. This tool, new in Office 2007, replaces the Detect and Repair feature in earlier Office versions and adds the capability to automatically check for hardware errors in memory and hard disks.

To run this utility, click the Microsoft Office Diagnostics shortcut in the Microsoft Office Tools group on the All Programs menu. As Figure 1.10 shows, it's an all-or-nothing proposition; you can't select individual tests to run.

Figure 1.10
The Microsoft Office Diagnostics tool checks for solutions to common problems with hardware and software.

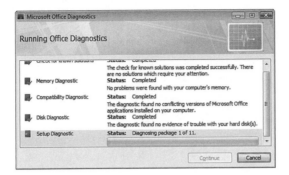

After the Diagnostic utility runs, you get a chance to review its results and make any necessary changes. It does not make any changes without your consent.

Uninstalling Office 2007

When you re-run Setup, the final option in Change Installation is Uninstall Office. When you choose this option, you see one and only one dialog box asking you to confirm that you want to remove Office completely. If you click OK, the Windows Installer begins the uninstall process immediately, removing all Office 2007 programs and all associated features and components.

TIP

> Thanks to the Windows Installer's rollback capability, you can abort the uninstall process at any time before completion, and Setup restores your system to its previous state. A progress bar moves from left to right as the Windows Installer removes components; if you click the Cancel button, watch the progress bar move from right to left as the Windows Installer undoes its actions and restores the original configuration.

You should be aware of two caveats when uninstalling Office:

- The Uninstall Office option effectively deletes virtually all program files and associated Registry entries. However, it leaves behind a considerable number of Registry entries associated with user settings and preferences, as well as some files that contain user settings. If you attempt to reinstall Office later, the new installation will use these settings. For instance, if you've defined alternate locations for documents, these will appear in your new installation, as will Excel macros in a leftover Personal Macro Workbook.

- If you upgraded over an earlier version of Office, removing Office 2007 will not bring back the previous version. The only way to preserve older Office versions is to specifically choose that option by performing a custom install of Office 2007 in the first place.

GETTING HELP

As in previous versions, each Office 2007 program includes detailed help content for Office users at any level, regardless of technical sophistication or experience.

The Help interface for programs in the Office 2007 family is completely rewritten. For programs that use the Ribbon interface, you ask for help by clicking the Help icon at the far right of the Tab bar—look for the white question mark in a blue circle. (For OneNote, which still uses old-style menus, click the Help menu and look for that same icon at the top of the list of commands.)

TIP

Or use the keyboard. As in every version of Office since the beginning of time, F1 still summons Help for the current program.

Think of the new Help window (shown in Figure 1.11) as a small, stripped-down web browser, with five buttons at the left of its toolbar that mirror functions in a web browser. The active topic always appears in the main window. You can show or hide the Table of Contents for the current program by clicking a button on the toolbar. Click the button with the pushpin icon to set the Help window so it's always on top.

Show/hide Table of Contents

Table of Contents | Keep On Top

Figure 1.11
The Table of Contents pane (left) allows you to browse Help topics. The selected topic appears in the viewer pane on the right.

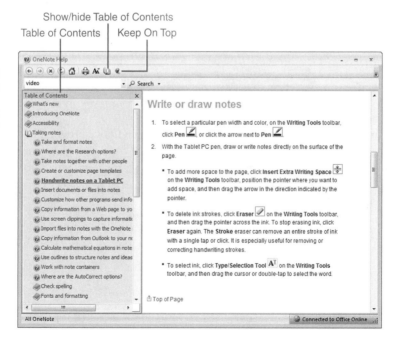

1

You can enter any text in the Search box to find topics containing that term. Use the drop-down Search list to change the scope of the search. By default, your search request looks for up-to-date content using Microsoft's Office Online servers. You can restrict your search to specific types of content, as in Figure 1.12; or, if you're working offline or have a slow Internet connection, specify that you want to use only locally stored content. To view only topics from the locally stored Help files, click the Show Me Offline Results from My Computer link in the contents pane, or choose any of the options from the Content from This Computer heading on the Search list.

Figure 1.12
The drop-down search list enables you to specify the scope of a search. The left side of the status bar shows the current search scope.

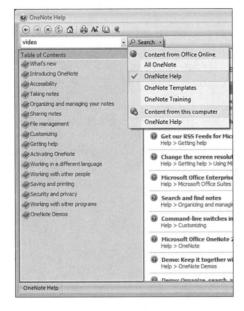

You can open multiple Help windows, one for each Office program in use. Some Help settings are shared among programs. For example, if you use the Change Font Size button to make text in the Help window larger or smaller, your choice applies to the current window and to any Help windows you open in the future, even in another Office program; it doesn't affect any other currently open windows.

CHAPTER 2

MAKING OFFICE 2007 WORK YOUR WAY

In this chapter

POINT, CLICK, AND CUSTOMIZE

The first time you encounter the new Ribbon interface in Word, Excel, and PowerPoint, we predict you'll experience a mixture of delight and confusion. The delight comes when you discover useful features that you never knew were in Office because they were previously buried under obscure menu choices and hidden dialog boxes. The confusion occurs when you realize the arrangement of commands is fundamentally different from any previous Office version, and all your experience with those earlier versions won't help you find them.

For would-be power users, one change will be particularly shocking. If you learned how to customize toolbars and menus in previous Office versions so they matched up perfectly with your working style, you'll no doubt be disappointed to learn that Office 2007 has one and only one customizable toolbar, and shortcut menus that appear when you right-click an object aren't changeable at all. If you want a custom Office interface, you'll need to find a third-party program to help you do it.

→ For an introduction to Office add-ins, including tools that can help you customize the Ribbon interface, **see** Chapter 24, "Extending Office with Templates, Macros, and Add-ins," **p. 687.**

In this chapter, we focus on the things you can do to make Office tasks easier. We start with the Quick Access toolbar, which is the one and only customizable toolbar in Office. We also show you how task panes and galleries work, how to set up spell-checking options, and how you can get a dictionary definition or a quick translation of a foreign phrase without leaving the friendly confines of your Office program. All in all, learning the techniques in this chapter can save you time and make Office easier to use. Good news: Most Office programs work in identical fashion, so after you learn how to tweak a toolbar and modify a menu in Word, you can use the exact same techniques in Excel and PowerPoint. (We also explain the differences between the new-fangled Ribbon and the old-school menus and toolbars found in OneNote.)

You might be tempted to skip over this chapter and go straight to one that's directly related to the program you're trying to use right now. That's fine. But be sure to come back and read this one after you've used a program for a while. With experience, you learn which features are most important to you, and that's the perfect time to begin tweaking.

HOW THE OFFICE INTERFACE WORKS

With its pull-down menus and a never-ending supply of toolbars, the venerable interface from older versions of Microsoft set the standard for a generation of Windows programs. And now it's gone. Well, almost. Those menus and toolbars live on in OneNote (for now), but the other three applications in Office 2007—Word, Excel, and PowerPoint—share a new, radically different interface called the Ribbon, which combines menus, command buttons, and an assortment of preview tools. This section incorporates a piece-by-piece look at the new interface.

USING THE OFFICE MENU

In the top-left corner of every Office program window is the Office button, an orb that bears the four-color Office logo and no text. Clicking this button displays the Office menu (shown in Figure 2.1), which includes many of the choices found on the File menu in previous Office versions.

Figure 2.1
Choices on the Office menu allow you to open, save, or print files. The Options button at the bottom leads to a dialog box where you can change program settings.

TIP

Want proof that the Office menu is a replacement for the old-style File menu? Just learn its keyboard shortcut: Tap the Alt key and then press F.

The Office menu is divided into three distinct zones. On the left is the main menu. To its right is the Recent Documents list, which is replaced by an expanded list of menu options if you hover the mouse pointer over an item in the main menu that has an arrow to its right. At the bottom of the Office menu is an Options button that leads to a dialog box where you can find practically every customization option for the current program.

With one exception (the Recent Documents pane) the choices on the Office menu are not customizable. Here's what you need to know about the choices listed here:

- The three basic file commands—**New**, **Open**, and **Save**—are at the top of the menu. Each has its own keyboard shortcut as well—Ctrl+N, Ctrl+O, and Ctrl+S, respectively.

- Click **Save As** if you want to save the current document, workbook, or presentation in a format other than the default. Figure 2.2 shows the Save As options available in Excel.

→ For more details about opening and saving files, as well as a complete discussion of alternative file formats, **see** Chapter 3, "Keeping Track of Your Files and Settings," **p. 55.**

- Options on the **Print** menu allow you to preview a document before printing it, as well as choose a printer, change the number of copies, and adjust other print-related settings.

- The **Prepare** menu, shown in Figure 2.3 and new in Office 2007, brings together options that are useful before you save a document and send it to other people. When you select the Mark as Final option and then save a document, for instance, all editing commands (including the Save menu) are disabled, making it truly read-only.

- Use the **Send** menu to attach the current file to an email message for review by other people, or to deliver it to a fax machine. If you choose the Internet Fax option without first setting up a fax service, Office opens a web page where you can sign up for an online fax account with a third-party provider.

- The Document Management and Document Workspace options on the **Publish** menu are useful only if you have a SharePoint server on your network (most home users don't). But that's not to say this option is completely irrelevant: In Word, you can

Figure 2.2

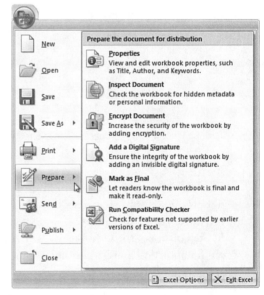

Figure 2.3

choose to publish a document to a weblog, and in PowerPoint you can package a presentation for saving to a CD or create handouts in Word, as shown in Figure 2.4.

→ For more details on creating PowerPoint handouts with Word, **see** "Extra Credit: Creating Top-Notch Notes and Handouts," **p. 592.**

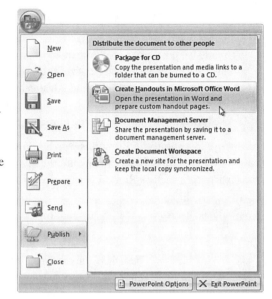

Figure 2.4

■ The **Close** command closes the current document (prompting you to save it if you've made any unsaved changes) but does not disturb any other open documents. If this is the only current document, this option leaves the program window open. Its keyboard shortcut is Ctrl+F4.

■ The **Recent Documents** pane displays a list of documents you've opened or saved recently. Click any entry in the list to reopen that document. The pushpin icon to the right of each entry locks that entry so it won't be replaced by a new entry. This feature is handy when you're working on a long-term project.

> **TIP**
>
> In previous Office versions, the number of entries on the Recent Documents list at the bottom of the File menu was set to four by default and could be increased to nine. By contrast, in Office 2007 this number defaults to 17 and can be set to a maximum of 50. To adjust this setting, open the Options dialog box for the program and click Advanced; the Show This Number of Recent Documents setting is under the Display heading.

■ The **Options** button (Word Options, Excel Options, and PowerPoint Options, respectively) opens a tabbed dialog box with an enormous number of settings for that program—some are momentous, others are picky in the extreme. We'll cover the features that are common across all programs later in this chapter in the section, "Configuring Common Office Features."

■ The **Exit** button closes the program and all open documents, prompting you to keep or discard any unsaved changes.

USING AND CUSTOMIZING THE RIBBON

As we noted in Chapter 1, "Getting Started with Office 2007," the Ribbon mixes icons, menus, and galleries of commands on tabs that roughly correspond to the old top-level menus. Despite its apparent size, the Ribbon occupies little more space than the combination of menu plus standard and advanced toolbars in earlier Office versions. The different sizes of command buttons help to highlight features that are more important or commonly used, making it easier to perform many common tasks.

One fact about the Ribbon is worth knowing right up front: it offers no customization options. The only way to change the layout of buttons, groups, and tabs is to use a third-party tool such as Ribbon Customizer.

→ For information about how to find and install Ribbon Customizer and other Office add-ins, **see** "Using Add-ins to Create Your Own Ribbon Customizations," **p. 693.**

> **TIP**
>
> The only way to change the look and arrangement of elements on the Ribbon is to shrink the program window so it is narrower than the full width of the current tab. When you do this, Office resizes commands it deems less important, without hiding any groups and without changing the order of groups. At its narrowest, the Ribbon consists of the group names, in the same font as the tab names on the top row. An arrow beneath each group name displays the choices within that group, menu-style.

If you find the colorful icons on the Ribbon distracting, you can make them go away so that all you see are the tab names along the top row. In this configuration, the Office 2007 interface looks almost like its predecessor, with a "menu bar" that displays the contents of each tab only when clicked.

To minimize the Ribbon, use any of these techniques:

- Double-click the name of any tab.
- Click the arrow to the right of the Quick Access toolbar and select the Minimize the Ribbon Menu option.
- Use the keyboard shortcut Ctrl+F1.

Figure 2.5 compares the height and appearance of the Ribbon in its full and minimized states.

Figure 2.5
When you minimize the Ribbon, you hide the commands on each tab temporarily; click any tab to reveal the contents.

When the Ribbon is minimized in this fashion, you use the tab names like a menu. Click to reveal the commands on that tab; when you choose a command or click anywhere else in the document, the commands retreat into hiding again.

CUSTOMIZING THE QUICK ACCESS TOOLBAR

As mentioned earlier in this chapter, the Quick Access toolbar (QAT) is the only toolbar you can customize directly. The toolbar occupies a single row, with tiny buttons that can't be resized or labeled with text. You can put virtually any command on the QAT, and despite its limitations it should be the number one tool for making yourself more productive with Office.

By default, the QAT sits on the title bar, to the right of the Office button. This is a space-saving arrangement, but it makes your mouse hand move considerably further to get to buttons on the toolbar, and it begins crowding out the window title when you add more than a few buttons.

For those reasons alone, we suggest that the first customization you make to the QAT should be to move it below the Ribbon. To do so, click the arrow to the right of the QAT and click Show Below the Ribbon, as shown in Figure 2.6.

Figure 2.6
If you use the Quick Access toolbar regularly, move it from its default position on the title bar, shown here, to below the Ribbon.

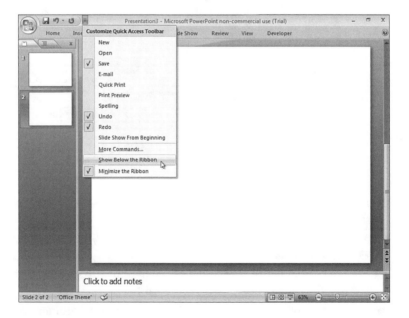

The Customize Quick Access Toolbar menu for each program includes a list of the 10 most popular commands for that program, as determined by Microsoft's usability testing group. You can add any of these commands to the QAT by selecting that command from the list. To add any other command available in the current program, find its command on the Ribbon or in the Office menu, right-click, and choose Add to Quick Access Toolbar. If the command you want isn't available on the Ribbon or the Office menu, click More Commands on the Customize Quick Access Toolbar menu to open the Customize dialog box shown in Figure 2.7.

The basic technique for customizing the QAT is simple: choose a category to filter the list of available commands, choose a command, and click Add. Here are some suggestions to help you be more productive with the QAT:

- Start with the Popular Commands list, which is likely to contain at least some of the commands you want to use. Add other commands directly from the Ribbon, where you can right-click and choose Add to Quick Access Toolbar.

Figure 2.7
From this dialog box, you can select any command and add it to the Quick Access toolbar.

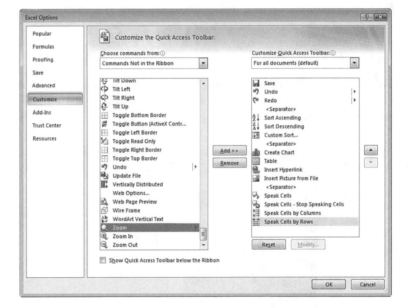

- Divide your additional commands into groups and use separators (available at the top of the list on the left) to arrange them visually.
- To add a new command in a specific position, first click a command in the list on the right. The command or separator you add appears below the command you selected. Use the Up and Down arrows to move commands you've already added. Keep the ones you use most often at either end of your customized toolbar.
- Can't find a command? Look in some of the specialized locations on the Choose Commands From list. Try Commands Not in the Ribbon or All Commands if you're certain that a feature is available but you can't locate it on any tab.

NOTE

For some commands, the only way to add a command button to the QAT is to find its entry in one of these long lists of commands. That's true in Word, for example, of just about anything related to fields, including the Unlink Fields and Update commands.

- The Reset button removes all customizations from the QAT and restores it to its default settings. You must click OK to one confirmation dialog box before making this change.

- To remove a command from the customized QAT, select it in the list on the right and click Remove.

TIP

Any changes you make to the QAT are normally saved as part of the default template for the program with which you're working. However, you can also save QAT customizations as part of individual documents or templates. This feature is useful if you want a specific set of tools, such as those for working with footnotes and endnotes, to be available when you're working with long research papers, but you don't want them cluttering up the screen when you write a letter.

To create a supplemental set of QAT settings, choose For <*document name*> from the drop-down list above your list of custom commands. That clears the list of commands and allows you to begin adding new commands that appear only when that document is open. If you save a group of custom commands as part of a template, those settings appear on the QAT for every document you create using that template. Note that these per-document custom commands appear in addition to those on the For All Documents list, so make sure you don't duplicate any commands in the two lists.

The QAT isn't perfect. Two frustrations are worth special note: You can't change the size of buttons, and you can't use more than one row.

BYPASSING MENUS WITH KEYBOARD SHORTCUTS

Are you a touch typist, or do you have an accessibility issue that makes it difficult to use the mouse? If so, you probably grit your teeth every time you have to take your hands off the keyboard to mess with the mouse. Well, we have good news for you: You don't have to leave the keyboard for most tasks. All you have to do is learn about the many, many Office keyboard shortcuts.

Office applications are remarkably consistent in their use of keyboard shortcuts. In every Office program, for example, you use Ctrl+F and Ctrl+H to display the Find and Replace dialog boxes, respectively. Some shortcuts use mnemonic devices to make it easier for you to remember what they do—Ctrl+B (Bold), Ctrl+U (Underline), and Ctrl+I (Italic) are common to every Office application. Others follow Windows standards, such as the universal Ctrl+X (Cut), Ctrl+C (Copy), and Ctrl+V (Paste) shortcuts, as well as Undo (Ctrl+Z) and Redo (Ctrl+Y). Still others give you access to commands that are nearly impossible to access any other way. For example, no menu choice in Word converts field codes to their results (or Unlinks them, in Word-speak); you have to know the shortcuts: Ctrl+6 (from the numeric keypad, not the row of numbers above the QWERTY keys) or Ctrl+Shift+F9.

No one expects you to memorize every Office keyboard shortcut, but learning a select few can dramatically increase your productivity, especially for commands and functions you use regularly.

TIP

> You don't need to hunt for cheat sheets to make discovering keyboard shortcuts for a particular Office program easier. Just aim the mouse pointer at a command on the Ribbon and see if the ScreenTip includes a shortcut. This option is on by default. To turn it off (or to enable it after it has been turned off), click the Office button, click *<Program name>* Options, select Advanced, and select the Show Shortcut Keys in ScreenTips check box under the Display heading.

Of all the Office-wide keyboard shortcuts, one stands out as by far the most useful. F4 is the Repeat key, which repeats the previous action; it is useful in a wide variety of situations. For example, you can use F4 to apply a new style to a series of paragraphs scattered throughout a Word document. Click in the first paragraph and select the style from the drop-down list. Click in the next paragraph and press F4 instead of going back to the Style menu; F4 continues to apply that style until you perform another action, such as typing or formatting. Add or delete a row in an Excel worksheet and then move the insertion point and press F4 to add or delete another row, again without using menus.

You can also use the keyboard to navigate from tab to tab on the Ribbon, selecting commands without ever touching a mouse button. Tap the Alt key to display keyboard equivalents for each clickable target on the Ribbon and the QAT, as shown in Figure 2.8.

Figure 2.8
Tapping the Alt key displays keyboard equivalents for each clickable target in the Office interface.

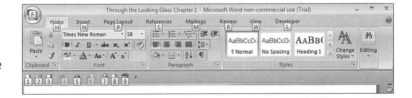

While these labels are visible, tapping any key has the same effect as clicking the object that it labels, and if that choice opens another tab or menu, it's labeled with keyboard equivalents as well. So, in Word, tapping Alt, M, S, W switches to the Mailings tab, selects the Start Mail Merge menu, and then selects the Step by Step Mail Merge Wizard option.

We do not highlight every keyboard shortcut in the text of this book because there are so many of them that the text would be practically unreadable. If we think a keyboard shortcut is important enough for you to consider memorizing, we'll call it out in the text. Printing out an exhaustive list of shortcut keys for each Office application would take hundreds of pages. To see a generally complete list organized by category, search in each program's online help for *keyboard shortcuts*.

Of all Office programs, only Word enables you to easily customize keyboard shortcuts. On the Customize dialog box (shown earlier in Figure 2.7), click the Customize button to the right of the Keyboard Shortcuts label. Select Tools, Customize, and then click the Keyboard button to select a command, a macro, an AutoText entry, a font, a style, or a common symbol. The Customize Keyboard dialog box (shown in Figure 2.9) displays the current key combination assigned to each item you select.

Figure 2.9
In Word (and only in Word), you can assign custom keyboard shortcuts to commands, macros, styles, and even fonts.

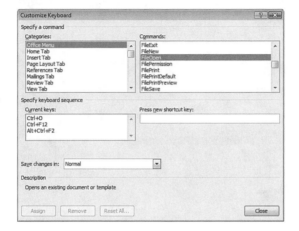

To add or change a key combination, first select the item you want to customize from the list on the left; then click in the Press New Shortcut Key box and press the key combination. Look at the text just below this box to see whether the key combination you've selected is already assigned to another function; if the option is available, click Assign. Look in the Current Keys box to see whether a key combination is already assigned to that function; to remove that definition, select the item and click Remove.

 For details on how to restore default keyboard shortcuts if you inadvertently reassign the wrong key, see "Restoring Default Shortcut Keys" in the "Troubleshooting" section at the end of this chapter.

CUSTOMIZING TOOLBARS AND MENUS IN ONENOTE

As we've noted in the preceding sections in this chapter, the old-style menus and toolbars are gone for good in Word, Excel, and PowerPoint, replaced by the Ribbon and QAT. That's not true for OneNote, however, where the old Office interface is alive and well.

In the previous edition of this book, we spent a dozen or so pages discussing the many ways you could customize toolbars and menus throughout Office. Those techniques still work in OneNote, but there's far less need for that sort of rich customization in a program that's made for freeform note-taking. If you used these capabilities extensively in a previous Office version, everything you learned still works in OneNote 2007. In this section, we've condensed the customization instructions for OneNote to a handful of key tasks.

For the most part, these customization options are all accessed through the Customize dialog box, which contains three tabs. To open this dialog box, choose Tools, Customize.

MANAGING TOOLBARS

OneNote includes 10 default toolbars, most of them hidden initially. You can show or hide any toolbar at any time; you can also create new custom toolbars and populate them with your favorite commands.

To show or hide an existing toolbar, right-click the top-level menu bar or any visible toolbar and select its entry from the list. To manage custom toolbars, click Customize from the bottom of the list of toolbars (or just click Tools, Customize). The Toolbars tab is shown in Figure 2.10.

Figure 2.10
From this dialog box, you can create new toolbars and then manage any custom toolbar.

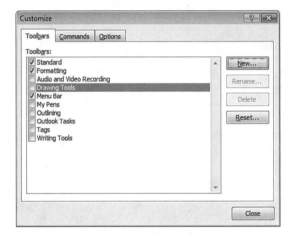

Select or clear the check box to the left of any item in this list to show or hide the toolbar in question. Click New to create a new, blank toolbar. (We'll explain how to fill it with command buttons in the next section.) The Rename and Delete buttons are available only for custom toolbars and are grayed out for built-in toolbars, which cannot be removed or renamed.

CUSTOMIZING TOOLBARS

OneNote's Standard and Formatting toolbars are packed with commands, including some for which you probably have no use. So why not customize the built-in toolbars to contain the buttons you use and remove those you don't need? It's easy to get rid of any command on an existing toolbar. Click the Toolbar Options arrow (the slim, down-pointing arrow at the right side of every toolbar), select Add or Remove Buttons, and choose the name of the toolbar to display the list of available buttons, as in Figure 2.11 (if you add a button, it appears on this list as well). A check mark next to any item on the list means that the button is currently visible; click to toggle this check mark and display or hide the button.

Figure 2.11
Click the arrow at the right of any toolbar to add or remove buttons easily.

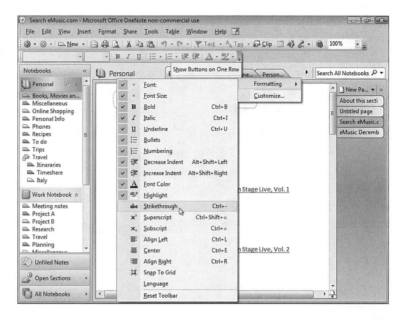

When customizing the selection of buttons on a OneNote toolbar, you're not limited to choices on the Add or Remove Buttons menu. You can add any command or existing menu to a toolbar. If you want the Extra Writing Space option to be on the toolbar instead of hidden at the bottom of the Insert menu, you can add that button to any toolbar (including a custom toolbar you create from scratch).

To add a command to a visible menu or toolbar, follow these steps:

1. Select Tools, Customize (or right-click any toolbar or menu and choose Customize from the bottom of the shortcut menu). The Customize dialog box opens.

2. If the toolbar you want to customize is not visible, click the Toolbars tab and click the check box for that toolbar.

3. Click the Commands tab, select an entry from the Categories list on the left, and then select the command you want to add from the Commands list on the right, as shown in Figure 2.12.

4. Drag the command from the Customize dialog box to the toolbar where you want to add the button. When you see a thick black I-beam in the correct position, drop the button to add it.

5. Repeat steps 3 and 4 to add more buttons to any toolbar.

6. When you've finished working with the toolbar, click Close to put away the Customize dialog box.

Figure 2.12
Select any command from the list on the right side of this dialog box and drag it onto an existing toolbar to add that command as a new toolbar button.

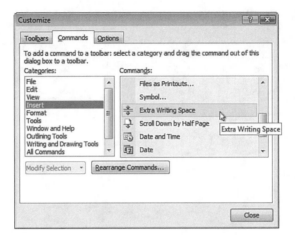

If you never use certain toolbar buttons, clear them away to make room for the buttons you do use. It's ridiculously easy to remove a button from a toolbar: Point to the button you want to remove and then hold down the Alt key as you drag it off the toolbar—when the pointer displays a tool icon with an X, release the mouse button to delete the item. If the Customize dialog box is open, you can remove any button or menu item by dragging it off the menu bar, without having to hold down the Alt key.

TIP

Use these same drag-and-drop techniques to move buttons and menu items, either on the same toolbar or between toolbars. From any editing window, hold down the Alt key and drag a button to move it to a different place on the same toolbar or to a different toolbar altogether. With the Customize dialog box visible, hold down the Ctrl key and drag any button to create a copy. And here's an undocumented shortcut we guarantee you haven't read anywhere else: Hold down the Alt key as you drag a button onto the same toolbar or on another toolbar. Then (while continuing to hold down the Alt key) press the Ctrl key and release the button. This shortcut creates a copy of the button, without opening the Customize dialog box. This technique is especially effective if you want to create slightly different versions of the same toolbar for different tasks: Create a new toolbar based on an existing toolbar, and then drag buttons from the old toolbar to the new copy. Switch between the two toolbars for different tasks.

CUSTOMIZING THE APPEARANCE OF TOOLBAR BUTTONS

For many toolbar buttons, you can decide whether to show its icon, a text label, or both.

For buttons you use infrequently, the default icon might not give you a very good clue as to what that button actually does. By showing both the icon and the text, you don't have to constantly hover the mouse pointer over the button so you can use the ScreenTip to remind you what it does. To change this setting for one or more buttons, you have to first open the

Customize dialog box (select Tools, Customize). You don't need to use any controls within the dialog box itself—drag it out of the way so you can see the toolbar containing the button you want to change and then right-click the button to display the shortcut menu shown in Figure 2.13.

Figure 2.13
Use this shortcut menu to change the text and icon that describe a toolbar button or menu choice.

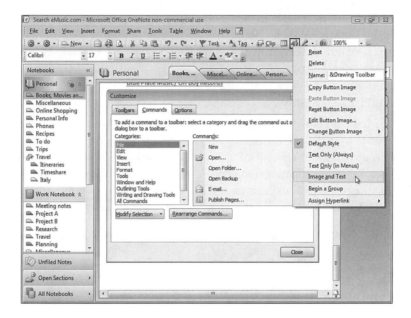

The four choices on this menu let you decide whether to show icons only, text only, or a combination of both. (The Default Style choice uses the setting that Microsoft's interface designers have determined is most appropriate for most users. That might or might not match what *you* want.)

TIP

Most built-in commands include their own images that Office programs can use as the icon on a toolbar button. You can change the image on any button, and if you're a decent icon designer, you can use the built-in Button Editor to create your own custom button images.

Although you can create an icon from scratch, it's usually best to start with an existing button image. If you see an image that you like on a built-in toolbar button, copy it to your custom icon using the Copy Button Image and Paste Button Image choices on the shortcut menu for each icon; then edit the pasted image. If you make a mistake, click Reset Button Image and start over.

When you have a group of buttons that work together, use a separator line to define the group. On the Standard toolbar in OneNote, for example, the Cut, Copy, and Paste buttons are all in a group with a separator line at either side. If the Customize dialog box is open, right-click the icon that begins the group and select Begin a Group from the shortcut menu. To quickly add a separator line without leaving the normal editing window, hold down the Alt key, click the button to the right of the place where you want the line to appear, and drag slightly to the right. To remove a separator line without having to go through a dialog box, hold down the Alt key, click the button to the right of the line, and drag the button to its left, over the line.

CUSTOMIZING OTHER MENU AND TOOLBAR OPTIONS

The last tab in the Customize dialog box, Options, includes one of the more controversial settings from the old Office interface. At the top of this dialog box, shown in Figure 2.14, is a group of options under the Personalized Menus and Toolbars headings. The Show Standard and Formatting Toolbars on Two Rows check box tells OneNote whether to display the two default toolbars on a single row or on two rows; the Always Show Full Menus check box has a significant impact on the menus and toolbars you see.

Figure 2.14
We recommend selecting both check boxes in the top portion of this dialog box.

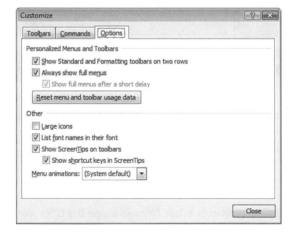

With the Always Show Full Menus check box cleared, menus and toolbars in OneNote change dynamically as you use the program. When you click a menu, you see a short list of available choices instead of the full menu. To make matters even more confusing, the short list changes over time, as each Office program monitors your usage patterns and "personalizes" menus and toolbars. The idea is to reduce clutter and simplify your work by showing you only the menu choices and toolbar buttons you use regularly, rather than overwhelming you with a long menu that contains many choices.

In our experience, most people find this constant shifting of menus and toolbars more confusing than helpful. If you agree, you can disable personalized menus and toolbars. Select Tools, Customize, click the Options tab, and make sure that both check boxes are selected.

CONFIGURING COMMON OFFICE FEATURES

As we noted at the beginning of this chapter, a button at the bottom of the Office menu in every Ribbon-based program leads to a dialog box where you can change just about any setting for that program. Some of these settings are specific to the type of data in that program—but many are common to all programs.

CHANGING THE LOOK AND FEEL OF OFFICE

The top selection in each of these dialog boxes is called Popular. As the name suggests, these options have a major impact on the overall look and feel of each program and deserve at least a quick glance. Figure 2.15 shows this dialog box for Excel.

Figure 2.15
In all three Ribbon-based programs, the Popular set of options have a major impact on the operation of Office programs.

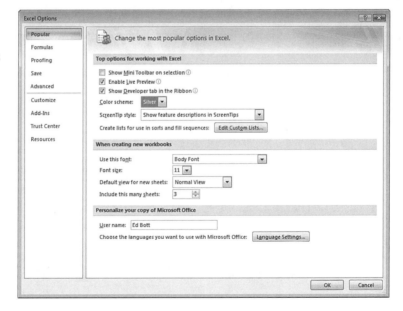

Several of the options in this section affect all Office programs when adjusted. If you change the color scheme in Word, for example, your change is reflected in all Office programs (including OneNote). Likewise, showing or hiding the Developer tab and changing settings for ScreenTips in one program affects all others.

If your copy of Office was preinstalled with a new PC, be sure to change your username (and initials in Word and PowerPoint) from the generic default entry.

SETTING UP SPELL-CHECKING AND RELATED OPTIONS

Unless you're the National Spelling Bee champion, chances are you need occasional help with a tricky word. That goes double if your fingers insist on hitting the wrong keys every so often. All Office programs have access to a powerful spell-checking module. No matter what program you're working in, you can check the spelling of a word, paragraph, or whole document with a few clicks. And if you use technical terms or proper nouns that aren't in the built-in dictionaries, you can add those words to your custom dictionary. Your changes are stored in a single text file, which you can easily open and edit, and when you add a word using one Office program, the term is available to the spell-checking feature in every other Office program.

To adjust spelling options in Office, use the following techniques.

For Word, open the Word Options dialog box and click Proofing in the left column. Use the dialog box shown in Figure 2.16 to adjust options.

Figure 2.16
Word's spelling options are by far the richest of any Office program.

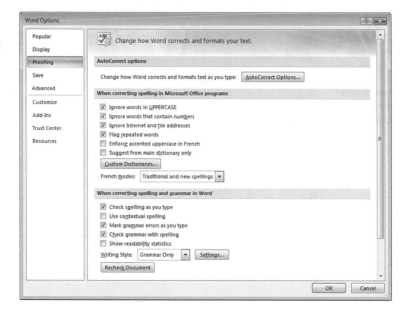

The options under When Correcting Spelling in Microsoft Office Programs are found in Excel and PowerPoint as well. PowerPoint shares three additional options with Word but not Excel, including the capability to check spelling on the fly and to hide spelling errors in a document or presentation.

Word has the most extensive set of spelling options, including the capability to add supplemental dictionaries for specialized vocabularies, such as those used in a medical or legal practice.

To tame some of Word's aggressive spell-checking tendencies, see "Word Changes Text Mysteriously" in the "Troubleshooting" section at the end of this chapter.

→ For more details on how Word automatically uses suggestions from the spelling-checker, **see** "Checking Spelling and Grammar," **p. 188.**

All Office spelling tools share the following dictionary files:

- A main dictionary, as determined by your language settings; on a system configured for U.S. English, for example, this file is `Mswds_en.lex`, and is typically found in %program-files%\Common Files\Microsoft Shared\Proof, where it is available for all users of the computer.

- A custom dictionary, which stores words you add while spell-checking; the default name for this file is `Custom.dic`.

> **TIP**
>
> Why are some words enclosed between percent signs in these locations? Those are called *environment variables*. If you type **%userprofile%** in the Windows Start menu's Search box and then click OK or press Enter, Windows opens an Explorer window and displays the contents of your user profile. You don't have to know the drive letter or any other details.

The custom dictionary file, on the other hand, should appear in a personal data folder, such as %appdata%\Microsoft\Proof. Because the custom dictionary file is a simple text file, shared by all applications, you can use any text editor to edit it. The easiest way to do this is with the help of Word. Open the Word/Excel/PowerPoint Options dialog box, select Proofing from the column on the left side, and click the Custom Dictionaries button to display the dialog box shown in Figure 2.17. Select the correct file from the list, if necessary—normally you'll have only the one Custom.dic file—and click Edit Word List. This opens up a neat dialog box where you can add one word at a time.

Figure 2.17
To edit the Office-wide Custom dictionary, click the Edit Word List button in the Custom Dictionaries dialog box, which is available from any Office program.

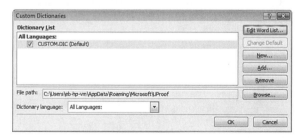

ADJUSTING ADVANCED OPTIONS

The Advanced tab on the Options dialog box allows you to customize dozens of settings in Word, Excel, and PowerPoint. For example, you can control whether you see and hear animation and sound effects when you use menus and other interface elements. If sound effects annoy you, turn them off here. You can also hide or show rulers, scrollbars, and other inter-face elements.

→ For a discussion of text entry, editing, and formatting options used throughout Office, **see** Chapter 4, "Entering, Editing, and Formatting Text," **p. 81.**

CUSTOMIZING TASK PANES

Task panes are small windows that dock within an Office program window (typically along the right side) to provide easy access to commands and program functions. Task panes give you access to common features such as the Office Clipboard, clip art, and research tools, as well as program-specific features such as styles in Word and PivotTable field lists in Excel.

Despite their widespread use, task panes are mostly fixed and barely customizable.

Most task panes can be docked to the left or right side of the program window. You can also dock a task pane on the top or bottom of the window, although this arrangement rarely makes the contents of the task pane easier to work with. You can even allow the task pane to float over the current document, undocked. To move the pane, point to the sizing handle at the left of the pane's title bar; when the mouse pointer changes to a four-headed arrow, click and drag the pane to its new position. You can also change the width of the pane by drag-ging the edge that's next to your document; this option is especially useful with the Clip Art task pane.

CUSTOMIZING SMART TAGS

Smart Tags are tiny button/menu combinations that appear automatically after certain types of actions. For example, a Smart Tag appears whenever you paste something (text, a picture, whatever) into any Office document. If the results of the paste operation aren't what you expect, you can use options on the Smart Tag menu to change the way the data appears. Smart Tags assist in error checking in Excel worksheets and are used for layout functions in PowerPoint. They can also automatically identify words or phrases that meet certain crite-ria. For instance, you can configure Word to automatically recognize the names of persons (as in Figure 2.18), or ask Excel to recognize stock ticker symbols.

Figure 2.18
Word automatically adds a Smart Tag to names in a document. Click the button to send and e-mail mes-sage or perform other tasks.

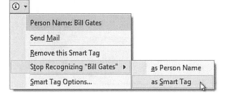

Subtle indicators mark the positions of each Smart Tag in an Office document. In a Word document, a faint purple line under a name means a Smart Tag is buried there. In Excel, a triangular indicator in the corner of a cell marks the presence of a Smart Tag. Hover the mouse pointer over the Smart Tag to display an Action button; click the button to see a list of actions you can take in response to the tag.

A wide array of options is available for customizing Smart Tags. To adjust these options for any Office program, open the Office program's Options window by clicking the Office button and then clicking the Options button. Click to display the Proofing tab and click the AutoCorrect Options button. When you click the Smart Tags tab, the full range of Smart Tags options will appear, such as the one in Figure 2.19. Using this dialog box, you can specify which types of data will be recognized or you can turn off Smart Tags completely.

Figure 2.19
Smart Tags are disabled by default. Use this dialog box to enable them for certain types of data.

TIP

Because Smart Tags use a standard format called XML, software developers can create Office-compatible add-ins that work as Smart Tags. The Office Update website lists a selection of available Smart Tags you can purchase or download free. Most of these add-ins are intended for businesses, but it's still worth checking to see if you might find one useful. For quick access to this site, open the Options dialog box and click AutoCorrect Options on the Proofing tab. In the AutoCorrect dialog box, click the Smart Tags tab, and click the More Smart Tags button.

If an Office program insists on incorrectly recognizing a word, phrase, or name and assigning a Smart Tag to it, use the actions menu to clean up the clutter. You can remove a single

2

Smart Tag, stop recognizing a certain word or phrase in a particular type of Smart Tag, or tell Office to completely ignore a particular word or phrase when checking for Smart Tags.

CONFIGURING THE RESEARCH TASK PANE

Office 2007 gives you access to an extensive collection of reference books and online research services. All of them are available whenever you're working in any Office program. To quickly find the definition of a word or phrase, select the text, right-click, and choose Look Up from the shortcut menu. The Research task pane opens, with the Encarta dictionary definition of the word you selected in place. Scroll down through the list to see other information, such as synonyms, or to translate the word or phrase into another language. Click the drop-down list below the search term to look in additional reference books, such as the Encarta Encyclopedia, as shown in Figure 2.20.

Figure 2.20
Information from a built-in dictionary and thesaurus and from online services, such as the Encarta Encyclopedia shown here, appear in the Reference task pane.

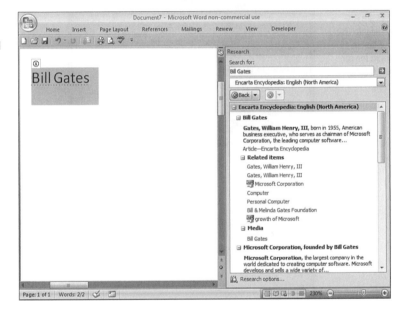

To go beyond the basic look-up tools, open the Research task pane and enter a name or phrase to look up using any of several online references. The MSN Search option enables you to look up any word or phrase on the Internet without having to leave the document on which you're working. It's free, but other services are typically available only with a paid subscription. The MSN Encarta encyclopedia, for example, provides a small amount of basic information free of charge, but you'll need to pay extra to get full details about the topic you selected. In most cases, clicking a link in the Office Research pane opens Internet Explorer, where a Research sidebar mirrors the results found in the Office task pane. The results of the online search appear in the browser window.

The list of books and services shown in the Research task pane is customizable. This is especially useful for anyone studying a foreign language; if you're writing papers in French, add the French-language Encarta dictionary and thesaurus to your Research pane. You can remove any existing service or add new services by visiting the Microsoft Office website. To access these options, open the Research task pane and click the Research Options link at the bottom. Figure 2.21 shows the complete list.

Figure 2.21
Select or clear these check boxes to add or remove services in the Research task pane.

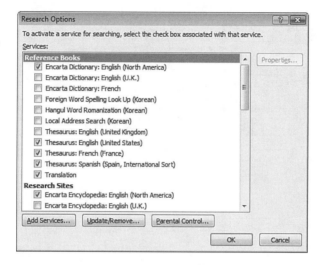

> **TIP**
>
> Parents who are setting up Office for use by young people should strongly consider enabling the Parental Control features in the Research task pane. From a Windows Administrator account, click the Parental Control button on the Research Options dialog box and click the Turn On Content Filtering to Make Services Block Offensive Results option. You'll need to enter a password before clicking OK; this prevents your kids from changing these settings without your permission.

SETTING SECURITY AND PRIVACY OPTIONS

Security isn't just for Windows. Office 2007 has an assortment of security and privacy settings as well, all designed to protect your computer and your identity from being compromised by viruses, hackers, and other ne'er-do-wells.

The default security settings in Office programs are designed to protect you, and we don't recommend that you change them unless you are sure you know the consequences. In general, the only reason to make changes is to enable features such as macros that are disabled by default. These features are discussed in more detail in Chapter 24, "Extending Office with Templates, Macros, and Add-ins."

To adjust the privacy options for any Office program, open the Options dialog box, click Trust Center in the column along the left side, and click Trust Center Settings. Figure 2.22 shows this dialog box for Word, which offers a few more options in this category than any Office program.

Figure 2.22
You'll find Office security settings in the new Trust Center. Word's privacy options are more extensive than other programs.

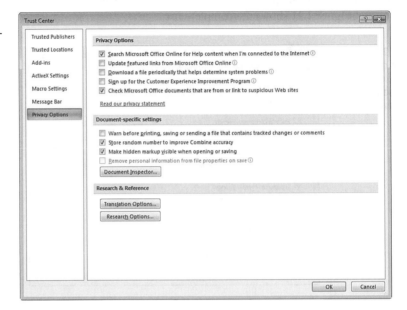

Settings in the Privacy Options category apply across all Office programs and affect how Office programs interact with the Internet. Document-specific settings typically include information about a document's creator and company, as well as other details that might be added during editing. For documents you intend to publish outside your organization, you might want to delete this information. Word, Excel, and PowerPoint allow you to specify that you want to be warned before printing, saving, or sending (via fax or email) such a file, so you can remove this information. Word also offers the option to show hidden markup (comments, revisions, and so on) when you open or save a file, giving you a chance to remove potentially embarrassing content before sending a document to someone else.

TIP

> Word embeds a random number in every document. This feature, originally intended to improve mail merge accuracy, can inadvertently affect your privacy by adding a unique identifier to a document. In theory, someone could use this random number as a "fingerprint" to identify you as the author of a document. Clear the Store Random Number to Improve Combine Accuracy check box under Document-Specific Settings to remove this possibility.

→ For more details on macro security issues, including a discussion of when it's safe to lower security levels, **see** "Configuring Macro Security," **p. 708.**

TIP

> If you don't use antivirus software, you're simply begging to lose data or suffer catastrophic loss. The best antivirus programs integrate tightly with Office to protect you from infection when you open a document from the Internet or receive one as an email attachment. Check with the maker of your antivirus software to determine whether you need an update for compatibility with Office 2007. If you're not sure which antivirus program to use, start by visiting ICSA Labs at http://www.icsalabs.com. Browse its list of ICSA-certified programs and find the one that represents the best match for your needs and budget.

TROUBLESHOOTING

RESTORING DEFAULT SHORTCUT KEYS

After assigning a shortcut key to one function, you discover that the keyboard combination you used applies to a useful system shortcut, and you want to reset it.

When you assign a keyboard shortcut to a specific function, Office removes that shortcut for any other function that uses the same combination. To restore the shortcut, select the original function and reassign the key combination that's normally associated with it. To restore every default Word key combination (and wipe out any custom shortcuts you've created), click the Office key and open the Options window. Select the Customize tab and click the Customize button.

WORD CHANGES TEXT MYSTERIOUSLY

As you create a document, you discover that Word is consistently changing some words or abbreviations you type. You've checked thoroughly, and you know the text being changed is not in the AutoCorrect list. What's up?

Word thinks you're mistyping the text in question, and it is convinced that it knows exactly what you meant to type. This behavior is controlled by a well-hidden spell-checking option. To stop it, click the Office button and open the Options window. Select the Proofing tab and click the AutoCorrect Options button. Click the AutoCorrect tab and clear the check mark from the Automatically Use Suggestions from the Spelling Checker box.

EXTRA CREDIT: CUSTOM BUTTONS FOR QUICK HIGHLIGHTING

While working on this book, we regularly used Word's yellow and green highlighters to mark text for specific tasks and then cleared the highlighting when the task was complete. Using the highlighter is an ideal way to remind yourself of a paragraph that needs to be rewritten, or to call out a sentence that needs a little more research. Because Word's

2

Highlighter icon remembers the last color you select, this routine often takes three clicks—one click to make the highlighting tool visible, a second click to display the drop-down list of available colors, and a third click to select a color (or None, to erase highlighting).

To make highlighting a one-click process, we first created three nearly identical macros. We started in Word by pressing Alt+F11 to open the Visual Basic Editor, double-clicked ThisDocument in the Microsoft Word Objects folder in the Normal Project, and then typed the following code:

```
Public Sub NoHighlight()
Selection.Range.HighlightColorIndex = wdNoHighlight
End Sub
Public Sub YellowHighlight()
Selection.Range.HighlightColorIndex = wdYellow
End Sub
Public Sub GreenHighlight()
Selection.Range.HighlightColorIndex = wdBrightGreen
End Sub
```

After carefully proofing our work, we clicked File, Save Normal (Ctrl+S) and then clicked File, Close and Return to Microsoft Word (Alt+Q).

(For more details on how macros work as part of the Normal document template, see Chapter 26, "Using Macros to Automate Routine Tasks.")

We then assigned each macro to a button in a group on the QAT and gave each new button its own easy-to-recognize icon, using these steps:

1. Click the drop-down arrow at the right side of the QAT and choose More Commands.

2. Click the Choose Commands From menu and choose Macros.

3. Select the NoHighlight macro and click Add. Do the same for GreenHighlight and YellowHighlight.

4. Add a separator and adjust the position of the new buttons, if necessary.

5. In the list of installed buttons, select the NoHighlight macro and click Modify. This opens the Modify Button dialog box shown in Figure 2.23.

Figure 2.23

6. Click the blank color box (the 10th item in the fifth row) and then click OK.

7. Repeat steps 5 and 6 for the yellow and green highlighters, using the color buttons on the sixth row of the Modify Button dialog box.

8. Click OK to save your changes.

Figure 2.24 shows the new buttons in position at the end of the QAT.

Although you can't tell it from this page, the button next to each toolbar label is the same color as the highlighting choice.

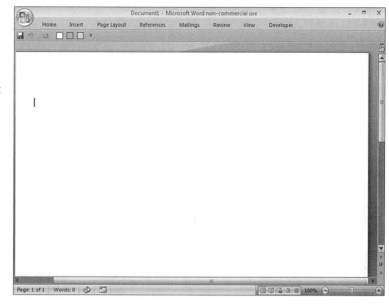

Figure 2.24

CHAPTER 3

KEEPING TRACK OF YOUR FILES AND SETTINGS

In this chapter

GETTING ORGANIZED (AND STAYING THAT WAY)

You're about to start working on a new report or presentation. What's the best way to get started? How do you avoid reinventing the wheel when you want to begin a new project? Where should you save your file? How do you find that file tomorrow, or next week, or next month? How do you protect yourself from the inconvenience (to put it mildly) of losing a document you've worked on for hours, days, or weeks?

Those are the questions we tackle in this chapter. Relax—we're not going to force you to change the way you handle your homework or your projects. It helps if you can stick to a sensible file-naming strategy, and you'll have best results if you have a clear understanding of where and how Office stores files. Whether you file every scrap of paper that goes across your desk or just throw everything into a shoebox, Office has a set of tools for you to use, as well as a rich trove of ready-made templates that others have already created. At the end of this chapter, we introduce you to an amazing search tool that can help you pick out any Office document, even if all you can remember is a word or phrase it contained.

For the most part, this chapter is concerned only with the three Office programs that use individual files to store your work: Word, for document files; Excel, for workbooks; and PowerPoint, for presentations. As we explain in Part V, OneNote's storage system doesn't rely on individual files, so it's not relevant in this chapter.

WHERE SHOULD YOU KEEP YOUR FILES?

In Windows Vista and Windows XP, the files you create for your personal use belong in one place: the subfolder set aside for document storage in your personal profile, which is created when you set up your user account. In Windows XP, this folder is called My Documents; in Windows Vista, it's simply called Documents. (And if you don't like either name, you can rename this system folder.) Regardless of the name, using this folder as the default location for your personal data files makes it easier for you to find and back up files you create.

The icon for your Documents folder is never more than two clicks away—it's located at the top of the right column in the Start menu. When you click the File menu and choose Open or Save As from within any Office program, the resulting dialog box takes you straight to the Documents folder.

TIP

> Although most of your files are stored in the Documents folder, you might need to store files elsewhere under certain conditions. For example, if you've created a PowerPoint presentation and you want someone else to be able to work with it, you might choose to save it in the Shared Documents folder (in Windows XP) or the Public folder (in Windows Vista). Files in these folders can be opened by anyone who logs on to the same computer, even if they do so with a different user account. If you've enabled file sharing on your computer, those files can also be accessed over a network.

The Documents icon in Windows Explorer windows and on the Start menu is a virtual folder, not an actual physical location. Opening this shortcut opens the folder that's registered as the Documents location for the user who's currently logged on. The exact physical location of the Documents folder varies, depending on which Windows version you have installed and whether it was a clean installation or an upgrade. On most computers running Windows Vista, the Documents folder appears in your *user profile*, normally `C:\Users\<username>\Documents`.

If you currently store data files in other locations and you're willing to reorganize your storage system, you can substantially increase the odds that you'll find files you're looking for when you need them. Doing so also makes it easier to back up data files.

You can change the default location that individual Office programs use for data files. Why would you want to reset the default working folder? Maybe your family has a home server where all family members keep documents, music, photos, and other files. In that case, you might want to define your Documents folder on the home server as the default working folder; whenever you choose File, Open or File, Save As, the dialog box displays the contents of this folder. Follow these steps, for example, to adjust the default document folder in Word:

1. Click the Office button, click Word Options, and select Save from the list on the left side of the dialog box, as shown in Figure 3.1.

Figure 3.1
Use the Options dialog box to adjust the default working folder for any Office program.

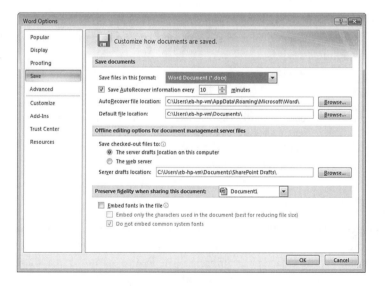

2. Click the Browse button to the right of the Default File Location entry.
3. Browse through drives and folders to select the correct folder and click OK.
4. Click OK to close the Word Options dialog box and save your change.

Follow the same basic procedure for Excel and PowerPoint, clicking the Excel Options and PowerPoint Options buttons, respectively.

The default file location setting for each application is independent. If you set Word's default Documents folder to a location on your home server, for example, Excel and PowerPoint continue to open to the default location—the Documents folder on your computer.

Behind the scenes, Office creates and uses an additional group of subfolders in the Application Data folder within the user's personal profile. These subfolders represent standard locations where Office stores customization data.

OPENING AND SAVING FILES OVER A NETWORK

Office 2007 enables you to work with files over a network in much the same way that you access files and folders on a standalone PC. If you are connected to a network at your home or school, you can open and save files in shared folders on the network, provided your user account has been granted the appropriate permission to read or write files. You can browse to shared folders using Windows Explorer or a common dialog box by starting in the Network folder (My Network Places in Windows XP). You can also enter the name of a shared network folder directly using *UNC syntax* (\\`Computer_name`\\`Share_name`\\). Unless the network administrator has restricted your rights, you can create and manage your own subfolders in this location.

Aside from the additional navigation steps, virtually no difference exists between using network shares and using local drives, assuming that you have proper authorization from your network administrator.

NOTE

On the Save tab in the Options dialog box for each Office program, you'll find options for document management server files. You can safely ignore these settings unless you have your own SharePoint server at hand; most homes and schools don't use this feature, which is found in high-end Windows server operating systems.

CREATING NEW FILES

When you click the Office button and choose New in an Office 2007 program, the New Document, New Workbook, or New Presentation dialog box opens (the exact name varies depending on the Office program in use). As Figure 3.2 illustrates, these dialog boxes are well organized and fairly self-explanatory.

In each Office program, the New dialog box is divided into three vertical sections. On the left is a category list that allows you to filter the list of available templates, which in turn appear in the center section. The pane on the right shows a full-page preview of the template selected in the center pane. Use the search box above the center pane to find a template that contains the search term in its name or description.

Figure 3.2
Every Office program except OneNote offers a variation of this dialog box, which gives you options for creating a new blank file or one based on a template.

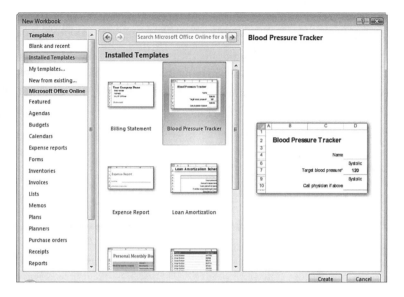

3

> **TIP**
>
> Do you have a large monitor? If so, drag the borders of the New dialog box to make it larger. The list of templates and the preview region on the right remain fixed in width, but the center section, which displays available choices in the category you've selected, gets wider to accommodate more templates. The larger window is especially useful when you choose a category that has a large number of entries, such as those found at Microsoft Office Online.

The choices available in the Templates list are similar in all three file-based Office programs:

- **Blank and Recent**—The Blank Document/Workbook Presentation option creates a new file using the default template for that program. This category also includes the last few templates you've used when creating new documents in that program, on the theory that you might want to create another one just like the previous one.

> **TIP**
>
> Although the name of this option includes the word *blank*, there's no reason that files created using this option have to be completely empty or unformatted. By modifying the default template for each program, you can turn the blank option into one that's at least partially filled.

- **Installed Templates**—This list shows all templates for the current program that are installed on your computer. The templates in this list are stored along with the program files in the Microsoft Office\Templates subfolder and are available to all user accounts on your computer.

- **Installed Themes**—You'll find this option in PowerPoint only; it has the same effect as creating a new blank presentation and then applying a theme from the Design tab.
- **My Templates…**—This option opens a dialog box like the one shown in Figure 3.3. Its contents include all templates you have created and saved or downloaded from Microsoft Office Online. This list of templates is stored in your personal profile and is not shared with other users of your computer.

Figure 3.3
Templates you save or download are stored in your personal profile and are available for use via this dialog box.

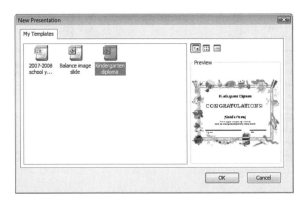

- **New From Existing…**—The last choice in the list gives you the option to turn any document into an instant ad hoc template. Browse to the document you want to use as your model and then click Create New. The Office program opens a copy of the selected file without disturbing the original; give it a name and you're ready to get to work.

CREATING AND SAVING YOUR OWN TEMPLATES

The default collection of Office templates is stored in a subfolder that corresponds to the system's current language settings; on a default U.S. English installation, this is `%programfiles%\Microsoft Office\Templates\1033`. All users of the current system see these templates. Each user's custom templates are stored in the location specified for User Templates. By default, this is `%appdata%\Microsoft\Templates`.

> **TIP**
>
> In the previous paragraph, %appdata% refers to an environment variable that uniquely identifies a system folder on a computer running Windows Vista or Windows XP. Typing this variable, complete with the surrounding percent signs, opens the target folder. Using this variable saves you keystrokes and enables you to create shortcuts that work for different users without modification and without having to worry about the exact drive or folder location. You can use environment variables in the Run dialog box, in the Search box at the bottom of the Windows Vista Start menu, in an Open or Save dialog box, or in the Target box of a file or program shortcut, for example. Other useful Windows environment variables that we use in this book include %localappdata% (which opens files in your personal profile's Local subfolder) and %userprofile% (which goes directly to the personal profile of the currently logged-on user). To see a full list of environment variables, open Control Panel's System option and click the Advanced tab.

If you're having trouble finding templates that you've saved, see "Putting Templates in Their Place" in the "Troubleshooting" section at the end of this chapter.

Although you can manage the contents of template folders in an Explorer window, the easiest and safest way to make new templates available to an Office program is to save the file in Template format. After creating the Word document, Excel workbook, or PowerPoint presentation that you want to use as a template, follow these steps:

1. Click the Office button and then click Save As.

2. From the Save as Type drop-down list, choose Word Template, Excel Template, or PowerPoint Template. The dialog box displays the contents of the Templates folder in your user profile.

> **NOTE**
>
> If your template includes macros (or if you think you might want to add them later), choose the Macro-Enabled Template option. To create a template that works with older versions of Office, choose the Word/Excel/PowerPoint 97–2003 Template option instead.

3. To add the new template to an existing tab in the New dialog box, click Templates in the Favorite Links list and then click the matching folder. To create a new tab, click the New Folder button and add a folder with the name you want the tab to use. If you don't select a subfolder here, your new template will appear on the My Templates tab in the New dialog box.

4. Type a name for the template and click Save.

> **TIP**
>
> If you want all users on a computer or a network to have access to a set of templates, you need to designate a shared folder as the Workgroup Templates folder and then configure each machine or user account to access that location. You'll find the dialog box with these settings in the Word Options dialog box. Click Advanced, scroll down to the General section, and then click File Locations. From this same dialog box, you can change the location where your personal templates are stored.

DOWNLOADING TEMPLATES FROM OFFICE ONLINE

At the bottom of the Templates list is a long series of categories representing templates available from the Microsoft Office Online website. Because this list draws its content directly from the web, it requires an Internet connection to work properly.

To browse through all available choices in a particular category, click the category name; in some cases, as in the calendars shown in Figure 3.4, you might have to select a subcategory first.

Figure 3.4
The Office Online template collection offers a particularly rich collection of ready-made calendars.

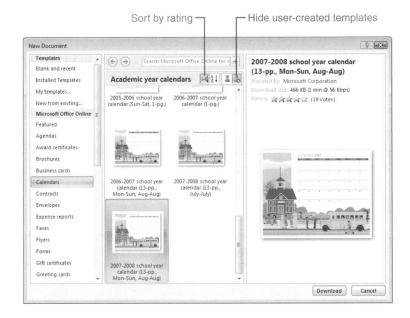

Before you can download and use an Office Online template, you have to go through a validation process that verifies that your copy of Office is not pirated. After you successfully pass the validation test, you can download the template you selected.

The Office Online collection is interesting because it includes templates created by other Office users, not just those from Microsoft. If you'd prefer to hide templates created by other users, click the Hide Customer Submitted Templates button just above the contents pane.

Templates available from Office Online are also rated by users, giving you another option to help you make your selection. The ratings (on a scale of 1 to 5 stars) are displayed in the preview pane for each template. A button above the templates list lets you sort by rating instead of alphabetically.

NAMING DOCUMENTS

After you create a new file, the first thing you should do is save it, and as you work on it you should get in the habit of saving it regularly. What's the best name to use? If the file is for your own personal use, you can make up your own file-naming system. If you're working as part of a group, you'll want to devise a standard that everyone can agree on and then follow that standard.

Whether the file-naming system is just for you or for an entire team, the most important guideline is to be consistent. As we explain in this chapter, you can use the search tools built into Windows and Office to find just about any file. But a file with a descriptive name is much easier to pick out of a list. Some people begin each filename with a keyword (*report*, *homework*, *budget*) that helps define the type of content. You might want to add the creation date (using a format *YYYYMMDD*) to help you see at a glance which version of a file is the most recent one: "Homework-English 101-20071031" is pretty descriptive, wouldn't you say?

Regardless of how you choose to name files, be sure you know the file-naming rules that apply to all Office documents:

- A filename can contain any *alphanumeric* character, including the letters A to Z and numbers from 0 to 9.

- A filename can be as short as 1 character and as long as a total of 255 characters, including the full path—drive letter, colon, backslashes, and folder names included.

> The rules governing maximum length of a filename include the full path. For this reason, moving a file with a long name can cause problems, especially when the destination folder is deeply nested. In practice, you can avoid this problem and still have descriptive names if you keep filenames to a maximum length of about 40 characters.

- The following special characters are allowed in a filename: $ % - _ @ ~ ` ! ( ) ^ # & + , ; =.

- You may use spaces, brackets ([ ]), curly braces ({ }), single quotation marks, apostrophes, and parentheses within a filename.

- You may not use a slash (/), a backslash (\), a colon (:), an asterisk (*), a question mark (?), a quotation mark ("), or angle brackets (< >) as part of a filename. These characters are reserved for use with the file system, and you'll see an error message if the name you enter includes any of these characters.

- Office files typically include a three- or four-letter *extension*, which is added automatically by the application that created the file (such as .docx for files created using the default Word 2007 format). File extensions define the association between a document type and the program that is used to create it. However, a file extension is not required, nor are file extensions restricted to a specific length. We don't recommend changing extensions unless you understand the full consequences of doing so. To force an Office program to use the exact name and extension that you specify, enter the full name, including the extension, between quotation marks. (Filename extensions are normally hidden; to make them visible, open Control Panel, Folder Options, click the View tab, and clear the Hide Extensions for Known File Types check box.)

> If you use a nonstandard file extension, you might be unable to open the file from an Explorer window. Also, files that include unregistered file extensions do not appear in the Open dialog box unless you choose All Files from the drop-down list of file types.

■ A filename may contain one or more periods. Windows treats the last period in the name as the dividing line between the filename and its extension.

NOTE

> Windows filenames are not case sensitive. Office ignores all distinctions between upper- and lowercase letters when you enter a filename in an Open or Save As dialog box.

USING AND CUSTOMIZING COMMON DIALOG BOXES

Every time you open or save a file in an Office program, you work with one of two common dialog boxes. The exact operation of the Open and Save As dialog boxes varies, depending on which version of Windows you're using:

Common dialog boxes in Windows XP have a series of shortcut icons on the left side, called the Places Bar, which are designed to speed navigation through common file locations. With a small amount of effort, you can easily customize these icons in dialog boxes used in all Office programs. To add a shortcut to the current folder to the Places Bar, right-click any empty space on the bar and choose the option at the top of the menu, as shown in Figure 3.5.

Figure 3.5
Customize the Places Bar by adding short-cuts to commonly used data folders; to see more choices, right-click the Places Bar and choose Small Icons from the short-cut menu.

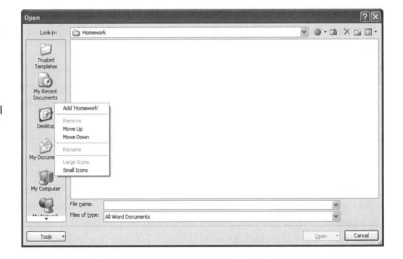

The default icons in Windows XP include links to the My Documents folder, to the Templates folder, and to the desktop. There's also a My Recent Documents icon, which contains shortcuts to files and folders with which you've worked. When you click this icon from within an Office program, Office displays only shortcuts appropriate to the program you're using.

NOTE

> Don't confuse the Office Recent folder with the Windows system folder of the same name. Office manages a separate Recent folder for each user profile on a system. To manage the Office shortcuts from an Explorer window, enter `%appdata%\Microsoft\Office\Recent` in the Run dialog box or in the Address bar of an Explorer window.

TIP

> The Recent folder is just one of many Most Recently Used (MRU) lists in Windows. Some people prefer not to keep this list, either for privacy reasons or out of a desire to reduce clutter. You can empty the Recent folder at any time by opening it in Windows Explorer, pressing Ctrl+A to select all files, and then pressing Shift+Delete (use the Shift key to bypass the Recycle Bin and permanently delete the selected shortcuts).

In Windows XP, the Places Bar in Office 2007 programs is different from the one found in common dialog boxes for other Windows programs. In Windows Vista, by contrast, the Open and Save As dialog boxes are identical to those found in other programs. In fact, these common dialog boxes work exactly like Windows Explorer. Instead of a Places Bar, you have a Favorite Links list to the left of the file contents. You can drag the icon for any folder, drive, or network location into this area to make it available for use anywhere in Windows or Office.

In Open and Save dialog boxes, Office includes two features that make it easier to find a file by name:

- As you type in the Filename box, the *AutoComplete* feature suggests names that match the characters you've typed so far. Keep typing, or use the down arrow to select an entry from the list, and then press Tab or Enter to accept it.

- If you click in the list of files and then type a character, Office selects the first file that begins with the letter or number you typed. If you quickly type several characters in rapid succession, the selection moves to the first file that begins with those characters. If you pause for more than a second between characters, this type-ahead feature resets. As you select files in this fashion in Windows Vista, Office fills in the Filename box for you.

To adjust the display of files in the Open and Save As dialog boxes, use the Views button. The drop-down arrow lets you choose from a list of views, or you can click the button to cycle through the different icon arrangements, which match the choices available to you in Windows Explorer:

- In Windows Vista, you can choose Icons view in a wide range of sizes; Windows XP offers a fixed-size Icons view and a Thumbnails view that is equivalent to Large Icons view in Windows Vista.

- Tiles and List views mirror their counterparts in Windows Explorer.

- Details view displays the filename, the date it was last modified, its type, and other information, as shown in Figure 3.6; click any heading to sort the list by that category. Click the down arrow to the right of the column heading to display a drop-down list or date control that you can use to filter or group items.

Figure 3.6
In Details view, you can click any heading to sort by that column, or click the down arrow to filter the list using dates or other criteria.

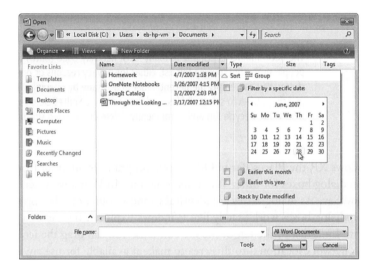

Three additional choices are accessible in different ways, depending on whether you're running Windows XP or Windows Vista:

- To see summary information about the selected document in Windows Vista, click Organize, Layout, Details Pane, which opens a horizontal pane above the Filename box. In Windows XP, choose Properties from the Views menu and a similar pane appears on the right side of the dialog box.

- To preview the contents of files without opening them, click Organize, Layout, Preview Pane, which displays a thumbnail version of the document in the right half of the dialog box as you move from file to file in the list. To enable this feature in Windows XP, choose Preview from the Views menu.

CAUTION

> In general, you should avoid this option on slower computers because of the performance penalty you pay: As you scroll through a dialog box, the program you're working with has to open each file; find an import filter, if necessary; and generate the preview. On a modern, reasonably fast computer, this concern is no longer a pressing issue.

- In the unlikely event you have access to a SharePoint server (most people don't), you can enter its URL (including the http:// prefix) address directly in the Open dialog box to display the contents of the Shared Documents folder. In Windows XP, this switches to a special view (called WebView on the Views menu).

TIP

> To manage files in Open and Save As dialog boxes, select the filename and right-click. Shortcut menus here work just as they do in an Explorer window. You can move, copy, delete, or rename a file, for example, as long as the file you select is not currently open.

USING ALTERNATIVE FILE FORMATS

By default, Office applications save data files in their own binary formats. When you double-click the icon for the saved file, it opens using the program with which you created the file. That's the correct choice if you use Office programs exclusively for your own personal productivity. However, when you share files with friends, neighbors, and coworkers who don't use Office 2007, you need to think carefully about how they will deal with the files you create.

The most important issue to consider is that all Office 2007 programs, by default, use new XML-based formats. (You can tell the difference by looking at the filename extension—the new, XML-based format for Word 2007 uses the .docx extension, whereas older files created using the format for older versions of Word use the .doc extension. The same is true of Excel, with .xlsx and .xls extensions, and PowerPoint, which uses the .pptx extension instead of the older .ppt extension.

The new formats have a variety of benefits, including decreased file size and a lower likelihood that you'll encounter data-destroying file corruption. But if you send a file to a friend who is unprepared for it, they'll see an error message when they try to open it.

So what should you do to avoid this sort of problem?

If the people with whom you plan to share files use an earlier version of Office (Office 2000, Office XP, or Office 2003), send them a link to the Microsoft Office Compatibility Pack, http://office.microsoft.com/en-us/products/HA101686761033.aspx. After they install this add-in, they can use their older version of Word, Excel, or PowerPoint to open, save, and edit files (with the obvious restriction that any features specific to Office 2007 won't be available for their use).

If your friends don't use Office at all, they can still open the files you send them by downloading and installing *viewer programs* that are compatible with the new formats, and then installing the Office Compatibility Pack. These lightweight programs allow anyone with a computer running Windows XP or Windows Vista to view, but not change, documents created in Office. (Don't be alarmed by the 2003 label on the Word and Excel viewers. The Compatibility Pack takes care of updating these two programs to handle the Open XML formats.) Find the viewers here:

- Word Viewer 2003 (http://office.microsoft.com/en-us/downloads/CD011197531033.aspx)
- Excel Viewer 2003 (http://office.microsoft.com/en-us/downloads/CD011347961033.aspx)

- PowerPoint Viewer 2007 (http://office.microsoft.com/en-us/downloads/CD102070641033.aspx)

Finally, you can head off all potential compatibility formats by saving any file you create in a format other than the Open XML default. To do so, click the Office button and choose Save As. In the Save As Type box, choose an alternate type that you know will work for all your recipients.

TIP

In previous Office versions, Rich Text Format (RTF) was often your best choice for saving a file created in Word and using it with other programs, especially from software companies other than Microsoft. No more. Nowadays you'll probably find that the easiest way to share data is to use the Web Page option, which is virtually guaranteed to be readable by any other person on any computer, because he can open it directly in his web browser. (Of course, he won't be able to edit the file, but if your goal is to share information, that shouldn't matter.)

Office includes an assortment of file converters to help open and convert files that were originally saved in other popular formats, including those for earlier versions of Office. Normally, Office programs open any file created in a compatible format without requiring any extra work on your part. The file you want to convert might not be visible in the Open dialog box if it ends with an extension that the Office program doesn't recognize. To see all files of a given file type, select the appropriate entry from the File Type drop-down list, which appears just to the right of the Filename box.

TIP

To see all files in the Open dialog box, regardless of their type, choose All Files from the Files of Type drop-down list. Some other distinctions in this drop-down list are less obvious but still useful. For example, selecting Word Documents filters the list to show only files with that file type and the *.docx extension, whereas All Word Documents includes web pages (*.htm, *.html, and *.asp), Word templates (*.dot and *.dotx), and Word 97–2003 documents (.doc), as well as Word documents saved in the Open XML format. Likewise, the All PowerPoint Presentations choice includes any web pages in addition to PowerPoint presentations and shows in old and new formats.

STORING EXTRA DETAILS ABOUT YOUR DOCUMENTS

The NTFS file system in Windows Vista and Windows XP keeps track of a few essential details about each file: its size, when it was created, and when you last modified it, for example. You can see all these standard details when you open Windows Explorer. So what happens when you save a document using an Office program? You get the option to store extra details called *properties*; these categorized bits of information include the author's name, a title and a subject for the file, and comments or keywords you can use to search for documents later. If you're an obsessive organizer, you can open a Custom properties sheet for any document and keep track of more than two dozen built-in categories or add your own. In addition, if you use Windows Vista, you can store freeform details called *tags*, which you can use for sorting, grouping, and searching any Office file type.

Some properties are filled in automatically by Office, but to really take advantage of this feature you need to go a little bit out of your way and fill in extra details for every document with which you work. Why should you bother?

- It helps you find stuff later—When you use the Windows search tools (or those offered by third-party developers), you can search for any property of any Office file. If you've trained yourself to enter details about a project or assignment in the Properties dialog box, it's trivially easy to locate all the files associated with that activity.

- It helps you keep projects organized—In Windows Explorer's Details view, you can add columns for many Office file properties. For example, in a folder filled with Word documents, right-click any column heading to display a list of available columns, and then click Title and Author to add those fields to the display. That way, you can scan through a list and see more than just the filename. (You can do the same with Search results.)

- It lets you reuse data—You can look up file properties in any document and then use those values in fields and in macros. Using fields, you can automatically fill in data within a document based on the values you enter in the Properties dialog box.

→ For more ideas and techniques using VBA, **see** Chapter 26, "Using Macros to Automate Routine Tasks," **p. 721.**

To view and edit the properties of a file currently open in an Office program, click the Office button, choose Prepare, and click Properties. This opens the Document Information Panel, which appears below the Ribbon and above the editing window, as shown in Figure 3.7.

The Document Information Panel displays a limited set of properties that are identical for all types of Office documents, including a free-form Comments box where you can enter notes about a file. To see the full list of available properties, click the Document Properties menu in the top-left corner of the panel and choose Advanced Properties. This opens a dialog box like the one shown in Figure 3.8, which organizes information in five tabs.

TIP

> The Comments field is particularly useful because the comment text appears in the status bar at the bottom of any Windows Explorer window when you select the saved file. It also appears in the ScreenTips that appear when you hover the mouse pointer over a filename in Windows Explorer.

Figure 3.7
The Document Information Panel displays summary information about the current document.

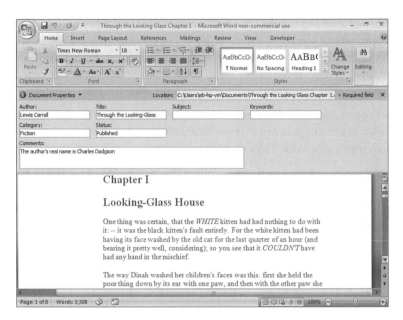

Figure 3.8
Each tab in the Advanced Properties dialog box displays different sorts of information; the Contents tab is the only one that can't be changed directly.

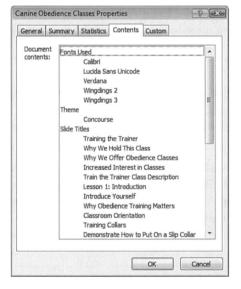

Each of the five tabs contains a different type of information.

- **General**—Basic information from the Windows file system: name, location, size, and so on.

- Summary—Information about the current file and its author, including fields for company name, category, and keywords. The check box at the bottom of this tab allows you to configure Word so it saves a thumbnail of every file of that type.

- Statistics—Details about the size and structure of the file, such as the number of words in a document or the number of slides in a presentation; also displays revision statistics and total editing time. If you rely on these statistics to stay within a specific word count when working on a homework assignment, always inspect them from within the document itself, using the Word Count indicator on the Status bar, to guarantee that the information is up to date.

- Contents—The parts of the file, such as the outline of a Word document, based on heading styles; worksheet titles in an Excel workbook; or slide titles in a PowerPoint presentation. The only way to change the information shown here is to change the contents of the file itself.

- Custom—Twenty-seven built-in fields that are useful when creating business documents, including Client, Document Number, and Date Completed. In addition, you can enter a field of your own creation, such as the name of a class or a teacher. Custom fields can contain text, dates, numbers, or Yes/No information; they can also be linked to Word bookmarks, named Excel ranges, or PowerPoint text selections.

NOTE

> You can inspect most Office file properties by right-clicking a filename in Windows Explorer and choosing Properties from the shortcut menu. Information in this dialog box is arranged differently from what you see within an Office program, and many properties are not available when the file is open for editing.

For simple projects, you might choose to ignore file properties and just give each document a descriptive filename that tells you everything you need to know about the file. For more complicated documents, however, adding file details—including keywords, categories, and free-form comments—can help you quickly find a group of related data files, even months or years after you last worked with them.

To enter additional details about an Office file, you must open the Document Information Panel or the Advanced Properties dialog box, fill in the appropriate fields, and then save the file. To close the Document Information Panel, click the X in its upper-right corner.

DEFAULT DOCUMENT PROPERTIES

If you just click the Save button without entering any additional data, Office programs save only a few document properties along with the saved file. Windows stores the standard file details, of course, including the name and size of the file as well as the date and time the file was modified. All Office programs add your name (using whatever name the program finds on the Popular tab of the Options dialog box) in the Author field. PowerPoint fills in the Title field as well, using the contents of the title slide.

CAUTION

> In previous versions of Word, the opening line of your document automatically appeared in the Title field as soon as you saved the document for the first time, leading to potentially embarrassing revelations if your initial draft started with language that you deleted from the final document. That's changed in Word, but not in PowerPoint. If you change the title of a presentation on the title slide, the Title property remains as it was when you first saved the presentation. The moral? It's always a good idea to check saved properties before you share a document with anyone else.

USING CUSTOM PROPERTIES TO ORGANIZE FILES

Custom properties make it easier to keep track of files in an environment where many people create and share files on a shared source such as a file server. Most of the ready-made fields here are designed for use in an office, where you might use the Client, Status, and Recorded Date fields to track the progress of Word documents. But you can also add your own fields to keep track of specific information you find useful. Figure 3.9 shows a Word document that includes several custom properties.

Figure 3.9
Record additional file properties on the Custom tab; later, use Search tools to find files containing these details.

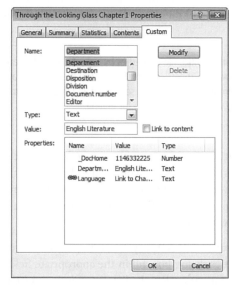

To enter custom criteria for any Office file, follow these steps:

1. Click the Office button, choose Prepare, and click Properties.
2. Click Document Information, Advanced Properties; click the Custom tab to display the dialog box shown previously in Figure 3.9.
3. Choose a field from the Name list. To create a new field, type its name here.

4. Choose one of the available data types from the Type drop-down list.

5. Type the data for the selected field in the Value text box.

CAUTION

> If you specify Number or Date as the data type for a custom field, you must enter the value in a matching format. If you enter dates in a nonstandard format or you include text in a field that should contain only numbers, Office enters the value as text.

6. Click Add. The new entry appears in the Properties list at the bottom of the dialog box.

7. Repeat steps 3–6 for any additional custom fields. To remove an item from the Properties list, select its entry and click Delete. Click OK to close the dialog box and return to the program window.

The Link to Content check box is grayed out and unavailable unless you're working with a Word document that contains bookmarks, an Excel workbook that contains named ranges, or a PowerPoint presentation containing linked text. In any of those cases, you can enter a custom field name, select the Link to Content check box, and then choose the bookmark or named range. In a PowerPoint presentation, you must select the text you want to link to a custom field before opening the Properties dialog box.

USING WINDOWS EXPLORER TO VIEW FILE PROPERTIES

To view any Office file's properties without opening the file itself, open a Windows Explorer window, right-click the file's icon, and then choose Properties. In Windows XP and Windows Vista, you can edit some file properties for Word documents, Excel workbooks, and PowerPoint presentations directly from an Explorer window.

In Windows XP, you can see some Office file properties, such as the author's name, in the info pane along the left side of a Windows Explorer window. In Windows Vista, this information appears in the details pane at the bottom of the window, as shown in Figure 3.10.

You can also see a thumbnail of the file itself in this region. The thumbnail appears for PowerPoint presentations only if you select the Save Preview Picture check box on the Summary tab of the Advanced Properties dialog box. For Word documents and Excel workbooks, this check box turns on thumbnails as a global option. After choosing the Save Thumbnails for All Word Documents (or Excel Workbooks) option, a thumbnail is automatically created when you save a file.

In the details pane of Windows Explorer, you can edit properties directly without opening the file. To increase or decrease the number of properties available in this pane, drag the horizontal divider between the contents pane and the details pane.

Figure 3.10
In Windows Vista, information drawn from an Office file's properties appears in the details pane at the bottom of a Windows Explorer window when the file is selected.

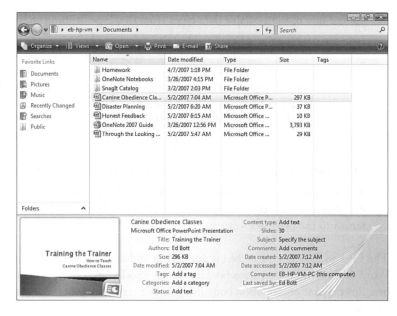

In Windows Vista, you can right-click the icon for an Office file in Windows Explorer and choose Properties. This view consolidates all Office-specific properties onto a single Details tab. If the file is not open in the Office program that created it, you can fill in or change some of these properties directly. Click in the area to the right of the property you want to change as in Figure 3.11 and enter the information.

Figure 3.11
Some properties of an Office file are editable directly from this Properties dialog box.

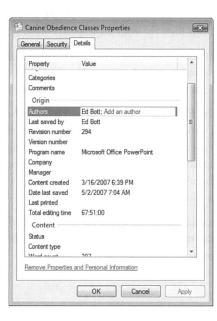

REMOVING PERSONAL INFORMATION FROM OFFICE FILES

Information in saved documents, workbooks, and presentations can sometimes reveal more about you than you like. If you plan to post a document to a public website, you might prefer to have traces of potentially personal information, such as your username, removed. All Office 2007 programs make this task simple. Click the Office button, choose Prepare, and click Inspect Document. Select the Document Properties and Personal Information check box (and any others that you might find useful) and then click Inspect.

If the inspection finds any optional properties saved with the file, you see a report like the one shown in Figure 3.12.

Figure 3.12
If you're concerned about personal information "leaking" out into the world, inspect your documents before publishing them.

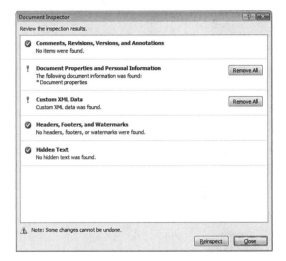

To remove all properties, click the Remove All button. To select individual properties for removal or editing, click Close and then open the Document Information Panel.

SEARCHING FOR OFFICE FILES

The Open dialog box displays a list of all files and subfolders in a single folder. Searching for a specific file can be tedious if the folder is full of files with similar names, or if it's organized into many subfolders. And in some cases you might have no idea where the file you're looking for is stored. So how do you find a file fast?

In Windows Vista, Search tools built into the operating system are available directly from Office common dialog boxes and from Windows Explorer. In Windows XP, similar capabilities are available from the Windows desktop and from Windows Explorer after you install Windows Desktop Search. If you can remember a few scraps of information about the file—part of the name, a date, or even a word or phrase that you remember using in the document—you can probably find it.

For example, you might look in your Homework folder for all files that you created or updated in the past week. You might search for files that include the word *report* and that are not marked as completed. If you're trying to clean out clutter in your Documents folder, you can search for all Office files that were last modified more than six months ago, and then burn them to a CD or move them to an archive folder.

In Office 2007 with Windows Vista, the file search tools are tightly integrated into Office programs. In Open and Save As dialog boxes, a Search box appears in the top-right corner of the dialog box. Enter a word or phrase here to find any file that contains that text in the title, body, or in any property. For a more robust set of search tools, start in Windows Explorer, as we explain in the Extra Credit section at the end of this chapter.

Basic searches in a common dialog box are quick and simple. Start in the location you want to search and enter your search text. You don't need to click a button to continue; Windows Vista performs the search on the fly as you type. Basic searches follow these rules:

- The search looks for any files that contain the search text, whether that text appears in the filename, the body of the file, in keywords or tags, or in file properties.

- Search results also include files that contain forms of the words you entered as search text, such as plurals or alternate verb forms (*looked* instead of *looking*, for example).

- The * is supported as a wildcard character. If you type `gla`, for example, you'll find a file that includes the word *glass* or *glamour*. If you type `lass`, however, you get a match only with words that begin with that string. Adding an asterisk at the beginning—`*lass`— finds files containing *glass* and *class*.

- You can restrict searches to specific fields using advanced search syntax. For example, to find files where you've filled in the Status field, preface your search text with the field name followed by a colon. The search terms `status:published` and `title:alice` return only items where the exact search term appears in the Status or Title field, respectively, and ignores documents containing those words in the body or in other fields.

In Windows Vista (but not in Windows XP), an arrow appears to the right of the column heading in any common dialog box. (If a particular column isn't available, right-click the list of headings and select from the drop-down list to add it to the display.) Choosing check boxes from this list allows you to filter the list of results to make it easier to find files.

WORKING WITH MULTIPLE FILES

In Word, Excel, and PowerPoint, you can open and view or edit more than one file at a time. To open multiple files using the common dialog boxes, follow these steps:

1. Click the Office button and choose Open (or press Ctrl+O) to display the Open dialog box.

2. Hold down the Ctrl key and click to select multiple filenames individually, or select one filename and then hold down Shift and click another filename to select all filenames between those two entries.

3. Click the Open button or press Enter to open all selected files.

To open multiple files from an Explorer window, hold down the Ctrl key and click each icon; then right-click and choose Open.

You can also open any file by dragging its icon from an Explorer window into an Office program window. When you drag an Excel or PowerPoint icon from an Explorer window into an open program window, Office opens the new file in its own window. On the other hand, if you drop a Word icon into an open document window, Word assumes that you want to insert the file at the point where you dropped it. To open the document in a new window instead, drop the icon onto the title bar of the Word program window.

Each data file gets its own button on the Windows taskbar, and you can switch between document windows the same way you switch between programs.

Unfortunately, the techniques for handling multiple document windows are inconsistent among Office programs, which can cause you no end of confusion. Unless you change its default behavior (see the following tip), each Word document exists in its own window; there's no way to display two or more Word documents in the same window, and closing one Word document has no effect on other windows. Using Excel and PowerPoint, on the other hand, you can rearrange two or more document windows within a single program window (choose Arrange All from the Window group on the View tab).

TIP

You can have Word put multiple documents inside its window like the other Office applications do (the so-called multiple document interface, or MDI). With Word in this condition, you can, for example, choose Window, Arrange All to have multiple documents appear inside Word without multiple copies of the menus and toolbars hanging around cluttering up the screen. To do so, click the Office button and choose Word Options; click Advanced in the categories list, scroll down to the Display section, and clear the Show All Windows in the Taskbar check box. Unfortunately, when you do this, individual documents no longer appear in the Windows taskbar.

SETTING UP AUTOMATIC BACKUP AND RECOVERY OPTIONS

No roller coaster can compete with the sinking feeling you get when an Office program hangs, crashes, or simply disappears. With most programs, you can kiss your unsaved work goodbye. But Office 2007, like its predecessors, comes with "air bags" designed to make crashes less frequent, to make them less devastating when they do occur, and to increase your chances of recovering a document when Office does crash.

If an Office program crashes while you're working on an open file, chances are good that you'll be presented with the Office Document Recovery task pane (see Figure 3.13) when you restart the program. Documents that are listed as [Original] probably aren't as up-to-date as those marked [Autosaved].

Figure 3.13
Office's Document Recovery task pane appears on the left side of the screen.

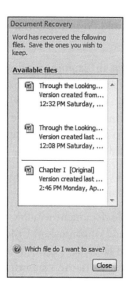

Every item that was automatically saved during Automatic Recovery gets its own entry in the Document Recovery task pane. In some cases, the recovery procedure actually repairs damage caused by file corruption. Click any entry to open it, examine its contents, and decide whether to save or discard it. If you're certain you know what to do with the item, click the arrow to the right of the item and choose whether to save it, view any repairs, or delete it. After you finish reviewing all recovered documents, close the Document Recovery task pane.

NOTE

> Office 2003 included a tool called the Microsoft Office Application Recovery program, which you were supposed to remember to run if an Office program stopped responding. Only a tiny percentage of people even knew it existed, and even fewer remembered to use it when it was needed. So, in Office 2007 the document recovery feature runs automatically whenever Office determines that a program has hung up.

It is often worthwhile to save several recovered documents and compare the versions to see which (if any) have changes you want to save. To do so, click the down arrow to the right of the [Autosaved] filename and choose Save As.

TIP

> Automatic Backup and Recovery–the "air bags for Office"–isn't foolproof. Sometimes it works; sometimes it doesn't. It's definitely not a substitute for saving your work regularly and keeping backup copies in a safe place. For projects that are especially important, burn your backups to a CD or copy them to a USB flash drive for extra protection.

TROUBLESHOOTING

PUTTING TEMPLATES IN THEIR PLACE

I created a group of templates and saved them along with the standard Office templates in the `%programfiles%\Microsoft Office\Templates\1033` *folder. But when I choose File, New, none of my custom templates are visible.*

Microsoft designed the folder that stores system templates so users cannot add templates to it. In Windows Vista, in fact, you'll be prohibited from saving files here by default file permissions. Instead, you should save your templates to the default User Templates location. The safest way to save templates to this location is one at a time. If you choose Template from the Files of Type list in the Save As dialog box, all Office programs will save your work to the correct location. If you want to add a large number of files to this location, open Word and choose Tools, Options; then click the File Locations tab and verify the User Templates location.

EXTRA CREDIT: FIND FILES FASTER WITH DESKTOP SEARCH TOOLS

You don't need to open an Office program to find a missing document. Desktop search utilities index the entire contents of your hard drive, including email messages, Office documents, music files, digital photos, and just about anything else. By entering a search term or two, you can display all matching documents and quickly zero in on the one you need.

Windows Vista includes an exceptionally well-designed and integrated search capability that is available within Office and practically everywhere within Windows. With Windows XP, you'll need to install a separate program to add this capability. Our two favorite programs in this category are both free and easy to install and use—Copernic Desktop Search (http://www.copernic.com) and Windows Desktop Search, which is included with the MSN Search Toolbar (http://desktop.msn.com/) and is based on the same program code as the search tools in Windows Vista.

One of the best features of Windows Vista's integrated Desktop Search is its capability to save searches based on multiple criteria. For example, you can search an entire folder and all its subfolders for Word documents that were saved since the beginning of last week and that contain the word *homework*. After running that search, you save it and then open the Searches folder to rerun it any time. Here's how:

1. Open your Documents folder in Windows Explorer and type *homework* in the Search box.

2. Click the arrow to the right of the Type heading and select the Microsoft Office Word Document check box. (If you also have documents saved in other Word formats, select those check boxes as well.)

3. Click the arrow to the right of the Date Modified heading and select Earlier This Week and Last Week from the calendar control.

You now have a filtered list that meets all your criteria. As the final step in the process, click the Save Search button on the Windows Explorer Command Bar and give your search a name, such as Recent Homework.

Now, any time you want to retrieve documents that match these criteria, click the Searches shortcut in the Favorite Links pane and then click the shortcut for your saved search.

3

CHAPTER 4

ENTERING, EDITING, AND FORMATTING TEXT

In this chapter

ENTERING TEXT: MORE THAN JUST TYPING

How hard can it be to enter text in an Office document? You click, you type. As long as your fingers hit the right keys, everything just happens, right? Well, not exactly. What happens when you need to enter a character that isn't on the keyboard: a currency symbol such as ¥, perhaps, or a Greek character such as Π?

In fact, Office 2007 contains full support for the Unicode standard, a universally recognized character set containing tens of thousands of letters, ideographs, and other symbols, which spans the majority of all written languages. If the operating system you are using supports the characters used in a specific language, those characters are available in Office. You won't find all those characters on your 102-key keyboard, of course, but they're only a few taps and clicks away, after you learn the secrets.

INSERTING SYMBOLS AND SPECIAL CHARACTERS

If you're writing a paper about world currencies, how do you enter the symbols associated with currencies other than your own? When you're citing sources written in a foreign language, how do you enter accented characters? Office supports three relatively easy methods to place a single symbol or other special character in an Office document:

- Your first stop should be the Symbol dialog box, which you open by clicking Symbol on the Insert tab. If you don't see the symbol you want in the gallery that drops down, click More Symbols to display the dialog box shown in Figure 4.1. There you'll find a comprehensive and easy-to-use list of every character available in normal or decorative fonts. The magnified preview makes it easy to select the correct symbol.

Figure 4.1
The frequently overlooked Subset list for Insert Symbol's normal text option offers quick access to different groups of characters.

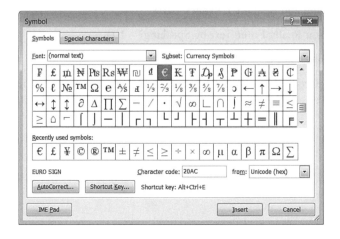

TIP

When you click a symbol, a short description of the character (as well as its character code) appears at the bottom of the Symbol dialog box. Most characters include a four-digit keyboard shortcut. To use the shortcut, hold down the Alt key while you type the four digits on the numeric keypad. When you release the Alt key, the symbol appears. Note that the numbers on the top row of the keyboard do not work for these shortcuts. You can use these shortcuts in any Windows program that handles text.

NOTE

After you insert a character, the Symbol dialog box remains open so you can insert additional characters, if necessary. To dismiss this dialog box, press Esc or click Close (X) or Cancel.

- The Special Characters tab in the Symbol dialog box (see Figure 4.2) gives you quick access to the most common punctuation characters (also known as *special characters*). The tab is only available in Word and Excel. If you are tired of scrolling through the Symbol dialog box's detailed lists, this is the place to turn. The shortcut-key reminders are visible in Word only.

Figure 4.2
The Special Characters tab includes only a small subset of the characters listed on the Symbols tab, but the ones that are there are easier to find.

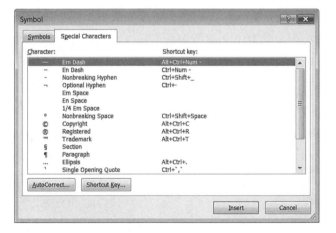

- If you know that you're going to be using a specific symbol or special character repeatedly, set up an AutoCorrect entry for it. For example, if you use the ¥ (Japanese Yen) symbol frequently, tell Office to AutoCorrect the two characters Y= to ¥. To set up AutoCorrect replacements in Word, click the AutoCorrect button in the Symbol dialog box. To create AutoCorrect items in Excel or PowerPoint, click the Microsoft Office button, choose Excel Options (or PowerPoint Options), click Proofing in the left pane of the Options dialog box, and then click AutoCorrect Options. To get to the AutoCorrect dialog box in OneNote, choose Tools, AutoCorrect Options. AutoCorrect entries that you set up in one Office program will also work in the others.

→ To learn more about saving and reusing text, **see** "Using AutoCorrect to Type Faster," **p. 90.**

NOTE

> To find various dashes, "curly" quotes, daggers, ellipses, and many more common marks quickly, open the Symbol dialog box and choose General Punctuation from the Subset list on the Symbols tab.

When it comes to inserting symbols into your documents, you have many more choices. For example, you can use the Windows Character Map applet (Charmap.exe). In Word and Excel, you can use the Symbol dialog box. In Word (but not Excel), you can take advantage of a long list of Math AutoCorrect options. (This is a great new feature in Word 2007. To use it, click the Math AutoCorrect tab in the AutoCorrect Options dialog box. Be sure to select Use Math AutoCorrect Rules Outside of Math Regions if you want these replacements to be available anywhere in your Word documents.) You can also choose from an endless assortment of keyboard macro and Clipboard management utilities designed for general-purpose use with Windows.

ENTERING ACCENTED AND INTERNATIONAL CHARACTERS

If you use the U.S. English version of Office 2007 and you have only occasional need for an accented, inflected, or otherwise altered character common in European languages, Word and OneNote recognize the shortcuts in Table 4.1.

TABLE 4.1   WORD AND ONENOTE'S ACCENTED CHARACTER SHORTCUTS

To Type Any of These Accented Characters	First, Press This Key Command	Then Type the Desired Letter
ÀàÈèÌìÒòÙù	Ctrl+`	AaEeIiOoUu
ÁáÉéÍíÓóÚúÝý	Ctrl+'	AaDdEeIiOoUuYy
ÂâÊêÎî'ôÛû	Ctrl+Shift+^	AaEeIiOoUu
ÄäËëÏïÖöÜüŸÿ	Ctrl+Shift+:	AaEeIiOoUuYy
ÃãÑñÕõ	Ctrl+Shift+~	AaNnOo
ÆæŒœ§	Ctrl+Shift+&	AaOos
Çç	Ctrl+,	Cc
Åå	Ctrl+Shift+@	Aa
Øø	Ctrl+/	Oo

To enter an inverted question mark or exclamation point (¿, ¡) for use with Spanish text, press Alt+Ctrl+Shift+? or Alt+Ctrl+Shift+!. These two shortcuts work in Word only.

ENTERING TEXT IN ANOTHER LANGUAGE

Office interprets the keys on your keyboard according to the settings you've established in Windows. To see what language layouts are available, or to add new ones, open Control Panel and click Change Keyboards or Other Input Methods (if you're having trouble finding it in Windows Vista, type **keyb** in Control Panel's Search box). On the Keyboards and Languages tab of the Regional and Language Options dialog box, click the Change Keyboards button. To add new language layouts, click Add and select items in the list that appears (see Figure 4.3). When you click OK or Apply, the languages you have selected become available. Before you leave the dialog box, though, be sure that the language you use most often is correctly identified in the Default Input Language drop-down. (This is particularly important if you occasionally use a right-to-left language but you work primarily in English.)

Figure 4.3
Office 2007 supports a wide variety of languages, even if you have only the U.S. English version.

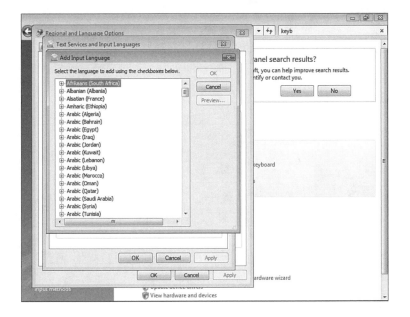

If you have set up your system to use more than one language, you can switch between languages by means of the Language Bar. Normally, this miniature toolbar is docked at the right side of the taskbar. Available languages are identified by two-letter codes (EN for English, for example, or HI for Hindi), and clicking the current two-letter code pops up a list of all the languages you've made available, allowing you to switch with a click of the mouse. If you prefer, you can make the Language Bar float on your desktop. To do this (or to re-dock the Language Bar), click the Language Bar tab in the Text Services and Input Languages dialog box.

TIP

> It's easy to set up a keyboard shortcut that changes languages. On the Keyboard applet's Language or Input Locales tab, use the Switch Languages (or locales) option. In Windows XP, you'll need to click Key Settings and then click the Change Key Sequence button in the Advanced Key Settings dialog box.

When you switch keyboards, Word automatically switches fonts to those that are designed for the language and sets the proofing language for spell checking and grammar checking.

Before you can edit text in those other languages, you need to have Office install the features demanded by that particular language. To do so, click Start, All Programs, Microsoft Office, Microsoft Office Tools, Microsoft Office 2007 Language Settings. On the Enabled Editing Languages tab (see Figure 4.4), select the languages you want Office to recognize.

Figure 4.4
Use the Editing Languages tab to enable editing features within a new language added to Word.

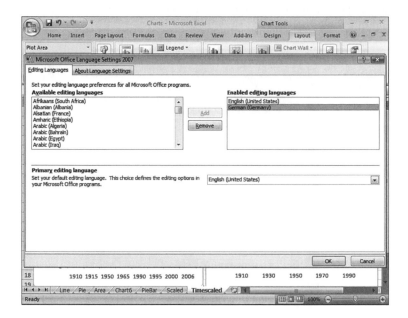

SELECTING TEXT

Text selection is one of the most fundamental Office activities, but the specific techniques used in each program vary widely. In fact, mastering the different shortcuts each Office application uses to handle text selection is a key step on the road to becoming an Office master.

When you select text with a mouse, the following shortcuts apply:

- Double-clicking a word selects the word in all Office applications. In the text-centered Office programs—Word, OneNote, and PowerPoint—double-clicking also selects the word's trailing space(s), if any; in Excel, it does not. That can be somewhat confusing when switching between programs.

- Triple-clicking selects an entire paragraph in Word, OneNote, and PowerPoint. Triple-clicking in Excel does not select an entire cell.

- In Word, moving the mouse pointer to the left margin changes it from an I-beam insertion point to an arrow that points up and to the right. When you see this pointer, you can click once to select the current line, twice to select the paragraph, or three times to select the entire document.

- In Word and PowerPoint (but not Excel or OneNote), the selection automatically extends to include entire words when you click and drag over more than one word. You can turn this feature off by clicking the Microsoft Office button, choosing Word Options (or PowerPoint Options), clicking Advanced in the left pane, and clearing the box marked When Selecting, Automatically Select Entire Word.

→ To learn more ways you can customize Word, **see** "Customizing the Word Interface," **p. 196**

- When working with text boxes in the drawing layer, Office takes on the clicking conventions of the underlying application: triple-clicking in a paragraph in an Excel text box does nothing, but the same action in Word or PowerPoint selects the entire paragraph.

→ For an explanation of how the drawing layer works, **see** "Working with the Drawing Layer," **p. 109.**

Many advanced Word users—especially proficient typists—prefer to use the keyboard to select characters and words. If you work with lots of documents that use special characters, memorizing a few simple commands can help you avoid the mouse and get to text on the screen much more quickly. Keyboard-selection techniques stay fairly uniform throughout Office (see Table 4.2).

TABLE 4.2   KEYBOARD SELECTIONS VALID IN ALL OFFICE PROGRAMS

To Select	Press
Next character to right	Shift+Right Arrow
Next character to left	Shift+Left Arrow
To end of word	Ctrl+Shift+Right Arrow
To beginning of word	Ctrl+Shift+Left Arrow
To end of line	Shift+End
To beginning of line	Shift+Home
Entire document	Ctrl+A

In addition, Word has two important shortcuts that you will want to memorize (see Table 4.3). These shortcuts come in handy when you're trying to select blocks of text in large documents, "from this point to the beginning" or "from this point to the end." No menu or toolbar button equivalents exist for either.

TABLE 4.3 KEYBOARD SELECTIONS VALID ONLY IN WORD

To Select	Press
To end of document	Ctrl+Shift+End
To beginning of document	Ctrl+Shift+Home

In Word, you can select noncontiguous characters—that is, characters that are not next to each other—by holding down the Ctrl and Shift keys simultaneously as you make your selections. (If you hold down Ctrl when you click, your initial selection extends to a complete sentence.) In Excel you can select noncontiguous cells the same way. In PowerPoint, you're allowed to select noncontiguous slides. But you can't select noncontiguous text in Excel or PowerPoint.

FINDING AND REPLACING TEXT

The quickest way to find or replace text in any Office application is to press Ctrl+F. This keyboard shortcut displays the Find and Replace dialog box (see Figure 4.5 for Word's version) in Word, Excel, or PowerPoint. OneNote does not include Replace capability, so pressing Ctrl+F takes you to a search box instead of a Find and Replace dialog box.

Figure 4.5
Word provides an extensive set of search options.

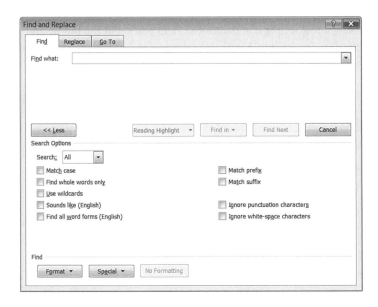

If you don't favor keyboard shortcuts, you can get to the appropriate dialog box in Word, PowerPoint, or Excel by clicking the Home tab and then clicking Find (in the Editing group, at the right side of the Ribbon). To get to the Search box in OneNote, choose Edit, Find. (Or just click the box; it's in the upper-right corner of the note-taking region.)

To find a particular text string, do the following after you're in the Find and Replace dialog box:

1. Type the text you want to locate in the Find What box.

2. Set up the criteria for your search. Depending on which Office application you are using, the process of setting up your search criteria will vary:

    • In Word, you can click the More button to choose whether you want to search Up (toward the beginning of the document) or Down (toward the end). In Excel (see Figure 4.6) or PowerPoint, you have no choice as to direction—the first Find uncovers the first occurrence of the string; subsequent Find Next selections move to later occurrences.

Figure 4.6
Excel's Find and Replace is remarkably different from Word's.

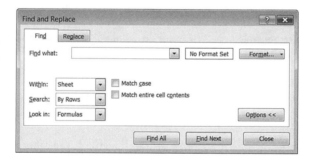

4

    • Excel enables you to choose whether you want to search *row-major* ("Search by Rows" going across the current row before dropping down to the next one) or *column-major* ("Search by Columns" going down the current column before looking at the next one to the right). Make your choice in the Search box. Excel also enables you to look at formulas or values (that is, formula results). If you have a cell that contains the formula =SUM(A1:B3), for example, searching the formulas for B3 results in a hit, whereas searching the values doesn't.

NOTE

> Excel allows you to easily search for text in comments. This feature can come in handy if you're scanning for comments from a specific individual or those that apply to a given topic. To do so, select Comments in the Look In box.

    • All the Office programs allow you to specify that you want to Match Case (as in the PowerPoint dialog box shown in Figure 4.7). With this check box selected, the capitalization shown in the Find What text box must match the capitalization of the text in the document precisely to get a hit.

Figure 4.7
PowerPoint's Find dialog box offers only these simple functions.

- Using the Find dialog box in Word and PowerPoint, you can select a check box that restricts the search to Find Whole Words Only. When this option is enabled, the text in the Find What field must appear in the document preceded and followed by a space or punctuation mark: `beast`, for example, will match *beast* but not *beasts*. Excel has a comparable check box that limits hits to cells where the entire cell's contents match the text in the Find What box.

3. With the find criteria established the way you want, click Find Next and the application selects the next occurrence of the text.

Word, Excel, and OneNote accept wildcards:

- `*` matches one or more letters. For example, `s*ap` will turn up hits on *snap* or *strap*, but not on *sap*.

- `?` matches one single letter. For example, `b?t` will match *bit* or *bat*, but not *boot*.

- In Excel only, the tilde character (~) followed by a ~, ?, or * matches ~, ?, or *. So `hop~*` matches `hop*`, but not `hop?` or `hope`, and `tr~?p` matches `tr?p` but not `tr*p`, `tr~p`, or `trip`.

Word has an enormous number of additional search features; the other Office applications pale in comparison.

→ To learn more about Word's powerful search features, **see** "Finding and Replacing Text and Other Parts of a Document," **p. 182.**

USING AUTOCORRECT TO TYPE FASTER

You see the result of AutoCorrect when you type a word such as *teh* and Word instantly transforms it into *the*. Don't take AutoCorrect's name too literally. Yes, it's true that AutoCorrect watches over you, correcting typos in Word or Excel—for example, type ***isn;t*** and AutoCorrect converts it to *isn't*. But it does much more:

- AutoCorrect works in all four programs in Office Home and Student 2007: Word, Excel, PowerPoint, and OneNote. Customized AutoCorrect entries you create in one program work in all the others (with one exception discussed later in this section); if you tell Word to change *mouses* into *mice*, the correction applies in all other Office applications.

- You can create your own AutoCorrect entries to supercharge your typing—say, changing your shorthand *tpfp* into *the Party of the First Part* or *otoh* into *on the other hand*.

- If you commonly work with boilerplate text, AutoCorrect can handle it for you. Do you have a description of the history and goals of your local civic organization that you put at the end of letters and email messages to potential new members? Set up a code you can remember—such as `history1`—so it automatically expands on demand. An AutoCorrect entry can consist of paragraphs, even pages, of text, footnotes, and the like.

- In Word, AutoCorrect entries can include graphics. This is handy if you frequently reuse the same graphic image. For example, you might want to scan your signature and turn it into an AutoCorrect entry called `mysig`. Then, wherever you type **`mysig`**, your scanned signature appears.

- AutoCorrect can even help you with odd capitalization. For example, if you're preparing a presentation about a company called ZapItInc, you might have trouble getting the caps right when you type the company name. Set up an AutoCorrect entry for `zapitinc` (all lowercase) and have it corrected to *ZapItInc*. Then every time you type **`zapitinc`**— or **`Zapitinc`**, **`ZapItinc`**, **`ZapitInc`**, or even **`zApitiNc`**—AutoCorrect automatically changes the word to *ZapItInc*.

Word has a similar feature, called AutoText, which can be more appropriate than AutoCorrect in certain situations.

→ To learn when you should use AutoText instead of AutoCorrect, **see** "Entering Text and Graphics Automatically with AutoText and AutoCorrect," **p. 178.**

TIP

> In all Office programs except Excel, a Smart Tag is available whenever AutoCorrect changes something you've typed. The Smart Tag enables you to undo the change that was just made, undo all subsequent changes of the same kind, or visit the AutoCorrect Options dialog box. You don't have to use the Smart Tag menu immediately. You can go on typing or editing your document and then return later to an item that was changed by AutoCorrect; the Smart Tag will still be available.

HOW AUTOCORRECT WORKS

The AutoCorrect engine watches as you type. Whenever you press the spacebar, type a punctuation mark, or press Enter, this Office component looks to see whether the preceding characters match an entry in your AutoCorrect list. (Because a closing parenthesis is a punctuation mark, AutoCorrect entries that respond to this character—such as (c), which AutoCorrect changes to a copyright sign—are activated immediately, even before you press the spacebar.) If AutoCorrect finds a match, it replaces the old text with the contents of the AutoCorrect entry.

We noted this earlier in the chapter, but it bears repeating here: To view the list of AutoCorrect items and adjust options in Word, Excel, or PowerPoint, click the Microsoft Office button, click *<program_name>* Options, click Proofing in the left pane of the Options dialog box, and then click AutoCorrect Options. To get to the AutoCorrect dialog box in OneNote, choose Tools, AutoCorrect Options.

In a default installation, the AutoCorrect list includes a large collection of commonly mis-spelled words and phrases. Figure 4.8 shows an AutoCorrect entry that changes *accomodate* to *accommodate*. Because of this entry, if you ever type **accomodate** followed by a space, punctua-tion mark, or paragraph mark, the misspelling will automatically be corrected.

Figure 4.8
The AutoCorrect dia-log box includes a ready-made list of commonly mistyped words and phrases.

The entry must match precisely. Using the default AutoCorrect list shown in Figure 4.8, Word would not change *accomodated* to its correct spelling. If you want plural and tense vari-ants corrected, you can expand the AutoCorrect list to include such items.

If AutoCorrect changes a word and you want the original back, click to position the inser-tion point within the changed word. Then let the mouse pointer hover over the underline beneath the changed word, click the lightning bolt icon to reveal the action menu, and choose the Change Back option to undo the correction. Alternatively—and much more quickly—you can immediately press Ctrl+Z or click the Undo button (look for it on the Quick Access toolbar). Either of these actions will reverse the change made by AutoCorrect and restore what you typed to its original state. The same action menu enables you to quickly remove an entry from the AutoCorrect Options list or stop AutoCorrect from per-forming a certain type of correction.

SETTING AUTOCORRECT OPTIONS

In addition to replacing one string of text with another, Office has four additional AutoCorrect settings:

■ When you select the Correct TWo INitial CApitals check box, AutoCorrect examines each word you type in an Office program; if it detects a word that starts with two consecutive capitals and that word appears in the dictionary, Office changes the second letter to lowercase. For example, if you miscapitalize **AHead**, Word changes it to *Ahead*; but if you type **JScript** or **IDs**, Word leaves it alone. You might want to override AutoCorrect on certain two-capital combinations. To do so, click the Exceptions button and add the entry manually.

You can bypass this dialog box and automatically add words that begin with two capital letters to the Exceptions list by immediately undoing the change. If you're writing a paper about a new club whose name is the GOphers, for example, and Word or PowerPoint "corrects" the entry to *Gophers*, click the AutoCorrect Smart Tag for the changed text and choose Stop Automatically Correcting GOphers from the action menu. (You can also press Ctrl+Z in any application to undo the change.) Office restores the second capital letter and adds the word to the Exceptions list in one operation. To disable this feature, click the Exceptions button on the AutoCorrect dialog box and clear the Automatically Add Words to List check box.

■ The Capitalize First Letter of Sentence box is built around the belief that Office can recognize when you're starting a new sentence. That's not an easy task. If this setting causes Office to make capitalization mistakes more frequently than you like, turn it off. Office generally assumes that you're about to start a new sentence when it detects the presence of a period followed by a space, but tempers that judgment by a lengthy list of exceptions, including *approx. and corp.*, which rarely signal the end of a sentence (see Figure 4.9).

Figure 4.9
A period usually signals the end of a sentence, but not when it follows one of these words.

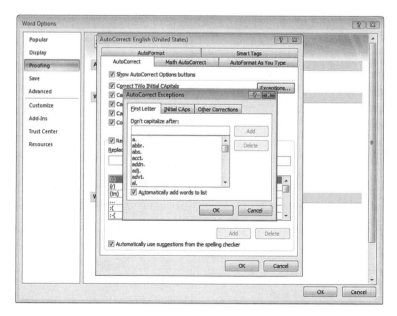

- The Capitalize Names of Days check box works as you would expect.

- The Correct Accidental Usage of cAPS LOCK Key check box, however, comes into play only when you type one lowercase letter, followed by pushing the Caps Lock key, and then continue typing. With this box checked, Office turns the first character into a capital, makes the other characters lowercase, and turns off the Caps Lock function.

Word offers two more AutoCorrect check boxes. The first, Capitalize First Letter of Table Cells, works much like the Capitalize First Letter of Sentences setting. The second option, Automatically Use Suggestions from the Spelling Checker, configures Word to consult the spelling checker if the usual AutoCorrect lookup doesn't find the word in question in the AutoCorrect list. If the spelling checker comes back with one—and only one—suggested correct spelling, the word you typed is replaced with the one offered by the spell checker.

CAUTION

> You could have an embarrassing mistake if Word substitutes the absolute wrong word for a misspelled one. However, Word's automatic substitution routines don't seem to generate vulgar expressions. In addition, AutoCorrect will not change proper nouns and other capitalized words (so, for example, if you type `Mr. Turkye`, it remains Turkye, and is not AutoCorrected to Turkey).

→ To learn more about Word's spelling checker, **see** "Checking Spelling and Grammar," **p. 188.**

If you type `tiime`, and there's no entry for *tiime* in the AutoCorrect list, Word consults the spelling checker. The spelling checker offers only one correct spelling—*time*—so, with this box checked, *tiime* is replaced by *time*.

CUSTOMIZING THE AUTOCORRECT LISTS

Office maintains three AutoCorrect lists. The first includes all unformatted Word AutoCorrect entries, plus all entries for the other Office applications. The second is a list of Math AutoCorrect options. These convert text expressions, such as \approx, to mathematical symbols, such as ≈. The Math AutoCorrect list operates only in Word, and—by default—only in math contexts (such as equations). If you want Word to use them in general text as well, select the check box labeled Use Math AutoCorrect Rules Outside of Math Regions, on the Math AutoCorrect tab of the AutoCorrect dialog box (see Figure 4.10). The third AutoCorrect list exclusively handles formatted entries available in Word.

Use a formatted AutoCorrect entry whenever it's important that formatting be applied in the replaced text. For example, if you're writing a paper for your civics class and you always want the term *Congressional Record* to appear in italic text, you might set up a formatted AutoCorrect entry called cr that always produces *Congressional Record* (see Figure 4.11).

Figure 4.10
Word's Math
AutoCorrect rules
normally apply only
in mathematical con-
texts.

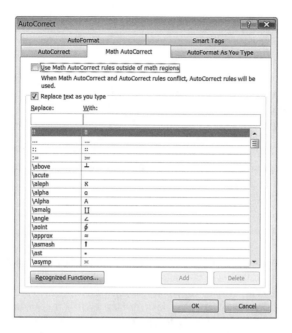

Figure 4.11
Formatted
AutoCorrect entries
are available only in
Word.

Adding your own formatted entries to the AutoCorrect list is easy:

1. Select the text you want AutoCorrect to produce. Apply whatever formatting you want.

2. Open the AutoCorrect Options dialog box. The text you've selected appears in the With box. Click the Formatted Text radio button.

3. Type the text you want to trigger an AutoCorrect replacement in the Replace box. In Figure 4.11, we instructed Office to replace cr with *Congressional Record*.

4. Click Add.

Formatted AutoCorrect entries apply only to Word. If you add the formatted cr entry shown earlier in Figure 4.11 and then type **cr** in Excel or PowerPoint, nothing happens. The text *cr* is AutoCorrected only in Word.

To add an unformatted AutoCorrect entry, click the Microsoft Office button, choose Word Options (or the corresponding command for a different Office program), click Proofing in the left pane, and then click AutoCorrect Options. In the AutoCorrect dialog box, type the entry name in the Replace box and the replacement text in the With box. Click Add.

CAUTION

> When Word searches for AutoCorrect entries, it looks for formatted entries first. Building on the previous example, if you create a formatted entry for cr in Word and then create an unformatted (plain text) entry for cr in another program, typing cr in Word will bring up the formatted entry, but typing cr in Excel or PowerPoint will bring up the unformatted (plain text) entry. To make things even more confusing, only the unformatted entry will show in the Word AutoCorrect list, although the formatted entry will still be used. If you can't make sense of a specific AutoCorrect entry, your best bet is to first remove the unformatted entry from Excel or PowerPoint, then remove the entry from Word, and start over.

You can also add AutoCorrect entries while performing a spell check. Right-click a word with a red squiggly underline, choose AutoCorrect, and select the correct spelling. Office corrects the misspelling and adds a matching AutoCorrect entry automatically.

Deleting AutoCorrect entries is as easy as adding them. Open the AutoCorrect dialog box, select the entry you want to remove, and click Delete.

If you type the name of the entry you want to delete in the Replace box, Office jumps immediately to that part of the list.

Word fields can appear in AutoCorrect entries, but only as formatted text. If you switch to plain text when creating an AutoCorrect entry that contains a field, Word converts the field to its field result before storing the entry.

Unformatted AutoCorrect entries are stored in a file that includes the extension .acl in the %appdata%\Microsoft\Office folder. In a default U.S. English installation, this file is called MSO1033.acl. The file can be moved from one computer to another along with other Office personal information. Formatted AutoCorrect entries are stored in Word's global template, Normal.dot.

Also consider adding words you commonly type that have odd punctuation—Yahoo! comes to mind—so the capitalizing routine will operate properly. You might have other abbreviations that appear frequently in your writing: tb. or exec., perhaps. To add these exceptions, go to the AutoCorrect dialog box and click the Exceptions button. Type **Yahoo!** and click Add. Type **tb.** and click Add again; type **exec.** and click Add one last time.

The AutoCorrect list is filled with hundreds of entries—not all of which might be to your liking. Consider removing the ones you find obtrusive. For example:

- Several combinations of colons, semicolons, dashes, lines, and parentheses are automatically turned into smiley faces. If you don't want smiley faces to appear in your documents, delete those entries from the AutoCorrect list. They're all near the beginning of the list.

- If you commonly create numbered lists by hand and use (a), (b), (c), and so on within the numbers, you'll quickly discover that (c) is automatically turned into a copyright symbol. To override that behavior, use the lightning bolt icon that appears when you hover over the copyright symbol and choose Stop Automatically Correcting "(c)".

- Another AutoCorrect entry turns a standalone lowercase *i* into an uppercase *I*. That, too, can be problematic if you create numbered lists by hand. To get around it, click the AutoCorrect Smart Tag (the lightning bolt icon) and use the action menu.

- One AutoCorrect entry changes three consecutive periods (. . .) into an ellipsis. The ellipsis is a single character that looks like three periods, squished close together (…). As long as your documents are destined to be used only by other Office programs, the ellipses pose no problem. But when you copy the text into an email message, for example, or post the document on the Web, the ellipsis character can turn into something totally inscrutable. To keep Office from changing three periods to an ellipsis, use the AutoCorrect action menu.

ADVANCED AUTOCORRECT TECHNIQUES

Any situation that involves boilerplate text is a likely candidate for AutoCorrect. If you commonly construct letters that contain five or six paragraphs selected from a pool of many dozens—or hundreds— of paragraphs, you can set up AutoCorrect entries for each of the possible paragraphs and, based on a printed list that's memorized or easily accessible, construct the letter rapidly.

In fact, by using {fillin} fields, you can prompt for specific pieces of text to further customize the boilerplate text.

→ To learn more about creating user input forms using Word fields, **see** "Prompting for Input," **p. 344.**

This feature is handy if you're starting several classes in which you're required to produce weekly papers that use standard elements, such as a title page, an abstract, and a bibliography.

4

You can set up each of these elements as an AutoCorrect entry with custom text that includes the class and teacher name—*title101, abstract101,* and *biblio101,* for example; then you can "type" that entire letter with three simple lines:

```
title101

abstract101

biblio101
```

In addition, if you set up the {fillin} field at the indicated location in the first paragraph, when you type title101, Word prompts you for the date of the letter. You type in the date and it appears in place of the {fillin} field.

By customizing these elements for different classes and changing the AutoCorrect entry names to match, you can make the process of getting started with a paper that much easier. These techniques are also useful in business, for writing form letters and other documents that use mix-and-match blocks of text.

AutoCorrect Do's and Don'ts

The most common problem with AutoCorrect entries arises when you create an entry that has unexpected side effects. For example, while working on a paper for a civics class you might create an entry called *econ* that AutoCorrects to *Council of Economic Advisors*. Then, a few days or weeks later, you might be writing a letter to a friend and include this line:

```
I'm thinking of signing up for Econ 101...
```

and the AutoCorrect entry kicks in:

```
I'm thinking of signing up for Council of Economic Advisors 101...
```

 If you find it difficult to locate some AutoCorrect entries, see "Finding Obscure AutoCorrect Entries" in the "Troubleshooting" section at the end of this chapter.

To minimize the chances for side effects like these, many Office experts use punctuation marks in their AutoCorrect entries. You might be tempted to set up an AutoCorrect entry called usr, for example, to "correct" into United Steel & Resources, Inc. Unfortunately, every time your finger slips on the keyboard and you misspell *use* as *usr*, AutoCorrect kicks in and you get gibberish. If you define the entry as usr., on the other hand—note the trailing period—you can type the entry almost as quickly as usr, and the chance for accidental side effects is greatly reduced.

Using and Managing Fonts

The first law of typography: Don't use more than three different fonts (typefaces) in any single document—one for the body text, one for headings, and at most one more for the masthead or main titles. Using these guidelines, you might settle on Garamond for body text, Arial for headings, and Verdana for the title page.

The second law of typography: Nobody follows the first law.

Unless you have a compelling reason to flout convention, most business letters and memos use at most two fonts: one font for the logo, return address, or any other fixed text at the top and bottom of the first sheet; and a second font for all the rest. Most teachers insist on having papers printed out in a standard format designed for readability, not good looks. In the United States, it's customary to use a *serif* font as the main font (for body text), and *sans serif* fonts are commonly used for heading text; in Europe, sans serif is almost as common as a body font, with serif fonts frequently used in headings.

TIP

> A serif font, such as Times New Roman, has curlicues on the ends of the letters, some-times referred to as feet; a sans serif font, such as Arial, has straight ends.
>
> For example
>
> This is Serif.
>
> This is Sans Serif.
>
> You can mix and match as you like, of course, but be aware that each font you add to a document increases the likelihood that typography will obscure, not enhance, your mes-sage. The sure sign of an amateur document designer is a wild mixture of fonts, of vary-ing sizes, with *lots* of italic and **even more** bold italic.

When you include the fonts that come with Windows and the fonts included with different Office programs, you have more than 150 fonts at your disposal. Third-party programs add still more fonts, sometimes by the hundreds. That's enough to overwhelm anyone who isn't a design expert.

4

COMMON FORMATTING OPTIONS

The three presentation-oriented programs in your Office suite—Word, Excel, and PowerPoint—provide a great assortment of tools for creating attractively formatted, high-impact documents. New in this version of Office are *themes*—named collections of fonts, colors, and backgrounds that give your documents a consistent, professionally designed appearance. Twenty themes are available out of the box, and you can download more from the Office Online website or create your own to augment the standard set. The themes not only make your Word, PowerPoint, or Excel documents internally consistent and pleasing (because the same themes are available in all three programs), they also give you a way to create a consistent look when creating groups of documents with different Office programs.

Themes are not the only way to create attractive documents, of course. Other advanced tools include styles and templates. For details about using all of these features, see Chapter 10, "Mastering Styles, Templates, and Themes."

Naturally, you can also format words, paragraphs, spreadsheet cells, and so on, individually, without depending on styles, templates, and themes. The methods you use to do this vary somewhat between Office applications.

CHANGING CHARACTER ATTRIBUTES

To change character formatting, follow these steps:

1. In all Office programs, select the characters you want to change. In Word, OneNote, or PowerPoint, if you don't make a selection, your changes apply to the entire word in which the insertion point is located.

2. In Word, PowerPoint, or Excel, you can get to the Font dialog box by clicking the Home tab on the Ribbon, and then clicking the button at the lower-right corner of the Font group (see Figure 4.12). (In Word and PowerPoint, this takes you straight to the Font dialog box; in Excel, it takes you to the Format Cells dialog box, in which you might need to click the Font tab to arrive at the font-formatting options.) Figure 4.13 shows the Font dialog box for Word.

Figure 4.12
Click the button in the lower-right corner of the Font group to open the Font dialog box.

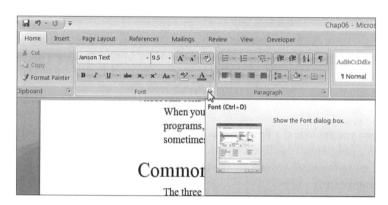

Figure 4.13
Word offers the greatest variety of font formatting options of any Office application.

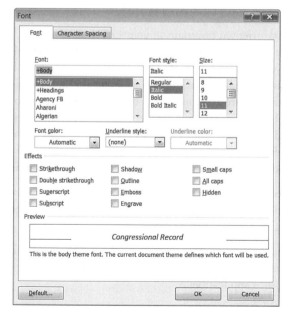

TIP

> Most of the font-formatting options in Word, Excel, and PowerPoint are available individually in the Font group of the Ribbon, so most of the time you won't need to display the Font dialog box. If you want the dialog box and find it awkward to click that tiny button in the corner of the Font group, learn the keyboard shortcuts Ctrl+D and Ctrl+1. Ctrl+D produces the Font dialog box in Word and the Font task pane in OneNote. Ctrl+1 summons the Format Cells dialog box in Excel (provided your selection currently is a cell, not a graphic object).

3. Set the characteristics. All Office programs enable you to change the font (that is, the typeface), size (in fractional increments), style (regular/roman, bold, italic, or bold italic), color, and single-line underline. Excel has several kinds of underline, strikethrough, superscript, and subscript. PowerPoint enables you to specify the super/subscript distance, shadow, and emboss.

4. Click OK to change the selected text.

→ To learn more about adding different formatting to your text in Word, **see** "Changing Text Formatting," **p. 221.**

Word and Excel both include check boxes that refer to the Default or Normal font. These boxes work differently in the two programs, however:

- In Word, the Default button sets the properties you want to use for the default font in all future documents created from the current template. When you click the Default button, Word asks whether you want to use the font settings for all new documents based on the current template. Click Yes. That sets the character formatting for the Normal style in the current template.

- In Excel, by contrast, when you click the Normal Font check box, Excel sets the font, style, and size of the current selection to match the characteristics of the current workbook's Normal style. To change the standard font used in Excel—in other words, to set the font for the Normal style in new workbooks you create—click the Microsoft Office button, click Excel Options, and click Popular in the left pane. Then select a font from the drop-down list labeled Use This Font.

USING BULLETS AND NUMBERS TO SET OFF LISTS

Bulleted and numbered lists come in handy both to emphasize and to organize. In general, you'll use bulleted lists to draw attention to important members of collections, and you'll want to save numbered lists when there's some sort of internal hierarchy (for example, a top-ten list) or when the sequence of points is important (for example, when describing each step in a complex procedure).

Word, OneNote, and PowerPoint enable you to create bulleted and numbered lists in a variety of styles and numbering methods. In each of these programs, the features are accessible via buttons; in Word and PowerPoint, the buttons are in the Paragraph group of the Home

4

tab. In OneNote, which doesn't use the Ribbon, you'll find buttons similar to those of Word and PowerPoint near the right side of the toolbar (in OneNote, you can also choose Bullets and Numbering commands on the Format menu).

To the right of the Bullets and Numbering buttons, you'll find tiny drop-down arrows. Click these to arrive at the full set of formatting options. You won't see the same choices in all three programs—or even the same style of dialog box (in OneNote, for example, you'll get a task pane instead of a dialog box). But the choices are plentiful and the dialog boxes pretty self-explanatory. To change the bullet style or number format in Word, look for a Define New option at the bottom of the bullet or numbering gallery (see Figure 4.14). In PowerPoint, the comparable option is called Bullets and Numbering. Among other things, you can use these commands to turn any character, symbol, or graphic image into a bullet.

Figure 4.14
You can choose from a variety of numbering styles or define your own.

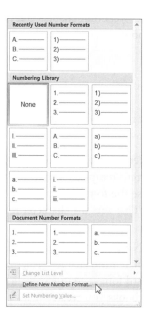

In all three programs you can apply bulleting or numbering to existing text by selecting the text and clicking the appropriate Ribbon or toolbar button. In Word and OneNote, you can also start a numbered list by simply typing a number followed by some text (the program will make the appropriate alignment adjustments to make your typing list-like, and it will increment the numbering automatically each time you press Enter). Similarly, you can begin a bulleted list by typing an asterisk, greater-than, hyphen, period, or other similar character, followed by a space or a tab.

Word and OneNote will also create multi-level numbered lists (outlines) automatically. Simply press Tab at the beginning of a line to create a sub-entry or Backspace to revert to a higher outline level.

→ To learn more about constructing customized numbering schemes in Word, **see** "Formatting Simple Lists with Bullets and Numbers," **p. 234.**

→ To learn how to create effective bulleted and numbered lists in PowerPoint, **see** "Working with Bulleted and Numbered Lists," **p. 568.**

UNDOING AND REDOING CHANGES

All Office programs include Undo features. If you make a mistake, press Ctrl+Z or click the Undo button (it's on the default Quick Access toolbar in Word, PowerPoint, and Excel). All four programs in your suite support multiple levels of Undo, enabling you to reverse a whole sequence of edits or commands. In Word, PowerPoint, and Excel, you can see what actions are available for undoing by clicking the drop-down arrow to the right of the Undo button (see Figure 4.15). By dragging your mouse pointer across this list, you can undo a whole sequence of edits or commands in a single action.

Figure 4.15
In Word, PowerPoint, and Excel, a drop-down list beside the Undo button shows you exactly what actions you can reverse.

If you discover you made a mistake five minutes ago, you might be able to recover by clicking the Undo button repeatedly. If you close your file, however, all bets are off—all Office programs clear the Undo history when you close the document.

Word includes a virtually unlimited number of Undo levels. As long as you don't close the document, you can undo anything you've done. (The size of the Undo file has some physical limitations, but in practice they aren't significant.) Word's tremendously powerful Undo capability enables you to bring back material that you might have thought was lost. For example, if you're working on a paper and you decide the opening paragraph you started with is better than the one you ended with, you can easily restore it. First, save your current document! If anything goes wrong while using Undo in this way, you can exit without saving and reopen your document to start over.

In Excel, the Undo feature used to be limited to 16 actions. Thankfully, that limit has been removed in Excel 2007. In PowerPoint, you can specify the number of actions you want to be undoable. To do this, click the Microsoft Office button, click PowerPoint Options, and click Advanced in the left pane. Then use the control labeled Maximum Number of Undos. (The default is 20.)

TIP

> An Office document's Undo history is cleared when you close the document. If you are running Windows Vista Ultimate Edition or Business Edition, however, you might be able to return a document to an earlier state by using the operating system's Previous Versions feature. To see if a previous version is available, right-click the document in Windows Explorer, choose Properties from the shortcut menu, and click the Previous Versions tab in the Properties dialog box.

CAN YOU REALLY ENTER TEXT BY SPEAKING?

If you've tried using speech-recognition technology in earlier versions of Office, you might well have concluded (as we did) that it wasn't worth the trouble. Provided you're running Windows Vista, however, it's dramatically better now. Windows Vista has brought speech recognition out of infancy into toddlerhood. If you're a person who communicates more effectively with tongue than with fingers, you should give the new speech tools a try.

You'll need the following:

- Any edition of Windows Vista.
- A high-quality headset microphone that comfortably sits within an inch of your mouth. USB microphones perform best, and a noise-cancellation microphone will be invaluable if you don't happen to have a sound studio for an office.
- A half hour to run the interactive Speech Tutorial (investing a little more time to train the system, after you have run the initial tutorial, pays a dividend in accuracy).
- Patience. The system learns and improves as you work with it. Each time you correct a mistake, you reduce the likelihood that the system will make the same mistake again.

To start using speech recognition, click the Start button and type **speech** in the Search box. The Windows Speech Recognition command appears at the top of the Start menu. When you run this command the first time, you are led through the steps of setting up a microphone and running the interactive tutorial. By the time you finish the tutorial, you are able to orally open programs and files, navigate through documents and dialog boxes by speech, and dictate text.

As you work, you can easily move between dictation and conventional interaction by saying "Start listening" or "Stop listening." Thus, you can find whatever combination of typing and talking best works for you. At any time, you can give your system an extra dose of training by typing **speech** in the Start menu Search box, choosing Speech Recognition Options, and clicking Train Your Computer to Better Understand You.

TIP

> If you are British, or if you learned English in British-style schools, you'll have more success with speech recognition using the UK speech engine. Open Control Panel, type **speech** in the Search box, click Speech Recognition Options, and then click Advanced Speech Options in Control Panel's task pane. Then, in the Language drop-down, select Microsoft Speech Recognizer 8.0 for Windows (English-UK).

TROUBLESHOOTING

FINDING OBSCURE AUTOCORRECT ENTRIES

A rogue AutoCorrect entry is causing unwanted text to appear in my documents, but I can't find the offending entry in the AutoCorrect list.

Most of the time, it's fairly easy to figure out which entry is causing the problem. Unfortunately, AutoCorrect isn't always so simple. In particular, note that AutoCorrect entries can have embedded spaces; so, for example, an entry for *any where* might correct to *anywhere*. That behavior can be puzzling until you realize that you might be the victim of an AutoCorrect entry that begins with *any*.

CUTTING TEXT CLEARS THE REDO LIST

I used Word's multiple-level Undo capability to roll back a large number of changes and then cut a block of text. But when I wanted to restore my document to its previous state, the Redo button was grayed out.

Did you save your changes before you performed the Undo operation? If so, exit the document without saving, and restore your saved copy. If not, you're out of luck. When you use Word's multilevel Undo, you can copy anything you want to the Clipboard; if you use the Cut command, however, you wipe out the Redo list, and nothing will bring it back.

EXTRA CREDIT: USING AUTOCORRECT TO ADD A SCANNED SIGNATURE TO WORD DOCUMENTS

If you have a scanner, it takes only a few minutes to set up an AutoCorrect entry that will replace the text you type in Word with a scanned image of your signature. For example, you can have Word replace the text `mysig` with a scanned image of your signature. A signature slug can be useful for "signing" daily correspondence, and it's indispensable if you want to sign a fax that is sent out electronically.

Start by scanning the signature and saving it as an image file. Next, use the Picture option on the Insert tab to insert it into a Word document. Select the scanned image and open the AutoCorrect Options dialog box (click the Microsoft Office button, select Proofing from the list on the left, and click AutoCorrect Options). On the AutoCorrect tab, you'll see a new entry waiting for you to assign replacement text. Make sure the Formatted Text button is selected, and type the text entry in the Replace box.

Make sure you don't allow others to use the scanned signature without your permission.

4

USING PICTURES AND DRAWINGS IN OFFICE

In this chapter

GOING BEYOND PLAIN TEXT

Documents that consist of only words are, frankly, boring. Photographs add visual interest to reports. Charts and diagrams can help you instantly tell a story with numbers that would otherwise be lost in a table. Even whimsical illustrations do wonders to make printed documents more readable, web pages more accessible, workbooks more lively, and presentations more engaging. Office 2007 includes a full set of drawing tools you can use, even if you aren't a trained graphic designer, plus a few features expressly aimed at making digital photos and scanned images easier to use.

In this chapter, you'll find a thorough explanation of the often-confusing drawing tools used throughout Office. If you're not sure of the difference between a shape and a SmartArt graphic, or if you can't tell the difference between a drawing canvas and a drawing object, you should read this chapter closely.

In this chapter we look at the graphics features included in three of your Office programs— Word, Excel, and PowerPoint. The fourth program, OneNote, is perfectly capable of displaying graphic images (you can insert pictures from files, transfer images directly from your scanner, or create freehand drawings on your Tablet PC), but because OneNote is not a presentation-oriented program, it doesn't have the features for creating diagrams, smart shapes, and charts that the other three programs have.

We also look at Microsoft Picture Manager, a handy program that's undeservedly buried under several layers of subfolders on the Start menu. Microsoft Picture Manager enables you to pull together even enormous collections of digital photos. Using its healthy assortment of editing tools, you can crop, resize, compress, and generally tweak those images so they fit perfectly in Office documents.

Office 2007 also includes an assortment of tools and techniques for working with clip art, and it offers you the capability to download additional clip art from the Office Online website. In this chapter, we explain how to use these cool (and often underrated) tools.

WHAT'S NEW IN OFFICE GRAPHICS TOOLS

If you have worked with graphics and charts in earlier Office releases, you'll be interested to know the following:

- To add any kind of graphic to an Office document, you start by clicking the Insert tab on the Ribbon. The Drawing toolbar is gone; you won't miss it.

- Word, Excel, and PowerPoint now share a common charting engine. Microsoft Chart, the primitive graph-making tool that was available in Word 2003, is gone; you *really* won't miss that.

- Office 2007 includes a new set of SmartArt tools that give you more powerful ways to create attractive diagrams. The AutoShapes of Office 2003 are now simply called Shapes. With these and with the SmartArt tools, you can easily insert a prebuilt diagram directly into Word, Excel, or PowerPoint; you can take your pick of diagrams chosen from six basic categories, each with many options. You can add geometric shapes, lines, arrows, and text boxes to a document, worksheet, or presentation and then add colors, shadows, and backgrounds to create images with impact. These aren't simple one-dimensional shapes, either—you can stretch, layer, and combine Office Shapes to create complex flowcharts and diagrams.

WORKING WITH THE DRAWING LAYER

Before you can even hope to harness the power of graphics in Office programs, you need to come to terms with a fundamental concept: Word, Excel, and PowerPoint documents are *layered*.

NOTE

When we use the term *document* in this chapter, we're referring to any Office data file that includes a drawing layer, including Word documents, Excel worksheets, and PowerPoint presentations.

It's tempting but misleading to think of an Office document as two-dimensional and directly analogous to a piece of paper or a computer screen. Actually, that finished product is only a snapshot of the real document, which consists of multiple layered drawings in addition to the main layer of the document itself; by changing the order, grouping, and arrangement of these drawings and the main layer, you can dramatically change a document's appearance.

The main layer is called the *text layer*. The graphic material is in a *drawing layer*, which exists independently of—but can interact with—material in the text layer. Technically, just one drawing layer is present; however, because you can position each object within the drawing layer independently, from front to back—and the text layer can be set at any depth—it's more useful to think of each object as a layer unto itself.

Think of the layered transparencies that have been used for several generations in high school biology classes. As you peel back each layer, a dissected frog appears, with each layer revealing some additional aspect of the frog's anatomy. The drawing layer works like that: Objects in the drawing layer are arranged from top to bottom (called the *Z order*), as if each drawing were on its own sheet, and each drawing can be moved independently toward the top or sent toward the back.

When you begin working with the drawing layer, it helps to visualize a complex document as consisting of many transparencies, each with its own data and properties:

- Because each layer, including the text layer, is transparent, you can see the contents of any one layer through all other layers.
- Although the text layer is normally at the bottom of the stack, with individual drawing objects in front of it, you can also position a drawing object behind the text layer.

5

- The contents of the text layer can be wrapped around a drawing layer.
- You can reorder and reposition virtually every object in the drawing layer; you can also group drawing items together and treat them as a single object, and then ungroup them to work on each individually.

Virtually all of the text-formatting and data-management capabilities we discuss elsewhere in this book—everything from search-and-replace to master formatting functions—apply only to the text layer. If you enter text in the drawing layer of a long report, it does not appear in the table of contents, nor does the appearance of the drawing layers change if you alter the formatting of your document.

As mentioned, your entrée to the graphics features in Excel, Word, and PowerPoint is through the Insert tab on the Ribbon. The Illustrations group of the Insert tab includes buttons for the various kinds of graphics with which you can work: Picture, Clip Art, Shapes, SmartArt, and Chart (see Figure 5.1). Because charting is such an essential activity in Excel, in that program you'll find a separate Charts group on the Ribbon, directly to the right of the Illustrations group. Instead of a single Chart command, you'll see seven commands for various types of charts—Column, Line, Pie, and so on. Although these subcommands don't appear directly on the Ribbon in Word and PowerPoint, all of the charting features of Excel are available in these two other programs.

Figure 5.1
The starting point for Office graphic objects is the Illustrations group of the Insert tab.

While you're working with graphic objects, the Ribbon displays additional commands appropriate to the type of object you're manipulating. If you select a picture, for example, a Picture Tools tab appears, from which you can select commands to edit and format your picture.

WORKING WITH A DRAWING CANVAS IN WORD

When you add graphic objects to a document in Word (and only in Word), you have the option of placing those objects on a drawing canvas. The drawing canvas, which looks initially like an empty rectangular frame with a dotted border, performs the following functions:

- It enables you to keep a set of shapes together. If you move the canvas, everything on the canvas moves with it. If you wanted to move a set of shapes together without a canvas, you would need to select each one before performing the move. Having a set of shapes framed by a canvas also ensures that those objects will not be separated by a page break when you print.

- It gives you an easy way to draw lines that connect shapes, so that the shapes remain connected even if you move them individually. (For more about this, see "Connecting Shapes," later in this chapter.)
- It allows you to easily add a formatted background to a set of objects. For example, if you want a set of graphic objects to appear against a light blue background, you can create a drawing canvas, fill it with light blue, and then add your objects to the canvas.

Earlier versions of Word created a canvas for you whenever you began working with the drawing layer. Word 2007 does not do that by default, but if you like the old way, you can change the default. Click the Microsoft Office button, click Word Options, and click Advanced in the left pane. Under Editing Options, select the check box labeled Automatically Create Drawing Canvas When Inserting AutoShapes. (Disregard the fact that Word 2007 no longer uses the term *AutoShapes*.)

If you don't choose to have a drawing canvas appear automatically when you work with the drawing layer, you can always add one manually. Click the Insert tab, click Shapes, and then click New Drawing Canvas (it's at the bottom of the Shapes gallery).

Drawing canvases are not available in Excel or PowerPoint. In these programs, however, lines drawn between objects can be connected automatically; that is, you don't need a canvas to carry out that function.

INSERTING SHAPES

To add a shape to an Excel, PowerPoint, or Word document, click the Insert tab on the Ribbon and then click Shapes. The Shapes gallery will descend, as shown in Figure 5.2. (The figure shows the Shapes gallery for Word; there are minor differences in the other two programs.) The Shapes gallery is divided into clearly labeled sections, with a section at the top devoted to the shapes that have been used most recently. If you're not sure what a shape in the gallery is or what it does, you can simply insert it and check it out. Alternatively, you might want to hover your mouse pointer over the shape before you click it; a descriptive tip appears.

TIP

If you have trouble remembering what all the different flowchart symbols mean, hover your mouse pointer over each in turn. The tips that appear will refresh your memory.

Figure 5.2
Clicking Shapes on the Insert tab unfurls a categorized gallery of drawing options.

After you've found the shape you want, click it and then click and drag on your document. When you've finished, your shape appears. While it's selected, useful handles appear along its perimeter. These handles perform the following functions:

- The round green handle in the upper center of the shape allows you to rotate the shape. Two-dimensional shapes (lines) don't get this handle. To rotate a line, drag either end.

- The square blue handles expand or contract a shape along a particular side. The round blue handles (in the corners) expand or contract in two directions at once.

- The yellow diamond-shaped handle, which appears only with certain shapes, does various things, depending on the shape (for example, you can use it to change a smiley face to a frowny face). Drag it to see what happens, and remember that you can reverse any maneuver by pressing Ctrl+Z.

> **TIP**
>
> To move a shape, drag any part other than one of its handles.

USING SHIFT AND CTRL TO CONSTRAIN SHAPES

Holding down the Shift or Ctrl key while dragging a shape constrains the shape in useful ways:

- Holding Shift while dragging a line allows the line to appear only at multiples of 15 degrees.

- Holding Shift while dragging a two-dimensional shape expands or contracts the shape equally in the vertical and horizontal directions. Thus, for example, you can create a square by clicking the rectangle tool and holding down Shift while you drag. You can expand or contract an existing rectangle without changing its aspect ratio by holding Shift while you drag a corner.

- Holding Ctrl while you drag expands or contracts a shape while keeping its center fixed.

Drawing Curves, Freeform Shapes, and Scribbles

The last three tools in the Lines section of the Shapes gallery—identified by their tips as Curve, Freeform, and Scribble, deserve a few additional words of explanation:

- As you drag with the Curve tool, each time you release the mouse button you create an *inflection point*—that is, the line you draw will bend at the place where you release the mouse button. You can create as many inflection points as you want. To terminate the shape, double-click. To close the shape, connecting its end with its beginning by means of a straight line, right-click it and choose Close Path.

- The Freeform tool allows you to create shapes with a mix of straight and curved lines. If you move the mouse without holding down the button, you get a straight line. If you hold down the button, you can draw as though you were using a pen. Each time you release the button, you get an inflection point. Double-click to complete the shape; right-click and choose Close Path to tie the ends together.

- The Scribble tool turns your mouse into a pen. As long as you hold the button down, you can scrawl and squiggle to your heart's content.

TIP

> If you're not happy with a shape you create using the Curve, Freeform, or Scribble tool, you can use the Edit Points command to reposition its inflection points. You'll find this command on the shortcut menu if you right-click a curved shape. Alternatively, select the shape, click the Format tab, and then click the Edit Shape command in the upper-right corner of the Insert Shapes group. The Edit Points command appears on the Edit Shape menu. Either way, Office redisplays the inflection-point handles and lets you drag to alter the shape.

5

Connecting Shapes

Most of the tools in the Line section of the Shapes gallery—all but Curve, Freeform, and Scribble—can be used as connectors as well as standalone shapes. To connect two shapes, follow these steps:

1. If you're using Word, start by creating a drawing canvas.

2. Insert the shapes you want to connect.

3. Click one of the lines in the Shapes gallery—with or without arrows, elbows, or curves, as you choose.

4. Hover the mouse pointer over one of the shapes you want to connect to reveal the red handles that mark available connection points. Click a handle.

5. Repeat step 4 for the other shape.

After they are connected, shapes can be moved at will, and the connector follows. If rearranging the shapes creates an awkward connection line, click the connector and drag it to a different connection point (the handles reappear when you click the connector). Or right-click the connector and choose Reroute Connectors.

USING THE SNAP AND GRID FEATURES

In addition to the connector capability, Excel and PowerPoint also include *snap* and *grid* settings—crucial tools for placing lines and other shapes. Word offers similar capabilities, although they are implemented differently.

When you use the drawing layer, you can take advantage of a hidden layout grid. By default, drawing objects align to this grid. Although it's usually a helpful shortcut, this *Snap to Grid* feature can be a problem when you're drawing a line manually. Because the edges of shapes are tied to grid positions, they might not line up visually with other shapes that are arranged in slightly different positions on the grid. The fix is to use the Snap Objects to Other Objects setting (in Excel it's called S*nap to Shape*) so, for example, the end point of a line connecting two shapes ends up at a reasonable point on each shape.

NOTE

> The capability to snap objects to other objects is off by default in Word and PowerPoint, but Snap to Shape is enabled in Excel.

To set the Snap options in Word, Excel, or PowerPoint, select an object on the drawing layer. On the Format tab, which appears at the right side of the Ribbon when a drawing object is selected, click Align in the Arrange group. Then, in Word or PowerPoint, choose Grid Settings in the Align menu. A dialog box presents your options (see Figure 5.3). In Excel, you have fewer options. Instead of using a Grid Settings dialog box, you can select options directly from the Align menu.

Figure 5.3
Word (left) and PowerPoint (right) offer similar grid options, although they differ in implementation.

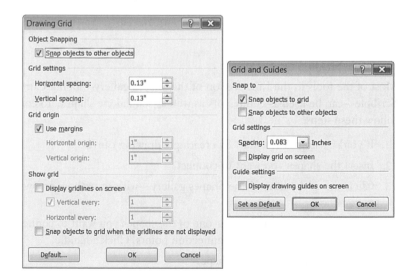

To set the Snap to Grid and Snap to Shape values in Word (and to perform other tasks, such as making the grid visible or resetting the grid), choose Draw from the Drawing toolbar, and then choose Grid. In Word, you see the Drawing Grid dialog box shown in Figure 5.3.

It's possible to move one or more objects in very fine increments without completely disabling the grid. Hold down the Alt key as you drag the object, and it moves freely rather than following the grid. You can also use the keyboard to move objects. Normally, when you select one or more objects and press any arrow key, the selection moves to the next point on the grid. If you make a selection and then hold down the Ctrl key while pressing any arrow, the selection moves in much finer increments.

FORMATTING SHAPES

After you've created a shape, you'll probably want to adjust its appearance to make it look good in the context of your document. When you select a shape, a Format tab appears on the Ribbon (it's the last tab on the right, under the heading Drawing Tools). Three command groups in this tab—Shape Styles, Shadow Effects, and 3-D Effects—give you a zillion ways to dress up your shapes (the choices are somewhat different in PowerPoint, but the range of options is comparable). We won't even try to describe them all, but a bit of experimentation will give you an idea of the formatting power at your disposal.

Your first stop should be the gallery of styles in the Shape Styles group (see Figure 5.4). Like other styles in Office (table styles in Excel, to cite just one example), these are pre-packaged combinations of formatting attributes. Some have solid backgrounds, some have gradient fills; some have simple solid borders, others are dotted; some have shadows, some do not; and so on. You can save yourself a good deal of tweaking time if one of the gallery styles happens to work for you.

Figure 5.4
The shape styles gallery provides 70 pre-packaged formatting combinations.

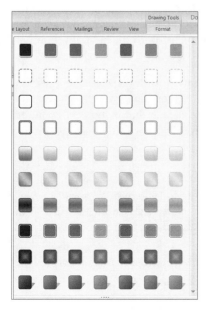

5

Like other styles in Word and Excel, the shape styles are keyed to your document's current theme. If you change the theme (by clicking Themes, at the left edge of the Page Layout tab in Word or Excel), the appearance of the items in the styles gallery changes accordingly. Themes are intended to ensure that you use pleasing combinations of colors and fonts in your documents. They also give you an easy way to achieve a consistent look in your Word documents and Excel spreadsheets.

If you decide not to use the style gallery (or to modify a style after you've applied it), look next to the Shape Fill and Shape Outline commands, which appear directly to the right of the styles gallery on the Ribbon. Each of these opens a large menu of fine-tuning commands. The outline commands affect the borders of your shapes and include options to apply, remove, or alter arrowheads on line shapes. The fill options govern everything within the borders of your shapes.

Directly below the Shape Outline command in Excel and PowerPoint (but not in Word), you'll find a Shape Effects command. This one is full of cool stuff—options to add glows, reflections, soft edges, bevel effects, shadows, and so on. You can lose yourself in this collection of options for a full day if you're easily distracted!

Farther to the right on the Ribbon are more detailed shadowing commands, options to add lighting effects, rotation commands, and so on. Experiment—and remember to save before you tweak (or press Ctrl+Z to retrace your steps).

USING TEXT BOXES AND CALLOUTS

The first two shapes in the Basic Shapes section of the gallery are text boxes. When you create one of these shapes, Office displays an insertion point inside the shape, and you can enter or paste text. The difference between the two text boxes is that the first is designed for horizontal text, the second for vertical. The shapes in the Callouts section are text boxes as well—ones with nonrectangular shapes. The callouts come with connectors designed to point to something else on your document. With the help of yellow handles, you can format these connectors independently of the rest of the callout shape.

Need text inside a shape other than a standard text box or callout? No problem. Right-click the shape on your document and choose Add Text from the shortcut menu. For example, the Flowchart shapes are not text boxes by default, but if you need to put text inside one, you can. (If you want to change horizontal text to vertical, select the text and then click Text Direction, near the left side of the Format tab.)

TIP

> To format the text in a text box—for example, to change its size or pick a different font—select the text, click the Home tab, and then use standard text-formatting commands.

Note that Word (but not Excel or PowerPoint) also includes an elaborate gallery of preformatted text boxes in a separate part of the Ribbon (click Text Box in the Text group of

Word's Ribbon). These stylish text boxes, designed for adding pull quotes and sidebars to documents, are discussed later in this chapter (see "Creating Pull Quotes and Sidebars").

ALIGNING AND GROUPING GRAPHIC ELEMENTS

Depending on the naked eye to center shapes in a drawing isn't always reliable. Office has built-in drawing tools with the capability to bring symmetry out of chaos. When *aligning* objects, the key is to do it one step at a time, carefully planning out what you need to do to redistribute or align them, and in which order.

If you have four objects on the drawing layer above an Excel worksheet and you want to organize them as shown in Figure 5.5, follow these steps:

Figure 5.5
Use the alignment tools to make graphics line up neatly, as shown here.

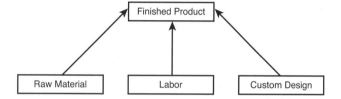

1. Select the bottom three rectangles by holding down the Shift key as you click each one.
2. To evenly space the three shapes, click the Format tab, click Align (in the Arrange group), and then choose Distribute Horizontally.
3. To line up the three shapes, click Align Top.
4. Now align the top rectangle with the middle one. Select both shapes, return to the Align menu, and choose Align Center.

After you have properly formatted, connected, aligned, and distributed all your shapes, you can take one more step to *group* them into a single graphic object. This step is crucial; it enables you to preserve the relationships between objects and it helps prevent the chance that you'll accidentally move or resize a shape.

Select all the elements you want to group, click the Format tab, open the Group menu (in the Arrange group), and then choose Group.

TIP

When you're creating complex drawings that consist of several shapes, it's easy to leave one out accidentally. After selecting multiple items for grouping, it's always a good practice to drag the collection left and right just a little; you can see whether any odd pieces are hiding behind other shapes. If you missed one, press Ctrl+Z to undo the move and regroup.

The individual elements in a group can't be edited independently. For example, if you have a text box in a group, you won't be able to change the text in the box as long as it remains grouped.

If you find you need to make a revision, you can ungroup, make your edits, and then regroup. To ungroup a composite graphic, select the graphic, return to the Group menu, and choose Ungroup.

WRAPPING, LAYOUT, AND STACKING

Graphics don't always appear where you want them—at least not without a bit of persuading. When you insert a complex graphic into a Word document, for instance, the graphic shoves the text in your report out of the way. In this case, you might prefer to *wrap* the text around a drawing object.

The solution? Use layout options (which are available only in Word) to adjust the placement of graphics relative to the text layer. Select the graphic object (or the drawing canvas, if all your drawing objects are enclosed in a drawing canvas), click the Format tab on the Ribbon, and then open the Text Wrapping menu:

- To lay out your graphic so it appears as a background to the document, choose Behind Text or In Front of Text. When using this option, use only very light-colored graphic objects; otherwise, the graphic will overwhelm the text on the page and make it unreadable.

- Use the standard Square method to wrap text around the rectangular borders of the graphic. This option is most appropriate when the graphic has a defined border.

- Use Tight wrapping if the graphic object or drawing layer does not have a rectangular border. For example, if you're wrapping text around an oval shape, the Tight option positions your text right up to the oval; the Square option aligns text vertically against the oval's selection handles.

In Word, Excel, and PowerPoint, you can also change the order of objects so that one is in front of another. By default, when you create or position a graphic object so that it overlaps another graphic object (including a drawing canvas), the new element appears on top of the old one. To change the front-to-back ordering, right-click the graphic element or drawing canvas you want to move, and choose Order. At that point, you can

- Float the graphic all the way to the top (Word calls it Bring to Front) or sink it all the way to the bottom (Send to Back).

- Bring the graphic up one level (Bring Forward) or push it down one level (Send Backward).

- Move the graphic so it's on top of the text layer (Bring in Front of Text), or place it behind the text layer (Send Behind Text). These options are not available in Excel or PowerPoint.

ADDING PICTURES TO OFFICE DOCUMENTS

Clip art has its place, especially in presentations and informal documents, where you want to make your audience laugh or just provide some visual relief. But certain types of reports require realistic graphics such as photographs or image files produced by professional graphic artists. A report for an art history class might benefit from photographs of paintings or sculptures, with enlarged detail pictures for sections that discuss specific details. For a geography or history paper, you might include maps or photographs that help the reader visualize the locations under discussion.

Pictures can be useful outside the classroom as well. When you submit a claim to your insurance company, for example, your letter will have a lot more impact if you embed digital pictures of the damage. And your annual holiday letter will be much more interesting if you can show, not just tell, what's been going on with your family throughout the year.

To add a picture to an Office document, click the Insert tab and then click Picture. An Insert Picture dialog box focused on your Pictures folder will appear. You can choose an image in any of the following formats:

- Compressed Macintosh PICT
- Compressed Windows Enhanced Metafile
- Compressed Windows Metafile
- Computer Graphics Metafile
- Encapsulated PostScript
- Graphics Interchange Format
- JPEG File Interchange Format
- Macintosh PICT
- Portable Network Graphics
- Tag Image File Format
- Windows Bitmap
- Windows Enhanced Metafile
- Windows Metafile
- WordPerfect Graphics

By default, pictures arrive in Word as inline objects—that is, without text wrapping. To wrap text around your picture, select it, click the Format tab, and then click Text Wrapping (in the Arrange group). You can also make one of the text-wrapping options the default for new pictures. To do this, click the Microsoft Office button, click Word Options, and then click Advanced in the left pane. Under the heading Cut, Copy, and Paste (you'll need to scroll down to get there), select the option you want from the drop-down list labeled Insert/Paste Pictures As.

Choosing Embedding or Linking

As Figure 5.6 shows, Office gives you choices about how to insert a picture:

Figure 5.6
Word enables you to Insert, Link to File, or Insert and Link a picture in a file.

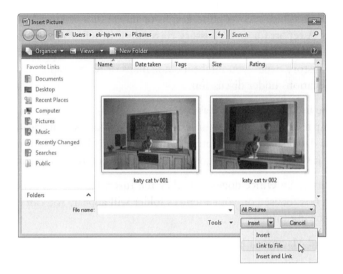

- Insert—This choice *embeds* the picture, physically placing it in the document. This is the default option in all Office programs. If you aren't overly worried about file sizes, don't need any history telling you where the picture came from, and don't care whether the picture gets updated, this is your best choice.

- Link to File—This choice puts a pointer to the picture at the place in the document where you want the picture to appear. The picture itself is not stored in the document. Instead, it's brought in as needed to display on the screen or print on the printer. If there's a chance the picture will be changed and your document *must* reflect those changes, this is your only option.

- Insert and Link—This hybrid option puts a copy of the picture in the document, but maintains a link as well. When the picture is needed, Office first looks for the linked file. If the picture file is unavailable, it reverts to the copy stored in the document. This option isn't generally useful for use in a home or school environment; it's more important for business documents stored on portable computers, because it ensures that graphics will be available when the computer is unplugged from the office network but can still be updated when you reconnect.

(In some circumstances you might see a fourth option, Show Previous Versions. This menu choice, available only when you have previously edited the selected image and saved it under the same name, invokes the Previous Versions feature that's available in Windows Vista Ultimate and Windows Vista Business Edition. As the name suggests, this feature can show earlier versions of a picture, in the event that the picture has changed.)

Office frequently uses fully qualified filenames as the links, which can cause problems if you move either the picture file or the document. If you link the picture `%userprofile%\Pictures\Corplogo.jpg` in a document and then send the document as an email attachment, the picture must be located in the exact same folder hierarchy or Office won't be able to find it, and will substitute a disconcerting placeholder.

When should you embed graphics and when should you link? Follow these guidelines:

- If you repeatedly use the same graphic in printed documents—for example, a letterhead logo—link to it and make sure it doesn't move. This helps reduce the size of all your saved documents.

- If you're connected to a network or using Office on a computer that is shared by several members of your family, linking works if the graphic is in the Shared Documents folder or in a *shared network folder* that's accessible to everyone who wants to use the document. If you don't have ready access to the shared folder, insert the graphic.

- If you plan to distribute documents externally, either as email attachments, on a CD, or via other media, you must insert the graphics. (Documents you save on a CD will show linked graphics if you save all the files in the same folder as the document, but the links will be broken as soon as the document is copied to another location.)

 If you discover broken image links in your document, see "Fixing Broken Image Links" in the "Troubleshooting" section at the end of this chapter.

FORMATTING PICTURES

When you select a picture in an Office document, your application adds a Format tab under the Picture Tools heading at the right side of the Ribbon. The largest chunk of this new tab, the Picture Styles group, offers a gallery of framing options; you can use items in this gallery, for example, to display your picture in a stylish oval frame. For even more offbeat ways to present a picture, click the Picture Shape command, just to the right of the styles gallery. As you'll see, you can constrain your picture to any of the standard Office shapes— parallelograms, triangles, flowchart symbols, you name it. The two commands directly below Picture Shape provide border options and effects. The latter include glows, soft edges, rotations, and so on.

WORKING WITH SCANNED IMAGES

In previous Office versions, Word, Excel, and PowerPoint directly supported scanners and digital cameras using the Insert, Picture, From Scanner or Camera option. This option is no longer available in Office 2007. Use your scanning software to save the image as a graphic file and then insert the saved file into a document, worksheet, or presentation.

5

TIP

> Office's graphics layer, in combination with a scanner, provides a solution to a modern problem: How do you neatly fill out a printed form when you don't have a typewriter anymore? The answer: Scan the form, save it as a file, and then insert the saved file as a picture in the document header. Crop and resize the image as needed, and format the picture layout as Behind Text. Exit from the header, and you can type over the form.
>
> Alternatively, scan the form and place the image in the main text layer. Crop and resize as needed, and then format the graphic object by using the Behind Text option. Add a text box on top of each field in the form; use the ordering options to place this layer in front of the form and make the box semitransparent.

VIEWING, EDITING, AND MANAGING PICTURES

Digital pictures usually need a bit of manipulation—and sometimes major surgery—before they fit properly into a document. For most tasks, you can use the internal image-editing tools that are installed along with Office 2007. Using commands in the Adjust group of the Format tab (the tab that appears on the Ribbon when you select a picture), you can crop, compress, lighten, darken, rotate, and colorize digital images. When you do this sort of manipulation, the original image file remains untouched; your changes affect only the image included in the Office file.

If you have a full-featured image-editing program, you can use it to manipulate pictures, save the results, and then insert the edited image files into your documents. If you don't have a favorite image-editing program (or if you're unhappy with the one you're using), take a look at Microsoft Picture Manager. This standalone program, which is included with Office, helps you organize collections of image files from local hard disks and shared network folders, including pictures you take with a digital camera as well as those you save from websites. You can perform most of the same image editing and compression tasks as you can with the built-in Office tools, and then some. On images afflicted with red eye, for instance, you can get the red out with one click. You can also convert images to alternative formats (from the space-hogging Bitmap format to the more efficient JPEG or GIF format, for instance), a trick that is impossible with the built-in Office tools.

To open Picture Manager, click Start, All Programs, Microsoft Office, Microsoft Office Tools, and finally click the Microsoft Office Picture Manager shortcut. (If you're using Windows Vista, you can find it much more quickly by clicking Start, typing `pic` in the Search box, and then clicking the shortcut that appears at the top of the search results list.) The Picture Manager main window is divided into three parts, as shown in Figure 5.7:

- Picture Shortcuts pane—Gather shortcuts to folders that contain pictures in this pane. Your pictures remain in their original location. By default, the list includes the Pictures folder and any folders you browse for pictures. Click the Add Picture Shortcut link to manually add a shortcut to the list; choose File, Locate Pictures to search for picture files in other folders on your computer or on shared network folders.

- Preview pane—View pictures in this center pane. Use the Preview toolbar at the top of the pane to switch between thumbnails, filmstrip, and individual picture views. Use the Zoom Slider control to make the image appear larger or smaller.

- Edit pane—Editing tools appear in this pane, including compression options, red-eye reduction, and cropping tools.

Figure 5.7
Image shortcuts appear in the left pane, with image-editing tools in the task pane on the right.

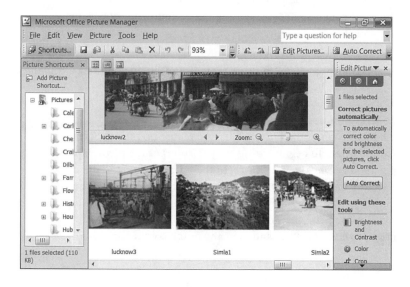

CAUTION

Watch out for one interface "gotcha" in Picture Manager's Picture Shortcuts pane. Yes, it's true that every folder listed here is a shortcut to an external location. However, if you right-click the shortcut and choose Delete Folder, the program really does delete the underlying folder and all of the files in it, not just the shortcut! To get rid of a shortcut in this pane, right-click and choose Remove Shortcut.

When you use Picture Manager to make any changes to image files, the resulting changed files appear in the Unsaved Edits folder at the bottom of the Picture Shortcuts pane. For instructions on how to save those changed files, see "Editing Image Files," later in this chapter.

RESIZING AND CROPPING PICTURES

When you insert a picture into a document, it appears full size. If the picture file is six inches wide, that's what you'll see in your document. More often than not, you'll need to make some adjustments to fit the picture to the document. You can *crop* the picture—that is, cut away portions of the image to show only the parts you want to see in your document. Or you can *resize* the picture, leaving the image intact but changing its height and width (and thus the number of pixels it occupies). You can also combine the two operations, cropping to the correct proportions and resizing to fit the page. (Although you can expand a small image to fit a larger space, the more typical task in Office documents is to shrink large digital images to a manageable file size.)

You have two choices:

- Make a copy of your original picture and then crop or resize it using Picture Manager or another photo editor. If you use the photo editor to adjust the image to the exact size and shape you need, you can import it into your document without requiring any additional work.

- If you want your original picture to remain the same, or if you're still designing your document and you think you might want to do additional cropping or resizing, use the built-in Office tools.

To crop an image within an Office document, first select the image and then click Crop in the Size group of the Format tab. The mouse pointer changes to match the icon on the Crop button. To begin cutting away portions of the picture, point to any of the eight cropping points (one on each corner of the image and one in the center of each side) and then click and drag toward the center of the image. Hold down the Ctrl key and drag the handles in the center of any side to crop identical amounts from the top and bottom or left and right; to maintain the exact same *aspect ratio* and crop equal amounts from opposing sides, hold down the Ctrl key and drag any of the corner handles in.

TIP

> In Word, you can avoid some sizing hassles by drawing a text box where you want to place the graphic and then inserting the graphic into the text box. The graphic is resized automatically. If the picture is already in the document, click it once, and then click the Text Box button on the Drawing toolbar to surround the image with a box.

If you make a mistake while cropping, press Ctrl+Z (Undo) and start over.

Commands in the Adjust group, at the left edge of the Format tab, allow you to make a few adjustments in picture quality: contrast, brightness, color, and the like. Again, any changes you make here affect only the picture in the document, not the original source file.

EDITING IMAGE FILES

If you want to start a raging debate, gather a bunch of graphics professionals in one place and ask them to name their favorite image-editing program. Then duck. Web designers and desktop publishers are typically passionate about their editing tools, and you'll probably get an earful.

The Picture Manager utility can't compete with professional-strength editing packages. However, its collection of features matches those found in many freeware and shareware image-management programs. If you're already experienced with one of these tools, you should at least look at Picture Manager and decide whether you want to make the switch.

To use Picture Manager's editing tools, first select one or more images, and then click the Edit Pictures button to open the task pane shown in Figure 5.8.

Figure 5.8
Click any of the editing options shown here to open a new task pane with specialized tools for that task.

The Auto Correct button adjusts brightness, contrast, and color automatically. For images that appear washed out or dull, you should always try this option first (if the results are unsatisfactory, press Ctrl+Z to undo the changes and start over). Use any of the following editing tools to alter specific parts of an image:

- Brightness and Contrast—Use this feature to correct pictures that appear too light or too dark. Try the Auto Brightness button first and then adjust manually.

- Color—Click to adjust the hue and saturation of the image. This option is useful for "punching up" dull pictures or fixing images where poor lighting caused unnatural tints.

- Crop—Remove extraneous portions of an image. You can crop out unnecessary elements or choose from the drop-down Aspect Ratio list to select a specific size—3×5, for instance. This option is not available when multiple images are selected.

- Rotate and Flip—Change an image from landscape to portrait orientation, and vice versa, or use the By Degree control to fix a scanned image that's slightly crooked or a digital photo that's askew.

- Red Eye Removal—This feature allows you to remove those ghostly red dots caused by your camera's flash. This option is available only when a single image is selected.

5

- Resize—Change the dimensions of a picture without cropping out any information by choosing a predefined or custom height and width or selecting a percentage of the original size. This feature is most useful for reducing file size for images you plan to use in email messages or on web pages.

As you edit images, Picture Manager keeps track of the changes you make. Click the Unsaved Edits icon in the Picture Shortcuts page to see any changes you have not yet saved. If you close Picture Manager, you are given the chance to save your changes, discard the changes, or cancel. Be careful! Choosing Save Changes overwrites the original images; if you don't have backup copies, those originals are gone for good.

When in doubt, open the Unsaved Edits folder and review your changes. Then click the File menu and choose any of the following options:

- Save—Accept the changes for a selected image or images and overwrite the original file.
- Save As—Specify a new name or location for the changed file. This option is available only when a single image is selected.
- Save All—Accept changes for all images and overwrite the original files. This operation cannot be undone.
- Export—Offers a wide range of options using the Export task pane (see Figure 5.9). You can change the name, location, file format, and size of one or more files.

Figure 5.9
The Export option offers the most options for saving images you edit with Picture Manager.

TIP

> Picture Manager offers one especially elegant way to add a consistent naming strategy to a disorganized folder made up of image files gathered from many sources. Add the folder to the Picture Shortcuts pane and press Ctrl+A to select all images in the folder. Then click the Rename Pictures link in the Getting Started task pane. Choose from the impressive array of options for using names and numbers to bring order out of chaos. This option is also available when you click Rename Pictures in the Export task pane.

COMPRESSING GRAPHICS FOR WEB PAGES AND PRESENTATIONS

Unless you're going to print a graphic on a high-resolution printer—in which case you can probably use all the detail you can get—chances are good that you will want to squeeze down the size of external graphic files for use in Office documents. This is especially true with images that were originally captured with high-resolution digital cameras in an uncompressed format, where file sizes can be 3MB or more.

To cut image files down to size outside of Office, use the Compress Pictures button in Picture Manager. To shrink a photo or graphic image that is already inserted in an Office document, use Office's built-in Compress feature. Although this option does remove data from the selected image, the practical effect is rarely noticeable and the reduction in document size can be profound. To compress a graphic in Word, Excel, or PowerPoint, follow these steps:

1. Click to select the graphic object.
2. Click Compress Pictures in the Adjust group of the Format tab.
3. In the Compress Pictures dialog box, select the check box (unless you want to compress all the pictures in this document). Then click Options. The Compression Settings dialog box appears (see Figure 5.10).

Figure 5.10
Office includes built-in tools to shrink the size of embedded graphics, thus reducing the size of a document or presentation.

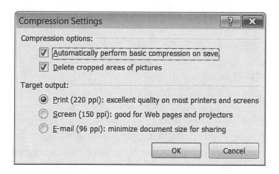

4. Choose Screen (150 ppi) for web pages or projectors or E-mail (96 ppi) to shrink the picture to a size suitable for mailing. Alternatively, leave the selection at Print (220 ppi) if you have used the built-in Office tools to crop portions of a picture and you want to

delete the cropped data without affecting the resolution of what remains visible. Be sure to select the Delete Cropped Areas of Pictures check box.

5. Click OK.

CREATING PULL QUOTES AND SIDEBARS

One well-known technique for livening up text is to throw in a pull quote—a usually provocative excerpt from the text that is enclosed in a box and formatted with large type. Newspaper editors and magazine designers use pull quotes as visual cues to "draw in" readers who are casually flipping through the pages looking at headlines and pictures without reading the body text. Word includes a gallery of gorgeously formatted text boxes that make it easy to add pull quotes to a document. To open this gallery (see Figure 5.11), click the Insert tab and then click Text Box in the Text group (near the right end of the Ribbon).

Figure 5.11
The position of the text in the Text Box gallery gives you an idea of how your document will flow around the pull quote.

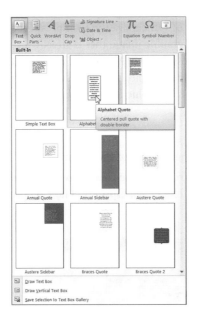

The simplest way to create a pull quote is to select the text you want to quote, press Ctrl+C to copy it to the Clipboard, open the Text Box gallery, select the option you want, and then immediately press Ctrl+V. The selected text box item appears initially with dummy text; pressing Ctrl+V replaces that text with the words you intend to quote. Figure 5.12 shows an example of the Alphabet Quote item (the item highlighted in Figure 5.11).

Several of the items in the Text Box gallery are identified as *sidebars*. The only difference between these and the ones labeled *quote* are that the sidebars are positioned at one edge of the document instead of in the middle. You can use sidebars either to quote text from your document or to display related information.

Figure 5.12
When you select an item from the Text Box gallery, Word flows your document around it; all you need to do is replace the dummy text with the text you want to quote.

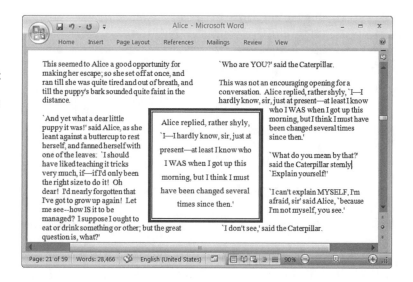

As an alternative to using one of the preformatted gallery options, you can use the Draw Text Box and Draw Vertical Text Box commands (at the bottom of the gallery) to create simple text boxes that you position and format yourself. You have to select some text in your document before you issue either command (or else nothing happens), and the select text is cut and pasted into the new text box. If you're using this method to create a pull quote, be sure to copy the text within your document before you create the text box; otherwise, you'll have a quote with no source.

After you create any text box using the Text Box gallery, Word displays a new Format tab on the Ribbon. With its Text Box Styles, Shadow Effects, 3-D Effects, and other command groups, you can season to taste.

USING WORDART FOR LOGOS

WordArt is an Office feature you can use to manipulate TrueType fonts and save the result as a graphic image. The resulting picture can be dropped into the drawing layer of documents, charts, or slides. Don't let the name fool you into thinking this utility is just for Word—WordArt is available in Excel and PowerPoint, too (although, as we'll see, you have a little extra work to do if you want to take full advantage of WordArt's capabilities in Excel and PowerPoint).

For the small business without a graphic arts department, WordArt can form the basis of a simple logo. You can use WordArt to lay text out vertically, curve it, and add 3-D effects.

To create a WordArt picture in an open document, worksheet, or presentation, follow these steps:

1. Click WordArt in the Text group of the Insert tab. Office responds with the WordArt Gallery; Figure 5.13 shows the version of the gallery that appears in Word.

Figure 5.13
WordArt makes for attention-getting text effects or easy logos.

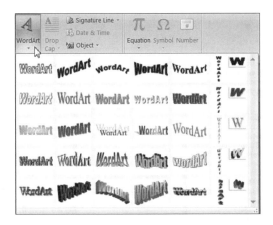

2. Click one of the styles in the WordArt gallery.

3. In the Edit WordArt Text dialog box, type the text you want to use as WordArt; select the font, font size, and treatment (bold or italic), and click OK.

> **TIP**
>
> Start with a simple font, such as a basic serif font. Decorative fonts generally produce horrible WordArt.

4. After the WordArt object appears in the drawing layer, click and drag any of the sizing handles to change its appearance, or use any of the commands in the Format tab (which now appears under the heading WordArt Tools) to make further adjustments to the appearance of your WordArt object.

The WordArt toolbar includes a large collection of shapes under the WordArt Shapes button that you can use to further bend, stretch, and modify existing pieces of WordArt. Additional buttons enable you to move and size text and adjust character spacing. A shortcut also exists for wrapping text around the WordArt. If the WordArt toolbar isn't visible, right-click any toolbar or the main menu bar and choose WordArt from the list of available toolbars.

Oddly enough, the WordArt gallery in Excel and PowerPoint lacks the options to create curved or slanted text. You can still get all the other great WordArt effects in these two programs, but if you want the bends, so to speak, create your WordArt in a Word document, and then cut and paste it into your Excel or PowerPoint document. After it's landed there, you can stylize it further, just as you would in Word. Why the 2007 editions of Excel and PowerPoint offer a scaled-back WordArt gallery (this was not the case earlier) is a mystery.

USING CLIP ART

Clip art—reusable drawings, photos, and the like—derives its name from the not-so-distant past, when designers actually clipped images from books and pasted them onto layout boards to produce master images for printed documents. The electronic versions of these tools are easier to use, but the effect is the same—they enliven an informal document. Much depends on the audience you want to reach and the effect you want to achieve.

A dynamite piece of clip art can tell a story worth a thousand words. A really poor piece of clip art hinders communication, leaving people scratching their heads and wondering, "What's *that* all about?"

Gratuitous clip art—that is, clip art that doesn't relate to the topic at hand or otherwise impedes the flow of your documents—distracts your audience and often detracts from the point you're trying to make.

In Office 2007, the clip art collection is accessible through its own task pane. The built-in clip art collection includes more than 1,600 graphic images, bullets, lines, and a few media files. The Clip Art task pane is tightly connected to the Office Online Clip Art and Media page, where you can download thousands of additional images, sounds, video clips, animated graphics, and the like. The result is organized in a fully indexed and searchable graphics database, sorted into collections, categorized by keywords, and eminently customizable.

At its simplest, you can search for relevant images by category or keyword. From any Office program, click Clip Art on the Insert tab to open the Insert Clip Art task pane. Then proceed in this order:

1. Click the drop-down arrow to the right of the Search In box to display the list of available collections.

2. Select or clear check boxes to choose the collections you want to search. This list includes three main groups:

    • My Collections—This group consists of clips you've added to your personal collection. In a default Office installation, it is empty.

    • Office Collections—These are the files installed on your hard disk with the initial Office setup, plus any files you've added from the Office Online site.

    • Web Collections—This group consists of content available from the Microsoft Office Online website.

3. In the Results Should Be box, choose the media type you're looking for (see Figure 5.14). Click the plus sign to the left of each category heading to display the full list of options and narrow your search to very specific types of media (for example, photographs in JPEG format and clip art in Windows Metafile format).

4. Type keywords in the Search For box and click Go.

Figure 5.14
To keep from being overwhelmed with results, select the specific types of clip art files for which you're looking.

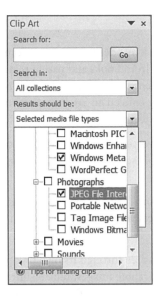

The results of your search appear in the scrolling pane at the bottom of the Clip Art task pane. If one of the images meets your needs, click to insert it in the current document, worksheet, or presentation. To see additional choices, click the drop-down arrow at the right side of every clip. You can copy an item to the Clipboard for use in another program, for example, or make it available offline in one of your personal collections. You can also preview the clip in a larger window that shows additional properties, as shown in Figure 5.15.

Figure 5.15
To see a larger view of search results, open this dialog box. Scroll through all search results by using the left and right arrows beneath the large preview.

The keywords and other saved details for clips that are part of Office clip art collections, whether they're stored locally or pulled from the Web, are not available for editing. In clips that are stored in your personal collections, however, you're free to customize the built-in keywords and captions. To set your own keywords for a particular clip, follow these steps:

1. Right-click the clip and choose Edit Keywords. The Keywords dialog box opens (see Figure 5.16).

2. In the Caption box, type a descriptive name for the clip. The caption can be virtually any length, and may include punctuation marks and other special symbols. The caption text appears as a ScreenTip when you hover the mouse pointer over the clip in the task pane.

3. In the Keywords for Current Clip box, add or remove keywords for the particular clip.

Figure 5.16
Add your own keywords and descriptive captions for clips in your collections.

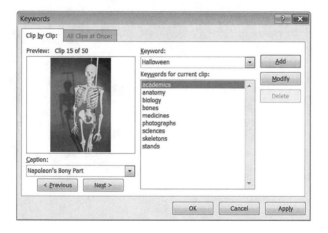

TIP

Office helps you maintain consistency in your keywords by use of the drop-down list. If you're careful to use uniform keywords, your efforts will pay off later with more effective searches.

You can also add photographs and graphic images to your personal collection from files on an individual computer or on a network, with the option to move or copy a graphic onto your computer or link the item in the collection to the original file location. If you regularly produce graphics-intensive documents using a library of images you've collected from many sources, you might find it useful to make those images available in the Clip Art pane.

To open the Clip Organizer, click Organize Clips… at the bottom of the Insert Clip Art task pane. You can also open the Clip Organizer on its own, without having to go through the Clip Art task pane—its shortcut is in the Microsoft Office Tools group on the All Programs menu. Then choose File, Add Clips to Organizer. You can have the Clip

Organizer automatically scan your disk for compatible files, or click the On My Own option to specify a location from which you want to import graphics files.

The Clip Organizer is also the ideal way to add files from the Office Online collections. Click the Clips Online button to visit the website and select clips you want to download. The Office Online site installs an ActiveX control that makes it easy to import new clips, which show up in the Downloaded Clips category (see Figure 5.17).

Figure 5.17
Clips you download from Office Online show up in your Personal Collection.

Images you download from Office Online go into the Microsoft Clip Organizer subfolder in your Pictures folder. The index to your personal collection is stored in a Media Catalog file (with the extension *.mcg) in the %appdata%\Microsoft\Clip Organizer folder.

CREATING CHARTS

To add a chart to a Word document or PowerPoint slide, click Chart in the Illustrations group of the Insert tab. Office responds with the Insert Chart gallery, shown in Figure 5.18. To insert a chart into an Excel worksheet, click one of the basic chart types in the Charts group of the Insert tab. As Figure 5.19 shows, Excel provides individual galleries for each of its chart types (the figure shows the gallery for Column charts). But an All Chart Types command, at the bottom of the type-specific gallery (see Figure 5.19), leads to the same composite gallery shown in Figure 5.18.

After you select a chart type from the gallery in Word or PowerPoint and click OK, Office opens an Excel worksheet with dummy data (see Figure 5.20). Replace the dummy data with something real, close this Excel worksheet, and you're back in Word or PowerPoint with a new chart.

Figure 5.18
The Insert Chart gallery in Word and PowerPoint provides one-stop access to all of Office's many chart types and subtypes.

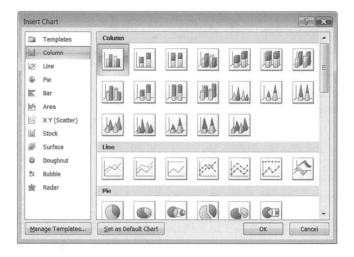

Figure 5.19
Excel offers separate galleries for each of the basic chart types, but the All Chart Types command at the bottom of these galleries presents the composite gallery shown in Figure 5.18.

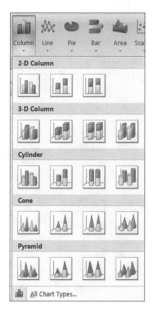

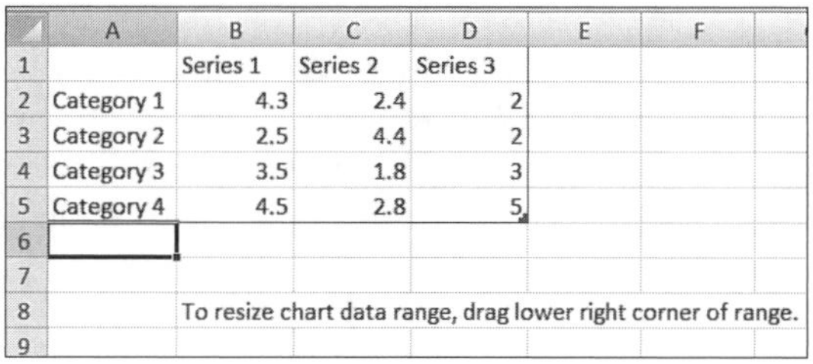

Figure 5.20
If you start the chart-creation procedure in Word or PowerPoint, Office displays an Excel worksheet with dummy data.

	A	B	C	D	E	F
1		Series 1	Series 2	Series 3		
2	Category 1	4.3	2.4	2		
3	Category 2	2.5	4.4	2		
4	Category 3	3.5	1.8	3		
5	Category 4	4.5	2.8	5		
6						
7						
8		To resize chart data range, drag lower right corner of range.				
9						

5

If this seems like a convoluted way to create a chart, go to the head of the class. It's simpler just to start in Excel. Build your chart there, and then copy it and paste it into your Word document or PowerPoint slide.

Because charting is integral to Excel and because the Office 2007 charting engine is elaborate and feature-rich, we'll defer the detailed discussion of chart creation and formatting to an Excel-specific chapter (see Chapter 16, "Turning Data into Charts").

CREATING DIAGRAMS WITH SMARTART GRAPHICS

Earlier versions of Microsoft Office included a program called Microsoft Organization Chart that allowed you to create various kinds of hierarchical diagrams. That program has been replaced in Office 2007 by a more versatile set of tools, called SmartArt, which is integrated into Office programs and accessible via the SmartArt button on the Insert tab. (If you really want the old utility back, click the Help button in an Office application and look for the topic "Where Can I Find Microsoft Office Organization Chart?")

Clicking SmartArt on the Insert tab opens a gallery of diagramming options organized into seven categories (see Figure 5.21). Pay particular attention to the right pane of the gallery, which provides a concise description of each diagramming option. (Ignore the colors; they make the gallery pretty but bear no relationship to how your diagram will look.)

Figure 5.21
The SmartArt gallery offers more than 100 types of diagrams in seven basic categories.

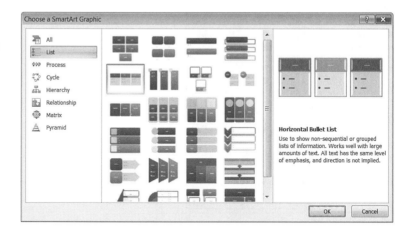

After you have selected a diagram and clicked OK, the diagram appears in your document adorned with dummy text (see Figure 5.22). You can replace the text by typing directly into a diagram block, or you can use the separate Text pane, which ordinarily appears alongside the new diagram. (If it's not there, click Text Pane in the Create Graphic group of the Design tab.)

Figure 5.22
The Text pane, to the left of the new diagram, simplifies replacement of dummy text.

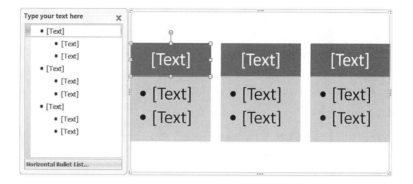

As the Text pane in Figure 5.23 shows, SmartArt diagrams can handle multiple levels of text, with subordinate levels indented, outline-style. As you enter text into the outline, SmartArt formats it intelligently in your diagram. What might not be obvious is that you can add entries and levels in the Text pane. Press Enter in the Text pane to create a new entry at the current outline level; press Tab to subordinate the current entry. Figure 5.23 shows a horizontal bullet list (the type of diagram begun in Figure 5.22) with three outline levels.

Figure 5.23
You can add text to a SmartArt diagram at various outline levels.

FORMATTING A SMARTART DIAGRAM

When you select a SmartArt diagram, Office adds two tabs to the Ribbon, under the heading SmartArt Tools. Using the Layouts group of the Design tab, you can switch from one type of diagram to another without starting over. With the SmartArt Styles group, you can take advantage of numerous cool 3D and rotation effects, among other things. On the Format tab, meanwhile, you'll find WordArt effects, fill and outline effects, and many other worthy enhancements and diversions.

TIP

To add pictures to a SmartArt diagram—handy for organizational charts—select a diagram element, click Shape Fill in the Shape Styles group of the Format tab, and then choose Picture from the Shape Fill menu.

5

TROUBLESHOOTING

FIXING BROKEN IMAGE LINKS

I created a link to an image stored on a networked computer and everything worked fine. When I opened the document later, however, the image link was broken.

If links get messed up, you have two options:

In Word or PowerPoint (but not in Excel), you can manually edit links. Click the Microsoft Office button, click Prepare, and then choose Edit Links to Files. Then, in the Links dialog box, click Change Source.

An even simpler option (the only one in Excel) is to re-create the link. If a linked graphic goes missing, double-click the box containing the ugly red X. This opens the Picture Tools Format tab. Click Change Picture, browse to the image you want to link, select it, and choose Link to File.

EXTRA CREDIT: A PROFESSIONAL FLOWCHART

Office shapes give you the opportunity to create almost any kind of basic process-related diagram. Note how this flowchart below emphasizes clean, simple phrases and places them in color and shape-coded boxes. A simple, clean flowchart can do wonders for explaining an otherwise difficult procedure. And with the use of standard Office drawing tools, the flowchart is equally at home in a PowerPoint presentation, a Word document, or an Excel workbook.

Figure 5.24

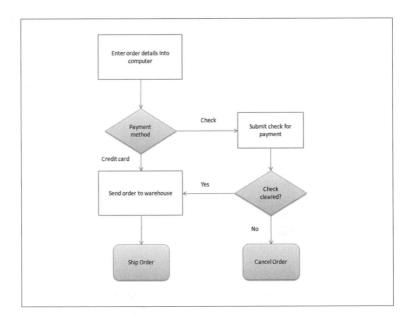

CHAPTER 6

USING OFFICE PROGRAMS TOGETHER

In this chapter

SHARING DATA BETWEEN OFFICE PROGRAMS

Every Office program produces its own type of data files. Each has its strengths and weaknesses, and sometimes creating the best document means snipping a piece from a data file produced by one program and dropping it into a document from a completely different source. Done poorly, this process can result in Frankenstein's monster. But when you know how to use each program properly, the final document can be much greater than the sum of its parts.

The possibilities are limited mostly by your imagination. The most common scenario is to use Excel's superb analytical tools to create eye-catching charts and tables and insert them into a Word document or a PowerPoint slide. You can even save the resulting file as a web page so that anyone can view it, with or without their own copy of Office.

The fundamental tool for shifting data from one program to another, the Windows Clipboard, is as old as Windows itself. In Office (starting with Office 2003), Microsoft has enhanced the capabilities of the venerable Clipboard. The result—a Clipboard task pane that holds up to 24 items—is a mixed success at best. In this chapter, we'll show you how to use the Office 2007 Clipboard.

The second most popular technique for moving and copying data is dragging it from place to place with the mouse. In Word and Excel, it's easy to compare two documents in side-by-side windows. Click the View tab, choose View Side by Side (in the Window group), and specify which documents you want to compare. After your documents are arranged in side-by-side windows, you can compare their contents and drag data between them easily.

USING THE OFFICE CLIPBOARD

The Windows Clipboard holds one item at a time. Period. When you cut or copy something, it immediately and irrevocably displaces the current item in the Windows Clipboard. That makes some cut-and-paste jobs almost unbearable. To borrow bits and pieces of one document to use in another, you have to copy the first bit, switch to the second document, paste, and then return to the first document to do it again, repeating the process until your mouse finger finally screams in protest.

Using the Office Clipboard, you can gather as many as 24 Office objects and then paste them—one at a time or all at once—into a Word document, Excel workbook, or PowerPoint presentation (see Figure 6.1). The enhanced Clipboard can hold any data type that will fit in the Windows Clipboard, including text from a Word document; graphics (even the animated variety) for use in PowerPoint presentations; and Excel charts or ranges. With only a little extra effort, you can also gather objects from applications outside of Office onto the Office Clipboard and then paste them into your Office documents.

Choose an item to insert

Figure 6.1
Use the Office Clipboard to copy up to 24 items and then paste them, one at a time or all at once, into any Office document.

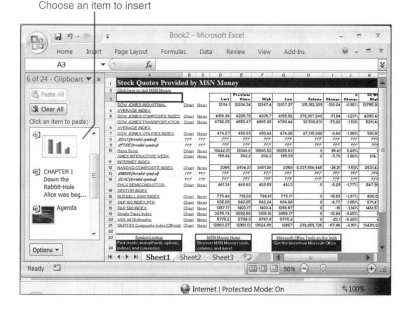

Using the Office Clipboard, you can tackle any of the following tasks:

- Pull together excerpts from a large report to create a summary or digest.
- Gather background information from scattered files and assemble the appropriate parts into the first draft of a report or presentation.
- Take a collection of notes, one from each member of a group, and stitch them together into a single report.
- Quickly collect a list of names or figures you expect to use repeatedly in a document.

DISPLAYING THE OFFICE CLIPBOARD

The contents of the Office Clipboard appear in a task pane, at the left side of your Word, Excel, or PowerPoint window (see Figure 6.1). To display the task pane, you can do any of the following:

- Click the arrow in the lower-right corner of the Clipboard group on the Home tab (see Figure 6.2). This method always works, regardless of how you have configured the Office Clipboard. Note that the window that drops down when you hover the mouse over this arrow does not actually show a preview of the Clipboard's contents; it just looks like it does.
- Press Ctrl+C twice in quick succession with the same text or object selected. This method works only if you have configured the Office Clipboard to respond to this signal (see "Configuring the Office Clipboard").

6

■ Double-click the Office Clipboard icon in the notification area of your taskbar (see Figure 6.3). This method works if you have configured the Office Clipboard to display the taskbar icon (it is configured this way by default). Hovering the mouse over the icon will tell you how many items the Clipboard contains.

TIP

By default, the Clipboard task pane is docked to the left side of your application window. You can make it "float" by clicking the down arrow at the top of the pane, choosing Move, and then dragging the pane.

Each item on the Office Clipboard is represented by an icon that depicts the program from which the item was copied. The Clipboard task pane also displays a thumbnail view of the copied item, whether it consists of text, numbers, or a graphic.

When you start an Office program, the first entry on the Clipboard task pane consists of the current contents of the Windows Clipboard. Whenever an Office program is running, any item you cut or copy using the standard Windows Clipboard techniques (even from a non-Office program) creates a new entry on the Office Clipboard. The Windows Clipboard keeps discarding its contents every time you cut or copy something new, but the contents of the Office Clipboard remain available as long as any Office program is running.

Each new item appears at the top of the Office Clipboard pane. When the Office Clipboard is visible and reaches its maximum of 24 items, cutting or copying another item drops the oldest item from the Office Clipboard.

PASTING FROM THE OFFICE CLIPBOARD

The Office Clipboard lists items in chronological order, from the newest item (at the top of the task pane) to the oldest (see Figure 6.2). To paste an item, just click it. To paste everything, click Paste All (at the top of the pane). When you paste the whole works, Office pastes the oldest item first, followed by the next oldest, and so on. You also can display the Office Clipboard task pane by double-clicking the Clipboard icon in the notification area (see Figure 6.3).

Figure 6.2
Click the arrow in the lower-right corner of the Clipboard group to display the Office Clipboard task pane.

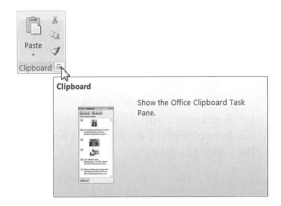

6

Figure 6.3
You can also display the Office Clipboard task pane by double-clicking the Clipboard icon in the notification area.

Clipboard icon

 If you're frustrated because the Paste All button is grayed out, see "Paste All and the Office Clipboard" in the "Troubleshooting" section at the end of this chapter.

CONFIGURING THE OFFICE CLIPBOARD

You have some choices about how the Office Clipboard works. To see them, click Options at the bottom of the Clipboard task pane (see Figure 6.4).

Figure 6.4
Default options include displaying a taskbar icon and a brief pop-up message when items are added to the Clipboard.

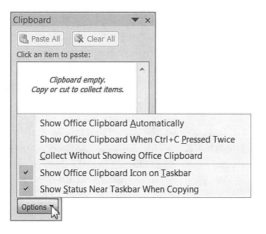

The default options, Show Office Clipboard Icon on Taskbar and Show Status Near Taskbar When Copying, are useful and unobtrusive, so you might as well leave them alone. (The second of these causes a brief message to pop up near your notification area whenever you add anything to the Clipboard. The message says something like "1 of 24" to let you know how many items you have added to the Clipboard.) The option labeled Show Office Clipboard When Ctrl+C Pressed Twice is not on by default, but it's also useful and harmless. Remember that the Ctrl+C signal is effective only when you press that combination twice in succession in the same place. There's also a time threshold involved here. If you select something, press Ctrl+C, wait a few seconds (without typing or moving the mouse), and then press Ctrl+C again, nothing happens. In other words, have no fear that turning this option on will make the pane appear by accident.

You can turn the Ctrl+C option on by selecting it in the menu or by selecting Show Office Clipboard Automatically (it's always on when you select the latter option). Note, however, that the Show Office Clipboard Automatically option does not do what you would probably

6

expect—it does not make the pane appear whenever you copy something in an Office application. In fact, it appears to do nothing at all; we suggest you ignore it.

Whether or not you activate the Collect Without Showing Office Clipboard option really does affect the system's behavior, however. The choices are as follows:

- If you leave this option unchecked (its default state), the Office Clipboard is inactive until you display the Clipboard task pane.
- If you turn on the Collect Without Showing Office Clipboard option, the Office Clipboard is always active. Any time you copy something in Word, Excel, or PowerPoint, what you copy is added to the Office Clipboard.

In other words, if you think the Office Clipboard is a totally useless frivolity, leave the feature in its default state, never display the Clipboard pane, and Office will behave as if the feature doesn't exist. If you want to use it only now and then, leave the feature off (its default state) and then display the Clipboard task pane on those occasions when you want to work with multiple Clipboard items. If you absolutely love the Office Clipboard and you want to have it working all the time, select Collect Without Showing Office Clipboard. Anything you copy from an Office application will land on the Office Clipboard, and any time you want to paste an item other than the latest addition, just display the Clipboard task pane and select that item.

TIP

> To stop the Office Clipboard from collecting any additional items, right-click the icon in the system tray and choose Stop Collecting from the shortcut menu. This immediately closes the Clipboard pane and removes the tray icon. It does not, however, clear the contents of the Office Clipboard.

The Windows Clipboard continues to operate just as it always does, without regard to the contents of the Office Clipboard. Every time you cut or copy a new item, it replaces the current item in the Windows Clipboard. Whenever you use the Paste command in a non-Office program, the Windows Clipboard uses the last item you cut or copied.

Don't expect miracles from the Office Clipboard. Among its many limitations worth noting are the following:

- You're limited to 24 items, period.
- It works only with Office programs. Although you can copy text and graphics from programs outside the Office family onto the Office Clipboard, you can't paste clips to those programs.
- Your saved clips stay in memory only as long as you have an Office program open. The Office Clipboard contents vanish when you close the last Office program in memory, and you can't save the list.
- You can't edit clips, nor can you see any more than the tiny preview in the Clipboard task pane.

6

TIP

> The Office Clipboard is useful, but for power users its limitations are all too apparent. If you really want to put some power in the Windows Clipboard (which you can then use in Office and any other Windows program), we recommend replacing it with a third-party utility. Mike Lin's Clipomatic (http://mlin.net/Clipomatic.shtml) is free and useful. For shareware utilities with a full set of features, try ClipCache Pro, from XRayz Software (http://www.xrayz.co.uk), or ClipMate, from Thornsoft Development (http://www.thornsoft.com). Unlike the Office Clipboard, these add-ons work with any Windows program. You can save hundreds or even thousands of clips for reuse later—when filling in forms, for example—and assign keyboard shortcuts to those you use regularly. You can even clean up clips—removing the >>> used as email forwarding indicators, for instance, or converting the case of text in a clip.

CONVERTING CLIPBOARD DATA INTO ALTERNATIVE FORMATS

When you paste an item from the Clipboard into an Office document, the Office program examines the item to determine its data format—simple text, HTML, formatted text (so-called Rich Text Format), worksheet data, or one of many picture formats, for example. Before the Office program pastes the Clipboard contents, a negotiation takes place in which the program attempts to discover the format that's most appropriate for the current contents.

Most of the time, Office makes the correct decision about what to do with the Clipboard's contents. In some cases, however, you might want to convert the Clipboard contents to an alternative format when pasting into another program (or even within the same program). For instance, when copying formatted text from one Office program to another—for example, the contents of an HTML-based email message into Word—you typically don't want the original formatting to appear in the document where you're pasting the data. Instead, you want to transfer just the text, letting it take on the paragraph formatting defined in the Word document.

In Office 2007, you have two opportunities to override the defaults and switch formats when using the Clipboard:

- Instead of using the default format, click the down arrow below the Paste command in the Clipboard group of the Home tab and then choose Paste Special. In the Paste Special dialog box, select from the available formats (see Figure 6.5). In this case, Unformatted Text is the best choice.

TIP

> As an alternative to using the Ribbon in Excel, you can choose Paste Special from the shortcut menu that appears when you right-click a cell. This handy shortcut menu item is not available in Word or PowerPoint, unfortunately.

6

Figure 6.5
Use Paste Special when you want to choose the format of copied data before pasting it into a new document.

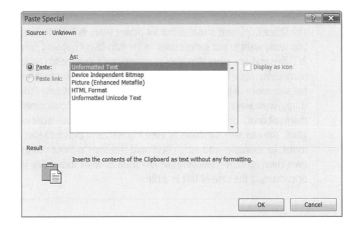

- After pasting the data, you can change its format by choosing from the Paste Options action menu, available by clicking the Smart Tag (see Figure 6.6). In this example, we copied a range of cells from an Excel worksheet and pasted them into a Word document. The Smart Tag shows additional formats available for the pasted data.

Figure 6.6
After pasting data into an Office program, click the Paste Options Smart Tag to change the format of the data.

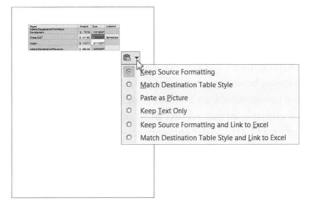

TIP

> The Paste Options Smart Tag might seem like a little thing, but it's one of the most useful improvements in Office in recent years. Whenever you use the Clipboard to copy data from one place to another within Office, it pays to click the Smart Tag to see which options are available on the action menu.

With an Excel worksheet range on the Clipboard, for instance, you can choose any of the following formats when using Paste Special to paste the data into a Word document:

- Microsoft Excel Worksheet Object—Used with the Paste Link option, this is a good choice if you plan to update the data in the worksheet and you want to ensure that the latest numbers appear in the Word document whenever it's opened.

- Formatted Text (RTF)—This option converts the Excel range to a Word table, retaining text formatting such as fonts and colors from the original data.

- Unformatted Text, Unformatted Unicode Text—These options force the text to take on the surrounding formatting in Word. Use the Unicode option if your original text includes any characters outside of the normal alphanumeric character set.

- Picture, Bitmap, Enhanced Metafile—Choose one of these formats to enable scaling and cropping, and to allow other kinds of picture formatting. You won't be able to edit text after pasting it in this format.

- HTML Format—Select this option if you intend to use the resulting Word document on a web page.

You can generalize from these formats to other options in other situations. Various Object types enable you to link or embed data from one program into another (an option discussed in more detail in "Combining Two or More Data Types in One Document," later in this chapter). Unformatted text options strip all the original formatting away, so the pasted data picks up whatever formatting is applied to the destination. Pasting in a picture format can cause formatting to become distorted, and you'll make the distortion worse if you try to resize the pasted-in picture after the fact. The good news with all these options is that you're free to experiment. Try a Paste Special format—if you don't like the results, click the Undo button and try another until you get the results you want.

DRAGGING AND DROPPING DATA

All Office programs support standard Windows drag-and-drop actions. Dragging with the left mouse button within a document, worksheet, or presentation moves the item from one place to the other. Word, Excel, and PowerPoint also enable you to drag with the right mouse button; when you do, you see a shortcut menu from which you can choose the correct action. For example, in Word, right-dragging a selected item enables you to choose whether to copy or move it to the new location, or to insert it as a shortcut or hyperlink (see Figure 6.7).

Excel allows right-drags and provides even more choices than Word: Move Here, Copy Here, Copy Here as Values Only, Copy Here as Formats Only, Link Here, Create Hyperlink Here, Shift Down and Copy, Shift Right and Copy, Shift Down and Move, Shift Right and Move, and Cancel.

6

Figure 6.7
Word, Excel, and PowerPoint allow you to drag text or objects with the right mouse button; in Word, use this technique to move text.

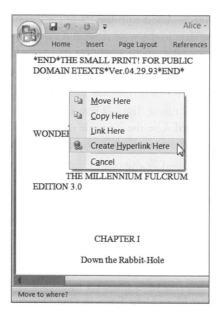

TIP

> One way to convert an Excel cell from a formula to its calculated value is to right-click an edge of the cell, drag it away, and then drag it back to its original location. When you release the mouse button, choose Copy Here as Values Only.

If you hold down the Ctrl key while dragging, the default action changes. In Excel, for example, use this technique on a worksheet tab to create a copy of the sheet. In PowerPoint's Slide Sorter view, Ctrl+drag copies the slide.

→ To learn more about moving and copying Excel data, **see** "Moving, Copying, Inserting, and Deleting Worksheets," **p. 356.**

Drag and drop is not limited to single documents or even single programs. By arranging document windows on your screen, you can easily drag and drop data from one window to the other. (For our advice on the best ways to work with multiple documents, see "Extra Credit: Side by Side with Office," at the end of this chapter.)

Dragging text between Word documents is a powerful and quick way to reuse material from one document in another. For example, if you select a phrase in one document, right-drag it to another document, release, and choose Create Hyperlink Here, you'll create a fully functional hot link between the two documents.

PowerPoint has terrific drag-and-drop capability in Slide Sorter view (see Figure 6.8). Drag or Ctrl+drag a slide from one presentation to another and you not only copy the slide, but it also automatically takes on the master style of the target presentation.

6

Figure 6.8
When you drag and drop in PowerPoint's Slide Sorter view, slides you copy between presentations are transformed to the target presentation's style.

To drag and drop between Office programs, arrange the windows on your screen so you can see both and then drag some Word text into an Excel cell or a PowerPoint slide into Word.

> **TIP**
>
> If you have a Word outline that's properly formatted, you can import it directly into PowerPoint and turn it into a presentation. But if your Word document doesn't conform to the official formatting rules, you can still assemble a presentation quickly: Set up a Word window next to a PowerPoint window and click and drag text from Word to the PowerPoint outline.
>
> When you want to drag between Office programs, but you want to work with each program at full size, use the Windows-standard drag-and-hover technique. Select the data from the original program, click, and then drag your mouse pointer over the target document's button on the Windows taskbar. Don't release the mouse button. Instead, allow the pointer to hover over the button for a moment, until the target window appears. Move the pointer to the correct location and release the mouse button to complete the drop.

COMBINING TWO OR MORE DATA TYPES IN ONE DOCUMENT

After you get beyond simple letter writing and number crunching, you get to the really interesting aspects of Office as a unified system. Using a few simple techniques, you can build *compound documents* by combining data created in a variety of sources—starting with a Word document and integrating an Excel worksheet into it, for instance, or incorporating an Excel chart into a PowerPoint presentation.

The most common use of compound documents is in business, where you can incorporate data from a "live" database into a Word document. Every time you open the document, the document goes out to the database and updates itself, so it's always up to date.

If you're using Office at home or in the classroom, of course, you're not going to be connecting to a corporate database, so these fancy techniques don't apply. But you can still benefit from creating compound documents. For example, if you're managing a list in Excel, you can link the range containing your list to a Word document so that the document is automatically updated when you make changes to the worksheet. Using this strategy, you don't have to remember to copy the Excel data into your report when it changes; the link between the two Office documents handles this chore automatically.

This all works because Office has an *object design*: Each Office document is essentially a container into which several kinds of information can be poured.

You'll see references to *OLE objects*, *COM objects*, and *ActiveX objects* in the online documentation and elsewhere. For everyday use, these terms all refer to the same thing. For simplicity's sake, we call them *objects* in this book.

NOTE
You'll also see the terms *OLE container*, *ActiveX container*, and *COM container* in the Help files and online articles. Don't be confused. These terms refer to Office files—documents, workbooks, and presentations.

EMBEDDING VERSUS LINKING

Office offers two very different methods for putting objects (such as text, charts, pictures, or a worksheet range) into a Word document, Excel worksheet, or PowerPoint presentation. The two methods are called *embedding* and *linking*:

- Embedding stores the data as an object inside the document, including an indication of which program made the object. So, if you embed an Excel chart in a Word document, all the data for the chart resides inside the Word document and Word "knows" it can be edited with Excel. The data for the chart is not available as an external file; thus, you can't start Excel and edit the chart directly. Instead, you must start with your Word document to edit the chart.

- Linking, on the other hand, inserts a pointer to data stored in an external file. When you create a link, the container document (the one that contains the link) might include a snapshot of the data, but it also attempts to update the link whenever necessary. Thus, if you insert a named range from an Excel worksheet stored in the file `C:\Users\Ed\Documents\Members.xlsx` into a Word document, the document stores a code that instructs Word to retrieve that range from the file in that exact location whenever you open or print the document. Because the data exists in an external file, you can use Excel to update `Members.xlsx` at any time, and your changes will be reflected the next time you open or print the Word document that contains the link.

Pictures frequently appear in documents as, simply, pictures—they're neither embedded nor linked.

Embedded objects are edited in place: If you double-click an Excel worksheet embedded in your Word document, for example, Excel's Ribbon replaces that of Word's—even though you're still working in the Word window (see Figure 6.9).

Figure 6.9
When editing an embedded Excel worksheet in Word, note that the window title says Word, but Excel takes over the Ribbon.

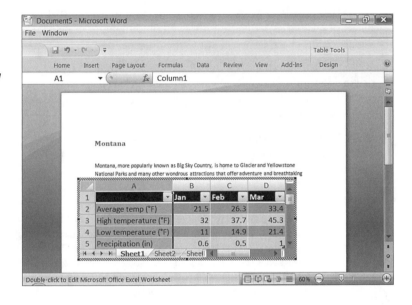

On the other hand, if you double-click a linked object, the originating program opens and loads the data from the linked external file. If you double-click an Excel chart linked in a PowerPoint presentation, Excel opens, loads the file containing the linked chart, and lets you begin working with it.

When you consider whether to link, embed, or place objects in documents, you must juggle three competing considerations:

- File Size—Will the objects make the document file too large? An embedded Office object (an Excel chart, say) can take up twice as much room as a picture of that same object. This isn't as much of an issue as it used to be, thanks to CD burners and USB flash memory keys.

- Update Capability—Will the object change? If so, you need to keep your options open. Yes, you can paste an Excel range into a Word document as a table and then convert it back to an Excel range for updates. But if you plan to update the data frequently, it's easier to embed or link the data.

6

- Portability—Will the document and objects stay on a single computer? If you think you'll distribute the file to one or more people over email, or if you plan to work on the file at your school's computer lab, you'll need to include all linked files. If one or more of the linked files are missing, anyone who opens the original document won't be able to see the updates and will have to deal with annoying error messages.

With those three goals in mind, here's how to select the best method for putting an object into a document:

- If you're not particularly worried about file size, and you won't need to update the object or change its formatting, forget about linking or embedding. Insert the data— picture, table, chart, whatever—into the document.

- If file size is the overriding concern and you don't expect to move documents from their original locations, use links to external data such as pictures and charts. If you need to move documents from one computer to another, just be sure to duplicate the folder structure for documents and linked objects.

- If portability is the main concern, and it's possible that you'll need to update the object or move the file that contains the source data, use embedding. That way, you'll always have the object at hand—the object and its data travel with the document.

> **TIP**
>
> You can quickly tell whether an object in Word is embedded or linked. Click the Office button, click Word Options, and choose the Advanced option in the left-hand pane. Under the Show Document Content heading, select the Show Field Codes Instead of Their Values check box . An embedded object appears with an {Embed} field code; a linked object appears as a {Link} field code. Pictures that are part of the file won't have any field code, and you can see the picture.

CREATING AND EDITING EMBEDDED OBJECTS

The easiest way to embed an object from one Office program into a document from another Office program is to use the Clipboard. For example, if you've created a table in Excel and you want to embed that table in Word, follow these steps:

1. Select the range that you want to use in your Excel worksheet.
2. Press Ctrl+C, or choose Copy from the Clipboard group on the Home tab.
3. Switch to the Word document, click the arrow below the Paste command on the Clipboard group of the Home tab, and choose Paste Special.
4. Choose the Paste (not Paste Link!) option and select Microsoft Office Excel Worksheet Object from the As list. (Note that the entry for this item in the Paste Special dialog box will look slightly different if the Excel file was not saved in the Excel Workbook format.)
5. Click OK.

Under some circumstances, you might want to create a brand new embedded object. If you're adding a simple table to a Word document, for instance, you might want to take advantage of Excel's new table features without creating a new worksheet. By creating a new object, you can enter your data and create the table object directly. The general method for creating any kind of new embedded object in Word or Excel is as follows:

1. Click to place the insertion point where you want to add the object.

2. Click the Insert tab, and then click Object (near the right side of the Ribbon, in the Text group). Then click Object on the drop-down menu. You'll see the Object dialog box shown in Figure 6.10.

Figure 6.10
Use the Object dialog box to create a new embedded object.

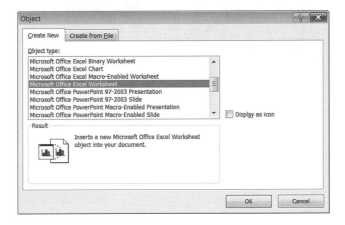

3. Scroll through the Object Type box until you find the type of object you want to insert. Select it and then click OK. The new object appears, ready for editing, using the menus and toolbars for the program associated with that object.

4. Edit the object as needed. When you're done, click outside the object area to return to the main document.

When you're back in the container document, right-click the object and select Format Object to set text wrapping, colors, size, layout, cropping, and the like.

PowerPoint works similarly, although you can get to the Object dialog box directly from the Ribbon, without going through an Object menu.

→ If you become frustrated trying to format or resize an embedded object, see "Formatting or Resizing Embedded Objects" in the "Troubleshooting" section at the end of this chapter.

In some cases, you can right-click and drag to create an embedded object. For example, if you right-drag a picture file from Windows Explorer and drop it onto a Word document, Word displays a shortcut menu. Choose Copy Here to embed the picture.

6

CREATING AND EDITING LINKED OBJECTS

You can create a link to an existing object in many ways. The easiest way to reliably create a link to an entire file is to follow these steps:

1. Click to position the insertion point at the location in the document (worksheet, presentation, and so on) where you want to add the link.

2. Click Object in the Text group of the Insert tab. Then choose Object from the drop-down menu and click the Create from File tab. You'll see the Object dialog box shown in Figure 6.11.

Figure 6.11
If the object already exists, you can embed or link to it from this dialog box.

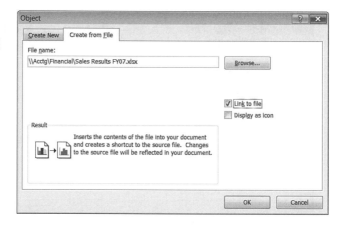

3. Use the Browse button to find the object, make sure the Link to File box is selected, and click OK.

Other ways to link to objects include the following:

- Use Ctrl+C to place the object on the Clipboard. Then click in the document where you want the link to appear, click the Paste button in the Clipboard group of the Home tab, and choose Paste Special. Select a format, choose the Paste Link option, and click OK.

- Click Picture in the Illustrations group of the Insert tab. In the Insert Picture dialog box, open the Insert drop-down list and choose Link to File.

In Word, if you choose Insert and Link from the Insert drop-down list, you get an embedded picture that's linked to the source file. A copy of the picture travels with the document, but each time the link is updated, Word goes out to the linked file and refreshes the picture.

It's all done with something called an {includepicture} field, which implements this strange hybrid of embedding and linking you won't find anywhere else in Office.

T I P

> If you're trying to link to a picture using the Clip Art task pane, you're out of luck. Office doesn't offer any direct way to link to clips stored in a Clip Art collection. If you insist on doing so, you need to track down the location where the underlying file is stored and then create a link directly to that file.

MANAGING LINKS BETWEEN DOCUMENTS AND OBJECTS

Try as you might to keep it from happening, links break easily. Because a link is just a pointer—a fully qualified filename, possibly with some ancillary information such as a range name—any time the path to the file changes, the link goes kaput. If you change the name or folder location of the object, the link breaks. If the link extends over a network and you lose the connection to the server or the shared folder on which the object is stored—for whatever reason—the link breaks as well. This is a particular concern on portable computers.

 If you have placeholder links instead of the pictures that should be in your document, see "Broken Links to Image Files" in the "Troubleshooting" section at the end of this chapter.

When you work with a Word document, Excel workbook, or PowerPoint presentation that includes one or more linked items, an Edit Links to Files command becomes available. To get there, click the Microsoft Office button and then choose Prepare (see Figure 6.12). Choosing Edit Links to Files displays the Edit Links dialog box, which lists all linked items in the current document, as shown in Figure 6.13.

Figure 6.12
To fix a broken link, choose Prepare on the Microsoft Office menu and then choose Edit Links to Files.

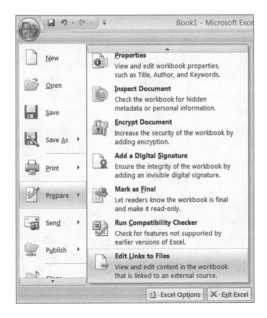

6

Figure 6.13
When a link breaks, use the Edit Links dialog box to fix it.

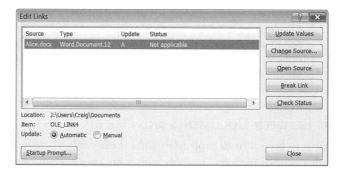

From the Edit Links dialog box, you can change the object (using the Change Source button), update the linked object manually, or break the link altogether. If you're planning to send a document to someone via email and they don't need to edit it, you should consider breaking the links first so they don't get any confusing error messages.

When you break the link, a format conversion takes place, changing the linked object into a picture, which is then placed in the document.

TROUBLESHOOTING

PASTE ALL AND THE OFFICE CLIPBOARD

Why is the Paste All button on the Office Clipboard grayed out?

When you click the Paste All button, the effect is the same as if you were to paste each item individually, pressing Enter (if necessary) between items. In some cases, some or all of the data types are incompatible with the current location of the insertion point. For example, if you've clicked in a cell within an Excel worksheet, you won't be able to paste a collection that contains a mix of text and graphics items. In that case, Office disables the Paste All button. Delete the incompatible data types from the Clipboard task pane, or paste the items one at a time.

FORMATTING OR RESIZING EMBEDDED OBJECTS

An embedded object is the wrong size, but there are no obvious options for reformatting or resizing it.

Formatting, resizing, and cropping an embedded object is difficult because embedded objects use formatting from their native program and generally ignore formatting from the host program. To complicate matters, the inserted object is frequently sized arbitrarily. In Word, try selecting the object and then enclosing it within a text box. If you can't get the formatting correct from outside the object, double-click it and see whether you can change settings in the program that created it.

Broken Links to Image Files

My document has placeholder icons instead of the pictures that should be visible there.

Those placeholder icons represent broken links to image files. If the links point to files on shared drives, check the permissions on the shared drive or folder. If it's necessary to move the linked files, you might need to re-create the links.

Extra Credit: Side by Side with Office

You have two copies of a document—an early draft and one that includes comments and annotations from a teacher or reviewer. You want to arrange both documents on the screen so you can compare their contents and move or copy data from one to the other. Here's how.

In Word or Excel, click the View tab and then click View Side by Side (in the Window group). This is absolutely, positively your preferred option when you need to see two documents alongside one another (see Figure 6.14).

The View Side by Side option is grayed out and unavailable until you have at least two documents or workbooks open. If you have more than two documents or workbooks open, a Compare Side by Side dialog box appears, enabling you to choose the document to which you want to compare the current document.

After you choose the View Side by Side command, a Synchronous Scrolling command also becomes available (directly below the View Side by Side command). This command allows you to synchronize scrolling of the two documents, so you can compare them without constantly switching back and forth.

If you maximize one of the documents to make some changes or take a closer look, click Reset Window Position to restore the side-by-side view. Click View Side by Side again when you're through with your comparison.

This option is ideal for occasional work with multiple documents. But if you regularly find yourself needing to arrange Office documents side by side, we have an even better suggestion: Get a second monitor (it's possible you'll also need to replace your display adapter, although most computers capable of running Windows Vista support two monitors). With two monitors, you can devote one full monitor to each window, without having to worry about squinting or painstakingly arranging windows on a single screen.

Figure 6.14
Viewing two documents side-by-side is just two clicks away.

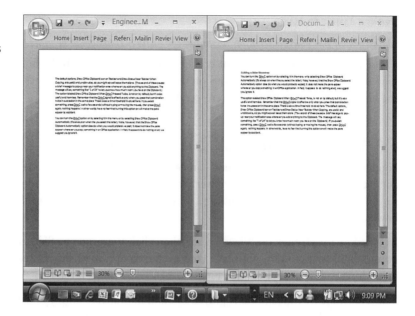

PART

II

USING WORD

CHAPTER 7

GETTING STARTED WITH WORD

In this chapter

WORD ESSENTIALS

When most people begin working with Microsoft Word, they open a new document and just start typing. Although that strategy has the advantage of producing immediate results, it doesn't allow you to take advantage of the power of Word. In fact, many of the most useful features of Word aren't immediately obvious, a failing we try to remedy in this chapter. Give us a few minutes of your attention and we'll explain why Word has so many different views, how to navigate effectively through even the longest documents, what you should know about printing, and how to enter and edit text using some of Word's most effective (and occasionally well-hidden) techniques.

Starting with Word 2007, the Ribbon, enhanced status bar, and zoom slider control all work harder so you can work less. We show you how to customize the Word interface so you can be more effective, and in the Extra Credit section at the end of this chapter we introduce a useful tool that can protect you from accidentally publishing personal or private information in a Word file.

CHOOSING THE RIGHT DOCUMENT VIEW

In previous versions of Word, you could switch views using buttons on the status bar or use options on the View menu to change the way your documents appeared onscreen. In Word 2007, the View menu is replaced by a View tab on the Ribbon, which incorporates most of the functions previously found on the View menu and throws in a few useful treats from the Window menu as well. The View buttons, meanwhile, have been rearranged and moved to the right side of the status bar, where they sit alongside a useful new Zoom slider.

These View buttons, shown in Figure 7.1, provide five ways to display the text, graphics, and other contents of your documents. Depending on the task at hand, you want to choose the view that provides the most appropriate mix of these features. Most experienced Word users find themselves switching views as they work on documents—particularly more complex documents—depending on what they're trying to accomplish. The view buttons are, from left to right, Print Layout, Full Screen Reading, Web Layout, Outline, and Draft.

> **TIP**
>
> In addition to using the status bar buttons, you can change to any of the five document views from the Ribbon. You'll find them in the Document Views group on the View tab.

DRAFT VIEW

Draft view (see Figure 7.2) shows section breaks, fonts and other character attributes, page breaks (shown as a dotted line), and, optionally, the names of paragraph styles. Draft view simplifies page layouts, hiding some elements to make editing easier.

Figure 7.1
Click one of the five View buttons to see your document from different perspectives.

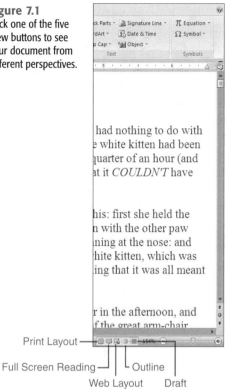

Print Layout
Full Screen Reading
Web Layout
Draft
Outline

Figure 7.2
Draft view shows most formatting, but reduces overhead by not showing pictures in their ultimate location.

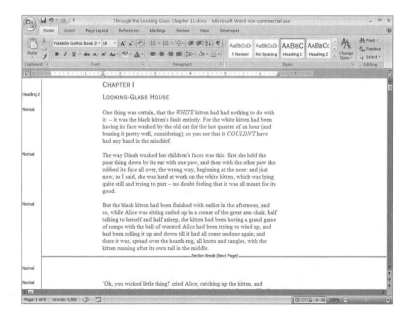

7

Draft view has three advantages that appeal to advanced users:

- You can see section breaks. If you have more than one section in a document, you should seriously consider working in Draft view when formatting or entering text.

- You can see style names for all paragraphs in a column to the left of the document. Normally, this area is hidden; to make it visible, click the Office button and choose Word Options, click Advanced, and finally change the Display section's option labeled Style Area Pane Width in Draft and Outline Views to a width greater than zero inches. When you click OK to close the Word Options window, each paragraph's style name appears to the left of each paragraph. With the style area visible, you can quickly scroll through a document to ensure that style standards are being observed. (This option is also available for Outline view.)

> **TIP**
>
> After you make the style area visible, you can use the mouse to drag it to a new width. If you drag the style area back to a width of 0 inches, the only way to make it visible again is with the Word Options dialog box.

- Draft view hides certain layout elements, including headers and footers, background images, drawing objects, and any picture that doesn't use the In Line with Text wrapping style. As a result, you can scroll through complex documents much faster in Draft view than in Print Layout view. When editing an exceptionally large file on a computer with limited resources, the difference in scrolling speed can be considerable.

WEB LAYOUT VIEW

If your document's ultimate destination is not paper but a website, it's important to see how the document will look when viewed as an HTML file. That's where Web Layout view comes in.

In Web Layout view, Word wraps text to fit the window, shows backgrounds, and places graphics on the screen the same way they would appear in a browser.

> **TIP**
>
> If you want to see how the document will appear in your default web browser—after all, each browser shows pages differently—click the Office button and select Save As. Choose the drop-down option labeled Web Page (*.htm; *.html) from the Save as Type option, click to display the Tools options at the bottom of the dialog box, and select Web Options. You can select the target browser that you want to view your document in (the list doesn't, alas, include popular non-Microsoft options like Firefox) as well as other options that determine how your document will look in that browser. You then can load the document inside your browser and review its appearance. Word 2007 is good at rendering web pages, and the browser's version should hardly differ from the document inside Word's Web Layout view.

PRINT LAYOUT VIEW

Print Layout view (see Figure 7.3) shows the document precisely as it will be printed, with page breaks, headers and footers, and pictures arranged correctly onscreen. (In Office versions previous to Office 2003, this view was called Page Layout view.)

Figure 7.3
Print Layout shows a true WYSIWYG (What You See Is What You Get) view of your document.

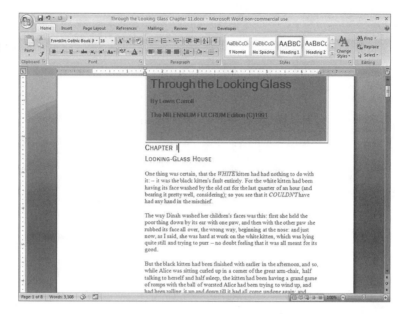

Picky Word users work in Print Layout view (unless they specifically need one of the tools available in the other views) because there are no surprises. The rendition on the screen closely mimics what will appear on paper.

OUTLINE VIEW

Outline view (see Figure 7.4) allows you to see an outline of your document while you're working on it. This view can be particularly helpful for rearranging sections of large documents, or promoting and demoting headings.

> **TIP**
> If you use Word's default Heading styles, outline levels are maintained for you. Otherwise, you can assign your own outline levels to individual styles. Click the dialog box launcher in the lower-right corner of the Paragraph group on the Home tab and make your choices from the Outline Level list. If you use the built-in Heading styles, Word changes the style applied to a given heading as you promote or demote it using the buttons in Outline view.

7

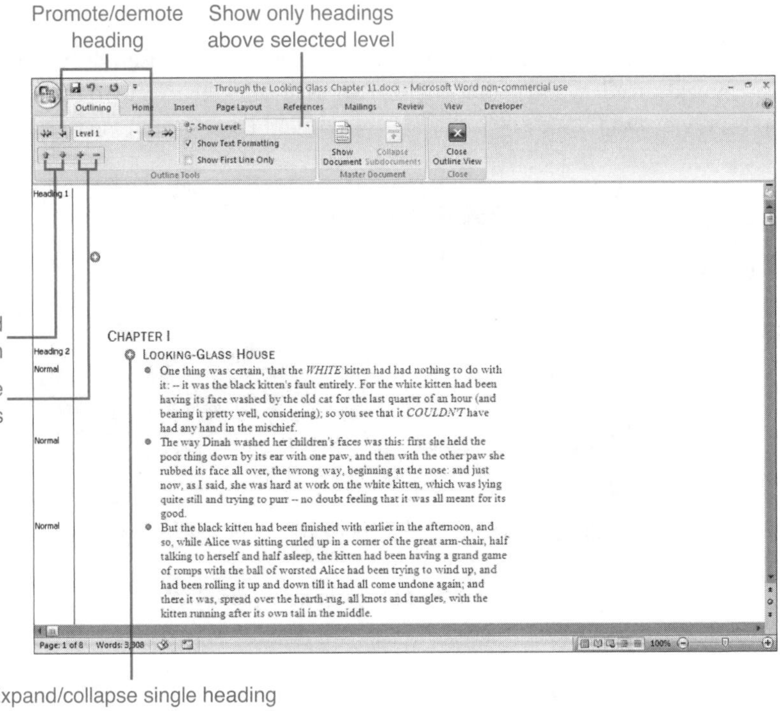

Promote/demote heading

Show only headings above selected level

Figure 7.4
Outline view shows the document's structure and enables you to freely move elements.

Move selected item up/down

Expand/collapse selected headings

Expand/collapse single heading

Of course, all the normal editing techniques are available in Outline view: You can select, drag, copy, cut, and paste as you would in any other view.

FULL SCREEN READING VIEW

In the Full Screen Reading view, Word uses the same fonts as in the original document; however, the display uses ClearType technology to make text easier on the eyes, and you can easily increase or decrease the size of the fonts without changing the formatting of the document itself. Unlike the Web Layout and Print Layout views, which are designed to display pages exactly as the designer intended them to be viewed in a browser or on paper, pages in Full Screen Reading view are rearranged to fit well on the screen, as shown in Figure 7.5. To see the document as it will appear in print, click View Options and select Show Printed Page.

To switch to Full Screen Reading view, click the Full Screen Reading view button on Word's status bar or the Ribbon's View tab. In Full Screen Reading view, you can show the Document Map and the Thumbnails pane (both of which are described in the next section). Word hides all toolbars except the Full Screen Reading and Reviewing toolbars. Many viewing options are available by clicking the View Options drop-down list from the top of the Full Screen Reading view screen.

Figure 7.5
Full Screen view alters the arrangement of text so pages are easier to read on the screen.

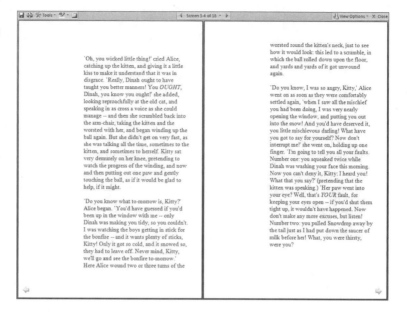

Page breaks show as gaps between pages in the Full Screen Reading view. Some users prefer that the page breaks show as a solid line instead, which gives them more screen real estate. Double-click the gap between any two pages while inside Full Screen Reading view and Word closes the gap and uses a heavy, solid line to indicate page breaks. Without the gap you'll gain a line or two more of text on your screen for your document. Double-click the page break line once more if you want the gap returned between your pages.

TIP

> A quick way to change the size of text in this view is to press and hold the Ctrl key and scroll your mouse or trackball wheel. The text increases or decreases in size depending on which direction you scroll.

Although this view is designed for reading, you have full access to editing tools, and you can add comments from the Tools drop-down menu. To exit Full Screen Reading view, click the Close button or just press Esc.

7

TIP

> When you double-click a Word document you receive as an attachment to an email message, Word automatically opens it in Full Screen Reading view. To change this default setting, click the Office button, select Word Options, and select the Open Email Attachments in Full Screen Reading View check box in the Popular section. If you're in Full Screen Reading view already, click View Options and then click Don't Open Attachments in Full Screen.

NAVIGATING WITH THUMBNAILS AND THE DOCUMENT MAP

Word provides two tools for keeping track of a document's navigation structure while you edit it. In all views except Full Screen Reading view, you can display a thumbnails pane that appears along the left side of the document window. This pane gives you a big-picture look at long documents and provides clickable links you can use to jump to a specific page. To make this pane visible, click the Ribbon's View tab and then select the Thumbnails option. To resize the thumbnails pane, click and drag its right edge; to make it disappear quickly, double-click the right edge.

The Document Map (see Figure 7.6) shows an alternate view of the document's outline, using the same outline levels employed in Outline view. It occupies the same space as the thumbnails pane, and in fact you cannot configure Word to show both elements at once.

To view a Document Map, click the Ribbon's View tab and then click the Document Map option. Right-click the empty space below the currently visible Document Map or right-click the plus or minus sign to the left of a heading to expand or collapse a specific heading or to hide headings below a selected outline level.

Figure 7.6
If you have enough room on the screen, Document Map offers one-click navigation to any heading in a document.

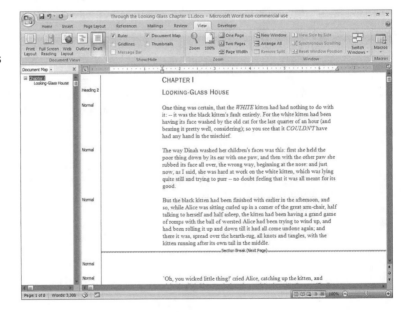

The Document Map is "hot" in the sense that you can click anywhere in the map and be transported to that location in your document. Unlike Outline view, it is not designed to offer interactive editing features—you can't promote or demote headings in the Document Map—but experienced Word users who commonly deal with long documents can readily navigate with it.

→ For more details on how to use the Document Map to get around in a long document, **see** "Navigating with the Document Map," **p. 172.**

ZOOM OPTIONS

Word enables you to zoom a document, making it appear larger or smaller on the screen. Microsoft introduced the zoom slider in Word 2007 and it's one of the best user enhancements in the upgrade. Just drag the zoom slider to the left or right to zoom out or in to your document from any view except Full Screen Reading view. The Zoom button on the View tab also allows access to the Zoom dialog box (see Figure 7.7) where you can control the amount of the zoom with the more traditional approach. To quickly display the Zoom dialog box without using the Ribbon, click the Zoom percentage value to the left of your status bar's Zoom Slider control.

Figure 7.7
Zoom in (higher percentage number) to see more detail; zoom out to see more of the page.

TIP

> Fine-tune the Zoom percent to make your fonts more legible. For day-to-day use, you want the largest zoom factor that lets you see your most commonly used fonts without straining. Also, double-check that you can easily distinguish visually between normal, bold, and italic characters with your zoom setting.

From the Ribbon's Zoom group, you can use the Zoom dialog box or the other Zoom options to choose automatic scaling options: Zoom the display to the width of a page, fit just the text on the page, view an entire page, or see two pages side by side. The Zoom dialog box includes one additional control that you can use to view multiple pages. Holding

7

Ctrl and moving your mouse's scroll wheel is usually the fastest way to zoom in or out of a document in 10% increments, although you won't get the precision you can obtain from the Zoom group on the Ribbon's View tab.

TIP

> Remember that you can select the Full Screen Reading view when you want more room on your screen to see your document without changing the magnification, as you do when you use one of the zoom controls.

SPLITTING A DOCUMENT WINDOW

Word allows you to split the document window, giving you two independently scrollable panes looking at the same document, one over the other (see Figure 7.8). Although each of the panes operates independently—you can even have Draft view in one pane and Outline view in the other—it's important to realize that you have just one copy of the document open: Changes made in one pane are reflected immediately in the other. This can be useful because it allows you to compare parts of a document directly, even when they're widely separated in the document.

Figure 7.8
Split the document window into two separately maintained panes to view different parts of the same document simultaneously.

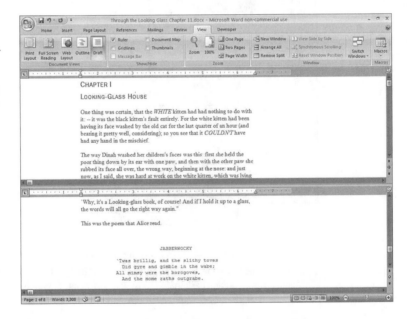

To split the document window, click the Ribbon's View tab, click the Split button, and click where you want the split to appear. Click and drag the split bar to resize the document panes. Double-click the split bar to restore the window to a single pane. (The Insert tab's Split button becomes a Remove Split button, so you may also click it to restore a split screen back to a single viewing window.)

NOTE

> You cannot split the document window if the Document Map or thumbnails pane is active.

NAVIGATING THROUGH A WORD DOCUMENT

Word offers an enormous number of ways to move through a document, and most people can increase their productivity by learning some of the shortcuts.

You needn't memorize dozens of key combinations or obscure mouse tricks to boost your productivity, and the amount of time you need to invest is negligible. If you concentrate on reducing the effort you expend on the two or three navigational techniques you use most, your productivity will soar.

Not all the best navigation tricks are well known, either. Some of them aren't even documented. In this chapter, we promise we won't just throw lists of shortcuts at you; instead, we'll teach you some tricks for memorizing the most important ones.

USING THE KEYBOARD TO MOVE THROUGH A DOCUMENT

Aside from the obvious up, down, left, and right arrows, the most useful keyboard shortcuts for navigating around a document are listed in Table 7.1.

TABLE 7.1 NAVIGATION KEYS IN WORD

To Move	Press
Next word to right	Ctrl+Right Arrow
Next word to left	Ctrl+Left Arrow
One paragraph up	Ctrl+Up Arrow
One paragraph down	Ctrl+Down Arrow
To beginning of line	Home
To end of line	End
Up one screen	Page Up (PgUp)
To beginning of first line of current screen	Alt+Ctrl+Page Up
Down one screen	Page Down (PgDn)
To end of last line of current screen	Alt+Ctrl+Page Down
To beginning of document	Ctrl+Home
To end of document	Ctrl+End

7

Most experienced Word users benefit from memorizing three groups of shortcut keys from those in Table 7.1, and they're all based on the Ctrl key. Here are the combinations and the way the Ctrl key changes the keys you're probably accustomed to:

- Ctrl+Home/Ctrl+End—Go to the beginning/end of the document (instead of beginning/end of line)
- Ctrl+Left/Right Arrow—Move by words (instead of characters)
- Ctrl+Up/Down Arrow—Move by paragraphs (instead of lines)

TIP

> Possibly the most useful, but obscure, key combination in Word is Shift+F5. Word keeps track of the last three locations where you edited text. Pressing Shift+F5 cycles through those three locations. This setting is persistent, too. When you open a document and you want to return to the last location you edited, press Shift+F5.

USING THE MOUSE TO MOVE THROUGH A DOCUMENT

Word follows most of the standard Windows mouse navigation techniques, with a few interesting twists. All of them are based on proper use of the scrollbars and the scroll box (the rectangular element within the scrollbar that defines which portion of a document is visible within the window) as described in Table 7.2.

TABLE 7.2 MOUSE NAVIGATION TECHNIQUES IN WORD

To Scroll	Do This...
Up one screen	Click above the scroll box
Down one screen	Click below the scroll box
To a specific page	Drag the scroll box and watch the ScreenTips for page numbers
In Draft view, scroll left, into the margin	Press Shift and click the arrow at the left of the horizontal scrollbar

If you have a mouse with a scroll wheel or extra buttons, additional mouse navigation options might be available. See the documentation that came with your mouse for more details. No matter what extra features the manufacturer provides, always remember that you can zoom in or out of your document by combining the use of the Ctrl key with your mouse wheel.

NAVIGATING WITH THE DOCUMENT MAP

By far the most powerful way to navigate through a long document with the mouse is via Word's Document Map. It's particularly valuable for advanced Word users who have to navigate through documents that are more than, say, five pages in length.

The Document Map is a "hot" outline of the document's contents—similar to a Table of Contents—which appears in a pane to the left of the document itself. If you take a little care in applying heading styles, the entire structure of your document appears in the Document Map, and each important point is directly accessible.

7

Because the Document Map is "hot," you can click a heading and jump immediately to the corresponding point in the document. You can use section headings or chapter numbers, for instance, to navigate using the Document Map. As you edit and add to your document, the Document Map updates as well.

Word constructs the Document Map based on outline levels, as defined in paragraph styles. If you stick to the standard Word heading styles—Heading 1, Heading 2, and so on—the outline levels are automatically applied by Word (level 1, level 2, and so on). If you use your own styles, they can have whatever outline level you want to apply.

→ For more details on styles, **see** "Formatting Documents with Styles," **p. 291.**

→ For details on changing the outline level and other paragraph format settings, **see** "Adjusting Paragraph Alignment and Outline Level," **p. 225.**

TIP

> Want to change the look of the text in the Document Map? No problem, as long as you know where to look. Word doesn't make this setting easy to locate! This setting is controlled by a hidden style; if you make it visible, you can adjust it. Open the Apply Styles task pane (Ctrl+Shift+S) and click the Styles button below the Style Name drop-down list. Click Options and select All Styles in the Select Styles to Show drop-down list. Click OK. Your floating Styles window (also called the Styles task pane) now displays all the styles available to you. Close the dialog box, saving your changes. The Document Map style should now be visible in the task pane, where you can change the font, font size, color, and other settings.

USING THE KEYBOARD AND MOUSE TO SELECT TEXT

In general, Word parallels the rest of Office in methods for selecting blocks of text. The wonders of Extend mode, however, remain unique to Word.

Word allows you to select multiple, noncontiguous blocks of text. Hold down the Ctrl key as you drag across the text you want to select, and then repeat the process to select the second and subsequent blocks (or double- or triple-click as you would with a single selection).

TIP

> You can change one single selected block of text without deselecting everything. Hold down the Ctrl key and click once inside a previously selected block. That specific selection, and only that selection, is deselected.

In addition, Word enables you to extend the current selection:

1. Click once at the beginning of the text block you want to select.
2. Hold Shift and click again at the end of the text block you want to select. If you make a mistake, continue holding Shift and click until you select exactly what you want to select.
3. Click once anywhere in the document, or press Esc, to remove the selection.

7

This technique can be particularly useful if you need to select large blocks of text. Although you can always click and drag across the text you want to select, Word sometimes scrolls so quickly that it's hard to stop.

If you hold down the Alt key and drag to select text, you'll find that Word selects a rectangular block of text without regard for sentences and paragraphs. This feature comes in handy in oddball circumstances—for instance, when you want to trim leading spaces from an imported text list. Click at the beginning of the text block, hold down Alt, and drag down to select the "column" of spaces. Then press Delete. Mastering this technique might take some practice; if you don't get it right the first time, press Ctrl+Z to undo your work and start over.

BOOKMARKS

In the classroom or the den, a bookmark is a piece of paper that marks a location in a document. In Word, a *bookmark* is a selection—a piece of text, a picture, or just an insertion point—with a name.

Bookmarks come in handy in two situations:

- They provide a location to which you can navigate. For example, you can put a bookmark in a document called "StartOfChapter17." Then you can tell Word "go to the bookmark called StartOfChapter17" and you're transported to that location. Similarly, you can use bookmarks as the destination for hyperlinks, setting up a link, say, to the bookmark called PopulationTable in a document saved as Economic History of Florence.docx.
- Word provides several tools for retrieving the text covered by a bookmark. For example, if you create a bookmark called MemberName in a form letter you're creating for the Swim Club, you can sprinkle {REF MemberName} fields throughout the contract, and everywhere the field appears, that person's name will show up.

To set a bookmark, do the following:

1. Select the text you want to have bookmarked, or click in your document to position the insertion point at the location you want to bookmark.
2. Click the Ribbon's Insert tab and then click Bookmark (or use the keyboard shortcut Ctrl+Shift+F5). The Bookmark dialog box appears (see Figure 7.9).
3. Type a bookmark name. Names must start with a letter and can include letters, numbers, or the underscore character (_), but not spaces.
4. Click Add. Word establishes a bookmark with that name at the indicated location.

Figure 7.9
Bookmarks can cover text, pictures, paragraph marks, and almost anything else in a document—or they can be as small as an insertion point.

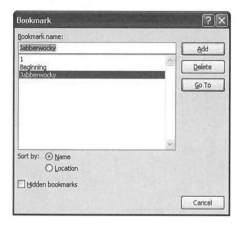

How can you spot existing bookmarks in a document? Normally, bookmarks are invisible. You can configure Word to display bookmarks with a subtle (maybe too subtle) indicator. Click the Office button, select Word Options, and then click the Advanced tab. Select the Show Bookmarks check box in the Show Document Content section and then close the Word Options dialog box. Word displays bookmarks as faint gray brackets surrounding the bookmarked text or location. You might need to squint to see these indicators, and you will look in vain for any further help—Word offers no ScreenTips or other indications that could help identify the bookmark.

If you move a block of text that includes a bookmark, the bookmark goes along. If you delete a block of text that includes a bookmark, the bookmark is deleted. If you copy a block of text that includes a bookmark, the bookmark stays in its original location, and the copy does not contain a bookmark.

Word has no built-in method for renaming bookmarks. You must take the long way around: Use the Bookmark dialog box to select the existing bookmark, create a new bookmark with a new name, and then delete the old bookmark.

Be careful when adding or deleting text near a bookmark. Text you enter at the beginning of a bookmark is added to the bookmark. Text you enter at the end of a bookmark is not added, unless the bookmark ends with a paragraph mark.

NAVIGATING THROUGH DOCUMENTS WITH THE SELECT BROWSE OBJECT MENU

In the lower-right corner of the Word window—down below the vertical scrollbar's down arrow—you'll find a remarkable collection of three buttons that allow you to browse through your document by jumping from object to object. In this case, the objects can be any of a dozen common types of Word data, including fields, comments, pictures, pages, and headings.

7

Browsing by object generally works best if you use it this way:

1. Click the circle in the middle (the Select Browse Object button, shown in Figure 7.10) and select one of the 12 Browse By boxes.

Figure 7.10
Word offers several ways to browse through your documents.

2. Click the Next button (the double down arrow, just below the Select Browse Object button) to search toward the end of the document for the next occurrence (the next picture, for instance, if you chose Browse by Picture). Click the Previous button (the double up arrow just above the Select Browse Object button) to search toward the beginning of the document. If you have trouble clicking these undersized buttons, use the keyboard shortcuts instead: Ctrl+Page Up and Ctrl+Page Down.

You can search for the following "objects":

■ Fields—Word moves from field to field, although it skips hidden fields (such as {XE}, the field that creates entries for a document's index).

→ To learn how you can empower your documents with fields, **see** "Using Fields Intelligently," **p. 332.**

■ Endnotes—An endnote is typically used to cite sources in a research paper or other formal document. It consists of a note reference mark, which is embedded in text, and the note itself, which appears at the end of the document. If you start in the body of the document, Word jumps through the document, stopping at each note reference mark. If you start in an endnote, Word cycles through each of the endnotes.

■ Footnotes—Footnotes are constructed like endnotes, except that the note portion appears at the bottom of the page containing the note reference mark. If you start in the body of the document, Word jumps from one note reference mark to the next. If you start inside a footnote, each click selects the next footnote.

■ Comments—The Next button works differently, depending on whether comments are visible on the page (as they are when you click the Ribbon's Review tab, click Show Markup, and choose Comments). If you position the insertion point inside a comment and click the Next button, you'll go to the next comment. If comments are hidden, clicking the Next button goes to the next comment marker. Using the Previous button jumps through the body of the document, from one comment marker to the next, regardless of whether comments are visible.

■ Sections—Word moves from the beginning of one document section to the next.

→ Ever used sections before? Many Word users haven't, at least knowingly. **See** "Page/Section Setup Options," **p. 210.**

- Pages—Word moves to the top of the next or previous page.
- Go To—This is the most interesting of the Browse By options. When you click the Go To box on the Select Browse Object menu, Word opens the Go To dialog box, as shown in Figure 7.11. Go To includes most of the other options on the Select Browse Object menu (Page, Section, Field, and so on), as well as Line, Bookmark, Equation, and a confusingly named Object option, which goes to the next embedded object.

Figure 7.11
Use the Go To box with the Select Browse Object menu to navigate in unconventional ways; these settings jump forward 10 lines at a time when you press Ctrl+Page Down.

Using the Go To box and the Select Browse Object menu together make it easy to navigate through a document in creative ways. To see all the bookmarks in a document, one after the other, click the Select Browse Object menu, and then click Go To (or press the keyboard shortcut Ctrl+G). In the Go to What box, select Bookmark. Click the Go To button. From that point on, each time you click the Previous button or press Ctrl+Page Down, you'll go to the next bookmark in the document. If you want to review all the second-level headings in an important term paper, you can choose Heading from the Go to What box, type **2** in the Enter Heading Number box, and begin browsing. Choose Line and enter **+10** to move through a document exactly 10 lines at a time.

- Find—Same as using the Find dialog box (available from the Ribbon's Home tab). We discuss the Find dialog box at length later in the section named, "Finding and Replacing Text and Other Parts of a Document."

  After you've set up a Find or Replace, the easiest way to repeat the Find or Replace is to exit the dialog box and use the keyboard shortcut Ctrl+Page Down (or Ctrl+Page Up to search backward).

- Edits—Word automatically keeps track of the last three locations where you've made changes. This setting enables you to cycle among the three edits (the same as the Shift+F5 keyboard shortcut). Note that these changes may be in different documents.
- Headings—Cycles to the beginning of each paragraph in the document that is formatted with a Heading *n* style, where *n* is any integer between one and nine.
- Graphics—Moves to the next or previous picture in the document (whether linked or embedded), or to the next or previous drawing canvas. This option ignores pictures and drawing canvases in the drawing layer.
- Tables—Cycles through all the Word tables in the document.

7

ENTERING TEXT AND GRAPHICS AUTOMATICALLY WITH AUTOTEXT AND AUTOCORRECT

Word has two main features for entering text and graphics automatically: AutoText and AutoCorrect.

→ To learn how to speed up repetitive text entry, **see** "Using AutoCorrect to Type Faster," **p. 90.**

When you type an AutoCorrect entry followed by pressing the spacebar, Enter key, or any punctuation mark, Word swaps out the text you've typed and replaces it with the indicated text (and graphics) in the entry. For example, you can set up an AutoCorrect entry to change dfre into The Decline and Fall of the Roman Empire. You see no warning that the change will take place; it just happens.

On the other hand, when you type an AutoText entry, such as octo, for example, Word replaces the octo with October only after you press F3. The AutoText entry, requiring the F3 to activate, is therefore less automatic. AutoCorrect is best-used for words you commonly misspell and for setting up abbreviations that you want Word to change into their full meaning as you type. AutoText is best used when you have a larger, formatted set of text you want to insert such as a common, formatted name and address closing at the end of a letter.

Many users agree that AutoText is one feature made more cumbersome in Word 2007. For example, if you don't know the AutoText shortcut code (such as octo), you'll need to select from a list of AutoText entries you've created. You can locate and insert an AutoText entry into a document by clicking the Ribbon's Insert tab, clicking on the Quick Parts button, selecting Building Blocks Organizer, locating the AutoText field you want to insert, and clicking the Insert button. As you can imagine, pressing F3 after typing the AutoText entry is much faster but if you've forgotten the shortened code that reflects the AutoText entry, you'll have to resort to the Building Blocks Organizer. AutoText is just one of several building block items available. Other building block items are cover pages, headers, footers, and page number formats (see Figure 7.12).

> **TIP**
>
> If you use AutoText entries regularly—and any productivity-obsessed Word user should— we suggest that you add the AutoText button to the Quick Access toolbar. Click the down arrow to the right of the Quick Access toolbar, select More Commands, and choose All Commands from the Choose Commands From drop-down list. Scroll to the AutoText entry, click Add, and then click OK. An AutoText button now appears on your Quick Access toolbar and you won't have to access the Building Blocks organizer to quickly choose any AutoText entry you've created from a convenient drop-down list. An option at the bottom of the list allows you to make a selection and save it as a new AutoText entry.

The current date, days of the week, months of the year, your company name, your username, and your initials are all picked up automatically by Word and turned into AutoText entries.

Figure 7.12
You'll find a list of AutoText entries, as well as other building blocks that save you typing time and effort, in the Building Blocks Organizer dialog box.

AutoText entries are stored in templates, so you can have separate global entries stored in the Normal document template (Normal.dotm or Normal.dotx) and local entries that apply only to documents based on specific templates.

In most cases, you'll find AutoCorrect easier to use than AutoText, thanks to the following advantages:

- Unformatted AutoCorrect entries are available to all Office programs.

- After AutoCorrect makes a change, you can hover your mouse pointer over the AutoCorrect entry and the AutoCorrect action menu (the lightning bolt icon) gives you access to the full array of AutoCorrect options, both for this individual entry and for AutoCorrect in general. That's handy.

- It takes at least one extra keystroke (F3) and possibly several mouse clicks if you use the Building Blocks Organizer to put an AutoText entry into a document. Many typists, especially fast typists, find that distracting.

However, in some circumstances AutoText is preferred:

- You can create AutoText entries for words without fear of accidentally triggering a replacement. For example, you could create an AutoText entry called pater that expands into The Paternal Order of Ornery Fellows. If you had an AutoCorrect entry with the same name and you typed the Latin phrase *pater familias*, you would end up with The Paternal Order of Ornery Fellows *familias*.

- AutoCorrect entries are global. Super-global, in fact, in that they take effect throughout Office. AutoText entries can be localized to specific templates.

7

To create an AutoText entry, follow these steps:

1. Type and, optionally, format the replacement text (or graphics) that you want.

2. Select the text. Include the paragraph mark, if you want, and the paragraph's formatting in the AutoText entry. (You might need to click the Show/Hide button in the Paragraph group of the Ribbon's Home tab to see paragraph marks if you don't normally work with them turned on.)

3. Display the Quick Parts drop-down list by clicking the Quick Parts button on the Ribbon's Insert tab. Select the Save Selection to Quick Part Gallery option to save your selection (including its format and any graphics that might be selected with it) to the Quick Part Gallery that you can then manage with the Building Blocks Organizer. The Create New Building Block window appears (see Figure 7.13).

4. The shortcut text goes in the Name field. Select AutoText from the Gallery drop-down list, add an optional description, and select how global you want the AutoText to be (choose Normal.dotm if you want the AutoText entry available to all documents you create with the Normal.dotm template).

5. Click OK and your new AutoText entry is saved.

After selecting the text you want to store as an AutoText entry, click the Quick Access toolbar's AutoText button (if you added it there) and choose Save Selection to AutoText Gallery at the bottom of the AutoText list to open the Create New Building Block window instead of going through the Ribbon's Insert tab.

Figure 7.13
You can save a selection as a new AutoText entry in your Building Blocks Organizer dialog box.

USING HYPHENS AND DASHES

A hyphen is a character on any standard keyboard. Dashes are longer than hyphens and are used for specific purposes in keeping with rules of typography and grammar. Word automatically changes some hyphens into em and en dashes (an em dash, as the name implies, is the width of a lowercase m, and an en dash is the width of a lowercase n). For example:

- Type a letter, two hyphens, and another letter, and then press the spacebar, add a punctuation mark, or press Enter. Word changes the hyphens to an em dash. It's nicely done, because the em dash has a little space to the left and right, and a line can break before or after it.

7

- Type any letter, a space, a hyphen or two, and any other letter, and Word transforms the hyphen(s) into an en dash.

This behavior is controlled by Word's AutoFormat as You Type feature.

→ For instructions on how to disable this and other AutoFormat options, **see** "Disabling AutoCorrect and AutoFormat Settings," **p. 199.**

In addition, you can always type an em dash into a document by pressing Alt+Ctrl+- (minus) on the number keypad. An en dash is Ctrl+- (minus) on the number keypad.

CAUTION

> Don't use the - (minus, or hyphen) that's located on the top row, to the right of the zero, on most keyboards.

When you use narrow columns, good hyphenation becomes crucial. On a term paper or letter that uses the full width of a letter-sized page, hyphenation isn't necessary. But in a highly formatted document where you use all of Word's designer-level typographical tricks—columns, text boxes, and so on—you need to pay close attention to line length. Unhyphenated or poorly hyphenated text is easy to spot—just look for the vast expanses of white space in the right margin. Word offers three methods for hyphenating:

- Automatically—Most experienced Word users who work in Print Layout view avoid this method because the constant sliding of lines makes it hard to concentrate on the screen; choose this option when you're copying text from another source into a formatted document. To turn on automatic hyphenation, click Hyphenation on the Ribbon's Page Layout tab and select Hyphenation Options to display the Hyphenation dialog box (see Figure 7.14). In the Hyphenation dialog box, click the Automatically Hyphenate Document check box. Hyphenation takes place immediately when you click OK, and Word continues to automatically hyphenate as you type or edit text. The Hyphenation Zone is the maximum allowable white space at the end of a line; the Limit Consecutive Hyphens To box specifies the maximum number of consecutive lines that can be hyphenated.

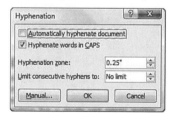

Figure 7.14

- Manually, Whole Document—Click Hyphenation on the Ribbon's Page Layout tab and select Manual. Word steps you through each hyphenation, allowing you to accept or reject each.

NOTE

> Generally, you'll want to undertake a manual hyphenation only after the text is in its final form. Making any changes to the text will probably throw off the hyphenation, at least in any changed paragraphs.

7

- Manually, One Word at a Time—You needn't turn on automatic hyphenation to have Word hyphenate an occasional word. Instead, use a soft or optional hyphen: Click where you want the soft hyphen to appear and then press Ctrl+-. Word uses the hyphen if it's required to balance out the line; if not, the hyphen won't appear.

Sometimes you want to prevent Word from breaking a line at a hyphen. For example, you decide in a paper on computer storage technology that the word CD-ROM should never be broken. Tell Word that you don't want it to break at that point by using a hard or nonbreaking hyphen: Ctrl+Shift+-.

TIP

Do you want to tell Word not to hyphenate a particular paragraph? You can accomplish that goal by using one of two formatting options. You'll find the more explicit option in the Paragraph dialog box, found by clicking the dialog box launcher at the right of the Paragraph group on your Ribbon's Home tab and then selecting the Don't Hyphenate check box. For a more indirect option, open the Language dialog box (choose Set Language on the Review tab) and select the Do Not Check Spelling or Grammar check box. Although it isn't immediately obvious, this option also prevents hyphenation.

FINDING AND REPLACING TEXT AND OTHER PARTS OF A DOCUMENT

If you want to find something simple, the standard Find features used throughout Office should suffice. You can look for literal text by typing any word or phrase into the Find What box on the Find dialog box. After selecting the Use Wildcards check box, you can have Word perform fuzzier searches: m?ne matches mane and miner, but not manner, and bo*t matches boats or bought, but not bat.

→ To sharpen your text-finding skills with techniques that work in any Office program, **see** "Finding and Replacing Text," **p. 88.**

Sometimes you need even more powerful search capability. Perhaps you're looking for all the words in a document that end with *ing*. Or you can get complex—say you have a list of license plate numbers and need to find the ones starting with the number 1 through 9, followed by the letters *QED*, and then four numbers ending in 9.

Word contains a flexible, powerful mini-language, a close cousin of the widely used *regular expression* syntax, that enables you to specify precisely what to find. To begin creating your own search expressions, choose Edit, Find, click the More button, and select the Use Wildcards check box (see Figure 7.15).

As detailed in the next section, this search string will find all those license plates:

```
<[1-9]QED[0-9]{3}9
```

Figure 7.15
The search string shown here uses wildcards and expressions to solve the license plate number problem described in the text.

Each part of the search string performs the following tasks:

- The < signifies that the following characters have to start a new word (in this case, a word is a license plate number).
- The [1-9] matches any single number between 1 and 9.
- The QED forces an exact match on the letters *QED*.
- [0-9] matches any single number.
- The {3} that immediately follows [0-9] means that the previous element is repeated three times; thus, you must have three consecutive numbers to match this search term.
- Finally, the 9 on the end matches only a 9.

FINDING TEXT

In addition to the ? and * wildcards, Word recognizes the symbols in Table 7.3. (See the preceding section for a detailed example using this syntax.)

TABLE 7.3   WILDCARDS FOR FIND

Symbol	Meaning
[xyz]	Matches exactly one of the listed characters. b[aioe]g matches bag and bog, but not bug.
[A-Z]	Matches any single character in the range. Case sensitive. b[A-W]g matches bAg and bUg, but not bug or bARge.
[!xyz]	Matches any single character except the ones listed. b[!au]g will match big and bog, but not bag, bug, or bring.
[!A-Z]	Matches any single character that doesn't lie in the range. Case sensitive. b[!a-m]g matches bog or bug, but not bag or big.

continues

TABLE 7.3   CONTINUED

Symbol	Meaning
<	The character(s) that follow this symbol must appear at the beginning of a word. `<[a-c]` matches `act` and `cat`, but not `react`. `<bl` matches `blue` and `blech`, but not `able`.
>	The character(s) that precede this symbol must appear at the end of a word. `ing>` matches `hiking` and `writing` but not `singer`. `[a-c]>` matches `Alma` and `tab` but not `read`.
{n,m}	The preceding character or expression must appear between *n* and *m* times. If the *m* is omitted, the character must appear *n* or more times. Thus, `blec{3,7}h` matches `blecccch` and `bleccccccch`, but not `blecch`, and `b[an]{2,}g` matches `bang` but not `bag`.
@	Same as {1,}. The preceding character must appear one or more times. `bo@t` matches `bot` and `boot`, but not `bat` or `boat`.
\	Search for the literal character that follows the backslash, even if it's a wildcard. `wh[ae]t\?` matches `what?` and `whet?` but not `whether` or `whatever`.

Word also includes a handy list of special symbols—tab characters, em and en dashes, page and section breaks, and so on—under the Special button of Figure 7.15, shown previously.

All this wildcard-matching business can be confusing, but it gets worse: Word supports two kinds of pattern matching. All the wildcard matching discussed so far in this chapter applies when you select the Use Wildcards check box, as shown in Figure 7.15. A different set of symbols is available if you do not check the Use Wildcards box.

Perhaps the easiest way to illustrate the difference is with the paragraph mark. If you leave the Use Wildcards box unselected and then type `^p` in the Find What box, Word will dutifully find the next paragraph mark.

However, if the Use Wildcards check box is selected, there is no apparent way to tell Word to find the next paragraph mark! If you type `^p` in the Find What box and the Use Wildcards box is checked, Word stops only if it finds a literal match in the document—that is, a caret followed by a `p`.

It's difficult to tell, offhand, whether a particular character or symbol is included in one group or the other. If you're trying to match a character that you can't type directly, the best approach is to start by clicking the Special button on the Find and Replace dialog box. If the character is on the drop-down list, click to select it and add the code to the Find What box. If that doesn't work, select the Use Wildcards check box, click Special, and look again.

Although the online documentation encourages you to paste text from a document into the Find What box, some characters (most notably paragraph marks) can't be pasted.

There are two more search options that you should use with caution:

- Sounds Like catches some simple homonyms (*new*, *gnu*, *knew*, for example, or *fish* and *fiche*), but it also makes odd matches (*rest*, according to Word, sounds like *reside*) and bizarre mistakes (*oh* sounds like *a*, according to Word, but not *owe*). It also fails the Woody test: According to Word, *Leonard* does not sound like *Leonhard*. Woody's parents would beg to differ.

■ Find All Word Forms is supposed to catch noun plurals, adjective forms, and verb conjugations: Tell Word to replace *heavy* with *light* and, with Find All Word Forms checked, *heavier* will be replaced by *lighter*, *heaviest* will be replaced by *lightest*. This, too, has problems. For example, tell Word to replace *bring* with *take* and, with Find All Word Forms checked, "I have brought it" will be replaced by "I have took it."

REPLACING TEXT

Replace behaves much the same as Find, except the entry in the Find What text box is replaced by the entry in the Replace With text box (see Figure 7.16).

Figure 7.16
The Replace tab of the Find and Replace dialog box enables you to build expressions using Word's powerful wildcard syntax.

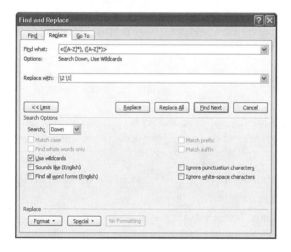

When performing a replace, you can use parentheses in the Find What box to specify groups of characters, which are then referenced in the Replace With box. The contents of the first pair of parentheses in the Find What box becomes \1 in the Replace With box, the second becomes \2, and so on.

This can be handy if, say, you want to replace all the occurrences of American-style dates (perhaps 10-20-51) with their European day-first equivalents (20-10-51). Make sure the Use Wildcards box is selected, and then in the Find What box, type

`<([0-9]*)-([0-9]*)-([0-9]*)>`

to force Word to recognize the American style date: the day (inside the first set of parentheses) becomes \1, the month (in the second set of parentheses) becomes \2, and the year becomes \3. In the Replace With box, type

`\2-\1-\3`

and the dates are swapped around.

Few people realize that you can use Word to change a list of names that looks like this:

`Lastname, Firstname`

Into a list that looks like this:

`Firstname Lastname`

To do so, click Use Wildcards and in the Find What box, type

`<([A-Z]*), ([A-Z]*)>`

and in the Replace With box, type

`\2 \1`

> **TIP**
>
> You can tell Word to use the contents of the Windows Clipboard in the Replace With dialog box. That can be handy if, for example, you want to replace a word, such as *STOP*, with a picture (perhaps a stop sign) throughout a document. To make it so, clear the Use Wildcards check box, and then type ^**c** in the Replace With box. Word interprets ^c as being the contents of the Windows Clipboard.

FINDING AND REPLACING FORMATTING

Word doesn't limit you to searching for and replacing text. You can specify formatting, as well—replace all occurrences of the italicized words *current annual dues* with the bold number **$100**. Here's how:

1. Click the Replace button on the Home tab. Click the More button to expose the Format selections.

2. In the Find What box, type **current annual dues**.

3. With the insertion point still in the Find What box, click the Format button and choose Font. Under Font Style, click Italic, and then click OK.

4. In the Replace With box, type **$100**. With the insertion point still in the box, click the Format button and choose Font. Under Font Style, click Bold, and then click OK (see Figure 7.17).

5. You can now proceed with the replace. Click Replace to verify each match individually, or click Replace All to make the update throughout the document.

> **TIP**
>
> If you're handy with keyboard shortcuts, you can use them to great effect in the Find/Replace dialog box. Click in the Find What or Replace With dialog boxes and then use any relevant keyboard shortcut to bypass the Format dialog boxes. Click Ctrl+I or Ctrl+B to toggle between italic and bold fonts, for instance. (This option also makes available a third option, Font: Not Italic or Font: Not Bold, where you can search only for matching text that *doesn't* have a particular attribute.) You can also search for paragraph attributes, such as centered or justified text or those with a particular line spacing specified.

Figure 7.17
In formatted searches, Word tells you that you're searching for formatted text by including the Format: line under the Find What or Replace With boxes.

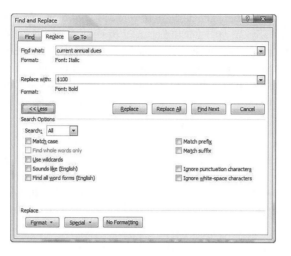

If you need to find and replace multiple instances of a particular word or phrase, it's easier to find the first instance, change it if needed, and then close the dialog box. That way, you can click the Next button (just below the Select Browse Object button) or press Ctrl+Page Down or Shift+F4 to find the next instance. Closing the dialog box clears clutter off the screen, and you can better see what you're doing. You can also quickly edit the found text without having to click outside the dialog box, and then press Ctrl+Page Down to continue searching. Press F4 to repeat the previous change, or use the contents of the Clipboard to replace the found text by pressing Ctrl+V.

In addition to Font formatting, you can specify Paragraph formatting, Styles (either character or paragraph), Tabs, Language, Frame type, or Highlight.

If you want to clear the formatting for either the Find What or Replace With boxes, click once inside the box and then click the No Formatting button at the bottom of the dialog box.

Both the Find and Replace formatting settings are "sticky." If you set Find to look for Heading 1 style paragraphs, for example, the next time you perform a Find or Replace, Word continues looking for Heading 1 style paragraphs.

NOTE

When you're done looking for a particular kind of formatting—or replacing with a particular kind of formatting—you must manually clear the formatting. Click to position the insertion point in the Find or Replace box and then click the No Formatting button.

INSERTING FOOTNOTES

Footnotes in Word are straightforward, although the terminology can be a bit difficult to fathom.

7

To put a footnote in a document, click the References tab on your Ribbon. Click Insert Footnote. A Footnote section opens at the bottom of your document and you can type your footnote. (To insert an endnote, click the Insert Endnote button. The endnote appears at the end of the current section or at the end of your document if no section changes take place between the current position and the end of the document.) Word automatically numbers the footnotes (or endnotes) for you, or you can specify your own footnote reference character.

Word draws a horizontal line between the text on a page and the first footnote. The line is called a Footnote Separator. If the footnote is too long to fit on one page, Word continues it onto the next page and uses a longer horizontal line, called a Footnote Continuation Separator. You can work with the separators by switching into Draft view and then selecting either Footnote Separator or Footnote Continuation Separator from the footnote's drop-down list.

→ If you need to create two references to the same footnote, **see** "Inserting Cross-References," **p. 276.**

Checking Spelling and Grammar

Word contains one of the most sophisticated spell-checkers you can find. The spell-checking module, which Word shares with the rest of Office, contains rich tools for custom dictionaries and "exclude" dictionaries, and easy right-click access to suggested spellings for words highlighted with the infamous red squiggly line.

→ To find out how to supercharge Word's spell-checker, **see** "Setting Up Spell-Checking and Related Options," **p. 44.**

Some people find the red squiggly lines distracting—as if they're being forced to correct spelling mistakes as they type. Word includes a batch spell-checker, so you can turn off the squiggly lines and run a spell-check after you're done typing. To turn off the squiggly lines, click the Office button and choose Word Options. Click the Proofing tab and clear the Check Spelling as You Type check box. To run a batch spell-check, click the ribbon's Review tab and select the Spelling and Grammar button—or press F7.

TIP

> If you don't want Word to spell-check a specific word or paragraph, select the text or paragraph, choose Set Language on the Review tab, and select the Do Not Check Spelling or Grammar check box.

The grammar checker's advice, on the other hand, can be overly simplistic. Why? Because it's rule-based, and grammar (whether in English, French, Spanish, or any of the other commonly used languages that also use the Word grammar checker) is far too complex to fit neatly into a small set of rules. If you know you need help with basic (and we do mean basic) grammar issues, you can get a great deal of benefit from the grammar checker. Most advanced users, however, find the squiggly green lines distracting and turn them off (click the Office button and choose Word Options; click the Proofing tab and clear the Mark Grammar Errors as You Type check box).

If you want the grammar checker to help improve specific aspects of your writing (such as flagging sentences that are too long or in passive voice, or *their/there* mistakes), you can customize Grammar Checker to respond only to violations of those rules. To do so, click the Office button and choose Word Options. Click the Proofing tab and click the Settings button to find dozens of grammatical problem areas; you can then instruct Word to watch for the ones most important to you.

To use Word's built-in Thesaurus, position the insertion point inside the word you want to look up, click the Ribbon's Review tab, and click Thesaurus. Alternatively, you can bring up the spelling checker by pressing F7, and the Thesaurus with Shift+F7.

PRINTING WORD DOCUMENTS

Most Word documents are destined for the printer. Word offers many features to give you extensive control over how pages print.

PREVIEWING PRINTED PAGES

If you're looking at one page, Word's Print Preview mode offers no real advantage over the standard Print Layout view. But Print Preview is extremely useful in two situations. Move the Zoom Slider control to show as few as two pages or several dozen at one time (the maximum number of pages allowed in Print Preview mode depends on your hardware). This view is especially helpful when you want to see at a glance where headlines, graphics, tables, and other nontext elements fall in your document. Although it's possible to edit text and move objects on the Print Preview screen, this screen is most appropriate for getting a bird's-eye view of your entire document.

To enter Word's Print Preview mode (see Figure 7.18), click the Office button, point to Print, and select Print Preview from the list of choices.

In Print Preview mode, you also have access to the Shrink to Fit button in the Preview group. Use this feature when the last page of your document includes two or three lines, and you want to force those leftovers to fit on the previous page.

Click the Shrink One Page button (identified in its ScreenTip by the old name Shrink to Fit) and Word alters font sizes to reduce the number of pages in the document by one. Note that changing the font size sometimes doesn't affect the spacing between paragraphs, so the resulting document might have an inordinate amount of white space. Also, the Shrink operation makes no changes to margins. Word won't reduce font sizes below the range of 6 or 7 points.

CAUTION

> While in Print Preview mode, you can click the Undo button or press Ctrl+Z to reverse the Shrink to Fit operation, but after you've closed and saved the document, it's impossible to return the document to its original state.

7

Figure 7.18
Word's Print Preview mode shows you precisely how the printed page will appear—but Print Layout view does almost as well, with none of the limitations.

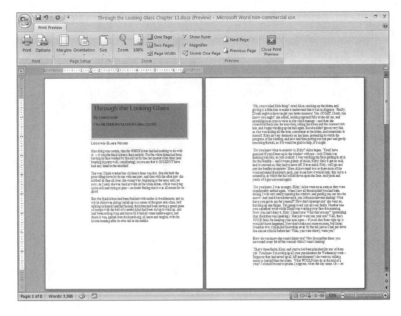

CHOOSING WHAT TO PRINT

If you want to print one copy of the current document using the defaults established on the Print dialog box (which you can review by selecting Print from the Office button's menu), press Ctrl+P. You can add the Print button to your Quick Access toolbar if you often find yourself accepting the Print dialog box's default options.

Word also allows you to print the currently selected page(s), or to specify the pages you want to print by page number. To invoke either of those options, click the Office button (or press Ctrl+F) and choose Print. Select Current Page or type in the page numbers in the Pages box (see Figure 7.19).

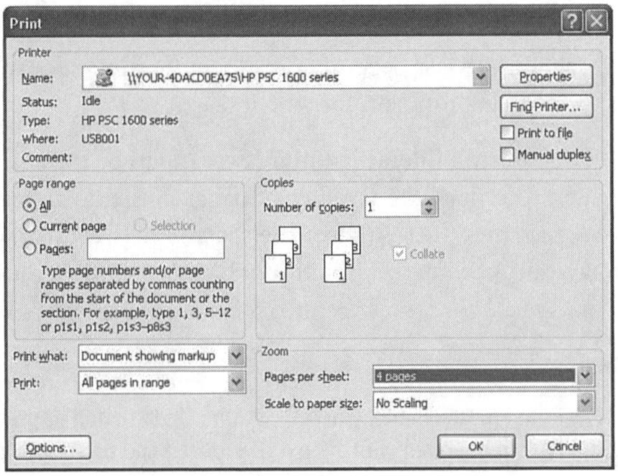

Figure 7.19
Word's Print dialog box allows you to print thumbnail images, two or four (or more) to a page, and gives you other options you'll find throughout the Print dialog after clicking Properties.

The Print box enables you to print all pages, or odd or even pages only. If you know how your printer feeds sheets, you can use this setting to print "duplex"—where pages alternate on the front and back of each sheet.

TIP

> If you check the Print to File box in the Print dialog box, Word prompts you for a filename. If your printer is currently unavailable, but you want to produce a hard copy of a document you're working with now, it can be a good option. Later, when the printer is available, you don't need to reopen Word; just copy the file you created directly to your printer by dragging it onto the printer icon in Windows Explorer.

Ever wonder what AutoText entries you have set up in a particular document or template? How about the styles or many other hidden parts of your document, for that matter? Choices in the Print What drop-down list help you find out these bits of information (see Table 7.4).

TABLE 7.4   PRINT DIALOG BOX'S PRINT WHAT CHOICES

Option	What Prints
Document Properties	Some of the information found in the dialog box that appears when you choose File, Properties; all the Summary information; some of the General and Statistics information
Document Showing Markup	Prints the document with changes, including comments, tracked in the margin; it does *not* print the style area
List of Markup	Prints a list of markups made to the current document
Styles	All the styles that you can see if you choose Format, Styles, and select Styles in Use
Building Blocks Entries	All Building Blocks entries available in the document, whether they originate in the document's template or the Normal global document template, Normal.dotm (or Normal.dotx)
Key Assignments	Only custom keyboard assignments for the current document, current template, and global template

PRINTING THUMBNAILS

The Pages Per Sheet list in the Print dialog box (shown previously in Figure 7.19) offers you the opportunity to print thumbnails of your documents—2, 4, 6, 8, or 16 pages—on a single sheet of paper.

7

TIP

> If your primary reason for printing is to file away a hardcopy record of your documents, consider printing 2-up or 4-up (available from the Print dialog box's Properties button), duplex if possible. Although you might need a magnifying glass to read the resulting printout, the storage space savings are enormous. If you regularly need to print double-sided pages and booklets, we highly recommend a wonderful program called FinePrint (http://www.fineprint.com), which handles those tasks and much, much more with aplomb.

COLLATING

If you choose to print more than one copy of a document, Word's default settings *collate* the copies for you—printing one copy from start to finish, and then printing the next copy from start to finish, and so on. That's convenient if you want to pull the pages right out of the printer and pass them around without any additional work.

SHARING DOCUMENTS

As the coauthors of this book can attest, collaborating on a writing project isn't easy. When two or more people work together to produce a document, disagreements inevitably arise over the right words to use and the best way to communicate concepts. To smooth the bumps in the collaborative process, Word includes a set of workgroup features that make it easier to track changes in a document.

In this section, we discuss Word's traditional collaboration features, all of which entail different people opening and editing a document. In a business setting, the shared document is typically stored in a shared network folder; in this book, we assume that you're most likely to pass around drafts of a document in progress via email.

TRACKING CHANGES TO A DOCUMENT

When more than one person can make changes to a document, pandemonium can ensue. The surest way to maintain the integrity of a document is to ensure that changes—if they're allowed at all—are clearly identified. That way, anyone reviewing the edited document can see each specific change and review the reasons for that change with the person who made it.

When you use Word to track changes made to a document, Word keeps a careful record of insertions, deletions, and changes in formatting, attaching a set of initials to each change. You and your partners can insert comments that aren't included with the text of the document. At the end of the process, you can go through the document one change at a time, accepting or rejecting each change, or you can accept every change with one click of the mouse.

To specify that you want Word to track changes made to the current document, click the Review tab and click Track Changes.

The Reviewing pane gives you one convenient location for working with all document changes. You can display the Reviewing pane either vertically or horizontally depending on whether you click Reviewing Pane Vertical or Reviewing Pane Horizontal from the Ribbon's Review tab. The drop-down list in the Review tab's Tracking group enables you to look at any of the following, depending on the options you've set in the Review tab:

- Final Showing Markup—This view shows the final state of the document. In Print Layout, Web Layout, Outline, or Full Screen Reading views, inserted text appears underlined and in a different color and deleted text appears in balloons in the margin. In Draft view, deletions appear as strikethrough text and insertions appear in color with the underline attribute.

- Final—The end result of all revisions without the intermediate insertions and deletions explicitly appearing.

- Original Showing Markup—In all views except Draft view, this option shows the original document, with insertions appearing in the margin and deletions marked with the strikethrough attribute. In Draft view the format changes don't appear in the margin.

- Original—What the document looked like before Track Changes was turned on.

Shifting back and forth among the different views gives you a quick idea of the effect of changes. If you're rewriting a first draft prepared by someone else, for instance, you might prefer to work in Final view, where Word behaves exactly as if you were editing the document without tracking changes. If you're reviewing an edited document, you can switch to Final Showing Markup so you can see what was deleted. Figure 7.20 shows a document that is currently under revision.

Figure 7.20
Using the Final Showing Markup view, you can see additions in the body of the document and deletions in the margin.

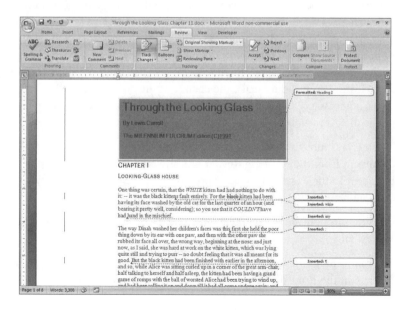

Use the Tracking group on your Ribbon's Review tab to fine-tune which changes Word tracks and how it displays them on the screen. If you find the balloons distracting in one of the non-Draft views, for example, click the Balloons button, and then click Show All Revisions Inline. Use the Show Only Comments and Formatting in Balloons option to show deletions and additions in the body of the document and comments in the margin. If you'd rather not keep track of formatting changes, click the Track Changes button. (Balloons are only visible in Print Layout and Web Layout view. If you're working in Draft view, changes appear in the document itself, and comments appear in a pane at the bottom of the document editing window.)

When reviewing a document, use the Accept, Reject, Previous, and Next buttons in the Changes group on the Review tab to jump from revision to revision, accepting or rejecting individual changes as you go.

What if you didn't turn on change tracking before passing a Word document along to someone else for their input? If the other person saved changes to a new document and you still have the original document, you can have Word compare the two documents and mark the differences between them. Open the original document and click Compare on the Ribbon's Review tab and then click Combine. Open the second document. This feature automatically generates revision marks, noting the pieces that have been added or deleted from the original document, along with formatting changes. Use the buttons in the Changes group on the Review tab to view and accept or reject changes.

ADDING COMMENTS TO DOCUMENTS

When you're collaborating on a document with other people, it's helpful to leave comments along the way, explaining why you made a specific change or suggesting places where additional changes might be necessary. When editors or reviewers make changes to a document for which you have final responsibility, it's relatively easy to accept or reject their additions or deletions. Don't fall into the trap of using comments to suggest changes, however; transferring those comments into the document requires multiple steps and takes a fair amount of time. Instead, you should make the change in the document itself (highlighting it with a bold color, if necessary) and add a comment inviting the original author to reject the change if he or she disagrees with it.

To enter a comment, select the text that pertains to the comment and choose New Comment from the Ribbon's Review tab. (If you don't make a selection, Word attaches the comment to the word immediately preceding the insertion point.) Type your comment in the comment box.

To cycle through all the comments in a document, use the Next button on the Ribbon's Review tab.

You can print all the comments attached to a document by selecting Document Showing Markup in the Print dialog box's Print What drop-down menu.

RESTRICTING CHANGES TO A SHARED DOCUMENT

For change tracking to work, all the people working on a document have to keep this option turned on. Otherwise, their changes won't be explicitly shown, and you'll have to go through the additional step of comparing your original document with their modified versions to figure out what has changed. In addition, you might want to pass around a document so that other people can read it without making any changes. To handle either of these scenarios, you can *protect* the document from unwanted changes. Word uses a special task pane to help you specify editing restrictions.

To set editing restrictions for the current document, follow these steps:

1. Click the Protect Document button at the far right side of the Review tab. This opens the task pane shown in Figure 7.21.

2. Under Editing Restrictions, select the Allow Only This Type of Editing in the Document check box.

3. Select an editing option from the drop-down list. To force everyone making changes to a document to have Word track their changes, choose Tracked Changes. To prevent any changes to the document, select No Changes (Read Only).

4. Click the button labeled Yes, Start Enforcing Protection.

5. In the next dialog box, enter an optional password if you don't want people to be able to override this setting. Click OK to finish.

Figure 7.21
Use the Protect Document task pane (backed up with a password, if necessary) to force other team members to track changes to the current document.

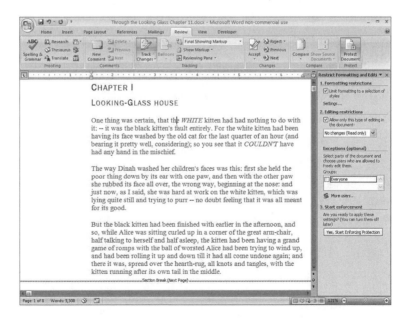

From that point on, anyone who opens the document has to abide by the restrictions you specified. To remove the restrictions, click the Protect Document button again to remove the protection.

STRATEGIES FOR NON-WORD ENVIRONMENTS

Do other people in your circle of coworkers use non-Microsoft word processors? Although Word is still the most popular word processor by a huge margin, WordPerfect has a loyal base of users, thanks to widespread bundling on inexpensive new computers. In addition, the StarOffice suite and the free OpenOffice suite have attracted fans who are either on a tight budget or want to make an anti-Microsoft statement. Many new computers come with Microsoft Works, which uses document format that Word 2007 can read and write.

To exchange documents with people who use these and other word processors, the simplest solution is to save your files in a format the other person can open. (Click the Office button, choose Save As and select from the Save as Type list.) The default Word 2007 file format is an XML-based format that will probably, someday, become the de facto standard for formatted business documents, as has happened with all Word formats to date. If none of these options is satisfactory, consider Rich Text Format as an option.

CUSTOMIZING THE WORD INTERFACE

Many components of the Word interface—toolbars, keyboard shortcuts, and the like—work precisely the same way as the other Office programs.

→ For the Office-wide overview, **see** "Point, Click, Customize," **p. 28.**

In this section you learn how to take control of features that are specific to Word. If you find that a feature in Word gets in your way, more often than not there's a simple check box that will disable the feature—or enable an alternative that might work better for you.

Word's customizing settings fall into two main groups: Options settings and AutoCorrect settings. You'll find choices for both throughout Word's Options dialog box, which is available when you click Word's Office button and choose Word Options. You'll also see an action menu (the lightning bolt icon that appears whenever AutoFormat makes a change) which allows you to delve directly into the AutoCorrect settings, by choosing the Control AutoCorrect Options item. Although most of the settings are quite obvious, we cover the most important (and confusing) ones in the following sections.

CONTROLLING HOW WORD DOCUMENTS APPEAR ON THE TASKBAR

Word normally produces one taskbar icon for each open document. If you prefer to see a single window for Word, with each open document appearing within that window, right-click a blank area of your taskbar and select Properties. Click to uncheck the Group Similar Taskbar Buttons option.

7

OPTIONS SETTINGS

Settings you make on the Display tab of the Word Options dialog box control the appearance of the Word editing window. When you create a new document, it takes on the settings defined here. You can subsequently change settings for the document, and they "stick" when you open and close the document. The main considerations for adjusting these options are

- Consider showing tab characters, so you can see why and how text lines up on tab stops.
- Some people prefer to see paragraph marks when they're copying, moving, and deleting blocks of text. If paragraph marks aren't shown on the screen, it's difficult to tell when you have selected one.
- If you have trouble with drawing layer items moving around on a page, show object anchors to see where the drawings are tethered.

The Advanced tab contains a long list of settings:

- If a specific document has links that you want to update only manually (perhaps because the updating takes a long time), clear the Update Automatic Links at Open check box.
- There is no penalty in rolling the Recently Used File list to nine, aside from a little lost screen space when you click the Office button.

SETTING EDITING OPTIONS

The Editing Options section on the Advanced tab controls how Word reacts when you edit text:

- If you select Typing Replaces Selected Text, Word overwrites any selected text whenever you press a key on the keyboard. Many advanced users turn off this option, to avoid accidentally deleting text.
- Normally, the Insert key toggles Word into and out of Overtype mode (where characters you type at the keyboard overwrite characters on the screen). You can turn off that behavior by making sure the Use the Insert Key to Control Overtype Mode check box is cleared. This is the default setting in Word 2007, but if you notice this behavior, this is the setting to check.
- The Use Smart Paragraph Selection option drives many advanced Word users nuts. If you select this check box, and you select only part of a paragraph but include the paragraph mark, Word drops the paragraph mark automatically and without warning.
- Select the Use Ctrl+Click to Follow Hyperlink check box to ensure that you never accidentally chase a hot link by inadvertently clicking it.

7

- By default, the When Selecting, Automatically Select Entire Word setting is on. It forces Word to select an entire word plus the following space when only part of a word is actually selected. For most people, this is a usability improvement. If you routinely select portions of words and sentences, clear this check box (or learn to hold down Ctrl+Shift when you want to select text that contains a portion of a word).

SETTING PRINT OPTIONS

In the Word Option dialog box, the Display tab contains a Printing Options section that enables you to set default printer settings:

- Consider selecting the Update Fields Before Printing check box if you want Word to automatically update all the fields in a document before it's printed. In some cases, it's beneficial to update all the fields so they have the most recent information (times, dates, and so on). But in other cases, you might want Word to skip the updating—for example, if you've manually modified several field results (perhaps Table of Contents or Index entries).

→ To learn about fields in depth, **see** "Using Fields Intelligently," **p. 332.**

- Specify whether hidden text should appear on the printout by selecting or clearing the Print Hidden Text check box.

> **TIP**
>
> Printing hidden text can come in handy if you need to print two versions of a document. For example, a teacher might set up an exam so the questions are in regular text and the answers are marked as hidden. Printing hidden text would produce a key for graders.

SETTING OPTIONS ON THE SAVE AND POPULAR TABS

The Save tab includes settings for both saving and AutoRecover:

- Select a different file-saving format by selecting from the Save Files in This Format option. If, for example, you must share documents with people who only have Word 2003, you can change the default file type to Word 97-2003 Document (*.doc).
- Word can automatically save an AutoRecover backup copy of the currently active document—a *.wbk file—at time intervals you specify in this dialog box. If Word crashes or freezes, the next time it starts, it automatically looks for and opens any *.wbk files. With a little luck, the automatically recovered file will contain all your edits, up to the most recent AutoRecover time. This protection is in addition to the built-in crash protection. If you're a fast typist, consider setting the interval to as little as two or three minutes.

> Don't disable AutoRecover unless you find the backup process terribly onerous. And if you do disable it, make sure you periodically save the current file. Word *does* crash—it isn't a question of whether, only of when.

The Popular tab contains the user's name and initials. These settings are used for identifying tracked changes, comments, envelope return addresses, and much more. Take a moment to make sure they're correct.

DISABLING AUTOCORRECT AND AUTOFORMAT SETTINGS

Advanced Word users should also periodically examine their AutoCorrect settings to ensure they aren't getting in the way. To open this dialog box, click the Office button and then click Word Options. Click the Proofing tab and click the AutoCorrect Options button to display the AutoCorrect dialog box. You'll find five tabs in the AutoCorrect dialog box:

- The AutoCorrect tab consolidates all AutoCorrect entries.

→ For an overview of how AutoCorrect works, **see** "Using AutoCorrect to Type Faster," **p. 90.**

- The AutoFormat as You Type tab contains several settings that advanced users, in particular, might want to disable, per Table 7.5. This tab also contains the setting Word uses to automatically detect web addresses and email addresses and turn them into hyperlinks. If you're planning to publish your document on the web or share it in electronic format with other people, that can be useful. In the case of printed documents, it isn't necessary. To turn off this intrusive setting, clear the Internet and Network Paths with Hyperlinks check box.

TABLE 7.5   GETTING RID OF AUTOFORMATTING

To Disable This Kind of AutoFormatting	Clear This Checkbox
* - - - > -> => symbols or pictures to create bulleted paragraphs	Automatic Bulleted Lists
0 1 I i A a to create numbered lists	Automatic Numbered Lists
Three or more - _ = * ~ # to put a border on a paragraph	Border Lines
+- - - -+- - - -+ to create a table	Tables
1st, 2nd, 3rd, and so on converted to 1st, 2nd, 3rd	Ordinals (1st) with Superscript
1/4, 1/2, 3/4 converted to ¼, ½, ¾	Fractions (1/2) with Fraction Character (½)

- The AutoFormat tab controls what Word does when you choose Format, AutoFormat.

→ To learn more about Word's AutoFormatting features, **see** "Formatting All or Part of a Document Automatically," **p. 236.**

- The Smart Tags tab controls whether Word looks for something that appears to be an Outlook Contact as you type. The only downside to enabling the full look-up capability is the performance hit: If you feel that Word is unnecessarily sluggish, try disabling these settings to see if performance perks up.

- The Math AutoCorrect tab includes a long list of text strings you can enter, which will automatically be replaced by math symbols. Normally, this substitution takes place only in math regions, which are created when you click the Equation button on the Insert tab and choose one of the many options available there.

WORD STARTUP SWITCHES

You can control how Word starts with *command-line switches*. These switches work from a command line, from the Run box, and as switches in Windows shortcuts. For example, to start Word with the /a switch enabled, press the Windows logo key+R, type `winword /a` in the Open box, and press Enter.

The available switches are listed here:

- /a keeps Word from running any Auto macros stored in the Normal document template, Normal.dotm. It also keeps Word from loading any add-ins in the Startup folder. Use this switch if you are having trouble getting Word to start.

- /n starts Word normally, but doesn't load the usual "Document1" first document.

- /mMacroname starts Word, and then runs the specified macro. (Note that there is no space between the *m* and the macro name.) For example, the following line starts Word and runs the macro File1, a built-in macro which loads the most recently used document:

```
winword.exe /mFile1
```

Similarly, you can use /mFile2 to open the second file in Word's most recently used list, and so on. This line

```
winword.exe /mFile1 /mFile2
```

starts Word and opens both the first and second files on the most recently used list.

Of course, you can always put the name (or names) of one or more documents on the command line, and Word will load them when it starts:

```
winword.exe %UserProfile%\Documents\"My English homework.docx"
```

TIP

> If the filename—including the path—includes any spaces, be sure to put quotes around the entire filename. Otherwise, Word won't interpret the command line correctly.

EXTRA CREDIT: PROTECT YOUR PRIVACY WHEN SAVING AND SHARING DOCUMENTS

Do you know what's hidden in your Word documents? The answer might surprise you. Every document you create using Word contains your name, for starters. It might contain the names of other people who reviewed the document. It might also contain comments, annotations, changes from previous versions (including text that has been deleted), data about your computer and network, email headers, and even text from other documents that might have been open at the same time. If you're the only person who will ever see this document, or if you intend to print it out and pass the printed copies around at a meeting, your secrets are safe. But as soon as you send the document file to someone else via email or publish the document file on a website, your secrets become accessible.

In some cases, the results can be embarrassing, to say the least. In recent years, several high-level government officials have been embarrassed when Word experts took a closer look at documents that had been made publicly accessible on a website; in at least one case they discovered comments from an earlier draft that contradicted the public statements being made by the affected agency!

Even if you're not creating top-secret documents, you should be careful with any document that you plan to make publicly available. Beginning with Office 2007, Microsoft added a tool called the Document Inspector, which you can use to clean your documents (including Word, Excel, and PowerPoint 2007 documents). It's recommended that you first save a copy of your original document, and then save it under a different name that you want to clean and send to others. That way, if you do need to modify revisions or otherwise use the hidden data, you'll have your original document safely tucked away.

When you've finished editing a document and you're ready to publish it without the hidden contents, click the Office button and choose the Prepare option. Select the Inspect Document option. The Document Inspector dialog box shown in Figure 7.22 opens.

After you select the hidden extras you want to scrub from your document, the Document Inspector will strip away all hidden data you've selected, including comments, tracked changes, and personal information stored with the document's properties. After it finishes its work (a job that typically takes only seconds), it displays a text file showing what was removed.

7

Figure 7.22
Use the Document Inspector to clean up your files before you send them to others.

One word of warning: Heed the advice to use the Document Inspector only on copies of your documents because this tool is ruthlessly effective at its job, and if you save a document under its current name you'll find that what has been removed cannot be recovered!

CHAPTER **8**

CREATING GREAT-LOOKING DOCUMENTS

In this chapter

UNDERSTANDING YOUR FORMATTING OPTIONS

The point of formatting is to make documents look good for printing (or onscreen viewing). This attention to design details also has an impact on readability; a carefully designed document, with bold headings, well-laid-out pages, and proper typography, is also easy to read or scan. Word's formatting toolkit includes options for specifying pages (paper size and orientation), margins, pre-formatted styles, themes, fonts, paragraph formatting, tab stops, bullets, and numbering. But before you click any of those buttons, you need to understand how formatting works.

Every Word document consists of components arranged in a strict hierarchy that is unrelated to the way you create a document. Inside a Word document, data is stored in one or more *sections*, which in turn contain one or more *paragraphs*, each of which consists of one or more *characters*. Although it's possible to select an entire document and apply formatting to it, Word doesn't actually format at the document level; instead, it applies your changes individually to characters, paragraphs, and sections within the document.

Word enables you to apply formatting directly, by making a selection and then selecting a pre-formatted style or theme from the Ribbon. You may also use formatting dialog boxes to modify the way your document looks. You may also define collections of character or paragraph formatting choices, save them as named styles and themes, and then apply the formatting to selected characters or paragraphs.

The most fundamental format is a character format, so it's best to start there.

CHARACTER FORMATS

Character formats apply to letters, numbers, and punctuation marks. The most common formatting options that apply to characters are font-related: the font name, size, and color, for example, as well as attributes such as bold, italic, underline, and strikethrough. If you copy or move a formatted character from one part of a document to another, the formatting travels with it.

→ To learn more about formatting, **see** "Common Formatting Options," **p. 99.**

Three special characters merit close attention:

- Each space is a character. Although you can't see its color, you can easily note its size: A 10-point space takes up much less room on a line than a 48-point space. (A single point is 1/72nd of an inch. Points are the standard measurement units used for character spacing.)

- Within a Word document, a tab is a character. When Word encounters a tab character, it shifts to the next tab stop before continuing to lay down text.

- A paragraph mark is technically a character as well, although you can't print a paragraph mark. By default, Word does not show paragraph marks on the screen, but they're always there. You can select, copy, move, or delete paragraph marks.

To make paragraph marks and other formatting characters visible, you can click the Show/Hide button in the Paragraph group on the Home tab.

→ You can also selectively show or hide spaces, paragraph marks, tabs, and other special characters, as we explain in "Options Settings," **p. 197.**

The most common character treatment options are available via buttons on the Home tab and keyboard shortcuts. For example, you can click the Bold, Italic, or Underline buttons in the Font group on the Home tab, or use the shortcut key combinations Ctrl+B, Ctrl+I, Ctrl+U, respectively, to toggle these formatting options for selected text.

TIP

> Here's a formatting shortcut even many experienced Word users don't know about. If you position the insertion point within a word and click a formatting button or key combination, the formatting applies to the entire word. In this case, a "word" is any series of characters delimited on each end by a space or punctuation mark. Use this option to change the font, size, or attributes of a word without having to select it first. Another related quirk is worth noting: If you place the insertion point within a word and choose a paragraph style, Word applies the style to the entire paragraph; but if you select the entire word and change the style, the style is applied only to that word.

Depending on your Word settings, when you start typing in a new, blank document, Word's default setup uses 12-point Times New Roman. To change the default font and size, click the arrow to the right of the word *Font* at the bottom of the Home tab's Font group. The Font dialog box opens (see Figure 8.1). Click Default and then OK to set that font as the default font for subsequent editing sections.

Figure 8.1
Change the default font for all documents by selecting the font you prefer and then clicking the Default button (bottom left).

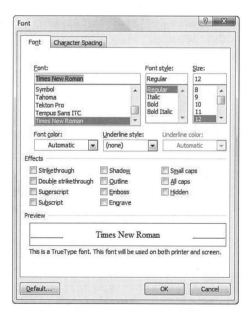

For normal correspondence, consider changing the font—Garamond, for example, is much more striking visually—and reducing the point size down to 11, or even 10. Although 12-point is the Word default, many people find it too large for ordinary correspondence. In our opinion, 11-point type is an excellent compromise.

TIP

> If you usually share documents with other users instead of printing them, make sure you pick a default font that others are likely to have, such as one of the default Windows or Internet Explorer fonts. Don't select an exotic custom font that you've specially installed.

Character spacing can be changed in any number of ways: moving characters above or below the baseline (superscripting and subscripting), magnifying or reducing selected groups of characters (scale), and even squishing together predefined pairs of letters that fit well together—such as VA—to minimize the white space between them (a process called *kerning*). All these techniques are discussed in the next chapter.

→ To learn more about fonts and character formatting, **see** "Using and Managing Fonts," **p. 98** and "Changing Character Attributes," **p. 100.**

Word also supports *highlighting*, a method of changing the background color of selected text much as you would mark up a paper document with a highlighting pen. Although highlighting is rarely used in final documents, it's a handy way to draw attention to text that you want someone else to review closely, or to emphasize pieces of text that are incomplete or need additional editing.

If you're exchanging drafts of a document with a coworker, for example, use a yellow highlighter to flag sections where you have questions or comments. If several people are reviewing the same document, each one can use a different color so others can see at a glance who marked up specific sections. Although you can formally track changes to a document, highlighting comes in handy in informal situations.

→ To work with documents in a group, **see** "Sharing Documents," **p. 192.**

Although highlighting isn't, strictly speaking, a character format (because it really affects the character's background), it behaves much like a character format: If you copy or move highlighted characters, for example, the highlighting travels with the character.

CAUTION

> Highlighting is not removed when you click the Clear Formatting button on the Ribbon's Home tab or when you press the Ctrl+Shift+N shortcut to restore the Normal character style to selected text. Internally, Word does not treat highlighting as if it were character formatting.

To apply highlighting to characters within a document, you can either make a selection and then click the Highlight button on the Ribbon's Home tab, or click the Ribbon's Highlight button first and then "paint" the highlighting on characters. Click the drop-down arrow to the right of the Highlight button to choose one of 15 available colors. The pointer changes to a highlighting pen with an insertion point. To turn off highlighting and return to normal editing, click the Highlight button again, or press Esc. To turn the tool into an eraser that removes highlighting from existing text, click the drop-down arrow to the right of the Highlight button and choose No Color for the highlight color.

→ For advanced formatting tips, **see** "Changing Text Formatting," **p. 221.**

If you open a document that contains fonts that are not installed on your computer, Word provides a way to specify which fonts should be substituted for the missing ones. Click the Office button and select Word Options. Click the Advanced tab, scroll down to the Show Document Content section, and click the Font Substitution button. In the Missing Document Font box, select the font you want to change. Then, in the Substituted Font drop-down list, choose the replacement font.

TIP

> Normally, the fonts you specify in the Font Substitution dialog box are not literally substituted for the missing ones. The document file itself isn't changed; Word uses the fonts you pick to display the document onscreen and to print it. If you want to make the substitution final, replacing all references to a particular font with a font of your choosing, click the Convert Permanently button after specifying the substitutions.

PARAGRAPH FORMATS

Each time you press Enter, Word inserts a paragraph mark and starts a new paragraph. By definition, a paragraph in Word consists of a paragraph mark, plus all the characters before the paragraph mark, up to (but not including) the preceding paragraph mark. Paragraph marks are a crucial part of Word, because they contain all paragraph formatting. When you copy, move, or delete a paragraph mark, the paragraph formatting goes with the mark.

Paragraph formatting includes alignment (left, center, right), indenting, bulleting, numbering, and spacing—both between lines within a paragraph and between paragraphs. It also covers background colors and shading, as well as boxes and lines drawn around and between paragraphs. Tab stops are also considered paragraph formatting—you don't specify a set of tab stops for each line on a page; instead, tab stops remain uniform throughout an entire paragraph.

When you press Enter to create a new paragraph, the new paragraph usually takes on the formatting of the paragraph immediately preceding it. For example, if you position the insertion point within a right-justified paragraph and press Enter, the new paragraph will also be right-justified. (The exception to this rule is if the style of the first paragraph specifies that a new style is to be used for following paragraphs; this setting is stored in the Style for Following Paragraph property.)

8

DIRECT FORMATTING VERSUS STYLES

For simple, short documents, it's often easiest to apply formatting directly to paragraphs and characters through the buttons on the Ribbon's Home tab. But when a document extends beyond a few pages, or when consistent formatting is crucial, you should use styles instead. Styles have one great advantage over manually applied formatting: When you change a style, your changes ripple throughout the document and are applied to all other text formatted with the style of the same name.

Word supports two kinds of styles: *character styles*, which include only character formatting; and *paragraph styles*, which combine paragraph formatting information with character formatting.

→ To learn more about styles, **see** "Formatting Documents with Styles," **p. 291.**

For example, while working on a thesis or dissertation you might establish a paragraph style called ChapterTitle, defining the style as Arial 24-point bold (that's the character formatting part), with 6 points of space after the heading (the paragraph formatting part). As you're typing, every time you start a new chapter, you type in the title of the chapter and apply the ChapterTitle style. The day before you're supposed to hand in your thesis, you decide it will be easier to read if you change the chapter titles to Garamond 20-point italic with 12 points of space after the heading.

Because you carefully formatted every chapter title in the thesis with the ChapterTitle style, you can change all the chapter titles in a matter of seconds by changing the settings for the ChapterTitle style. On the other hand, if you had applied formatting manually, you would have to scan the entire document and change the formatting of each chapter title manually; in doing so, you run the risk of missing a chapter title, which results in a sloppy look for your document—and could have an effect on your final grade.

→ Line and page breaks, indents, tabs, and other paragraph formatting are covered in depth in "Changing Paragraph Formatting," **p. 224.**

APPLYING AND MODIFYING FORMATS

Word includes two nifty task panes that make it easy to understand why and how formatting has appeared in your document, and to apply formatting quickly and reliably.

REVEALING FORMATTING WITHIN A DOCUMENT

Beginning with Word 2003, Word includes a feature that's meant to mimic the "reveal codes" capability found in WordPerfect.

After selecting any text—from a single character to an entire document—press the keyboard shortcut Shift+F1 to display the Reveal Formatting task pane. Word responds with a comprehensive list of all formatting applied to the current selection (see Figure 8.2). If you move the insertion point to a different location, Word updates the Reveal Formatting task pane to reflect the format of whatever text you're on.

8

The more you use the Reveal Formatting task pane, the more you're likely to discover what a tremendous help it can be in troubleshooting formatting problems. Here are three ways to squeeze extra information out of the task pane:

- Select the Distinguish Style Source check box at the bottom of the Reveal Formatting task pane. When you do so, Word shows you the source of each specific type of formatting in the selection. For example, in Figure 8.2, you can see that the base font for the paragraph is 12 point, as defined in the Normal style, and the font (Times New Roman) has been applied directly to the selection. This kind of detail can be useful if you're trying to sort through exactly why and how text appears in a particular format.

- Hover the mouse pointer over the Selected Text box at the top of the task pane to reveal a drop-down arrow on the right side of the box. Click this arrow to reveal a menu that enables you to select similarly formatted text elsewhere in the document, clear all formatting from the selection, or change the formatting of the selection to match the surrounding text.

- After selecting some text, click the Compare to Another Selection check box. When you select this option, a second box opens beneath the original Selected Text box. You can now navigate to another part of the document and make a second text selection. The contents of the Reveal Formatting task pane change to show just the differences in formatting between the two selections.

Figure 8.2
Word can show you full formatting information for any part of a document.

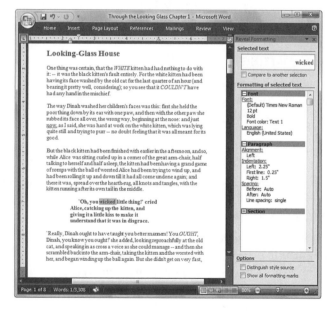

8

COPYING FORMATS

Three ways to copy specific formatting from one place in a document to another are

- Set up a style to reflect the formatting, and apply the style (either character or paragraph) to the text you want to change. This is the most consistent and reliable approach, and it enables you to change formatting throughout a document by modifying the style. If you add the style to the list of Quick Styles that appears on the Home tab, applying that style is always just a click away on the Ribbon. (You save a style to the list of Quick Styles by clicking the down arrow to the right of the Home tab's list of styles and selecting Save Selection as a New Quick Style.)

- Use the Format Painter icon on the Ribbon's Home tab. Select the text (or paragraph) that includes the text that's formatted to your liking, click the Format Painter button, and then "paint" the formatting elsewhere in your document. This process is most effective when copying character formatting to a very limited selection. If your hand-eye coordination is less than perfect, the process can be cumbersome and error-prone, especially if you accidentally select a paragraph mark prior to "painting."

- Use the floating Styles window. If your document already contains the formatting you want, select the text you want to format, and then click the dialog box launcher in the lower-right corner of the Styles group on the Ribbon's Home tab. Note that the Styles window isn't limited to formally defined styles; it also includes entries for all the manually applied formatting that exists in your document. You can see all styles available by clicking the Options link in the Styles window's lower-right hand corner.

REMOVING TEXT FORMATTING

Novice users can make a thorough mess of a document by randomly applying direct formatting to characters and paragraphs. To remove all manually applied character and paragraph formatting from a selection so you can start fresh, bring up the Styles window and choose Clear All. To selectively remove character or paragraph formatting and styles from a selection, click the Style Inspector button at the bottom of the Styles window. This incredibly useful little dialog box displays formatting information and includes four separate "eraser" buttons to clear manual formatting or styles at the character and paragraph level.

PAGE/SECTION SETUP OPTIONS

Most simple Word documents contain just one *section*. Usually, you'll add sections to a document when you want to use a different header or footer on certain pages of a document, or to alter the number of columns—perhaps to print a long list. You can also change sections to switch from one paper size or orientation to another—for example, to print a table in landscape orientation in the middle of a document.

Each section in a document has its own headers and footers, page size, margins, number of snaking newspaper-like columns, and paper source—a designated paper bin on your printer.

→ To properly format sections, **see** "Formatting Documents by Section," **p. 262.**

Sections are separated by section break marks, which are visible only in Draft view (see Figure 8.3).

Figure 8.3
To see section breaks, switch to Draft view.

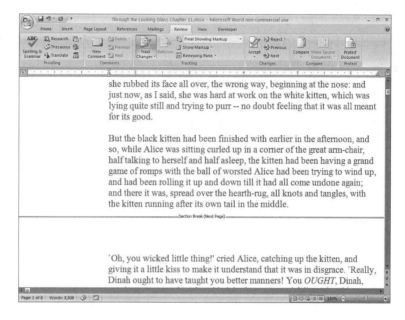

Section formatting is stored in the section break mark; the formatting for the final section in a document is in the document's final paragraph mark. When you select a section break mark and copy, move, or delete it, the section formatting stored in the mark goes with it.

The safest way to add a new section to a document is to insert a new section break manually—surprisingly, you won't find a way to do this on the Ribbon's Insert tab. Click the Page Layout tab, choose Breaks from the Page Setup group, and choose from the list of available section break types:

- Next Page starts the next section on a new page.
- Continuous enables the new section to follow the current one, without a page break.
- Even Page forces the next section to start on an even-numbered page.
- Odd Page forces the next section to start on an odd-numbered page.

NOTE

> The first three options on the Breaks button's drop-down list—Page, Column, and Text Wrapping—are not section related.

Word automatically inserts section break marks in a document if you click the Page Layout tab, click the dialog box launcher in the lower-right corner of the Page Setup group to open the Page Setup dialog box, and choose This Point Forward (see Figure 8.4). Word adds the section break as a consequence of changing the layout. Similarly, if you click Columns from the Page Layout tab and select More Columns, you can choose This Point Forward in the Apply To drop-down list and Word automatically inserts a section break to mark the point where the number of columns changes.

Figure 8.4
Choosing This Point Forward inserts a section break mark in the document and then formats the newly created section.

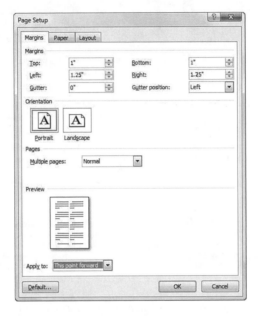

TIP

Editing and formatting documents with multiple sections can be extremely confusing. If you inadvertently move or delete a section break mark, you can make a mess of the document's headers and footers, for example, and it's nearly impossible to recover except by starting over. When you work on documents with more than one section, we strongly recommend that you work only in Draft view and that you insert section break marks manually from the Breaks drop-down list in the Page Setup group on the Page Layout tab.

The most common reason for using multiple sections in a document is to alter headers and footers. Each section in a document has its own headers and footers, although you can specify that a section link to the preceding section, and carry forward the preceding section's headers and footers.

→ To customize headers and footers, **see** "Creating and Editing Headers and Footers," **p. 271.**

Sections also enable you to organize snaking newspaper-like columns, whether they're for an entire document or for a list of items you want to appear in the middle of a document.

→ If you need to change the number of columns, **see** "Formatting a Document with Columns," **p. 269.**

8

FLOATING VERSUS INLINE OBJECTS

Like other Office applications, Word includes a *drawing layer*, which can contain pictures, text boxes, and other drawing objects. When you specify that text should wrap around a picture, for example, Word places the picture in the drawing layer.

→ To change text-wrapping options when you use floating objects in the drawing layer, **see** "Working with the Drawing Layer," **p. 109.**

Word also enables you to insert an object called a drawing canvas onto the drawing layer. The canvas constitutes a sanctuary for drawings: Everything you place on a canvas sticks together. Objects on the canvas stay in the same relative location, and the canvas as a whole is not allowed to break across a page. To place a canvas on a page, click where you want the illustration. Display the Ribbon's Insert tab, click Shapes, and then select New Drawing Canvas from the drop-down menu that appears.

→ For a discussion of the intricacies of the drawing canvas, see "Working with a Drawing Canvas in Word," **p. 110.**

AUTOMATIC FORMATTING

Unless you make a special effort to turn them off, Word applies automatic formatting in a wide variety of situations, sometimes for no apparent reason. The effect is guaranteed to annoy anyone except a Microsoft marketing manager, for whom these automatic changes are a trademarked feature called IntelliSense. The most obvious paragraph AutoFormatting options are listed in Table 8.1.

TABLE 8.1 PARAGRAPH AUTOFORMATTING

If You Type Any of These...	Followed by This...	You'll Get...
* - -- > -> =>	A space or tab, and then text, and Enter	A paragraph formatted as bulleted, using a bullet that matches the characters you typed
A symbol from a symbol font such as WingDings (click Symbol on the Insert tab)	Two or more spaces, or a tab, followed by text, and Enter	A paragraph formatted as bulleted, using the symbol as the bullet character
A picture (Insert tab, Picture) slightly larger than the height of the line	Two or more spaces, or a tab, and then text and Enter	A paragraph formatted as bulleted, using the picture as the bullet character

continues

8

TABLE 8.1   CONTINUED

If You Type Any of These...	Followed by This...	You'll Get...
0 1 I i A a	A period, hyphen, closing parenthesis, or > sign, then a space or tab, and then text and Enter	A paragraph formatted as numbered, using standard, Roman, or alphabetic numbers
Three or more - _ = * ~ #	Enter	Applies a border to the paragraph above (or below)
Series of plus signs and hyphens, ending in a plus sign; for example, +----+----+	Enter	Creates a one-row table, with columns defined by the plus signs

As soon as Word applies AutoFormatting, you're presented with an action menu (indicated by a lightning bolt icon) that gives you quick access to various options for undoing what Word hath wrought (see Figure 8.5).

Figure 8.5
Word's action menu lets you undo AutoFormatting as soon as any piece of text has been changed.

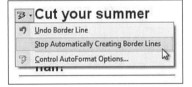

TIP

To undo automatic paragraph formatting promptly, press Backspace or Ctrl+Z immediately after Word applies the AutoFormatting.

In the case of AutoFormatted numbered or bulleted lists, if you press Enter twice, the bulleting/numbering is removed from empty paragraphs. To turn on bullet/numbering formatting again, either start the list numbers over or go back to the end of the last bulleted or numbered paragraph where you left off, and press Enter. Auto bulleting and numbering can also be turned off by clicking the appropriate button on the Home tab.

The most obvious types of character AutoFormatting are:

- If you type an ordinal, such as 1st, 2nd, 3rd, 4th, 30th, 175th, and so on, Word super-scripts the characters: 1st, 2nd, 3rd, 4th, 30th, 175th.

- The specific fractions 1/4, 1/2, and 3/4 are changed into ¼, ½, and ¾.

- Internet addresses such as http://www.quepublishing.com and ed@example.com are automatically converted into hyperlinks. The hyperlinks are "hot," so Ctrl+clicking a web address brings up your web browser and takes you to the site; Ctrl+clicking an email address invokes your default email program and creates a blank message addressed to the name in the mail link.

If you click the Undo button or press Ctrl+Z immediately after Word performs its AutoFormatting in all three of these cases, the formatting returns to normal. In addition, automatically created holinks come with full drop-down instructions on the various means of their removal.

→ To turn off this kind of character AutoFormatting, **see** "Disabling AutoCorrect and AutoFormat Settings," **p. 199.**

LOCKING A DOCUMENT'S FORMATTING

Few tasks are more frustrating than having to undo someone else's formatting follies. The syndrome is all too common: You carefully format a Word document, crafting styles and applying them consistently throughout a document. Then you send it to a friend for comments and discover, to your horror, that the returned document contains a mishmash of mangled styles and haphazard direct formatting.

In one of its most useful features, Word offers a solution. You can lock formatting options in a document so that it can't be accidentally undone. This capability is a welcome add-on to the capability to restrict a document so that it can't be changed at all.

To turn on this option, click the Review tab, click Protect Document, and then click Restrict Formatting and Editing. As Figure 8.6 shows, this option opens a task pane that walks you through a simple three-step process.

1. Under Formatting Restrictions, select the Limit Formatting to a Selection of Styles check box. Click the Settings link to open a dialog box that enables you to choose which, if any, styles are available. Choose one of the following three options from the Formatting Restrictions dialog box (see Figure 8.7):
   - All—Allows anyone editing the document to choose from currently defined styles but eliminates the ability to add new styles or modify existing ones.
   - Recommended Minimum—Selects standard Word styles. Use this option as a starting point and select additional styles from the list, if you want.
   - None—Clears all selections from the list of styles. With this option selected, users cannot modify any formatting.

2. After setting formatting restrictions, you can restrict available editing options in the Editing Restrictions section. Make any necessary changes.

Figure 8.6
Use this task pane to prevent other people from tampering with document formatting.

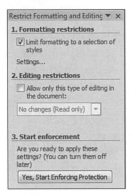

Figure 8.7
Styles you select in this dialog box can be applied to a protected document, but cannot be modified.

3. When your changes are complete, click the Yes, Start Enforcing Protection button in the Start Enforcement section. You'll be offered the option of adding a password and removing any existing direct formatting or any style-based formatting that does not match the restrictions you just specified.

When you enable the Formatting Restrictions option, you eliminate the ability for anyone (including you!) to make any direct formatting changes. When this document is opened, the Protect Document task pane appears, warning the person viewing the document that formatting restrictions are in effect. Clicking a link in this task pane opens a customized version of a Styles task pane, containing only those styles that are available for use.

CHANGING PAPER SIZE AND ORIENTATION

The Size button on the Ribbon's Page Layout tab enables you to choose from several common paper sizes (Letter, Legal, or A4, for example). Select the More Paper Sizes option at the bottom of the Size menu to open the Paper dialog box shown in Figure 8.8, where you have complete control over the paper you wish to print to. Also on the Page Layout tab, click the Orientation button to pick whether you want the printing to run from left to right along the short edge of the paper (Portrait orientation) or the long edge (Landscape orientation).

Figure 8.8
Word gives you complete control over paper size and the printer bin.

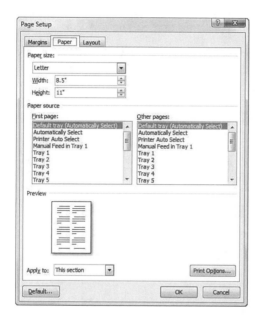

As with margins, the settings for paper size and orientation apply to sections. If your document has only one section, the size and orientation you choose applies to the entire document.

By judiciously choosing the page size, you can use a few tricks for special effects.

Word can print to within 1/8 inch of the bottom of the sheet on a Hewlett-Packard LaserJet printer—an important discovery if you're trying to print labels that extend to the bottom of the sheet. To fool Word into using the full space at the bottom of the page, open the Page Setup dialog box by clicking the More Paper Sizes option on the Size button's drop-down list. On the Paper tab, select a Paper Size of Legal, with a width of 8.5" and a height of 14". Then in the Paper Source box, pick Manual Paper Feed in both the First Page and Other Pages boxes. If you manually feed a regular letter-sized sheet, the print nearly touches the bottom of the sheet.

Other effects are possible as well. For example, when printing envelopes, adjust the page size to extend beyond the borders of the envelope, and you can frequently print all the way up to the edge, or even bleed over the edge. Experiment a bit. Remember that envelopes can often be fed either short-end first or long-end first.

ADJUSTING MARGINS

In the world of pen and paper, margins are lines that define white space at the left, right, top, and bottom of each page; if your penmanship is neat, you avoid crossing over those lines and thus preserve the pristine appearance of the page.

Word's margins are similarly straightforward in concept if you're setting routine margins, which you'll be doing most of the time. Just click the Margins button on the Page Layout tab and choose the margin setting you want to change. Some margin settings can be complex—especially when paper size, margin, and header and footer areas need to work in unison. If you've been having trouble with margins, follow along closely.

To view and change the margin settings for a document with a single section, click the Page Layout tab's Margins button and select Custom Margins from the drop-down list. Word responds with the Page Setup dialog box shown in Figure 8.9.

Figure 8.9
Margins appear to be simple, but they're not.

The Left margin setting works as you would expect: It specifies the distance from the left edge of the paper to the left margin of text. So, if you set a left margin of 1 inch, any left-aligned paragraph with an indent of 0 inches will start precisely 1 inch from the left edge of the paper. Similarly, the Right margin setting gives the distance from the right edge of the paper to the rightmost character in right-aligned or fully justified paragraphs, with 0 right indent.

→ For an explanation of how indents work, **see** "Indenting Paragraphs for Emphasis," **p. 226.**

If you're going to print on both sides of each sheet of paper (called *duplex printing*) and bind the sheets in a book or some kind of binder, you might want to allow extra room along the bound side—the left side on odd-numbered pages, and the right side on even-numbered pages. If you look at this book, you'll see how the additional white space, alternating left and right, improves the balance of the pages. To allow extra room, alternating left and right, choose Mirror Margins from the Multiple Pages drop-down list. Word adjusts the Page Setup dialog box—instead of Left and Right margins, you now see Inside and Outside margins, with the inside margin being the one closer to the binding (see Figure 8.10).

Figure 8.10
Use mirror margins when you create a bound document with printing on both sides of each sheet of paper.

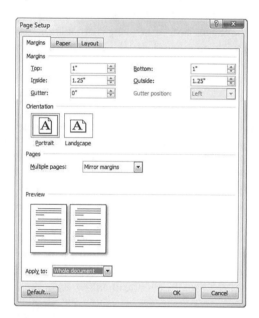

Similarly, you can choose the 2 Pages per Sheet option from the Multiple Pages drop-down list to print two half-size pages on a sheet (if your original pages are in portrait mode, be sure to select Landscape orientation for the new layout, so that the pages maintain their original orientation).

Choose the Book Fold option to print in booklet sequence so the pages can be stapled down the middle. If you choose Book Fold for a document, the pages print in landscape orientation, two to a page. If you change your mind and choose Normal from the Multiple Pages drop-down list, Word leaves your document in landscape orientation. You'll have to change it back to portrait manually.

TIP

Although Word's capability to arrange multi-page documents in booklet form is somewhat useful, it requires a lot of careful preparation on your part, and if you miscount the number of pages, your booklet can be unreadable. For maximum control over printed pages, we recommend a marvelous third-party program called FinePrint. It handles booklets, double-sided pages, and other fancy printing options from any Windows program, not just Word, and its ease of use is unparalleled. If you print a few hundred pages a month, we predict you'll save enough in paper alone to pay the software's modest cost in a few months. Check it out at http://www.fineprint.com.

A *gutter* is the additional amount of space left on each sheet for binding pages. If you're going to print on only one side of each sheet of paper, the gutter distance is added to the left edge of each sheet. If you're going to print on both sides of each sheet of paper and chose Mirror Margins in the Multiple Pages drop-down list, Word adjusts the gutter accordingly— adding it to the left margin on odd-numbered sheets and the right margin on even-numbered sheets.

NOTE

Word also has a provision for gutters at the top of each sheet; just choose Top in the Gutter Position drop-down list. This is a rather odd setting because it won't be mirrored if you plan to print on the front and back of each sheet. (You might expect the gutter to appear at the top of odd-numbered pages and at the bottom of even-numbered pages, but it doesn't work that way.) You might use it for legal briefs that are bound at the top, or for single-sided pages that are destined for flip-top binders.

To control the amount of white space at the top of each sheet, you must juggle three settings: the Top setting on the Margins tab in the Page Setup dialog box, the Header setting on the Layout tab, and the contents of the header itself. After exhaustive testing, we have determined that Word lays out the top of each document by using the following rules:

- Word takes the Header measurement in the Layout tab of the Page Setup dialog box and goes down that far from the top edge of the page, placing the top of the first line of the header (if a header exists) that distance from the top of the paper.

- Word then lays out the rest of the header, including pictures, before and after spacing, and the like. So, for example, if the last paragraph of the header has an After spacing of 24 points, Word reserves an additional 24 points of space at the bottom of the header.

- Finally, Word assembles the first line in the body of the document, placing it below the header in the location it would normally occupy if there were no distinction between header and body text. Word then measures the distance from the top of this first body line to the top of the paper. If that distance is less than the Top value on the Margins tab of the Page Setup dialog box, Word moves the line down so at least the Top amount of space is between the top of the first line and the top of the sheet.

Using the terminology commonly associated with paragraph distances, the Header distance is an "exactly" measurement; and the Top distance is an "at least" measurement.

Bottom margins work the same way but in reverse, with the bottom of the last line of the footer exactly the Footer distance from the bottom of the sheet, and the bottom of the last line of body text at least the Bottom distance.

Click the Default button at the bottom of the Page Setup dialog box, and Word offers to alter the template attached to the current document, giving it all the page-formatting options specified on the three tabs in the dialog box.

You can also change margins for individual sections within a document.

→ For more information about your options when setting up a document, **see** "Page/Section Setup Options," **p. 210.**

CHANGING TEXT FORMATTING

When you're typing, each new character you type takes on the formatting of the character before, unless you do something to change it (such as pressing Ctrl+I to turn on italic formatting). The first character you type in a paragraph takes on the formatting of the paragraph mark.

To remove all manually applied character formatting—that is, to make it match the formatting of the current paragraph style—bring up the Styles window (press Ctrl+Shift+Alt+S or click the dialog box launcher in the lower-right corner of the Styles group on the Home tab), select the text, and click Clear All. (Equivalently, you can press Ctrl+Spacebar.)

Select a character or characters and click one or more buttons in the Font group on the Ribbon's Home tab. For more control, click the arrow to the right of the Font group name (or right-click and choose Font), and you will see Word's main font formatting options (see Figure 8.11). Most of the character (Word says "font") formatting you'll commonly encounter is applicable to all the Office applications.

→ To learn more about character formatting, **see** "Changing Character Attributes," **p. 100.**

Word has a few formatting options that aren't quite so straightforward. On the Font tab:

- Superscript reduces the size of the characters about four points and moves them above the baseline by about three points; Subscript also reduces about four points and moves the characters below the baseline about two points.

- Small Caps shows and prints lowercase letters as capitals, reduced about 2 points (so, for example, a lowercase letter in 11 point will print as a capital letter in 9 point). Some fonts have specific small caps characters, in which case those will print.

- Hidden text is displayed onscreen and/or printed only when you specifically request it (controllable from the Office button's Word Options window; click the Display tab to see the Hidden Text option).

Figure 8.11
Most of the Font dialog box's options match up with options in other Office applications.

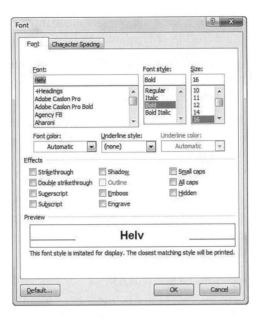

TIP

Hidden text can be useful when you want to keep details handy but show them only occasionally. For example, teachers frequently type exams in Word and place the answers inside the document as hidden text. That way, they can print the exam normally for distribution to students, but then print a second copy with answers for graders.

The Hidden Paragraph Mark

Sometimes Word forces you to have a paragraph mark, whether you want one or not. For example, if you have a document that ends in a table, Word insists on placing a paragraph mark after the table. Sometimes those extra paragraph marks get in the way—in the worst case, Word might print an extra, blank page at the end of the document to accommodate the invisible paragraph mark.

If that should happen to you, remember that the paragraph mark is just like any other character. In particular, you can format it as hidden. A hidden paragraph mark won't print and won't show on the screen, and one at the end of a document won't force Word to print an extra, blank page.

Formatting options on the Character Spacing tab of the font dialog box (see Figure 8.12) include the following:

- Scale applies a zoom effect to the selected text. This option is particularly useful when you're trying to squeeze a headline into a tight space and it just won't quite fit. Adjust the scale to 95% or so and see if the problem goes away.

- Spacing controls the distance between characters. In particular, it allows you to add a uniform amount of space after each of the selected characters (expanded spacing) or uniformly reduce the amount of space between characters (condensed spacing). Use this option to unobtrusively expand lines that need to be longer, or shorten lines that are too long.

Figure 8.12
Character spacing enables you to squish, elevate, lower, and push together fonts.

- Position controls how far above or below the baseline of text the selected characters will appear. This is similar to Superscripting and Subscripting, discussed earlier in this section, except it doesn't change the font size, and this box gives you fine control over the positioning.

- Kerning squishes matched pairs of letters together. The most dramatic example in English is AV. If AV is not kerned, there's a considerable amount of white space between the letters. If it is kerned, they're squished together so the leftmost part of the V appears to the left of the rightmost part of the A. Kerning is best used sparingly, with display type such as headlines. It doesn't have much effect at smaller point sizes and, for letters smaller than 10 points or so, it even inhibits your ability to read the type. If you want to kern letters, select them and tell Word the point size at which you want kerning to begin.

 Are you having trouble getting kerning to work? See the "Troubleshooting" section, "When You Can't Kern," at the end of this chapter.

Word has one more automatic character-formatting capability that some people love and others hate: If you type an asterisk, followed by text, followed by another asterisk, the text between the asterisks is made bold. Similarly, if you type an underscore, text, and another underscore, the text between the underscores is made italic. This feature exists for compatibility with long-standing formatting conventions in text documents exchanged over the

8

Internet. In Word 2007, this option is off by default. If you upgraded from an earlier version of Word, however, you might find that it is enabled. To turn this feature on or off, click the Proofing tab in the Word Options dialog box and click the AutoCorrect Options button. Click the AutoFormat As You Type tab and select or clear the *Bold* and _Italic_ with Real Formatting box.

In fact, this option is a bit more complex than it first appears. When Word detects the asterisk-text-asterisk combination, it formats the text between the asterisks using the formatting defined by the Strong character style. (The text remains in Normal style—it isn't turned into Strong—but the formatting defined by the Strong style is applied to it.) The underscore combination is formatted with the formatting of the Emphasis character style.

> **TIP**
>
> The Strong and Emphasis styles exist for compatibility with the corresponding HTML tags, <strong> and <em>. If you don't use Word to create web pages that use these tags, you can change the characteristics of the Strong and Emphasis styles; for example, you can change the style so that *text* makes the text red, or _text_ makes the text Arial 14 point.
>
> If you select the *Bold* and _Italic_ with Real Formatting box and then use asterisks to create bold text, the style Strong suddenly appears in your Apply Styles task pane. From that point, it's easy to change the style definition. This works similarly for Emphasis.

→ To learn more about working with styles, **see** "Saving Formats as Named Styles," **p. 297.**

CHANGING PARAGRAPH FORMATTING

Word enables you to change the indenting and spacing of paragraphs. Word also gives you control on a paragraph-by-paragraph basis over whether to keep entire paragraphs together or to force one paragraph to "stick to" the next, so they both appear on the same page.

The key concept: Paragraph formatting is stored in the paragraph mark. When you copy or move a paragraph mark, the formatting goes with it. When you delete a paragraph mark, any text following the paragraph mark becomes part of the current paragraph, and the new, combined paragraph takes on the formatting of the deleted paragraph mark.

> **TIP**
>
> It's almost impossible to tell whether you've selected a paragraph mark unless you have paragraph marks showing on the screen. Some Word users (Woody, for instance) keep paragraph marks and tabs visible at all times. Others (like Ed) find these marks distracting and keep them hidden except when working with paragraph formats. To make these marks visible temporarily, click the Show/Hide + button on the Ribbon's Home tab. To make them visible at all times, open the Word Options dialog box, click the Display tab, and select the Tab Characters and Paragraph Marks check boxes.

To restore default paragraph formatting—that is, the formatting mandated by the paragraph's style—select the paragraph and click the style name on the Styles task pane (available by clicking the arrow to the right of the Ribbon's Home tab's Styles group name or by pressing Ctrl+Shift+Alt+S).

ADJUSTING PARAGRAPH ALIGNMENT AND OUTLINE LEVEL

Word includes simple tools for aligning your paragraphs to the left, center, or right, or justifying paragraphs so they line up neatly along both left and right margins. Several paragraph-related buttons are available on the Home tab. For example, you can use the Align Left, Center, Align Right, or Justify buttons in the Paragraph group to set alignment.

Click the arrow to the right of the Paragraph group name to display the Indents and Spacing tab of the Paragraph dialog box, as shown in Figure 8.13. Set the Alignment box to reflect the alignment you like.

Figure 8.13
Use the Paragraph dialog box to adjust a paragraph's alignment, indentation, and spacing.

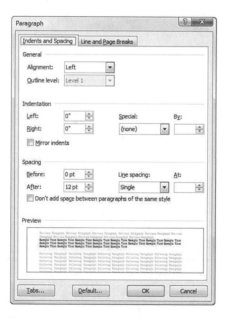

→ Word helps you navigate through large documents by using headings. To learn more, **see** "Outline View," **p. 165** and "Navigating with Thumbnails and the Document Map," **p. 168.**

Word has a text-aligning technique called Click and Type, which allows you to click anywhere on the screen and start typing text. Although it should be called Double-click and Type, the paragraph alignment part of the concept is straightforward:

- If you double-click somewhere near the middle of an empty line (that is, halfway between the left and right margins), Word converts the line to center alignment. You can tell the area is "hot" because Word puts centered lines below the usual I-beam pointer.

8

- If you double-click somewhere near the right end of a line (that is, near the right margin), Word converts the line to right-justified. Again, you know the area is hot because Word changes the I-beam pointer so it has lines to the left. This feature makes it especially easy to put left- and right-justified text on a single line.

CAUTION

> Unless you're careful and watch the lines around the I-beam closely, Word might insert tabs and tab stops instead of changing the entire paragraph's alignment. Although the tab stops might fool a novice, paragraphs with tabs don't act like aligned paragraphs, as a few moments' work will demonstrate. This is yet another reason for showing paragraph marks and tab characters on the screen.

Normally, the outline level is set along with the paragraph style. In fact, if you select one of the built-in heading styles (Heading 1, Heading 2, and so on), the Outline Level option will be grayed out and unavailable. Adjust this level manually for a paragraph if you want that specific paragraph to be visible in Outline view or in the Document Map without affecting other paragraphs that use the same style.

INDENTING PARAGRAPHS FOR EMPHASIS

You might think of it as a margin change, or a way to set off quotes or other material for emphasis. In Word terminology, an *indent* moves the left edge of a paragraph to the right or the right edge of a paragraph to the left. The paragraph shown in Figure 8.14 has been indented on the left and the right.

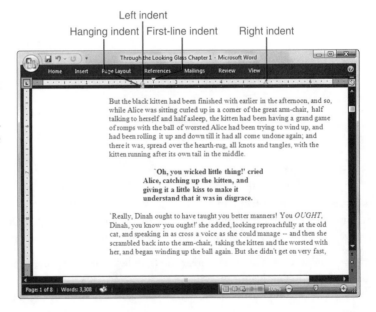

Figure 8.14
Use Word's ruler to indent the left or right margin of a paragraph. To move only the first line of a paragraph to the right, use a first-line indent.

Left and right indents are often used to set off blocks of quoted text. Another common type of indenting, typically used in informal letters, moves only the first line of a paragraph; not surprisingly, this is called a *first-line indent*. Its counterpart—where the first line juts out to the left—is called a *hanging indent*. Used sparingly, this is a good way to emphasize the first few words of a paragraph. (It's also common for bulleted and numbered paragraphs, which are discussed later in this chapter.)

Although it takes a bit of practice, Word's ruler offers the fastest, most accurate way to control indents. Learn what each of the four widgets on the ruler does, and you're well on your way. The downward-pointing triangle at the left controls the first-line indent for the current paragraph; the upward-pointing triangle just below it controls the hanging indent. Click the rectangle (below both triangles) to adjust the left indent by moving both the first-line indent and the hanging indent simultaneously. The triangle at the right controls the right indent.

> **TIP**
>
> As you drag these widgets, a faint dotted line appears on the document to show where the indented text will end up. And if you absolutely can't remember which widget is which, let your mouse hover over each one and read the ScreenTips.

You can also use the Paragraph dialog box to set indents. To adjust the left and/or right indent, use the Left and Right boxes of the Paragraph dialog box. To change the left indent only, in half-inch increments, you can also use the Increase Indent and Decrease Indent buttons on the Paragraph group of your Ribbon's Home tab. To create a first-line indent, select the paragraphs you want to indent, display the Paragraph dialog box by clicking the arrow to the right of the Paragraph group name, and select First Line in the Special box.

When you press Tab at the beginning of a new paragraph, Word adds a tab character. When you position the insertion point at the beginning of an existing paragraph and press Tab, however, Word adds a first-line indent. If you actually wanted a tab instead, you can use the AutoCorrect action menu (the lightning bolt icon just below the indented text) to cancel the change.

To create a hanging indent, select the paragraphs you want to indent, open the Format dialog box, and select Hanging in the Special drop-down list.

ADJUSTING LINE AND PARAGRAPH SPACING

Word has controls for three kinds of spacing:

- The amount of blank space before the first line of a paragraph
- The amount of blank space after the last line of a paragraph
- The amount of space internally, between the lines of a paragraph

The spacing between paragraphs adds up just as you would think: The after spacing from the first paragraph is combined with the before spacing of the second paragraph. Word ignores the after space if a paragraph will fit at the end of a page; but it includes the before space when a paragraph starts on a new page.

Internal line spacing isn't so simple:

- If you set Line Spacing to Exactly (say, Exactly 12 points), Word makes the distance between all the lines in the paragraph equal to whatever measurement you choose. If you put a large character on a line—say, an 18-point character—the top of the character might be cut off.
- If you set Line Spacing to Single, 1.5 Lines, Double, or some other Multiple, Word calculates the distance between each line of the paragraph separately. It takes the tallest character (or graphic) on each line and adjusts to single, 1.5, or double spacing, as appropriate. If you have one 18-point character in the middle of a paragraph consisting of 12-point characters, the distance to the line containing the 18-point character will be 50% greater than the distance between the other lines.

NOTE

> Normally, the height of invisible characters—spaces, paragraph marks, tabs, and the like—is not taken into account when calculating Single, 1.5, Double, or Multiple spacing. The exceptions are that if the paragraph is empty, the calculation is based on the size of the default font for that paragraph; if it contains only invisible characters, the height of those characters counts.

- If you set Line Spacing to At Least (say, At Least 12 points), Word treats it the same as single spacing but sets spacing to a minimum of the height you specified, even if all characters in a given line are smaller than that size.

Generally, you'll want to use Exactly spacing if you use two or more fonts in a paragraph: By setting the internal spacing to Exactly a given figure (typically one or two points more than the largest font used in the paragraph), all the lines will be equally spaced, even if the different font normally calls for more white space.

CONTROLLING PAGE BREAKS

Each paragraph can also be formatted to control the way Word breaks pages. The Line and Page Breaks tab in the Paragraph dialog box (see Figure 8.15) holds these settings:

- Widow/Orphan Control, when selected, keeps Word from printing *widows* (the last line of a paragraph all by itself at the top of a new page) and *orphans* (the first line of a paragraph all by itself at the bottom of a page). It's on by default.
- Keep Lines Together ensures that all the lines of the paragraph appear on a single page.

- Keep with Next forces Word to put this paragraph and the next paragraph on the same page.
- Page Break Before makes Word start the paragraph on a new page.

Figure 8.15
You can control each paragraph individually to determine whether it flops onto a new page.

Word can't always follow your instructions, of course: If you format all the paragraphs in a long document to Keep with Next, the pages have to break somewhere. Word makes a valiant effort to follow your instructions but, if they're impossible, lays out the pages as best it can.

In almost all cases, you'll want to enforce widow and orphan control. If you have a paragraph in a report whose visual impact depends on the whole paragraph appearing on one page (a mission statement, for example, or a quotation), you will probably want to keep the lines together. And headings should generally be formatted Keep with Next so they don't get separated from the text they head.

USING DROP CAPS FOR EMPHASIS

Drop caps add emphasis and distinction to a paragraph. Used sparingly, they make a good visual break at the beginning of major sections in a report. Word makes drop caps easy: Click once inside the paragraph that's to have its initial letter turned into a drop cap, and then click the Drop Cap button on the Ribbon's Insert tab. For added control, click Drop Cap on the Insert tab and select Drop Cap Options from the bottom of the menu (see Figure 8.16).

8

The default height of the drop cap is three lines, which is about right for most paragraphs. If the drop cap appears to be crowding the text that follows it, increase the value in the Distance from Text box. You're not limited in your selection of fonts, either. Some "fancy" fonts are particularly well suited to drop-cap treatment. Take a look at the Algerian font, which is installed with Office, or Old English Text MT.

To remove a drop cap, click to the left or right of the drop cap and click the Ribbon's Drop Cap button; select None from the Position box.

Figure 8.16
Drop caps work best in decorative fonts. Fonts that you wouldn't normally use in a business report make eye-catching drops.

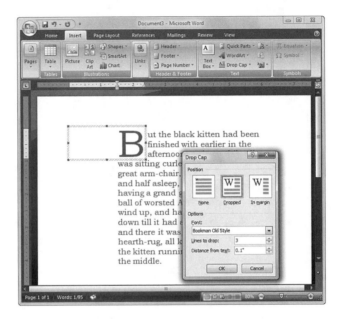

POSITIONING TEXT WITH TABS

To fully understand the way tabs work in Word, you first must realize that a tab consists of two parts. First, there's the tab character—which, like any other character, is placed in a document when you press the Tab key. Second, there's the tab stop, which is a location, or series of locations, on the page. In Word, you set up tab stops for each paragraph, not for each line; in other words, every line in a paragraph has identical tab stops.

Strangely, Word 2007's help system includes this statement: "Office Word 2007 provides predesigned pages, such as cover pages and various page layout options, which make tab stops unnecessary."

The previous statement is true as long as your document needs exactly fit those that Microsoft designed for you. Unfortunately, some people's documents don't fit into Microsoft's pre-designed formulas.

> **TIP**
>
> It's nearly impossible to work with tabs unless you make them visible on the screen. To do so, click the Show/Hide ¶ button on the Ribbon's Home tab.

When Word encounters a tab character in a document, it advances to the next defined tab stop. Tab stops come in four varieties: left-aligned, right-aligned, centered, and decimal-aligned (which aligns numbers so the decimal point appears at the tab location). In addition, you can specify a leader character (pronounced "leeder")—a character that will appear, repeated, in the blank area leading up to the tab stop. You've no doubt seen them in tables of contents.

This is a leader of periods........<Tab stop>

The next section contains a detailed example of how leaders can be used to create a fill-in-the-blanks form.

When working with tabs, it's always much easier to plan on having just one line per paragraph, and one paragraph per line. You'll see how that makes a big difference in the example in the next section.

To set a tab stop, do the following:

1. Select the paragraph(s) where you want to set new tab stops.

2. Click the dialog box launcher at the lower-right corner of the Paragraph group on the Home tab to open the Paragraph dialog box. Click the Tabs button to display the Tabs dialog box as shown in Figure 8.17.

3. Type the location of the first tab stop in the Tab Stop Position box. (The location is the distance from the left margin of the document to the position of the tab stop, regardless of where the left edge of the paragraph might fall.)

Figure 8.17
Use the Tab dialog box to add, remove, and adjust your document's tab stops.

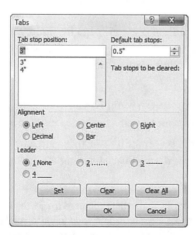

NOTE

> The default Normal paragraph style starts out with no explicitly defined tab stops. In this case, Word uses the Default Tab Stops setting of 0.5 inches, which treats the paragraph as if it contained a left-aligned tab stop every half-inch. As soon as you specify one or more tab stops, Word stops using the default tab stops preceding the ones you create. So, if you set a tab stop at 3 inches and another at 4 inches, pressing the Tab key once advances to 3 inches from the left margin; pressing Tab again goes to the right another inch. After it reaches the last user-defined tab stop, Word goes back to its default setting of left-aligned tab stops—in this case, at 4.5, 5.0, 5.5, 6.0, and so on, until you reach the right margin. You can change the Default Tab Stops setting to any value between 0.01 and 22 inches.

4. Choose the alignment and leader you want for the tab stop. Click the Set button and Word establishes a tab stop at the location you specify.

CAUTION

> The Bar tab type in the Tabs dialog box creates a vertical rule—an up-and-down line—in the paragraph at the indicated tab location. This setting is a throwback to an early version of Word that didn't have borders. If you need a vertical line, use tables or borders, but avoid this setting.

The tab stops you create are stored in the paragraph mark along with other paragraph format settings; copy or move a paragraph mark, and the tab stops go with it. If the insertion point is in a normal paragraph with custom tab stops and you press Enter, the new paragraph inherits the same tab stops. Many Word users—even advanced Word users—find that confusing. To restore a paragraph to the default (left-aligned tab stops every half inch), select the paragraph, press Ctrl+Shift+S to open the Apply Styles task pane, and click the original style's name.

USING THE RULER TO SET TAB STOPS

Although the Tabs dialog box (shown on the previous page in Figure 8.17) gives you much greater control over the location and characteristics of tab stops, many people use the Word ruler to set and move tab stops. To set a left-aligned tab stop at 2 inches using the ruler, you might try this approach:

1. Select the paragraphs that need tab stops. (You'll be able to see the results of setting tab stops immediately if you've already put the tab characters in the paragraphs.)

2. Bring up the ruler at the top of the screen, if it's not there already, by clicking the View Ruler button at the top of the vertical scroll bar at the right of your Word screen.

TIP

> If you want the ruler to remain hidden until you need it, click the View Ruler button again to hide it and then slide the mouse pointer up to the top of the editing window, to a razor-thin line below the Ribbon (and the Quick Access toolbar, if you've moved it there). Allow the pointer to remain there for a second or two and the Ruler slides down. Move the pointer again and it slides back up.

3. The icon on the far left of the horizontal ruler tells you what kind of tab is available: left-, center-, right-, or decimal-aligned. Click the icon to cycle through each of these tab types until you get the one you need.

4. Click the ruler where you want the new tab to appear. All default tabs to the left of the new tab are destroyed in the process. Click and drag the tab icon left or right to position it precisely where you want it. To get rid of a tab, click it and drag it off the ruler.

It's impossible to set the leader character directly from the ruler. For that task, you need to use the Tabs dialog box. Skip the menus, though; if the ruler is visible, just double-click on any tab stop to open the Tabs dialog box and fine-tune the settings.

USING TABS TO CREATE A USER-INPUT FORM

Suppose you want to create a fill-in-the-blanks form, with room for respondents to write (or type) information such as their name and address.

If you've used Word for any time at all, you have probably tried to create just such a form, most likely by typing underscore (_) characters and trying to line up columns that never look right. By far the easiest way to create such a form is by using tabs, with the underscore leader. Here's how:

1. Type the text, that will comprise the final form. Enter a tab character wherever you want a fill-in-the-blanks line to appear. In this case

```
Last Name <tab> First Name <tab>
Address <tab>
City <tab> State <tab> Zip <tab>
```

2. Position the insertion point inside the first paragraph, and display the Tabs dialog box by clicking the Paragraph dialog box's Tabs button. Set two tab stops—a left-aligned tab at 3 inches, with underscore leader (Type 4); and a right-aligned tab at 6 inches with underscore leader.

> **TIP**
>
> The default Word page layout—8.5-inch paper width, with 1.25-inch margins left and right—places the right margin at 6 inches, using the tab-measurement method.

3. Position the insertion point inside the second paragraph, and set a right-aligned tab at 6 inches, with underscore leader.

4. Position the insertion point in the third paragraph and set three tabs: left-aligned at 3 inches, left-aligned at 4.5 inches, and right-aligned at 6 inches, all with underscore leader.

5. If you want to fine-tune individual lines, click inside the line and then drag tab stop icons on the ruler to whatever position you like.

8

Word also enables you to double-click a "hot" spot on a line and insert a tab stop at the double-click location. This variant of Click and Type is notoriously inaccurate and much harder to use than either the Tabs dialog box or the ruler.

→ To learn more about Click and Type, **see** "Adjusting Paragraph Alignment and Outline Level," **p. 225.**

FORMATTING SIMPLE LISTS WITH BULLETS AND NUMBERS

By far, the simplest way to create a bulleted or numbered list is to use one of the many shortcuts for starting and continuing such lists. For example, if you type a number or letter, followed by a period, a space, and then text, Word begins a numbered list, provided that you haven't disabled the options on the AutoFormat as You Type tab in the AutoCorrect dialog box. Dozens of combinations are available.

→ To have Word handle some of the formatting chores for you, **see** "Automatic Formatting," **p. 213.**

Numbering and bulleting are paragraph properties. As such, they're stored in the paragraph mark and travel along with other paragraph settings if the paragraph mark is copied or moved. Position the insertion point inside a numbered or bulleted paragraph and press Enter, and the bulleting or numbering is inherited by the new paragraph.

NOTE

AutoNumbered and AutoBulleted lists are slightly different because Word lets you bail out of bulleting or numbering by pressing Enter twice in succession. In other words, if the insertion point is inside a bulleted or numbered paragraph, and the paragraph is empty, when you press Enter, Word removes the bulleting and formatting from both the old and new paragraphs.

Bullets and numbers maintained by Word aren't "real" characters. You can't select them, much less delete or change them. Instead, they are generated automatically by Word, as a consequence of their paragraph formatting. That's a big help when you're working on a document and want the freedom to add new items to a list or reorder existing items without having to worry about renumbering or manually applying bullet characters.

Many advanced Word users disable Word's AutoBulleting and AutoNumbering feature and apply bullets or numbers to lists by using the three buttons along the top of the Paragraph group on the Home tab or similar options on the shortcut menu.

→ AutoFormat driving you crazy? The good news is that you can disable it. **See** "Disabling AutoCorrect and AutoFormat Settings," **p. 199.**

You can always create a simple bulleted or numbered list by selecting the paragraphs you want to bullet or number and then clicking the Bullets icon or Numbering icon on the Ribbon's Home tab.

To take advantage of Word's extensive bulleting and numbering options, select the paragraphs you want to bullet or number and then click the arrow on the right of the Bullets or Numbering buttons on the Ribbon's Home tab. The options for modifying your bulleted lists are shown in Figure 8.18.

Figure 8.18
From simple bullets to complex outline-style numbering schemes, Word has a solid (but far from complete) array of options.

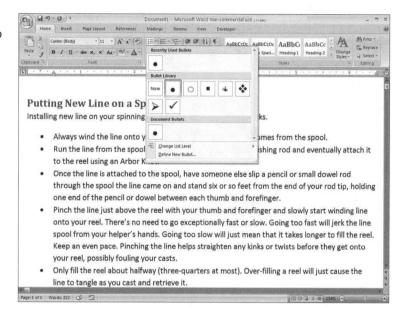

Select from the prebuilt bullet or numbering schemes, or click the Define New Bullet option in the Bullets or Numbering drop-down list to establish your own.

Consecutive paragraphs need not be numbered consecutively. For example, you could have paragraphs numbered 1, 2, and 3, then two paragraphs with no numbering, and pick back up at 4, 5, and so on. To stop the numbering sequence, select the paragraph(s) you don't want to have numbered, right-click on the incorrectly numbered paragraph, select Numbering from the shortcut menu, then select None. To continue numbering where you last left off, select the first paragraph after the break, change it to a numbered paragraph, right-click the number, and select Continue Numbering.

TIP

You can associate numbering with a specific paragraph style, making Word put a sequential number in front of each paragraph formatted with that style. If your chapter headings are formatted with a custom ChapterTitle style, for example, associating numbering with the ChapterTitle style automatically generates chapter numbers. To make the association, instead of clicking the Bullet or Numbering buttons on the Ribbon's Home tab, click Multilevel List button. Select Define New Multilevel List and select a numbering style. In the Link Level to Style box, choose the ChapterTitle style.

8

Because bulleting and numbering is a paragraph property, if you place the insertion point inside a bulleted or numbered paragraph and press Enter, the newly created paragraph "inherits" the bulleting or numbering.

It also means that you can move, drag, or rearrange numbered paragraphs at will, and Word renumbers them, on-the-fly, as appropriate.

FORMATTING ALL OR PART OF A DOCUMENT AUTOMATICALLY

If you feel intimidated by all of Word's formatting options, you can leave your document's destiny in the hands of Word's occasionally useful, but frequently awful, batch AutoFormat capability. Because Word 2003 and earlier users are accustomed to using AutoFormat, Microsoft kept the feature in Word 2007, although it's not an easy feature to find. It's often easiest to use the Quick Styles that you'll learn about in Chapter 10, "Mastering Styles, Templates, and Themes," but in case you still want to use AutoFormat, here is how you can make the feature easier to access:

1. Click the Office button and click Word Options.
2. Click the Customize tab to display a list of commands you can add to your Quick Access toolbar. (You can shortcut steps 1 and 2 by clicking the down arrow to the right of your Quick Access toolbar and selecting More Commands.)
3. In the Choose Commands From drop-down list, select All Commands.
4. Scroll to AutoFormat and click to select it.
5. Click Add to add the AutoFormat command to your Quick Access toolbar.
6. Close the Word Options dialog box. When you want to use AutoFormat, click the AutoFormat button that now appears on your Quick Access toolbar.

When you run it, AutoFormat scans your document, identifies the AutoFormat As You Type kinds of changes—changing straight quotes to curly ones, creating headings, AutoNumbering and AutoBulleting lists, and the like—and adds some general formatting changes (changing paragraphs that use the Normal paragraph style to Body Text, for instance). You can simply let the process happen, or you can tell Word you want to review each suggested change and decide whether to apply it or ignore it.

→ To learn more about the perils and pitfalls of AutoFormatting, **see** "Automatic Formatting," **p. 213.**

Because you have the option to review the changes onscreen and vote yea or nay on each, you really have nothing to lose by running AutoFormat. An AutoFormat run can be useful if you've just opened a plain-text document and need to format it quickly, or if you're having trouble getting the hang of Word's formatting capabilities. If you select a portion of a document, AutoFormat works only on your selection.

TIP

> Word's built-in AutoFormat choices include settings designed for cleaning up email messages. Using AutoFormat removes extra carriage returns and emphasizes marked reply text. Using AutoFormat with email messages requires that you first save the message in HTML or Text Only format and then open the saved file in Word.

Before using AutoFormat, save a copy of the file. If anything goes wrong, you can restore your backup copy and be right back where you started. To run AutoFormat, follow these steps:

1. To format the entire document, make sure no text is selected. To format a portion of the document, select that portion first.

2. Click the Quick Access toolbar's AutoFormat button (assuming you added the button there at the beginning of this section) or use the Word 2003-compatible shortcut Alt+O, A. If you want to review changes, select the AutoFormat and Review Each Change option.

3. Tell Word whether you're AutoFormatting a plain document (General Document), a letter, or an email message. Slightly different rules are applied in each case.

4. To see which AutoFormat rules will be applied to your document, click the Options button. If necessary, select or clear any options.

5. Click OK to perform the AutoFormat. If you chose the option to review changes, you can accept or reject any or all of them (see Figure 8.19).

Figure 8.19

Out of the box, AutoFormat can cause as many formatting headaches as it cures. Starting with Word 2007, the AutoPreview styles are much simpler to use as long as a Quick Style exists that you want to apply to your document. You can tame the AutoFormat beast and actually make it useful by following these tips:

- Try to clean up documents before using AutoFormat. Headings should be separated by line spaces, if possible, so that they aren't mistaken for short paragraphs.

- If you have any custom styles you want to use, apply those first. The default AutoFormat settings preserve manually applied styles.

- AutoFormat automatically applies heading styles, list styles, and paragraph styles (using the Body Text style for anything that isn't a heading or a list, for instance). To suppress any of these changes, click the Options button and clear the appropriate check box under the Apply section.

- If you don't like the results, press Ctrl+Z to undo them immediately and then try again using different options. Word treats AutoFormat as a single action so no matter how much your text changes in a single AutoFormat action, Ctrl+Z undoes all of the most recent AutoFormat conversion.

When you review AutoFormat changes, Word offers you access to the Style Gallery, which allows wholesale (and frequently disastrous) substitution of styles. The Style Gallery is most useful if you have created a library of standard templates based on the default Word templates, using different fonts and format settings for identically named styles. In that case, you can safely experiment with the Style Gallery to adjust the look of a document to match your styles. Most Word users, even advanced users, don't take this much care with templates, of course, making the Style Gallery a hindrance rather than a help.

TROUBLESHOOTING

WHEN YOU CAN'T KERN

When I select a block of text and use the Font dialog box to set kerning options, nothing seems to happen.

Kerning must be defined in the font itself—the people who design the font have to set up pairs for kerning and tell Windows how much space can be squeezed out between each pair. Most common text fonts have defined kerning pairs; many fonts do not.

If you tell Word to kern selected text, and you can't see any effect on obvious kerning pairs such as AV, first check to make sure the type size is equal to or larger than the points setting on the Character Spacing tab. If it is, chances are good that the font you're using doesn't support kerning.

Extra Credit: Straight Quotes or Curly Quotes?

One of the most useful AutoFormat as You Type options is the default setting that changes straight quotation marks to curly quotes (referred to as *smart quotes* in Word) as you type. The effect gives printed documents a more professional look, as the figure here shows.

The straight quotes at the top of the figure are exactly what you'd see if you used an old-fashioned typewriter. The curly quotes are typographic characters used for centuries by professional printers and publishers.

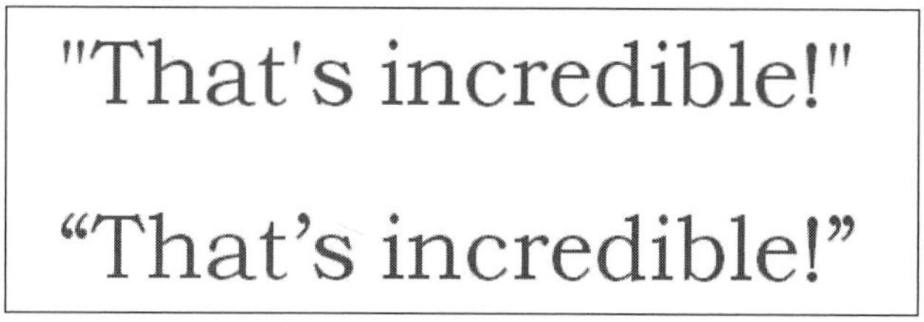

"That's incredible!"

"That's incredible!"

Figure 8.20

If your goal is to produce a printed page, you'll want to use the default option to automatically replace straight quotes with curly quotes. But there are a few cases where straight quotes are more appropriate. If you need to save a Word document as a plain text file, for example, you'll have better results with straight quotes. Also, some email programs and desktop publishing programs can't process curly quotes properly.

When you know that the ultimate destination of your document is more suited to straight quotes, disable this feature in the Word Options dialog box. Click the Proofing tab and then click the AutoCorrect Options button. On the AutoFormat as You Type tab, clear the Straight Quotes with Smart Quotes check box under the Replace as You Type heading. Select this check box to reenable the setting.

What do you do if you've created (or inherited) a document whose contents need to be converted from straight to curly quotes, or vice versa? Simple. First, make sure that the straight quotes setting on the AutoCorrect Options dialog box matches the result you want to achieve in your final document. Then press Ctrl+H, enter a single quote character in both the Find What and Replace With boxes, and click Replace All. Repeat this process with double quotation marks.

CHAPTER 9

ORGANIZING COMPLEX DOCUMENTS WITH ADVANCED FORMATTING OPTIONS

In this chapter

GOING BEYOND BASIC FORMATTING

Word isn't a full-fledged desktop publishing program, but that doesn't mean you're limited to dull paragraphs of text with an occasional heading and graphic sprinkled in to relieve the tedium. As we explain in this chapter, you have a rich set of options available when you want to create professionally designed pieces using Word. For starters, you can use tables to arrange words and numbers in neat rows and columns. You probably didn't know, however, that you can also use tables to perform some sophisticated page layout tricks. We show you how to coax more out of plain old tables than you ever dreamed possible.

Want to add some zing to a flyer or brochure? Use lines, borders, shading, and background graphics to add an extra dimension to the page. You can even divide text into newspaper-style columns to create a quick, easy-to-read newsletter.

Word also has a collection of features that are tailor-made for working with longer documents. If you're working on an epic research paper, you can chop the project into sections, add headers and footers to make navigation easier, create a table of contents and index by tagging text, and even add cross-references that update themselves automatically.

USING TABLES TO ORGANIZE INFORMATION

You might take one look at the neat row-and-column arrangement of Word tables and dismiss them out of hand as a pale imitation of Excel worksheets. Big mistake.

In fact, Word tables are at their weakest when pressed into service as repositories for rows and columns of numbers. Word has a paltry selection of tools for working with numbers. If you want to do any sort of arithmetic in a Word document—anything more complex than an occasional sum or product on a small handful of data—you're far better off embedding or linking an Excel range inside your Word document, even if you have to learn Excel to do it.

So, what are Word tables good for? Obviously, they're tailor-made for organizing and presenting price lists, feature comparisons, schedules, and other orderly arrangements of text. But Word tables are also excellent page layout tools that can help you precisely place words, numbers, and pictures on a page. In Figure 9.1, it might be obvious to you that we used a table to create the list of auction results toward the bottom of the screen—after all, each cell has a line around it and the data is classically tabular. But it might not be so obvious that the Word template for this fax uses a table to organize the header. Gridlines are not visible when you display a Word document from Print Preview mode or inside a web browser. To display gridlines, click the Ribbon's Table Tools Layout tab and click the View Gridlines button. The Table Tools Design and Table Tools Layout tabs appear on the Ribbon only when you click on or select a table in your document.

Figure 9.1
A table without the gridlines makes it easy to create and maintain lists like this one.

You should consider using tables when you need to perform any of the following tasks:

- Line up paragraph headings on the left with text on the right. This type of formatting is especially useful if you're preparing a résumé or a curriculum vitae.
- Draw intersecting horizontal and vertical lines. Using tables is generally much simpler than trying to add borders around words or paragraphs.
- Create fill-in-the-blanks printed forms.
- Place text in a fixed location on a page. Anytime you're thinking about using tab stops to arrange text or graphics on a page, consider using tables (without gridlines) instead. In general, tables are faster and easier to set up, and much simpler to maintain.

You can draw one table inside another—a very handy trick if you use tables for page layouts. Each nested table appears, in its entirety, within a single cell in the larger outer table.

ADDING A TABLE TO A DOCUMENT

When creating a new table, you have two options: Word can draw the table for you or you can draw it yourself. When Word draws the table for you, you are subject to the following restrictions:

- You specify the number of columns (to a maximum of 63) and rows (up to 32,767).
- You define how the table fits on the page, using one of three options: the table can fill the width of the page, each column can have the same width, or each column can automatically expand to accommodate the contents of the widest cell.

- Rows start out one line tall but automatically get taller, if necessary, to hold text or graphics.

If you can live with those restrictions, Word will make your table quickly. If you want more control over the initial table design—if you want the table to occupy only part of the page width, for example, or if you have complex cell patterns—you can draw your table freehand. After you place a table in your document, the Ribbon changes to include a Table Tools tab that provides formatting options you'll use throughout much of this chapter.

CREATING QUICK TABLES

By far the fastest, easiest way to insert a table into a Word document is to click the Table button on the Insert tab and use the grid at the top of the menu to define your table at the current insertion point. As you move your mouse pointer across the grid (shown in Figure 9.2), the selection changes color and a label appears at the top of the list to indicate how many columns and rows you've selected. When you're satisfied with the results, click to insert the table.

Figure 9.2
As you drag the mouse pointer over the Insert Table grid, a Live Preview shows you what the resulting table will look like in your document.

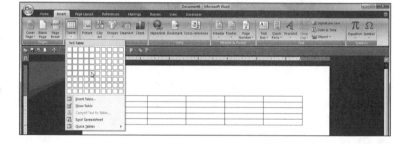

The resulting table is bland and generic, with absolutely no formatting. If you prefer something with a little more pizzazz (or a lot more, for that matter), click the Table button on the Insert tab and choose Quick Tables from the bottom of the menu. As Figure 9.3 shows, Word 2007 includes a selection of preformatted tables, including calendars, a matrix, a tabular list, and a pair of ready-made tables with subheadings. Select an existing Quick Table to insert it at the current insertion point, where you can work with it just like any other table.

TIP

> The predefined Quick Tables are interesting, but replacing the sample data with your own data takes a lot of the quick out of the process. If you like this feature, use it to create your own favorite table styles, using actual or sample data. Start with one of the predefined Quick Tables or with a blank table and modify it using the techniques listed in this chapter, changing the number of rows and columns, width, color, shading, and so on. Add sample text, if you want it. When you're satisfied with the results, select the entire table (click the Table Tools Layout tab, click Select, and choose Select Table). Then click the Insert tab, click the Tables button, click Quick Tables, and choose Save Selection to Quick Tables Gallery. Fill in the blanks in the Create New Building Block dialog box and click OK to add the table to the list.

Figure 9.3
Quick Tables include predefined formats and sample data that you'll need to replace in your document.

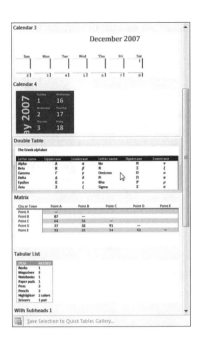

9

To have Word draw a table for you and set some basic AutoFit options as part of the same process, follow these steps:

1. Click in an empty paragraph where you want the upper-left cell of the new table to be located.

2. On the Insert tab, click Table, and then click Insert Table from the menu below the table grid. The Insert Table dialog box appears (see Figure 9.4).

Figure 9.4
Use the Insert Table dialog box to request a table.

3. In the Table Size section, choose the number of columns and rows. If you're not sure how many columns or rows you'll need, don't worry; you can easily increase either number later.

4. In the AutoFit Behavior section, tell Word how to determine the width of the table and its columns.

5. Click OK to add the table to your document (see Figure 9.5).

By default, every new table uses a generic Table Grid style. As soon as your table resides in your document, you will see the Table Tools tab appear on the Ribbon that has two sub-tabbed pages labeled Design and Layout. Click the Design tab, run your mouse pointer over the table styles, and Word's Live Preview changes your table's appearance accordingly. Click the down arrow at the right of the table style section to see more. When you find a table style you like, click it to change your table's appearance to that style.

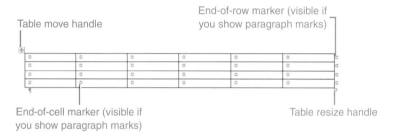

Figure 9.5
Quick, cookie-cutter tables from the Insert Table dialog box are easy to format.

After you insert a table, you can change its style by selecting another one from the Table Tools Design tab. You can also change other elements of the table's design such as the border, shading, line widths, and more.

The table move handle appears in the upper-left corner of the table in Print Layout view when you click anywhere in the table. Click this handle to select the entire table; drag it to move the table to a new location. When the entire table is selected, you can right-click and use the shortcut menu to make changes; a different set of shortcut menu options appear when you click within a cell. In either case, you'll find that most common table-editing tasks are much easier to accomplish if you stick with the Table Tools Design and Layout tabs.

DRAWING A COMPLEX TABLE

Unless you specifically want a table that conforms to Word's Insert Table restrictions, drawing one by hand is often simpler and makes the table look exactly the way you intend from the beginning. Follow these steps to do so:

1. On the Insert tab, click Table and choose Draw Table. The mouse pointer turns into a pencil.

2. Click where you want the upper-left corner of the table to appear. (You can even click inside a table cell to create a nested table within that cell. For details, see "Nesting Tables Within Tables," later in this chapter.)

3. Drag the pencil down and to the right, to the lower-right corner of the new table. Word creates a table with a single, large cell.

4. Using the pencil, click an existing table line and drag to the opposite edge to form a row, column, or individual cell. You can even click a cell corner and drag to the opposite corner to create a diagonal line.

If you don't like the position or size of a line you've drawn, use the Eraser button on the Table Tools Design tab to remove it. The mouse pointer turns into an eraser. Position the mouse pointer on the line you want to erase and click. To restore your usual mouse pointer, press Esc or click the Draw Table button.

TIP

> Don't worry about being neat when drawing rows and columns within a table. Just concentrate on getting the number of rows and columns right. You can use the Automatically Equalize Row Spacing option and move column borders later.

CONVERTING TEXT TO A TABLE

As you type text into a Word document, you might decide that what you've been typing would work better as a table. You might be tempted at that point to create a new table and then to cut and paste the text into it. Before you go through that labor-intensive exercise, consider doing the job in a few clicks with Word's built-in text-to-table converter.

For the conversion to work properly, your text must include a *delimiter* (paragraph mark, tab, comma, or some other character) so that Word can figure out what data goes in which cell. The number of delimiters must be consistent, too, or Word will be unable to figure out how many columns to use in each row. The lines shown in Figure 9.6, which include a single tab character to delimit cells, work fine.

Figure 9.6
If you're careful about using delimiting characters (such as the tab here), Word can readily convert text to a table.

TIP

> By far the simplest and most reliable way to delimit text for easy conversion to a table is with tabs separating the values that will go in each column, and paragraph marks at the end of each row. Although you can use commas, hyphens, or just about any other character, you're more likely to run into problems when these characters appear in the data and throw off the conversion.

To convert properly delimited text to a table, follow these steps:

1. Select the text you want to convert.

2. On the Insert tab, click Table, and then click the Convert Text to Table link. Word presents the Convert Text to Table dialog box shown previously in Figure 9.6.

3. Choose the delimiter in the Separate Text At section at the bottom of the dialog box. If the number of rows and columns doesn't match your expectations, click Cancel and take another careful look at your selected text. Chances are you picked up a stray line along the way.

4. Click OK to create the new table using the text you selected. After the table appears, you can select a table style to format the table to your needs.

 If you can't make the last row of your table match the last row of your data, see "Check for Stray Delimiters" in the "Troubleshooting" section at the end of this chapter.

TIP

> One of the hardest characters to find is a tab character that's squished between two pieces of text—or, worse, two or more tab characters in succession that aren't entirely visible because text surrounds them. Word does a bad job at displaying tab marks in such cases. You can select the text and use Find to search for single or double tabs—look for ^t or ^t^t.

You can convert a table back to text using the Convert to Text button on the Table Tools Layout tab. As part of the conversion, you can choose which character you want to use as a delimiter.

NESTING TABLES WITHIN TABLES

Word enables you to create tables within tables. *Nested tables* can be handy if you're using tables to perform advanced formatting tricks, such as creating side-by-side headings in a résumé, in which you need to put a table inside one of the cells.

NOTE

> You can move a table anywhere on a page by clicking and dragging the table move handle at the upper-left corner of the table. To put two tables side by side, for example, you don't need to create a table inside a table. Just drag the two tables into position.

To create a table within a table, click in the desired cell and use the menu or freehand drawing tool as explained earlier in this section. For an example of nested tables and their application in a common document type, see "Extra Credit: Nested Tables for Superior Layout" at the end of this chapter.

WORKING WITH TABLES

Table cells behave much like Word paragraphs. Text within a cell can be formatted, centered, indented and spaced, bulleted and numbered, with borders and shading, and each cell can have its own tab stop settings. All cell formatting is stored in the end-of-cell marker, which you can see only when paragraph marks are showing (click the Show/Hide ¶ button on the Ribbon's Home tab).

SELECTING CELLS, ROWS, AND COLUMNS

Select data within a cell just as you select data in a paragraph; if you want to transfer cell formatting, make sure you pick up the end-of-cell marker. Alternatively, you can select everything in a cell (including the end-of-cell marker) by letting the mouse pointer hover over the left side of the cell. When the mouse pointer turns into a thick arrow pointing up and to the right, click to select the whole cell.

One of the easiest ways to select table text is to use the buttons on the Table Tools Layout tab (see Figure 9.7). Click the Select button to choose from Select Cell, Select Column, Select Row, and Select Table. The buttons are easiest to use when your table spans more than the width or length of your screen.

Figure 9.7
The Select menu on the Table Tools Layout tab makes it easy to select parts of a table.

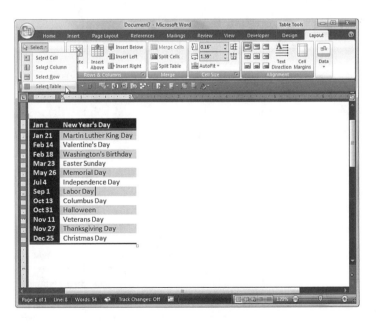

Other selection techniques include the following:

- To select an entire row, including the end-of-row marker, move the mouse pointer to the left of the row. Click when it turns into the shape of a hollow arrow pointing to the upper right. Equivalently, drag your mouse from the leftmost cell to the right to select the entire row.

- To select an entire column, let the mouse pointer hover near the top of the column. Click when it turns into a black solid arrow pointing down. Or you can select the entire column by dragging your mouse.

- To select the whole table, let the mouse pointer hover over the table move handle at the upper-left edge of the table until the pointer turns into a four-headed arrow, and then click to select the table. Alternatively, you can drag your mouse through all the cells to select them.

ENTERING AND EDITING DATA

You can type in a table cell precisely the same way you would type in a paragraph. If you press Enter, Word creates a new paragraph for you—in the same cell. Single cells can contain text, graphics, linked items, and embedded items—basically anything you can put in a document.

To move from one cell to the next, press Tab. To move back one cell, press Shift+Tab. To move backward or forward one character at a time, jumping from cell to cell at the beginning and end of each cell's contents, use the left- and right-arrow keys. To move up or down one cell, press the up- and down-arrow keys.

> **TIP**
>
> To enter the Tab character in a table cell, press Ctrl+Tab.

If the insertion point is in the last cell in a table, pressing Tab creates a new row, formatted the same as the current row, and moves the insertion point to the first cell in that row.

Many of the special navigation key combinations described in Chapter 4, "Entering, Editing, and Formatting Text," work inside tables. For example, Shift+Right Arrow selects text one character at a time, Ctrl+Shift+Right Arrow picks up a word at a time, and so on.

→ To learn about Word's extensive text-selection techniques, **see** "Selecting Text," **p. 86.**

> **TIP**
>
> You can add text above a table at the top of a document. With the insertion point in the first row of the table, press Ctrl+Shift+Enter to insert a paragraph above the table. The insertion point moves into that new paragraph and allows you to begin entering text. Use this same shortcut to split a table in two—position the insertion point in the row you want to use as the first row of the new table and then press Ctrl+Shift+Enter.

MOVING AND COPYING PARTS OF A TABLE

All the usual copy, cut, and paste routines you're accustomed to in Word work equally well within tables and cells. If you've copied cells from an existing table, Word adds new entries in the shortcut menu that appears when you right-click on all or part of a table: Paste Cells, Paste Columns, Paste Rows, and Paste as Nested Table. (Some or all of these options also appear on the Home tab's Paste menu when you've cut or copied table data.)

If you select a portion of a table first, Paste Cells replaces the selected cells with the contents of the copied cells. The table itself expands only if there are too many copied rows or columns to fit in the existing table. If you choose Paste as Nested Table, Word creates a new table as needed and fills it with the contents of the Clipboard. If you click inside a cell and then insert directly from the Clipboard task pane, Word assumes that you want to insert the columns, rows, or table on the Clipboard as a nested table within the current cell.

CAUTION

> When you paste cells, Word overwrites the contents of the current cells without warning, and without giving you an opportunity to change your mind. If that happens, click the Undo button (or press Ctrl+Z), and try again.

You can click and drag cells, columns, and rows, just as you do elsewhere in Word—with one exception. If you're going to move an entire row, you must select the end-of-row marker.

If you copy or move a single cell, with or without the end-of-cell marker, to an area outside a table, Word copies only the contents of the cell. If you copy two or more cells and paste them to an empty space in a document, Word creates a new table using those cells.

 If you are frustrated with cell contents or the row markers disappearing, see "Disappearing Cell Contents and Row Markers" in the "Troubleshooting" section at the end of this chapter.

CHANGING COLUMN WIDTHS AND ROW HEIGHTS

To adjust a column's width, you have four choices:

- Eyeball it—Move your mouse pointer so that it's near a vertical line in the table. When the pointer changes into a double-headed arrow, click and drag the line. If you move left, the column to the left becomes narrower and the column to the right becomes wider. If you move right, the column to the right becomes narrower and the column to the left becomes wider.

TIP

> If you want to change the width of the column only on the left (shrinking or expanding the size of the entire table as you go), hold down the Shift key as you drag.

- Measure it—Right-click inside the column you want to change, and then choose Table Properties from the shortcut menu. In the Table Properties dialog box, click the Column tab (see Figure 9.8). From that point, you can precisely specify the width of each column.

Figure 9.8
To get precise column measurements, nothing beats the Table Properties dialog box.

- Fit the contents—If you want the column width to grow or shrink depending on the width of the contents, right-click in the column, and then choose AutoFit, AutoFit to Contents from the shortcut menu.

TIP

> To AutoFit a single column, select the entire column and then double-click its right border.

- Fit the margins—You can also have Word automatically calculate how wide the table must be to extend all the way from the left to the right margin. To do so, right-click inside the column, and then choose AutoFit, AutoFit to Window from the shortcut menu. When you use this option, Word replaces the fixed widths for each column with percentages that match the current table, expanding each column so that it retains its same relative width.

The Table Tools Layout tab includes an AutoFit button with all the AutoFit options for those who find that selecting from a drop-down menu is easier than right-clicking a column or row. If you need to restore some uniformity to the table, you can always make all the columns the same width by selecting the columns and choosing Distribute Columns Evenly from the right-click shortcut menu.

TIP

> Yes, you can use the ruler to adjust column widths, as you'll discover with some experimentation (try dragging each little widget left and right, and then try the same operation while holding down the Shift, Ctrl, or Alt key, for instance). You can also use the vertical ruler to adjust row heights. If you double-click any of the markers that denote breaks between columns, you open the Table Properties dialog box. In our experience, though, trying to figure out and remember the exact function of each little slider and triangle is more trouble than it's worth. It's much easier to manipulate a table directly.

By default, rows expand and contract to hold the tallest item in the row. You can adjust row height in much the same way as column widths: Eyeball it with a click and drag or measure it in the Table Properties dialog box that you see when you right-click the upper-left corner of a table and select Table Properties. Click the Row tab, select the Specify Height check box, enter a height in inches, and select At Least or Exactly. You can also make two or more rows the same height by selecting the row and clicking Distribute Rows Evenly on the right-click shortcut menu.

TIP

> If you're creating a Word form for data entry, using Exactly for the row height prevents the cell from expanding if the user types in too much text. That prevents entries from pushing information from one page onto the next.

To change the width of individual cells, select the entire cell (including the end-of-cell marker) and then click and drag. As long as you've selected an entire cell (or group of cells), only those cells are resized.

 If you can't see all the contents of a table cell, see "Properly Setting the Row Height for Word Tables" in the "Troubleshooting" section at the end of this chapter.

ADDING AND DELETING ROWS AND COLUMNS

Sometimes, you want to keep your table formatting intact, but replace existing data in the table. For example, if you create a monthly status report showing the progress of your school's fund-raising efforts, you can copy the table from last month's report into a new document, and then delete the old data and replace it with this month's numbers. Here are a few tricks you need to know:

- If you select a cell and press Delete, the cell contents are deleted. Even if you include the end-of-cell marker, the cell formatting stays intact.

- If you select a column or row and press Delete, the contents of all the cells in the column or row are deleted—but the column or row itself stays and, again, the end-of-cell markers and their formatting remain. It doesn't matter whether you select the end-of-row marker.

- If you select an entire table and press Delete, the contents of all the cells in the table are deleted, but the table skeleton remains, formatting intact.

- If you select an entire table plus one or more characters after the table (including, for example, a paragraph mark) and press Delete, the entire table and selected character(s) are deleted completely. No skeleton remains.

To truly delete a cell, row, column, or table, click to select the cell, row, column, or table that you want to delete, and choose the appropriate Delete command.

To insert a cell, row, or column (or a table, for that matter), right-click to select the cell, row, or column to the left, right, above, or below the place you want to put the new cell, row, or column, and then choose Insert followed by the appropriate item you want to insert. The Table Tools Layout tab also has Insert buttons that you might find easier to work with depending on the size of your table.

ROTATING TEXT

It's easy to rotate text in a table by 90°, clockwise or counterclockwise. To do so, select the cell(s) you want to rotate, right-click the selection, and then choose Text Direction. The Text Direction – Table Cell dialog box enables you to choose orientation (see Figure 9.9). Clicking the Text Direction button on the Table Tools Layout tab rotates the text in the currently selected cells 90°. Click it again to rotate the text 90° to the left, and once more to return to normal orientation.

Figure 9.9
As long as you want your text aimed straight up or straight down, Word can accommodate.

If you want table headings at any other angle than 90°, consider embedding or linking an Excel range. It's much easier to rotate text to any desired angle in an Excel worksheet.

MERGING AND SPLITTING CELLS AND TABLES

If you insert a table into a cell, you have two tables, one inside the other, which are nested tables. Most of the time you don't need—or want—two separate tables; usually, when you run out of room in a table, what you really need is the capability to split an existing cell into two, four, or six cells.

Only a few subtle differences exist between, say, nesting a four-column one-row table inside a cell and manually splitting the cell into four smaller cells. The main difference is in spacing—unless you change the spacing settings, nested tables take up an additional amount of space inside the cell to accommodate the outside of the table itself, whereas split cells require no additional spacing. Use a nested table when you want to manipulate the contents of a portion of the table as a unit. You can click and drag a nested table outside its confining cell, for example, but moving four subcells is considerably more complex.

→ To learn more about using nested tables, **see** "Nesting Tables Within Tables," **p. 248.**

The easy way to split a cell into multiple cells is to use Word's table-drawing tools. Select the Draw Table option on the Ribbon's Insert tab's Table button. Use the pencil-shaped pointer to draw horizontal or vertical lines inside the cell or cells you want to split. Use the Split Cells button on the Table Tools Layout tab if you want to rearrange a group of selected cells and their text—converting four cells in one column into four cells in a single row, for example.

In some cases, you might want to merge cells. In a table that has one or more rows that function as headings, as in Figure 9.10, merging the cells from that row makes the heading easier to see. To merge two cells together, use the Eraser icon when in the table-drawing mode. To merge cells in a row that contains many columns, select the cells and click the Merge Cells button on the Layout tab or select Merge Cells from the shortcut menu that appears when you right-click over selected cells.

Figure 9.10
You might want to merge the cells in one row of a table to accommodate headings, as shown here.

CPU Components	
Disk Drives	4 (320GB, 250 GB)
Sound Card	One
CRT Ports	Two
Software	
Op Sys	Windows Vista
Productivity	Office 2007
Games	Spider-Man, Tetris
Cables	
USB	2
FireWire	1

To split a table horizontally—between two rows—click once in the row that will become the top row in the new table. Click the Table Tools Layout tab's Split Table button. A paragraph mark appears between the two tables. (As noted earlier, you can also press Ctrl+Shift+Enter to split a table.)

TIP

> You can easily split a table vertically as well. Select the columns you want to split away from the original table. Right-click the selection and choose Cut from the shortcut menu (or press Ctrl+X). Move the insertion point to wherever you want the new table to appear, right-click, and select Paste from the shortcut menu. You can then place the two tables side by side by using their drag handles.

SORTING DATA WITHIN TABLES

Although it doesn't hold a candle to Excel's sorting capabilities, Word can sort using as many as three keys, including dates. Within a table that contains student records, for instance, you can sort by Grade, and then by LastName, and then by FirstName. Word can also handle case-sensitive sorts as well as nonstandard sorting sequences (for languages other than English).

Sorting in Word can come in handy in many situations. You might want to sort a table of names to put it in alphabetical order by last name, and then copy the table and sort it again by grade point average or test score. Or perhaps you created a table with the data sorted by last name, but you later decide that it would be more useful if sorted by first name. That kind of sorting is easy in Word.

NOTE

In fact, you needn't put data in a table to sort it. Word does just fine if you have clean data with delimiters—precisely in the same way that's required for converting text to a table. You can also sort simple lists (say, a list of state names, each in a single paragraph) because the paragraph mark is a delimiter.

TIP

Entire chapters and sections can be sorted (using their headings) in Outline view.

→ To learn more about automatically converting your text into a Word table, **see** "Converting Text to a Table," **p. 247.**

You can also sort by individual words within cells—for example, if you have a row with names in FirstName LastName order, you can tell Word to sort by LastName, the second word in the column, followed by FirstName, the first word in the column (see Figure 9.11). To sort data, do the following:

1. Click once to position the insertion point inside the table (or data).
2. On the Ribbon's Table Tools Layout tab, click the Sort button. You see the Sort dialog box shown in Figure 9.11.

Figure 9.11
Although not as comprehensive as Excel's sorting capabilities, Word does rather well and you needn't convert your data to a table to sort it.

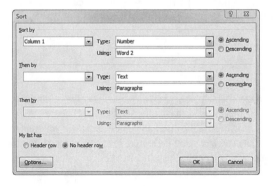

3. If your table (or data) has a header row—that is, if the first row describes the data below it—start by clicking the My List Has Header Row option. That way, Word uses the names from the header row instead of the generic Column 1, Column 2, and so on. (This also prevents your column headings from mixing in with your data when you sort.)

4. Choose your sort conditions. If you're planning to sort by LastName FirstName, you need to click Options, choose Other under the Separate Fields At heading, and enter a space as the field delimiter. (You will also use this dialog box for nontable data, when specifying a case-sensitive sort, or when choosing a sorting sequence other than standard English.)

5. When you're ready to perform the sort, click OK.

TIP

In unusual circumstances, you might want to sort just one column of a table, while leaving the other columns untouched. A teacher might construct a table with two columns, one containing scientific terms, the other containing definitions. By sorting just one column, the teacher could create a "connect the definitions" test, in which the students have to associate terms with definitions. To sort just one column of a table, select the column prior to starting the sort , click the Sort dialog box's Options button, and then check the Sort Column Only box. Click OK, and the single column is sorted independently.

POSITIONING TABLES ON THE PAGE

Although you might think that tables exist in the drawing layer because you can click the dragging handle to move them around, they are in the main part of the document. Thus, you can put captions inside tables and reference them via the Cross-reference dialog box, which appears when you click the Cross-reference button on the Insert tab. Paragraphs can be numbered and the numbering continues from the main part of the document, through the table, and into the rest of the document; and entries in tables are picked up for indexes and tables of contents.

Although you'll most often want a table to appear flush left with text above and below it (not wrapping around), from time to time, you might want the table to appear flush right or centered. You also might want main body text in the document to wrap around the table, especially with smaller tables. Follow these steps to make it happen:

1. Create the table by using any of the methods explained in this chapter.

2. Right-click inside a table (or on the icon that appears when you click outside the upper-left corner of the table) and choose Table. On the Table Tools Layout tab, click Properties. You see the Table Properties dialog box (see Figure 9.12).

Figure 9.12
The Table Properties dialog box enables you to align tables on a page and specify whether you want text to wrap around the table.

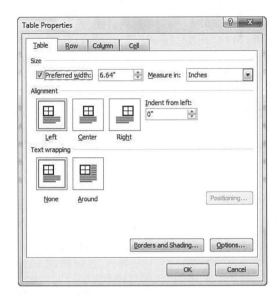

3. Click the Table tab and set Left, Center, or Right alignment in the Alignment section. If you want to control the distance from the left edge of the box to the left margin of the page, use the Indent from Left spinner.

4. Allow document body text to flow around the table by clicking the Around box. If you want finer control over text wrapping—for example, the distance from text to the table edges—click the Positioning button.

ADVANCED TABLE FORMATTING OPTIONS

A properly formatted table helps the reader absorb and understand the contents. You know your table hasn't been formatted well when a reader has to pull out a ruler to tell which numbers belong on what rows.

LETTING WORD DO THE WORK WITH TABLE STYLES

Word provides a diverse selection of table styles, available from the Table Tools Design tab (which appears when you click anywhere inside a table). Table styles define whether the table is formatted as a list or a grid, and the ready-made styles mix different colors, types of shading, and borders that give you a good start on your way to table perfection. As with other Gallery-based formatting options, you can run your mouse over the table styles to see a Live Preview of the style in the current table. After you find the table style you want to use, click that style and Word changes your table appropriately.

If you routinely create tables of a certain size, shape, and format, you can save those settings for reuse. After creating a table using any of Word's table-creation methods, select the table and click the Table Tools Design tab. Click the down arrow to the right of the row of ready-made table styles to open the full Table Styles gallery and select Modify Table Style. Word opens the Modify Style dialog box (see Figure 9.13) where you can fine-tune various aspects of your table and name the new table style you want to create. The next time you display the Table Styles Gallery, your style appears in the Custom section. Click that style and Word instantly changes your selected table to the saved table style. To delete a custom table style, right-click the table style in the Custom section and select Delete Table Style.

Figure 9.13
Be sure to select the entire table before choosing Modify Table Style. Enter a custom name and click OK to save your formatting as a new table style.

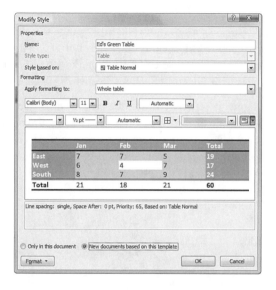

Using Borders and Shading

The options for adding borders, shading, and background colors in table cells are identical to their counterparts in the Paragraph group on the Home tab. Position the insertion point within a table or select a cell, row, or column and choose from the Table Tools Design tab to change the border, shading, or line color and thickness; click the Borders button to open the Borders and Shading dialog box and apply multiple changes to the current selection.

→ To learn more about the common drawing tools used throughout Office, **see** "Adding Lines, Borders, Shading, and Backgrounds," **p. 265.**

Word normally displays a faint gray gridline, corresponding to cell borders, even if you format the cells so that their borders are invisible. Tables viewed by a web browser never show gridlines, regardless of the Show/Hide Gridlines setting.

TIP

If you're creating a table that will be viewed onscreen in Word, you can hide the gridlines by clicking the View Gridlines button; click again to view the gridlines.

9

ALIGNING TEXT IN CELLS

Left-aligned text in cells might work for certain types of text tables, or tables where the columns are narrow. Frequently, however, you'll want to right-align numbers or center text. Right-aligned numbers are much easier to read and compare. If you're using a two-column table to simulate columns (in a résumé, for example), right-align the text in the left column to help show the connection with the matching blocks of text in the right column. For small amounts of text, centered text—even if it's just centered headings over a column—looks better than left-aligned almost anywhere in a table, except the first column.

You can click once in a cell, or select a series of cells, and change the alignment from left-justified to centered to right-justified by clicking the Align Left, Center, and Align Right buttons on the Ribbon's Home tab. Because end-of-cell markers behave much like paragraph marks, that formatting travels with the end of cell marker when it's copied or moved.

Word also allows you to align text vertically inside the cell. To do so, select the cells you want to format and then select one of the nine options in the Alignment group on the Table Tools Layout tab or in the fly-out Cell Alignment menu on the right-click shortcut menu (see Figure 9.14). You can choose from any combination of top, center, or bottom positioning with left, center, or right text alignment. Click Properties in the Table group and then click the Options button to tell Word how much whitespace you want between the cell edge and the text inside the cell (see Figure 9.14).

Figure 9.14
All nine combinations of text and vertical alignment appear on the cell's context menu.

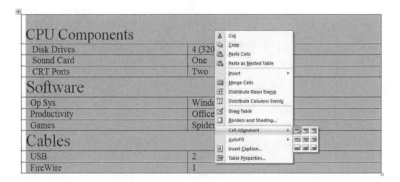

WORKING WITH BIG TABLES

When you work with large tables, you'll commonly encounter three distinct problems. Fortunately, each has a simple solution:

- Too wide—When adjusting column widths or adding columns, sometimes the table extends beyond the page margins. If you're working in Print Layout view, you won't be able to see (or work with) the rightmost columns.

 If you lose the final column, refer to "Can't See Final Column(s) in a Table" in the "Troubleshooting" section at the end of the chapter.

- Repeating titles—If your table will print on more than one page, readers might lose track of what's in each column; you might want the title row(s) to appear at the top of each additional page. Select the row(s) you want to use as the repeating titles (you must include the first row of the table), and click the Repeat Header Rows button on the Table Tools Layout tab.

- Page breaks in cells—By default, Word keeps all of a cell's contents on one page, allowing a page to break only when a new cell starts. If you're writing a résumé using a table, for example, you might want to relax that restriction so that page breaks can fall more naturally.

 If you want to relax the way Word breaks cells in a table, see "Allow Page Breaks in a Table Cell" in the "Troubleshooting" section at the end of the chapter.

Taking Control of Page Breaks

We cringe every time we see a Word beginner try to control pagination by clicking at the beginning of the paragraph that should start a new page and then pressing the Enter key— over and over again—until the text appears at the top of a new page. The result is almost always a mess that spirals out of control with even the simplest changes.

In long, highly formatted documents, the best way to control page breaks is through the use of paragraph styles—set a page break before each paragraph with the Chapter Heading style, for example, or force all the text in a Quote style paragraph to appear on one page. That kind of page break setting belongs in the paragraph style. Press Ctrl+Shift+S to display the Apply Styles pane and select the style you want to modify; then click the Modify button, click Format, Paragraph, and click the Line and Page Breaks tab. Even with well-designed paragraph styles, however, sometimes you'll want to force Word to start a new page at a location of your choosing.

To force Word to start a new page in a specific place, don't use the Enter key. Instead, click once where you want the new page to begin, click the Ribbon's Insert tab, and click the Page Break button. (Alternatively, you can press Ctrl+Enter.) In Draft view (see Figure 9.15), each page break appears as a dotted line. In other views, the break markers are visible only if you click the Home tab's Show/Hide ¶ button.

The problem with manually inserted page breaks, of course, is that they don't change when the text changes. If you add or delete a few lines in several places in a document, you might need to adjust every manual page break—a dreary prospect indeed. To delete all manual page breaks, follow these steps:

1. Click the Replace button on the Home tab (or press Ctrl+H).

2. Clear the contents of the Find What and Replace With boxes, if necessary, and then click the More button. Clear all check boxes and all formatting.

Figure 9.15
Manually inserted page breaks are visible as dotted lines in Print Layout and Draft view, as shown here.

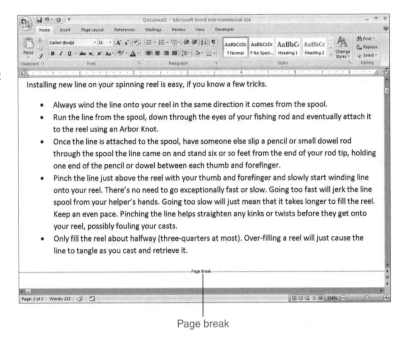

Page break

3. Click the Special button and choose Manual Page Break. Word adds the ^m character to the Find What box. (If you remember this character, you can enter it yourself without going through the Special menu.) Leave the Replace With box empty.

4. Choose Replace All to remove every manual page break in the document.

FORMATTING DOCUMENTS BY SECTION

Although most Word documents contain only one section, if you want to change headers or footers, page size or orientation, margins, line numbers (used in some legal documents), page borders, or the number of newspaper-like columns in different parts of a document, you have to use sections.

Perhaps the most common situation arises when you want to change headers or footers in the middle of a document. In that case, you have to add a new section; there's no alternative. Likewise, you might need to add a section if you have a wide table in the middle of a long report. Most of your pages will be printed in portrait orientation, but you'll need to add a section break before and after the table so that you can print it in landscape orientation. You could print the table separately and collate it by hand, but using section breaks removes your layout hassles with just a few clicks.

→ For a description of other page setup settings, **see** "Page/Section Setup Options," **p. 210.**

TYPES OF SECTIONS

Word recognizes four types of section breaks:

- Next Page—The most common type of section break, a Next Page section break not only defines a new section, it forces Word to start the section on a new page.

- Continuous—Defines a new section but does not force a page break. Continuous section breaks are used almost exclusively for changing the number of newspaper-like columns in a document or resetting line numbering (typically in legal documents).

- Odd Page—Like the Next Page break, except Word can add one blank page (if necessary) to force the new section to begin on an odd-numbered page.

- Even Page—Like the Odd Page break, but Word starts on an even-numbered page.

Section breaks are visible in all views when you click the Show/Hide ¶ button to make special formatting characters visible.

Just as paragraph formatting is stored in the paragraph mark at the end of a paragraph, so Word stores section formatting in the section break mark at the end of the section. Formatting for the final section in a document is stored in the last paragraph mark in the document. If a document has only one section, the document's final paragraph mark holds the section formatting for the entire document.

INSERTING AND DELETING SECTION BREAKS

To insert a new section break into a document, follow these steps:

1. If the document does not yet include one, we strongly recommend that you put a dummy manual section break at the end of the document. To do so, click once in front of the final paragraph mark in the document. Press the Enter key a few times. Then click the Page Layout tab, and click the Breaks button (in the Page Setup group) to see a menu of available options. From the Section Breaks group (see Figure 9.16), choose Continuous.

2. If all the headers and footers in the document will be the same, you'll find it much easier to establish them now. Follow the instructions in the "Creating and Editing Headers and Footers" section later in this chapter.

3. Carefully determine what section breaks you'll need in your document, what type they should be, and where they will occur. In particular, if you plan to change the number of newspaper-like columns for a short run in the middle of the document, you'll want continuous section breaks both before and after the change.

4. Starting at the beginning of the document, create the section breaks, one at a time, by using the Page Layout tab's Breaks button.

Figure 9.16
Before you insert that first section break, you can save yourself hours—days!—of trouble by placing a dummy section break at the end of the document.

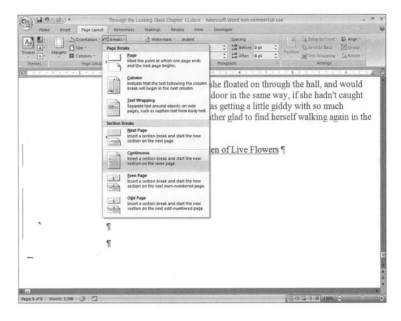

The dummy section break at the end of the document can help you salvage important formatting information because you can copy or move the section break, although copying or moving the final paragraph mark won't have any effect on section formatting. See the next section for details.

After establishing all sections, carefully go back into each section and apply the section formatting you require.

TIP

> You'll find it much easier to work with sections if you plan ahead and then go through each section in order, from beginning to end, applying the section formatting. By working from beginning to end, you simplify problems—massive problems—associated with changing headers and footers, and whether a section is linked to the previous one. If you start at the beginning, you can see the effect each change has on subsequent sections. If you start in the middle, it can be infuriatingly difficult to see why or how a header or footer has changed.

If you must delete a section break, select the break and press Delete. The newly merged section takes on the settings of the section break at the end. Immediately examine the document for odd formatting changes. If you find any unwelcome formatting, press Ctrl+Z or click the Undo button to restore the section break.

Copying Formatting Between Sections

Section breaks store the settings for the section. You can select, delete, copy, or move these settings at will. By far, the simplest way to copy section formatting from one section to another is by copying the section break. If you want to copy the section formatting from, say, section number 6 to section number 3, follow these steps:

1. Select the section break at the end of section 6 and press Ctrl+C to copy it to the Clipboard.
2. Click just in front of the section break at the end of section 3.
3. Press Ctrl+V to paste the section break you copied previously.
4. Press Delete to delete the old section break at the end of section 3.

> **TIP**
>
> If you created an extra dummy section break at the end of the document, all the document's original section formatting is stored in that section break. To restore the document's original formatting to a specific section, copy that dummy section break to the end of that section.

Adding Lines, Borders, Shading, and Backgrounds

Word enables you to draw border lines and apply colors and other forms of shading to specific pieces of text, cells in tables, paragraphs, entire tables, or entire pages. When you draw a line around a page, it's called a *page border*. When you apply colors or shading to an entire page, it's called a *background*. And when you place a picture or text behind the text on a page—say, to print DRAFT diagonally across the page or to brand the page with the word CONFIDENTIAL—that picture or text is called a *watermark*.

> **TIP**
>
> To add a watermark to a document, click the Page Layout tab and click Watermark to display a menu of predefined and custom watermark options. When you select a watermark, the watermark is inserted as part of the document's (actually, the section's) header. By working directly with the header (use either the Print Layout or the Full Screen Reading view to see the header and footer), you can manually change the watermark—move it, resize it, or even delete it.

Quick Ways to Create Lines

The easiest way to draw a horizontal line across a page is to type any of the horizontal line AutoFormat characters three or more times and press Enter (see Table 9.1). The line appears above the characters you typed.

TABLE 9.1   AUTOFORMAT CHARACTERS FOR HORIZONTAL LINES

Character	Type of Line
- (hyphen)	Light single line
_ (underscore)	Heavy single line
= (equal)	Heavy double line
# (number sign)	Thick line with thin lines above and below
~ (tilde)	Wavy line
* (asterisk)	Horizontal line of small squares

The horizontal line (also called a *rule*) is actually a lower border for the paragraph above the one where you typed. If you click to position the insertion point in that paragraph and then click the Borders and Shading option from the bottom of the Borders menu in the Paragraph group on the Home tab, you'll see what formatting has taken effect by viewing the details inside the Borders and Shading dialog box (see Figure 9.17 in the next section). If you find this automatic line-drawing behavior annoying, you can turn it off.

→ To eliminate unwanted AutoFormat behaviors, **see** "Automatic Formatting," **p. 213.**

You can also use the tools on the Shapes menu (in the Illustrations group on the Ribbon's Insert tab) to draw lines, or use the Draw Table button on the Insert tab's Table menu and use Word's table-drawing tool. Neither of these approaches, however, quickly creates lines that extend all the way across a page and move with their associated text as easily as using one of the AutoFormat options.

BORDERS AND BOXES

You can draw borders—essentially rectangles—around characters, paragraphs, table cells, or pages. To create a border for characters, paragraphs, or cells, follow these steps:

1. Select the characters, paragraphs, table cells, or tables you want to format.

2. Click the Borders and Shading button (on the Home tab) to open the Borders and Shading dialog box. On the Borders tab (see Figure 9.17), make sure that the Apply To box shows the correct setting: Paragraph, Text, Cell, or Table.

3. Choose from the common settings along the left, or draw your own border in the Preview pane on the right. You might want to use the Preview pane if, say, you want to have lines appear to the left and above a paragraph but not to the right or below. Choose the line style, color, and width in the center pane.

TIP

> If you want borders of different types (to add double lines on the top and bottom but single lines at the left and right, for example), start by clicking the Custom box. Then build the first border type by selecting from the Style, Color, and Width boxes. Finally, tell Word where you want this particular border type to appear by selecting the locations in the Preview pane. Go back and build your second border type, apply it in the Preview pane, and repeat as needed.

Figure 9.17
The Borders and Shading dialog box enables you to draw lines around characters, paragraphs, and cells.

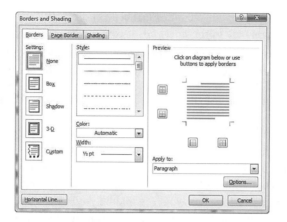

9

4. To set the distance between the text and the border, click Options and fill in the amounts. Click OK and the border appears.

The procedure for applying page borders is similar:

1. If you want only a specific page (or pages) in your document to have a border, set up section breaks at the beginning and end of the page (or pages). Then click once inside the section you want to have page borders.

2. Click the Ribbon's Page Layout tab and click the Page Borders button.

3. To choose from a selection of more than 150 border options, click the down arrow in the Art box. Page border formatting options are similar to general border formatting, except pages can also use artwork for their borders.

N O T E

Unfortunately, you can't add your own page borders to Word's collection.

4. If you don't want the border to encompass the header or footer, click the Options button, choose Measure from Text, and clear the Surround Header and Surround Footer boxes. Click OK and the border will be visible in Print Layout view.

To understand how borders can move around a document and appear suddenly as if out of nowhere, it's important to know where the formatting is stored:

■ Character borders are stored in the characters themselves. If you move or copy a character with a border, the border goes along with it.

■ Paragraph borders are stored in the paragraph mark. If you copy, move, or delete a paragraph mark, the border goes with it. If you press the Enter key while inside a paragraph with a border, the new paragraph inherits the border settings from the previous paragraph.

- Table cell borders are stored in the individual cell's end-of-cell marker. Borders that apply to the entire table are in the final end-of-row marker.

- Page borders are stored in the section break mark. If your document has only one section, page borders are stored in the final paragraph mark in the document.

→ For an explanation of how to format cells, rows, and tables, **see** "Working with Tables," **p. 249.**

SHADING CHARACTERS, PARAGRAPHS, AND PAGES

A little shading goes a long way. Black text on a light shade of gray (or a pale yellow) can be quite legible. On forms, in particular, a little shading can actually enhance the appearance of text and make the form easier for users to fill in. White text on a very dark background makes a striking visual impression. But avoid the middle ground: Dark shading with dark characters can be virtually illegible, even if you never print the document—colors vary widely from monitor to monitor, as well.

Character, paragraph, table cell, and entire table shading works much like borders. Select the items you want to shade and then click the Home tab's Borders and Shading button. Click the Shading tab to see the Shading options shown in Figure 9.18.

Figure 9.18
Color and shading are both applied from the Shading tab.

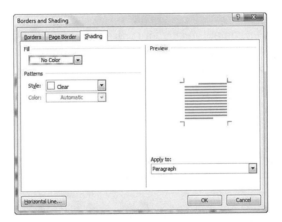

The interaction of the various parts of the Shading dialog box can be confusing. Think of it this way: If you want to apply a solid color, use the Fill box at the top of the dialog box. If you want to apply a shade—say, a 5% gray background—use the Patterns area at the bottom. Selecting No Fill in the Fill box on the top means there's no solid background color. Selecting Clear in the Style box near the bottom means there's no shading.

If you absolutely must have a background color, with a shade of gray on top of the color, pick the color in the Fill box and the shade in the Pattern box. Finally, just to guarantee that you stay thoroughly confused, shades aren't confined to shades of gray. In fact, you can shade with any color; choose it in the Color box at the bottom.

If you want to apply a shade or a fill color to the entire page, you're in the wrong place. You'll have to go back to your document, click the Page Color button on the Page Layout tab, and select a color from the current themes. If you select Fill Effects, Word opens the Fill Effects dialog box shown in Figure 9.19. Using fill effects, you can perform one- or two-color gradient fills; use a repeating picture called a *texture* to give your document a background that looks like stone, wood, or fabric; create cross-hatched patterns in a wide variety of styles and any color; or bring in your own picture, which will be repeated like a tiled Windows wallpaper.

Figure 9.19
Word has an extensive collection of fill effects, but they can be applied only to pages, and all the pages in a document must have the same effects.

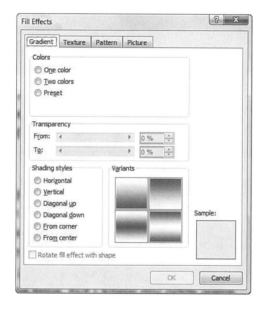

Page backgrounds apply to the entire document; they cannot be changed from section to section, like page borders. In addition, the fill effects available on pages are not available to characters, table cells, or paragraphs.

FORMATTING A DOCUMENT WITH COLUMNS

Another section-formatting option controls the number of newspaper-like snaking columns within the section. You might be tempted to use multiple columns for laying out newsletters and brochures, or (not surprisingly) newspapers. Text arranged in relatively narrow columns is often easier to read than the same text that uses the full width of a letter-size page; the human eye can take in a narrow column all at once and allow the reader to scan down quickly, whereas the eye has to move from left to right and back again for a wide column.

Before you begin using columns, take a closer look at the pluses, minuses, and gotchas. Snaking newspaper-like columns might not work the way you're expecting: They run from top to bottom, and there's no rebalancing for a page break. If you have, say, 12 items in a section that's set up with three columns, they'll appear arranged as in Table 9.2.

TABLE 9.2 SEQUENCE OF SNAKING COLUMNS

Item 1	Item 5	Item 9
Item 2	Item 6	Item 10
Item 3	Item 7	Item 11
Item 4	Item 8	Item 12

However, if you add a page break between, say, the second and third lines in Table 9.2, items 2, 6, and 10 will appear on the first page, and items 3, 7, and 11 will end up on the second page.

If you need greater control over the appearance and layout of snaking columns, use tables instead of column formatting. Place each item in its own table cell and hide the table's gridlines. With Word's capability to draw custom tables with any number of cells, including nested cells, it makes little sense to work with columns if the layout is complicated.

To set up snaking columns in the middle of a document, follow these steps:

1. Switch to Draft view, click to position the insertion point where you want the columns to begin, and then click the Breaks button on the Page Layout tab. Add a continuous section break immediately before the beginning of the text or the first item in the list.

2. Add another continuous section break immediately after the end of the text block or the last item in the list.

3. Click once between the two section break marks, click the Columns button on the Page Layout tab, and select the number of columns you want to use. For added control, instead of selecting a number of columns, select the More Columns option at the bottom of the list and choose the column layout you like (see Figure 9.20). Note that you can set column widths and intercolumn whitespace manually.

Figure 9.20
To avoid confusion, set up the before and after section breaks manually: Click inside the area you want to format in snaking columns, and choose This Section from the Apply To box.

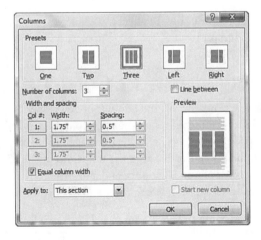

CREATING AND EDITING HEADERS AND FOOTERS

Headers appear at the top of each page; footers at the bottom. Word lets you specify "first page only" headers and footers, so the first page of a report or letter can have headers and footers different from those in the body of the report. That's useful if your first page is a decorative title page and you don't want it to contain a page number or the title. In addition, Word enables you to set up different headers and footers for odd-numbered and even-numbered pages. That comes in handy if you're going to be printing on the front and back of each sheet of paper and then binding the final document into a book format. (Look at the headers in this book for an example.)

CREATING HEADERS AND FOOTERS

Headers and footers exist on every page in a Word document. Until you put something in them, however, they're invisible. Word reserves room for them but doesn't print anything (or show anything on the screen) in the reserved area. To create a header, follow these steps:

1. Click the Insert tab and click the Header (or Footer) button to display a drop-down list of predefined headers (or footers) from which you can select. When you select a header, Word switches to Print Layout view (if necessary), displays the Header & Footer Tools Design tab on the Ribbon, turns the body text of the document gray, and highlights the header area of the page (see Figure 9.21).

Figure 9.21
When you add a header—or just click in the empty header area—Word adds descriptive labels and a dashed dividing line.

Header area

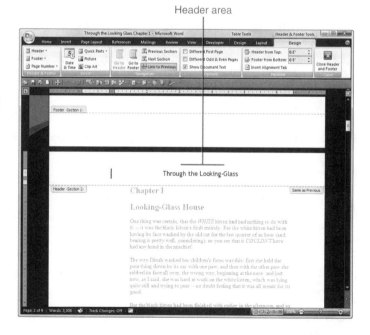

9

2. Enter text and format the header as you need. Note that the paragraph is formatted with the Header style, which includes two tab stops: a centered stop at the middle of the page and a right-aligned stop on the right margin. If you've changed margins, you also need to change the locations of these tab stops.

3. When you finish with the header, click the Close Header and Footer button. If you'd rather work with the footer, click the Ribbon's Go to Footer button. (As you might expect, the Go to Header button puts you right back in the header.) Word moves the insertion point to the footer for the current page.

4. Enter text, graphics, or whatever else you want in the footer.

5. Click the Close Header and Footer button to return to the body of the document.

If you have created a header or footer for a page, you can see it when you're in Print Layout view as a grayed-out shadow of how the header or footer will appear on the final printed page. To edit a header or footer that you can see on the screen, double-click it.

To force Word to use a different header and footer on the first page than in the rest of the document, or to alternate headers and footers for odd- and even-numbered pages, select the Different First Page or Different Odd & Even Pages check boxes on the Header & Footer Tools Design tab. After selecting the Different First Page check box, you can navigate to the first page in your document and double-click the header or footer area to customize the first-page header and footer as you like.

With the Different Odd & Even Pages check box selected, any changes you make in the header or footer of any even-numbered page appear on all even-numbered pages; thus, if you change the header on page 6, your changes also appear on pages 2, 4, 8, and so on. Similarly, changing the header or footer on any odd-numbered page changes all the odd-numbered pages, with the possible exception of page 1, which remains unaltered if you've selected the Different First Page check box.

The actual locations of a header or footer on the page are determined by the margins.

→ For an explanation of how headers and margins work together, **see** "Adjusting Margins," **p. 218.**

TIP

> To remove a header, click the Header button on the Headers & Footer Tools Design tab and click Remove Header at the bottom of the menu.

NUMBERING PAGES

By far the most common use for a header or footer is to show the page number. Word gives you several options:

- Use one of the predefined headers or footers that include page numbers when you first insert a header or footer.

- Click the Page Number button on the Insert tab or on the Header & Footer Tools Design tab to show the available predefined page numbers (see Figure 9.22). By scrolling through the list of Page Number button options, you'll see the various page number formats available to you, whether you want to place the page numbers at the top or bottom of the page, in the margins, or at whatever position you clicked first to insert the number.

- To gain control over how your page number will look, click the Page Number button and select Format Page Numbers to display the Page Number Format dialog box. This option allows you to add chapter numbers as well, based on heading styles.

Figure 9.22
Word makes it easy to insert page numbers into your headers and footers.

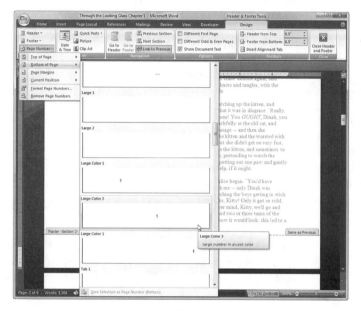

- Type any text or use fields to create a completely custom page numbering scheme. If you choose one of the predefined Page x of x headers or footers, Word actually adds a {Page} field in the header or footer; the Insert Number of Pages icon adds a {NumPages} field. By inserting your own fields, you can create and edit custom page number formats—to track sections, chapters, or other divisions, for example.

ADDING DATES AND DOCUMENT DETAILS

The Header & Footer Tools Design tab also includes a button that enables you to insert the current date or time. You can accomplish the same result manually by creating your own fields to show, say, the document's filename or the date and time it was last printed. (To insert a field, click Quick Parts on the Insert or Header & Footer Tools Design tab and then choose Field.)

One of the most important fields—called {StyleRef}—allows you to put text from the document into a header or footer. You can use {StyleRef} to add the title or number of the current chapter to a header, for example, or to produce "Able–Autry" page indexes in the header, as in a telephone book.

HOW SECTION BREAKS AFFECT HEADERS AND FOOTERS

Headers and footers are section-level settings; if you have more than one section in a document, each section can have its own set of headers and footers. Headers and footers are stored in the section break marks. If a document has just one section, the headers and footers are stored in the final paragraph mark in the document; that is an important detail if you find yourself trying to unravel inscrutable headers and footers in a multisection document.

→ To decipher the mysteries of sections, **see** "Formatting Documents by Section," **p. 262.**

To format a section so that it uses the same headers and footers as the preceding section, you don't need to do anything more than insert a section break. Word automatically formats the headers and footers in the new section by using the Link to Previous button on the Header & Footer Tools Design tab.

If you want to break the Link to Previous link between the current section and the preceding section, click the Link to Previous button. When you break the Link to Previous link, you effectively break the document into two separate pieces. With this setting in effect, any changes to a header or footer in the first section affect pages only in that section. Likewise, changes to a header or footer in the second section affect only that section.

CAUTION

When you break and restore the Same as Previous link, or add, delete, move, or copy section breaks on the fly, the effect on existing headers and footers can be extremely unpredictable. It's always best to lay out your document and establish section breaks first, before you begin modifying text, headers, or footers.

Sometimes you need to restart the page numbers in a section. Perhaps you want to start the numbering at 1 again, as many books do following the introduction. Maybe you need to advance a handful of numbers to accommodate sheets you plan to print and interleave manually. To restart page numbers, follow these steps:

1. Switch to Draft view and click the Breaks button on the Page Layout tab. Choose Next Page on the drop-down list that appears to create a section break where you want the new page-numbering sequence to begin.

→ For an explanation of how each type of section works, **see** "Types of Sections," **p. 263.**

2. The insertion point should be positioned immediately after the Next Page section break. Click the Page Number button in the Header & Footer group on the Insert tab, and select Format Page Numbers.

3. In the Page Number Format dialog box, choose the number format that you want to appear in your header or footer.

4. In the Page Numbering section, select the Start At option and specify the section's starting page number. Click OK to close the dialog box to save your changes.

KEEPING LONG DOCUMENTS UNDER CONTROL

Effectively using Word to handle long documents—100 pages or more in length, or more than a megabyte or two in size—requires forethought and planning. If you *can* break a very long document into several smaller ones, you probably should. If you need some of Word's advanced features, such as a table of contents or page numbering, use some of the strategies we outline in this section.

ONE FILE OR MANY?

As your documents get larger, you have several choices:

- Continue to work with a single large file—An effective backup strategy is always valuable, but it's especially important when working with large files, where a single misstep can wipe out huge amounts of work.

- Cut the large file down to size—If your file contains multiple graphics, save the pictures in separate files and create links instead of embedding them.

→ To learn more about when embedding is better than linking, **see** "Embedding Versus Linking," **p. 150.**

- Use fields to include the contents of one file in another—Click the Ribbon's Insert tab and click Object. Click the Create from File tab and use the Browse button to select the name of a second file, click Link to File, and click OK. Word adds a {LINK} field to your document that automatically reads in the contents of the second file. This technique is especially useful for boilerplate text. For example, if you have a legal disclaimer that you are required to use in all documents you create on behalf of your homeowners association or nonprofit group, you can use this technique to ensure that this block of text always contains the latest version.

- Break the large document down into smaller files—The best way to perform this task is manually, employing techniques described in this chapter to keep everything together.

CAUTION

> All the approaches that involve linking pictures or using multiple documents depend on hard-coded filenames that include the full pathname. That can pose problems when moving a complex document from one machine to another. Replicating folder structures is almost a prerequisite for moving large documents from one machine to another.

Using Bookmarks

One of the largest problems facing those who maintain large documents is maintaining the integrity of references. For example, the title of Chapter 3 in your dissertation might be "The Birth of the Industrial Revolution." When you refer to Chapter 3 in other parts of the document, you might be tempted to type that text. But if you later change the title of Chapter 3, you'll have to search through your document and change every reference. For a long, complex document that undergoes many changes, keeping cross-references synchronized manually is a nightmare. The simplest way to keep text in sync is to use bookmarks with the {REF} field.

→ To create and work with bookmarks, **see** "Bookmarks," **p. 174.**

In this example, you could select the text "The Birth of the Industrial Revolution" and give the bookmark the name Chapter3Title. Then, anyplace you wanted to refer to the title of Chapter 3, you could click the Insert tab, choose Field from the Quick Parts list, choose Ref from the Field Names list, and add Chapter3Title from the list of available bookmarks to tell Word you want to insert the field {Ref Chapter3Title}.

→ For details on the {Ref} field, **see** "Using Fields Intelligently," **p. 332.**

That way, anytime the title changes—that is, anytime the contents of the Chapter3Title bookmark changes—all the {Ref} field references to the title will change, too, automatically.

You can maintain page number references in the same way, using the {PAGEREF} field. For example, the field {PAGEREF Chapter3Title} gives the page number of the bookmark Chapter3Title. So, a line such as "See {Ref Chapter3Title} on page {PageRef Chapter3Title}" will yield a valid reference, no matter what the bookmark Chapter3Title might contain or where it might be located, as long as the bookmark, {Ref} field, and {PageRef} field are all in the same document.

If you break a long document into multiple files, the bookmark options aren't quite as good. You can reference bookmarks in other documents by using the {IncludeText} field, but the references retrieve only the contents of the bookmarks; you can't get at the page number. For example, this field

```
{INCLUDETEXT "D:\\MyName\Documents\\Annual Report.docx" Chapter3Title}
```

retrieves the contents of the Chapter3Title bookmark in the indicated file and places it in the current document.

Inserting Cross-References

Word includes extensive support for *cross-referencing*—everything from "See Figure x-y above" kinds of references to "as defined in paragraph IV.B.7.a." Each type of cross-reference has its own requirements and quirks, so a little bit of planning goes a long way.

These references persist even if the document changes. That's what makes them so powerful and useful. Say you have a reference in your homeowners association agreement that says "as defined in paragraph IV.B.7.a." Then, after reviewing the draft, the board of directors adds an additional numbered paragraph, and that new paragraph has to go ahead of the current paragraph IV.A. All you need to do is insert the paragraph, press Ctrl+A to select the document, and press F9 to update fields. Automatically, the old paragraph IV.B.7.a becomes paragraph IV.C.7.a, and the old reference to it turns into "as defined in paragraph IV.C.7.a."

Many kinds of cross-references interact with captions. Say you have a picture in a document with a caption that says "Figure 17," and a reference to it such as "See Figure 17." You decide to add a figure immediately before figure number 17. If you used cross-references and captions correctly, the next time you update fields, the old figure number 17 will get the caption "Figure 18," and the old reference will be updated so that it says "See Figure 18." The connections persist even in the face of complex restructuring in the document. So, if you moved this new Figure 18 to the beginning of the document, for example, it would get the caption "Figure 1" and the reference would change to "See Figure 1." Captions and references throughout the document would change to match the new numbering scheme—and all you have to do is update fields.

To see Word's Cross-reference dialog box (see Figure 9.23), click the Insert tab's Cross-reference button.

Figure 9.23
Word's cross-reference capabilities key off precisely defined styles, bookmarks, and sequences located inside the document.

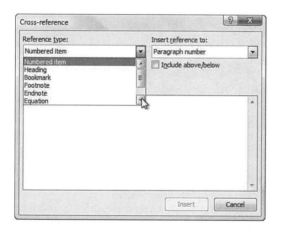

Choices in the Reference Type drop-down list link to specific elements in the document. Reference Type: Numbered Item refers exclusively to paragraphs formatted with Word-applied numbering. (If you number your paragraphs manually, they won't appear here.) There's a fair amount of native intelligence in the cross-reference. For example, if you refer to paragraph IV.B.7.a from inside paragraph IV.B.6.c, you can tell Word to use the reference "7.a." Reference Type: Heading choices include only those paragraphs marked with the built-in Word heading styles: Heading 1, Heading 2, Heading 3, and so on.

Say you're preparing an itinerary for an upcoming group excursion. You've created a document in which the name of each destination appears in a paragraph formatted as Heading 2. You've written a description of the glorious beaches and resorts of Thailand that appears on page 17. Throughout your document, you would like to insert references that follow the format "For more information about *destination*, see page *nn*" (where *nn* is the actual page number on which that content appears). No problem. Follow these steps to add cross-references:

1. Click once where you want the reference to appear. Type your introductory text—in this example, **For more information about** (don't forget the trailing space)—and then click the Cross-reference button on the Ribbon's Insert tab. Choose Heading from the Reference Type drop-down list and Heading Text from the Insert Reference To list (see Figure 9.24).

Figure 9.24
It's easy to insert a reference to a heading, if you use the built-in tools.

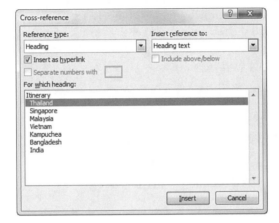

2. In the For Which Heading box, choose the item for which you want to create a cross-reference—Thailand, in this example. Click Insert, and then Close.

3. Type **, see page** (with a comma, a leading space, and a trailing space) and then click the Cross-reference button again.

4. In the Reference Type drop-down list, choose Heading; in the Insert Reference To drop-down list, choose Page Number. In the For Which Heading list box, choose the same item you selected in step 2. Click Insert, and then Close.

The cross-reference in your document now reads, "For more information about Thailand, see page 17."

Reference Type: Bookmark includes any bookmarks you've defined in the document. By using the Insert, Cross-reference feature, you can put the bookmarked text or the bookmark's page number in the document, and it updates should the contents of the bookmark—or its location—change.

Reference Type: Footnote, Endnote is tied to footnotes and endnotes in the document. If you want to create an additional reference to an existing footnote, click the Cross-reference, and in the Reference Type drop-down list, choose Footnote.

→ To work with footnotes in general, **see** "Inserting Footnotes," **p. 187.**

Reference Type: Figure refers exclusively to paragraphs in the document that contain the {SEQ Figure} field. When you choose Insert, Cross-reference, and select Figure from the Reference Type drop-down list, Word scans the document for {SEQ Figure} fields and puts the paragraphs containing those fields in the For Which Heading list. See the next section ("Wrapping Text Around Graphics") for several examples of how to use figure cross-references. In particular, when you use Word's built-in Insert, Caption feature (you'll find this button on the References tab), it can generate an {SEQ Figure} field that's picked up by the Cross-reference dialog box.

Reference Type: Equation, Table similarly refers exclusively to {SEQ Equation} and {SEQ Table} fields.

9

CAUTION

> Captions that appear in the drawing layer aren't detected by Word's Insert Cross-reference feature. If you place a caption in a text box, or if your figures "float" over text with an attached caption, you must first move the caption into the document itself before your cross-references will work properly.

Cross-references work only on references inside the current document, or inside a master document.

CREATING INDEXES

Creating an index for your document is a straightforward two-step process:

1. Mark index entries in the document by selecting text to be indexed and clicking Mark Entry on the References tab. Adjust the index text in the Mark Index Entry dialog box, click Mark, and then click Close. Keep selecting text and clicking the Mark Entry button through the entire document, marking index entries where they occur.

2. When you're done marking the entries, generate the index by placing the insertion point where you want the index to appear, clicking the Insert Index button on the References tab to display the Index dialog box (see Figure 9.25), and clicking OK.

Like so many other advanced Word features, indexing is driven by field codes. In this case, the {XE} field code, generated previously in step 1, marks the location of index entries. The index itself, generated in step 2, is really just an {Index} field. To understand how indexes are built, you first must understand Word fields.

→ To learn more about fields, **see** "Using Fields Intelligently," **p. 332.**

Unfortunately, Word's indexing feature is not as intuitive as one might hope. Although it appears that indexes built with the standard Mark Index Entry dialog box can run only two entries deep, there is a workaround. Even though the Mark Entry dialog box has only two boxes for entry levels (Main Entry and Subentry), you can enter up to seven levels in either of these boxes by separating your entries with colons—for example, you could enter Flowers:Roses:Red. With that caution in mind, you can use a few tricks to make indexing faster and easier.

Figure 9.25
The Index tab allows you to both mark index entries and generate the index itself.

To create an index entry for a particular word in a document, double-click the word to select it, and then press Alt+Shift+X. If you want to use the word as the main (highest level) entry, press the Enter key. If you want to use something different for the main entry, press Ctrl+X to cut the selected word, type in your main entry, press Tab, and then press Ctrl+V to make the selected word a subentry. For example, if you see the word *Rose* in a document and want to create an entry for Flowers:Rose, here's a quick way to do it:

1. Double-click Rose to select it.
2. Press Alt+Shift+X to bring up the Mark Index Entry dialog box.
3. Press Home to move the insertion point to the beginning of the Main Index Entry box.
4. Type the word **Flowers:** (note the colon).
5. Press Alt+M and then Enter (or click Mark and then click Close). Word inserts an {XE "Flowers:Rose"} field into your document.

Although the key sequence is a bit convoluted, you'll quickly master it with practice.

{XE} fields are hidden. If you insert them via the Mark Index Entry dialog box, Word turns on the Show All feature so that you not only can see the fields, but you also get paragraph marks, dots for spaces, and so on. To turn off Show All, click the Show/Hide ¶ button on the Home tab.

If you're willing to trust the computer to construct your index, consider using an Index AutoMark concordance file. You set up this file as a two-column table, with entries you want to index in the first column (say, Roses), and the index you want to use in the second column (say, Flowers:Rose). You apply an index concordance file to a document via the AutoMark button in the Index dialog box, as shown in Figure 9.24.

Now for the gotcha. When Word updates the {Index} field, you're given two options: Update the page numbers only (in which case new index entries are ignored), or update the entire index (in which case any entries or formatting you've manually entered into the index get wiped out). The lesson to learn is not to make any manual changes to an automatically generated index. Fortunately, you can pour Word documents into high-end desktop publishing programs, which include all the tools necessary to generate decent professional-grade indexes.

If you're frustrated because your edits to the compiled index are lost whenever you update the index, see "Updating Index Entries" in the "Troubleshooting" section at the end of this chapter.

If you've spell-checked your index but still find spelling errors, see "Spell-Checking an Index" in the "Troubleshooting" section at the end of this chapter.

CREATING A TABLE OF CONTENTS

If our explanation of the difficulties of creating an index scared you off, take heart. The Table of Contents (TOC) generator in Word works quite well:

1. Make sure that you've applied styles to all the heading paragraphs you want to appear in the TOC. You can use Word's default Heading *n* styles, or you can create your own.

2. If you want to add more entries—say, free-form text entries that will appear in the TOC even if they aren't in paragraphs with appropriate styles—click the Insert tab and choose Field from the Quick Parts list, and then use the Field dialog box to put {TC} fields in your document.

3. Put the insertion point where you want the TOC to appear, click the References tab, and then click the Table of Contents button. Choose one of the predesigned table of contents formats, or select the Insert Table of Contents option and use the Table of Contents dialog box (see Figure 9.26) to design your own format.

Figure 9.26
You can build a table of contents based on any set of styles.

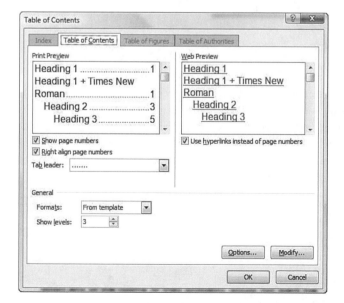

4. If you're using styles other than the standard Heading *n* set, click Options and map each style to a TOC heading level. When you're done, click OK, and Word builds the TOC.

A table of contents (even a large one) is just a Word field—a {TOC} field, to be precise. To see the field, choose Tools, Options, click the View tab, and select the Field Codes check box.

TIP

> If you regularly work with field codes, memorize the ViewFieldCodes keyboard shortcut, Alt+F9. Or add the View Field Codes command to the Quick Access toolbar, using the techniques explained in "Customizing the Quick Access Toolbar," **p. 33.**

{TOC} behaves just like any other field, with one exception. When you update it, Word might ask you whether you want to update page numbers only or update the entire table. Although the default response is Update Page Numbers Only, you should accept this choice only if you are absolutely certain that none of the TOC entries have been deleted or changed, and no new entries have been added. Word generally keeps good track of your headings, and if it detects that a heading has been added or deleted, it won't even ask whether you want to Update Page Numbers Only.

Word can also produce TOC-like tables for figures, or any of the special {SEQ} fields. Click Insert Table of Figures from the References tab to get started. The entire Table of Figures engine is based on the labels in {SEQ} fields, in a manner similar to the cross-reference hooks described earlier in this chapter. In fact, a Table of Figures is nothing more than a {TOC} field with switches added to indicate which {SEQ} field should be indexed.

A table of contents, index, or other kind of reference table can be generated only for entries inside the current document.

WRAPPING TEXT AROUND GRAPHICS

Word makes it easy to wrap text around a graphic. Insert the graphic into your document (for example, by clicking the Picture button on the Ribbon's Insert tab), right-click the graphic, and choose Format Picture (or Format AutoShape if you inserted a shape). Click the Layout tab and choose how you want the text to wrap. (You'll find additional options when you click the Advanced button.) You can also use the Ribbon to modify the picture. Click Position from the Picture Tools (or Drawing Tools) Format tab to adjust the graphic's layout as shown in Figure 9.27.

If you want to wrap text tightly around an odd-shaped graphic, start with the Tight option when you adjust the text-wrapping layout.

Figure 9.27
Word does a decent job of wrapping text tightly around a picture, but you can do better.

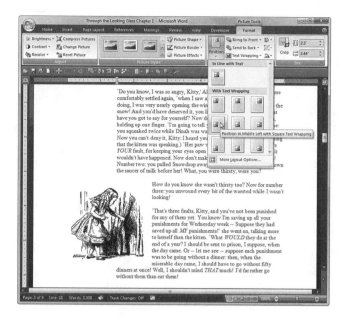

TROUBLESHOOTING

CHECK FOR STRAY DELIMITERS

When I use Word's Convert Text to Table feature, occasionally it does the conversion incorrectly and the table is off by a cell or two.

Immediately after converting text to a table, look at the last row of the table and verify that it matches the last row of the selected data. If you're off by one or two cells (typically, one or two cells will be dangling at the bottom of the table), you probably have a stray delimiter character somewhere in the selected text. Scan the table to see whether you can locate it. Click the Undo button or press Ctrl+Z, fix the data, and try the conversion again.

DISAPPEARING CELL CONTENTS AND ROW MARKERS

I selected a row and dragged it to a new location, but instead of moving the whole row, as expected, Word replaced the contents of the existing cells in the destination row.

Although you thought you selected the entire row, you actually selected all the cells in the rows. To select an entire row, place the mouse pointer in the margin to the left of the row until the pointer turns to an arrow that points up and to the right, and then click. To make sure you select the entire row, configure Word so that you can see the end-of-row markers—which are visible only if you show paragraph marks (open the Word Options dialog box and select the Paragraph Marks check box on the Display tab). If you want to click and drag a table row to a new location, select the entire row—including the end-of-row marker—and then click and drag, as you would with any other Word component.

PROPERLY SETTING THE ROW HEIGHT FOR WORD TABLES

When I insert a lot of text (or graphics) in a table cell, I can't see all of it. The bottom is chopped off.

Chances are good you did something to make Word set the row height using the Exactly option. To restore the default setting—in which rows grow and shrink to fit the contents—open the Table Properties dialog box (click Properties on the Table Tools Layout tab), click the Row tab, and clear the Specify Height box.

CAN'T SEE FINAL COLUMN(S) IN A TABLE

When I add a column to a table (or adjust the width of a column), I can no longer see the last column.

The table is too wide to fit in the defined margins, and if you try to view the document in Print Layout view, you won't see the portion that falls off the page. Click the status bar's Draft View button and use the horizontal scrollbar to move to the right. You can also take advantage of Word's Zoom Slider (in the lower-right corner of the Word window, next to the View buttons), which enables you to zoom further out from your document and see more columns on one screen.

ALLOW PAGE BREAKS IN A TABLE CELL

In one of my documents, Word insists on waiting until the end of a cell before it triggers a page break. As a result, my tables flip-flop all over the page. Some pages have only one row showing, and it looks horrible.

You must have changed Word's default setting, which allows page breaks to occur at logical points. You might want all the data in a row to stay together, especially when the cells all contain fairly modest amounts of text. But in your case, this setting is getting in the way. To get Word to relax a bit, click anywhere in the table, click Select on the Table Tools Layout tab, click Select Table, and then click Properties. In the Table Properties dialog box, click the Row tab and select the Allow Row to Break Across Pages box.

UPDATING INDEX ENTRIES

After inserting an index, I edited the entries by directly typing over them within the index itself. But when I updated the index, all those edits were lost.

Always make changes to the index entries in the body of the document—that is, change the contents of the {XE} fields themselves. That way, when you update the index (or table of contents), the new index reflects your changes. The process doesn't work in reverse, as you discovered the hard way. If you type over an item in the index itself, you eliminate the reference to matching index fields within the document.

SPELL-CHECKING AN INDEX

Even though I spell-checked my index, there are still spelling errors in the index.

Index entries—that is, {XE} fields—normally are hidden. Word doesn't check hidden text when you run a spell-check. To spell-check your index entries, first display hidden characters (click the Hidden Text check box on the Display tab of the Word Options dialog box). Next, run the spell-check. Misspelled words in {XE} fields appear with a red squiggly underline.

EXTRA CREDIT: NESTED TABLES FOR SUPERIOR LAYOUT

Nested tables provide great flexibility in setting page layout. In Figure 9.28, we've modified the standard Word Professional Résumé with a table across from the Community Service Activities entry, making it easy to enter multiple items. The gridlines are visible only when editing; they won't appear on the final, printed document.

A nested 2-row, 2-column table

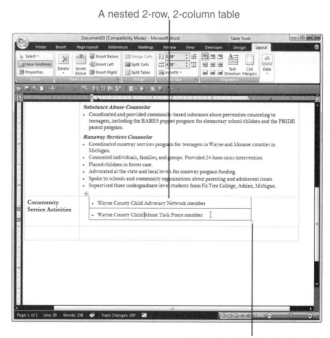

The nested table's drag handle

Figure 9.28

CHAPTER **10**

MASTERING STYLES, TEMPLATES, AND THEMES

In this chapter

MOVING BEYOND MANUAL FORMATTING

Most Word users work too hard. They start with a set of boring default formats for every new document and then manually adjust those formats for every document. Manual formatting works, but at a high price in time and inconsistency. Doing the same work over and over again is unnecessary, especially when you learn how to save formats and reuse them.

To unlock this power, it's important that you understand how Word handles formatting. The secret resides in a handful of key concepts that are not immediately obvious. When you understand how much time and effort you can save with a minimal investment of work, you'll never go back to manual formatting again.

USING STYLES, TEMPLATES, AND THEMES TO MANAGE FORMATS

10

Word allows you to apply multiple formatting settings at one time by using *styles*. You gather character and paragraph format settings together and give them a name. Then, when you want to use all the formatting at once, you apply the style. For example, you could tell Word that you want the NewsHeadline style to consist of centered paragraphs, with Arial 18-point, italic blue characters. Then, every time you apply the style NewsHeadline to a paragraph, Word formats it as centered, Arial 18-point, italic blue. Word contains many predesigned styles and makes a selection of the most popular available in a Quick Style Gallery on the Home tab. In addition, you can adjust and create new styles from the floating Apply Styles task pane (by pressing Ctrl+Shift+S) and the Styles window (by pressing Ctrl+Shift+Alt+S).

Think of styles as an easy and fast way to organize the format settings you see on the Home tab. Although you can scroll through the Styles pane with the Show Preview option selected to locate a style that appears to be an Arial 18-point, italic blue entry, it's generally simpler to create your own style that matches your needs and name it something you'll recall, such as NewsHeadline. Styles also tie parts of your document together to ensure the formatting is consistent: If you decide to change formatting for all your product names to Arial 18-point, bold blue, you can change the style and watch your changes ripple through the document to every piece of text that uses that style. Looking for the old formatting and replacing it by hand is a tedious, cumbersome, error-prone task.

Styles are stored in *templates*. When you create a new document, you must base it on a template. You can use the default Normal document template (Normal.dotm), or one of the cookie-cutter prototypes installed with Word, or you can create and save your own custom template and use it as the basis for new documents. Word dutifully copies all the text that resides in the template into the new document—even if the template contains only a single paragraph mark—before it presents the document to you for editing. It also loads all the styles, macros, AutoText entries, and other saved elements from that template.

Behind every document sits at least one associated template. Unless you've taken steps to change it, the main template attached to a document is the same one you used to create the document in the first place. To see the name of the template associated with the current document, open the Word Options dialog box and select the Add-Ins tab. Click the Manage drop-down list, select Templates, and then click Go. The Templates and Add-Ins dialog box appears. Your current document's template is visible in the list (see Figure 10.1).

Figure 10.1
Word tells you the name of the template attached to the current document, as well as the names of any global templates (other than Normal.dotm) that were loaded when Word started.

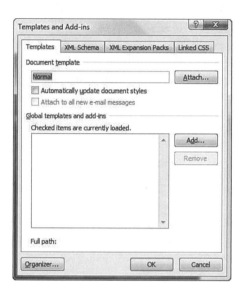

NOTE

A *global template* is a template that's available to all open documents. Specifying a global template gives you access to styles, special-purpose macros, and AutoText entries throughout Word, without having to change the template for a given document. Because the Normal document template (Normal.dotm) is always loaded and made global each time Word starts, it's always available to every open document. You'll hear Normal.dotm called "the" global template, but it isn't the only one: You can have multiple global templates available if you want.

Now say that you apply the style NewsHeadline to a paragraph. Word first checks the document to see whether it includes a style by that name. If the style isn't there, Word looks in the document's template. If the style isn't in the template (or if no custom template is attached to the document), Word looks in the default template, called Normal, which is always available.

The Normal document template includes dozens of predefined styles, including the ubiquitous Heading 1, Heading 2, and Heading 3 styles, the Normal paragraph style, and a plethora of styles used for formatting table of contents entries, footnotes, bulleted and numbered lists, index entries, tables, and more. To make matters even more confusing, sometimes Word takes it upon itself to automatically apply a style to text you've typed. We discuss these automated escapades elsewhere in this chapter, but here are the major culprits:

- Word might apply a Heading style to your short sentences or sentence fragments. To enable or disable this behavior, open the Word Options dialog box, click the Proofing tab, click the AutoCorrect Options button, and on the AutoFormat as You Type tab, select or clear the Built-in Heading Styles box.

- Word might change the properties of styles when you position the insertion point in manually formatted text and then use the Style drop-down box. To stop this behavior, open the AutoCorrect Options dialog box and, on the AutoFormat as You Type tab, clear the Define Styles Based on Your Formatting box.

- If you manually apply formatting to one paragraph, Word might apply that change to your entire document. To prevent this from happening, you need to modify your Normal paragraph style so that it stops automatically updating every time you make a change.

 See "Word Keeps Changing My Entire Document" in the "Troubleshooting" section at the end of this chapter for instructions on how to make the change.

- Word automatically applies the Hyperlink character style (blue, underlined, and clickable) to text you type that appears to be a web address—for instance, www. quepublishing.com. To disable this setting, open the AutoCorrect Options dialog box, and on the AutoFormat as You Type tab, clear the Internet and Network Paths with Hyperlinks box.

In addition to named styles and templates, Word also supports *themes*, which are prepackaged sets of background colors, graphical bullets, and other design elements. Beginning with Word 2007, themes have changed completely from their predecessors. As noted elsewhere, themes are used consistently throughout the Office family to apply professionally designed collections of colors, fonts, and other formatting. Using themes, you can ensure that Word documents, PowerPoint presentations, and Excel workbooks have an identical look and feel. In previous versions, themes weren't so much integrated with Word as they were tacked on. They were suitable only for online viewing (in web pages and email messages, for example), and you could not create or change a theme using Word. Themes in Word 2007 are much easier to use and now you can design your own. The Page Layout tab includes a Themes group where you can apply, modify, and create themes.

Styles, templates, and themes are a powerful way to manage formatting. You'll have best results if you follow these basic guidelines:

- Change global preferences and styles—those you want to use in all documents, all the time—in the Normal document template, Normal.dotm.

- If you plan to reuse custom styles, store them in their own templates, not in individual documents or in the Normal document template.

- Be extra careful when creating custom styles in individual documents. In particular, avoid customizing any styles that use the same names as Word's built-in styles—the Normal and Heading 1 paragraph styles, for instance. It's too easy to accidentally replace your customized styles with the default style, wiping out your careful formatting work. If you must create a custom, one-off style, use a descriptive name that is unique to that document.

- Develop a consistent naming strategy for custom styles, especially those that use inheritance to pick up attributes from other styles.

- Back up every custom document template you create. At a minimum, you should have safe copies of your customized Normal.dotm file and any special-purpose templates you've created. Be sure to update these backup copies whenever you make changes.

→ To learn where Word and other Office programs store your customized files, **see** "Where Should You Keep Your Files?," **p. 56.**

FORMATTING DOCUMENTS WITH STYLES

A style is nothing more or less than shorthand for formatting: Put a bunch of formatting specifications together, give it a name, and you have a style. If you find yourself applying the same formatting to text throughout a document, styles can help ensure a consistent and professional appearance that's easily modified. Use styles to control the formatting of the following:

- Heading paragraphs—Whether the headings are chapter titles, section names, class numbers, departments, or committee and subcommittee names, it doesn't matter. If your documents include multiple paragraphs that are used for a specific purpose and are always formatted the same way, create a style for that type of paragraph.

- Repeating body text—If your document includes multiple blocks of text that require formatting different from normal body text, use a style to format it. For example, if your school district name always appears in Arial 12 point, bold, create a style for it. If your homeowners association documents consistently apply bold formatting to **Acme Homeowners Association**, use a style. Similarly, you can use a style to format italicized telephone numbers in a phone directory, to highlight student names in an article for the yearbook or the school paper, or to call attention to negative numbers in a report on fund-raising activities.

Defining and using styles consistently provides two great benefits. First, it ensures that all similar items in a document are formatted consistently—say, all the student names will appear in Garamond 12-point, bold. Second, if you need to make a change to the appearance of a style—say, you decide that all the student names should appear in 14-point instead of 12-point—changing the style (which requires just a few clicks) changes the appearance of everything formatted with that style all the way through the document.

PARAGRAPH VERSUS CHARACTER STYLES

Paragraph styles control all the characteristics of a paragraph. Settings available as part of a paragraph style include centering, spacing, widows (that is, whether a single line that begins a paragraph should be allowed to appear alone at the bottom of a page), orphans (whether a single line that ends a paragraph should be allowed to appear alone at the top of a page), and

10

other settings in the Paragraph dialog box (to open, click the launcher visible in the lower-right corner of the Paragraph group on the Home tab.) Paragraph styles also dictate bullets and numbering, borders and shading, tab stops, and the language Word uses for proofing tasks, such as checking spelling and grammar.

> **TIP**
>
> One well-hidden check box in the settings for a paragraph style allows you to tell Word to skip over all text formatted with that style when using the spelling checker. This option is a time-saver in documents that contain lots of proper names and other words that normally trip up the spelling checker.

In addition, paragraph styles define *character formatting* for all characters within the paragraph. When you establish a paragraph style, you must also specify the default character format for the paragraph. Unless you specifically override the default character format with direct formatting or a character style, all text within a paragraph will appear in the paragraph's default character format.

Say you have a paragraph style called NewsHeadline that specifies centered paragraphs, with Arial 18-point, italic blue characters. If you apply the NewsHeadline style to a paragraph, all the characters turn Arial 18-point, italic blue. But if you then select the last word in the paragraph and make it red, the formatting you applied manually—the red—takes precedence over the default character formatting specified in the NewsHeadline style.

Character styles behave similarly, except they carry only character formatting. That includes the font, font size and style, color, super/subscript, underscore, and other attributes available in the Home tab's Font group. Character styles can also define borders and shading and proofing settings.

Say you have a character style called PhoneNumber that specifies the Courier New font in 10-point. If you apply the PhoneNumber style to some text, that text loses its previous formatting (which probably originated as the default character formatting of the underlying paragraph style) and picks up the formatting defined by the character style—Courier New 10-point.

> **TIP**
>
> How can you tell the difference between a character style and a paragraph style? In the Styles window (Ctrl+Shift+Alt+S), look for the little symbol to the right of the style's name. A paragraph mark (¶) indicates a paragraph style, and an underlined lowercase letter a points out a character style.

When it comes to character formatting, Word's hierarchy is strict. First comes the paragraph style, which you can modify by applying formatting directly (for example, you can format a Normal paragraph to be right-aligned without changing its style). Then comes the character style, which takes precedence over the paragraph style settings. Finally, you can apply formatting directly to a character. That formatting takes precedence over both the character and the paragraph styles.

You can see the hierarchy at work by bringing up the Reveal Formatting task pane as shown in Figure 10.2 (press Shift+F1), and then selecting the Distinguish Style Source option at the bottom of the pane. The full hierarchy of formatting applied by both the paragraph and character styles and by directly applied formatting is shown.

Figure 10.2
Using the Distinguish Style Source option on the Reveal Formatting task pane gives you all the formatting details about the selected text, along with an explanation of where the formatting originated.

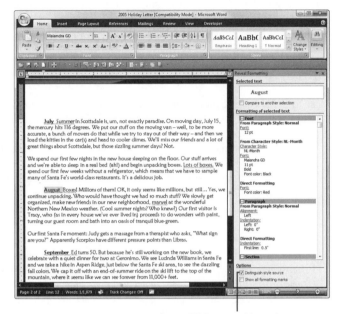

Click to see hierarchy

Every paragraph has exactly one paragraph style. Every character has exactly one character style. If no character style is defined for a particular piece of text, the style is Default Paragraph Font, in which case Word applies the character formatting defined in the paragraph style. If you don't explicitly define a paragraph style when you begin a new paragraph, Word uses the default paragraph style for the document. Typically, this is the Normal style, but you can set any paragraph style as the default. To do so, format at least one paragraph in the current document using the style you want to set as your new default. Then click the Office button, click Word Options, click the Advanced tab, and select that style from the Default Paragraph Style drop-down list.

LIST AND TABLE STYLES

Word has two built-in sets of styles that you might find useful when applying complex formatting:

- List styles enables you to directly specify the level of a list item by choosing the style and applying it to your selected paragraph. For example, if you want a bulleted list item that appears at the third indent level, you can apply the List Bullet 3 style, and Word takes care of the details. List styles are available for standard indented lists with no bullets or numbering (called, simply, List), standard lists with extra space inserted below the list item (List Continue), bulleted lists (List Bullet), and numbered lists (List Number).

- Table styles include all the formatting options available in Word's Table AutoFormat dialog box. Dozens of styles exist, all with names beginning with the word *Table*.

TIP

To see all available built-in styles, display the Styles window, click Options, and select All Styles from the Select Styles to Show list. This setting also controls which styles are available from the drop-down Style Name list on the Apply Styles task pane. (Remember, the Apply Styles task pane appears when you press Ctrl+Shift+S and enables you to select and modify styles.) The Styles window, which can be docked as a task pane or float, is available when you press Ctrl+Shift+Alt+S or when you click the Apply Styles task pane's Styles button. There you can control styles that display, modify, and create new styles.

CAUTION

When you use the Table Styles Gallery, your changes apply to all the rows in a table, whether or not they've been selected. Trying to edit table styles manually can trip up even experienced users. Make sure that you review formatting changes made by the Table styles before moving on to other parts of a document. To remove all table formatting (a drastic step), select the entire table and apply the Table Grid format button, which is the first option in the first row of the Tables Styles Gallery.

APPLYING STYLES MANUALLY

Assuming that you don't want to use a Quick Style (see "Working with the Fastest and Easiest Styles: Quick Styles" later in this chapter on p. 300), you can apply a paragraph style by following these steps:

1. Click once inside the paragraph whose style you want to change, or select one or more paragraphs.

2. Press Ctrl+Shift+S to display the Apply Styles task pane. Choose a style from the task pane's Style Name list and Word changes the paragraph's style to mimic the style you select.

To apply a character style, follow these steps:

1. Select the characters whose style you want to change.

2. Choose the character style from the Apply Styles task pane.

If you select text and apply a paragraph style, Word looks at what you've selected before applying the style. If you have chosen all the text in a paragraph (with or without the paragraph mark), Word applies the paragraph style, just as you would expect. If one or more paragraph marks are in the selection, all the selected paragraphs have the chosen paragraph style applied.

You can assign styles to a selection manually, if you prefer, by clicking in the Style Name box on the Apply Styles task pane. Word AutoCompletes this entry for you (if the AutoComplete Style Names option is set), so you might need to enter only a few characters. When you see the correct style name, press the Enter key to apply it to the selection.

CAUTION

> If you type a style name that does not exist, the Apply Styles task pane's Reapply button changes to a New button. If you click New, Word saves the paragraph's (or character's) formatting under a new style name.

For touch typists, Word includes the keyboard shortcuts shown in Table 10.1 that enable you to assign common styles to paragraphs.

TABLE 10.1   DEFAULT KEYBOARD COMBINATIONS FOR STYLES

Style	Shortcut Key
Normal	Ctrl+Shift+N
List Bullet	Ctrl+Shift+L
Heading 1	Ctrl+Alt+1
Heading 2	Ctrl+Alt+2
Heading 3	Ctrl+Alt+3

You don't have to assign keyboard shortcuts in Word through the tedious Word Options dialog box. Here's a much faster way: Open the Apply Styles task pane, select a style, and click the Modify button. Click Format, Shortcut Key. The insertion point is already positioned in the Press New Shortcut Key box; all you have to do is hold down the key combination you want to assign to the style. Click Assign to save the new shortcut key.

TIP

> You can quickly add any style to your Ribbon's Quick Style Gallery by right-clicking any style name in the floating Styles window and selecting Add to Quick Style Gallery.

USING THE APPLY STYLES TASK PANE

The Apply Styles task pane is much more than a static list of available styles. It represents both a window on your document's formatting and a central place from which to apply, modify, and manage styles in your documents and templates. From the Apply Styles task pane, you can display the Styles window for further style-management features.

When you select a style in the task pane's Style Name list box and click Modify, you'll see the source of the character formatting for the current selection (if no text is selected, this box shows the formatting at the insertion point). Beneath a sample text box that displays the current selection, you might see a style description that looks something like this:

```
Font: (Default) Janson Text, 9.5 pt, Indent: Left: 0.33", Line Spacing: Exactly
12.5 pt, Space After: 6 pt, Widow/Orphan Control, Keep Lines Together,
Following Style: NL
```

If no direct formatting is applied to the selection, this box shows the style that is the source of the character formatting.

10

> **NOTE**
>
> The Reveal Formatting task pane is more detailed in its description of the current selection's formatting. Press Shift+F1 to display the Reveal Formatting task pane. Both the Reveal Formatting task pane and the Apply Styles task pane can be open at the same time. You can also click the Styles button in the Apply Styles task pane to open the Styles window. By dragging the floating Styles window to the left or right edge of your Word document, you can anchor the window to act like a task pane.

With the Styles window open, you can select all the text in a document that shares a particular type of formatting—whether it's direct or applied by a style. To select all text that matches the formatting of the current selection, right-click any style and choose Select All *nn* Instance(s). (Conveniently, Word tells you exactly how many times that particular bit of formatting is used in the current document.) If the style you want to select is not used in the current document, Word grays out this option for that style.

This technique is the preferred way to change styles applied to a particular type of text. If you've used direct formatting to make all headlines appears as Arial 20-point, bold blue, you might decide you want to apply the NewsHeadline style instead. No problem. Select all text with the direct formatting (as shown in Figure 10.3), and then click the NewsHeadline style to instantly reformat every instance.

As you'll see in the following section, you can also use this task pane to create a new style, modify an existing style, or delete a custom style that's no longer needed. You cannot, however, delete any of the built-in styles in the Normal document template, such as Normal, Heading 1, and Body Text.

Figure 10.3
Use the Styles window to select all instances of a particular type of manual formatting so you can apply a named style instead.

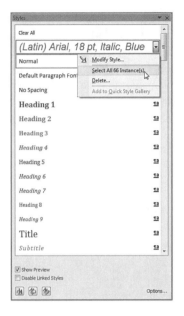

TIP

If you don't see any manual formatting in the Styles list, click Options, and then from the Select Formatting to Show as Styles list, and select the types of formatting you know you want to see. You can also use the Select Styles to Show list here to limit the potentially overwhelming list of visible styles.

SAVING FORMATS AS NAMED STYLES

Although Word ships with more than 100 defined styles—they're built into the Normal template—as well as 20 themes and a matching collection of Quick Styles, you'll quickly find that they don't always apply to your documents and your specific needs. If your needs are simple, you can set up a paragraph style by formatting a paragraph the way you want and telling Word the name of the style to be based on that formatting. To do so, follow these steps:

1. Format an entire paragraph to have all the attributes you want—both character and paragraph formatting apply.

2. Click once inside the paragraph. If you've used multiple fonts or font styles in the paragraph, the new paragraph style will use the font formatting at the point where you click.

3. Press Ctrl+Shift+S to display the Apply Styles task pane and type a new name for your style. The Reapply button changes to New.

4. For more control over your new style's creation, click the Styles button at the bottom of the Apply Styles task pane to display the Styles window and click the New Style button at the bottom of that window. The Create New Style from Formatting dialog box opens (see Figure 10.4). In the Style Type box, choose Paragraph to create a paragraph style, or Character for a character style. You can also choose a table or list style, although it would be inappropriate in this example.

Figure 10.4
Creating a new style can be tricky. Make sure that you understand what all the options mean before using them.

5. In the Style Based On box, choose the style on which you want your new style to be based. Any changes you make to the style listed here will also apply to your new style. If you want your style to stand on its own, choose (No Style) from the top of the list.

TIP

> Managed properly, an inheritance scheme is a wonderfully effective way to help you keep a complex design in perfect order with styles. You can create hierarchies of styles based on a small number of base styles, and then change the overall design of your publication by adjusting just the base font. For example, you might define a Catalog Base style that contains only the basic font formatting—Arial 12-point, with single-line spacing. You can then define styles for catalog headings, catalog product descriptions, and catalog captions, varying the size, color, and weight of the font. Using this organization, you can change the font used throughout your publication—from Arial to Arial Narrow, say—just by modifying the Catalog Base style. If you decide to create a highly structured style scheme like this one, be sure to document it thoroughly!

6. The Style for Following Paragraph box tells Word which style it should use for the next paragraph when you press Enter.

10

TIP

> By defining a chain of styles in your document, you can automate a lot of routine formatting. After using the Illustration style, for example, you might want the next paragraph to be formatted with the Caption style, and the paragraph after that to be formatted with the Body Text style. By adjusting the Style for Following Paragraph settings for each style, you can format a paragraph as Illustration and then apply the following styles effortlessly, just by pressing Enter.

CAUTION

> The Style for Following Paragraph setting kicks in only if the insertion point is immediately in front of a paragraph mark when you press Enter. If you leave even a single space between the insertion point and the paragraph mark when you press Enter, Word gives you a new paragraph with the same formatting and style as the current paragraph.

7. Select the Automatically Update box if you want every change you make to a paragraph formatted with this particular style to be automatically applied to every paragraph in the document with that style. Clear this check box if you want the style's formatting to remain fixed as you define it.

CAUTION

> In almost all circumstances, Automatically Update is a disaster waiting to happen. You should use this option only on those rare occasions when you are absolutely certain that you never want to apply any direct formatting to text formatted with a particular style without changing all other paragraphs that use the same style.

8. Click the Format button to apply any additional formatting options. For a paragraph style, you can adjust virtually any type of formatting; for a character style, you can adjust only font, border, and language settings. You can also assign a shortcut key from this menu.

9. Click OK. If no style with that name exists, a new one is created for you and is placed in the document. Click the style name in the Styles window to apply the newly created style to the current paragraph or any other existing paragraphs.

If you want to modify a style's definition, click the drop-down button next to the style's name in the Apply Styles task pane, and then choose Modify. You'll have all the foregoing formatting options at your disposal. For simple changes, such as changing the font, font size, or spacing of a paragraph style, you can modify a style by example: Format some text using the style you want to modify and make your changes; then click the style name and the Modify button in the Apply Styles task pane.

If your custom styles disappear when you open a document, see "Automatically Updating Styles" in the "Troubleshooting" section at the end of this chapter.

WORKING WITH THE FASTEST AND EASIEST STYLES: QUICK STYLES

The default Normal document template includes hundreds of predefined styles, but you'll probably work with only a handful of them at any given time. That's the philosophy behind the Quick Style Gallery, which sits in the Styles group on the Home tab and allows you to, well, quickly apply a style.

As in all Office 2007 galleries, the Ribbon holds the contents of only the first row and is limited to the number of options that will fit in the width of the current window. To scroll through the gallery row by row, use the up and down arrows to the right of the Quick Style buttons; to see the full gallery, click the More button, which opens the gallery display shown in Figure 10.5.

Figure 10.5
Each style in the Quick Style Gallery is listed by name, with a sample that shows what its formatting will look like.

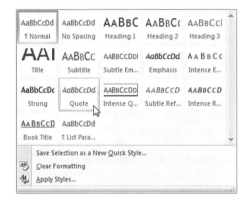

There's nothing special about the styles in the Quick Style Gallery. The buttons here represent a simpler, less cluttered view of the Styles collection. Here's what you need to know about Quick Styles:

- When you point to a button in the Quick Style Gallery, Word's Live Preview feature temporarily applies that style to the current selection. If no text is selected, paragraph styles are applied to the current paragraph, and character styles are applied to the word at the current insertion point. To remove the preview, move the mouse pointer. To apply the style, click the Quick Style button.

- You can right-click any Quick Style button and use the shortcut menu to modify that style, rename it, or select all instances of that style in the current document. These options work exactly as if you had used the Apply Styles task pane or the Styles window.

- To add a style to the Quick Style Gallery, open the Styles window (Ctrl+Alt+Shift+S), right-click its entry in the list of available styles, and choose Add to Quick Style Gallery.

- To remove a style from the Quick Style Gallery, right-click its entry in the Quick Styles Gallery (or in the Styles window) and choose Remove from Quick Style Gallery.

As with the full Styles window, you can make a selection in a document and save the manually applied formatting from that selection as a Quick Style. To take advantage of this feature, first make a selection, right-click, and then choose Save Selection as a New Quick Style from the Styles menu at the bottom of the shortcut menu.

As noted elsewhere in this chapter, themes and styles work together. When you change the theme, you also change the styles associated with the current document. As part of each, you can choose from a selection of style sets (see Figure 10.6), which apply different sizes, styles, and paragraph formatting to the fonts used in that theme. The benefit of style sets is that they use the built-in style names and are designed to work together. When you choose a new style set, the changes apply to body text, headings, lists, and so on. To choose a different style set, click the Change Styles button in the Styles group on the Home tab and choose an option from the Style Set menu.

10

Figure 10.6
Style sets allow you to change the overall look of your document using standard style names; fonts and other settings are drawn from the current theme.

Click the Set as Default button after you select a style set that you want to use as the default style set for all subsequent documents you create.

CUSTOMIZING THE NORMAL DOCUMENT TEMPLATE

When you create a new, blank document—by clicking the Office button and selecting New—Word creates a new document based on the Normal document template, Normal.dotm. The Normal template is always available when Word is running.

As noted at the beginning of this chapter, Word looks for styles starting with the document, moving up to the document's template and, if the style name can't be found there, looking inside the Normal template.

NOTE

> If the document is based on the Normal template, there's no intermediate step—the search progresses directly from the document to Normal.

Actually, the Normal document template is no more "normal" than any other template. A more accurate name would be the *default* document template, the one Word uses when you create a new blank document without specifying a template. Normal.dotm is frequently called the global template because it's always available. Although other templates can be global in the sense that they're loaded when Word starts (refer to the Templates and Add-Ins dialog box shown in Figure 10.1), no other template is tied directly to the New Blank Document icon on the Office menu or the Blank Document choice in the New Document dialog box.

In Windows Vista, Word starts new blank documents with the Calibri 11-point font, with no paragraph indenting, 1.15 lines of spacing within paragraphs, and an additional 10 points of spacing after each paragraph. If you open Normal.dotm, you'll see why: It contains a single paragraph mark formatted in the Normal style, and the Normal style is defined as Calibri 11-point, line and paragraph spacing defined explicitly. When Word creates a new document based on Normal.dotm, it copies everything in the template into the new document—just as it does when creating a document from any template—and you end up with a new document with a single paragraph mark, with Normal style formatting.

TIP

> If you want to change the default font for new blank documents, you don't need to mess with Normal.dotm. Instead, use this hidden shortcut: Create a new blank document, and then format all the font characteristics you want your new template-based documents to have (say, Garamond 11-point) from the Font dialog box. (Open the Font dialog box by clicking the arrow to the right of the Font group name on the Ribbon's Home tab.) After you've formatted the initial character in the document the way you want it, click the Default button. From that point on, any new blank document you create will use the Garamond 11-point font for its Normal style.

If you want to change more than the default font on new blank documents, the simplest way is this:

1. Create a new blank document.

2. Press Ctrl+Shift+S to display the Apply Styles pane and select the Normal style. Click the Modify button.

3. Make whatever changes you want to make to Word's defaults for new blank documents. Click the Format button to adjust more advanced formatting options. You can change the font, paragraph formatting, tabs, borders and shading, proofing language, frame, bullets, and numbering, and even add a shortcut key to the style so that you can access it later with one keystroke from any document based on the current template.

4. After making all the changes you want, select the New Documents Based on This Template check box, and click OK. All the modifications you made to the Normal style are reflected in this document's template—which just happens to be the Normal document template, Normal.dotm.

 If you've made a colossal mess of your Normal document template and want to start over, see "Restoring the Default Normal Template" in the "Troubleshooting" section at the end of this chapter.

USING WORD'S BUILT-IN TEMPLATES

Word ships with scores of templates, and hundreds more are available to download from Microsoft's Office Online website. You can visit the Office Online website and search for these templates manually, but you'll get much better results using the categorized view of those same templates, which is available via the New Document dialog box.

→ For more details on how to find and use templates from the Office website, **see** "Extending Your Office Expertise with Third-Party Templates," **p. 688.**

Although the generic "click here and type" templates can come in handy in a pinch, you'll want to customize any generic template that you expect to use more than a few times. It's well worth your while to replace the "click here" instructions with text appropriate to your particular situation—your name, phone number, and so on. Here's how to customize Word's Professional fax template and make it your own. You can use the same basic techniques with any of Word's canned templates.

1. Click the Office button (you can also press Alt+F) and select New.

2. In the list of templates in the left column, click Faxes. Figure 10.7 shows the start of all the fax-based templates you'll see. Select Fax Cover Sheet (Professional Design) and click Download to create a new document based on that template. Note that you'll be required to complete Microsoft Office Genuine Advantage validation before the download begins.

10

Figure 10.7
Numerous professional templates come with Office so that you can create eye-catching documents, preformatted for you.

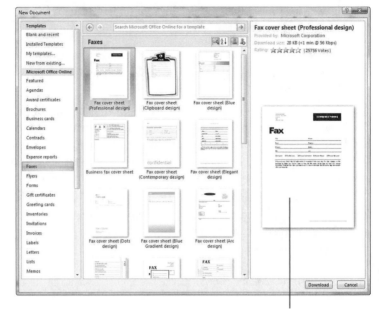

Preview of template

3. Fill out the appropriate portions of the fax template—the information that won't change from fax to fax—such as the company name, address and phone number, and possibly the From: entry.

4. Click the Office button (Alt+F) and select Save. In the Save as Type box, choose Document Template. Give the template a descriptive name and click the Save button.

5. The next time you want to use the template, open the Templates dialog box and select the template name you assigned from the offerings on the General tab.

CHANGING DOCUMENT FORMATS GLOBALLY

When Word creates a new document, it copies the entire contents of the template to the new document—text, pictures, headers and footers, and so on—and then establishes a link between the document and template (so, for example, styles in the template become available in the document). With one possible exception, nothing from the template gets copied into the document after a document is created. For example, if you change the Normal template so that its default font is Garamond 11-point, all new blank documents will have Garamond 11-point—but all old documents based on the Normal template will stay just as they are.

TIP

> There's one huge exception to this rule: If you open the Tools and Add-Ins dialog box from the Word Options Add-Ins tab (select Templates from the Manage list and click Go), and then click the Automatically Update Document Styles check box, Word updates a document style if one exists in the template with the same name. This option is good news if you always, without exception, want template styles to control the look of a document, as you might in a corporate environment, where maintaining a standard design is essential. But if you sometimes create styles within a document, avoid this option.

So, unless the Automatically Update box is checked, you can make all the changes you want to a template, and the documents already associated with that template won't change a bit. Changes to the template affect only new documents based on the template.

How do you make global paragraph and character formatting changes to a document—that is, make global changes to the appearance of a document—without going into each style, each paragraph, and making the changes manually? Word gives you three options:

- Allow Word to make changes for you, either piece by piece (in the AutoFormat feature) or wholesale (by using the Quick Style Gallery). Neither of these options is likely to improve the appearance of the document.

→ To learn how you can put Word's AutoFormatting features to work for you, **see** "Automatic Formatting," **p. 213.**

- Change the template applied to the document and then force Word to update all the styles in the document so that they conform to the styles in the new template. You might want to do this if, for example, you're updating an old document with a new template that handles all the styles you commonly use.
- Apply a theme.

To attach a new template to a document and update the document's styles, follow these steps:

1. If the document has any styles defined inside it (that is, at the document level), save a copy of the document. This process can completely overwrite styles in the document, and you can't bring them back.
2. Open the Word Options dialog box and select the Add-ins tab. Click the Manage drop-down list, select Templates, and then click Go. The Templates and Add-ins dialog box appears. Click the Attach button, navigate to the template you want to attach to the document, and click Open.
3. Select the Automatically Update Document Styles check box. Click OK.
4. Close the document (saving it if prompted) and then reopen it. With the Automatically Update Document Styles check box selected, the act of opening the document flushes out any styles with identical names in the document—overwriting the document's formatting with the new template's formatting.

5. If you don't want to update the document with future style changes in the attached template, immediately go back into the Templates and Add-ins dialog box and clear the Automatically Update Document Styles check box.

MANAGING STYLES AND TEMPLATES

As you can see from the discussion in this chapter, styles and templates are inextricably related. Because many of the styles you use are stored in templates, managing styles boils down to managing the templates that contain them.

CREATING A NEW TEMPLATE FROM SCRATCH

To create a new template from an existing file, click the Office button (or press Alt+F) and click the New from Existing link in the left column. Select the file you want to use as the starting point for your new document. To start with an empty document based on the current Normal.dotm template that you might want to tweak into a different template, select the default, Blank Document, to start from scratch.

Before you make any changes, it might be helpful to store the document as a template now so that you don't overwrite the document you might have used as the basis for the new template. Click the Office button and select Save As. Select Word Macro-Enabled Template (.dotm) and type a name for your template. Click the Templates entry in the Favorite Links list to the left to ensure that the template file is stored with the rest of your templates.

A Word template is nearly identical to a Word document, except that it also contains AutoText entries. (The Normal template also contains formatted AutoCorrect entries.) That's the only difference. By default, Word templates are identified with the filename extension *.dotm. A more limiting template extension that does not support macros is .dotx, but your templates are more robust if you create templates that support macros. In addition, you can save document templates in the Word 97-2003 Template format, which uses the *.dot extension. Only files with the *.dotm, *.dotx, or *.dot extensions appear in the Templates dialog box.

WHERE DOES WORD STORE TEMPLATES?

When you save a new template in the Templates entry of your Save As dialog box's Favorites list, Word attempts to save it in your Templates folder—that's the location marked User Templates in the File Locations dialog box available when you open the Word Options dialog box, click Advanced, and click the File Locations button at the bottom of the dialog box. Figure 10.8 shows the File Locations dialog box.

Figure 10.8
The User Templates folder holds your template files.

Unless you specifically change the location on the File Locations tab, custom templates you create are stored in this standard location. As noted in Chapter 3, "Keeping Track of Your Files," you can open this folder directly by typing `%appdata%\Microsoft\Templates` in the Start menu's Search box, in the Run dialog box (Windows logo key+R), or in the Address bar of Windows Explorer. If you want to create a new tab for the Templates dialog box and place your template on that tab, do this: From the Save As dialog box, choose Document Template from the Save as Type list, and then click the Create Folder icon button on the toolbar. Give the new folder the name you want to appear on the new tab, and then choose Save. To add a template to a Letters and Faxes folder, for instance, you need to create a new folder called Letters and Faxes and save your template to that folder. To use files you create and save in this fashion, click the Office button, click New, and choose My Templates at the top of the categories list on the left.

→ To learn the tricks of the trade when it comes to creating new files throughout Office, **see** "Creating New Files," **p. 58.**

CUSTOMIZING WORD TEMPLATES

When you open a template (as opposed to creating a new document based on a template), you can modify it in precisely the same ways as you would change a document. You can add text, pictures, headers and footers, hyperlinks, macros—in short, everything that goes in a document (plus AutoText entries and styles).

Remember, any text you place in the document itself is considered boilerplate, and is copied into any new documents you create based on that template. If you attach a template to an existing document, however, saved items in that template are available, but the boilerplate text is ignored.

COPYING STYLES AND SETTINGS BETWEEN TEMPLATES

Word includes a handy tool called the *Organizer* that allows you to copy styles and macros between documents and templates. To make use of the Organizer, follow these steps:

1. Display the Styles window by pressing Ctrl+Shift+Alt+S or by clicking the Styles button on the Apply Styles task pane if the task pane is displayed. Click the Styles window's Manage Styles button to open the Manage Styles dialog box and click the Import/Export button to display (finally) the Organizer dialog box (see Figure 10.9).

Figure 10.9
The Organizer copies, deletes, and renames styles.

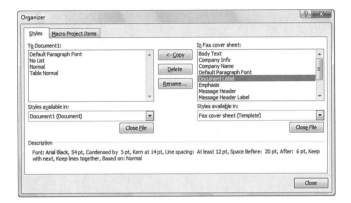

2. Make sure that the "from" and "to" files—documents or templates—are referenced in the Styles Available In boxes. If you have the wrong files, click Close File, and then Open File, and select the correct ones.

3. Select the individual items and click Copy, Delete, or Rename, as appropriate. Note that if you click to select an item in the box on the right, the direction arrow changes to indicate that your selection will be copied to the template or document on the left.

TROUBLESHOOTING

WORD KEEPS CHANGING MY ENTIRE DOCUMENT

Every time I select a paragraph and make even the tiniest change to it, Word changes my entire document. If I want to boldface a paragraph, my entire document turns bold. If I add a bullet character, every paragraph in the document gets a bullet. I figured out that I can press Ctrl+Z to undo the global change, but this is getting ridiculous. What's going on?

Word is only following orders. Somewhere along the line, you told Word that you wanted it to automatically update the Normal paragraph style every time you made a change to it. When you select a paragraph formatted with the Normal style, Word dutifully applies the change to every other paragraph using that style. Although this option is incredibly useful for custom styles you create, we can't think of a single good reason to have this option turned on for the Normal style. To turn it off, open the Apply Styles task pane, select the Normal style entry, and click Modify. Clear the Automatically Update check box and click OK.

REVEALING CHARACTER FORMATTING

As a former WordPerfect user, I'm accustomed to WordPerfect's reveal codes command, which displays formatting directives hidden in a document, much like HTML tags. When I search through online help, however, there's no mention of Word's reveal codes command.

The new document format in Word 2007 uses XML tags that are similar in function to the WordPerfect-style codes, but they're not intended to be edited directly. Instead, the Reveal Formatting task pane (Shift+F1) displays the names of styles and direct formatting applied to any character. If you saved in the new (*.docx) format using a plain text editor, you can see the XML codes. Just don't try to modify them directly. Word saves formatting instructions as XML tags, but these bear no resemblance to WordPerfect codes.

AUTOMATICALLY UPDATING STYLES

When I opened a document that contained a number of custom styles, the formatting changed unexpectedly, and clicking the Undo button didn't bring them back.

Styles in the document template are overwriting styles in the document itself. If you create a set of formats in named styles and save them in a document, you might find that your styles get wiped out by styles of the same name stored in the document template every time you open the document. To make sure that you don't encounter this problem with a specific document, click the Office button, select Word Options, and click the Add-ins tab. Open the Manage drop-down list box and select Templates. Click Go to display the Templates and Add-ins dialog box and clear the Automatically Update Document Styles box. To avoid the problem in the future, do not use standard style names (Normal, Heading 1, and so on) when creating custom styles within a document.

RESTORING THE DEFAULT NORMAL TEMPLATE

I've made a mess of the Normal template, and every new document I create inherits formatting I don't want.

You have three choices. The easy (but drastic) option is to exit Word, rename Normal.dotm to something else (for example, Old-normal.dotm), and start Word again. When Word can't find Normal.dotm, it creates a new Normal document template; in the process, however, you'll lose all your toolbar customizations, keyboard shortcuts, formatted AutoCorrect entries, and much more.

If you just want to reset the Normal paragraph style and other standard styles to their defaults, you can use the Apply Styles task pane's Modify dialog box to work through each style in the template until you have the Normal style back to where it started. Make sure that you click New Documents Based on This Template when you're done. It's more work, but you won't lose any of your customizing.

If that sounds like too much work, combine the two strategies. Create a fresh copy of Normal.dotm using all Word's defaults, and then use the Organizer to selectively move custom styles, toolbars, macros, and other items from the backed-up Old-Normal.dotm to your new file. Just don't overwrite the standard styles!

CHAPTER 11

LETTERS, MAIL MERGE, AND "SMART" DOCUMENTS

In this chapter

PUTTING WORD TO WORK

In previous chapters, we've discussed how you use Word to create documents, generally starting from a blank page. In this chapter, we explain how to get Word to do some of the work for you, starting with letters and advancing to documents that can literally fill in the blanks on your behalf.

One of the most common uses of Word is to create letters. This chapter starts by explaining how to create simple letters using templates and widgets called *content controls*, which allow you to pick dates from a drop-down calendar and choose snippets (or large blocks) of text using menus that you customize yourself. We also explain how to use Word to print matching envelopes and labels.

What if you want to create multiple letters, all starting from the same basic text, to a long list of recipients? For that task, use Word's mail merge feature (a topic known to cause migraine headaches even for experienced Word users). Mail merge isn't just for junk mail; we explain how to use its features to create directories, sheets of labels and postcards, and other unconventional outputs.

The secret weapon that makes mail merge possible is a complex Word feature called *fields*. After we explain how to create basic mail merge projects, we end with a detailed discussion of more advanced uses of fields.

11

CREATING AND EDITING LETTERS

Previous versions of Word included a feature called the *Letter Wizard*, which offered a seemingly simple way to build a simple letter by filling in a series of dialog boxes. The Letter Wizard was a fine idea, terribly executed, and we're delighted to report that it is completely gone in Word 2007. If you want to write a letter to a single recipient, you can use any of the following options:

- Write it from scratch. This is the most labor-intensive option, suitable only if you want absolute control over the look and feel of your letter. You have to apply formatting manually or build your own styles (do yourself a favor and save the formatted letter as a template so that you can reuse it later).

- Use a ready-made template from the Office Online collection. You'll find literally hundreds of options, neatly categorized and searchable, with canned text that you can adapt to your own purposes. These downloadable documents use a few simple techniques to help you fill in essential data fields. In this section, we explain how to work around the limitations and gotchas of these templates.

- Use one of the new Word 2007 letter templates to build letters from scratch. These templates use a Word 2007 feature called content controls to add date pickers, fill-in text boxes, and custom drop-down lists to help you assemble a great-looking letter with minimal effort. We show you how to customize one of these templates (or build your own from scratch).

USING CANNED LETTERS FROM OFFICE ONLINE

When you click the Office button, choose New, and then select Letters from the list of categories under the Microsoft Office Online heading, you open a list that includes literally hundreds of letters on a breathtaking range of topics, including some you never even thought of. Use the search box to filter the list using the term "complaint," for instance, and you'll end up with complaints about floral deliveries, teachers, lost luggage, hotels, overbooked flights, and even—we are not making this up—a complaint about a complaint resolution. Watch out for these gotchas:

- Although this collection might change over time, at this writing all the letter templates are saved in the Word 2003 format. If you want to use themes or content controls (described in the following section), save the downloaded file in Word 2007 format first.

- The letters are, in many cases, excruciatingly specific, with details that you're expected to delete and replace with your own writing. Very few of these templates can be used without modification. If you try, you'll almost certainly be embarrassed.

- All of these templates use a special type of element called a DoFieldClick Macro Button, which highlights a text element you're expected to click and replace. If you plan to use these templates regularly, open the Word Options dialog box, click the Advanced tab, and select Always from the Field Shading box under the Show Document Content category. This option makes it easy to spot the fill-in fields and lessens the likelihood you'll miss one.

USING THE WORD 2007 LETTER TEMPLATES

For some reason, Microsoft has buried its most valuable letter-writing tools. To unearth them, click the Office button, click New, and choose Installed Templates from the list of categories on the left. That opens the window shown in Figure 11.1, which includes templates for common types of documents using five of the themes installed with Office 2007. The ones we're interested in are the letter templates.

Each of the five installed letter templates is named after an Office theme. Don't be fooled by that naming scheme, however. You can mix and match any theme with any of the default letter templates—click the Page Layout tab and click the Themes button to see the full gallery of available themes.

No, the real distinction between the different letter templates is their design. Each one includes the same elements: date, sender's and recipient's addresses, and a salutation, followed by body text and a signature. The arrangement of those items on the page varies from template to template. The Urban Letter template, for example, uses tab stops to align the sender's address in a block in the top-right corner of the page. The Origin Letter (shown in Figure 11.2) achieves the same look using a table, and the Oriel Letter rotates the sender's address 90 degrees and puts it in a colorful vertical bar that runs along the right side of the page.

11

Figure 11.1
Word's collection of installed templates includes five classic business-style letters, each named after its assigned theme.

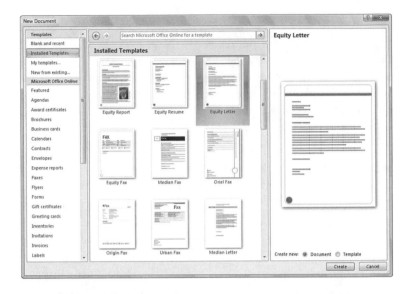

Figure 11.2
The Origin Letter template uses a table to lay out the address blocks at the top of the letter.

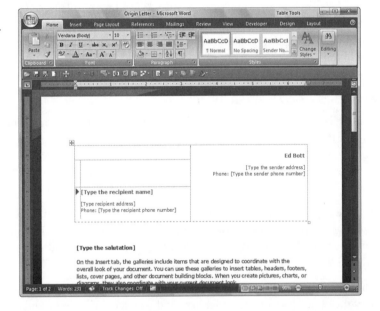

TIP

If you like the basic layout of a template, customize the template to meet your needs and save it with a name that's meaningful to you. Fill in the sender's address block with your name and address, add graphics, choose a preferred theme, and save your changes as a document template with a descriptive name, such as *Ed's Family Letter*.

You can roll your own letter template without basing it on one of the ready-made templates. If you choose this option, make sure that your letter contains the following blocks of data with matching styles:

- The date block is formatted using the Date Text style. (In templates created for older versions of Word, you might see the Date style used here.)

- The sender address might appear at the top of the letter, in the same font as the body, or it might reside in a text box designed to look like preprinted stationery.

- The recipient address normally appears just above the one-line salutation.

- You can adjust the indents and spacing for body text, which might extend for many paragraphs.

- The closing and signature lines are usually separated by a space large enough to accommodate your pen-and-ink signature on the printed page. If you're not planning to use a physical signature, adjust this space accordingly.

- Older templates might include a Cc:/Enclosure line, although none of the new Word 2007 designs includes this area. If you regularly send copies or attach additional documents, you'll want to add this line.

ADDING CONTENT CONTROLS

Even if you normally shun prefabricated document templates, it's worth looking at these letter templates—and, for that matter, at all the related templates in the Installed Templates section—to learn how they take advantage of content controls to guide you through the process of creating a letter (or a report or fax or résumé). These customizable controls are tiny input blocks that allow you to click and type in a box that automatically resizes to fit your text, or choose from a drop-down list you create, or pick a date from a drop-down calendar, as shown in Figure 11.3.

Before you can add a custom control to your own documents or templates or customize an existing control on an existing template, you have to make the Developer toolbar available. Click the Office button, click Word Options, and select the Show Developer Tab in the Ribbon check box on the Popular tab. With that accomplished, switch to the Developer tab, where you'll find the group of controls shown in Figure 11.4.

11

Figure 11.3
The Date Picker control allows you to embed a calendar any place where you would normally type a date. Each bracketed block of text in the right column is also a custom control.

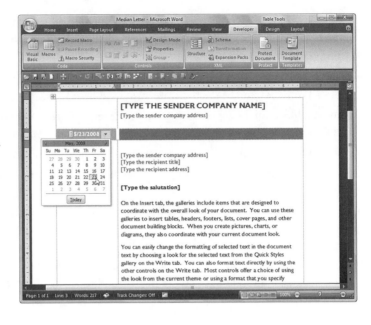

Figure 11.4
Position the insertion point where you want your content control to appear and then choose one of the controls shown here.

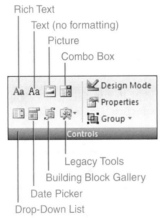

You can add a content control anywhere in your document, including in headers or footers. For example, if you mail out a weekly update on your newborn baby to email-challenged friends and relatives, you might include a picture content control in the template so that you can easily add the latest adorable photo of Junior. Use Text and Rich Text controls for address blocks and body text, Date Pickers for datelines, and the Building Block Gallery to enter saved AutoText entries.

→ For more details on how to manage AutoText and other Building Block Gallery entries, **see** "Entering Text and Graphics Automatically with AutoText and AutoCorrect," **p. 178.**

To customize the appearance and operation of a content control, select the control and click Properties, in the Controls group on the Developer ribbon. Figure 11.5, for example, shows the Properties dialog box for a Drop-Down List control.

Figure 11.5
By assigning properties to a content control, such as the entries in this drop-down list, you control its appearance and operation.

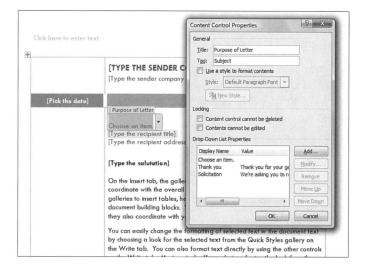

Even if the basic control does everything you need it to, you still might want to adjust some of the properties shown here. Whatever text you enter in the Title box will show up in the gray title bar above the content control, which you can use to prompt yourself for the correct data. You can also use the check boxes to set the format for dates inserted via the Date Picker control and to specify that you want a Text or Rich Text control to go away after you finish entering text.

TIP

For the most powerful automation technique, embed the Building Block Gallery content control in your letter where the body text would normally go. For example, you might have different opening paragraphs for each letter you send in response to inquiries to a nonprofit organization, depending on whether the correspondent is a new prospect, an existing member, or a longtime member whose annual fee is due. Save the paragraphs you use as boilerplate text for these different situations as items in the Quick Parts Gallery and assign a unique category to those items. Then, from the Properties dialog box for the Building Block Gallery content control, assign that same category under Document Building Block Properties. When you create a new letter using that template, you can pick saved blocks of boilerplate text and have Word do most of the work of assembling each letter for you.

CREATING ENVELOPES AND LABELS

Word includes an extensive set of features that allow you to address and print a single envelope, use mail merge to generate a large number of properly addressed envelopes, and format single and multiple labels using addresses from a variety of sources.

PRINTING ENVELOPES

To print an envelope, click the Mailings tab and then click Envelopes. The Envelopes and Labels dialog box appears. Fill in the Envelopes and Labels dialog box shown in Figure 11.6 and then click the Print button. Insert a blank envelope in your printer's manual feed, and you should get the results you expect.

Figure 11.6
Type or paste the delivery and return addresses for an envelope in this dialog box; Word positions each block in the correct place on the printed envelope.

The first time you print an envelope, make sure that you click the Options button to set up the proper envelope size, fonts, paper source, and other printing options.

TIP

Although Word usually does a good job of figuring out what kind of printer you're using—and thus how to orient an envelope so it prints properly—it rarely (if ever) correctly identifies an envelope paper tray. If you have an envelope tray for your printer, you'll have to click the Options button and specify that your printer includes this tray.

If you select an address before opening the Envelopes and Labels dialog box, Word grabs the selected text and inserts it in the Delivery Address box, sparing you the need to type or paste. In addition, Word is frequently smart enough to identify an address if it appears near the beginning of the document, as is common for business and other correspondence. If your document contains multiple addresses, just clicking anywhere inside one causes Word to grab that address and use it for the delivery address.

When you click the Add to Document button in the Envelopes and Labels dialog box, Word creates a new section at the beginning of the document and stores the envelope in that section, numbered as Page 0. When you subsequently print the letter, both the letter itself and the envelope will print (unless you manually specify that you want to print only Page 1 and later). That can be helpful if you aren't ready to print the letter, but want to set up the envelope ahead of time. It can also be helpful in creating a template with an envelope attached to the document. Finally, you can use this technique to place a logo, text box, or other graphic element on the envelope prior to printing.

→ For more details on how to merge addresses with envelopes, **see** "Merging Envelopes," **p. 331.**

TIP

> Want to automatically add graphics to an envelope? Word recognizes two AutoText entries, EnvelopeExtra1 and EnvelopeExtra2, which it uses exclusively for this purpose. Define one or both of these entries and they'll be added automatically to the return address portion of your envelopes when you click Print (or when you click Add to Document) on the Envelopes tab. You might add a logo and return address (in a text box) and define it as EnvelopeExtra1—you don't need to set up custom templates, and you can use the Envelopes dialog just as you normally would.

11

PRINTING LABELS

For mass mailings, labels are often easier to work with than envelopes. Typically, peel-and-stick labels are sold in sheets that match a standard paper size. You can also buy heavier stock that is perforated rather than adhesive-backed; this type of label is used for business cards, postcards, and so on. When you click the Labels button on the Mailings tab, the Envelopes and Labels dialog box opens with the Labels tab selected (see Figure 11.7), which allows you to create single labels or an entire sheet of labels. Click the Options button to tell Word the label position (row and column) you're using. (If you use standard labels, you can let Word set these options automatically. The dialog box includes settings for virtually all Avery labels, for example.) Then fill in the label number if you want to print only one label, and click Print.

Figure 11.7
Word's label format includes grids for all the major label (and business card) sizes.

You can also generate mailing labels for an entire list of recipients, via a mail merge.

→ For details on how to merge data and labels, **see** "Merging Labels," **p. 331.**

CUSTOMIZING LABELS

The major shortcoming in Word's bag of labeling tricks is its incapability to let you customize what prints on labels. If you're running standard Avery 8810 labels, with three labels per row and 10 rows per sheet, there's no room on the label to print anything interesting. But if you have larger labels (or business cards), you don't have to limit yourself to a plain-vanilla name and address.

For example, some predefined settings use six labels per page. More than enough room is available on labels that big to include your return address and a picture or logo.

TIP

If you have an odd-sized label, Word makes it easy to add it to the list of available labels, with extensive tools to help you get the layout just right. On the Labels tab of the Envelopes and Labels dialog box, choose Options. Then on the Label Options dialog box, choose New Label. Use a ruler that can handle fine measurements, and you should have no trouble filling in the details.

If you want to print larger, fancier labels, your best choice is to create a template that includes all the design elements—logo, return address, and so on—except the addressee's name and address. If you have such a template handy, you can create a new document based on the template, copy the addressee's details into it, and print. If you want to get even fancier and print just one label at a time, you can create a collection of templates, each with the design elements for just one label. Give the template a descriptive name ("AV5164 lower-right label") and you can generate precisely the right document for the right location.

The easiest way to make a template for a specific type of label is to use the Envelopes and Labels dialog box. In Figure 11.7 (shown previously), leave the Address box blank, choose the Full Page of the Same Label option, and click the Options button. Pick the manufacturer and product number from the Label Information section and click OK to return to the Envelopes and Labels dialog box. Finally, click New Document. Word creates a grid of labels for you, completely blank and ready for your customizing. Add your return address logo and other custom details and then save the document as a document template.

TIP

> Because the labels are just a table, you can use all the table formatting tricks, including dividing the label into subcells to better place graphics and text.

→ To read more about how to create and modify templates, **see** "Customizing Word Templates," **p. 307.**

MERGING DATA TO CREATE CUSTOM REPORTS AND LETTERS

Most Word users think of *mail merge* as a synonym for "form letters" or "junk mail." Although it's true that Word can churn out form letters and bulk mailings until the cows come home, the term *mail merge* only hints at what you can do with this capability.

At its most basic, a mail-merge operation consists of two parts—a database and a document—and the "merge" just brings the two together. The database can contain just about anything—names and addresses are the most common contents, of course, but you can also stuff the database with product names, court case citations, serial numbers, website addresses, test scores, or anything else you can fit into a database record.

The document, too, can take just about any imaginable form—yes, the first thing you think of is likely to be a form letter, but you can also add fields from your database to an envelope, catalog, email or fax message, telephone book, web page, financial report, stock inventory, or time log. For that matter, the document could simply be a text file, enabling you to use a mail merge to create a new database from an old one.

Word doesn't have the extensive merging capabilities of a full-strength database manager (such as Microsoft Access, which is included in some of the more expensive Office 2007 packages). But it's the best tool to choose when you need to produce a document or series of documents based on data in a reasonably clean list.

Word's mail merge features come in handy in a variety of circumstances. When you're working with form letters going out to a mailing list, Word allows you to sort and filter the incoming data, removing records according to field-level criteria you establish (for example, you could specify "Only include people in my ZIP Code"). You can also force the merge process to pause at each record to enable you to type in custom information. Use this technique if you're producing a holiday newsletter, for example, and you want to add some unique content for each recipient. When you move beyond basic form letters, Word's mail merge capabilities let you

- Send similar, but customized, email messages or faxes to a large number of people
- Create a product catalog, parts list, or price sheet from a list (or database) of individual products
- Create an organization membership roster or telephone book from a list (or database) of members

TIP

> Most Office users tend to think of mail merge as producing one page (or form letter) per data record, but Word isn't so constrained. As long as you tell Word that you want to create a directory, it will place data records on a page until the page gets full, and then go on to the next page. Therefore, if you have a data file for your coin collection, home inventory, paid checks, office carpool, VIP donors, or best-selling books, you can use Word's mail merge to create a professional-looking, well-formatted report. Just call it a directory.

Word contains extensive support for running mail merges, embodied in the Mail Merge Wizard (which looks just like a task pane). To get to it, click the Mailings tab and then click the Start Mail Merge button to display a drop-down menu. Choose Step by Step Mail Merge Wizard. The wizard handles almost every merge problem you're likely to encounter (see Figure 11.8).

Figure 11.8
The Mail Merge Wizard—the first wizard Microsoft ever created—appears as a task pane.

Although the wizard has its share of idiosyncrasies, it makes perfect sense after you've learned how to use it.

> **TIP**
>
> The first few times you run a mail merge, keep a detailed log of the steps you take—especially problems you encounter with Word or your printer. Chances are good you'll hit similar problems when using mail-merge capabilities sometime in the future, and good notes can save you precious troubleshooting time.

Each of the major types of mail merge is a bit different, so we're going to deal with each one separately.

USING MAIL MERGE TO PERSONALIZE FORM LETTERS

By far the most common mail merge scenario involves a form letter, a database, and a printer. You have a database of names and addresses, most likely in an Excel table, but possibly in the form of a simple text file in tab- or comma-delimited format, and you have a form letter or at least an idea of what you want to write. That's all you need: In Word-speak, you have a data source and a main merge document. The rest is just juggling.

> **NOTE**
>
> As we noted in Chapter 1, Office Home and Student 2007 doesn't include Microsoft Outlook, which is included in every other Office edition. You'll notice the difference when you use Word's mail-merge and envelope/label features. When Outlook is installed, an Address Book button appears above the Sender and Delivery Address boxes in the Envelopes and Labels dialog box, allowing you to select a name from your Outlook Contacts folder and insert the associated address with a single click. That button is missing from a normal installation of Office Home and Student 2007. In the Word Mail Merge Wizard, choosing the E-Mail Messages option from the Start Mail Merge menu appears to work, but the final step—actually sending the email messages—fails silently with any email program other than Outlook. Likewise, the Select Recipients step includes a Select from Outlook Contacts option that produces only an error message if you try to use it.

The Mail Merge Wizard walks you through six steps, each of which is neatly labeled at the bottom of the Mail Merge task pane (we provide additional details and useful suggestions for each of these steps later in this chapter). The following six descriptions match up with each of the numbered steps in the Mail Merge task pane.

TIP

If you're comfortable with the art and science of mail merge, you can handle each step individually, using the buttons on the Mail Merge tab. Work from left to right to choose a document type (Start Mail Merge), define a data source (Select Recipients and Edit Recipient List), and insert merge fields using the buttons in the Write & Insert Fields group. Preview the results and then click the Finish & Merge button to complete the job.

1. After you start the wizard and the Mail Merge task pane appears, choose the type of document on which you're working. For this example, select Letters.

2. Pick an existing document, or create a new one, to use as the *merge document*—the boilerplate skeleton that will drive the merge.

TIP

If you choose one of the installed Word 2007 Merge Letter templates, most of the work of placing merge fields is done for you. These templates are similar to their Letter counterparts, described earlier in this chapter, and they can be customized in similar fashion.

3. Attach a data source—the list or database to be merged—to the form letter. The wizard lets you create a new list from scratch, draw from an Outlook Contacts folder, or use an existing list.

4. Use the Mail Merge Wizard to place merge fields in the form letter. They'll appear something like this: <<Address Block>>, or <<First Name>> <<Last Name>>.

NOTE

You can't just type the << and >> marks: Word has to insert them for you, via buttons in the Mail Merge Wizard.

5. Use the wizard to preview how the first few merged letters will appear. If you want to exclude certain records from the merge or sort them so that the letters print in a particular sequence (ZIP Code order, for example), use the Mail Merge Wizard's Edit Recipient List option to set them up.

6. On the Mail Merge Wizard's final pane, click the Edit Individual Letters option so that Word merges the form letters to a new file, and save the new merged file. Before you print the file, go through it and make sure that it doesn't contain any surprises. When you're satisfied that everything is correct, start printing.

> Long merge print jobs can pose all sorts of mechanical challenges, from toner cartridges running down, to buffer overflows, to massive paper jams. If the merged file contains more than a few hundred pages, consider printing a hundred or two at a time. Click the Office button (or press Alt+F), select Print, and enter a range in the Pages box.
>
> For important mailings, keep the merged file handy until the mailing has been delivered to the post office—or better yet, until you're certain that most addressees have received their copies.

The merged document consists of multiple sections—one section per input record. That can cause unexpected problems if you try to use an advanced technique to get particular pages to print.

→ If you get stuck working on multiple sections, **see** "Formatting Documents by Section," **p. 262.**

CREATING THE FORM LETTER

When creating a main merge document, all Word's tools are at your disposal. You can adjust formatting, insert pictures, create headers and footers, add tables and fields, and work with objects in the drawing layer. For example, you might choose to insert your company's logo in the letter or use a callout AutoShape to draw attention to a specific selling point. Starting with a template, as we've done in Figure 11.9, simplifies things greatly.

Figure 11.9
In the second step of the Mail Merge Wizard, you put together a main merge document—or use a ready-made template as we've done here.

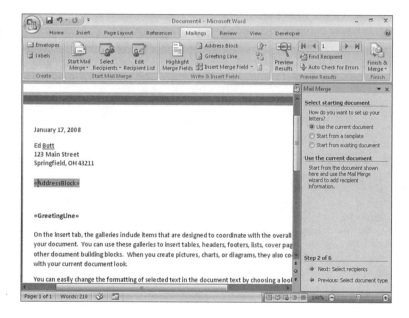

When you're satisfied with the content of your form letter, choose Next: Select Recipients at the bottom of the task pane and begin adding merge data.

SPECIFYING A SOURCE FOR NAMES AND ADDRESSES

After you have the static part of the form letter complete, you have to tell Word where to pick up the data that will be merged. In fact, at this point, Word just needs the data field names—last name, first name, address, and so on—but the Mail Merge Wizard takes advantage of the moment to have you select the data source.

TIP

> It's an often-overlooked point, but the biggest problem you're likely to encounter at this juncture is the lack of a specific data field or a poorly defined field. For example, if your form letter demands an "Amount Due" in each letter, you'd better have a data file handy that includes an "Amount Due" for each recipient.

The Mail Merge Wizard gives you three choices:

- Use an Existing List—If you have an existing data source, whether it's a table in a Word document, a list in an Excel workbook, or a database stored in any compatible format, use this option. If the first row of the Word table or Excel list includes field names (Last Name, First Name, and so on), you'll be able to merge immediately. Click Browse and retrieve the list.

- Select from Outlook Contacts—As noted earlier, this choice produces an error message in a default installation of Office Home and Student 2007. If you have separately installed Outlook 2003 or Outlook 2007, click Choose Contacts Folder and pick the Contacts list you want to use.

- Type a New List—Select this option and click Create to bring up a useful Data Form (see Figure 11.10) that allows you to create your own merge database and add names and addresses on the fly. If you want to modify the field names and their order, click the Customize button.

Figure 11.10
The New Address List dialog box allows you to build a merge data document on the fly. The address list is stored using an *.mdb extension.

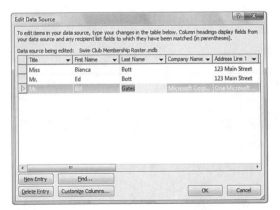

NOTE

> When you save or open a file you create using the Type a New List option, Office describes these file types as Microsoft Office Address Lists. In actuality, these files use the same format and file name extension as those created by Microsoft Access, the database manager found in high-end corporate versions of Office. If you copy one of these files to a computer running Access, you can open and edit the file there as well.

PLACING DATA FIELDS WITHIN YOUR DOCUMENT

Now that Word knows what data you're going to use, it can help you put merge data into your document. Data fields represent the link between your form letter and the data source. For example, if you have a data source field called *Last Name*, Word replaces every occurrence of the field <<Last Name>> in the form letter with the Last Name data in the current record of the data source.

The easiest way to insert data fields into your form letter is via step 4 of the Mail Merge Wizard. Place the insertion point wherever you want a data field to appear, click Insert Merge Field on the Mailings tab, and choose the field you need. Instead of entering every single element of the name and address, click the Address Block button to display the dialog box shown in Figure 11.11. This dialog box inserts an especially helpful merge field called Address Block, which does a graceful job of importing Outlook contacts, Access tables, and other data into Word. The various check boxes and options allow you to tweak the display so that it's appropriate for formal business letters or more informal personal mass missives.

Figure 11.11
This dialog box adds the Address Block field to your merge document and customizes its appearance.

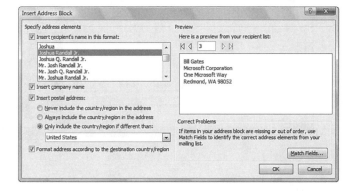

From the Mail Merge Wizard, click the Greeting Line link to add an opening to your letter. Click the More Items link to insert other fields throughout the letter. Remember that you have to provide the punctuation if it isn't included in the data source. A typical letter opening might look like this:

```
<<AddressBlock>>

Dear <<Title>> <<LastName>>:
```

TIP

> You can put the same data field in the form letter as often as you like. If you're preparing a letter to parents in a specific school district, for example, you might include the <<City>> field in the text of the letter as well as in the address block: "This meeting will discuss issues that are of particular interest to families of school age children who live in <<City>>."

PREVIEWING MAIL MERGE RESULTS

To see how the merge will progress, start by having Word show you what the result will be when you merge live data with your form letter. To do so, go to step 5 of the Mail Merge Wizard and click the Next Record button repeatedly to see how the records appear (see Figure 11.12).

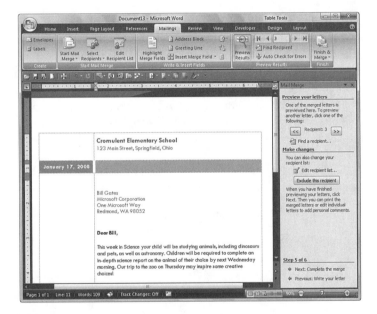

Figure 11.12
Word lets you preview your form letter with live data, stepping through each data source record.

Use this preview to check for gross errors:

- Look for incorrect fields—for example, those using <<First>> where you really wanted <<Last>>.

- Identify unreliable data source information; if half of your data source records don't have an entry in the <<Title>> field, for example, you need to find a way to work around the problem.

- If you see any parts of the merge that just don't look right—if some of the merged letters flop over to two pages, for example—click Edit Recipient List and try to tweak the data so it fits.

When all looks well, go to step 6 in the wizard, and click Edit Individual Letters. Before you print the resulting document, which has all the merged letters head-to-toe, examine it closely for any unexpected and unwelcome merge results.

> TIP
>
> In general, you should avoid merging directly to the printer. Creating a merge file first lets you easily recover from mechanical disasters—you can reprint letters 1378 to 1392, for example, if the printer runs out of toner or the person carrying the envelopes to the post office drops them in the mud.

CREATING DIRECTORIES

The only real difference between the way Word handles form letters and the way it handles merged directories (in pre–Word 2003 versions, they were called *catalogs*) lies in the way Word uses page breaks. In a form letter, Word inserts a page break (actually, a Next Page section break) after it finishes processing a record from the data source. In a directory, Word doesn't add page breaks; as a result, one record follows another in the finished document.

If you use Excel to create a membership list for a school club and save it as an Excel table, you can print a custom report in which several records appear on a page in a format like those used by a paper-based personal organizer. Here's how you do it:

1. Start a new document as described in the preceding sections, but in the first step of the Mail Merge Wizard, choose Directory. That tells Word you want to put more than one record on a page.

2. Add the fields by using step 4 of the Mail Merge Wizard, as before. A typical page might look like Figure 11.13.

Figure 11.13
Use this template in combination with the Directory option to print out a concise membership list.

«Student Name»
«AddressBlock»
Home: «Home_Phone»
Work: «Work_Phone»
Email: «Email_Address»

3. Adjust the document any way you see fit. In the case of Day-Timer–like reports, you might want to create multiple columns, change the page size, and set the paper source to print on special drilled sheets.

TIP

> To control page breaks in directory-style merges such as this one, use the paragraph formatting property Keep with Next. In this case, you might put an empty paragraph mark at the end of all the data lines. Then select the data lines (*not* the final paragraph mark), click the arrow to the right of the Home tab's Paragraph group to open the Paragraph dialog box, click the Line and Page Breaks tab, and select the Keep with Next check box to ensure that records don't break across pages.

4. Have Word merge to a new document. You'll probably want to print in duplex style— that is, using both sides of each sheet of paper. To do so, display the Print dialog box by clicking the Office button and choosing Print. Select the Automatic Duplex check box in the Print dialog box. If your printer supports manual duplexing, you'll need to check the Manual Duplex box and manually turn the paper over when you're ready to print the other side.

ADVANCED MAIL MERGE TECHNIQUES

Mail merge works by using Word fields specially designed for implementing a merge. To see those fields, open a main merge document and press Alt+F9; Figure 11.14 shows this view of the merge fields.

Figure 11.14
Main merge documents contain fields that dictate how the merge should happen.

```
{ MERGEFIELD "Spouse First Name" \m }
{ ADDRESSBLOCK \f "<< _TITLE0_ >><< _FIRST0_ >><< _LAST0_ >><< _SUFFIX0_ >>
<< _COMPANY_
>><< _STREET1_
>><< _STREET2_
>><< _CITY_ >><< , _STATE_ >><< _POSTAL_ >><<
_COUNTRY_ >>" \l1033 \c 2 \e "United States" \d }
Home: { MERGEFIELD "Home_Phone" }
Work: { MERGEFIELD "Work_Phone" }
Email: { MERGEFIELD "Email_Address" }
```

In many cases, you'll be able to get satisfactory results with a merge by using the Mail Merge toolbar to manipulate these fields. In some more advanced cases, however, you might find yourself operating on the fields directly.

→ To learn how to manipulate fields manually, **see** "Some Useful Custom Fields," **p. 340.**

MERGING ENVELOPES

Running a merge to generate envelopes that match one-for-one with a form letter run isn't difficult, as long as you go to great pains to ensure that the data source doesn't change between the time you run the form letters and the time you print the envelopes, and that the filters you specify are identical.

> **TIP**
>
> Beware of paper jams because one missing or one extra letter or envelope can throw off the entire sequence. If a jam should occur, mark that point in the run—with a paper clip or a sticky note, for example. After you've finished running both letters and envelopes, go back to the marked points and ensure that you have one—and only one—letter for each envelope.

To start an envelope run, start the Mail Merge Wizard and select Envelopes as the document type in the first step.

MERGING LABELS

Word's features for creating mailing labels work well enough for small labels—that is, labels specifically designed to comfortably accommodate a name and address. But if you're using preprinted labels, or if you have larger labels and want to print your return address or logo on them, or if you want to change the default font, you'll probably run into a few common problems (unless you know these tricks, of course). To run a mail merge and generate labels the usual way, do the following:

1. Start the Mail Merge Wizard by clicking Start Mail Merge on the Mailings tab. Choose Step by Step Mail Merge Wizard.

2. In the first step of the wizard, select Labels as the document type.

3. In the wizard's next step, click Label Options in the Change Document Layout section. Supply the details for your mailing labels in the Label Options dialog box. In most cases, you can select a manufacturer and product number; most common label products, including those from Avery, the 800-pound gorilla of the industry, are among the built-in formats listed here (see Figure 11.15).

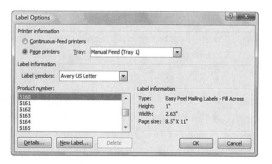

Figure 11.15

4. Follow Word's prompts to select a recipient list. Place the data merge fields in the first label position.

> **NOTE**
>
> Word automatically causes text in the label to "float up and down"—that is, to be centered vertically. If you want the printing on your labels always to appear at the same location, right-click and select Properties to open a Table Properties dialog box, click the Cell tab, and choose Top or Bottom.

5. When you're happy with the arrangement of merge fields on the first label, click the Update All Labels button in step 4 (Arrange Your Labels). This copies the layout to all labels on the template you've chosen.

6. When everything is ready for the merge, click the Ribbon's Finish and Merge button, select Print Documents, and the labels will print.

> **TIP**
>
> Because the label form is just a table, you can divide the existing cells to better position text, graphics, a return address, or anything else on the label.

USING FIELDS INTELLIGENTLY

As mentioned earlier in this chapter, the secret of mail merge, as with many of Word's other powerful features, is a peculiar document element called a *field*. Word fields are placeholders whose contents change dynamically; they are normally invisible and work in the background, displaying the correct data onscreen and in print, based on information within the current document, in other documents, or from external sources such as a database used for a mail merge. For example, if you put a {Date} field in your document, Word displays the current date in that location each time you open the document.

Word supports more than 70 types of fields. Use them when you want to accomplish tasks such as these:

- Show the current day in a document ({Date}, {Time}), or the time the document was last saved ({SaveDate}) or printed ({PrintDate}).
- Refer to the contents of bookmarked text. For example, you can place a bookmark on a chapter title and refer to that title throughout your document by using the {Ref} field. If the title changes, all the references change, too.

→ For details on all the nuances of using bookmarks, **see** "Using Bookmarks," **p. 276.**

- Insert information about a document into the document itself ({Info})—total number of pages, filename, author, file size, number of words, date when the document was last saved, and so on.

- Perform calculations, comparisons, and even elementary arithmetic. For example, the {Page} field produces the number of the current page, whereas a {{Page}+1} field results in the number of the next page.

There's even a {BarCode} field that converts a postal ZIP Code to a USPS bar code!

In addition to mail merges, fields also drive key built-in Word capabilities such as tables of contents, figures, tables, equations, and indexes. Although Word uses layers of wizards and dialog boxes to shield you from the field codes used to implement those features, sometimes the only way to tweak the feature—to limit a table of contents to a part of the document covered by a specific bookmark, for example—is by working with the field code itself.

NOTE

Fields are an enormous topic. In this chapter, we barely scratch the surface and only explain how to work with some of the more useful fields. If you need a detailed fields reference, see *Special Edition Using Microsoft Word 2007* (published by Que).

CAUTION

Many fields do not translate well into HTML-formatted files. If you must use a field on a web page, test it with all the commonly used browsers to ensure that it works properly.

INSERTING A FIELD INTO A DOCUMENT

By far, the easiest way to put a field into a document is to use one of the built-in Word features to do the dirty work for you. For example, if you click the Date and Time button on the Insert tab and then select the Update Automatically check box, Word inserts a {Date} field into your document, adding a formatting switch for the date format you choose (see Figure 11.16).

Figure 11.16
Selecting the Update Automatically check box here causes Word to insert a {Date} field instead of the date itself.

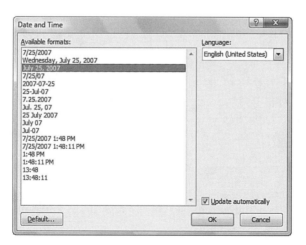

Similarly, putting a page number in a header or footer by using the Page Number button on the Header & Footer Tools Design tab inserts a {Page} field, as does inserting a table of contents or index, creating a caption or cross-reference, and inserting merge fields using the Mail Merge feature.

If you want to build a field from scratch, you can do it the hard way, by pressing Ctrl+F9 to create the field marks, and then manually typing the field name and any optional or required parameters. If you make even the tiniest mistake, of course, the field won't work as you expect. To be certain you get the syntax right, switch to the Insert tab, click Quick Parts, and choose Field. The Field dialog box (see Figure 11.17) offers context-sensitive help and immediate access to the most common field switches (the terms *properties* and *options* are somewhat arbitrary; don't get hung up on the terminology). If you want to work with the raw field code (or you just want to explore and preview the field's syntax), click the Field Codes button in the lower-left corner.

Figure 11.17
Word provides good support for fields via the Field dialog box.

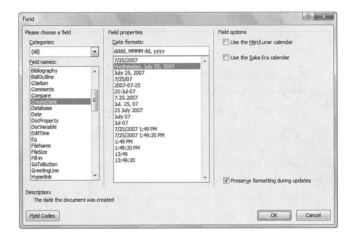

 If you consistently have trouble finding field codes you insert within a document, see "Hiding and Revealing Field Codes" in the "Troubleshooting" section at the end of this chapter.

SHOWING AND HIDING FIELD CODES

Word allows you to flip-flop between seeing the field codes themselves and field code results—for example, between seeing

`{Date \@ "d-MMM-yyyy"}`

and

`1-Jan-2008`

To show all field codes in the current document, press Alt+F9. To return to showing field code results, press Alt+F9 once again.

TIP

> If you're going to do much serious work with field codes, you might want to add the ViewFieldCodes command as a button on the Quick Access toolbar. Clicking the button toggles between showing field codes and showing their results. Click the arrow to the right of the Quick Access toolbar and select More Commands. From the Choose Commands From drop-down list, select All Commands, choose View Field Codes, click Add, and then click OK. Word sends the new button to your Quick Access toolbar.

FIELD CODE SYNTAX

Field codes can take many forms, but generally they look like this, with the field name and required or optional parameters enclosed in curly braces:

```
{Author \* mergeformat}
```

In this case, the field {Author} has one parameter, called a *formatting switch*. A formatting switch, if present, controls the way the field result is formatted inside the document. We discuss switches in the following section, "Formatting Field Results."

NOTE

> In this book, you'll always see field codes as they appear onscreen, surrounded by curly braces—something like this:
>
> ```
>     {Seq Figures \* mergeformat}
> ```
>
> Field codes are not case-sensitive, so you might see them in all capitals rather than uppercase and lowercase as we depict them here. Functionally, there's no difference. And of course, you can't type curly braces into a document and get a field code. There are only three ways to insert field marks (braces): Click the Quick Parts button on the Insert tab and choose Field; use one of the built-in Word functions that produces a field code; or press Ctrl+F9.

11

FORMATTING FIELD RESULTS

Unless you add a switch inside the field to change formatting, the field result takes on the formatting of the first nonblank character of the field.

For example, if you have a field that says {Author}, with the *A* in Times New Roman, 10-point italic, the result of the field takes on that formatting:

Douglas Adams

Word has three field switches that control the appearance and formatting of field code results.

GENERAL * FORMAT SWITCHES

The most common field switch is the general formatting switch:

```
\* mergeformat
```

This switch tells Word to ignore the formatting of the first character of the field, and instead to use whatever formatting you apply to the field itself.

For example, say you're typing along in 12-point Garamond, and you insert a {NumWords} field (which shows the number of words in the document), using the Field dialog box. If you click the Preserve Formatting During Updates check box, Word inserts a * mergeformat switch:

```
{NUMWORDS  \* MERGEFORMAT}
```

With that switch in place, every time you update the field, it takes on the original formatting—Garamond 12 point—unless you apply some different formatting directly on the field result.

By using formatting switches, you can exercise an enormous amount of control and flexibility over how a field appears in your document. For example,

```
\* dollartext
```

converts a number—say, 123.45—into the kind of text you put on a check: one hundred twenty-three and 45/100.

To capitalize the initial letters of each word in the field result, use

```
\* caps
```

Combine the two formatting switches with the = field, which evaluates numeric expressions, to get the field

```
{ = 123.45 \* dollartext \* caps }
```

that appears in your document as

```
One Hundred Twenty-Three And 45/100
```

The most useful formatting switches are detailed in Table 11.1.

TABLE 11.1   * FORMATTING SWITCHES

Switch	Action
* mergeformat	Retains the current formatting of the field result whenever it's updated.
* charformat	Uses the formatting applied to the first nonblank character of the field code.
* caps	Capitalizes the first letter of each word.
* firstcap	Capitalizes the first letter of the first word only.
* lower	Makes all letters lowercase.
* upper	Makes all letters uppercase.

Switch	Action
* cardtext	Converts a number to text: *12* becomes *twelve*.
* ordtext	Converts a number to the ordinal text: *12* becomes *twelfth*.
* Roman	Displays a number in capitalized Roman numerals: *12* becomes *XII*.
* dollartext	Spells out the whole part of the number, rounds the fraction, and appends "and xx/100": *123.456* becomes *one hundred twenty-three and 46/100*.

NUMERIC \# PICTURE SWITCHES

Word also allows you to specify a numeric "picture" switch to apply to numbers. This could come in handy if, for example, you calculate numbers in a table or bring them in for a merge, and you want to show negative numbers in parentheses. The basic building blocks of field numeric pictures are as follows:

- Decimal point
- Thousands separator (in the United States and Canada, this is typically a comma; in Europe, it's a period)
- Zero (digits that always appear)
- # sign (digits that are used only if necessary)
- Various combinations to format negative numbers
- Literal text, which appears in the field result

You could practically write an entire book on the nuances of numeric picture formatting. Rather than dwell on the details, examine the common numeric picture elements shown in Table 11.2.

TABLE 11.2   COMMON \# NUMERIC PICTURE ELEMENTS

Switch	Result
\# 00.00	Forces Word to display two digits to the left and two to the right of the decimal point, adding leading and trailing zeros as needed: *1.2* displays as *01.20* and *–1.2* shows up as *–01.20*. Use this format when you want numbers in a column to line up perfectly.
\# #0.000	One or more digits might appear to the left of the decimal point, but three must appear after: *1.23* displays as *1.230*, *–12.3456* becomes *–12.346*, and *1234.5* shows *1234.500*.
\# $,#.00	Shows a dollar sign, followed by the number with commas grouping each set of three digits, and two decimal places: *.12* appears as *$.12*; *12345.678* shows *$12,345.68*.
\# $,0.00	Same as the preceding, but always shows at least one digit for dollars: *.12* displays as *$0.12*.

11

Unless you specify a different format, Word always displays negative numbers with a leading minus sign. To force Word to show negative numbers in parentheses, you have to provide two formatting pictures, the first for positive numbers and the second for negatives, enclosed in quotes, separated by a semicolon. For example, this format

```
\# "$,#.00;($,#.00)"
```

shows *0.123* as *$.12* and *–1234.56* as *($1,234.56)*.

DATE-TIME \@ FORMAT SWITCHES

The date-time picture switch almost always appears in a {Date}, {Time}, {CreateDate}, {PrintDate}, or {SaveDate} field. (The last three fields show when the document was created, last printed, and last saved, respectively.) The switch tells Word how to format the date or time for display in the document. For example, add this field to a document:

```
{Date \@ "MMMM d, yyyy - h:mm:ss AM/PM"}
```

When you open the document on the morning of Bill Gates' 55th birthday, Word updates the field and displays text that looks like this:

```
October 28, 2010 - 8:33:05 AM
```

The most common date-time picture elements are shown in Table 11.3.

TABLE 11.3   \@ DATE-TIME PICTURE ELEMENTS

Element	Meaning
M	Month number without leading 0: *August* is *8*
MM	Month number with leading 0: *August* is *08*
MMM	Month as three-letter abbreviation: *Aug*
MMMM	Month spelled out: *August*
d	Day of the month without leading zero
dd	Day of the month with leading zero
ddd	Day of the week as three-letter abbreviation: *Mon*
dddd	Day of the week spelled out: *Monday*
yy	Last two digits of the year: *08*
yyyy	Four-digit year: *2008*
h	Hour on a 12-hour clock without leading zero
hh	Hour on a 12-hour clock with leading zero
H	Hour on a 24-hour clock without leading zero
HH	Hour on a 24-hour clock with leading zero
m	Minutes without leading zero
mm	Minutes with leading zero

Element	Meaning
s	Seconds without leading zero
ss	Seconds with leading zero
AM/PM	AM or PM (used with h and hh for 12-hour clock)
Text	Appears as literal text in the field result

DISPLAYING FIELD RESULTS CORRECTLY

When you first insert a field code into a document, or when you create a new document with a field code in it, Word calculates the value of the field code and displays its results. After the first time, however, field codes never update automatically, except when a file is opened. So, for example, if you create a new letter based on a template that has a {Date} field code, Word puts the current date in the new document. When you close and reopen the document, Word updates the field if necessary, but if you leave the document open overnight, the date won't change.

When you open a document containing a field, the field is updated automatically. The following are two common ways to update a field manually—that is, to have Word recalculate the field's value and display the new value in your document:

- Select the field (or position the insertion point anywhere within the field) and then press F9
- Select one or more fields, right-click, and choose Update Field

You can also specify that Word should automatically update all fields in a document immediately before printing the document. To set this option, click the Office button and select Word Options. Click the Display tab and click the Update Fields Before Printing check box. The setting is global, so it stays in effect for all documents until you change it.

You can permanently eliminate a field and have it replaced with the text that's currently showing in the document. For example, if you've printed and mailed a letter that you originally wrote using a {Date} field, you might want to replace the field with its results; that way, when you open the letter later, you'll see the date you sent the letter rather than the current date. This process is called *unlinking a field*, although it actually removes the field entirely, replacing it with the current value of the field. To unlink a field, do the following:

1. If you want to be certain the field result is current, update the field. In some circumstances, you might choose not to update the field; for example, if it shows an old date and time that you want to preserve.
2. Click to position the insertion point in the field. It doesn't matter whether field codes or field code results are showing.

11

3. Press Ctrl+6 (that's the 6 on the keyboard, not on the number pad) or Shift+Ctrl+F9. (The Ctrl+Z Undo shortcut key reverses this if you realize you've just converted the wrong field or change your mind.)

> **TIP**
>
> If you regularly work with fields, add an Unlink Fields button to the Quick Access toolbar, using the procedures described in Chapter 2, "Making Office 2007 Work Your Way."

To lock a field—that is, to prevent a field from being updated—select the field or place the insertion point in it and press Ctrl+F11. To allow the field to be updated again, select the field and press Shift+Ctrl+F11.

SOME USEFUL CUSTOM FIELDS

Word includes a wasp's nest of fields, many of which have become outdated over the years and remain available only so that documents created in older versions of Word will work in Word 2007. These fields and their switches and settings make up an entire programming language unto itself, buried inside Word, and completely separate from the language used in macros: Visual Basic for Applications.

> **TIP**
>
> Don't let the profusion of fields sway you. In general, if there's a way to accomplish your goal without using fields, that alternative is preferable. Many Word field codes are poorly documented, and you can expect to squander precious time and brain cells trying to make them work properly.

Although you can use the Field Properties and Field Options lists in the Field dialog box to assemble a field, some options aren't listed at all, and interactions among options are complex and confusing. And because error messages are few and far between, debugging field codes is usually a tedious, repeated trial-and-error process. Word's online help provides numerous field code lists that you might find useful.

SHOWING DATES AND TIMES

If you want to insert the current date and time in a document, click the Insert tab on the Ribbon and click the Date and Time button.

> **TIP**
>
> The date and time formats that appear when you click the Date and Time button are identical to the formats offered when you insert a field from the Quick Parts menu and then choose Date from the Field Names list. If one of the formats listed in the Date and Time dialog box is close to the one you want, use the Date and Time entry, and click the Update Automatically check box to insert the field code in your document. Then press Alt+F9 to show field codes and edit the field manually. It's much easier than constructing a field from scratch.

Table 11.4 lists Word's date and time fields. They're all formatted by using the \@ date-time format switches, discussed in the "Date-Time \@ Format Switches" section earlier in this chapter.

TABLE 11.4   DATE AND TIME FIELDS

Field	Meaning
{Date}	The current date and time
{Time}	The current date and time
{CreateDate}	The date and time the file was created
{PrintDate}	The date and time the file was last printed
{SaveDate}	The date and time the file was last saved

So, for example, the field

```
{PrintDate \@ "d-MMM-yy h:mm AM/PM"}
```

in a document last printed on September 29, 2008, might have a field result that looks like this:

```
29-Sep-08 10:45 AM
```

The only significant difference between {Date} and {Time} is in the default formatting—that is, the format of the field result if no \@ date-time format switch is used:

- For the {Date} field, if you've clicked Date & Time on the Insert tab and set a default date format using the Default button on the Date and Time dialog box, Word uses that format. Otherwise, Word looks to the Windows Short Date style; to adjust this format, open Control Panel and adjust the date settings under Regional and Language Options.

- For the {Time} field, if you've set a default time format in the Date and Time dialog box, Word uses that format. Otherwise, Word uses the Windows Time style setting; open Control Panel, double-click Regional and Language Options, click the Customize This Format button on the Formats tab, and then click the Time tab to adjust this format.

The {Date} field also takes a \l switch that isn't used in the {Time} field. When Word updates a {Date \l} field, it checks to see which date or time format you last used in the Date and Time dialog box and then applies that format to the field.

 If you enter a time field in your document, but when you update the field it displays a date, see "Time and Date Discrepancies" in the "Troubleshooting" section at the end of this chapter.

If no \@ date-time switch is in the {CreateDate}, {PrintDate}, or {SaveDate} fields, they show the date and time, formatted according to Date and Time defaults, as described previously, or the Windows date and time options.

11

CAUTION

Be careful using {Date} fields in templates. Date fields are useful in form letters, such as those you might use to reply to a request for information from a potential customer. However, these fields are potentially dangerous in correspondence where the date is an important part of the letter's content. When you create a new letter based on the template, Word puts the {Date} field in the document, and then updates the field so that it shows the current day. A week later, when you discover that you need an extra copy of the letter, you open the saved file and Word dutifully updates the {Date} field—leaving you no idea of when you actually created the letter.

To avoid allowing Word to insert the current date in a document each time you open it, you should use the {CreateDate} field in templates, and explicitly supply the \@ date-time format switch for it. That way, the date won't change if you open or print a letter sometime after its creation. For example, this field

```
{CreateDate \@ "MMMM d, yyyy"}
```

produces a result reflecting the day the document was created, with formatting like this:

```
May 23, 2008
```

PAGE NUMBERING

To show the current page number or the total number of pages in a document's header or footer, you don't have to enter the {Page} and {NumPages} fields manually. The Header and Footer Tools Design tab supports a Page Number button that drops down into a list to handle each of those.

If you aren't in a header or footer, however—or you have to use the {SectionPages} field, which displays the total number of pages in the current section—you should start by inserting a field from the Insert tab's Quick Parts button. You'll find {Page}, {SectionPages}, and {NumPages} in the Field Names box.

DISPLAYING DOCUMENT PROPERTIES

How many words are in your document? When was it last edited? What template does it use? Word allows you to retrieve these and other details and insert them in the current document (see Table 11.5). The most important of these details are also available in the Document Information Panel, which appears when you click the Office button and select Prepare, Properties; to see the full selection of properties for the current document, click Document Properties at the top of the Properties pane and click Advanced Properties.

TABLE 11.5 FILE PROPERTIES AVAILABLE VIA FIELDS

Field	Meaning
Author*	From the Document Information Panel and the Summary tab of the Advanced Properties dialog box.
Comments*	From the Document Information Panel and the Summary tab.
EditTime	Total editing time from the Statistics tab.
FileName	Filename from the Document Information Panel and the General tab. Click the Add Path to Filename check box in the Field dialog box to show the filename with full path.
FileSize	Size of the file from the Document Information Panel and the General tab. Click one of the check boxes in the Field Options section to show the size in KB or MB.
Keywords*	From the Document Information Panel and the Summary tab.
LastSavedBy	From the Statistics tab. Word keeps track of the registered username of the last person to save the file, regardless of the name in the Author field.
NumChars	Number of characters (excluding spaces) from the Statistics tab. Use DocProperty (described later in this section) to retrieve the number of characters with spaces.
NumWords	Number of words from the Statistics tab. Might or might not match your word count because of the way Word defines the term *word*.
Template	Name of the file's template, from the Summary tab. Check the Add Path to Filename box to return full path as well. If the file is a template, returns the name of the file.

11

CAUTION

> The first time Word updates the NumChars field, it is low by the number of characters in the NumChars field's result! To see a number identical to the one on the Statistics tab, you must update the field twice.

Fields with an asterisk in Table 11.5 can be set as well as referenced. For example, the field

```
{Author}
```

yields a field result that's identical to the contents of the Author box on the Summary tab of the File Properties dialog box. However, the field

```
{Author "Mark Twain"}
```

sets the Author value on the Summary tab to Mark Twain *and* displays that result in the document.

TIP

> There's a tricky, effective, and thoroughly undocumented (until now, anyway) method for prompting the user to fill in any of these modifiable file properties. For details, skip ahead to the "Prompting for Input" section that follows.

Several values that appear in the File Properties dialog box don't have fields associated with them directly. Most of them can be accessed through the `DocProperty` field. For example, this field

```
{DocProperty "Paragraphs"}
```

shows the number of paragraphs in the current document as it appears on the Statistics tab. (Like the `NumChars` field, this field must also be updated twice to get an accurate value.) To get to all the `DocProperty` settings, click the Ribbon's Insert tab, click Quick Parts, choose Field, and then choose DocProperty from the Field Names list.

NOTE

> Word has dozens of operators and functions that enable you to perform (almost) any kind of mathematical calculation, including the `Sum`, `Round`, `Count`, and `Average` fields. But just because the capability exists doesn't mean you should use it. In all but the most elementary cases, you're much better off working with a tool more suited to calculations, such as Excel 2007 or your trusty calculator.

PROMPTING FOR INPUT

Word supports two fields that prompt for user input. Typically, you would use the {Ask} and {Fillin} fields in a template or a mail merge document to request additional information from the person creating a new document or performing the merge:

- A {Fillin} field in a template can prompt the user to type in keywords or other data that can then be saved as properties of the current document. Each time a new document based on the template is created, the {Fillin} field updates and the user sees the prompt.

- An {Ask} field in a mail merge can pause the merge on every record, prompting the user to type in information specific to the record—say, a past-due amount or a personalized message in a greeting card—and have that information repeated several places in the merged document.

When you update an {Ask} field, it stores the results in a bookmark in the document. When you update a {Fillin} field, Word uses the typed text as the field result. So, the field

```
{ Ask DueDate "Enter the due date:" }
```

replaces whatever was in the DueDate bookmark with what the user typed. And the field

```
{ Fillin "Enter student name" }
```

displays whatever the user types as the field code's result.

The {Fillin} field, in particular, can be manipulated in many useful ways. For example, the

```
{ KeyWords "new key words" }
```

field can set the value of the Keywords box in the Document Information Panel. Say you have a template that you use all the time, but you often forget to fill out the Keywords box—making it difficult to search for documents. Put this field at the beginning of the template:

```
{Keywords {Fillin "Please enter document keywords"}}
```

Every time you create a new document based on the template, Word first updates the {Fillin} field by prompting you (see Figure 11.18).

Figure 11.18
When Word updates a {Fillin} field, it prompts the user for input.

Then Word updates the {Keywords} field, inserting the keywords typed by the user into the Keywords box in File Properties. Unfortunately, the result of the {Fillin} field shows in the new document. Fortunately, you can use the {Seq} field to hide it. To prompt the user for keywords in a new document, all you need is this nested field in the template:

```
{Seq \h {Keywords {Fillin "Please provide document keywords:"}}}
```

You can do the same for any of the file properties listed with an asterisk in Table 11.5 earlier in this chapter.

MANAGING CUSTOM NUMERIC SEQUENCES

Word supports a variety of built-in paragraph numbering schemes via the Numbering button on the Home tab. For custom numbering tasks, you can use two fields to create your own numbering schemes and maintain them throughout a document. If you work with legal documents, these capabilities might be the single most important feature in Word:

■ The {ListNum} field works wonders in custom-generated paragraph numbering schemes, particularly the type of numbering schemes you'll find in legal documents.

■ The {Seq} field, on the other hand, helps you maintain sequences of numbers that are (typically) independent of paragraph numbering.

USING {ListNum} TO CREATE SOPHISTICATED NUMBERING SCHEMES

{ListNum} fields can adhere to one of three numbering schemes (Number, Outline, and Legal), per Table 11.6.

TABLE 11.6 {ListNum} NUMBERING SCHEMES

Level	Number	Outline	Legal
1	1)	I.	1.
2	a)	A.	1.1.
3	i)	1.	1.1.1.
4	(1)	a)	1.1.1.1.
5	(a)	(1)	1.1.1.1.1.
6	(i)	(a)	1.1.1.1.1.1.
7	1.	(i)	1.1.1.1.1.1.1.
8	a.	(a)	1.1.1.1.1.1.1.1.
9	i.	(i)	1.1.1.1.1.1.1.1.1.

The {ListNum} field allows you to build complex and sophisticated numbering sequences that are sensitive to both other {ListNum} fields and to the position of the {ListNum} field in a sentence. Detailing the capabilities of {ListNum} could take a chapter by itself, but to get a glimpse of its power, try these experiments:

- Put a {ListNum} field at the beginning of a blank paragraph. Select the field, and use the Increase Indent or Decrease Indent buttons to change the level of the field—and thus the format of the number.

- Insert several {ListNum} fields in a paragraph, interspersed with text. Click and drag the text with its associated {ListNum} field. All the fields will be renumbered automatically.

- Put a bookmark on a {ListNum} field, and use a {Ref} field (or select Cross-Reference from the Insert Ribbon tab) to refer to the field. Then move the {ListNum} field and update the document. The reference is updated as well. This is the kind of approach you can use to keep references such as "see paragraph III (173) A (3) iii" in sync. If you set up the reference to use a {Ref} field, and the {Ref} field points to a bookmark over a (potentially quite complex) {ListNum} or series of {ListNum} fields, the reference changes automatically if you move the fields. So, if the previously mentioned paragraph is moved and suddenly becomes paragraph III (172) A (3) iii, the reference automatically updates to see paragraph III (172) A (3) iii.

- Experiment with two {ListNum} switches. The \s switch tells Word what number to start at (so that you can begin numbering at any point). Usually, {ListNum} senses its level in the list by its position within a paragraph, and the presence of {ListNum} fields before it. The \l switch allows you to manually override the level auto-sensing capabilities of {ListNum}.

USING {Seq} TO COUNT AUTOMATICALLY

By contrast, {Seq} fields are straightforward. You have to make up an identifier (or use one of the built-in identifiers provided by Word) to keep the various sequences in a document straight. For example, you might add this text with field codes at the start of a document:

```
Refer to folders {Seq FolderNumber} and {Seq FolderNumber}
```

The field results will look like this:

```
Refer to folders 1 and 2
```

> **NOTE**
>
> You cannot use {Seq} fields in headers or footers.

The next time Word encounters a {Seq FolderNumber} field, it will display the value 3, and then 4, and so on. This technique can be extremely useful if, for example, you want to number illustrations in a manuscript sequentially. If you use a field such as

```
Illustration Number {Seq IllustrationNo} - Monet
```

in the caption above or below each illustration, Word numbers the illustrations sequentially:

```
Illustration Number 77 - Monet
```

Then if you reorder the illustrations—move a few around, delete some, and add some others throughout the document—all you have to do is press Ctrl+A to select the entire document, and then press F9 to update the fields. Word renumbers the illustrations, starting at 1 and continuing sequentially throughout the document.

Moreover, if you use one of the three identifiers that Word recognizes—Figure, Table, or Equation—your {Seq Figure}, {Seq Table}, and {Seq Equation} fields can dovetail into Word's built-in features for generating cross-references, such as (See Figure 17 on page 22), and tables of figures. {Seq} fields recognize five switches; the three you'll commonly use are shown in Table 11.7.

TABLE 11.7   COMMON {Seq} FIELD SWITCHES

Switch	Meaning
\c	Repeat the previous sequence number; don't increment the counter
\h	Hide the field and its results
\r *val*	Reset the sequence number to *val*

So, for example, this series of {Seq} fields starting at the beginning of a document

```
{Seq MyId} {Seq MyId \c} {Seq MyId} {Seq MyId \r 8} {Seq MyId}
```

produces this as the field result:

```
1 1 2 8 9
```

TIP

> If you have a long document with more than one chapter, and you want to reset the figure sequence so that it starts at Figure 1 at the beginning of each chapter, put this field at the beginning of each chapter:
> `{Seq Figure \h \r 0 }`

TABLE OF CONTENTS AND INDEX FIELDS

Word creates tables of contents and indexes using fields, as well. A wealth of information about those fields—{tc}, {toc}, {ie}, and {xe}, and the like—is in the online help.

In general, the table of contents options are handled so well with the built-in TOC tools (click the References tab and then click the Table of Contents button) that dealing with individual fields is time-consuming and won't buy you much. By contrast, Word's indexing tools (click the Insert Index button on the Ribbon's References tab) are so woefully inadequate that all the field codes in the world won't accomplish much. Avoid them if you possibly can. If you're serious about indexing, buy an add-on package that can read Word files.

TROUBLESHOOTING

HIDING AND REVEALING FIELD CODES

My document is filled with field codes, but I sometimes have a hard time locating them. On more than one occasion, I've accidentally wiped out a crucial field code while editing some other text because I didn't know the code was there.

Normally, field codes are hidden onscreen, and their locations are invisible except for a gray shading that appears when you select the code's location. You can show all field codes in a document by pressing Ctrl+A and then pressing Alt+F9. To make the location of field codes visible at all times without showing the codes themselves, open the Word Options dialog box, click the Advanced tab, and change the Field Shading option in the Show Document Content section to Always (from its default value of When Selected). Note that this shading will appear in printed copies of pages that contain fields; you'll probably want to turn field shading off before printing a document.

TIME AND DATE DISCREPANCIES

I entered a {Time} field in my document, but when I update it, the field displays a date.

To solve the problem, remove the \l switches in your {Date} and {Time} fields. If you don't understand how the \l switch works, bizarre consequences like this are nearly inevitable. If you use the Date and Time dialog box to insert a time in a document, all the {Time \l} fields will show a time when updated. If you then use the same dialog box to insert a date in your document, all the {Date \l} fields will show a date when updated.

EXTRA CREDIT: CUSTOMIZING FORM LETTERS WITH FIELDS

As with so many other advanced Word features, merging data and documents occurs through the magic of Word fields. The various merge fields discussed in this chapter are just special types of Word fields—which in turn are a small subset of the fields available in Word. The Mail Merge Wizard simply puts a pretty face on the underlying fields: You get to use the merge fields without getting your hands dirty working with field codes, formatting switches, and the like. The fields themselves control all the nuances of merging. You can use any of Word's extensive collection of fields in mail merge documents.

Two fields are useful if you want Word to pause the merge at each record, and let you type in custom data. Both {Ask} and {Fillin} request data for each merged record. The former places whatever you typed in a bookmarked location on the form letter; the latter replaces the field with the text you fill in, at the point in the document where you place the field.

A {Fillin} field might be useful in a form letter, when you want the option to add a personalized paragraph at the end of every letter. As each merged letter pops up, you can enter your own customized text or just click OK to use the default text. You might use this feature to customize receipts you send to donors in your annual fund drive. For donors who have a special connection to your organization, you might want the option to insert a special, truly personal message of thanks instead of the generic text that goes to the bulk of the list. Here's how to create these semicustom letters:

1. Place the insertion point wherever you want the custom text to appear in the form letter.

2. Click the Mailings tab and click Rules. Select Fill-In from the menu.

3. In the Insert Word Field: Fill-In dialog box, type in a suitable prompt and default text, as shown in Figure 11.19.

Figure 11.19

NOTE

Although the input box in the Insert Word Field: Fill-In dialog box is small, you can type in lengthy default responses, providing they don't include carriage returns.

4. Perform the merge as usual. Each time Word encounters a {Fillin} field, once for each data source record, it prompts you for whatever custom text you want to provide, as shown in Figure 11.20. Note that the default text is highlighted. Click OK to accept the default text or begin typing to replace it with your preferred text.

Needless to say, you do not want to use this trick with databases that include more than a few dozen records!

For additional information on fields that apply specifically to mail merge, see the Help topics under the heading "Mail Merge Fields."

Figure 11.20

PART III

USING EXCEL

CHAPTER **12**

GETTING STARTED WITH EXCEL

In this chapter

WORKING WITH WORKSHEETS AND WORKBOOKS

Before you begin working with Excel, it helps to understand its basic building blocks.

An Excel document consists of one or more *worksheets*, which together comprise a *workbook*. A worksheet is the equivalent of a single two-dimensional sheet of paper divided into rows and columns; the intersection of a row and column is called a *cell*. A cell can contain text (called a *label*) or a formula. A formula can make reference to data contained in one or more other cells (for example, a formula in one cell might add up the values contained in various others), or it can simply calculate something by itself, without reference to other data (for example, a formula might calculate and display the current date).

NOTE

> If you create charts in Excel, those charts can either exist as objects on worksheets or as separate sheets, called *chart sheets*. Thus, a workbook might include one or more chart sheets as well as one or more worksheets. Earlier versions of Excel (much earlier) supported a macro language called XLM that entailed writing code on special sheets called *macro sheets*. Technically, a workbook can still hold one or more macro sheets, although the XLM language is ancient history now.

By default, each new Excel workbook starts out with three blank worksheets; an index tab at the bottom of each worksheet identifies the sheet by name. You can add a new worksheet, delete an existing worksheet, and rename or rearrange worksheets to suit your needs. You can also change the default so that new workbooks consist of more or fewer worksheets.

Multiple worksheets help keep complex projects organized within a single workbook. In a consolidated annual budget for a school district, for example, you might create a separate worksheet for the numbers reported by each individual school. In this case, you would use identical templates to make sure each sheet is formatted identically: Each budget category appears in the same row and each month is in the same column. You would then use an additional worksheet with the same structure to create a summary that totals each row and column for the entire district.

Placing related data tables on different sheets makes it easier to view, format, and print each type of data separately—for example, if you're researching loans for a new house, you might create a loan analysis form on one worksheet and then generate an amortization table on a separate sheet in the same workbook.

TIP

> In workbooks with a large number of worksheets, you won't be able to see all the sheet names without using the four arrow buttons to the left of the sheet names to scroll. Unless, of course, you know this secret: Right-click any of those arrow buttons to display a pop-up list containing the names of all the worksheets in the current workbook. Click any name to jump straight to that worksheet.

UNDERSTANDING EXCEL'S WORKBOOK FILE FORMATS

If you click the Microsoft Office button and choose Save As, you'll find that you can save your workbook in any of four file formats. Those formats are as follows:

- Excel Workbook (.xlsx)—The default in Excel 2007, this format is new with this version. Data is stored in industry-standard XML (Extensible Markup Language) and compressed, making it possible for you to transfer data in this format to other programs without a file-conversion step. But this format has two noteworthy disadvantages: Although files in this format are compact, they sometimes take longer to load than a binary (.xlsb) equivalent. (After it is in memory, the file performs as quickly as any other Excel format.) Also, the Excel Workbook format does not support macros.

- Excel Macro-Enabled Workbook (.xlsm)—Because Office macros have in the past been used to carry computer viruses, the default .xlsx format does not allow them. If you want to write or record macros, use the .xlsm option (or .xlsb) instead of .xlsx. Apart from the matter of macro support, .xlsm is identical to .xlsx; that is, it uses industry-standard XML and file compression.

- Excel Binary Workbook (.xlsb)—This is a non-XML format that supports macros. Its advantage is that it is likely to load more quickly than an equivalent XML format. Disadvantages mostly affect corporate users; at home or in an educational setting you shouldn't notice any difference. Because Microsoft clearly sees XML as the way of the future, it's conceivable—although unlikely—that some Excel version down the road might not support this format. The .xlsb format uses the same compression methods as the XML formats, so file size should be comparable.

- Excel 97–2003 Workbook (.xls)—If you need to share files with users of earlier Excel versions, you need to stick with this version. Features and enhancements that are new to Excel 2007 are, of course, unavailable in this format.

In short, if the data-portability advantages of XML don't interest you, you can save a little file-loading time by using the Excel Binary Workbook (.xlsb) format. If you want XML but you also want to be able to use macros, choose Excel Macro-Enabled Workbook (.xlsm). Otherwise, go with the default: Excel Workbook (.xlsx).

To change the default workbook file format, click the Microsoft Office button, choose Excel Options, and click the Save tab (in the left pane). Then make your choice in the drop-down menu labeled Save Files in This Format. To save a particular file in a non-default format, just use the Save As command.

TIP

Do you regularly work with a particular set of workbooks? If so, consider saving them as a *workspace*. With the entire set of files open, click the View tab and then click Save Workspace (in the Window group). Excel creates a workspace (.xlw) file that records the names and locations of each document in the set. At your next session, just open the workspace file, and all your workbooks arrive at once.

12

MOVING, COPYING, INSERTING, AND DELETING WORKSHEETS

In many cases, the easiest way to construct a workbook containing multiple sheets is to create the first sheet and then copy it. Although each new workbook starts with three blank worksheets (a setting you can change), you can add, copy, delete, and rearrange worksheets at will.

To add a new worksheet to an existing workbook, click the icon to the right of the last sheet tab (for example, to the right of the Sheet3 tab in a default workbook). Alternatively, right-click any sheet tab and choose Insert, click the Worksheet icon in the Insert dialog box, and click OK. The new worksheet will have a generic name and a number one higher than the highest numbered sheet in the current workbook.

To copy an existing worksheet, point to the sheet tab you want to copy, hold down the Ctrl key and drag the sheet tab left or right. (This Ctrl+drag technique is the same one you use to copy files in Windows Explorer.) As you drag, the mouse pointer changes shape and a small triangular marker with a plus sign appears above the sheet tab. When you release the mouse button, Excel creates a copy of the sheet you dragged, using its name followed by a copy number in parentheses: Sheet3 (2), for example.

To delete a worksheet from a workbook, right-click the sheet tab of the worksheet you want to delete and then choose Delete from the shortcut menu.

TIP

In some workbooks, you might want to hide a worksheet rather than remove it. This technique is especially useful when a worksheet contains static data you use in formulas on other worksheets but rarely need to edit. Hiding a sheet also makes it slightly more difficult for other users to examine (and possibly change) the data on one of these sheets. (But don't even think about using hidden sheets as a true security measure—anyone interested in unhiding the sheet can do so with a few clicks.) To hide a sheet, right-click the sheet tab and choose Hide. To display a list of hidden sheets in the current workbook so you can make them visible again, choose Unhide from the same menu.

To move a worksheet within a workbook, point to its sheet tab, click, and drag the triangular pointer along the sheet tabs until the black marker is over the location where you want to move the worksheet. Release the mouse button to drop the worksheet in its new location. Although it's possible to drag and drop worksheets between workbooks, it's much quicker and more accurate to use shortcut menus for this task. Follow these steps to move or copy a worksheet from one workbook to another:

1. Open the target workbook into which you plan to move or copy the worksheet. (Skip this step if you plan to move or copy the worksheet to a brand-new workbook.)

2. Switch to the workbook that contains the worksheet you want to move or copy. Point to the worksheet tab and right-click.

3. Choose Move or Copy from the shortcut menu.

4. In the Move or Copy dialog box (see Figure 12.1), select the name of the target workbook from the To Book drop-down list. To move or copy the sheet to a new, empty workbook, choose (new book) from the top of the list.

5. By default, Excel moves or copies sheets to the beginning of the target workbook. To select a different location, choose a sheet name from the Before Sheet list.

6. By default, using this dialog box moves the selected worksheet to the target workbook. To leave the original worksheet in place, select the Create a Copy check box.

7. Click OK.

Figure 12.1
The list of available workbooks in the top of this dialog box shows only workbooks that are currently open.

RENAMING A WORKSHEET

To navigate more easily through workbooks with multiple worksheets, replace the generic default worksheet labels (Sheet1, Chart2, and so on) with descriptive names such as "November Expenses," "Industrial Output," or "PivotTable." To rename a worksheet, double-click the worksheet tab (or right-click the tab and select Rename). Type a new name and press Enter.

Names you enter on worksheet tabs must conform to the following rules:

- Maximum length is 31 characters. (Many other size limits have been increased in Excel 2007, but this one has not.)

- Spaces are allowed.

- You can use parentheses anywhere in a worksheet's name, but brackets ([ ]) are not allowed.

- You cannot use any of the following characters as part of a sheet name: / \ ? * : (slash, backslash, question mark, asterisk, or colon). Other punctuation marks, including commas and exclamation points, are allowed.

12

If you plan to use references from one worksheet in formulas on another sheet, choose worksheet names carefully. Create names that are as short as possible without being needlessly cryptic; long names can make formulas particularly difficult to troubleshoot and edit.

NOTE

> Worksheet tabs automatically resize to accommodate the name you enter.

TIP

> Excel allows you to color code worksheet tabs (right-click the worksheet tab and choose the Tab Color option). This option is best used sparingly. Colorizing each worksheet tab doesn't help organize data. Instead, try using colors to identify sheets that are part of the same group (yellow for social studies, green for economics), or use colors to highlight summary sheets while leaving data input sheets with the default gray background.

Navigating in a Workbook with Keyboard Shortcuts

For touch typists, Excel includes a wealth of keyboard shortcuts. Some are obvious, but a few are less than intuitive, and some represent unusual ways to move through a worksheet and select cells with precision:

- Ctrl+Home returns to the top-left corner (cell A1) of the current sheet.
- The Home key moves to the beginning of the current row.
- The Page Up/Page Down keys take you one window in their respective directions.
- Ctrl+End jumps to the bottom-right corner of the data-containing part of the worksheet—a useful technique when navigating through a lengthy list.
- If you've selected a range, you can move clockwise through all four corners of the range by repeatedly pressing Ctrl+period. (The selection remains unchanged, but the active cell—the cell where Excel will accept data if you type—changes.) If you've highlighted multiple ranges, this shortcut works only in the currently selected range.
- To move through the current workbook one worksheet at a time, press Ctrl+Page Up or Ctrl+Page Down.
- Pressing the End key turns on *End mode*, an unusual (and somewhat confusing) way to move through the current worksheet. The End mode shortcuts were designed as a convenience for users whose finger habits were established with Lotus 1-2-3; they are also handy for people who are unable to press two keys simultaneously. Press End followed by an arrow key to jump along the current row or column in the direction of the arrow, to the next cell that contains data, skipping over any intervening empty cells. Press End and then Home to go to the cell that is at the intersection of the furthest data-containing row and column in the current worksheet. Press End and then Enter to move to the last cell in the current row, even if there are blank cells within the row— this is the most useful of the End mode shortcuts, because it has no matching Ctrl+*key* alternative. If you press the End key by accident, press End again to turn off End mode.

TIP

Don't forget all of the common shortcuts that Excel shares with Windows and other Office programs. In particular, F2 (Edit) positions the insertion point in the active cell and makes it available for editing, F4 repeats the previous action, and F6 switches between panes in a worksheet where you've used the Split command (in the Window group on the View tab).

WORKING WITH MULTIPLE WORKSHEETS

Working with multiple sheets simultaneously is how power users quickly create and format a complex workbook with a minimum of wasted effort. Use the following techniques to make working with multiple sheets easy:

- To select multiple worksheets, hold down the Ctrl key as you click each tab.

- To select a contiguous group of worksheets, click the first one in the group and then hold down the Shift key and click the last one in the group.

- To select all the worksheets in the current workbook, right-click any worksheet tab and choose Select All Sheets from the shortcut menu.

- If you've selected more than one sheet, you see the word *Group* in brackets in the title bar, and any data you enter appears in the corresponding cells on each worksheet in the group. So, if you have grouped Sheet1, Sheet2, and Sheet3, entering text in cell A1 on Sheet1 also enters the same text in the corresponding cells on Sheet2 and Sheet3.

- To quickly make any sheet active, click its index tab; to remove a sheet from a group, hold down Ctrl and click its tab.

- To remove the multiple selection and resume working with a single sheet, click any un-selected sheet; if you've selected every sheet in the workbook, right-click any worksheet tab and choose Ungroup Sheets.

- Likewise, any formatting choices you make—resizing columns, for example, or applying a numeric format—affect all the grouped worksheets identically. If you're building a master workbook with identically formatted sheets for each division or department, you can use these techniques to quickly enter the budget categories in the first column and months along the top of each sheet.

- You can't use the Clipboard to enter data into multiple sheets simultaneously. When you paste data, it appears only in the active sheet, not in any other sheets you've selected. To quickly copy formulas, labels, or formats from a single worksheet to a group of sheets within a workbook, follow these steps:

  1. Select the sheet that contains the data you want to appear in each sheet.

  2. Use Ctrl+click or Shift+click to select the group of sheets to which you want to add the data.

  3. Select the data itself and choose Fill, Across Worksheets from the Editing group on the Home tab. An additional dialog box enables you to choose whether to copy the formatted cell contents, just the data, or just the formats.

12

NOTE

> Watch out for one gotcha if you exchange workbook files with anyone who uses Microsoft Works. Although the Spreadsheet module in Works 7.0 can open Excel workbooks, it treats multi-sheet workbooks as though each sheet were a separate file.

USING CELL REFERENCES AND RANGE NAMES TO NAVIGATE IN A WORKBOOK

Excel's Name box (the combo box to the left of the Formula bar) enables you to jump straight to a specific cell or named range. Click in this box, enter a cell reference (H4, for example), and press Enter to jump straight to that cell. To pick from a list of all named ranges in the current workbook, even on different worksheets, click the drop-down arrow to the right of the Name box.

Excel's Go To dialog box offers the same capabilities, with a few extra twists, including the capability to return to a cell you previously selected, or to select all cells on a worksheet that match criteria you specify.

To open the Go To dialog box shown in Figure 12.2, choose Edit, Go To, or use the keyboard shortcuts F5 or Ctrl+G. To jump to a specific cell or range, type its address or name in the Reference box. In general, it's easier to use the Name box to jump around a worksheet in this fashion. The advantage of the Go To dialog box is that Excel keeps track of the four most recent cell addresses you enter here, including the cell from which you started. To return to any of these addresses, open the Go To dialog box and double-click the entry in the Go To list.

Figure 12.2
The Go To dialog box enables you to jump to cells or named ranges you've visited recently.

The list of references in the Go To dialog box also includes any named ranges in the current workbook. To jump to one of these ranges, select its name from the list and click OK. Because Excel saves range names with the workbook, that list is always available when you open the Go To dialog box. On the other hand, Excel discards the list of recent addresses each time you close the workbook.

TIP

> Using the Go To dialog box to jump to a specific cell or a named range is needlessly complex. Whenever possible, use the Name box instead. It's also easy to create a macro that jumps to a specific named range or cell address. Use the following code, for example, to jump to a range with the name ZipCodes in Sheet1 (the Scroll parameter positions the window so that the top-left cell in the range is at the top-left corner of the window):
>
> ```
> Sub GoToZipCodes()
> Application.Goto Reference:=Worksheets("Sheet1"),Range
> ("ZipCodes"),scroll:=True
> End Sub
> ```

→ For an explanation of how range names work in formulas, **see** "Using Range Names and Labels in Formulas," **p. 448.**

→ For details on the incredibly useful Special button, **see** "Selecting Ranges of Data with the Go To Dialog Box," **p. 363.**

USING RANGES TO WORK WITH MULTIPLE CELLS

Any selection of two or more cells is called a *range*. You can dramatically increase your productivity by using ranges to enter, edit, and format data. For example, if you highlight a range and click the Currency Style button, all the numeric entries in that range appear with dollar signs and two decimal places. Assigning a name to a range makes it easier to construct (and troubleshoot) formulas, and ranges make up the heart and soul of charts by defining *data series* and labels for values and categories.

The most common way to select multiple cells is to highlight a *contiguous range*—a rectangular region in which all cells are next to one another. But cells in a range don't have to be contiguous. You can also define a perfectly legal range by selecting individual cells or groups of cells scattered around a single worksheet.

Excel uses two addresses to identify a contiguous range, beginning with the cell in the upper-left corner and ending with the cell in the lower-right corner of the selection. A colon (:) separates the two addresses that identify the range—such as A1:G3. Commas separate the parts of a noncontiguous range, and you can mix individual cells and contiguous ranges to form a new range, as in the example A3,B4,C5:D8.

NOTE

> You can also reference a range that includes all the cells in a given row or column. The range A:A, for example, covers everything in column A. The range 3:3 means all cells in row 3, and so on.

SELECTING RANGES

To select a contiguous range, click the cell at any corner of the range and drag the mouse pointer to the opposite corner. To select a noncontiguous range, select the first cell or group of cells, hold down the Ctrl key, and select the next cell or group of cells. Continue holding

12

the Ctrl key until you've selected all the cells in the range. To select an entire row or column, click the row or column heading. To select multiple rows or columns, drag the selection or hold down the Ctrl key while clicking.

To select all cells in the current worksheet, click the unlabeled Select All button in the upper-left corner of the worksheet, above the row labels and to the left of the column labels.

> **TIP**
>
> Use this shortcut to select a contiguous range that occupies more than one screen: Click the top-left cell in the range and then use the scrollbars to move through the worksheet until you can see the lower-right corner of the range. Hold down the Shift key and click to select the entire range.

MOVING FROM CELL TO CELL WITHIN A RANGE

To enter data into a list in heads-down mode, select the range first. As you enter data, press the Enter key to move the active cell down to the next cell within the range, or press Tab to move to the right. (Press Shift+Enter or Shift+Tab to move in the opposite direction.)

When you reach the end of a row or column, pressing Enter or Tab moves the active cell to the next column or row in the selection. When you reach the lower-right corner of the range, pressing Enter or Tab moves you back to the upper-left corner.

ENTERING THE SAME DATA IN MULTIPLE CELLS

Occasionally, you'll want to fill a range of cells with exactly the same data in one operation, without using the Clipboard. For example, you might want to enter zero values in cells in which you intend to enter values later; you can also use this technique to enter a formula in several cells at once. To enter a formula in several cells at once, follow these steps:

1. Select the range of cells into which you want to enter data. The range need not be contiguous.
2. Type the text, number, or formula you want to use, and then press Ctrl+Enter. The data appears in all cells you selected.

> **TIP**
>
> When you enter a formula using this technique, Excel inserts *relative cell references* by default. If you want the formula to refer to a constant value, select the cell reference and press F4 to convert it to an absolute reference before pressing Ctrl+Enter.

→ For a discussion of the differences between absolute and relative cell references, **see** "Using Cell References in Formulas," **p. 441.**

→ For instructions on how to automatically fill in data using Excel's AutoFill feature, **see** "Automatically Filling In a Series of Data," **p. 480.**

SELECTING RANGES OF DATA WITH THE GO TO DIALOG BOX

The Go To dialog box is especially useful when you're designing or troubleshooting a large worksheet and you want to quickly view, edit, format, copy, or move a group of cells with common characteristics. In fact, mastering this dialog box can make it possible to do things even most Excel experts swear can't be done, such as copying a range of data while ignoring hidden rows and columns. Open the Go To dialog box as usual, and then click the Special button to display the Go To Special dialog box shown in Figure 12.3. When you select one of these options and click OK, Excel selects all the cells that match that characteristic.

Figure 12.3
Use the Go To dialog to select groups of cells.

When you select cells using the Go To Special dialog box, the effect is the same as if you had selected a range by pointing and clicking. If you select all constants, for example, you can use the Tab and Enter keys to move through all the cells in your worksheet that contain data, skipping over any cell that contains a formula.

> **TIP**
>
> If you select a range with the mouse or keyboard and then use the Go To Special dialog box to narrow the selection to particular types of data, the selection includes only cells within the range that you originally selected. That is, it refines the selection to the data type in which you're interested.

The following list describes the options available in the Go To Special dialog box:

- Comments—Selects all cells that contain *comments*. Use this option and then press the Tab key to move from comment to comment. (A better way to navigate between commented cells is to click the Review tab and then click either Next or Previous in the Comments group.)

- Constants—Selects all cells that contain text, dates, or numbers, but not formulas. Note that the four check boxes under the heading Formulas become available when you select Constants (as well as when you select Formulas). Use the Numbers and Text check boxes to restrict the selection to those data types. For example, select text only if you want to change the formatting of row and column labels while leaving the data area alone. Ignore the Logicals and Errors check boxes; they have no effect when you're selecting constants.

- Formulas—The opposite of the Constants choice, this option selects only cells that begin with an equal sign. The Numbers and Text check boxes enable you to restrict the selection by data type. Use the Logicals check box to find cells that contain a TRUE or FALSE value. Click the Errors check box to quickly select all cells that currently display an error value, and then use the Tab key to move from cell to cell and fix the misbehaving formulas.

- Blanks—A straightforward option that searches all cells between the top of the worksheet and the last cell that contains data, selecting those that do not contain data or formatting. This option is useful when you want to enter a default value (such as 0) or assign a default format to these cells.

- Current Region—Selects all cells around the active cell, up to the nearest blank row and column in any direction.

- Current Array—If the active cell is within an *array*, this option selects the entire array. (For more on array formulas, see "Using Array Formulas," in Chapter 14, page 446.)

- Objects—Choose this option to select all charts, text boxes, shapes, and other graphic objects on the current worksheet. This option is particularly useful when you want to change formatting for borders and shading, or when you want to group objects.

- Row Differences—Selects cells whose contents are different from those in a comparison cell. This is a challenging option to master. You must make a selection first, and then use the Tab or Shift+Tab key to position the active cell in the column you want to use for comparison. If you select multiple rows, Excel compares each row independently to the value in the column that contains the active cell. The example in Figure 12.4 shows what happens when you select B2:H12 and then position the active cell in column B and use the Go To Special dialog box with the Row Differences option. The highlighted result helps you readily identify rows (such as 2 through 6) where expenses are different each month, but it also pinpoints one out-of-the-ordinary value in cell D10. Press Tab to move through from one highlighted cell to the next within the results.

- Column Differences—Like the previous option, except it works on a column-by-column basis. This option is extremely useful for finding unexpected differences in a list.

- Precedents—Selects all cells to which the current selection refers (in other words, all cells that contribute to the result of the current cell). Use the Direct Only and All Levels options to find only direct references or all references. This option is useful when you're trying to trace the logic of a complex worksheet by working through a series of formulas.

Figure 12.4
Using the Row Differences command identifies values that are out of the ordinary; a cost-conscious manager might ask why the March cleaning bill was $275 higher than usual.

Position the active cell in column B

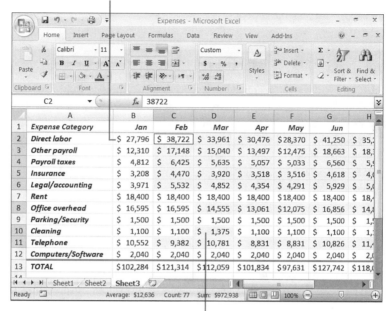

The Row Differences option selects the cells in gray because they contain values that are different from those in the comparison column

- **Dependents**—Similar to the previous option, except it selects all cells that directly or indirectly refer to the active cell or range.
- **Last Cell**—Jumps to the last cell on the worksheet that contains data or formatting.
- **Visible Cells Only**—Easily the most useful of all the options in the Go To Special dialog box. Use this type of selection to avoid the common problem of pasting more data than you expect. For example, if you copy a range of data that includes a hidden row or column, and then paste it into a new sheet, Excel pastes the hidden data as well. To avoid this problem, select the range you want to copy, and then use the Go To Special dialog box to select only visible cells. Copying and pasting that selection will have exactly the result you intend.
- **Conditional Formats**—Selects all cells that use any form of *conditional formatting*. Use the All option when you want to quickly find all cells that contain conditional formatting. Use the Same option if you just want to edit these options for cells that match the current cell.

→ For a detailed explanation of how and when to use conditional formatting, **see** "Using Conditional Formatting to Identify Key Values," **p. 430.**

- **Data Validation**—Similar to the previous option, except it selects cells with *data validation* rules.

If choosing the Last Cell option in the Go To Special dialog box causes you to jump to a blank cell far below your actual worksheet range, see "Resetting the Last Cell" in the "Troubleshooting" section at the end of this chapter.

HIDING ROWS AND COLUMNS

On some worksheets, you need to use rows or columns to hold data used in calculations, but you don't need to clutter up the rest of the worksheet by showing it. Click any cell within the row or column you want to hide (you don't need to select the entire row or column). Then click the Home tab, click Format (in the Cells group), click Hide & Unhide, and choose Hide Rows. To make a hidden row visible again, select cells in the row above and below the hidden row, go back to the Format command, click Hide & Unhide, and then choose Unhide Rows.

Use similar procedures to hide and unhide columns. To hide a column, for example, select one of its cells, click Format in the Cells group of the Home tab, click Hide & Unhide, and then choose Hide Columns.

If the first row or column of a worksheet is hidden, press F5 to open the Go To dialog box. Type **A1** in the Reference box and click OK; then choose Format, Row (or Column), Unhide.

FINDING, REPLACING, AND TRANSFORMING DATA

Just as in other Office applications, you can use simple drag-and-drop techniques to move or copy the contents of a cell or range. Using the Windows Clipboard and the Paste Special menu, you can also change the format of information or perform mathematical transformations as you move or copy it. Most of the options are self-explanatory, but a handful are unique to Excel and truly useful.

→ For an overview of standard Clipboard techniques you can use within and between Office programs, **see** "Using the Office Clipboard," **p. 140.**

FINDING AND REPLACING THE CONTENTS OF A CELL OR RANGE

You can use the Find and Replace dialog box to search for and replace strings of text. You can also find and change formatting, or use options to search across all sheets in a workbook or to restrict the search and subsequent changes to the current worksheet.

As in other Office programs, you use the Find and Replace commands (click the Home tab, and then click Find & Select in the Editing group) or the corresponding Ctrl+F and Ctrl+H shortcuts to open the respective dialog boxes. Figure 12.5 shows the Replace dialog box with formatting options selected. (If the additional settings aren't visible, click the Options button.)

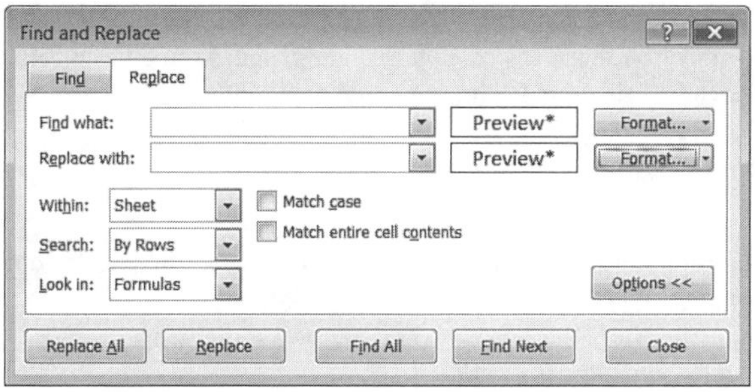

Figure 12.5
The Find and Replace dialog boxes enable you to change formatting globally across an entire workbook.

If you leave the Find What or Replace With boxes blank, Excel finds or replaces formatting in all cells where it finds a match. To enter formatting criteria using dialog boxes, click the Format button to the right of the Find What or Replace With text boxes. To find cells where formatting matches the settings of an existing cell, click the drop-down arrow to the right of the Format button and select the Choose Format from Cell option. After you select this option, the Find and Replace dialog box disappears and the mouse pointer changes to an eyedropper shape. Click the cell that contains the formatting you want to match.

Dragging and Dropping to Convert Data

As is true elsewhere in Office, you can take control of the options available when dragging cells from one place to another. For instance, if you aim at the border surrounding a selection of one or more cells, hold down the right mouse button, and drag the cell or range, a shortcut menu with paste options appears when you release the button. Two of these options are worth special note:

- Use the Copy Here as Formats Only option to quickly transfer cell formatting (fonts, shading, borders, and so on) without copying the contents of the cells.
- Choose Copy Here as Values Only to convert formulas to their results and paste the Clipboard contents as constants—numbers or text—rather than as formulas.

This technique is especially useful when you want to quickly convert a cell or range from a formula to a value. Say column A contains a list of ISBN numbers and book titles (all books use these; just look at the back cover of this one), imported from an external database. All you really need from each cell is the 10-digit ISBN number it starts with, so you've filled column B with a range of formulas, each of which uses the LEFT() function to extract the first 10 characters from the original cell—for example, =LEFT(A2,10).

So far, so good. But if you now delete column A, your list of part numbers will shift to the left and turn into a column full of error messages. Before you can safely delete column A, you must convert column B to its results. To do so, select the entire range that contains the formula, right-click the border of the selection and drag it a short distance in any direction (without releasing the mouse button), and then drag it back and release it over the original cells. Choose Copy Here as Values Only from the shortcut menu. The column now contains just the part numbers, and you can safely delete column A.

12

TIP

> To convert a single cell (as opposed to a range) from a formula to a constant value, select the cell, press F2, press F9, and press Enter.

NOTE

> You cannot use the Clipboard or drag-and-drop techniques to copy or move a noncontiguous range that consists of multiple selections.

TRANSFORMING DATA WITH PASTE OPTIONS

One of the most powerful ways to manipulate data on a worksheet is to copy it to the Clipboard first. Using the Clipboard, you can strip some or all formatting or manipulate values in the copied cells or range; you can then paste the data into the new location so it appears exactly as you want it.

The Paste Options Smart Tag allows you to quickly apply some common transformations. When you copy data to the Clipboard and then use Edit, Paste or the Ctrl+V keyboard shortcut to paste the data, you see a Smart Tag in the lower-right corner of the pasted area. Click the Smart Tag to choose from the menu options shown in Figure 12.6.

Figure 12.6
Smart Tag options enable you to tweak the appearance of data after pasting it; the Keep Source Column Widths option, for instance, fixes the truncated row labels in this example.

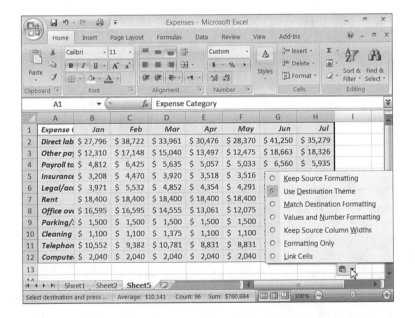

By default, data pasted from another Excel worksheet brings along its own formatting. If the data appears incorrectly when you paste it, click the Smart Tag and change the display of the pasted data in any of these ways:

- Click Keep Source Formatting to bring the original formatting into the new worksheet

- Choose Use Destination Theme to make the pasted data conform to the theme that's currently assigned to the destination worksheet.

- Choose Match Destination Formatting to strip all of the source-range formatting but preserve formulas.

- Choose Values and Number Formatting to keep numeric (and formula) cells looking the way they did in the source range, while removing formatting attributes from other cells. Choose Values and Source Formatting to preserve the original formatting.

- Click Keep Source Column Widths to copy all formulas, number formatting, and cell formatting along with column widths. This option is most useful when pasting a highly formatted table into a new worksheet, where all columns are the standard width.

- Choose Formatting Only when you want to copy the format of a table to a new worksheet and then enter data manually in the new location.

- Click the Link Cells option to convert the pasted data into a link to the other worksheet.

→ For more details on how to use links between worksheets and workbooks, see "Using Links to Automatically Update or Consolidate Worksheet Data," p. 374.

Choices available through the Paste Options Smart Tag are convenient for quick, uncomplicated transformations. But they have several limitations, most notably that each change undoes the changes from other Smart Tags. So if you paste in a range of formulas, you can use Smart Tags to convert formulas to values *or* to adjust column widths, but not both.

For more control over the results of a paste operation, use the Paste Special menu. Copy the contents of one or more cells to the Clipboard, click the arrow beneath the Paste command (in the Clipboard group of the Home tab), and choose Paste Special. (Alternatively, right-click the destination cell or range and choose Paste Special from the shortcut menu.) You'll see the Paste Special dialog box shown in Figure 12.7. A handful of these options are also available using the Paste Options Smart Tag, but Paste Special offers a much broader range of capabilities.

Within or between workbooks, you can selectively paste in the following ways:

- The Formulas option is poorly named. Use this option when you want to copy all the data from one range to another, including formulas, without copying any formatting. This option is most useful when you're trying to copy data from another worksheet without destroying the formatting of your existing worksheet. Use the Formulas and Number Formats option to copy number formatting without carrying over other cell formatting, such as borders and colors. Use All Except Borders when the source range has border attributes that aren't appropriate in the destination range.

- Select Values to convert formulas to their results and paste them as constant numbers or text. This has the same effect as the drag-and-drop technique described in the previous section. Use this option when you need to convert a noncontiguous range of formulas to its results. This option does not copy any formatting. Use the Values and Number Formats option to preserve number formatting without affecting other cell formatting.

12

Figure 12.7
Use the Paste Special dialog box to add or subtract two columns of numbers, or to multiply or divide a range of numbers by a value you copy to the Clipboard.

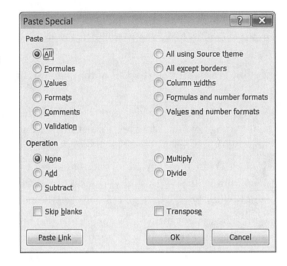

- Click Formats to copy all formatting from one cell or range to another. Use the All Except Borders option to skip cell borders, and the Column Widths option to duplicate column widths, especially from one worksheet to another.

TIP

> Using Excel's Paste Special options can test your creativity. It's often possible to save a ton of work by combining several operations in consecutive Paste Special actions. For instance, choose All Except Borders to copy formulas and cell formatting without adding underlines and table borders from the original data; then repeat the Paste Special option and choose the Column Widths option. This duplicates an entire table on a new worksheet, leaving out only borders and underlines.

- Choose the Comments option to transfer comments from one location to another.
- Use the Validation option to duplicate data-entry rules, especially between different worksheets or workbooks.

The options in the Operation area are some of the most interesting of all, because they allow you to perform mathematical transformations on a group of numbers without having to tamper with your existing worksheet structure. To use this technique, enter a number in one cell and copy it to the Clipboard, select the range you want to transform, and use the Paste Special dialog box to add or subtract the value on the Clipboard from each entry in the selection or to multiply or divide the selection by that number. This technique might come in handy if you're beginning to plan next year's family budget and you want to start by increasing this year's numbers by 6%. Follow these steps:

1. Click in any blank cell (even on another worksheet) and enter the value you want to use when transforming the existing data. In this case, enter **1.06** because you want to increase the values by 6%.

TIP

> You can also use this technique to add or subtract two ranges of numbers, or to multiply one range of numbers by another. If you have two worksheets formatted in exactly the same way, you can copy all the numbers from one worksheet and use this option to add them to the data in the other sheet, for example. Just make sure that the range you copy is the same size as the range to which you paste.

2. Press Ctrl+C to copy the value to the Windows Clipboard.

3. Select the range of data you want to increase.

4. Right-click and choose Paste Special from the shortcut menu. In the Paste Special dialog box, choose the Multiply option.

5. Click OK. Excel multiplies the selected range by the constant on the Clipboard, increasing each number by exactly 6%.

The final two check boxes in the Paste Special dialog box work with other options:

- Click the Skip Blanks option if you're performing a mathematical operation using two ranges of data. This setting skips pasting data for any cells that are blank in the original copy area.

- Click the Transpose check box to flip the contents of a row into a column, or vice versa. You can use this option to change the orientation of an entire region as well.

TIP

> Changing the orientation of an entire region is a trick that is especially useful when working with imported data. If your list has months along the side and categories along the top, for example, choose the Transpose option to rearrange the list so that each month's data appears in its own column and each category gets its own row.

12

CUSTOMIZING THE WORKSHEET WINDOW

Changing the size and configuration of a worksheet window can make it easier to work with data, especially in large worksheets. Zoom out or in to show more or less data, lock a row or column in place to maintain titles and headings, work in multiple panes, or open a new window on the same workbook.

USING THE ZOOM CONTROLS

Use the Zoom controls at the right side of the status bar (or their equivalents in the Zoom group of the View tab) to change the view of your worksheet. Most of the options are self-explanatory: You can shrink the worksheet to as small as 10% of normal size for an overview of the sheet's design, or enlarge it to as much as 400% of normal. (This option is inappropriate for entering numbers but is especially useful for close editing of complex grouped objects on a sheet.) If you choose a Zoom level of 39% or lower, your gridlines disappear. That's not a bug—at the lower magnification, the lines get in the way of your ability to edit, so Excel hides them on the screen.

The most useful Zoom option is one that even some expert users don't know about. You can resize and reposition the editing window so that it includes the current selection; Excel chooses the proper Zoom percentage automatically. After you make a selection, click the View tab and then click Zoom to Selection. Excel resizes the selection automatically. To return to normal view, click 100% in the Zoom group.

TIP

> If your mouse includes a wheel, you can use it to zoom in and out of your worksheet. Hold down the Ctrl key and spin the wheel down to zoom out; spin the wheel up to zoom back in.

LOCKING ROW AND COLUMN LABELS FOR ONSCREEN VIEWING

In a typical worksheet, labels identify the type of data in each column or row. For example, a common design for budget worksheets arranges data into one row for each budget category, with values for each month appearing in columns from left to right. In this model, a label at the left edge of each row identifies the category, and a label at the top of each column identifies the month. If the data in your worksheet occupies more than a single screen, row and column labels can scroll out of view, making it difficult to identify which data goes in each row and column. The lack of labels also makes it difficult to enter data in the correct rows and columns, unless you want to continually scroll to see the heading labels.

To keep the row and column labels visible at all times, *freeze* them into position. In Figure 12.8, for example, notice that you can see the row titles in column A at the left, as well as the columns for August and beyond at the right (starting at column I). As you click the horizontal scrollbar, columns on the left of the data area scroll out of view, but the labels in the first column remain visible.

To freeze rows, columns, or both, click in the cell below the row and to the right of the column that you want to lock into position. To freeze the first two columns and the first row, for example, click in cell C2. Click the View tab and then click Freeze Panes (in the Window group). A solid line sets off the locked rows and columns from the rest of the worksheet.

TIP

> One of the many conveniences offered by Excel 2007's new table features is that column headings in tables are automatically frozen. For more details, see Chapter 15, "Working with Tables and PivotTables."

Figure 12.8
When you freeze rows or columns in place, you can scroll through the worksheet without losing identifying labels.

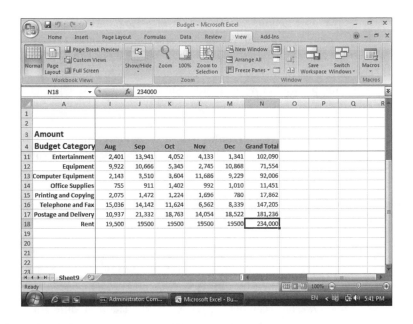

To navigate in a worksheet whose panes are frozen, use the scrollbars to move through the data in your worksheet. The panes are locked only on the screen; if you print the worksheet, rows and columns appear in their normal positions. To unlock the row and column labels, click the View tab and then click Freeze Panes, Unfreeze Panes.

→ To learn how to add row or column labels on each page of a printed worksheet, **see** "Using Repeating Titles for Multiple Page Printouts," **p. 386.**

SPLITTING THE WORKSHEET WINDOW

Split a worksheet into separate panes when you want to compare data in different regions of a worksheet side-by-side. A *split bar* divides the window into two panes, horizontally or vertically. You can drag both split bars onto the worksheet to create four panes. All changes you make in one pane are reflected in the other. You can drag cells and ranges between panes, and you can scroll and enter data in each pane independently.

To split a worksheet, use either of the following techniques:

- Click to select the cell below and/or to the right of where you want the split to appear, click the View tab, and then click Split. Select any cell in the column at the left of the current window to create side-by-side panes (also known as a vertical split). Select any cell in the top row to create a horizontal split, with one pane over another. If you choose the cell at the top left of the screen, Excel divides the window into four equal panes.

- Aim the mouse pointer at one of the two *split boxes*, which appear just above the vertical scrollbar and just to the right of the horizontal scrollbar, to create side-by-side panes (vertical split). When the mouse pointer changes to a double line with two arrows, click and drag in the direction of the worksheet to create a new pane. As you drag, the bar snaps into place at a row or column boundary. Release when you reach the right position.

To remove multiple panes and return to a single editing window, click the View tab and then click Split. Or drag the split bars to the right and top edges of the window.

USING LINKS TO AUTOMATICALLY UPDATE OR CONSOLIDATE WORKSHEET DATA

Use *links* to share data between cells or ranges in one worksheet and another location in the same workbook or a different workbook. Just as a formula displays the results of a calculation, a link looks up data from another location and displays it in the active cell.

Links offer a powerful technique for consolidating data from different sources into one worksheet without requiring that you re-enter or copy data. For example, a teacher might use separate worksheets in a single workbook to keep track of test results for each class, with a separate worksheet that organizes results into an alphabetical list by student.

NOTE

> You can use links (also known as external references) within formulas as well.

After you establish a link, data you enter in one location automatically appears in all linked locations. To create a link, follow these steps:

1. Open all the workbooks you plan to link.
2. In the source worksheet (the one that contains the data you want to reuse), select the cell or range to be linked, and press Ctrl+C to copy it to the Clipboard.
3. Switch to the dependent worksheet (the one in which you want to insert the link), and select the cell where you want to create the link.
4. Right-click the destination cell and choose Paste Special. In the Paste Special dialog box, click the Paste Link button.

In general, you should avoid creating links between cells or ranges that are contained in separate workbooks. If you move or delete the workbook that contains the external reference, you break the link and damage the integrity of your data and formulas. Excel updates linked cells automatically if the worksheet that contains the link is open. If you change the data in the source workbook when the workbook that contains the link is closed, the links do not update automatically. When you reopen the workbook that contains the links, Excel will ask whether you want to update the links. To update or change the source of links manually, click the Microsoft Office button, Prepare, Edit Links to Files.

RESTRICTING AND VALIDATING DATA ENTRY FOR A CELL OR RANGE

When designing a worksheet, you'll occasionally want to restrict the type of data users can enter in a specific cell or range. Excel enables you to define data-validation rules for cells and ranges to do exactly that. Examples of useful applications include the following:

- In a list of test scores formatted to show only month and date, restrict entry in a specific column to only dates within the past 14 days. This technique lessens the likelihood that you will inadvertently enter a date in the wrong month or year, or in the future.

- On a budget worksheet, require that the user enter a category and restrict allowed entries to a specific list. You can add a drop-down arrow to a cell with this type of restriction so users can pick from a list.

- For your personal budget, check the amount entered in an expenses column against a typical maximum value—say, $500. If the amount is over that limit, display an "Are you sure?" message.

- Provide a prompt when entering data to include a description of a list item; to keep data to a manageable length, restrict the total number of characters the user can enter and display a warning message if the description exceeds that length.

- On a form that you send to club members requesting payment of annual dues, allow the option to enter a discount, but only if the member first joined more than five years ago. Compare the entry in the Discount field with a formula that calculates the member's start date to validate the entry.

12

DEFINING DATA-VALIDATION RULES

Each *data-validation* rule has three components: the criteria that define a valid entry; an optional message you can display to users when they select the cell that contains the rule; and an error message that appears when users enter invalid data. To begin creating a data-validation rule, first select the cell or range for which you want to restrict data entry, click Data Validation in the Data Tools group of the Data tab, and then click Data Validation. You'll see a dialog box similar to the one in Figure 12.9.

On the Settings tab, enter the criteria that define a valid entry. First, choose the required data type in the Allow drop-down list; then define specific criteria. The available options in the Allow drop-down list (described in Table 12.1) vary depending on the type of data you select. Keep in mind that the options shown in the Data Validation dialog box change depending on the criterion you've selected in the Allow drop-down list. The dialog box shown in Figure 12.9 represents just one example.

Figure 12.9
When defining data-validation rules, you can enter values or formulas that evaluate to the correct data type. This example restricts valid entries to dates within the past 30 days.

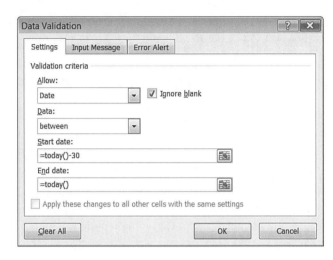

TABLE 12.1 DATA-VALIDATION SETTINGS

Data Type	Allowed Restrictions
Any Value	Default setting; no restrictions allowed. Select this option if you want to display a helpful input message only, without restricting data entry.
Whole Number or Decimal	Choose an operator (between, for example, or greater than) and values or formulas. The Whole Number data type produces an error if the user enters a decimal point, even if it's followed by zero. The Decimal choice allows any number after the decimal point.
List	In the Source box, enter the address or name of the range that contains the list of values you want to allow. The range can be on another worksheet (a hidden worksheet in the current workbook is your best choice) or in another workbook. For a short list, enter the valid items directly in this box, separated by commas (East, West, North, South). If you want users to be able to pick from a list, select the In-cell Dropdown check box.
Date or Time	Choose an operator and appropriate values. You can enter formulas here as well; for example, to allow only dates that have already occurred, choose Less Than from the Data box and enter **=TODAY()** in the End Date box.
Text Length	Choose an operator and then specify numbers that define the allowed length; you can also enter formulas or cell references that produce numbers as values for use with the selected operator.
Custom	Enter a formula that returns a logical value (TRUE or FALSE). Use this option when the cell that contains the rule is part of a calculation, and you want to test the results of that calculation rather than the cell value itself. On an order form with multiple items that you total in a cell named Total_Order, for example, enter **=Total Order < 500** as the rule for each cell used in the SUM formula; that prevents the user from exceeding a $500 total limit even though each individual item is under the allowance.

DISPLAYING HELPFUL INPUT MESSAGES

Rules that stop users from entering invalid data are good, but helpful messages are even better. As part of a data-validation rule, you can display messages that appear every time the user enters the cell that contains that rule. These messages appear in small pop-up windows alongside the cell. Use *input messages* to help users (including yourself!) understand exactly what type of data they should enter in the cell, especially if you are designing a data-entry sheet for less-experienced Excel users or one that you use infrequently.

To create an input message, click the Input Message tab in the Data Validation dialog box (see Figure 12.10) and enter the title text and message you want to appear. Your message should be as helpful and brief as possible; if you've restricted the user to a particular type of data, make sure they know exactly what they're allowed to enter.

Figure 12.10
The message you enter here can explain the purpose of the cell and warn the user of data restrictions.

ALERTING THE USER TO ERRORS

How do you want Excel to respond when users enter invalid data? In all cases, you can display an error alert. If the data type is wrong, or if the date or value is not appropriate, you can refuse to accept the input and force users to enter an acceptable value. You can also choose to accept the value; this can be an effective way to force users to double-check values that might be valid but are outside of a normal range. On a report listing contributions to your annual fund drive, for example, you might define valid entries as being below $100. If the amount users enter is more than that amount, you could display a message that asks them whether they're sure the amount is correct. If they accidentally added an extra zero, the message will give them a chance to correct their mistake; if the amount was from an exceptionally generous donor, the user can click OK and allow Excel to accept the input.

To define an error message and set options for handling data that is outside the defined range, click the Error Alert tab in the Data Validation dialog box (see Figure 12.11).

Figure 12.11
You define the error message users see when they enter invalid data; you can reject the data or allow them to enter it with a warning.

Select the Show Error Alert After Invalid Data Is Entered check box. Enter a title and text for the message you want users to see when they enter an invalid value. As with the input message, try to be as informative as possible so the user knows exactly what he or she must do to correct the error. Then select one of the following choices from the Style box to define how Excel should handle the input:

- Stop—Displays a Stop dialog box and lets the user choose Retry or Cancel.
- Warning—Displays the error message and adds Continue?. The user can choose Yes to enter the invalid data, No to try again, or Cancel.
- Information—Displays the error message. The user can click OK to enter invalid data or Cancel to back out.

DELETING, MOVING, OR COPYING DATA-VALIDATION RULES

To remove all validation rules from a cell or range, first select the cell(s) containing the validation rule; then click Data Validation, in the Data Tools group of the Data tab, and then click Data Validation from the drop-down menu. In the Data Validation dialog box, click Clear All.

What about the check box labeled Apply These Changes to All Other Cells with the Same Settings (on the Settings tab of the Data Validation dialog box)? When should you select that? When you create a set of validation rules for a range of cells, Excel stores those settings with the range. If you later adjust the settings for a particular cell in that range, you break the link to the range. Check this box while editing data-validation settings for a single cell, and Excel extends the selection and applies your changes to the entire range you originally selected. The check box has no effect on other cells for which you defined rules individually, even if the rules are absolutely identical.

12

TIP

When you copy or move a cell or range, data-validation rules travel with the cell's contents. To copy only data-validation rules from one cell to another, without affecting the contents or formatting of the target cell, use Paste Special. In the Paste Special dialog box, click the Validation option and click OK.

 Are you still finding invalid data in a user form in which you've created validation rules to protect data? See "Data Validation Limitations" in the "Troubleshooting" section at the end of this chapter.

TROUBLESHOOTING DATA ERRORS

Data-validation rules are not perfect. Users can bypass the rules and enter invalid data by pasting from the Clipboard, or by entering a formula that results in an invalid value. Also, Excel does not check the existing contents of a cell or range when you create or copy a validation rule.

To find cells containing values outside the limits you defined with data-validation rules, click Data Validation on the Data tab and then choose Circle Invalid Data from the drop-down menu (see Figure 12.12). Excel draws a bright red oval around any value that violates a validation rule. To remove the red ovals, choose Clear Validation Circles from the same drop-down menu.

NOTE

The Circle Invalid Data command finds a maximum of 255 cells. If you have more invalid entries, you'll need to correct the data in some of the invalid cells and then choose Circle Invalid Data again.

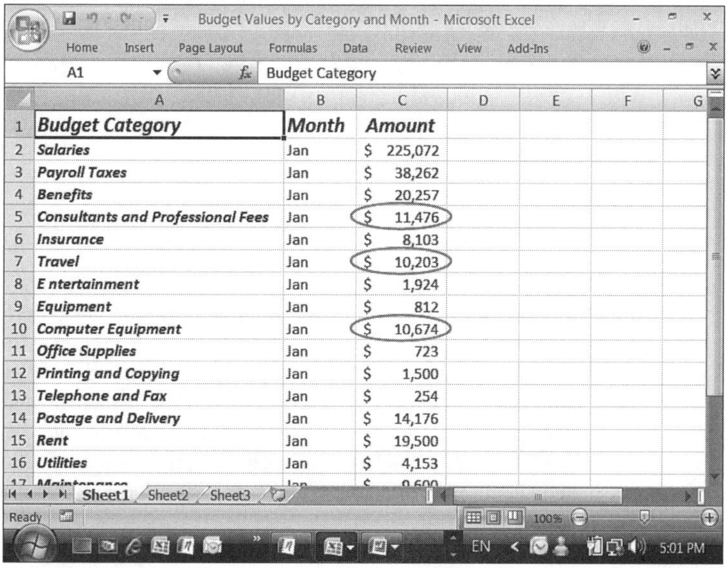

Figure 12.12
Choose Circle Invalid Data (Data tab, Data Tools group, Data Validation menu) to add these bold highlights around any cell whose contents violate a validation rule.

→ For an overview of other tools you can use to track down problems in formulas, **see** "Troubleshooting Formulas," **p. 462.**

PRINTING WORKSHEETS

Unlike Word documents, which typically are designed to fit on specific paper sizes, Excel worksheets are free-flowing environments that sprawl in every direction. If you press Ctrl+P and leave the formatting to Excel, you'll end up with page breaks that appear at arbitrary locations in your worksheet, with no regard to content. To properly translate a large worksheet into printed output takes planning and a fair amount of creative formatting.

If you don't specifically define a print area, Excel assumes that you want to print all the data in the currently selected worksheet(s), beginning with cell A1 and extending to the edge of the area that contains data or formatting. If necessary, you can divide a worksheet into smaller sections and print each region on its own page. As explained in this section, you can also shrink the print area to fit in a precise number of pages, and you can repeat row and column headings to make the display of data easier to follow.

TIP

> Don't overlook other techniques for rearranging data on a worksheet for the purpose of producing great printouts. On lists and tables, filtering commands can help you select and print only data that matches criteria you specify (see Chapter 15 for more details). Hiding rows and columns temporarily can help cut a large worksheet down to size. To print this quarter's grades without printing the grades from prior quarters, for example, hide the details before printing the selection. In some cases, the best way to print a complex selection from a worksheet is to translate it into another worksheet, using linked ranges or PivotTable reports (also covered in Chapter 15).

USING RANGES TO DEFINE THE DEFAULT PRINT AREA

You can force Excel to use a defined print area as the default for a worksheet. This technique is especially useful if you regularly print a complex worksheet that contains a number of nonprinting regions. On a worksheet that contains a list and a criteria range, for example, you'll typically want to print only the list. On a budget worksheet that includes monthly data by category and an executive summary region, you might want to define the summary as the default when you print.

TIP

> The Print button, a fixture on the Standard toolbar in earlier versions of Excel, has been removed from the default user interface in Excel 2007. Not to worry; you can add it by right-clicking the Quick Access Toolbar and choosing Customize Quick Access Toolbar from the shortcut menu. In the list of available commands on the left side of the dialog box, select Quick Print. Then click the Add button. Be aware that the Quick Print button (it has been renamed as well as removed) bypasses all printing dialog boxes, sending the current default output to the current default printer. For a safer, but almost as quick, way to print, press Ctrl+P. This approach does display the Print dialog box.

Start by selecting the range you want to print. The range need not be contiguous, but if you select a noncontiguous range, keep in mind that each selection will print on its own page, and the results might not be what you intended. All parts of the range to be printed must be on the same worksheet; each worksheet in a workbook gets a separate print area.

To define the selection as the default print area, click the Page Layout tab. Then click Print Area, in the Page Setup group, and choose Set Print Area from the drop-down menu. Excel creates a named range called Print_Area in the current worksheet.

TIP

> If you define a print area on each worksheet, you can preview or print the defined print area on all sheets in the current workbook. Choose File, Print (or press Ctrl+P) and select Entire Workbook from the Print What area of the Print dialog box.

To delete the current print area selection and start over, click the Page Layout tab. Then click Print Area in the Page Setup group and choose Clear Print Area from the drop-down menu.

When you define a specific print area, Excel prints only that area when you click the Quick Print button. If you define a print area and then add rows at the bottom or columns to the right of the data, the new data won't appear on the printed pages. Whenever you redesign a worksheet, make a special point to recheck the print area.

CONTROLLING PAGE BREAKS

When you print a worksheet, Excel automatically inserts page breaks to divide it into sections that will fit on the selected paper size. Excel doesn't analyze the structure of your worksheet before inserting page breaks; it simply adds a page break at the point where each page runs out of printable area.

To make multipage worksheets more readable, you can and should position page breaks by hand. The easiest way to do this is by using Page Break Preview mode. Click the View tab, and then click Page Break Preview in the Workbook Views group. Excel displays dashed blue lines to indicate where it currently intends to break the pages, and it displays page numbers to show you the order in which pages will be printed. In Figure 12.13, for example, the vertical dashed lines between columns D and E and columns I and J, as well as the horizontal dashed line below row 28, show that Excel will print this document on six pages. The page numbers tell you that the two segments encompassing columns A through D will be printed first, followed by the two segments encompassing columns E through I, and so on.

12

Figure 12.13
The dashed lines show where pages will break, and the numbers indicate the order in which pages will be printed. You can adjust the page-break positions by dragging the dashed lines.

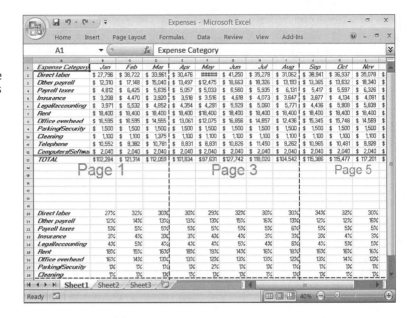

Dashed lines represent automatic page breaks inserted by Excel; solid lines represent manual page breaks. To adjust page breaks in this view, point to the thick line between two pages and drag it in any direction. To adjust the print area, drag the solid lines on any edge of the print area; cells that are not in the print area appear gray in Page Break Preview.

When using Page Break Preview, you'll have best results if you start at the top of the worksheet and work in the order it will print—normally from top to bottom and left to right, unless you've used the Page Setup dialog box to specify that you want to go across the worksheet before you work your way down. Move page breaks up or to the left only; moving them down or to the right can cause unpredictable results if you drag past the size of the page. In that case, Excel adds its own page breaks, undoing the effects of your painstaking page-breaking efforts.

As an alternative to using Page Break Preview to adjust page breaks, you can use the Insert Page Break command (in any worksheet view). Select the cell below and to the right of the last cell you want on the page and then click the Page Layout tab. Click the Breaks command in the Page Setup group and then choose Insert Page Break. To remove the page break, select the same cell, go back to the Breaks command, and choose Remove Page Break. To remove all manual page breaks from the current worksheet, choose Reset All Page Breaks.

TIP

To add only a horizontal page break, select any cell in column A; to add only a vertical page break, select any cell in row 1.

EXTRA ITEMS YOU CAN PRINT

Use Excel's Print dialog box to specify that you want to print additional parts of a worksheet, such as comments, gridlines, and row or column headings. You can also control the way Excel translates colors into shades of gray. To see these additional printing options, click the Page Setup tab, and then click the little arrow in the lower-right corner of the Page Setup group. In the Page Setup dialog box, click the Sheet tab.

Table 12.2 lists the options available for each worksheet.

TABLE 12.2   WORKSHEET PRINT OPTIONS

Print Option	What It Does
Gridlines	It's okay to show gridlines on draft worksheets; for final output, however, turn off gridlines and use borders to set off data areas.
Comments	By default, comments are not printed; select this check box to print them on a separate sheet or as they appear onscreen.
Draft Quality	This option, which prints cell contents but skips gridlines and graphics, is unnecessary when using a laser printer but might be useful for speeding up printing on color output devices or slow inkjet printers.
Black and White	Excel translates color backgrounds to shades of gray on the printed page. This option removes most gray shades; it can also speed up print jobs on color printers. Use Print Preview to print a small test page to check results before printing a large sheet with this option.
Row and Column Headings	Prints letters and numbers to help identify cell addresses. Use in combination with the option to view formulas (click the Office button, click Excel Options, click the Advanced tab, and select the Show Formulas in Cells Instead of Their Calculated Results check box under Display Options for This Worksheet) when you want to print out the structure of a worksheet so you can study it.
Print Titles	If the data in your worksheet spans several pages, you might lose your points of reference, such as the headings above columns of data or to the left of each row. Identify the Rows to Repeat at Top of each page or the Columns to Repeat at Left of each page. (See the following section for more details.)
Page Order	The graphic to the right of this option shows whether your sheet will print sideways first, and then down, or the other way around. Adjust this order if necessary to make page numbering work properly.

LABELING PRINTED PAGES WITH HEADERS AND FOOTERS

Any worksheet that spans more than one page should include a header or footer (or both). An assortment of preconfigured headers and footers enables you to number pages, identify the worksheet, specify the date it was created, list the author, and so on.

The easiest way to specify headers and footers is by using Excel 2007's new Page Layout view (see Figure 12.14). To get there, click the View tab and then click Page Layout in the Workbook Views group.

Figure 12.14
Page Layout view, new in Excel 2007, shows you how your pages will look on paper. It also makes it easy to create headers and footers.

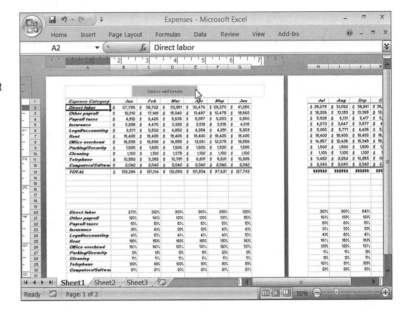

Think of Page Layout view as an interactive form of print preview; it shows you how your pages will look on paper. Rulers appear at the top and left edges of the window to help you gauge page fitting, and a header box at the top of the page provides a place where you can easily specify your header. (A similar footer box appears at the bottom of the page.) When you click in this box, the Ribbon changes to offer the options shown in Figure 12.15.

To choose one of the built-in headers or footers, use the drop-down arrows below Header and Footer at the left edge of the Ribbon. To add fields to the header—such as the current date or the name of your file—click the appropriate items in the Header & Footer Elements group. For additional options, click the Options button at the right edge of the Ribbon. While your mouse cursor remains in the header (or footer) box, you will see codes representing chosen fields. As soon as you click away, you'll see the calculated result of those codes—the current page number, for example.

The header (or footer) box initially appears in the center of the window, and specifications made there will be centered on the printed page. You can add flush-left or flush-right elements to your header or footer by clicking to the left or right of this box (the box moves accordingly).

Figure 12.15
Easy-to-use header options appear on the Ribbon when you click in the header box in Page Layout view.

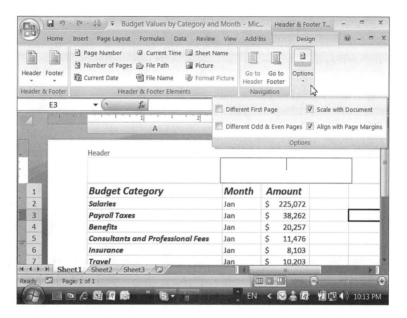

Using the Picture button in the Header & Footer Elements group, you can include graphic images, such as a company logo, in a header or footer. Click Picture and browse to any graphic file whose format is supported by Office. You can insert one and only one graphic in each section—left, center, and right. Click the Format Picture button to crop, compress, resize, or scale a picture file in a header or footer.

→ For general-purpose advice on how to work with graphics in Office, **see** Chapter 5, "Using Pictures and Drawings in Office."

By default, Excel allows a half-inch for a worksheet's header or footer. If you want to maximize the amount of data on each page and you're not using a header or footer, open the Page Setup dialog box, click the Margins tab, and set the Header, Footer, Top, and Bottom boxes to 0. (On some printers, you might need to adjust the top and bottom margins to match the unprintable area on the page.)

TIP

> If your custom header or footer doesn't look right on the page, see "Adjusting Header and Footer Margins" in the "Troubleshooting" section at the end of this chapter.

TIP

> If you want a custom header or footer to appear on every worksheet you create, add headers and footers to each sheet in the template Excel uses when you create a new workbook. (The specific instructions for creating and saving this template appear later in this chapter, in "Customizing Excel.") Remember that each sheet has its own header and footer; if you want the same header to appear on each sheet in the template, you must create each one individually.

USING REPEATING TITLES FOR MULTIPLE PAGE PRINTOUTS

For worksheets that span multiple pages, you can repeat one or more rows or columns (or both) as titles for the data on each new page. On a typical budget worksheet, for example, the first column might contain income and expense categories, with columns for each month's data extending to the right across several pages. In this case, follow these steps to repeat the entries in a particular column or row as titles at the left of each page:

1. Click the Page Layout tab and then click the small arrow in the lower-right corner of the Page Setup group. In the Page Setup dialog box, click the Sheet tab.

2. To specify a column for titles, click in the Columns to Repeat at Left box. To use a row as titles on each new page, click in the Rows to Repeat at Top check box.

3. Click in any cell in the column or row you want to specify as the title. You need not select the entire row or column. If you select multiple cells, Excel uses all selected rows or columns as titles. If necessary, use the Collapse Dialog button to the right of the input box to move the dialog box out of the way as you select.

4. Click the Print Preview button to ensure that you've configured the titles correctly. Click Print to send the worksheet to the printer immediately.

FORCING A WORKSHEET TO FIT ON A SPECIFIED NUMBER OF PAGES

Just as you can use the Zoom control to change the size of cells in a worksheet window, you can also reduce the size of data on a printout. Making the scale smaller lets you squeeze more rows and columns onto each page. If you want your printed worksheet to fit in a specific number of pages, Excel can calculate the *scaling percentage* for you:

1. Click the Page Layout tab and then click the small arrow in the lower-right corner of the Page Setup group. In the Page Setup dialog box, click the Page tab.

2. To scale the page to a fixed percentage, enter a value between 10 and 400 in the Adjust to % Normal Size box.

CAUTION

> Choosing a number that's too low can result in a completely unreadable printout. In general, you should choose a scaling percentage lower than 40 only when you want to see the overall structure of your worksheet, not when you want to actually read and analyze data.

3. To adjust the printout to a fixed height or width, select the Fit To option. Use the spinner controls to adjust the number of pages you want the printout to occupy; leave one number blank if you want Excel to adjust only the width or height of the printout. The settings in Figure 12.16, for example, will scale the worksheet to no more than one page in width but allow the sheet to print additional rows on multiple pages.

Figure 12.16
These settings force Excel to scale the current worksheet to one page wide for printing.

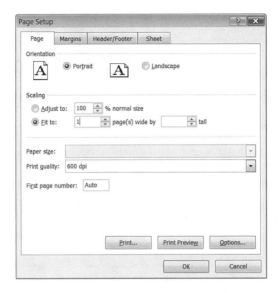

4. Click Print Preview to verify that your worksheet's print settings are correct.
5. Click Print to send the worksheet to the printer.

PROTECTING A WORKSHEET

If you store Excel workbooks only on your own PC, you can control exactly how and when you change the data and structure of each worksheet. But what if you need to share a workbook with other people? How do you maintain the confidentiality of sensitive data? How do you allow others to view the contents of a workbook without changing crucial data or formulas, either deliberately or by accident?

Excel's assortment of security options includes the following:

- You can set passwords that restrict access to the entire workbook. Excel allows you to specify separate passwords to open the workbook in read-only mode and to edit the workbook's contents.

- You can lock parts of a worksheet—such as cells that contain formulas—so that no one can make any changes to those cells without unlocking the entire worksheet.

- You can designate certain ranges as protected and allow editing only by individuals you specify.

- You can restrict access to specific elements of a worksheet, including sorting and filtering of lists, PivotTable reports, graphic objects, and chart sheets.

- You can protect a shared workbook so that it can't be returned to exclusive use or have its change history deleted. This prevents a user from deliberately or accidentally deleting a record of changes he or she made to the shared workbook.

12

USING PASSWORDS TO RESTRICT ACCESS TO A WORKBOOK

The simplest form of protection uses passwords to prevent unauthorized users from opening and/or modifying a workbook. You can specify this option at any time: Click the Microsoft Office button, choose Save As, and select the kind of file you're about to save (Excel Workbook, for example). In the Save As dialog box, click the Tools menu and choose General Options.

You can specify two different passwords, one for opening the file and one for modifying it. By setting up both, you can allow access to information while maintaining the integrity of data in a workbook. For example, you might assign different Open and Modify passwords to a budget workbook and then give other members of your committee the Open password, so they can see your calculations, but allow only the organization's Treasurer to have the Modify password. If anyone wants to make a change to the budget, they'll have to talk to you or the Treasurer.

> **TIP**
>
> If you leave the Open password blank but assign a Modify password, anyone with access to the folder in which the workbook file is stored can view, but not change, its contents.

Anyone who attempts to open a password-protected workbook will first have to enter the correct password. If the workbook is protected by a Modify password, you'll see a second dialog box, like the one shown in Figure 12.17.

Figure 12.17
If you don't know the password, click the Read Only button to view the workbook's contents. Without the password, you cannot save changes to the workbook unless you give it a new name.

Workbook passwords are an all-or-nothing proposition. After entering the correct Modify password, a user can make any changes. That unrestricted freedom can be disastrous in the hands of a sloppy or untrained user if you've carefully designed a worksheet and entered complex formulas. You can even do irreparable damage to your own workbooks or work-sheets if you're distracted or you simply don't notice that you're working with an original when you meant to create a copy. The following two sections describe how to protect yourself.

PREVENTING CHANGES TO A WORKSHEET

Excel allows you to exercise fine-grained control over what other people can do with a workbook or worksheet. You can prevent cell formatting, stop users from inserting or deleting rows and columns, and ensure that no one enters a hyperlink in a worksheet, for example.

To apply protection options to the current worksheet, click the Review tab and then click Protect Sheet in the Changes group. (Alternatively, click Format in the Cells group of the Home tab and then choose Protect Sheet.) In the Protect Sheet dialog box (see Figure 12.18), select options you want to apply to all users (including yourself). The Protect Worksheet and Contents of Locked Cells check box (at the top of this dialog box) turns on or off protection for the current sheet.

Figure 12.18
Use these options to restrict access to specific worksheet features.

You can require users to enter a password before entering data in specified ranges. To impose this level of control on a worksheet, choose Allow Users to Edit Ranges, in the Changes group of the Review tab. The resulting dialog box (see Figure 12.19) lists currently protected ranges and allows you to specify which users can edit those ranges.

Figure 12.19
Click the Permissions button to specify which users (including yourself) can edit data without a password.

12

To add a new range to this list, first unprotect the worksheet, if necessary, and then follow these steps:

1. From the Allow Users to Edit Ranges dialog box, click the New button.

2. In the New Range dialog box (see Figure 12.20), replace the generic description (Range1) in the Title box with a descriptive name.

3. Adjust the range shown in the Refers to Cells box, if necessary. By default, this box shows the address of the current selection.

4. Enter a password if you want only specific users to be able to enter data in the locked cells.

5. Click the Permissions button to choose the names of users who can enter data without supplying a password. For files stored on an NTFS-formatted drive in a Windows network, this option hooks directly into file system permissions.

Figure 12.20

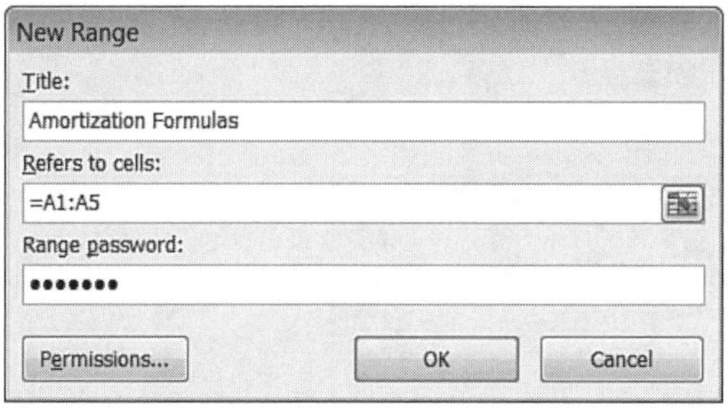

New Range
Title:
Amortization Formulas
Refers to cells:
=A1:A5
Range password:
•••••••
Permissions...   OK   Cancel

The biggest advantage of setting data-entry protection by range is that you can assign varying levels of protection to a worksheet. Lock especially important data with a supervisors-only password while opening the data-entry ranges with a password that's more widely distributed. After defining ranges that are locked for editing, you must protect the worksheet (click Format, in the Cells group of the Home tab, and then choose Protect Sheet).

You can also use cell formatting to protect cells. The Protection tab on the Format Cells dialog box (select any cell and then press Ctrl+1) includes two check boxes, which you can use, separately or in combination, to prevent changes to data and formulas in individual cells:

- Click the Locked option to lock a cell. This action prevents all users from deleting or changing the contents of that cell.

- Click the Hidden box to hide formulas within a cell. In a *hidden cell*, any user can see the results of the formula without being able to see the formula that produced that result. This option enables you to protect proprietary calculations and prevent users from being confused by particularly long and complex formulas.

→ To learn more about formatting numbers and text in your worksheets, **see** "How Cell Formatting Works," **p. 402.**

By default, all cells in a worksheet are formatted as locked but not hidden. So why can you enter data on a new worksheet? Because this formatting is disabled unless you specifically enable protection for a worksheet. To unlock a cell or range and allow editing, or to hide formulas within a cell or range, you first must make a selection and adjust its cell formatting. Because the Locked and Hidden formats are independent, you can lock a cell that contains a formula while still allowing the user to see that formula.

CAUTION

Although you can hide a formula without locking the cell in which it's stored, it's hard to imagine a scenario in which this option makes sense; with this formatting, the user could inadvertently wipe out the formula by typing in another value.

To protect the contents of the current worksheet, follow these steps:

1. Select the cells you want to unlock for editing, typically those used for data entry or notes. (Remember that all cells are locked by default on a worksheet.)

2. Click Format in the Cells group of the Home tab and then choose Format Cells (or just press Ctrl+1). In the Format Cells dialog box, click the Protection tab and clear the check mark from the Locked box.

3. Select all cells that contain formulas you want to hide.

4. Return to the Protection tab of the Format Cells dialog box and click the Hidden check box.

5. Repeat steps 1–4 for other worksheets you want to protect. Click OK to close the dialog box, and then save the workbook.

To enable protection for the current worksheet, click Format in the Cells group of the Home tab and choose Protect Sheet. The Protect Worksheet and Contents of Locked Cells box is selected by default. Add an optional password and click OK. Repeat this process for any other worksheets that you want to protect.

PROTECTING THE STRUCTURE OF A WORKBOOK

After you've assigned a password to a workbook, locked important cells, and turned on worksheet protection, your worksheet is perfectly safe, right? Wrong. A malicious or clumsy user can destroy all your careful work by deleting a worksheet from a workbook, even when it's otherwise fully protected. In fact, you can damage your own workbook if you forget the rules, and the results can be painful if you don't have a backup copy. To keep your data out of harm's way, you need to add one more level of protection.

To prevent users from changing the design of your workbook, click Protect Workbook in the Changes group of the Review tab. In the Protect Structure and Windows dialog box (see Figure 12.21), select one or all of these options:

12

Figure 12.21
Use workbook protection options to prevent users (including yourself) from deleting a worksheet or closing a window.

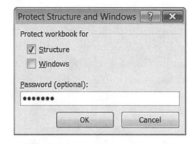

- By default, the Structure option is checked. This setting prevents users from adding or deleting worksheets, renaming sheets, or displaying sheets you've hidden.
- Click the Windows check box if your worksheet contains more than one sheet and you've arranged the individual sheets as windows in a particular size and position. When you select this setting, the Minimize, Maximize, and Close buttons on each worksheet window disappear. Any attempt to move or resize a window fails, and although users can select Arrange from the Window menu, this option has no effect.
- Add a password to prevent users from removing protection.

The Protect Workbook command in the Changes group of the Review tab becomes Unprotect Workbook after you have applied protection. To restore the capability to make changes to a workbook, click Unprotect Workbook and supply the password if required.

PUBLISHING EXCEL DATA IN WEB PAGES

Like Word and PowerPoint, Excel allows you to save files in HTML format so that you or anyone else can view them in a web browser. You can save a simple range of data, a chart, a worksheet, or an entire workbook in HTML format; when opened in a web browser, the resulting file will closely resemble the worksheet as seen in an Excel window. Some differences in formatting and appearance are inevitable because of the way that browsers display HTML code.

When saving a workbook as a web page, you must deal with the following noteworthy restrictions:

- HTML pages represent a static snapshot of the worksheet data; if you view worksheet data in a browser, you can't edit or rearrange cells or their contents.
- Gridlines and row or column headings do not appear in the browser window.

TIP

To set off rows and columns in an Excel-generated web page, don't rely on gridlines; instead, use borders to separate cells within the data area. Use shading and font formatting to set off headings, totals, and other distinctive elements.

- Some advanced features don't translate properly to HTML pages; for example, if you've saved multiple scenarios in a workbook, they'll be lost in translation, as will rotated text and some other forms of custom formatting.

 *You'll see an error message if you try to publish a password-protected workbook as a web page; **see** "Passwords Don't Work on Web Workbooks" in the "Troubleshooting" section at the end of this chapter.*

To save an entire workbook as an HTML page, click the Microsoft Office button, choose Save As, and then choose Other Formats. In the Save As dialog box, use the Save as Type drop-down list to select Single File Web Page. Give the page a name, choose a destination folder (on a local hard drive, a network server, or a web server), and click Save. Alternatively, if you want the web page to be updated automatically whenever you update the underlying worksheet, click Publish instead of Save. Select the AutoRepublish Every Time This Workbook Is Saved check box and click Publish to save the web page.

TIP

Don't forget the title. In the Save as Web Page dialog box, just above the Filename box, you'll see a space for the page title, which appears in the browser title bar and on the page itself. Excel doesn't add a title by default; click the Change button to add or edit the title.

NOTE

The option to publish web pages with interactivity has been removed from Excel 2007.

CUSTOMIZING EXCEL

One of the most useful ways to customize the Excel user interface is by modifying the Quick Access Toolbar (QAT). This toolbar, which appears initially directly above the Ribbon (you can move it below the Ribbon by right-clicking it and choosing Show Quick Access Toolbar Below the Ribbon), is intended to hold icons for the commands you use most often. Since Excel has no way of knowing what those might be, the toolbar, out of the box, has only three icons—Save, Undo, and Redo. To add or remove items, right-click the toolbar and choose Customize Quick Access Toolbar. As Figure 12.22 shows, the dialog box for tailoring the QAT includes a list of available commands on the left, and a list of commands currently on the QAT on the right. Add and Remove buttons transfer selected items from one list to the other.

Initially, the Choose Commands From drop-down menu is set to show Popular Commands. Lots of worthwhile commands are there (in the list to the left of the Add button), but many others are not. You might want to switch from Popular Commands to All Commands to see what's available. In any case, whenever you find an item that you're likely to use regularly, select it and click Add.

12

Figure 12.22
Tailoring the Quick Access Toolbar to make your most-used commands mouse-accessible should be your first customizing step.

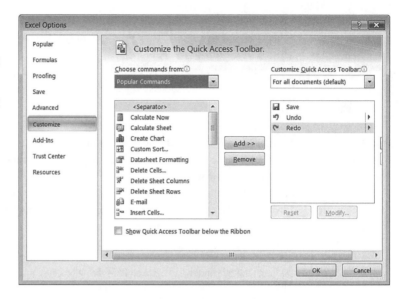

The options for tailoring the QAT appear on the Customize tab of the Excel Options dialog box. Other tabs provide dozens of additional options for adjusting the way Excel looks, acts, and works. To get to the Excel Options dialog box, click the Microsoft Office button and then click Excel Options.

Most of the options in this dialog box are self-explanatory, and many of them are variations on common features found in other Office applications. In this section, we highlight only the most useful:

→ For details of Office-wide configuration options, **see** "Configuring Common Office Features," **p. 43.**

■ To hide or show interface elements, such as the formula bar, status bar, gridlines, and scrollbars, look in the Display section of the Advanced tab. Note that options that apply to all workbooks and options that apply only to the current workbook appear in separate lists.

■ Options affecting calculation appear in two places: in the Formulas and When Calculating This Workbook sections of the Advanced tab, and also on the Formulas tab (the second tab from the top in the left pane). Don't ask why.

■ Options in the Editing Options section of the Advanced tab have a significant impact on nearly every move you make in Excel, so you should check these over carefully. Some users like the ability to edit directly in cells, for example, while others prefer the old-fashioned approach of editing only on the formula bar. Some users like the fact that Excel, by default, moves the selection down a row after you enter data in a cell; to others that's an annoyance. Spend a moment familiarizing yourself with all these choices.

TIP

> When entering currency values, such as entries in a check register, people with an accounting background often prefer to let Excel fill in the decimal point. If you choose the Automatically Insert a Decimal Point option and leave the default setting of 2 in place, entering 14398 will result in a value of 143.98. It's extremely unlikely you'll want to set this option permanently. If you use it frequently, however, create this simple toggle macro and assign it to a QAT button so you can switch into and out of fixed decimal mode on demand:
>
> ```
> Sub ToggleFixedDecimal()
>     Application.FixedDecimal = Not Application.FixedDecimal
> End Sub
> ```

- The Lotus Compatibility and Lotus Compatibility Settings For sections of the Advanced tab include options that were originally designed years ago to help Office users who had previously used Lotus 1-2-3. The Lotus Help option is gone in Excel 2007, although you can still choose to access menus Lotus-style, using the slash key.

- The option that specifies the number of worksheets that will be included in a new workbook (set by default to three) appears in the When Creating New Workbooks section of the Popular tab. You can choose any number from 1 to 255. Choose a smaller setting if you rarely use multiple sheets in a workbook or a larger one if you regularly create complex workbooks, such as consolidated budgets. In the same section of the Popular tab, you can also adjust the font that Excel uses for text and numbers in new worksheets.

TIP

> We recommend you leave the At Startup, Open All Files in the Specified Directory box (in the General section of the Advanced tab) blank. Templates and workbooks you want to load automatically should go in the XLStart folder in your personal profile instead. If you specify an alternative location, Excel loads any workbooks stored in that folder as well as those from XLStart. This feature is typically used in corporate settings to run macros and install Excel add-ins automatically from a network location.

12

- Set AutoRecover options on the Save tab. This feature works similarly to its Word counterpart.

→ For a discussion of Office AutoRecover features, **see** "Setting Up Automatic Backup and Recovery Options," **p. 77.**

- Use the Proofing tab to set spell-checking settings and AutoCorrect options.

- The Error Checking section of the Formulas tab includes settings that enable you to control background checking for common worksheet errors, including those in formulas. These options include check boxes that let you locate numbers stored as text (which can cause problems with formulas) and text dates containing two-digit years (which can result in Y2K-style date arithmetic errors).

→ For more details on how to check for errors in formulas, **see** "Troubleshooting Formulas," **p. 462.**

CHANGING DEFAULT FORMATTING FOR NEW WORKBOOKS AND WORKSHEETS

Every time you start Excel or create a new workbook without using a custom template, Excel uses its default settings. To change settings for the default workbook, create a new template called Book and save it in the XLStart folder. Follow these steps:

1. Create or open the workbook whose settings you want to use as Excel's defaults.

2. Set all formatting parameters to whatever you want to use as your new defaults. If you want to change the number of sheets or add headers and footers, go right ahead.

3. Click the Microsoft Office button, choose Save As, and choose Other Formats. In the Save as Type box, choose Excel Template, Excel Macro-Enabled Template, or Excel 97–2003 Template.

4. In the Filename box, enter **Book**. (Excel adds the appropriate extension automatically— `.xltx` for Excel Template, `.xltm` for Excel Macro-Enabled Template, or `.xlt` for Excel 97–2003 Template.) Do not save the file in the Templates folder; instead, save it in the XLStart folder. This folder is stored as part of your Windows profile, at the location %UserProfile%\AppData\Roaming\Microsoft\Excel\XLStart. It's actually easier to get there than you might think. When you start to save a template file, Excel proposes the folder %AppData%\ Microsoft\Templates. If you edit this path to replace \Templates with \Excel\XLStart, you'll be in the right place.

5. Click OK to save the template. Any future workbooks you create—after the next time you start Excel—will include the formats and content in this template.

> **NOTE**
>
> What's the difference between an Excel template and a worksheet? Structurally, the two file types are identical. Like a workbook, a template can include as many sheets as you want, with or without text, charts, and formatting. The key difference is this: When you open a workbook template from within Excel or from an Explorer window, Excel leaves the original template file undisturbed and creates a new, unnamed document that is an identical copy of the template.

EXCEL STARTUP SWITCHES

When you start Excel, it normally opens a new workbook using the default settings, runs any AutoStart macros in the Personal Macro workbook, and switches to the default location for data files. To change any of these settings, use one of the following startup switches with the Excel.exe command line. You can use any of the switches shown in Table 12.3 as part of a shortcut or type them directly at the command line.

TABLE 12.3   EXCEL STARTUP SWITCHES

Switch	Function
/e	Forces Excel to start without displaying the startup screen or creating a new workbook (Book1).
/p <folder>	Sets the active path to a folder other than the default file location; enter the folder name (with its complete path) in quotes.
/r <filename>	Forces Excel to open the specified file in read-only mode.
/s	Forces Excel to start in safe mode, bypassing all installed add-ins as well as files in the XLStart and Alternate Startup Files folders. Use this switch when debugging startup problems.

NOTE

You can use these switches in combination. For example, the command string `excel /s /r <filename>` starts Excel in safe mode with a particular file opened for read-only access.

TROUBLESHOOTING

RESETTING THE LAST CELL

I pressed Ctrl+End to go to the last cell in my worksheet, but I ended up with the insertion point in a blank cell below and to the right of the actual end of the sheet. How do I convince Excel to jump to the actual end of the sheet?

When you select the last cell in a worksheet, either by using the Go To Special dialog box or by pressing Ctrl+End, Excel actually jumps to the last cell that has ever contained data or formatting. As you've seen, that can produce unexpected results, especially if you've deleted a large number of rows or columns (or both) from a list or worksheet model, or if you once placed a range of data in an out-of-the-way location and then moved or deleted it. In that case, selecting the Last Cell option might position the insertion point in a cell that's far beyond the actual end of the sheet. To reset the sheet so you can truly jump to the last cell, all you need to do is save your file. Press Ctrl+S, and Excel recalculates the Ctrl+End target.

ADJUSTING HEADER AND FOOTER MARGINS

I created a complex custom footer for a worksheet, but when I try to print, the footer runs into data at the bottom of the sheet.

By default, Excel positions headers and footers a half-inch from the edge of the page and another half-inch from the worksheet's data. That's ideal for a one-liner, but if you try to add too much information in either place—for example, if you insert a long boilerplate paragraph required by a government agency at the bottom of each sheet—you'll quickly overrun that margin. If you decrease the Top or Bottom margins without also adjusting the

Header or Footer margins, your data might also collide. You can enter an exact measurement for any of these margins by using the Margins tab on the Page Setup dialog box (click Margins in the Page Setup group of the Page Layout tab). If you've already created the header and footer, however, it's much easier to set the margins visually. Click the Microsoft Office button, choose Print, and then choose Print Preview. In the Print Preview window select the Show Margins check box. Then drag the margin lines up or down until the preview looks right.

PASSWORDS DON'T WORK ON WEB WORKBOOKS

When I try to save a workbook as a web page, I get an error message warning that the workbook or sheet is password-protected.

For security reasons, Excel won't let you save a password-protected worksheet in HTML format. If any sheet is protected, you cannot publish that sheet or even a selection from it in HTML format. Temporarily remove the password protection by clicking Format, in the Cells group of the Home tab, and choosing Unprotect Sheet. After entering the correct password, you can publish the web page and then restore the protection.

DATA VALIDATION LIMITATIONS

I created a set of validation rules to protect data entry, but when users returned the filled-in worksheet, I found invalid data in those cells. I've triple-checked the data-validation rules, and I'm certain they're working properly. What's the problem?

Validation settings apply only when the user types data into a cell. If the user copies or cuts data from another source and pastes it into the cell via the Clipboard, Excel ignores the rule. There is no workaround for this problem, so you'll have to train your users not to use the Clipboard when filling in forms. Also, if any cell contains a formula as well as a data-validation rule, Excel ignores the rule.

If you want to triple-check the values in cells protected by data-validation rules to make sure they're correct, use the Go To dialog box. Press F5 and click the Special button, and then select the Data Validation option. Click All to see all cells with data-validation rules, or Same to see only cells whose rules match the currently selected cell.

EXTRA CREDIT: USE TEMPLATES AND CHECK OUT MICROSOFT'S TEMPLATE LIBRARY

If you create a stylish workbook that can serve as a model for future needs—a well-crafted expense-report form, for example—be sure to save that file as a template (click the Microsoft Office button, choose Save As, choose Other Formats, and then specify Excel Template in the Save as Type drop-down). You can reuse the saved template at any time thereafter by clicking the Microsoft Office button, choosing New, and selecting My Templates in the left pane of the New Workbook dialog box (your template appears in the big window at the right).

Before you go reinventing wheels, though, take a look at the library of templates available via Microsoft Office Online. You'll find attractive models there to suit all sorts of common purposes—expense forms, budget forms, calendars, purchase orders, memos, and much more (see Figure 12.23). In addition to meeting immediate needs, these templates might give you design ideas and broaden your perspective on applications for Excel.

The first time you use a Microsoft Office Online template, you'll need to download it from the web. Thereafter, the file is stored locally, and you are able to reuse it as easily as you use your own designs.

Figure 12.23
Microsoft Office Online offers a wide variety of free, down-loadable templates.

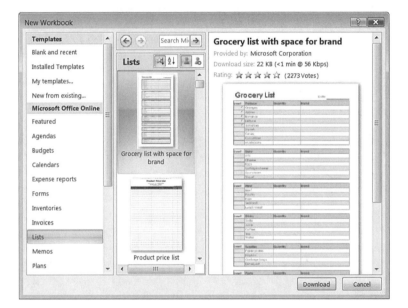

12

CHAPTER 13

MAKING GREAT-LOOKING WORKSHEETS

In this chapter

HOW CELL FORMATTING WORKS

In an Excel worksheet, what you see in a cell is not necessarily what's stored in that cell. If you enter a formula, for example, Excel stores the formula but displays its result. When entering numbers, dates, and text, you can go as quickly as you want, without too much regard for how they'll look in your worksheet; afterwards, use cell formatting instructions to specify how you want the cells' contents to display, including such details as decimal places, currency symbols, and how many digits to use for the year. Other cell formatting options enable you to adjust fonts, colors, borders, and other attributes of a cell or range.

A handful of buttons on the Home tab of the Ribbon enable you to bypass dialog boxes for some common tasks, such as choosing a font or changing a range of cells to bold. If you're building a financial worksheet, click the Currency button to ensure that every number in a given range lines up properly and includes the correct currency symbol. To see the full assortment of Excel formatting options, select a cell or range; then press Ctrl+1 to open the Format Cells dialog box. Alternatively, right-click a cell or range and choose Format Cells from the shortcut menu. (You can also get to the Format Cells dialog box from the Ribbon. On the Home tab, click the small arrow in the lower-right corner of the Font group.) All available cell formatting options are arranged on six tabs in the Format Cells dialog box.

USING THE GENERAL NUMBER FORMAT

On a new worksheet, every cell starts out using the General format. When the cell contains a constant value, Excel usually displays the exact text or numbers you entered; in cells that contain a formula, the General format displays the results of the formula using up to 11 digits—the decimal point counts as a digit. (Date and time values follow a special set of rules, as you'll see shortly.) If the cell is not wide enough to show the entire number, Excel rounds the portion of the number to the right of the decimal point, for display purposes only; if the portion of the number to the left of the decimal point won't fit in the cell or contains more than 11 digits, the General format displays the number in scientific notation.

To remove all number formats you've applied manually and restore a cell to its default General format, right-click, choose Format Cells, and then click the Number tab and choose General from the Category list.

NOTE

Although it's not particularly intuitive, there's also a keyboard shortcut that applies the General format instantly to the active cell or current selection: Press Ctrl+~ (tilde) to reset cells to General format.

CONTROLLING AUTOMATIC NUMBER FORMATS

When you enter data in a format that resembles one of Excel's built-in formats, Excel automatically applies formatting to the cell. In some cases, the results might be unexpected or unwelcome:

- If you enter a number that contains a slash (/) or hyphen (-) and matches any of the built-in Windows date and time formats, Excel converts the entry to a date serial value and formats the cell using the closest matching Date format. If the date you enter includes only the month and date, Excel adds the current year.

→ In some cases, Excel picks up formatting from your Windows version; for details of how this interaction works, **see** "Setting Date and Time Formats," **p. 411.**

 If you import data into a worksheet, Excel might convert values that look like dates or times. For suggestions on how to prevent this from occurring, see "Stopping Automatic Conversions" in the "Troubleshooting" section at the end of this chapter.

- If you enter a number preceded by a dollar sign, Excel applies the Currency style, and displays the value with two decimal places, regardless of how many decimal places you entered. (If you've used the Regional and Language Options in the Control Panel to specify a different currency symbol, Excel applies the Currency style when you enter data using that symbol.)

NOTE

> As explained later in this chapter, the Currency style is actually a variation of the Accounting format.

- If you enter a number that begins or ends with a percent sign, Excel applies the Percent style with up to two decimal places.

TIP

> Excel supports fraction formats as well, but entering data in this format is tricky. If you enter 3/8, for example, Excel interprets your entry as a date—March 8 of the current year—and formats it accordingly. To enter a fraction that Excel can recognize automatically, start with 0 and a space: 0 3/8. Excel correctly enters that number as 0.375 and changes the cell format to Fraction. Although Excel stores the number as 0.375, it is displayed as 3/8.
>
> Excel also supports compound fractions—fractions that include a whole number and a fractional number, such as 12 1/8. Enter the whole number part (in this case, 12) followed by a space and then the fraction part. Excel displays the entry as 12 1/8 but stores it as 12.125. You'll find this technique invaluable if you ever have to perform calculations involving historical stock market prices; although most major markets have now moved to decimal pricing, some historical data sources still contain data using archaic fractional pricing—16ths, 32nds, even 64ths of a dollar!

- When you enter a number that contains a colon (:), Excel converts it to a time format if possible. If the number is followed by a space and the letter *A* or *P*, Excel adds AM or PM to the display format.

- If you enter a number that contains leading zeros (as in part numbers, for example, which might need to fill a precise number of characters), Excel drops the leading zero.

13

- When you enter a number that contains the letter *E* anywhere in the middle (3.14159E19, for example), Excel formats the cell using the Scientific option, using no more than two decimal places. In this case, Excel would display 3.14E+19.

- If you enter a number that includes a comma to set off thousands or millions, Excel applies the Number format using the default thousands separator as defined in the Regional and Language Options for Windows. If the number you entered contains more than two decimal places, Excel stores the exact number you entered but rounds it for display purposes to no more than two decimal places.

To override any of these automatic number formats, you have four choices:

- After entering the data, press Ctrl+1 (or right-click the cell and choose Format Cells) and select a new format. This is your best choice if the underlying data stored in the cell is correct and you just want to use a different display format.

- Enter an apostrophe before entering the number. When you do this, Excel formats the number as text and displays it exactly as entered. Note that this solution might have unintended consequences in formulas that use the value shown in that cell!

- Enter a space character before entering the number. This prefix also tells Excel to treat the number as text or a value using the General format and display it exactly as entered. Note that this technique will not prevent Excel from converting a number to scientific notation nor will it preserve leading zeros. It will, however, work with all other automatic formatting described in the previous list.

- Click the Number format drop-down list and select Text. (The Number format drop-down is in the Home tab, at the top of the Number group. It indicates the format of the current cell; by opening it, you can quickly switch to a different format.)

AVOIDING ROUNDING ERRORS

It's tempting to assume that because numbers look so orderly in Excel's row-and-column grids, they're also unfailingly accurate. That's not exactly so. To squeeze data so that it fits in a cell, Excel rounds numbers and truncates cell contents, usually without telling you. And there's an absolute limit on the precision of Excel calculations that affects every calculation you make.

What's the difference between rounding and truncating? When Excel *rounds* a number, it changes the value displayed in the cell without affecting the underlying number stored in the cell. If you enter 3.1415926 in a cell and format it to display two decimal places, Excel displays 3.14. If you later change the display format to show all seven decimal places, your number will appear exactly as you entered it. When Excel *truncates* data, on the other hand, it chops off digits permanently. If you enter a number with more than 15 decimal places, for example, Excel lops off the 16th and any subsequent numbers to the right of the decimal point. Fortunately, Excel 2007 does not truncate characters after the 255th character in a cell if you copy a worksheet that contains cells with more than 255 characters to another. Previous versions of Excel truncated all data after the first 255 characters.

When Excel alters the display of a number, the most common cause is that the number is too long to fit in the active cell. Excel deals with this sort of data in one of the following three ways:

- When you enter data that is wider than the current cell, Excel automatically resizes the column. It does not resize a column if you have already set the column width manually. If the cell is formatted using General format, this automatic resizing stops when the number reaches 11 digits, at which point Excel converts it to scientific notation. If the cell is formatted using Number format, automatic resizing continues until the number reaches 30 digits.

- In cells using the default General format, Excel uses scientific notation to display large numbers if possible. The General format rounds numbers expressed this way to no more than six *digits of precision* (8.39615E+13, for example).

NOTE

It's no accident that the total number of characters in the preceding example—including the decimal point, plus sign, and E—is 11. Regardless of column width, cells using the General format are always limited to 11 characters.

- In cells using any number format other than General, Excel displays a string of number signs (####) if the column is too narrow to display the number in scientific notation. You must change the cell's number format or make the column wider before Excel can display the number correctly.

The second most common cause of apparent errors in a worksheet occurs when the number of decimal cells you specify in a number format doesn't match the number of decimal places stored in that cell or range. Figure 13.1, for example, shows two identical columns of numbers. Because column A uses the General format, each number appears exactly as entered. Column B, on the other hand, is formatted with the Number format to show zero decimal places. When Excel performs the calculation on the numbers in column B, it uses the actual amount stored in the cell, not the rounded version you see here. It then displays the result without any decimal places, exactly as specified in the cell format. If you calculate the sum of the rounded numbers in column B, you get 16. But in the cell beneath that column, Excel uses the SUM formula and rounds the actual result to 15 for display purposes. Because of the mismatch between the numbers and their formatting, Excel (and, by extension, the author of this worksheet) appears incapable of basic arithmetic.

That's a simple and obvious example, but subtle rounding errors can wreak havoc in an environment where you require precise results. To prevent rounding from making it look like your worksheet contains errors, always match the number of decimal places displayed with the number of decimal places you've entered in the row or column in question.

13

Figure 13.1
The values in these two columns are identical, except for the formatting. Because of cumulative rounding errors, the numbers in column B appear to add up to 16, despite what the SUM formula in B7 suggests.

	A	B
1	2.3	2
2	2.5	3
3	2.5	3
4	3.1	3
5	2.75	3
6	2.2	2
7	15.35	15

TIP

If you must use rounded numbers in a worksheet, indicate that fact in a footnote on charts and reports you plan to present to others. Rounding can cause apparent mistakes, and anyone who sees your worksheet—or a chart or presentation slide based on those numbers—might make unflattering judgments about your accuracy if totals in a pie chart, for example, don't add up to 100%.

THE LIMITS OF PRECISION

There's an overriding limit to the degree of precision you can achieve with Excel. If you enter a number that contains more than 15 significant digits, Excel permanently and irrevocably converts the 16th and subsequent digits to 0. (It doesn't matter which side of the decimal point the digits appear on—the total number of digits allowed includes those on both sides of the decimal point.) Although you can display numbers with up to 30 decimal places, your calculations will not be accurate if Excel has to store more than 15 digits.

Excel includes a useful, but extremely dangerous, option to permanently store numbers using the displayed precision. If you've increased the numbers in a budget worksheet by 8.25%, for example, you might end up with three decimal places for some entries, even though only two are displayed using the Currency format. In the Advanced section of the Excel Options dialog box (click the Microsoft Office button and then click Excel options), there's a Set Precision as Displayed check box. Selecting this check box (you'll find it under the heading When Calculating This Workbook) converts all numbers stored in the current workbook to the values actually displayed.

CAUTION

When you use the Set Precision as Displayed option, Excel displays a terse dialog box warning you that your data will permanently lose accuracy. Believe it. This option affects every cell on every sheet in the current workbook, and it remains in force until you explicitly remove the check mark from this box. If you forget you turned on this option, even simple formatting choices like changing the display of decimal places will permanently change stored data. Unless you're absolutely certain that using this option will have no unintended consequences, you should treat it like dynamite.

TIP

The Set Precision as Displayed option affects all cells in the current workbook, and there's no way to apply it just to a selected range. If you want to change the precision of a selection, use the Windows Clipboard to control this option precisely—in the process, you can also avoid any unintended ill effects. Open a new, blank workbook, copy the range you want to change from the original workbook, and paste it into the blank workbook. In the blank workbook, turn on the Set Precision as Displayed option. Click OK when you see the warning dialog box. Now copy the changed data to the Clipboard and paste it over the original data. Close the blank workbook without saving it, and you're finished.

WORKING WITH NUMBERS IN SCIENTIFIC NOTATION

Scientific (or exponential) notation displays large numbers in a shorthand form that shows the first few digits along with instructions on where to place the decimal point. To convert a number written in scientific notation to its decimal equivalent, move the decimal to the right by the number that appears after "E+"; if there's a minus sign after the E, move the decimal to the left. In either case, add extra zeros as needed. Thus, 8.23E+06 is actually 8,230,000, and 3.82E-07 is .000000382.

Numbers expressed in scientific notation are often rounded. When you see numbers in General format expressed in scientific notation, you'll see a maximum of six significant digits, even if the cell is wide enough to hold more. To display a number in scientific notation using more digits of precision, open the Format Cells dialog box and choose the Scientific option from the Category list. Use the spinner control to set a fixed number of decimal places, between 0 and 30.

ENTERING NUMBERS AS TEXT

Hands down, the most confusing option on the Number tab of the Format Cells dialog box is Text. Use this format when you want to enter numbers in a cell, but you want Excel to treat them as though they were text. You might use this format, for example, when entering a list of part numbers that you will never use in calculations.

If you apply the Text format to a cell and then enter or paste a numeric value into that cell, Excel adds a small green triangle in the top-left corner of the cell, indicating a possible error. Selecting that cell reveals a Smart Tag that warns you the number is stored as text. Use the Convert to Number option to change the cell's contents to a number format, or click Ignore Error to keep the text and make the green triangle vanish.

→ For more information about Smart Tags, **see** "Common Formatting Options," **p. 99.**

→ To learn how to check an Excel workbook for errors, **see** "Checking for Errors in a Worksheet," **p. 464.**

When you format numbers as Text, Excel ignores them in formulas such as SUM() and AVERAGE(). It also aligns the cell's contents to the left rather than the right. Unfortunately, applying the Text format requires that you work around an admitted bug that still exists in

13

Excel 2007. If you select the cells first, apply the Text format, and finally enter the numbers, Excel treats the data as text, just as you intended. However, if you try to apply the Text format to numbers that are already in your worksheet, Excel changes the alignment of the cell, but not the data stored there. After applying the Text format, you must click in each reformatted cell, press F2, and then press Enter to store the number as text. The error-checking tools in Excel 2007 do not identify cells formatted this way, either.

If you format a cell as text and enter a formula in that cell, you see the formula itself rather than its result. To fix the display, change the cell format back to General, select the cell, press F2, and then press Enter.

CHANGING FORMATTING FOR A CELL OR RANGE

In general, as noted previously, Excel stores exactly what you type in a cell. You have tremendous control over how that data appears, however. Number and date formats, for example, give you control over commas, decimal points, and whether months and days are spelled out or abbreviated. And if you can't find the precise format you're looking for, Excel enables you to create your own custom format.

SETTING NUMBER FORMATS

How should Excel display the contents of a cell? You have dozens of choices, all neatly organized by category on the Number tab of the Format Cells dialog box. Many of these are also available on the Ribbon in the Number group of the Home tab. To specify exactly how you want the contents of a cell or range to appear, follow these steps:

1. Select the cell or range you want to format. Then press Ctrl+1 to open the Format Cells dialog box.

   TIP

   > Few keyboard shortcuts in all of Office are as useful as Ctrl+1, which opens the formatting dialog box for whatever is currently selected. If a cell or range is selected, Ctrl+1 opens the Format Cells dialog box. If a chart element is selected, the shortcut opens the formatting dialog box for that chart element, and so on. When you're formatting a large or complex worksheet, this key combination can save a startling number of mouse clicks. Even if you generally don't use keyboard shortcuts, this one is worth memorizing. Note that you must use the number 1 on the top row of the keyboard; the 1 on the numeric keypad won't work.

2. In the Format Cells dialog box, choose an entry from the Category list on the left.

3. If the category you selected includes predefined display options, select one from the Type list. Adjust other format options (currency symbol, decimal point, and so on), if necessary.

TIP

> To quickly adjust the number of decimal points in a cell or range, make a selection and click the Increase Decimal or Decrease Decimal buttons, in the Number group of the Home tab. Each click adds or subtracts one decimal point from the selection.

4. Inspect the Sample box in the upper-right corner of the dialog box to see how the active cell will appear with the format settings you've selected. Click OK to accept the settings and return to the editing window.

The following number format categories are available:

- General, the default format, displays numbers as entered, using as many decimal places as necessary, up to a maximum of 11 digits. It does not include separators between thousands. No additional options are available.

- Number formats let you specify the number of decimal places, from 0 to 30 (the default is 2), as well as an optional separator for thousands, based on the Windows Regional and Language Options. (see Figure 13.2).

Figure 13.2

- Choices in the Currency category display values using the default currency symbol, as specified in the Regional and Language Options section of the Control Panel. (see Figure 13.3).

Figure 13.3

- Accounting formats are similar to those in the Currency category, except that currency symbols and decimal points align properly in columns and you can't choose a format for negative values. With Accounting formats, the currency symbol ($ in U.S. English installations) sits at the left edge of the cell. This effect can be odd in wide columns that contain small numbers; in that case, choose a Currency format instead, if possible (see Figure 13.4).

Figure 13.4

13

■ The Date category includes 15 formats that determine whether and how to display day, date, month, and year. All versions of Excel since Excel 2000 include a pair of Year 2000–compatible date formats that use four digits for the year (see Figure 13.5).

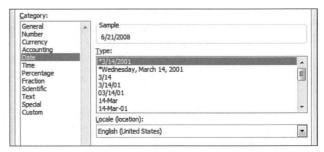

Figure 13.5

■ The Time category includes eight formats that determine whether and how to display hours, minutes, seconds, and a.m./p.m. designators (see Figure 13.6).

Figure 13.6

■ Applying the Percentage format multiplies the cell value by 100 for display purposes and adds a percent symbol; the only option here enables you to specify the number of decimal places, from 0 to 30 (the default is 2).

■ Fraction formats store numbers in decimal format but displays cell contents as fractions using any of 9 predefined settings; to display stock prices using 8ths, 16ths, and 32nds, click Up to Two Digits in the Type list (see Figure 13.7).

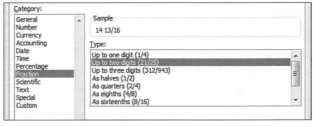

Figure 13.7

■ Choose Scientific to display numbers in scientific notation; you select the number of decimal places, from 0 to 30.

■ Applying the Text format displays cell contents exactly as entered, even if the cell contains numbers or a formula.

13

- The four choices in the Special category allow you to select formats for long and short U.S. ZIP Codes, phone numbers, and Social Security numbers. You enter the number without any punctuation, and Excel adds hyphens and parentheses as necessary for display purposes only (see Figure 13.8).

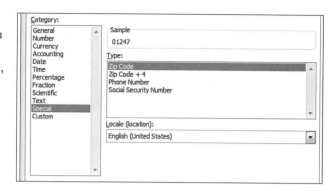

Figure 13.8

- Choose the Custom option to define your own display rules. Start with a built-in format and use symbols in the formatting instructions; see "Custom Number Formats" later in this chapter for more details on custom number formats.

SETTING DATE AND TIME FORMATS

Normally, Excel stores exactly what you type into a cell. That's not the case when you type a recognizable date or time, however; when storing date and time information, Excel first converts the value you enter into *serial date format*. This numeric transformation explains how Excel can perform calculations using date and time information. Understanding the following facts is crucial to working effectively with serial date formats:

- Excel converts the date to a whole number that counts the number of days that have elapsed since January 1, 1900. Thus, the serial date value of December 31, 2007 is 39447.

- When you enter a time (hours, minutes, and seconds), Excel converts it to a fractional decimal value between 0 (midnight) and 0.999988 (11:59:59 p.m.). If you enter a time of 10:00 a.m., for example, Excel stores it as 0.416667.

- If you combine a date and time, Excel combines the serial date and time values. Thus, Excel saves December 31, 2007 10:00 a.m. as 39447.416667.

NOTE

> When you enter only a date, Excel converts it to a serial value and uses 0 (or 12:00 a.m.) as the time value. If you enter only a time, Excel tacks on a date value of 0; if you later format this cell to show the date and time, Excel displays the nonsense date 1/0/1900.

13

The transformation to a serial value happens as soon as you enter a date or time value in a cell; at the same time, Excel automatically applies the default Date or Time format to your cell so that the data you enter displays correctly. You can choose a different Date or Time format to change the display format of date or time values. If you change the format of the cell to General or Number, however, you will see the serial values instead of the dates you expect.

Conversely, if you accidentally apply the Date format to a cell that contains a number, the result is likely to be nonsense, especially if the number is relatively low. Choose the General or Number format to display the cell's contents correctly.

TIP

> If the display of dates is important to you, be aware of the unusual interaction between Excel's date and time formats and those you define in the Regional and Language Options section of the Windows Control Panel. These linked formats appear at the top of the Date and Time lists in the Format Cells dialog box, with an asterisk in front of the format. When you change the date format in Windows, the format in your worksheet changes, too—if you've used one of these formats.

Excel transforms dates and times to serial values so you can use them in calculations. Because date and time values are stored as numbers, you can easily enter formulas that calculate elapsed time. If you include a student's birth date as part of a list, for instance, you can use a simple formula to compare that value to today's date and determine whether the student is old enough for a program that is restricted to children who are at least 13 years old. If you enter start and end times for each participant in a road race, you can easily calculate the total elapsed time and determine the top finishers.

After you enter the student's birth date in C1 and your report date in C2, for example, you can calculate the difference between the two dates by using the formula =C1-C2.

TIP

> Unfortunately, Excel outsmarts itself when you use this type of formula. Because it sees dates in both cells used in the formula, it automatically applies a date format to the cell containing the formula. As a result, the cell contents display as a nonsense date. Reset the cell's format to General or Number to correctly display the difference between the dates.

To use a date directly in a formula, enclose it in quotation marks first: =Today()-"1/1/2007" counts the number of days that have elapsed since January 1, 2007, for instance.

NOTE

> The Advanced section of the Excel Options dialog box includes a setting for the 1904 date system. This obscure option is necessary only when exchanging files with users of old versions of Excel for the Macintosh, which started the calendar at the beginning of 1904 rather than 1900. Mac Excel versions since Excel 98 handle this conversion seamlessly. Under normal circumstances, you should never need to use this option.

EXCEL AND YEAR 2000 ISSUES

The much-feared global Y2K crisis never happened. Planes continued to fly, power stations hummed along, and banks didn't run out of money. Yes, the world successfully entered the new millennium, but that doesn't let you off the hook when it comes to Year 2000 (Y2K) issues. Excel's default settings correctly handle most formulas that include dates from different centuries. But a few "gotchas" linger for the unwary:

- When you enter a date before January 1, 1900, in an Excel worksheet, the date appears as text. As far as Excel is concerned, dates before the 20th century simply don't exist— that's bad news for students of history, and scientists hoping to use Excel to plot dates that go back more than a century.

- On the other hand, dates after December 31, 1999, don't represent a problem. In fact, Excel worksheets will accept any date through December 31, 9999 (that's a serial date value of 2958465, if you want to try it for yourself).

TIP

> If you need to track timelines and perform calculations for dates before the beginning of 1900 (to chart long-term records of earthquake activities, for example), you'll need to provide some help for Excel. One solution is John Walkenbach's excellent Extended Date Functions Add-in (http://j-walk.com/ss/excel/files/xdate.htm). It handles date arithmetic all the way back to the year 100 C.E. If you're a student of ancient history, you'll need to use another program—or perhaps you can make do with clay tablets.

Because Excel stores dates as serial values, it is unaffected by most garden-variety Y2K problems. In practice, however, you might encounter Y2K problems if you enter or import data that includes only two digits for the year. When Excel encounters dates in this format, it has to convert the year to four digits; in the process, it's possible to select the wrong century. When translating two-digit years, Excel uses the following rules:

- Excel automatically converts dates entered using the two-digit years 00 through 29 to the years 2000 through 2029. Thus, if you enter or import the value 5/23/04, Excel stores it as serial value 38130, or May 23, 2004.

- When you enter the two-digit years 30 through 99 as part of a date, Excel converts the dates using the years 1930 through 1999. Thus, when you enter or import the value 9/29/55, Excel stores it as serial value 20361, or September 29, 1955.

On a new worksheet, Excel automatically displays dates using a four-digit format. However, if you design a worksheet so that some dates display only two years (or if you use an older worksheet that was designed using those formats), you might not realize that Excel has stored the wrong data. In that case, any calculations you make might be off by a full century. To avoid inadvertently entering or importing incorrect data, get in the habit of entering all dates using four-digit formats for the year: 5/23/2004. Excel stores this date correctly regardless of the Date format you've chosen for display purposes.

When importing data that includes dates with two-digit years, check the format of the original data carefully. You might need to manually edit some dates after importing. Pay special attention to worksheets that were originally created using pre-2000 versions of Excel for Windows or the Macintosh, because the algorithms those programs use to convert two-digit years are different from those in Excel 2000 and later versions.

The automatic date conversion routine is a clever workaround, but don't rely on it. Entering or importing two-digit years is guaranteed to cause problems in the following circumstances:

- In the banking industry, in which dates beyond 2029 are common in 30- and 40-year mortgages that begin in the year 2000 or later. If you enter the start date as 2/1/06 and the end date as 2/1/36, your loan will start out 70 years overdue.

- In any group that includes milestone dates—birthdays, graduation dates, and so on—for an older population. If you enter a birth date of 6/19/27, your worksheet might assume that the person in question isn't born yet.

TIP

> This can't be said strongly enough or repeated too often: Get in the habit of using four-digit years whenever you enter or display a date in a worksheet. Excel 2007 makes this easy, by automatically displaying dates you enter with a two-digit year in a four-digit format. If you must enter dates the short way, be sure to look at the result displayed in the cell to verify that it's what you intended.

CREATING CUSTOM CELL FORMATS

If the exact number format you need isn't in Excel's collection of built-in formats, create a custom format. Custom formats enable you to specify the display of positive and negative numbers as well as zero values; you can also add text to the contents of any cell.

TIP

> Excel saves custom number formats in the workbook in which you create them. To reuse formats, add them to the template on which you base new workbooks. To copy cell formats from one workbook to another, copy the cell that contains the custom format, click in the workbook where you want to add the format and choose Paste Special from the Paste drop-down, at the left edge of the Home tab. (Alternatively, right-click where you want to paste and then choose Paste Special from the context menu.)

The list of 35 custom formats in the Type box includes some that are already available within other categories, as well as a few you won't find elsewhere. It's almost always easier to design a custom format if you start with one that already exists. To create a custom number format, open the Format Cells dialog box and choose the format with which you want to start. Then click Custom at the bottom of the Category list. Excel displays the codes for the format you just selected in the Type box, ready for you to modify. The example shown in Figure 13.9, for example, shows the results when we chose a Currency format and changed the symbol from the U.S. dollar sign to the Euro. Although the switches for these codes are undocumented, this technique adds them to the Type box, making it easy to define a new format that uses this symbol correctly.

Figure 13.9
Enter custom format codes here. Note the Sample area, which shows how the contents of the active cell will appear.

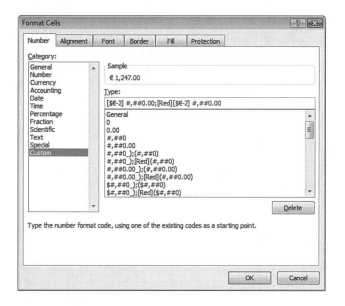

Custom formats use format codes to tell Excel how to display digits, decimal places, dates and times, and other details. Each custom format can include up to four sections, separated by semicolons. Using all four sections defines display formats for positive numbers, negative numbers, zero values, and text, respectively. If you enter only two sections, Excel uses the first set of instructions for positive numbers and zero values and the second for negative numbers. If you enter only one section, that format will apply to all numbers you enter. You don't need to enter a format for each section, but if you plan to skip a format option (specifying formats only for positive numbers and zero values, for example), insert a semicolon for each section you skip.

TIP

> When creating an extremely complex custom format, working with the narrow text box in the Format Cells dialog box can be difficult. To make life easier, select the contents of this box and then copy them to a friendlier editor, such as Notepad or Word. Edit the format codes and then use the Clipboard to paste the results back into the dialog box.

13

Creative use of custom number formats can help you deal with tricky data-entry challenges. For example, how do you make it easy to enter a serial number with leading zeros? Say you are building a list of serial numbers that must be exactly seven digits, with no exceptions. If the number you enter includes fewer than seven digits, you want Excel to pad the beginning of the entry with as many zeros as it takes to reach that magic number. Entering a number like 0001234 won't work, because Excel considers the leading zeros insignificant digits and strips them before storing the value in the cell.

The solution is to create a custom format that includes a zero for each digit you want to include in the displayed result—in this case, 0000000.

> **TIP**
>
> To guarantee that only correct data appears in the cell, combine this custom format with a data-validation rule. If a valid serial number must be larger than 1000, create a validation rule that restricts data entry to whole numbers (to prevent stray decimal points or text from messing up the list) between 1001 and 9999999. The all-zeros display format guarantees that any data within this range will display as exactly seven digits, with leading zeros if necessary.

CUSTOM NUMBER FORMATS

Custom number formats enable you to round or truncate numbers, control the number of decimal places or significant digits, and make sure amounts line up properly in columns. Use the codes shown in Table 13.1 to define the display format.

TABLE 13.1   CUSTOM NUMBER FORMAT CODES

Code	What It Does	How You Use It
#	Displays significant digits	Using the format #.# displays all significant (nonzero) digits to the left of the decimal point and rounds to one digit on the right of the decimal point; if you enter 0.567, this format displays .6.
0	Displays zero if the number has fewer digits than the decimal points; for numbers below 1, it includes a 0 to the left of the decimal point.	The format 0.000 always displays exactly three number to format.
?	Aligns decimal points or fractions	Click any of Excel's built-in Fraction formats and then choose Custom to see an example of how to use this placeholder.
.	Decimal point	To round the cell's contents to a whole number, leave off the decimal point.

Code	What It Does	How You Use It
,	Displays thousands separator or scales number by multiple of 1,000	Inserting two commas after a number scales it by a million; to display a large number (163,200,000) in an easier-to-read style (163.2 MM), enter this format: `#0.0,," MM"`.
%	Displays the number as a percentage of 100	If you enter 8, Excel displays it as `800%`. To display `8%`, start with a decimal point and a zero: `.08`.
[color]	Shows the cell contents in the specified color	Choose one of eight colors—Black, Blue, Cyan, Green, Magenta, Red, White, Yellow—for any section; you must use brackets and enter the color as the first item in each section, like this: `[Blue]#,##0;[Red] #,##0;[Black]0`.

CUSTOM DATE AND TIME FORMATS

Excel's selection of ready-made date and time formats is extensive, but you might want to create your own in several situations. For example, if you're doing volunteer work for an organization that uses a special date format to identify dates on reports, you can enter a format such as yyyymmdd to display a date as `20050321`.

Custom date and time formats are also useful if you need to keep track of time that volunteers spend on a project by the minute or hour, or if you've captured data from time sheets that include starting and ending times for shifts. Table 13.2 includes examples of date and time codes you can add to custom formats.

TABLE 13.2   CUSTOM DATE/TIME FORMAT CODES

Code	What It Does	How You Use It
d, dd, m, mm	Day or month in numeric format, with or without columns of dates	Use the leading zero when you want leading zeros to line up properly; to add a zero to the date only, use this format: m/dd/yyyy.
ddd, mmm, dddd, mmmm	Day or month in text format, abbreviated or full	Use ddd or mmm to show abbreviations such as Wed or Jan; use dddd and mmmm for the fully spelled out month or day: January and Wednesday.
mmmmm	Month as first letter only	Potentially confusing because it's impossible to distinguish between January, June, and July, or between March and May.
yy, yyyy	Year, in two- or four-digit format	If you're concerned about possible confusion caused by the year 2000, specify four-digit years.

13

continues

TABLE 13.2 CONTINUED

Code	What It Does	How You Use It
h, hh, m, mm, s, ss	Hours, minutes, or seconds, with or without leading zero	Use a leading zero with minutes and seconds; to store precise times, add a decimal point and extra digits after the format: `h:mm:ss.00`.
A/P, AM/PM	Show AM/PM indicator	Insert after time code to use 12-hour clock and display AM or PM (6:12 p.m.); otherwise, Excel displays the time in 24-hour format (18:12).
[h], [m], [s]	Show elapsed time in hours, minutes, or seconds	Add brackets to display elapsed time rather than a time of day. Add decimals for seconds; for instance, for a worksheet containing race times, use this format: `[m]:ss.00`.

ADDING TEXT TO A CELL

To display text in a cell that contains numbers, Excel includes a selection of special format codes. Use this type of format to add a word such as *shortage* or *deficit* after a negative number, for example. Because the format doesn't change the contents of the cell, the number you entered will still work in formulas that reference that cell.

You can add the space character, left and right single quotation mark, and any of the following special characters without enclosing them in double quotation marks:

$ - + / ( ) : ! ¢ & ~ { } = < >

To add other text to a cell, use the codes in Table 13.3.

TABLE 13.3 CUSTOM TEXT FORMAT CODES

Code	What It Does	How You Use It
*	Repeats characters to fill cell to column width	Enter an asterisk followed by the character you want to repeat. Use `*-` in the third position of a custom format to replace zero values with a line of hyphens, for example.
_ (underscore character)	Adds a space the width of a specified character	Enter an underscore followed by the character whose width you want to use. Several built-in formats use `_)` with positive number formats, for example, to make sure they line up properly with negative numbers that use parentheses.

Code	What It Does	How You Use It
\	Displays the character that follows the backslash	To add a space and the letter *P* or *L* after a positive or negative value, use this format: `#,##0_) \P;[Red] (#,##0) \L`.
"text"	Displays the text you enter inside the double quotation marks	Remember to add a space inside the quotes when necessary. For example, to display a negative amount as $514.32 Loss in red, enter this format: `$0.00" Profit";[Red] $0.00" Loss"`.
@	Displays the text entered in the cell	Use this code only in the fourth (text) section in a custom format to combine the entered text with other text. If you include a text section without the @ character, Excel hides any text in the cell.

TIP

> When creating a custom number format, first click in a cell that contains data you want to see in the new format. As you edit the custom format, the Sample region of the Format Cells dialog box shows you how the active cell's contents will appear in the new format.

ADDING CONDITIONS TO A DISPLAY FORMAT

You can also use *conditions* as part of custom number formats. Conditions use comparison operators and are contained in brackets as part of a format definition. Look at the built-in Phone Number format (in the Special category) to see how this option works:

```
[<=9999999]###-####;(###) ###-####
```

If you enter a number of seven or fewer digits in a cell that uses this format, Excel treats it as a local phone number and adds a hyphen where the prefix appears. If you enter a number greater than seven digits, Excel uses the second part of the format, displaying the last seven digits as a phone number and any number of digits prior to that number as an area code in parentheses.

The results of this format can be absurd if you enter a number that's smaller than 7 digits or larger than 10 digits. Here's how to use conditions to customize this format. The example shown here assumes you live or work in the 212 area code and want to add that code to the beginning of any 7-digit (local) number; if the number uses more than 10 digits, the default condition at the end kicks in, adding the international dialing prefix (+011) and splitting the digits before the number into country and city codes.

```
[<=9999999](212) ###-####;[<=9999999999](###) ###-####;"+011 "(#-##) ###-####
```

13

TIP

> Don't confuse these custom formats with conditional formatting, which is described later in this chapter, in the section "Using Conditional Formatting to Identify Key Values." If you want to change the font or color of text based on values displayed in the cell, use the Conditional Formatting option in the Styles group of the Home tab (described later in this chapter). The conditional display formats shown here are most useful when you want to subdivide a number with punctuation marks or change the number of digits displayed. You can effectively combine this type of format with conditional formatting—for example, if the user enters a phone number with six or fewer digits, you might display it in red to help it stand out as a possibly invalid number.

DESIGNING AND FORMATTING A WORKSHEET FOR MAXIMUM READABILITY

If you simply enter data into a new worksheet without adjusting any formatting first, every cell will look exactly the same, and anyone reading the worksheet will be forced to work to pick out the important details. Want to make it easier on your audience? Set off different regions of a worksheet by using custom cell formatting—larger, bolder fonts for headings, for example, plus borders around the data area with a double line to mark where the data range ends and the totals begin. Carefully resetting row heights and column widths, wrapping and slanting text, and adding background shading can make the entire sheet easier to follow.

CHANGING FONTS AND CHARACTER ATTRIBUTES

The default worksheet font is fine for basic data entry, but for any worksheet more complex than a simple list you'll probably want to adjust fonts to squeeze more data onto printed pages while beefing up titles, totals, and category headings with larger, bolder fonts.

If you select a cell or range, you can apply font formatting to the entire contents of the selection. You can also apply different fonts, font sizes, colors, and font attributes to different words or characters in the same cell. In either case, you can use the Font and Font Size drop-downs in the Font group of the Home tab. You can also open the Format Cells dialog box and click the Font tab (see Figure 13.10) for access to all font formats, including some options you won't find on the Ribbon, such as strikethrough and double underline attributes.

Most of the options on the Font tab of this dialog box are straightforward. The Normal font check box deserves some explanation, however. When you add custom font formatting in any way—for example, by switching to italics or adding a Strikethrough effect, you automatically clear the Normal Font check box. You can remove all such formatting at once by checking this box again.

 If you're having trouble restoring default font formatting to a cell, see "Click Twice for Normal" in the "Troubleshooting" section at the end of this chapter.

Figure 13.10
Options on the Font tab let you format an entire cell or selected words or characters within a cell.

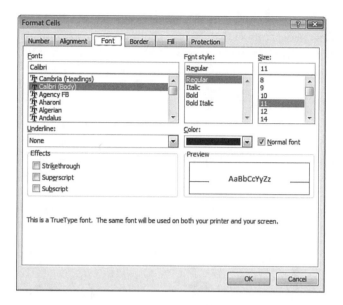

You'll find countless uses for rich formatting within cells. The range shown in Figure 13.11, for example, uses different font formatting for the ISBN number and title in a list of classic books. This feature is also a useful way to insert trademark and copyright symbols and other special characters within a cell.

Figure 13.11
You can mix and match font formatting within a cell to emphasize one type of data over another.

NOTE

To enter a manual line break within a cell, position the insertion point at the spot where you want the break to appear and press Alt+Enter. Unfortunately, there's no easy way to copy rich formatting from one cell to another. If you use the Format Painter or the Clipboard to copy formats, only the first font is copied.

An obscure check box on the Alignment tab of the Format Cells dialog box actually has a major effect on formatting. Click the Shrink to Fit check box when you want Excel to automatically adjust the font size when the contents of a cell are too wide to fit. This option doesn't change the formatting applied to the cell; it changes the scaling instead. If you enter more text or adjust the width of the column, Excel automatically changes the size of the font used to display the contents so that you can continue to see its contents. Use this option with care—if you format an entire column as Shrink to Fit and then fill it with data that varies in length, the results can look like a ransom note.

FORMATTING WITH CELL STYLES

The Cell Styles button, in the Styles group of the Home tab, opens a gallery of well-designed formatting options that you can apply to any cell or range. As Figure 13.12 shows, the gallery is divided, initially, into five groups, called Good, Bad and Neutral; Data and Model, Titles and Headings; Themed Cell Styles; and Number Format. (The last of these is a redundancy; the options here are equivalent to their namesakes in the Format Cells dialog box.) You can also create your own styles, using the New Cell Style command near the bottom of the gallery. If you do, a sixth category, called Custom, appears in the Gallery.

Figure 13.12
The Cell Styles gallery enables you to assign well-designed formatting attributes with a single mouse click. Live Preview lets you see the effect of styles before you leave the gallery.

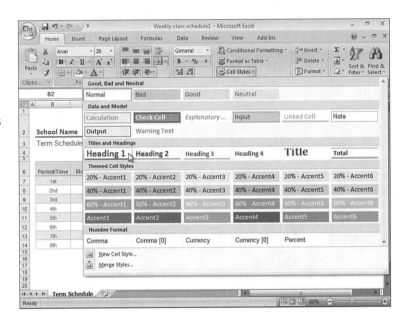

The principal reasons you might want to use cell styles are

- Cell styles make effective use of the colors and fonts specified in the current Theme. Therefore they can help you achieve design consistency within a workbook or across multiple workbooks.

- Cell styles are easy to use; a single click in the gallery applies a combination of formatting attributes.

- Cell styles make it easy to change your mind. If you have many headings in a worksheet that use the Heading 1 style, for example, and you decide you want all of these headings to be a little larger, you can right-click Heading 1 in the Cell Styles gallery, click Modify, and then express your preferences in the dialog box that appears. All cells to which you have assigned the modified style will be updated at once.

NOTE

> Cell styles are keyed to the current theme. If you change the theme (by opening the Themes drop-down at the left edge of the Page Layout tab), the formatting attributes of the cell styles change accordingly.

The biggest disadvantage to cell styles is that they can't be linked with Excel's conditional formatting rules. The styles in the Good, Bad and Neutral group, for example, are handy for flagging numbers that need—or don't need—attention. But you might find it more effective to flag such numbers with conditional formatting rules (a feature that is discussed later in this chapter). Cell styles are static; conditional formats are dynamic.

On the other hand, the styles in the Titles and Headings group, as well as those in the Themed Cell Styles group, generally don't suffer from being static, because they're generally applied to text rather than numbers. Using the Titles and Headings group is a great way to put attractive headlines on your worksheet, and the Themed Cell Styles can help you delineate various functional sections of a model.

ADDING YOUR OWN STYLES TO THE GALLERY

Using the New Cell Style command near the bottom of the Cell Styles gallery, you can create your own custom cell styles. The easiest way to do this is by formatting a cell or range on the worksheet with the desired attributes before you click the New Cell Style command. If you work this way—creating a "style by example"—the Style dialog box (see Figure 13.13) will be filled out correctly for you, and all you might need to do is provide a name for the new style and click OK. (Be sure to look over the check boxes first, though. If you don't need the Number format to be part of the style definition, for example, clear the Number check box before clicking OK.)

If your "style by example" specification doesn't perfectly exemplify the style you want to create, click the Format button in the Style dialog box. This takes you to the familiar Format Cells dialog box, where you can make the necessary adjustments.

MERGING STYLES

Custom cell styles are workbook-specific. If you want to reuse custom styles that you've defined in a different workbook, you can merge those styles with the styles of the current workbook. Open the workbook that includes the styles you want to reuse, switch to the workbook in which you want to reuse them, open the Cell Styles gallery, and click Merge Styles. The Merge Styles dialog box lists the names of open workbooks; select the one that has the style definitions you want to copy, and click OK.

13

Figure 13.13
You can create your own custom styles, either "by example" or by clicking Format in this dialog box and specifying the formatting attributes that will define your style.

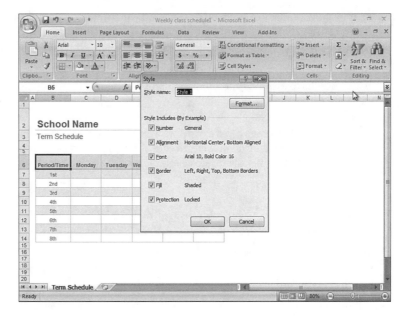

ALIGNING, WRAPPING, INDENTING, AND ROTATING TEXT AND NUMBERS

When you use the default General format, cells containing text align to the left, and those with numbers align to the right. You can change the alignment of any cell or range by using the Align Left, Center, and Align Right buttons in the Alignment group of the Home tab.

Use the Wrap Text button in the Alignment group (or on the Alignment tab of the Format Cells dialog box) to handle long strings of text that don't fit in a cell. Wrapped text is useful for column headings that are much longer than the data in the column. You can also use wrapped text to create tables, where each cell in a row holds an entire paragraph. Excel wraps text to additional lines automatically, maintaining the column width you specified. To control the location of each break, place your cursor where you want the break and press Alt+Enter. To use text wrapping, follow these steps:

1. Select the cell or range that contains the text you want to wrap.

2. Click Wrap Text, in the Alignment group of the Home tab.

3. Adjust the vertical alignment if needed, using the Top Align, Middle Align, and Button Align buttons, in the Alignment group of the Home tab.

Two other alignment options can help make worksheets easier to read. You can change the orientation of a column heading to any angle, including straight up or down. Slanting column headings can save space and give tables a professional look when you have narrow columns with lengthy titles. To help set off groups of items in a column, indent the cells in second and subsequent levels. (See the before and after worksheets at the end of this chapter for examples of all these alignment options.) This option is especially useful when you want to distinguish subheadings from headings at the beginning of a row.

To indent a cell or range of cells, follow these steps:

1. Select the cell or range you want to format, right-click, and choose Format Cells.

2. Click the Alignment tab. In the Text Alignment section, click the Horizontal drop-down list and choose Left (Indent).

3. Use the Indent spinner to select the indent level for the selection. For each number, Excel adds approximately as much space as a capital M (see Figure 13.14).

Figure 13.14
For the outline levels in column A, we used settings of 1 and 2, respectively.

	A
1	**Expenses**
2	**Payment & Benefits**
3	*Salaries*
4	*Payroll Taxes*
5	*Benefits*
6	*Insurance*
7	**Travel & Entertainment**
8	*Travel*
9	*Entertainment*
10	**Capital Budget**
11	*Equipment*
12	*Computer Equipment*
13	**Office Expenses**
14	*Office Supplies*
15	*Printing and Copying*
16	*Telephone and Fax*
17	*Postage and Delivery*
18	**Real Estate Costs**
19	*Rent*
20	*Liabilities*
21	*Maintenance*
22	**Consultants and Professional Fees**

4. Click OK to accept the changes and return to the worksheet.

TIP

Often the quickest way to indent a set of contiguous cells is to select them and click Increase Indent in the Alignment group of the Home tab.

To change the orientation of column headings so that they slant up or down, click the Orientation button in the Alignment group of the Home tab. The following angle options appear when you click the Orientation button:

- Angle Counterclockwise
- Angle Clockwise
- Vertical Text
- Rotate Text Up

13

- Rotate Text Down
- Format Cell Alignment

Use the last of these if none of the others meet your needs. When you choose Format Cell Alignment, Excel displays the Alignment tab of the Format Cells dialog box (see Figure 13.15). You can use the Orientation control in this dialog box to set your text at any angle you desire.

Figure 13.15
You can drag the Text line in the Orientation control to any desired angle. Or you can use the spinner to specify an angle in degrees. Click the vertical "Text" to stack letters above one another.

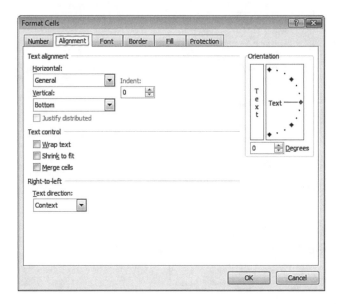

TIP

> Word doesn't allow you to position headings using any orientation except horizontal or vertical. If you want to add a table with slanted headings to a Word document, create the table in Excel and then use Paste Special and choose Microsoft Excel Worksheet Object to embed the worksheet range, complete with slanted headings.

13

USING BORDERS, BOXES, AND COLORS

You can create a distinctive identity for sections of a worksheet by using borders, boxes, and background colors. Dark backgrounds and white type help worksheet titles stand out. Soft, light background colors make columns of numbers easier to read. Use alternating colors or shading to make it easy for the eye to tell which entries belong in each row, especially on a wide worksheet that contains many columns of data.

TIP

> When preparing a worksheet that you intend to print on a black-and-white printer, test different color combinations. Use the printout to decide which colors are best for you. Sometimes, for example, it's easier to read black type on a light yellow background (which appears gray) than on a background on which you specify a shade of gray.

The Borders, Fill Color, and Font Color buttons in the Font group of the Home tab work much as you would expect. After selecting a cell or range, click the arrow to the right of each button to choose a specific option from the drop-down list.

These buttons don't give you access to every formatting option, however. For maximum control over borders and colors, first select the cells or range you want to format; then right-click and choose Format Cells. Click the Border tab (see Figure 13.16) to add and remove lines around the selection.

Figure 13.16
The Borders tab of the Format Cells dialog box gives you fine control over lines between and around cells or ranges.

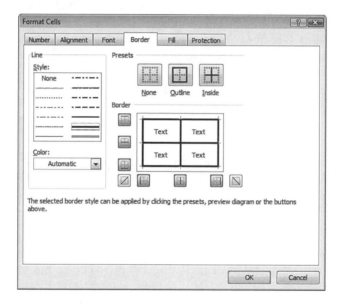

To create custom borders, follow these steps:

1. Before you add any lines, choose a line style—thick, thin, doubled, dotted, or dashed—from the Style box at the left.

2. Choose a different border color, if you like, from the Color drop-down list. Colors are most effective with thick lines.

3. Click the Outline button to add lines in the thickness and color you specified on all four sides of the active cell. If you selected a range, click Outline to draw a box around the range and click Inside to draw borders around every cell in the selection.

13

4. Click any of the buttons in the Border section to add one line at a time, on the left, right, top, or bottom of the cell, or diagonally. Click again to remove the line. The preview area shows which edges currently have borders.

NOTE

> You can also click directly on lines in the preview area to add or remove borders.

5. You can mix and match line styles and colors, even on different borders of the same cell. Click the line style or change the color and then click the button in the Border area to change the style.

6. Click OK to close the Format Cells dialog box and return to the worksheet.

Getting borders just right on a complex worksheet often takes multiple iterations. The trick is figuring out which regions need separate formatting and which have common borders. For example, you might need to select the entire data area first to add a thick border around the outside. Then select the heading rows to adjust their borders, which might be thinner and lighter. Select the data area next, to add, remove, and format interior rules between rows and columns that contain data. Finally, if your data area contains a totals row at the bottom, select that row (or the last row of data) to add a double line between the end of the data range and the totals.

MERGING CELLS

On a highly structured worksheet, merging cells can help you show the relationship between headings and subheadings. In a list where two or three rows have the same value in the first column, for example, you could merge those cells to make the common nature of those rows truly stand out. You can combine adjacent cells in a row, a column, or any contiguous range.

To quickly merge two or more cells, select the cells and click the Merge and Center button in the Alignment group of the Home tab. Excel displays a dialog box warning you that when you merge cells, you will lose all data except the contents of the top-left cell in the selection. Click OK to continue or click Cancel if you want to back out and move the data before you lose it.

To edit text in a merged cell, click in the cell and begin typing. You can also change the alignment of the merged cells to left or right, without changing the merge.

You might encounter problems when you try to cut and paste merged cells, or when you attempt to sort a list that contains a merged cell. To restore the merged cells to their normal position on the grid, click the drop-down arrow beside the Merge and Center button and choose Unmerge Cells.

13

CHANGING ROW HEIGHT AND COLUMN WIDTH

On a new worksheet, every row is exactly 12.75 points high, and every column is 8.43 characters wide. (If the default font is a proportional one such as Arial, Excel uses a lowercase x as the character to measure.) As you design a worksheet and fill it with data, however, you'll need to change the size of rows and columns. A column that contains only two-digit numbers doesn't need to be as wide as one that's filled with category headings, for example.

Some of these adjustments happen automatically. If you change the font size of text in a cell, the row automatically changes height to accommodate it. Likewise, when you enter data that's too wide to fit in the default column width, Excel expands the column.

→ For an explanation of how columns expand to accommodate data you enter, **see** "Avoiding Rounding Errors," **p. 404.**

You can also adjust row heights and column widths manually in any of three ways:

- Use Excel's AutoFit feature to set column widths and row heights automatically. Double-click the right border of a column heading to adjust the column width to fit the widest entry in the column. Double-click the bottom border of a row heading to resize a row to accommodate the tallest character in that row. If you select multiple rows or columns, you can adjust them all at once.

- Click and drag any column or row to a new size. Point to the thin line at the right of the column heading or the bottom of a row heading until the pointer changes to a two-headed arrow. Click and drag the column or row to the desired width or height, and release the mouse button.

TIP

> When you use the mouse to adjust column widths and row heights, ScreenTips show the exact height and width, in characters (for columns) or points (for rows). Curiously, both ScreenTips also show the measurements in pixels—use this scale if you're optimizing a worksheet for viewing in a browser at a specific resolution, say, 800×600 pixels.

- To set a precise height or width, use a dialog box. Right-click any row number and choose Row Height. Enter any number between 0 and 409 (points). Or right-click a column name and select Column Width. Enter any number between 0 and 255 (characters).

13

To adjust more than one row or column, select the group of rows or columns first. Then point to the border of any row or column heading in the selection and drag to the desired size. When you release the mouse button, Excel adjusts all selected rows or columns to the height or width of the column you selected. This technique is especially useful when you're putting together a budget worksheet with 12 columns, one for each month. After entering data, select all 12 columns and drag them to the correct width.

Here are some expert tips to help you when working with row heights and column widths:

- Most of the column- and row-sizing commands are available on the Format button in the Cells group of the Home tab.

- To hide any row or column, set its height or width to 0 (click the right side of a column heading and drag to the left, or click the bottom of a row heading and drag to the top). To make a hidden column or row visible, select the columns or rows on either side of the hidden one; then choose Format, Row or Column and click Unhide.

- To resize a column according to the contents of one or more specific cells in that column, select those cells, click the Format button (in the Cells group of the Home tab), and choose AutoFit Column Width.

- If you've customized column widths and/or row heights and you want to copy this information along with data, copy and paste the entire row or column, not just the individual cells. Use the Column Widths option on the Paste Special dialog box to duplicate the arrangement of columns from one worksheet to another.

- To change the standard width for all columns in the current worksheet, click Format in the Cells group of the Home tab, and then choose Default Width. Enter the new column width (in characters) in the dialog box. The new width will not apply to columns whose width you have already reset.

USING CONDITIONAL FORMATTING TO IDENTIFY KEY VALUES

Conditional formatting allows you to set font attributes, colors, and other formatting options that cause data to appear differently based on the value displayed in a cell. Most often, you'll use this feature to set an alarm that highlights data that is outside of an expected range. For example, you might attach conditional formatting to a row of totals on a daily sales report, displaying each cell's contents in bold red letters if it falls below a target level and in bright green if the number is significantly above average. In an employee roster, you might use bold formatting to identify the names of employees who are overdue for a formal evaluation.

> **TIP**
>
> Conditional formats are most effective when used sparingly. If every cell in a worksheet has "special" formatting, nothing stands out. The best use of this option is to highlight truly unusual conditions that require action—when you open a worksheet and see one or two items in bright red, they get your full attention.

Some predefined number formats automatically display negative numbers in red, but conditional formatting gives you far greater control. For cells whose contents match one or more conditions you define, you can specify a new font style (bold italic, for example), use the underline or strikethrough attributes, or change the borders and color of the selection. You cannot use conditional formatting to change fonts or font sizes.

To use conditional formatting, select a cell or range and then click Conditional Formatting in the Styles group of the Home tab. You'll see a list of ways you can conditionally format cell data. You could, for example, define a condition Cell Value Is Greater Than or Equal to 20000, and Excel would apply the special formatting if the value is 30,000 but would leave the standard format in place if the value is only 15,000.

To highlight cells when a certain condition becomes true, select the Highlight Cells Rules option. You'll select from these comparison choices: Greater Than, Less Than, Between, Equal To, Text That Contains, A Date Occurring, and Duplicate Values. Selecting any of these options displays a corresponding dialog box such as the one in Figure 13.17.

Figure 13.17
Specify the range that should trigger the conditional format and then choose a formatting option from the drop-down list at the right.

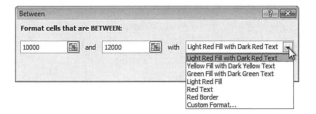

The drop-down list at the right side of this dialog box offers a half dozen formatting possibilities. You're not limited to these, however; if you want something else, click Custom Format at the bottom of the drop-down list. Excel responds with the Format Cells dialog box (with a few options—such as those involving fonts and sizes—unavailable).

For more control, click the Conditional Formatting button, select Highlight Cell Rules, and then select More Rules. Figure 13.18 shows the New Formatting Rule dialog box that appears. Here you can create conditional formatting rules that format data throughout your worksheet based on specific values, based on cells that contain certain values, based on the top- or bottom-ranked values in the entire worksheet (great for spotting exceptional values), based on values above or below the average of the cell values, based on the presence of duplicate values, and based on a formula you enter. Formulas in conditional formats can apply to any data on the worksheet, not just the data in the current cell; they can even apply to external data.

TIP

> If you enter a formula to trigger conditional formatting, that formula must use a logical function that evaluates to True or False.

The dialog box that appears when you click Conditional Formatting on the Ribbon includes four other categories in addition to Highlight Cells Rules. Here is an overview of those other categories.

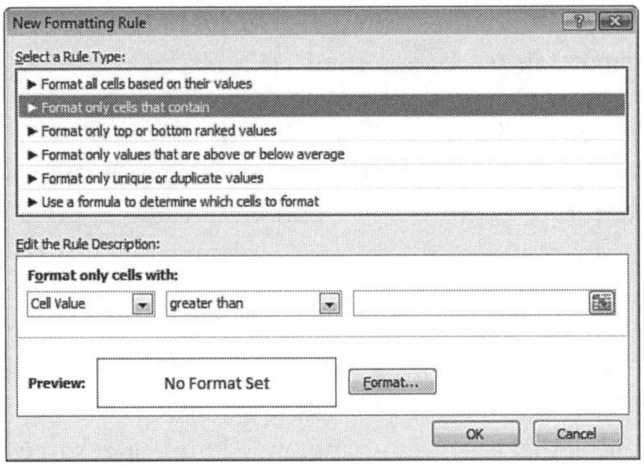

Figure 13.18
Create your own formatting rules.

USING TOP/BOTTOM RULES

The Top/Bottom Rules option conditionally formats cells that fall in the top *n*, top *n* %, bottom *n*, or bottom *n* % of all values in a selected range. You can also use this option to flag values above or below the average of values in a range.

Note that, although Excel's dialog boxes refer to the top 10, bottom 10, top 10 percent, and so on, you're not required to use *n* = 10. You can set *n* to any positive integer. To format the highest 5 values in a range, for example, you would select the range, click Conditional Formatting (in the Styles group of the Home tab), choose Top/Bottom rules, and then Top 10 Items. In the Top 10 Items dialog box (see Figure 13.19), you would use the spinner at the left to change 10 to 5, choose a format from the drop-down list at the right, and then click OK.

Figure 13.19
The command (as indicated by the title of this dialog box) is called Top 10 Items, but you can replace 10 with a different positive integer.

USING COLORED DATA BARS

Colored data bars, new in Excel 2007, display a colored bar graph based on the relative values in a selected range. When you select a range of cells, click Conditional Formatting, and then select Data Bars, a list of color choices appears. Select a color, and Excel places a colored bar chart behind the values in the range, so you can see at a glance how the values stack up against one another (see Figure 13.20).

Figure 13.20
Data Bars superimpose a bar graph over your data, showing the relative sizes of the values in the selected range.

	A
1	647,458
2	876,600
3	701,595
4	768,442
5	688,614
6	836,435
7	379,954
8	245,891
9	241,195

USING COLOR SCALES

The Color Scales option, also new in Excel 2007, uses colored shading to format cells. Higher-valued cells in the selected range get darker shading; lower-valued cells get lighter shading. Of the eight color options that initially appear when you click Conditional Formatting and choose Color Scales, some use two colors and others use three. You can see the effect on any of these options on the selected range immediately, thanks to Live Preview. If you want to design your own color bars, click More Rules.

USING ICON SETS

If you click Conditional Formatting and choose the Icon Sets option, Excel displays various icons next to the cells in the selected range, distinguishing values by icon type. In Figure 13.21, for example, we've chosen the first icon set from the Icon Sets gallery, and Excel has responded by marking the highest values in our selected range (A1:A9) with upward-pointing green arrows, the lowest values with downward-pointing red arrows, and the one middling value with a rightward-pointing yellow arrow.

Figure 13.21
You can use icon sets to mark high, low, and middle values in a range.

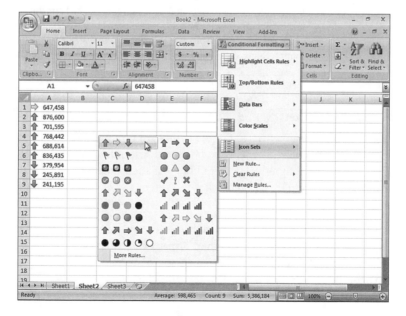

To see how Excel determines which values get which icons, or to change the way it makes that determination, click More Rules, at the bottom of the Icon Sets gallery. As Figure 13.21 shows, Excel initially divides the landscape into equal segments. For an icon set with three icons, such as the one shown in Figure 13.21, it uses the low icon for values falling in the lowest 33 percent of the range, the high icon for values falling in the top 33 percent, and the middle icon for everything else. You can adjust those divisions to suit your needs.

> **TIP**
>
> Maybe all you need to display on your worksheet is the icons. If so, you can hide the numbers and keep the icons, by selecting the Show Icon Only check box in the New Formatting Rule dialog box.

COPYING FORMATS WITH THE FORMAT PAINTER

Use the Format Painter button to quickly copy all formats—fonts, colors, borders, alignment...the works—from one cell to another. Select a cell that has the formatting you want to copy, click the Format Painter button, and click the cell to which you want to copy the formatting. (If you select a range of cells to copy from, Excel repeats the formatting in your selection.)

If you want to copy formatting to multiple cells, select the cell whose formats you want to copy and then double-click the Format Painter button to lock it in position. Click each destination cell to copy formatting. When you're finished, click the button again or press Esc to turn off the Format Painter.

> **TIP**
>
> If you select an entire column or row, you can use the Format Painter to copy column widths and row heights. After the pointer turns to the paintbrush shape, click the heading of the row or column you want to change. Note that this technique will also copy other formats (fonts, colors, and so on) from the selected row or column.

SAVING FORMATS AS NAMED STYLES

Use the Format Painter button in the Clipboard group of the Home tab to quickly copy all formats—fonts, colors, borders, data bars, color scales, icon sets, alignments, and so on—from one cell to another. Select a cell that has the formatting you want to copy, click the Format Painter button, and then click the cell or range to which you want to copy the formatting.

If you want to copy formatting to multiple discontiguous cells, select the cell you want to copy from and then double-click the Format Painter button. Then, with the Format Painter button "locked," click each cell to which you want to copy formatting attributes. When you have finished, click the Format Painter button again or press Esc.

TIP

> If you select an entire column or row, you can use the Format Painter button to copy column widths and row heights. After the pointer turns to the paintbrush shape, click the heading of the row or column you want to change. Note that this technique will also copy other formats (fonts, colors, and so on) from the selected row or column.

TROUBLESHOOTING

STOPPING AUTOMATIC CONVERSIONS

After importing data into a worksheet from text files and databases, I noticed that Excel converts some data to date serial values and other data to scientific notation. I want the information to appear in my worksheet exactly as it did in the database. Is there any way to change it back?

No, unfortunately. When Excel sees a value that looks like a date or time or scientific notation, either when you type a value into a cell or when you import a database, it converts the value automatically as you type or import. There is no way to reverse this conversion. If you have serial numbers that use the format ##X####, where each # is a number and the X is a letter, Excel converts any serial number that contains the letter *E* in that position to scientific notation. Your best option is to edit the text or database file, adding an apostrophe to the beginning of each field that contains values Excel will try to convert. In that case, Excel imports the data in text format exactly as it appears.

CLICK TWICE FOR NORMAL

I formatted text in a cell using more than one font, and I want to restore Excel's default font format. I opened the Format Cells dialog box, clicked the Font tab, and clicked the Normal Font box once, but my formatting stays exactly as it was. What's the secret?

When you have multiple font formats applied to different words or characters in a cell, the Normal Font check box is selected but it's grayed out. To restore the default formatting, click once to clear the box (exactly the opposite of what you normally do) and then click OK to close the dialog box. Now reopen the dialog box and click the Normal Font check box again. This time your change will stick.

WORKING WITH MULTIPLE CONDITIONS

I applied conditional formatting to a cell, but the formatting doesn't appear on some cells, even though the data in those cells meets the conditions I specified.

If you specify multiple conditions and more than one is true for a given cell, Excel applies the formats of the first true condition it encounters and ignores the second and third conditions. If you've defined conditions that have the potential to overlap, arrange them in order so that the most important one (or the one least likely to be true) is first in the list.

EXTRA CREDIT: REDESIGNING A WORKSHEET CLARIFIES THE INFORMATION

When you first create a worksheet, every cell uses the same fonts, every row is the same height, and there's no distinction between headings and the data they describe. With Excel's extensive selection of formatting tools, you can redesign a worksheet to make its organization crystal clear.

When we imported data from a database into a worksheet, the results looked like a data disaster, as the "Before" example in Figure 13.22 illustrates.

Figure 13.22
Before

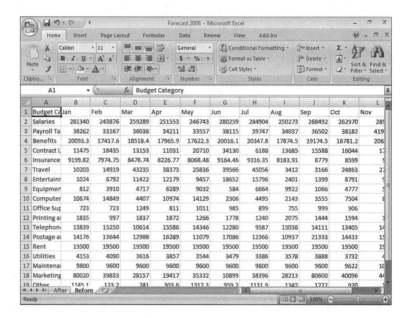

After some careful formatting, however, the results are much easier to read and follow. Here are the basic principles we followed when formatting the "After" worksheet shown in Figure 13.23:

- Adjust the formatting for every cell, especially those that contain numbers, dates, and dollar amounts. Pay particular attention to fonts, font size, and the number of decimal places displayed.

- Enter totals, averages, and other formulas as needed for analytical purposes.

- Make sure that all columns align properly and that rows and columns are the proper width.

- Make headings and titles bigger and bolder so they clearly define what type of data is in each row and column. Bold white type on a dark background is especially effective in column headings.

- Turn on text wrapping and merge cells as needed, especially in headings.
- Use the Borders button to add grid elements as necessary.
- Use the Fill Color drop-down menu to add light shading throughout the data section. In this worksheet, a soft green shading was added to alternate rows to make long rows easier to follow.

Figure 13.23
After

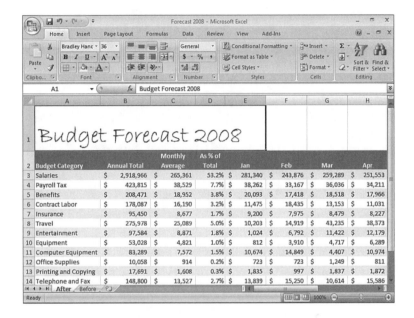

Note that, although the transformation of Figure 13.22 to Figure 13.23 was easy to accomplish with formatting features that have been part of Excel for many versions, the new Table Styles feature introduced with Excel 2007 makes it even easier to create attractive, readable worksheets. We discuss this feature in Chapter 15, "Working with Tables and PivotTables."

13

USING FORMULAS AND FUNCTIONS

ENTERING AND EDITING FORMULAS

Formulas add intelligence to a workbook. Using formulas, you can manipulate values (text, numbers, or dates), perform simple or complex calculations, and display alternative results based on logical tests.

With the help of formulas, you can perform any of the following common tasks:

- Manage home finances by tracking expenses
- Simplify coursework in advanced math and statistics classes
- Create "what-if" worksheets to help make financial decisions such as purchasing a home or leasing a car
- Manipulate text in lists
- Improve your success in hobbies by calculating handicaps from your golf or bowling scores, tracking statistics for players in a fantasy league, and so on

A formula can be as simple as a reference to another cell, or it can go on for hundreds of characters, with as many as 64 functions nested within other functions; regardless of its complexity, however, a formula must begin with an equal sign (=). If you start a formula with a plus sign (+) or minus sign (–), Excel adds an equal sign to the beginning of the formula.

Formulas consist of three basic building blocks: *operands* (the elements to be calculated), *operators*, and worksheet functions:

- Operands—The data to be calculated in a formula can include any combination of the following: *constant values* (numbers, text, or dates you enter directly in a cell or formula, for example); cell or range references; names that refer to cells or ranges; or worksheet functions. When you use a cell or range reference in a formula, Excel substitutes the contents of that address just as if you had typed it in directly.

- Operators—Formulas can use any of six basic arithmetic operators: addition (+), subtraction (–), multiplication (*), division (/), percent (%), or exponentiation (^). You can also use comparison operators to compare two values and produce the logical result TRUE or FALSE. The list of comparison operators consists of equal to (=), greater than (>), less than (<), greater than or equal to (>=), less than or equal to (<=), and not equal to (<>). Use an ampersand (&) to combine, or concatenate, two pieces of text into a single value.

- Worksheet functions—Predefined formulas that allow you to perform calculations on worksheet data by entering a constant value or a cell or range reference as the *argument* that a named function transforms. You can use a worksheet function as the complete contents of a cell, or you can use a function as an operand in another formula.

→ For a full discussion of worksheet functions and arguments, **see** "Manipulating Data with Worksheet Functions," **p. 451.**

14

USING CELL REFERENCES IN FORMULAS

You can enter any cell or range address directly in a formula. These addresses are not case-sensitive; if you enter a2:b8 in a formula, Excel converts the entry to A2:B8 when you press Enter. You can also point and click to enter any cell or range reference.

One of the simplest Excel formulas is a direct reference to another cell. If you click in cell I24, for example, and enter the formula =A5, Excel displays the current value of cell A5 in cell I24. This technique is most commonly used with worksheets that contain input cells in which you type data that you'll use throughout the worksheet. For example, cell A5 might contain the current interest rate you plan to use as part of a series of loan and payment calculations. If you use custom views to display different portions of your worksheet, this technique lets you see the underlying assumptions at a glance.

To enter a reference to an entire row or column, use the row number or column letter as both halves of the range reference: B:B for column B, 2:2 for row 2. You can also use this syntax for multiple rows or columns—B:K includes every cell in columns B through K, just as 10:13 includes every cell in rows 10 through 13.

USING 3D REFERENCES TO CELLS ON OTHER WORKSHEETS

Sometimes it's helpful to use references to cells and ranges on other worksheets within the same workbook—known as *3D references*. For example, in a worksheet analyzing the economic output of Western Europe since World War II, you might include a lookup table that lists industrial output statistics by country and by year on a separate sheet. Using the data from this table to create a series of calculations for each country makes your data accurate, yet keeps the main worksheet uncluttered. Likewise, in a loan worksheet you might want to perform all the data-entry and payment calculations on one sheet, but place the amortization table on its own sheet for display and printing.

To enter a 3D address, preface the cell address with the name of the sheet followed by an exclamation point. (If the sheet name contains a space, enclose it within single quotation marks.) If you have a sheet named Amortization Table, for example, you can refer to the top-left cell of that sheet by entering ='Amortization Table'!A1 on any other sheet in the same book. You can also click the appropriate sheet tab and then select the desired cell or range of cells to add references to cells or ranges on other sheets. When you use this technique, Excel automatically enters the sheet name, exclamation point, and cell references.

CONTROLLING THE CALCULATION ORDER IN FORMULAS

If a formula contains more than one operator, Excel performs calculations in the following order:

- Percent (%)
- Exponentiation (^)
- Multiplication (*) and division (/)
- Addition (+) and subtraction (−)

14

- Concatenation (&)
- Comparison (=, <, >, <=, >=, <>)

To override the default order of calculation, use parentheses; Excel evaluates all items within parentheses first, from the inside out, using the same order as listed previously. If a formula contains operators with the same precedence, such as addition and subtraction or any two comparison operators, Excel evaluates the operators from left to right. The number of levels of nested parentheses you can use within a single formula is not limited, although you are limited to 64 levels of nesting for a function.

TIP

> When you're trying to figure out the structure of a complex formula with many sets of nested parentheses, let Excel help. Click to make the cell that contains the formula active, and then use the arrow keys to move back and forth through the formula. As you move the insertion point to the right of a left parenthesis or to the left of a right parenthesis, Excel highlights its mate in bold. When you make any change to the formula, Excel displays each matched set of parentheses in a different color, making it easier for you to see which is which.

CONTROLLING THE TIMING OF CALCULATIONS

Normally, Excel recalculates all formulas every time you open or save a workbook. When you change a value in a cell, Excel recalculates all formulas that refer to that cell on any worksheet in the current workbook. Calculation takes place in the background, and on a typical uncomplicated worksheet, the process is essentially instantaneous.

You might want to control when Excel recalculates formulas in at least two circumstances:

- If your worksheet contains a very large number of complex formulas, recalculation can cause annoying pauses when you try to enter data. This is especially noticeable on computers with slow CPUs and low-memory configurations.
- When your formula contains cells that refer to themselves, as in some scientific and engineering formulas, Excel must repeat (iterate) the calculation—by default, each time you recalculate this type of formula, Excel goes through 100 iterations.

Unless you're working with one of these unusual worksheet configurations, you should leave recalculation settings alone. If you must turn off automatic recalculation, follow these steps:

1. Click the Microsoft Office button and then click Excel Options. In the left pane of the Excel Options dialog box, click Formulas (see Figure 14.1).
2. In the Calculation options section, choose Manual. (The Automatic Except Tables option is for use with worksheets that include a relatively obscure Excel feature called data tables. If your worksheet includes a one- or two-variable data table, Excel recalculates the entire table every time you edit any cell in the worksheet; checking this option lets you recalculate the table manually.)

14

3. If you want Excel to recalculate the workbook only when you explicitly choose to do so, remove the check mark from the Recalculate Workbook Before Saving check box.

4. Click OK to save the setting and return to your worksheet.

Figure 14.1
Adjust recalculation options with care. For most situations, the default automatic options are appropriate.

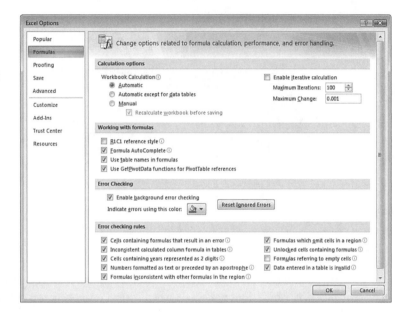

When you turn off automatic recalculation, you need to specify when Excel should recalculate formulas. To calculate all formulas in the current workbook, press F9. To recalculate only formulas in the current worksheet, press Shift+F9.

TIP

> Are you using a worksheet that was prepared by someone else using an older version of Excel? Excel 97, which was very popular in its day and is still used by some, includes several well-documented calculation bugs that can cause incorrect results under some circumstances. Beginning with Excel 2000, Microsoft made major changes to Excel's recalculation engine intended to fix these bugs. The first time you use a newer version of Excel to open a worksheet created in Excel 97, the program completely recalculates the worksheet. When you close the worksheet, you'll be asked whether you want to save your changes, even if you've done nothing more than look at the worksheet. We strongly recommend that you click Yes when you see this dialog box to avoid the possibility of being bitten by those old recalculation bugs.

ABSOLUTE VERSUS RELATIVE CELL REFERENCES

Normally, Excel interprets cell and range references within a formula as *relative references*. When you copy or move the formula, Excel automatically adjusts cell references to reflect their position relative to the new location. This capability is useful when you need to quickly copy a formula across several rows or columns. In the worksheet shown in Figure 14.2, for example, the formula in cell B7 totals the contents of column B. When you copy that formula across to the right, Excel assumes you want to total the numbers in the same relative position in each column, so it adjusts the formula accordingly, from =SUM(B2:B6) to =SUM(C2:C6), =SUM(D2:D6), and so on.

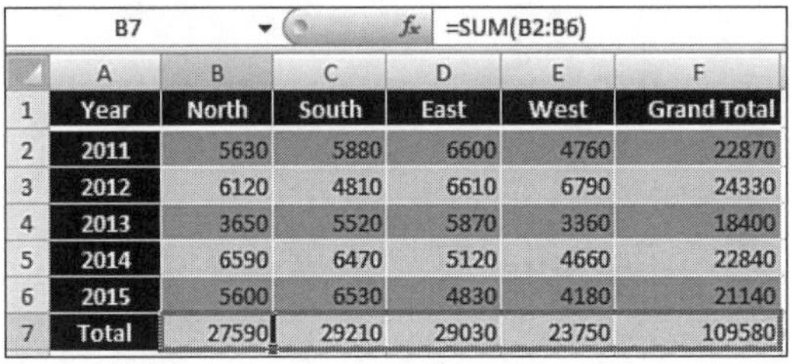

Figure 14.2
Relative cell addresses are automatically updated as they are copied from cell to cell.

	B7			f_x	=SUM(B2:B6)	
	A	B	C	D	E	F
1	Year	North	South	East	West	Grand Total
2	2011	5630	5880	6600	4760	22870
3	2012	6120	4810	6610	6790	24330
4	2013	3650	5520	5870	3360	18400
5	2014	6590	6470	5120	4660	22840
6	2015	5600	6530	4830	4180	21140
7	Total	27590	29210	29030	23750	109580

→ The easiest way to copy a row or column of formulas is with the help of Excel's AutoFill feature; **see** "Automatically Filling in a Series of Data," **p. 480.**

In some cases, however, you want to copy a formula so a cell or range reference in the copied formula points to the same cell or range as in the original. For example, if you enter the current interest rate in a cell near the top of a loan worksheet, you can refer to that cell in any formula that makes an interest-related calculation. To convert a relative reference to an *absolute reference*, which does not adjust when copied or moved, use dollar signs within the cell address. For example, when you copy the formula =B4*$A$5 to the right, Excel adjusts the first cell reference relative to its new location, but leaves the second reference unchanged: =C4*$A$5, =D4*$A$5, and so on.

TIP

When you want to include a reference to an input cell in several formulas, you're generally better off using a named range, which is always an absolute reference. If cell A5 contains an interest rate, name the cell Interest_Rate and use that name in formulas— =B6*Interest_Rate, for example. If you move or copy the formula, the reference to the named range will not change.

You can mix and match relative and absolute addresses in a formula, or even in the same address. Using a dollar sign in front of the column portion of the address ($A5) tells Excel to change only the row reference when the formula is moved or copied; likewise, a dollar sign in front of the row (A$5) changes only the column portion of the cell reference. In Figure 14.3, for example, you could enter the formula =B2/$F2 in cell B10 and then copy the formula down and to the right. The *mixed reference* to $F2 adjusts the references so that they always point to the Grand Total formula in Column F for the correct row.

Use the F4 keyboard shortcut to switch quickly between relative, mixed, and absolute references in a formula. Click in the active cell to enable editing, place the insertion point in a

14

cell or range reference (either in the Formula bar or in the cell itself), and press F4 to convert a relative reference to absolute. Press F4 again to enter a mixed reference. Keep pressing F4 to cycle through all four variations for the selection.

Figure 14.3
Formulas in the bottom table use mixed references that allows each percentage to be divided by the result in the Grand Total column as you copy the formula down and across.

	A	B	C	D	E	F
1	Year	North	South	East	West	Grand Total
2	2011	5630	5880	6600	4760	22870
3	2012	6120	4810	6610	6790	24330
4	2013	3650	5520	5870	3360	18400
5	2014	6590	6470	5120	4660	22840
6	2015	5600	6530	4830	4180	21140
7	Total	27590	29210	29030	23750	109580
8						
9	Year	North	South	East	West	
10	2011	24.6%	25.7%	28.9%	20.8%	
11	2012	25.2%	19.8%	27.2%	27.9%	
12	2013	19.8%	30.0%	31.9%	18.3%	
13	2014	28.9%	28.3%	22.4%	20.4%	
14	2015	26.5%	30.9%	22.8%	19.8%	

PREVENTING FORMULAS FROM DISPLAYING IN THE FORMULA BAR

When you design a worksheet that you intend other people to use for data entry, you might want to hide the formulas themselves and show their results. This technique can be useful if your formula contains confidential or proprietary information that you don't want to share with others. It's also a useful way to prevent other users from attempting to edit a formula.

To prevent a formula from appearing in the Formula bar, you must first set a specific formatting option for that cell and then turn on *protection* for the entire worksheet:

1. Right-click the cell that contains the formula you want to hide (to hide multiple formulas, select a range) and choose Format Cells from the shortcut menu.
2. Click the Protection tab and select the Hidden check box.

CAUTION

> Make sure you leave the check mark next to the Locked box as well. If you clear this box and check Hidden, anyone who can open the worksheet can replace the hidden formula with another formula or a constant value, undoing your attempt at protection.

3. Select other cells on the worksheet, if necessary, and adjust whether their contents are hidden or locked.
4. Click Protect Sheet in the Changes group of the Review tab. In the Protect Sheet dialog box, make sure the Protect Worksheet and Contents of Locked Cells check box is selected.

14

5. Click OK to close the Protect Sheet dialog box. Users will no longer be able to see hidden formulas in the Formula bar or in the cell itself, nor will they be able to edit formulas. The results of a hidden formula will display in the cell and on printouts.

→ For more details on how to prevent unauthorized changes to a workbook or worksheet, **see** "Protecting a Worksheet," **p. 387.**

USING ARRAY FORMULAS

Array formulas enable you to perform multiple calculations across a range of cells (an array) by using a function that normally works only on a single cell. To enter an array formula, construct the formula just as you normally would and then press Ctrl+Shift+Enter. Excel enters the formula in curly braces to indicate that it is an array formula.

An array formula can return either a single result or multiple results. Array formulas are a common way to combine the SUM and IF functions, for example. Under normal circumstances, an IF function compares one cell with another cell or a constant value. An array formula, on the other hand, enables you to compare a single value to every cell in an array and return a result you can work with, so you can compare a condition in an IF function and use all matching results in a SUM function, all in one formula.

 If you're having trouble editing an array formula, see "Editing an Array Formula" in the "Troubleshooting" section at the end of this chapter.

For example, say you keep a list of personal spending in an Excel worksheet with header information in row 1 and the first record in row 2, as in the example in Figure 14.4. If column B contains the amount of each purchase, and column C contains the category you've assigned to that purchase, you can use an array formula to keep a running total of all purchases by category. Assuming column D is blank, click in cell D2 and type this formula: =SUM(IF($C$2:C2=C2,$B$2:B2)). Press Ctrl+Shift+Enter to enter it as an array formula, and then use AutoFill to copy the formula to the remainder of the cells in column D. (Excel automatically adds curly braces at the beginning and end to indicate that this is an array formula. Do not enter the curly braces yourself, or the array formula will fail.)

Figure 14.4
In this example, the array formula allows you to keep a running total of all expenditures by category.

	A	B	C	D
1	Trans_Num	Amount	Category	Running total by category
2	1001	$64.23	Groceries	$64.23
3	1002	$11.56	Entertainment	$11.56
4	1003	$76.69	Dining Out	$76.69
5	1004	$79.56	Gifts	$79.56
6	1005	$63.67	Groceries	$127.90
7	1006	$46.12	Interest	$46.12
8	1007	$96.93	Dining Out	$173.62
9	1008	$26.26	Automobile	$26.26
10	1009	$1,532.48	Mortgage	$1,532.48
11	1010	$20.00	Healthcare	$20.00
12	1011	$67.52	Utilities	$67.52
13	1012	$88.44	Groceries	$216.34
14	1013	$76.84	Phone	$76.84
15	1014	$5.99	Coffee	$5.99
16	1015	$91.53	Computer	$91.53
17	1016	$31.46	Dining Out	$205.08

14

The first argument in this array formula compares each previous cell in column C to the contents of column C in the current row. The second argument returns a purchase amount to the SUM function for each cell in column C if the condition in the IF function is true. The copy of this formula in cell D13, for example, looks like this:

```
{=SUM(IF($C$2:C13=C13,$B$2:B13))}
```

This formula looks in the range from C2 to C13 for cells that match the contents of C13—the category "Groceries." It finds matching contents in C2, C6, C13, and C19, so it adds the purchase amounts in B2, B6, and B13 to produce its result, a running total of all amounts up to and including row 13 for the Groceries category.

USING THE WATCH WINDOW TO MONITOR CALCULATIONS

Normally, as you enter and edit values in a worksheet, formulas that reference those values change as well. If the formula is close to the cells you're editing, you can see the results immediately. But it's more difficult to track formula results when the formulas are widely separated—on the same worksheet or even on linked sheets in a different workbook.

Thanks to a little-known Excel feature, you can keep an eye on the results of specific cells, even when those cells are on different sheets. Use the *Watch Window* to track a list of cells; this window floats above the current worksheet, as shown in Figure 14.5. With this window open, you don't have to continually switch between worksheets to monitor your work.

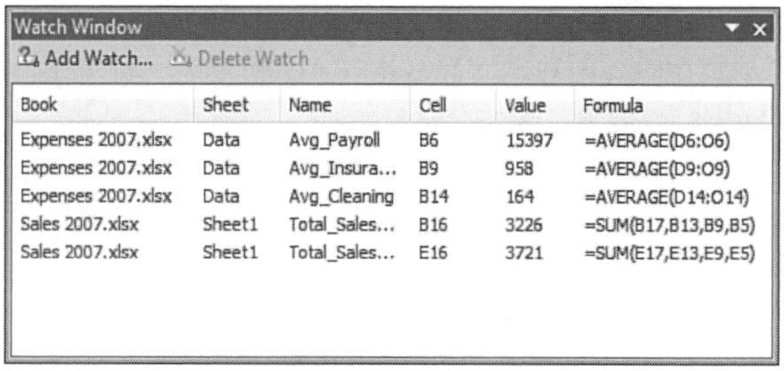

Figure 14.5
The Watch Window enables you to track formula results across multiple workbooks. Range names make it easier to identify why you added a cell to the list.

Book	Sheet	Name	Cell	Value	Formula
Expenses 2007.xlsx	Data	Avg_Payroll	B6	15397	=AVERAGE(D6:O6)
Expenses 2007.xlsx	Data	Avg_Insura...	B9	958	=AVERAGE(D9:O9)
Expenses 2007.xlsx	Data	Avg_Cleaning	B14	164	=AVERAGE(D14:O14)
Sales 2007.xlsx	Sheet1	Total_Sales...	B16	3226	=SUM(B17,B13,B9,B5)
Sales 2007.xlsx	Sheet1	Total_Sales...	E16	3721	=SUM(E17,E13,E9,E5)

To display the Watch Window, click Watch Window, in the Formula Auditing group of the Formulas tab. To add cells or ranges to the watch list, click Add Watch and then point to the cell or range on the worksheet that you want to add. (If you add a range, each cell in the range becomes a watch-list entry.) The Watch Window is resizable. And just as with any list-based control, you can click a column heading to sort by that column, or resize columns by dragging the line between column headings.

TIP

If you use the Watch Window a lot, we recommend that you define names for the cells you include on the Watch list. The Name column appears in the list, and a meaningful name such as May_Purchases makes it much easier to identify the value you're tracking than a cell address such as B10.

USING RANGE NAMES AND LABELS IN FORMULAS

Understanding the logic of a complex formula can be a challenge, even when you entered the formula yourself. This form of amnesia is especially common when you haven't opened a particular workbook in months or years.

To make it easier for you to understand a formula's purpose just by looking at it, you can enter cell references by using *named ranges*. This technique is especially useful with cells that contain constant values such as interest rates, loan amounts, sales tax rates, and discount formulas, because you can define a handful of input cells and then plug the contents of those cells into formulas on any worksheet within the workbook.

You can define range names explicitly, or you can enter cell references that are defined by the labels on rows and columns.

NOTE

Earlier versions of Excel included a feature called natural-language formulas, which allowed you to reference a cell by means of the labels above and to the left of that cell. If you had a cell at the intersection of a column named May and a row named Flowers, for example, you could reference that cell as May Flowers. Because there were numerous hazards and limitations attendant to this feature, Microsoft eliminated it from Excel 2007. If you use Excel 2007 to open a workbook that was created in an earlier version and that uses one or more natural-language formulas, Excel 2007 will convert those formulas to ordinary cell references. You will receive a potentially alarming message when you first open the file, but rest assured that your worksheet will function exactly as it used to function in the old version. You just won't have those natural-language cell references any more.

USING NAMED RANGES IN FORMULAS

For absolute control over cell and range references in formulas, use a range name instead of its row-and-column address. Unlike natural-language formulas, which rely on row and column headings, you explicitly define range names. When you refer to a named range in a formula, the effect is the same as if you had entered the absolute address of the named cell or range.

Using named ranges makes it easier for anyone looking at a worksheet to understand exactly how a formula works. That comes in handy when you share a workbook with a coworker, or when you look at a worksheet you designed long ago. On an invoice worksheet, for example, the following formula is instantly understandable:

```
=Quantity_Ordered*Unit_Price*(1+Sales_Tax_Rate)
```

The easiest way to name a cell or a range is to use the Name box, located just to the left of the Formula bar (see Figure 14.6). Select the cell or range you want to name and then click in the Name box. Type a legal name for the cell or range and press Enter to store the range name in the workbook.

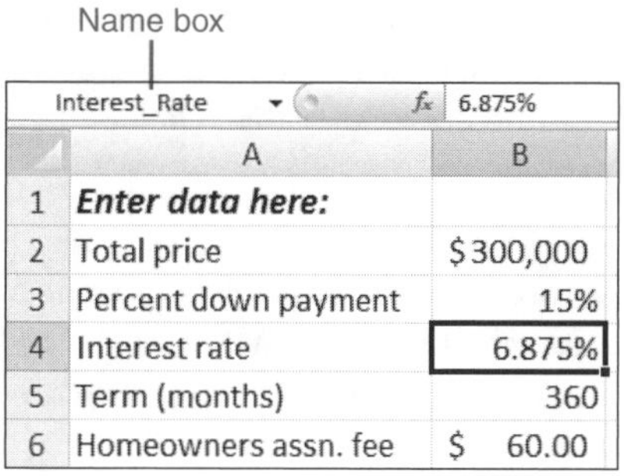

Figure 14.6
Select a range, and then click in the Name box and type the name you want to use for that range.

Name box

Interest_Rate	▼ ⌐ ⊙	f_x	6.875%

	A	B
1	*Enter data here:*	
2	Total price	$ 300,000
3	Percent down payment	15%
4	Interest rate	6.875%
5	Term (months)	360
6	Homeowners assn. fee	$ 60.00

The rules for assigning a legal name to a cell or a range are completely different from (and much more restrictive than) those that apply to the names of files and worksheet tabs:

- You can use a total of up to 255 characters in a range name.

TIP

The point of range names is to make worksheets and formulas easier to understand. For clarity's sake, try to keep range names under 15 characters—the width of the Name drop-down list.

- The first character must be a letter or the underline character. You can't legally name a cell or range 4thQuarterBudget, but Q4Budget is acceptable.

- The remaining characters can be letters, numbers, periods, or the underline character. No other punctuation marks are allowed in range names. Spaces are forbidden; use the underscore character instead to form a legal name that's also easy to read.

- A cell or range name cannot be the same as a cell reference or a value, so you can't name a cell Q4, FY2006, or W2, nor can you use a single letter or enter a number without any punctuation or letters.

NOTE

When you name a cell or range, that name attaches itself to the absolute address you specify. If you move or copy a formula containing a reference to the named range, the reference continues to point to the original address rather than adjust to a new relative address. For this reason, you should use named ranges in formulas only when you want the formula to refer to an absolute address.

When constructing a formula, you can choose from a list of all defined names in the current workbook. After typing an equal sign or clicking in an existing formula, click the Formulas tab on the Ribbon and then click Use in Formula. The drop-down list that appears will include all defined names on all sheets in the current workbook. If the name you select is on a different worksheet, Excel automatically enters it by using the correct syntax, including the sheet name.

14

If you insert a cell or range reference in a formula by clicking a cell or range, Excel enters the defined name of the cell or range, if one exists. If you don't want this automatic substitution to take place, type the cell address directly, rather than clicking to enter it.

MANAGING RANGE NAMES

To manage names of cells or ranges stored in a workbook, click Name Manager, in the Defined Names group of the Formulas tab. The Name Manager dialog box (see Figure 14.7) enables you to add a new name to an existing range, delete one or more range names, or change the reference for an existing name.

Figure 14.7
Use this list to manage named ranges in a workbook. To redefine an existing name, select a new cell or range in the Refers To box.

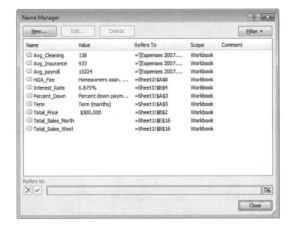

TIP

> You can assign more than one name to the same cell or range. Use different names if you intend to refer to the contents of a cell in several formulas, and you want the names to match the purpose of each formula. For example, on a loan worksheet, you might refer to the same cell as `AmountFinanced` and `AmountBorrowed` and then use the appropriate name in formulas on different parts of that worksheet.

→ You can also use the Go to Special dialog box to view and locate range names, a topic we cover in "Selecting Ranges of Data with the Go To Dialog Box," **p. 363.**

It's relatively easy to change the location that a cell or range name refers to: In the Names Manager dialog box, select the cell or range name. Select the contents of the Refers To box and click in the worksheet to select the new cell or range. When you use this technique, any worksheet formulas that refer to the range name automatically use the new location you defined.

In Excel 2007 (unlike previous versions), you can change a defined name. Display the Name Manager dialog box, select the name you want to change, and click Edit.

14

If some of the formulas in your workbook display error messages after you change or delete a range name, see "Checking Formulas Before Deleting Range Names" in the "Troubleshooting" section at the end of this chapter.

MANIPULATING DATA WITH WORKSHEET FUNCTIONS

Worksheet functions handle a broad array of tasks, from simple arithmetic to complex financial calculations and intricate statistical tests. Regardless of its complexity, every function consists of two parts: the function name and its *arguments*—the specific values the function uses to calculate a result. The *syntax* of a function defines what type of arguments it uses: text, numbers, dates, and logical values, for example. In most cases, you can substitute a cell or range address or another formula or function as an argument, as long as the data evaluates to the required data type. Some arguments are required, and others are optional. Arguments always appear to the right of the function name, inside parentheses; Excel uses commas to separate multiple arguments.

The following examples illustrate the syntax of some commonly used functions. Bold type means the argument is required. An ellipsis (...) means that the function accepts an unlimited number of arguments.

```
=TODAY()
=AVERAGE(number1,number2,...)
=IPMT(rate,per,nper,pv,fv,type)
```

TODAY, which accepts no arguments, is one of the simplest of all worksheet functions. Whenever you open, save, or otherwise recalculate a worksheet that contains this function, Excel updates the value of the cell that contains this formula to display the current date, as stored in your computer's clock chip. This function is extremely common in formulas that calculate elapsed time, such as the number of days that have passed since you mailed an invoice or received a payment.

AVERAGE accepts up to 255 arguments (but requires only 1) and calculates the arithmetic mean of all values in the list, ignoring text and logical values. Although you can enter constant values in this formula, it's most commonly used to calculate the average of a range of numbers, such as monthly sales or budget results. If you calculate a year's worth of monthly expenditures in cells B20 through M20, for example, =AVERAGE(B20:M20) displays the average of the 12 monthly totals.

To calculate the amount of interest you pay each month on a mortgage, use the IPMT function. As the syntax description shows, you must supply a minimum of four values as arguments. This function requires (in order) the interest rate per period (rate), the specific payment period for which you want to calculate interest (per, a number between 1 and nper), the number of payment periods (nper), and the present value (pv, the amount of the loan). The final two arguments—future value (fv) and the type of loan (type)—are optional. Here, too, you're more likely to include a reference to a cell than the actual number in a formula that uses this function.

> **NOTE**
> Although the Formula bar and Excel's help screens always display function names in capital letters, the names are not case sensitive. Use any combination of capital and lowercase characters; when you enter the formula, Excel converts the function's name to capitals.

ENTERING ERROR-FREE FORMULAS

For some functions, especially those with only a single argument, the easiest course of action is often to type them into a cell directly, using the mouse to select the cell or range address of any arguments.

When you begin to enter a new function or edit an existing one, Excel displays a ScreenTip just below the Formula bar. This yellow box displays all required arguments in bold type, with optional arguments in lighter type. After you enter an argument, the argument name serves as a link—click it to select the entire argument.

For functions with multiple arguments, however, especially those where you're not certain of the exact syntax, a fill-in-the-blanks form often ensures the proper results. The Insert Function dialog box allows you to enter any function and all its arguments quickly and accurately, by using a series of dialog boxes. The Insert Function dialog box is an expert Excel user's best friend: It makes errors nearly impossible, it provides constant feedback as you build a formula, and it includes hooks to surprisingly advanced help, including useful examples of some complex formulas.

You can use the Insert Function dialog box to build a function from scratch: You choose a function from a categorized list and then fill in the arguments using input boxes. Or you can enter part or all of the function and its arguments and use the Insert Function dialog box to edit specific arguments or debug a formula that isn't working as you expect.

To build a function from scratch, follow these steps:

1. Click to select the cell in which you want to add a formula and then click the Insert Function button (the *fx* just to the left of the Formula bar). Excel inserts an equal sign in the Formula bar, positions the insertion point to its right, and opens the Insert Function dialog box.

> **NOTE**
> When you type an equal sign in a cell or the Formula bar, Excel replaces the Name box (just to the left of the Formula bar) with the Function box. When you first use Excel, this list includes the 10 most popular functions; as you use the Insert Function dialog box, Excel replaces the entries on this list with the 10 functions you've used most recently. The last function you used is always the top selection in the Function box.

2. If the name of the function you want to use appears in the Select a Function box, click to select it. If the function you want to use is not on the Most Recently Used list, choose a category (see Figure 14.8).

3. The text at the bottom of the Insert Function dialog box offers a brief explanation of the selected function and its syntax (click the Help on This Function link for a more detailed explanation). When you've selected the correct function, click OK (see Figure 14.9).

Figure 14.8

4. Click within the first argument box and fill in the required data. Note that the help text at the bottom of the dialog box is specific to the argument you're currently working with, and the data type required for each argument appears to the right of the input box.

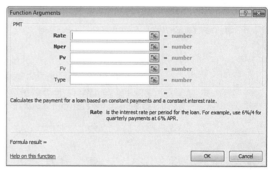

Figure 14.9

- Type text, numbers, and other constants directly in the input box.

- To add cell references by pointing and clicking, first click the Collapse Dialog button (at the right side of each argument input box) to roll most of the Insert Function dialog box up and out of the way. Next, select the cell or range to use for the selected argument and then click the Collapse Dialog button again to continue.

- To use a function as an argument within another function, click to position the insertion point within the box for that argument and then select the function from the Function box to the left of the Formula bar. (See "Extra Credit: Nesting Functions Within Functions" at the end of this chapter for more details.)

- When entering constant values, you can include the percent operator (%) and minus signs (–) with numeric data. Look to the right of the input box to see the current value of each argument you enter. If the data is not of the type required by the argument, Excel displays the word Invalid to the right of the input box.

5. Repeat step 4 for other required and optional arguments. Look to the right of the equal sign for each argument to see its current value, using the data you've entered so far. To see the result of the formula itself, look at the text along the bottom of the dialog box.

14

6. After entering all required arguments, click OK to paste the complete function into the current cell, or click Cancel to start over.

TIP

> Debugging a formula can be frustrating, especially when working with complex formulas containing several nested functions. Here's a backup strategy that allows you to freely experiment with formulas and functions without fear of losing your work or damaging a worksheet. Before editing a formula, remove the equal sign from the beginning of the formula and press Enter; then copy the formula to another cell. Without the equal sign, Excel treats the cell's contents as plain text and copies the formula exactly as it appears, with no adjustments. If your experiments are unsuccessful, copy the backed-up formula to the original cell and then restore the equal sign.

To use the Insert Function dialog box as a proofreading and reference tool, begin constructing your formula as usual, starting with an equal sign and the function name. After entering the first parenthesis, click the Insert Function button to open the Insert Function dialog box with the current function selected. Any arguments you've already entered will be in the dialog box as soon as it opens.

TIP

> If you are entering a function by hand, without using the Insert Function dialog box, and you find yourself in need of help with the arguments, press Ctrl+A. This takes you straight to the Function Arguments dialog box.

TOTALING ROWS AND COLUMNS AUTOMATICALLY

The most commonly used functions are also the easiest to enter. To insert a formula that adds a column or row of numbers automatically, click in a blank cell beneath any column of numbers (or at the end of a row of numbers) and then click the AutoSum button (in the Editing group of the Home tab). Excel inserts the SUM function with the argument already filled in and selected. Adjust the selected range, if necessary, and then click the Enter box in the Formula bar or press Enter to store the formula in the active cell.

Use the drop-down arrow to the right of the AutoSum button to select the AVERAGE, COUNT, MAX, or MIN functions for the adjacent row or column. Select the More Functions option from the bottom of the list to open the Insert Function dialog box with the adjacent row or column selected as the default argument.

Two quirks in AutoSum are worth noting:

- If the range above or to the left of the cell containing the SUM formulas contains any blank cells, the range to be totaled stops there.
- When the cell that holds the SUM function is at the end of a row and a column, AutoSum always selects the column.

In either case, the moral is the same: When using AutoSum, always check to be certain that the correct range is selected.

To automatically add totals for several adjacent rows or columns, select the cells directly beneath the columns or to the right of the rows and then choose an AutoSum function. Excel plugs in the selected formula for each row or column, just as if you had added each one individually. When you use the AutoSum button this way, you do not see a confirmation dialog box.

If you use AutoSum below a filtered table, the resulting formula uses the SUBTOTAL function instead. This syntax allows you to see a correct sum using only the filtered data; if you used the SUM function, the result would show all cells, including those hidden by the filter.

TIP

> You don't need to enter a formula to make quick calculations. When you select two or more numbers in a worksheet, Excel displays a summary of the selected cells in the status bar along the bottom of the worksheet window. The default calculation is a simple total; look at the right side of the status bar and you'll see SUM=, followed by the total of the selected cells. Right-click anywhere on the status bar to display a shortcut menu that lets you choose a different calculation, including Average, Max, Min, Count (which counts the number of selected cells), and Count Nums (which counts only the number of selected cells that contain numbers). Use this feature in conjunction with selecting a column in a list, for example, to quickly spot the largest and smallest values in that field.

PUTTING WORKSHEET FUNCTIONS TO USE

Excel has more than 300 functions, including those available in various add-ins. The following sections list some of the tasks you can accomplish by using functions in each category.

FINANCIAL FUNCTIONS

Excel includes a large number of financial functions—50 in all—covering everything from simple household budget problems, such as calculating a house payment, to complex tasks such as figuring the bond-equivalent yield for a U.S. Treasury bill (TBILLEQ) or the yield of a security that has an odd last period (ODDLYIELD).

Most of the more advanced financial functions, including those that calculate depreciation schedules (DB, DDB, SLN, SYD, and VDB) and internal rates of return (IRR and MIRR) are useful only if you have enough of an accounting or finance background to understand the underlying principles. However, a number of general-purpose functions are useful for a wide variety of calculations involving loans and investments. You can calculate the periodic payment for a loan or annuity using PMT, figure the net present value of an investment or loan with NPV, determine the interest and principal portion of a periodic payment with IPMT and PPMT, and calculate the future value of an investment with FV. These functions, and several more that cover the same ground, use some or all of the following common arguments:

14

- Future value (fv) is the amount that an investment or loan will be worth after all payments have been made. When dealing with investments, fv is usually positive; in the case of loans, fv is typically 0.

- Number of periods (nper) is the total number of payments or periods of an investment. Make sure the unit of measurement is consistent with the payment period; if you pay a 30-year mortgage monthly, nper is equal to 360 (30*12).

- Payment (pmt) is the amount paid periodically to an investment or loan. It cannot change over the life of the investment or loan. Typically, pmt includes principal and interest but no other fees or taxes. For a loan or investment, in which you are the one making payments, you typically enter pmt as a negative number; if you receive dividends or other payments (in other words, if you're the bank), pmt is generally a positive number.

- Present value (pv) is the value of an investment or loan at the beginning of the investment period. When you are the borrower, the present value of a loan is the principal amount that is borrowed, expressed as a negative number.

- Rate (rate) is the interest rate or discount rate for a loan or investment. Pay particular attention that nper and rate use the same scale as pmt. If you make monthly payments on a 30-year loan at 7.5% annual interest, use 7.5%/12 for rate (to convert the annual rate to a monthly rate, such as the payments) and 30*12 for nper (360, the number of monthly payments in a 30-year loan).

- Type (type) is the interval at which payments are made during the payment period, such as at the beginning of a month or the end of the month. In interest rate calculations over a long period of time, the difference can be substantial.

DATE AND TIME FUNCTIONS

Use date and time functions for simple tasks, such as displaying today's date or the day of the week for a given date. If you run an organization whose members pay dues annually on their birthday, how do you create a list of birthdays sorted by month? If you sort by birthday, you'll end up with a list that's sorted by the members' ages. To sort properly, you'll have to create a column in which each row contains a formula that uses the MONTH function to convert a date to a month.

NOTE

There's a profound difference between using a function to convert a value and using cell formats to change the display of a value. Functions return a different value from the value you use as an argument; when you change formats, on the other hand, the underlying value stored in the cell remains exactly the same.

→ For an overview of how Excel enters and manipulates dates as serial values, **see** "Setting Date and Time Formats" **p. 411.**

14

Date functions can help you perform even the most sophisticated calculations. For example, U.S. tax laws require that participants in some types of retirement accounts begin withdrawing funds and paying taxes as soon as they turn 70 1/2 years old. To calculate the first day of the month after a person reaches that age, enter the account holder's birth date in a cell named *Birth_date*, and then use the following formula to calculate the retirement date:

```
=DATE(YEAR(Birth_date)+70,MONTH(Birth_date)+7,1)
```

NOTE

> The formula just cited works even for birthdays in the second half of the year, because Excel's DATE function accepts "out of range" arguments. If the birth date is in November, for example, the MONTH(Birth_Date)+7 component of the formula evaluates to 18. Fortunately, Excel is intelligent enough to recognize that when the MONTH argument of a DATE formula is greater than 12, it should simply subtract 12 from the month and add 1 to the year.

Table 14.1 lists the most useful date and time functions, along with examples of how to use each one.

TABLE 14.1   DATE AND TIME FUNCTIONS

Function Name	Description	How to Use It
TODAY(), NOW()	Return the current date or time as a serial value.	No argument required; TODAY() returns current date; NOW() returns current date and time.
DATE(year,month,day)	Returns the specified day as a serial value.	Useful when one or more of the arguments is a calculated value or a reference to another cell; otherwise, it's simpler to enter the date directly on the worksheet.
YEAR(serial_number), MONTH(serial_number), DAY(serial_number)	Convert a serial date value to its year, month, or date.	Useful when you need to extract a component of a date—for example, to create a list of birthdays sorted without regard to year.
WEEKDAY(serial_number)	Converts a serial date value to a weekday.	Handy when you need to know the day of the week a day falls on; returns 1 (Sunday) through 7 (Saturday).

continues

14

TABLE 14.1 CONTINUED

Function Name	Description	How to Use It
HOUR(serial_number), MINUTE(serial_number), SECOND(serial_number)	Convert a serial date value to its hour, minute, or second.	Useful when you need to extract a time component of a date value.
EDATE(Start_Date,Months)	Returns a day equal to the start date, a specified number of months before or after the start date.	Useful for working with payments that are due monthly on the same date.
EOMONTH(Start_Date, Months)	Returns the last day of the month, a specified number of months before or after the start date.	Useful for working with payments that are due on the last day of a month.
WORKDAY(Start_Date,Days, Holidays)	Returns the serial value of the date a specified number of workdays before or after the start date.	Useful for planning work schedules. The Holidays argument (optional) should be a range listing dates to be excluded.
NETWORKDAYS(Start_Date, End_Date,Holidays)	Returns the number of workdays between two dates.	Works like WORKDAY, except that you supply two dates, instead of a date and an interval.

NOTE

EOMONTH, WORKDAY, and NETWORKDAYS are among a large group of advanced functions that used to be accessible only via an add-in called Analysis Toolpak. In Excel 2007, these functions are incorporated into the core program. You no longer need to install the add-in to use these functions.

STATISTICAL FUNCTIONS

Excel includes a huge number of statistical functions, including such widely used measures as standard deviation (STDEV), normal distribution (NORMDIST), Chi test (CHITEST), and Student's t-test (TTEST). As with the financial functions, these are most useful to students and teachers in high-level mathematics classes (or people who have a firm grounding in the principles of statistical analysis after having completed such a class), but a handful are applicable to users with a general business background.

Excel includes not one but three functions for working with a set of values. AVERAGE returns the arithmetic mean (the total of all values, divided by the number of entries in the list), MEDIAN returns the value in the middle of the list, and MODE returns the value that occurs most frequently. Depending on the distribution of data in a sample, any one of these three functions might be more or less appropriate.

MIN, MAX, and COUNT are straightforward functions that calculate the minimum, maximum, and number of entries in a list. These functions (and several others) have variants that end in the letter *A*—MINA, MAXA, and COUNTA. Use COUNTA, for example, when you want to work with not just numeric values in a list, but all arguments, including text and those that evaluate to a logical result such as TRUE or FALSE.

DATABASE FUNCTIONS

Excel includes a dozen functions you can incorporate into formulas to analyze information in a table. These functions work with the same techniques as advanced *filters*—for each function, you define a criteria range, specify the location of a list, and select a column on which to perform calculations.

To work with any of these functions, click the Insert Function button. In the Insert Function dialog box, select Database from the Select a Category list. Choose any entry from the list on the right to see a brief description in the same dialog box, or click the Help button for step-by-step instructions on how to use the function and enter parameters.

Note that all 12 of these functions begin with the letter *D* (for *database*). All the D-functions take three arguments:

- database—The first argument is the range that contains your list; it must include the header row that contains column labels.
- field—The second argument is the label over the column you want to summarize.
- criteria—The final argument is the range that contains a condition you specify.

Use these functions to analyze whether values in a list that meet specific criteria. For example, in a list that contains historical weather information organized by date, you can count all the rows in which the total rainfall for that period is greater than 0.1 inches.

MATH AND TRIGONOMETRIC FUNCTIONS

Given Excel's extensive mathematical capabilities, it's only natural that the list of worksheet functions includes 60 mathematical functions. Several handle advanced trigonometry calculations (COS, TAN, SIN, ACOS, ATAN, and ASIN, for example), and the PI function displays the value of Pi to 15 digits (14 decimal places).

Use the ROUND and TRUNC functions to transform values for use in calculations. For example, if cell C16 contains the value 23.5674, use =ROUND(C16,2) to convert that value to 23.57; the second argument defines the number of decimal places. Use =TRUNC(C16,2) to lop off all digits beyond the number of decimal places you specify in the second argument. Because this function truncates the value rather than rounding it, the result is 23.56 rather than 23.57.

14

NOTE
> Although you can use cell formats to change the way information is displayed in a cell, these formats don't change the underlying information stored in the cell. Use the ROUND and TRUNC functions when you want to perform calculations based on a specific level of precision.

The MOD function divides one value by another and returns a remainder. One interesting use of this formula is to determine whether a given year is a leap year. If cell A1 contains the year to be tested, enter this formula:

```
=IF(OR(MOD(A1,400)=0,AND(MOD(A1,4)=0,MOD(A1,100)<>0)),"Leap Year","Not a Leap Year")
```

This tricky formula uses the logical operators IF, OR, and AND to test whether cell A1 is divisible by 400 or is both divisible by 4 and not divisible by 100. If either condition is true, it returns the text "Leap Year"; otherwise, it returns the text "Not a Leap Year."

To display the *absolute value* of a formula, so the result is always a positive number, use the ABS function. =ABS(A14-A16), for example, always returns the difference between the values in these two cells as a positive number, even if A16 is larger than A14.

One of the most interesting functions in this group is SUMIF(range,criteria,sum_range); use it to total a range of numbers based on whether they meet criteria you define. For example, if the range B2:B20 contains the names of club members and the range C2:C20 contains individual donations in an annual fund-raising drive, use the following formula to calculate the total for all donations that were solicited by Bianca Bott:

```
=SUMIF(B2:B20,"Bianca Bott",C2:C20)
```

TEXT MANIPULATION FUNCTIONS

It's easy to think of functions in mathematical terms, but some of the most useful functions work strictly with text. You can use text functions to pull specific information from a single *text value*, split a text value into multiple cells, combine text values into a single string, or convert one type of data (such as a number or date) into text, using a specific format.

When you want to combine (or *concatenate*) the text from two cells, use an ampersand. The following formula adds a space between the values in two adjacent cells:

```
=A1&" "&A2
```

For more sophisticated manipulation of strings of text, use any of Excel's two dozen text functions. These functions are especially useful when you've imported text from another program or file. Simple text functions enable you to convert text from all capitals to lowercase letters (and vice versa) or convert a date value to text in a specific format. The following formula, for example, combines three functions to pull out just the last name from a complete name in cell A17:

```
=RIGHT(A17,LEN(A17)-FIND(" ",A17))
```

14

The task isn't as easy as it might first appear. Because the last name can be any length (Bott or Leonhard, for example), you first need to calculate the correct number of characters. For starters, use the FIND function to locate the space separating the first and last names. If the first name contains five letters, the formula FIND(" ",A17) returns the value 6. Next, use the LEN function to determine the total length of the name; by subtracting the value determined in the first step from this value, you can determine the exact length of the last name. Finally, use the RIGHT function to extract that number of characters from the input cell (A17), starting at the right side.

Table 14.2 lists the most useful text functions.

TABLE 14.2   COMMON TEXT FUNCTIONS

Function Name	Description	How to Use It
CONCATENATE(text1,text2,...)	Combine two or more text items	Generally, an ampersand (&) is easier.
UPPER(text), LOWER(text), PROPER(text)	Convert case of text, to all capitals, all lowercase	=PROPER("pearson technology group") changes the first letter of letters, or initial capitals each word to a capital letter—in this case, Pearson Technology Group.
FIND(find_text,within_text, start_num), SEARCH(find_text, within_text,start_num)	Find text in a cell	FIND is case-sensitive; SEARCH allows wildcard characters.
LEFT(text, num_chars), RIGHT (text,num_chars), MID(text, start_num,num_chars)	Extract text from a cell	Use to extract part of a text string—for example, a part number from a lengthy product code.
TEXT(value,format_text), FIXED (number,decimals, no_commas), DOLLAR(number,decimals)	Convert number to text	For the TEXT function, specify any number format (except General) from the Category box on the Number tab in the Format Cells dialog box. Be sure to enclose the format in quotation marks: =TEXT(TODAY(),"mmmm d,yyyy").
CLEAN(), TRIM()	Remove unwanted characters from text	TRIM removes extra spaces from imported text, and CLEAN removes unprintable characters, such as might be found at the top or bottom of a file that contains formatting information that Excel can't interpret.

14

If you have trouble concatenating two values, see "Converting Values to Text Before Concatenating" in the "Troubleshooting" section at the end of this chapter.

LOGICAL AND INFORMATION FUNCTIONS

Excel includes six *comparison functions*, which you can use to compare two values and define actions based on the comparison. Far and away the most popular and useful logical function is IF. The following is the syntax of the IF function:

```
=IF(logical_test,value_if_true,value_if_false)
```

Excel also includes 18 information functions, which give you information about cells, worksheets, and your system itself. For the most part, you'll use these functions to build error-handling and data-validation routines into a worksheet. Nine of these functions belong in a subgroup called the IS functions: ISTEXT, ISERROR, ISNUMBER, and so on.

By combining the IF function and the ISERROR function, you can avoid seeing error codes in a worksheet. The formula =IF(ISERROR(A5/A8)," ",A5/A8), for example, tests the value of the formula A5/A8 before displaying a result. If A8 is equal to 0, Excel displays nothing in the cell rather than the annoying #DIV/0! error message; if the value of A8 is other than 0 and the formula returns a valid result rather than an error message, Excel displays that result.

TROUBLESHOOTING FORMULAS

The more complex the formula, the more likely you are to need time to get it working properly. Excel 2007 includes a variety of tools you can use to troubleshoot errors in formulas and in worksheets. This section discusses the most useful options.

HOW FORMULA AUTOCORRECT WORKS

Under most circumstances, Excel won't let you enter a formula using incorrect syntax. If you make one of many common mistakes in formula syntax or punctuation, Excel offers to correct the mistake for you, and generally the correction is appropriate. This feature, called Formula AutoCorrect, can detect and repair any of the following errors within a formula:

- Unmatched parentheses, curly braces, or single or double quotation marks.
- Reversed cell references (14C instead of C14, for example) or comparison operators (=< instead of <=).
- Extra operators—for example, an extra equal sign or plus sign at the beginning of a formula or a dangling operator at the end.

TIP

> In a nod to its great spreadsheet predecessors VisiCalc and 1-2-3, Excel will allow you to begin a formula with a plus sign instead of an equal sign. (It will add its own equal sign before your plus sign.) If, for any reason, you find it easier to hit the plus key than the equals key, go right ahead; Excel won't mind.

- Extra spaces in cell addresses (A 14 instead of A14), between operands, or between a function name and its arguments.

- Extra decimal points or operators—in general, Excel uses the decimal point or operator farthest to the left and removes all others, so 234.56.78 becomes 234.5678, and =23*/34 becomes =23*34.

- Incorrect range identifiers, such as a semicolon or an extra colon between the column and row identifiers.

- Implied multiplication—if you omit the multiplication sign and enter 2(A14+B14), for example, or use an x instead, Excel adds the correct sign.

> **N O T E**
>
> Excel will fix one common type of formula error without even asking. If you omit the closing parenthesis on a simple function call, Excel will supply it for you. If there is any ambiguity about a missing parentheses, however, Formula AutoCorrect will intervene and propose a resolution.

RESOLVING COMMON ERROR MESSAGES

All Excel error messages begin with a number sign (#); in all, you might see any of seven possible error codes. To remove the error message and display the results you expect, you have to fix the problem either by editing the formula or changing the contents of a cell to which the formula refers.

If the cell in question contains an error message, a small green triangle will appear in the upper-left corner. Click to select the cell, and a Smart Tag with a yellow exclamation point appears. Click the Smart Tag to display a menu like the one shown in Figure 14.10.

The top line in the Smart Tag menu displays the name of the error and is not clickable. Use additional menu choices to find possible causes and solutions for the error.

Table 14.3 lists the seven error codes you're likely to see when an Excel formula isn't working properly, along with suggested troubleshooting steps.

Figure 14.10
Click the Smart Tag to find clues to the cause of an error message and possible solutions.

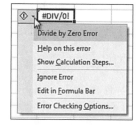

14

TABLE 14.3   COMMON FORMULA ERROR CODES

Error Code Displayed	What It Means	Suggested Troubleshooting Steps
#DIV/0!	Formula is trying to divide by a zero value or a blank cell.	Check the divisor in your formula and make sure it does not refer to a blank cell. You might want to add an error-handling =IF() routine or conditional format to the cell, as described earlier in this chapter.
#N/A	Formula does not have a valid value for argument passed.	#N/A means "No value is available." Check to see whether you have problems with LOOKUP functions. You can also manually enter the #N/A value in cells in which a value is temporarily unavailable, to prevent #DIV/0! errors.
#NAME?	Formula contains text that is neither a valid function nor a defined name on the active worksheet.	You've probably misspelled a function name or a range name. Check the formula carefully. In a natural-language formula created in an earlier version of Excel, this error means Excel cannot identify one or both labels.
#NULL!	Refers to intersection of two areas that don't intersect.	You're trying to calculate a formula by using labels for a column and row that have no common cells. Choose new labels for the row or column or both.
#NUM!	Value is too large, too small, imaginary, or not found.	Excel can handle numbers as large as 10^{308} or as small as 10^{-308}. This error usually means you've used a function incorrectly—for example, calculating the square root of a negative number.
#REF!	Formula contains a reference that is not valid.	Did you delete a cell or range originally referred to in the formula? If so, you see this error code in the formula as well.
#VALUE!	Formula contains an argument of the wrong type.	You've probably mixed two incompatible data types in one formula—trying to add text with a number, for example. Check the formula again.

CHECKING FOR ERRORS IN A WORKSHEET

As noted in the previous section, Excel tracks formula errors automatically as you work, displaying a green triangle in the upper-left corner of any cell that contains an error. You can also check for errors on a sheet manually, by clicking Error Checking in the Formula Auditing group of the Formulas tab. When you choose this option, Excel finds the first error (on the current sheet only) and displays a dialog box like the one shown in Figure 14.11. Use the Previous and Next buttons to highlight additional errors on the sheet.

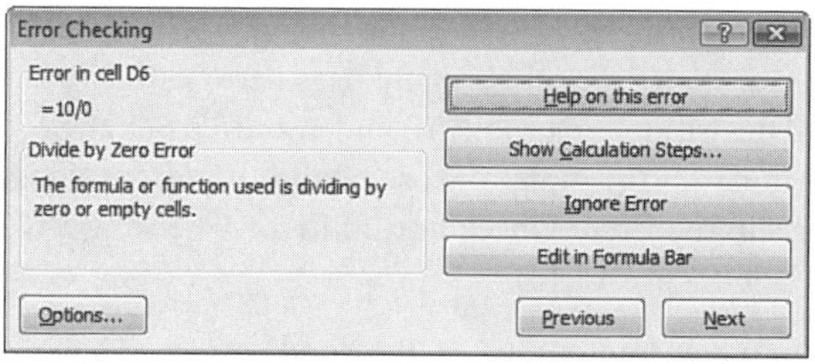

Figure 14.11
Click the Show Calculation Steps button to step through each operation and debug a complex formula.

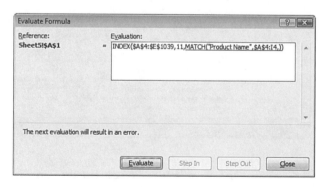

If the error is harmless and you don't want Excel to nag you about it any further, click the Ignore Error button. For simple errors where the fix is immediately obvious (a typographical error or a misplaced divisor, for instance), click the Edit in Formula Bar button to make the change directly, without closing the Error Checking dialog box.

For complex formulas, in which an error can be difficult to track down, click the Show Calculation Steps button. This button opens the Evaluate Formula dialog box (see Figure 14.12), which enables you to drill down into a formula to find and fix the problem.

The initial view shows each element in the formula, evaluated to the result just before the error. Click the Evaluate button to step through the error. Keep clicking and you'll eventually return to the formula as entered, where you can walk through each element of the formula, moving from left to right. With each click, Excel evaluates another part of the formula.

For formulas that refer to other formulas in other cells, click the Step In button to follow the chain of references through as many steps as it takes to find the error.

Figure 14.12
Clicking the Step In button allows you to drill down into a formula in search of errors from another cell.

TIP

> If you inherit a worksheet that someone else has developed and you want to quickly check it for errors, take this precautionary step: Open the Error Checking dialog box, click the Options button, and click the Reset Ignored Errors button. This option ensures that you'll see all possible errors that Excel can detect, even if a previous user hid the error indicators.

14

Click the Options button on the Error Checking dialog box to specify for which errors Excel should look. For instance, Excel normally flags dates with two-digit years as errors (because of possible date arithmetic problems) and also calls out any formula that is inconsistent with other formulas in the same row or column. If you get tired of false alarms, clear any of the check boxes in the Error Checking and Error Checking Rules section of the dialog box that appears (see Figure 14.13).

Excel dutifully catches many common types of formula errors as soon as you press Enter. For instance, if you click in cell E8 and enter the formula =SUM(E1:E7)/E8, Excel will warn you that you're about to create a *circular reference*, in which one part of your formula refers to itself. Because the act of calculating the formula changes one of the values in the formula, you'll get a different result each time you calculate a formula that contains a circular reference. More subtle forms of circular references incorporate intermediate calculations that depend on the value in the current cell. For instance, if a formula in A8 refers to a value in E8, adding a reference to A8 into the formula in E8 will create a circular reference.

Figure 14.13
Use the check boxes under the Error Checking and Error Checking Rules headings to prevent Excel from checking for particular types of errors.

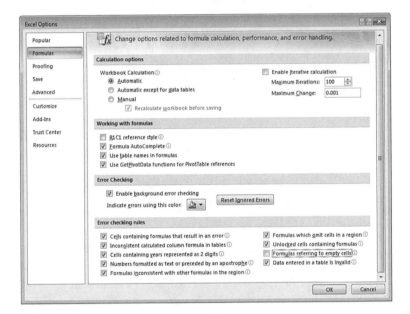

If you inadvertently create a circular reference, you can use the Circular Reference toolbar (click the drop-down arrow next to the Error Checking button in the Formula Auditing group of the Formulas tab and then choose Circular Reference) to display all circular references on the worksheet.

NOTE

> Some esoteric scientific calculations rely on circular references. In this case, you can specify the number of iterations you want to use when recalculating the formula. For a more detailed explanation, see the "Allow or Correct a Circular Reference" Help topic.

USING THE RANGE FINDER TO LOCATE PARTS OF A FORMULA

When a cell that contains a summary formula doesn't display the correct result, the first place to look is at the cell and range references in that formula. If you've added new rows or columns, it's possible that the formula references the old range and doesn't include the new cells.

To match cell references in any formula with the actual worksheet cells, use Excel's Range Finder. When you select any cell that contains a formula and make it available for editing, Excel highlights each cell or range reference in that formula with a different color and then adds an identically color-coded outline around the cells to which the range refers.

If you discover that a formula includes an incorrect cell or range reference, use the Range Finder to add or remove cells from the reference, or to select a completely different group of cells. Click the color-coded border on any cell edge to move the reference to a different cell; click and drag the square handle in any corner of the colored border to extend the selection. To record your changes, press Enter or click the green Enter Formula button next to the formula bar.

USING GOAL SEEK TO FIND VALUES

After you've constructed a worksheet and built several intricate formulas, you might discover that you can't easily get the answer for which you're looking. A formula that uses the PMT function, for example, is designed to produce the total monthly payment when you enter the price and loan details. But what if you've determined your maximum monthly payment, you've shopped around for the best interest rate, and now you want to calculate the maximum loan amount you can afford based on those values? Rather than construct a new formula or use trial-and-error methods to find the right result, use Excel's Goal Seek tool to perform the calculations in one operation:

1. Start by opening the worksheet that contains the formula with which you want to work. Then click What If Analysis in the Data Tools group of the Data tab. From the menu that descends, choose Goal Seek shown in Figure 14.14.

2. Fill in the three boxes to match the results you're trying to achieve. In the Set Cell box, enter the address of the formula whose results you want to control. In the To Value box, enter the amount the formula specified in the previous cell should equal. Finally, in the By Changing Cell box, enter the cell that contains the single value you want to change.

14

Figure 14.14
Excel displays the
Goal Seek dialog box.

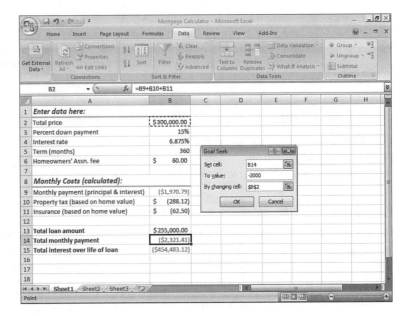

3. When you click OK, Excel runs through all possibilities and displays the Goal Seek Status dialog box, as shown in Figure 14.15.

4. Click OK to incorporate the changed data into your worksheet; click Cancel to close the dialog box and restore the original data.

Figure 14.15
If you look at the
worksheet itself, you'll
see the values have
changed to reflect the
result shown here.

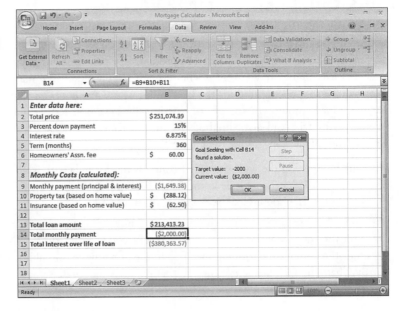

TROUBLESHOOTING

EDITING AN ARRAY FORMULA

I entered an array formula, but when I try to edit or copy it, the results change or I get an error message.

Editing an array formula is tricky. If the array formula was entered across multiple cells, you must select every cell that contains the array before you can edit it. If the array formula is contained in a single cell, you can edit it just as you would a conventional formula, but you must remember to press Ctrl+Shift+Enter to store your changes as an array formula. If you forget and press Enter, Excel stores it as a standard formula, with the wrong results. Finally, you'll notice some restrictions when you try to copy an array formula. If the destination range you select also contains the array formula, you'll get an error message; select a new destination range, or use AutoFill to copy the formula. Oh, and don't try to cheat by adding your own curly braces to create an array formula—the only way to enter an array formula is to press Ctrl+Shift+Enter and let Excel add the curly braces.

CHECKING FORMULAS BEFORE DELETING RANGE NAMES

After I deleted a range name in my worksheet, some of my formulas displayed error messages.

It's a frustrating fact of life: When you delete a range name from a worksheet, Excel does not automatically adjust any formulas that contain that range name. Even though it should, logically, be able to substitute the old cell address for the range name, it leaves the name there to taunt you. After deleting a range name, you will see a #NAME? error in any cell that contains a formula with a reference to the deleted range name. Unfortunately, there's no easy way to determine which cell goes with the defunct name. If you spot these errors immediately after deleting the range name, press Ctrl+Z to undo your change. If you remember this possibility before deleting a range name, you can easily change any cells before deleting or changing the defined name. Press Ctrl+F to open the Find dialog box, enter the name of the cell or range, choose Formulas from the Look In box, and click Find Next to jump to and edit each cell that contains that name.

CONVERTING VALUES TO TEXT BEFORE CONCATENATING

When I try to combine a cell that contains text with one that contains a date, the result is nonsense. The cell that holds the date is correctly formatted, but the resulting text says something like "Today is 38059" instead of displaying a date.

As you've seen, Excel ignores the formatting of the original cell when concatenating the two values and instead displays the serial date value. Before concatenating a date with text, you must convert the date to text and choose a format. Use the TEXT function followed by a format in quotation marks. If the date is in cell A15, for example, use this formula to get the result you're looking for: `="Today is "&TEXT(A15,"mmmm d, yyyy")`.

EXTRA CREDIT: NESTING FUNCTIONS WITHIN FUNCTIONS

In some cases, it's necessary to use one function as the argument for another. *Nesting* functions within functions this way is common with logical functions such as IF, for example. You might use a set of nested functions to help you decide how much to pay on a handful of credit cards and installment loans, where your goal is to pay off the debts with the highest interest rate first and make minimum payments on all others.

The sample worksheet shown in Figure 14.16 is built using the following principles:

- Column B shows the current balance for each debt.

- Column C lists the interest rate for each debt.

- Column D calculates the minimum payment you want to make on each balance, at 5% of the current balance.

- Cell E8 contains the total amount available for repaying your total debt load.

Figure 14.16
Nesting functions in a worksheet.

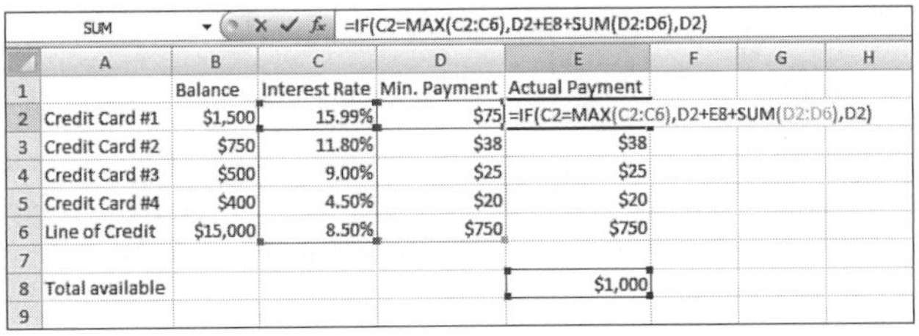

	A	B	C	D	E	F	G	H
SUM				=IF(C2=MAX(C2:C6),D2+E8+SUM(D2:D6),D2)				
1		Balance	Interest Rate	Min. Payment	Actual Payment			
2	Credit Card #1	$1,500	15.99%	$75	=IF(C2=MAX(C2:C6),D2+E8+SUM(D2:D6),D2)			
3	Credit Card #2	$750	11.80%	$38	$38			
4	Credit Card #3	$500	9.00%	$25	$25			
5	Credit Card #4	$400	4.50%	$20	$20			
6	Line of Credit	$15,000	8.50%	$750	$750			
7								
8	Total available				$1,000			
9								

- Each cell in column E contains a formula that enters the minimum payment for all rows except the one with the highest interest rate; for that value, the calculation adds whatever is left over from the Total Available amount after making all minimum payments.

The following formula performs the full calculation in a single step for the first row:

```
=IF(C2=MAX(C2:C6),D2+E8-SUM(D2:D6),D2)
```

Note that this example includes two levels of nesting, with the SUM and MAX functions nested within an IF function.

You can nest functions within functions within functions to create some clever effects. Say you want to add a date stamp to a worksheet, so whenever you print the worksheet, you'll see a large text label that includes your name and the current date. Enter this formula in a cell that is within the print range, substituting your name in the text string that begins the formula:

```
="Prepared by John Q. Smith, "&TEXT(TODAY(),"mmmm d, yyyy")
```

14

When nesting functions, note that the nested function must return the same value type (text, number, date, true/false) as the argument it's replacing. Unlike formulas containing constants or cell references, which can contain an unlimited number of nesting levels, Excel enables you to nest a maximum of seven levels of functions. If you need to perform more calculations than this, you'll have to break the formula into multiple steps and place each step in its own cell.

You can use the Insert Function dialog box to enter a nested function within another function. Begin entering the first function by using the Insert Function dialog box, as described in "Entering Error-Free Formulas," earlier in this chapter. Click in the input box for any argument and then choose another function from the Function box (this box is located to the left of the Formula bar, where the Name box normally appears; it is visible only when the Function Arguments dialog box is open). As you enter the formula, you can switch between functions at any time by clicking the function's name in the Formula bar. If you choose a function that contains a nested function as an argument (as in the example shown in Figure 14.17), the entire function appears in the input box, and the result of the function using current values appears to its right.

Figure 14.17

WORKING WITH TABLES AND PIVOTTABLES

In this chapter

15

SLICING AND DICING DATA WITH TABLES

Excel is absolutely, positively not just for accountants and other number crunchers. For proof, take a look at the extensive set of features you can use to track information stored in tabular format. You've probably already figured out that Excel makes it easy to enter a column of names or dates and quickly sort them, but its table-management features go much deeper. A table can include thousands of rows of data and dozens of columns, which you can use to filter, sort, and extract the details for which you're looking. Want to do sophisticated cross-tabulations of data? That's no problem when you use the amazing PivotTable features.

You can enter data manually by creating a table, defining columns, and typing each row. Or you can import data from other programs or from Web-based repositories and then perform your own research and analysis. For example, you can do any or all of the following tasks:

- Keep a list of students or club members and track attendance for a series of classes or events.
- Maintain an address list and use it to create mail-merge documents with Word.
- Perform detailed analysis of statistical information, such as weather, population growth, and industrial or agricultural output.
- Track your scores or times in a favorite hobby—golf or bowling scores, marathon times, and so on.

In this chapter, we cover techniques for working with both standard tables and PivotTables.

LISTS VERSUS TABLES

Any well-organized rectangular block of data might informally be called a table, but in Excel 2007, the term *table* has a formal meaning. It refers to a block of cells that you have explicitly chosen to format as a table. You do this by means of a simple Ribbon command or keyboard shortcut, and after you have done so, your table acquires the following highly useful attributes:

- Excel makes a gallery of *table styles* available to the table. Like cell styles, these are stylishly designed combinations of formatting characteristics, keyed to the current theme. (If you change the theme, by means of the Themes command on the Page Layout tab, the colors and fonts assigned to the table styles change as well.) But table styles are smarter than cell styles. Among other things, in many cases they provide banding (contrasting shading for alternate rows), which makes it easier to read across a set of columns without losing track of which row you're reading. Excel keeps the banding in place, even if you delete rows or shuffle the data by means of a Sort command.
- After you have declared a range to be a table, Excel expands its boundaries for you if you add rows or columns. Your table style automatically encompasses the new data. If you have created a PivotTable from your table, the new rows or columns are automatically made available to the PivotTable. If you have used one or more columns as data series in a chart, the chart expands right along with your expanding table.

- Formulas within the table are automatically replicated as the table expands. So, for example, if your table includes several columns of numbers plus a column that totals the values in the other columns, Excel creates a new formula for you if you add a new row.

- A simple Ribbon command can add a Total row to the bottom of your table. Cells in the Total row can apply any function to the values in the columns above. That is, they are not limited to totaling; they can compute averages, find maximums and minimums, count values, and so on.

- A simple Ribbon command becomes available to weed out duplicate entries in the table.

- If you scroll downward far enough in a table that the header row disappears, Excel displays the header text in the worksheet frame. The effect is equivalent to freezing the top row of the table, but the program performs this service for you automatically.

- Formulas that reference table elements can do so by means of *structured referencing*. For example, if your table includes columns with the header labels Jan, Feb, and Mar, and a column labeled Q1Total that adds the values in the first three columns, Excel can use the formula =SUM(*TableName*[[#This Row],[Jan]:[Mar]]) to create the formula (see Figure 15.1). Excel usually creates the correct structured references for you if you build your formulas by pointing with the mouse to the cells you want to reference. That's a good thing, because the structured-referencing syntax is somewhat complex, and it's easy to make mistakes. You are not required to use it; you can build formulas the old-fashioned way, with cell addresses or names. But structured-reference formulas have the potential to make your formula logic self-documenting.

Figure 15.1
You can, but are not required to, use structured referencing in table formulas.

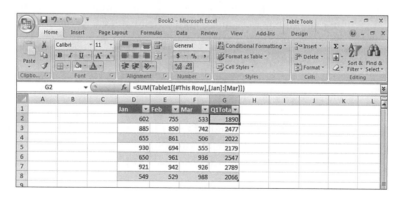

NOTE

> In Chapter 14, "Using Formulas and Functions," we noted that the natural-language formulas supported in earlier versions of Excel are no longer supported in Excel 2007. Structured references to cells and ranges within tables are intended to be a functional replacement for natural-language references.

15

Excel 2003 supported a construct called a *list* that was somewhat like a table in Excel 2007. In Excel 2003, you convert a range to a list by pressing Ctrl+L. Those old-style lists have many, but not all, of the features of Excel 2007 tables (in particular, they lack the formatting intelligence of Excel 2007 tables). If you open an Excel 2003 workbook containing one or more lists, those lists will be ordinary ranges in Excel 2007, but you can convert them quickly to tables. You can even continue to use the Ctrl+L shortcut to do this (as well as the new Ctrl+T shortcut). Because lists, as a formal object type, are gone in Excel 2007, we use the term *list* informally to signify a range that could become, but is currently not, a table.

Whether your range is a table or just a plain old list, you can sort it, filter it, chart it, use functions to analyze it, and use it as a source range for a PivotTable. But because all these operations are simpler to carry out in tables, there is seldom a good reason not to turn a list into a table.

ORGANIZING TABULAR INFORMATION

A well-organized table should adhere to the following guidelines:

- Each column in the first row should hold a label that describes, uniquely and unambiguously, the kind of information the column contains. This header row isn't absolutely required, but it makes life easier. And if you don't supply your own header labels, Excel simply creates them for you—using nondescriptive text such as Column 1, Column 2, and so on.

- Each column should contain one kind of information. In a team roster, for example, one column might hold last names, another first names, a third telephone numbers. Be sure that any element that you might want to manipulate independently gets its own column. If your telephone list contains numbers in more than one area code, for example, and you want to be able to sort or filter on the basis of the area codes, don't bundle the area codes in with the numbers; give them their own column.

- The table should occupy a contiguous block of cells; that is, it should not include any blank rows. If you think you might ever filter the table (that is, restrict it to showing only those rows that meet some criterion), don't put any data to the right or left of the table. Filtering hides rows, without regard to anything that might lie alongside the table.

TURNING A LIST INTO A TABLE

To turn a cell range into a table, select any cell within that range and press Ctrl+T. Alternatively, select a cell in the range and click Format as Table in the Styles group of the Home tab. If you do the latter, the Table Styles gallery drops down (see Figure 15.2), enabling you to select a style at the same time you create the table. If you use the keyboard shortcut instead, Excel gives your new table a default style; you can select a different style at any time. In either case, before Excel creates the table, it prompts you to confirm the range of the table and the presence or absence of a header row (see Figure 15.3). Ordinarily Excel gets these details right; the only exception might be if you accidentally select more than one cell in the table range (but not the entire range) before creating the table. In that case, Excel assumes that the cells you selected constitute the whole table.

Figure 15.2
Excel provides a gallery of more than 60 table styles.

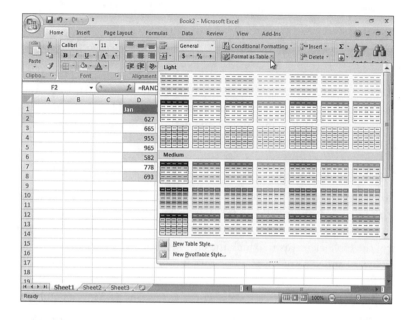

Figure 15.3
Use the Create Table dialog box to confirm the range of your table and whether that range includes a header row.

After creating the table, Excel adds a new Design tab to the right side of the Ribbon, under the heading Table Tools. This tab is available whenever the selection lies within a table.

NAMING THE TABLE

Like charts and drawings, tables in Excel are named objects. Excel assigns a default name to your table when you first create it. That name appears in a box in the Properties group at the left end of the Design tab (see Figure 15.4). You can change the name by clicking in the box and typing.

15

Figure 15.4
Excel gives your table a default name, but you can change it.

Click here to change the table name

Click here to open the Table Styles gallery

You don't need to change the table's name, but if you use structured-referencing formulas, you might find those formulas easier to read if the table is indicated by a descriptive name, rather than a default name. You should definitely provide a descriptive name if you intend to write macros that refer to the table.

CHOOSING A TABLE STYLE

To change the table style, select a cell within the table and then open the Table Styles gallery at the right side of the Design tab. Directly to the left of the Table Styles gallery in the Table Style Options group are six check boxes. By selecting or deselecting items here, you can control the table elements to which the current style will apply. For example, if the current style includes banded rows but you don't want them banded, deselect Band Rows.

USING THE TOTAL ROW

To add a total row to your table, select any cell in the table and then select the Total Row check box in the Table Style Options group of the Design tab. The check box is a toggle. You can remove the total row by clearing the check box.

Initially, Excel puts the label TOTAL in the first cell of the total row, and it sums the last column. You can add summary formulas to any of the other columns, and any formulas in the row can use any function. For example, in Figure 15.5, we added a Count to column B, to have a running total of the number of donors as well as a running total of the amount donated. To add or change a summary formula, click in the cell where you want the formula to be. A drop-down arrow appears. Open the drop-down list and choose the function you want to use.

Because the statistical functions in the total row drop-down list actually apply variants of the SUBTOTAL function, if you filter the table to show particular rows only, the total row summarizes only the visible rows. Normally, that's exactly what you want. If you filtered the table in Figure 15.5, for example, to show only those donations that arrived on 6/22/07, the numbers on the total row would change to 3 (in column B) and 1990 (in column D).

Figure 15.5
Formulas in the total row can use any function.

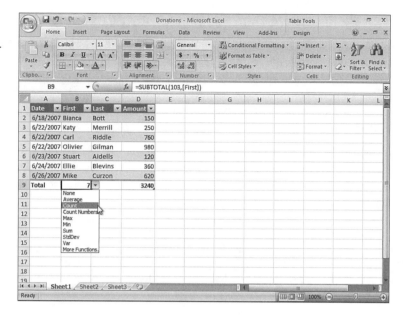

TIP

When you turn a list into a table, Excel adds filter controls to the headers in each column (see Figure 15.5, for example). These filter controls are invaluable when your table is more than a few rows deep. They enable you to focus your attention on those rows in the table that you're interested in at any given time. But if you find them inconvenient, you can remove them by clicking Filter, in the Sort and Filter group of the Data tab. Click the same button again to restore the filters.

ADDING ROWS TO A TABLE

To add a new row to a table that is not currently displaying the total row, simply select a cell in the row directly below the table and type. Excel expands the table to include your new row. If the total row is displayed, this approach won't work. To add new data in this case, select the rightmost cell in the row above the total row and then press Tab. Excel adds a new row to the table, in the process moving the total row down to accommodate the new data.

ENTERING DATA IN TABLES AND LISTS

Excel provides a number of features that simplify data entry. The features described in the following sections work equally well in ordinary lists and ranges that you have formally declared to be tables.

SPEEDING UP REPETITIVE DATA ENTRY WITH AUTOCOMPLETE

Excel's default setup enables an option called *AutoComplete*, which is designed to speed up entering data in lists and tables. As you type, Excel compares each character that you enter with other entries in cells directly above the active cell. If the opening characters match those of any other entry, Excel assumes that you want to repeat that entry and fills in the rest of the label. (This comparison applies only to cells that contain text; AutoComplete ignores numbers, dates, and times.)

If you want to repeat the previous entry, press Enter (or Tab or any arrow key) to insert the AutoComplete entry in the cell. Keep typing to enter a new value in the cell. Excel does not suggest an AutoComplete entry unless the string you have entered matches a unique entry in the list above the active cell.

TIP

> Instead of waiting for Excel's suggestion, you can select from a list of entries already in the column. To display the list, press Alt+down arrow, or right-click the cell and then choose Pick from List from the shortcut menu.

Some users find AutoComplete disconcerting, dangerous, or merely annoying because if you don't pay close attention, you risk accidentally entering the wrong data. You can easily disable AutoComplete: Click the Microsoft Office button, click Excel Options, and then click Advanced in the left pane of the Excel Options dialog box. Then, under the heading Editing Options, clear the check mark from the Enable AutoComplete for Cell Values box. Click OK to save the new setting and continue editing.

If you have a love-hate relationship with AutoComplete, create a macro that toggles this feature on and off. Assign a keyboard shortcut to the macro so you can turn the feature on and off quickly and easily. Here's all the code you need:

```
Sub ToggleAutoComplete()
    Application.EnableAutoComplete = Not Application.EnableAutoComplete
End Sub
```

→ For details on how to use macros, **see** Chapter 26, "Using Macros to Automate Routine Tasks," **p. 721.**

→ Don't confuse AutoComplete with AutoCorrect; for more details about this and other Office-wide Auto features, **see** "Using AutoCorrect to Type Faster," **p. 90.**

AUTOMATICALLY FILLING IN A SERIES OF DATA

One common and tedious data-entry task is entering a sequence of numbers or dates in a column or row. Excel's *AutoFill* feature can handle this chore automatically by filling in information as you drag the mouse along a column or row. Use AutoFill to copy formulas or values; enter the days of the week, months of the year, or any series of numbers or dates; and even fill in custom lists of departments, category names, part numbers, and other information you define.

Because of its tremendous number of options, even Excel experts sometimes have trouble coaxing the correct results out of AutoFill. Using Smart Tags makes this task somewhat easier. If using AutoFill has the wrong result, click the AutoFill Smart Tag to see a list of other options that enable you to select a different result, such as changing a simple copy to a series.

→ For more details about Smart Tags, **see** "Customizing Smart Tags," **p. 46.**

In general, using AutoFill has one of the following results:

- Copy data from one or more cells—If the selection is not a sequence that Excel recognizes—for example, if you select a single cell that contains text—AutoFill copies the selection in the direction that you drag.

> TIP
>
> Using AutoFill is an excellent way to copy a formula from one cell across a row or down a column. This technique is especially useful for copying formulas that total columns or rows. As you drag, AutoFill copies the formula, adjusting relative references as needed.

- Copy formatting or values across a row or down a column—Normally, AutoFill copies both formats and values from the cells with which you start. To choose one, make a selection and then hold down the right mouse button while dragging the fill handle. When you release the mouse button, choose Fill Formatting Only or Fill Without Formatting. If you select a formula in the starting cell, either option copies the formula, with or without formatting.

- Fill in a series of dates—If you enter a date in any recognizable format, such as 4/10 or 5-23-08, AutoFill extends the series in one-day increments. AutoFill also recognizes long and short versions of days of the week and months. If you enter Jan in the first cell, for example, AutoFill continues the list with Feb, Mar, Apr, and so on; start with Wednesday, and AutoFill extends the list with Thursday, Friday, Saturday, and so on. Excel also recognizes calendar quarters. If you enter Q1 in a cell and use AutoFill, you get Q2, Q3, and Q4, at which point the series starts over with Q1.

> TIP
>
> When you reach the end of a finite AutoFill sequence, such as days of the week or months of the year, the sequence repeats. If you start with Monday, for example, the sequence starts over again after the seventh cell.

- Fill in a series of numbers—This is probably the trickiest AutoFill option. If you start with a single cell that contains the number 1 and use AutoFill to extend it, Excel copies the number 1 to the rest of the cells you select. To instruct Excel to AutoFill a series instead of copying the number, hold down the Ctrl key as you drag, and then choose Fill Series from the shortcut menu. Alternatively, enter 1 in the first cell and 2 in the second. Then select both and drag the fill handle.

TIP

> When you insert a sequence of numbers, Excel assumes that you want to increment them by 1. Thus, if you start with 100, the sequence continues with 101, 102, and so on. To use a different sequence, enter values in at least two cells so the sequence is apparent and then select those cells and use AutoFill. For example, if you enter 100 and 200 in the first two cells and then select those cells and use AutoFill, Excel continues the series with 300, 400, and so on. You can also use this technique to enter a date series, such as every other day (Monday, Wednesday, Friday), every third month (Feb, May, Aug), or the 10th of each month (1/10, 2/10, 3/10). Enter the first two or three cells in the sequence, select the cells you entered, and then extend the selection using AutoFill.

- **Fill in a series of numbered items**—If you enter any text plus a number (Chapter 1, Item 1, or Area 51, for example), AutoFill extends the selection by one (Chapter 2, Chapter 3, and so on). Confusingly, this AutoFill option works exactly the opposite as it does on a series of numbers without text: In this case, hold down Ctrl to prevent Excel from extending the selection and copy the values instead.

- **Fill in a custom list**—If you've created a custom list (see the following section for step-by-step instructions), enter any item from that list in any cell, and then use AutoFill to add the remaining items in the list.

- **Fill in a trend series**—For this option, you must select a number of cells first and then drag with the right mouse button for more options. You can choose a *Linear Trend* series, in which Excel calculates the average difference between each value in the series that you selected and then adds it to (or subtracts it from) each succeeding value in the AutoFill range. Choose a *Growth Trend* series to have Excel calculate the percentage of difference between items in the series and apply that amount to each new value. These options are useful when you're trying to project future patterns, such as population growth, based on existing data.

To use AutoFill, follow these steps:

1. First, enter the initial value or values for the range. If the list begins a unique sequence—months of the year, for example, starting with Jan or January—you need to enter a value in only one cell. To AutoFill a sequence of numbers or dates with an increment value other than one, enter the first two or three values in the series.

2. Point to Excel's *fill handle*—the small black square in the lower-right corner of the currently selected cell or range. When you point at the fill handle, the mouse pointer turns into a thin black cross.

3. Drag in any direction (up or down in a column, left or right in a row) to begin filling in values (see Figure 15.6). Hold down the Ctrl key as you extend the selection to switch the AutoFill action from copy to fill series, or vice versa.

Figure 15.6
As you drag, Excel
automatically fills in
values in your series—
dates, in this example.

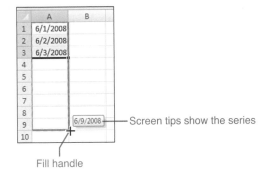

— Screen tips show the series

Fill handle

> **NOTE**
>
> AutoFill works only in one row or column at a time. To extend a selection down and to
> the right, you must perform the AutoFill action in two steps.

4. ScreenTips display the value that will appear in each new cell as you extend the series. When you reach the final cell, release the mouse button to fill in the data.

5. If the AutoFill results are not what you expected, click the AutoFill Smart Tag to display a menu with additional options (see Figure 15.7).

Figure 15.7

For maximum control over AutoFill options, hold down the right mouse button while dragging. When you release the mouse button, you can choose the appropriate option from the shortcut menu. Choose the Series option at the bottom of the shortcut menu to display a dialog box that lets you choose any option, including starting points and step values for a series, as in Figure 15.8.

> **TIP**
>
> You can also use AutoFill to remove items from a range without removing formatting.
> Select the entire range that contains the series. Aim the mouse pointer at the lower-right
> corner, but instead of dragging the fill handle down or to the right, as you normally
> would do to extend a series, drag it up (for a column) or to the left (for a row). This
> action makes the range smaller, removing those items that are no longer selected with-
> out affecting the formatting applied to those cells.

Figure 15.8
If Excel can't recognize the progression in an AutoFill series, use this dialog box to specify series settings manually.

CREATING CUSTOM AUTOFILL LISTS TO FIT YOUR PROJECTS

You can also create a custom list, such as names of countries, budget categories, or department codes, and add the list to Excel. Excel adds custom lists to the Windows Registry, with each list appearing in the precise order in which you enter individual items. The result can be tremendous time savings for you if you regularly insert the same list into worksheets. AutoFill can insert any custom list in any row or column, anytime (and, as we'll demonstrate in the next section, you can also use a custom list as a sort key for the rest of your list).

> **TIP**
>
> To copy a custom list from one computer to another, use the original custom list to fill in a range on a blank worksheet and then save the resulting workbook. On the computer where you want to import the list, open the saved workbook, select the list range, and use the Import button on the Custom Lists tab of the Options dialog box, as described in this section. It takes a few minutes at most, and it's foolproof.

To add a custom list to Excel, use either of the following procedures:

- If the list is short, you can type it directly into a dialog box. Click the Microsoft Office button and click Excel Options. Click Popular in the left pane of the Excel Options dialog box. Then click Edit Custom Lists. Select New List in the Custom Lists dialog box, and start entering items in the List Entries box, as shown in Figure 15.9. Be sure to enter each item in the correct order and press Enter at the end of each line. When the list is complete, click the Add button.

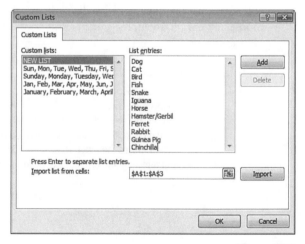

Figure 15.9

- If the list is already available in a worksheet, the process is even easier. Say that you've created a worksheet that contains all of your family budget categories in the exact order you want to enter them every time. Open that sheet and select the worksheet range (column or row) that contains the list. Open the Custom Lists dialog box (see the previous paragraph), select New List, and then click Import.

Your list is now available in any Excel worksheet you open on this machine. To automatically add the custom list to a worksheet range, enter the first list item, use the fill handle to complete the list, and click OK.

SORTING TABLES AND LISTS

Excel's sorting capabilities enable you to view data in almost any order, regardless of the order in which you entered it. To quickly sort a list, first click a single cell in the column by which you want to sort and then click the Sort Ascending button in the Sort and Filter group of the Home tab. Excel selects all the data in your list or table and sorts it alphabetically, using the column that contains the active cell. Click the Sort Descending button to sort in reverse order, using the same column. If you want to sort only a portion of the table or list, make a selection first and then use the Tab key to move the active cell to the correct column. This option, used incorrectly, can make a mess of your data, so use it with caution.

> **TIP**
>
> If the order in which you enter data is important, add a column to your list and fill it with numeric values that you can use to identify each row and then increment it by one for each new record. Re-sort using the values in this column to return the list to its original order. Don't use a formula for the data in this column, however—when you sort the list, the values will change and you won't be able to return to the original sort order.

When you choose ascending order, Excel always sorts numbers first, then most punctuation characters, and then letters, in ascending (A–Z) order, without regard to whether the letters are uppercase or lowercase. Excel generally ignores apostrophes and hyphens when sorting; if two entries are otherwise identical but one contains a hyphen, it will appear after the one that does not contain a hyphen. The precise order for punctuation follows the same order as the Unicode character set, as follows:

```
(space) ! " # $ % & (°) * , . / : ; ? @ [ \ ] ¢ _ ` { ¦ } ˜ + < = >
```

SORTING BY MULTIPLE COLUMNS

By using the Ascending Sort and Descending Sort buttons in the Sort and Filter group of the Data tab, you can perform a multicolumn sort without ever using a dialog box. Perform each column sort in sequence, working your way up in reverse order to the sort order you want to see; Excel preserves the order of other columns in the list when you sort each succeeding column. In a budget worksheet for a large organization, for example, you might click in the Month column and click a sort button, and then do the same with the Category

15

column and finally with the Department column. The result is to sort your list by department, then by category, and then by month.

The Sort dialog box enables you to sort multiple columns at one time; to open the dialog box (see Figure 15.10), click Sort, in the Sort and Filter group of the Data tab. Excel 2007 lets you specify up to 64 columns for your sort order (in contrast to earlier versions, in which only 3 were permitted), using ascending or descending order for each one.

Figure 15.10
This Sort dialog box shows three sort keys, each corresponding to a column label in the list.

SORTING BY DATES OR CUSTOM SERIES

By default, Excel's sort options reorder data alphabetically or numerically. However, a basic A–Z or 1–10 sort isn't always appropriate. Dates and weekdays in text format represent a particular problem. For example, a list of modules for a school curriculum might include a column, formatted as text, that identifies the month in which a particular lesson should be taught. Or, a list of shift assignments for volunteers at the local community center might include a column of weekdays. Using the default sort order would put the month names and weekdays in alphabetical order—April, August, December, February, or Mon, Sat, Sun, Thu—when you actually want to sort the list in calendar order. You might also want to sort your list using a custom AutoFill list—by region, for example, or by budget category (see the previous section for details about how to create one of these lists).

Sorting by date or a custom series is available only when you use the Sort dialog box. To sort by text dates or a custom series, follow these steps:

1. Click in the list you want to sort, or select the region to be sorted.

2. Click the Sort button on the Data tab and identify up to 64 columns for sorting.

3. Click the down arrow in the first Sort By option, select the column that holds the series you want to sort by, and select Custom List. The default selection includes four built-in lists—days of the week and months, in long and short versions. In addition, any custom lists you've created appear here. You see your customized sort list in the Order field, as Figure 15.11 shows.

4. Click the down arrow in the first Order list box and select the appropriate series. The default selection includes four built-in lists—days of the week and months, in long and short versions. In addition, any custom series you've created appear here. You can also choose a different orientation here—for most lists, the default setting, Sort Top to Bottom, is the correct choice.

5. Click OK to confirm the sort order you selected; then click OK again to perform the sort.

Figure 15.11
You can easily sort according to a custom series you've defined.

NOTE

By default, Excel does not distinguish between lowercase and capital letters when sorting. To change this setting, click the Options button in the Sort dialog box and check Case Sensitive. With this option enabled, Excel sorts lowercase letters ahead of capital letters.

Excel now allows your date or custom sort series to appear as any column in the table or list you're sorting. Earlier versions required a sort by date or custom series to be applied to the first column.

FINDING AND FILTERING DATA IN A LIST OR TABLE

When working with tables or lists, you can use the Find shortcut (Ctrl+F) to search for any value. That technique is useful if you want to jump quickly to a specific unique value. More often, however, you'll want to extract details from a table or list instead of simply jumping to a single record. In that case, use *filters* to hide all records except those that match criteria you specify. In a table or list that contains hundreds or thousands of rows, defining a filter helps you see a small number of related records together, making it easier to compare data and identify trends.

For example, in a table of daily high, low, and closing stock prices that includes data for many companies, you might want to see only those records in which the entry in the Symbol column is equal to KO. Or, if you import product inventory information from a database into an Excel list, you can use filters to show only items that are currently out of stock, making it easy to build a reorder list.

Filter options enable you to select information by choosing from drop-down lists of unique items in each column. You can also create custom filters using multiple criteria and combining criteria from multiple columns, or you can display only the top 10 (or bottom 10) entries in a list, by number or percentage, based on the contents of a single column.

15

> **NOTE**
>
> Unlike sorts, which rearrange data in a list, filters do not change the underlying data. When you define a filter, you hide records that don't match the criteria you define.

→ For an overview of Office-standard Find and Replace tools, **see** "Finding and Replacing Text," **p. 88.**

USING FILTERS TO FIND SETS OF DATA

The easiest way to build a filter is with the help of Excel's Filter capability. (In previous versions of Excel, this feature was called AutoFilter.) When this option is enabled, you can define criteria by choosing values from drop-down lists. When you understand how filters work, you can use them to narrow even massive lists.

If the range you're working with is defined as a table, filter controls (drop-down arrows) appear automatically in your header row. Otherwise, you can enable these controls by clicking Filter, in the Sort and Filter group of the Data tab. The Filter button is a toggle; click it again to remove the controls. (Filter controls can also be removed this way from the header row of a table.)

To filter a list or table, click the arrow to the right of the column label you want to use as the first condition in the filter. The menu that descends includes sorting commands, along with check boxes for each unique value in the selected column (see Figure 15.12).

Figure 15.12
Filter controls enable you to narrow your selection by choosing from all unique values in a column.

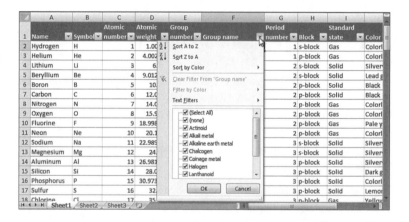

To display only the rows that meet particular criteria, first clear the Select All check box. Then select one or more of the remaining check boxes. Excel applies your criteria immediately, hiding all rows except those that contain the value(s) you selected.

NOTE

Excel generates the drop-down list of Filter values for each column automatically by pulling out all unique values from that column. As a result, every item on the drop-down list is guaranteed to be in that column, making it impossible to select an incorrect value. Items in the Filter lists always appear in ascending order.

USING TEXT FILTERS, NUMBER FILTERS, AND DATE FILTERS

Along with the check boxes for each unique item in a column, a filter control includes an additional command, called Text Filters, Number Filters, or Date Filters—depending on the type of data Excel finds in the column. If your column contains text, for example, clicking Text Filters displays the submenu shown in Figure 15.13. You can use this menu to find groups of records, such as all items that begin with a particular letter combination.

Figure 15.13
Text filtering options enable you to locate groups of items without having to select several individual check boxes.

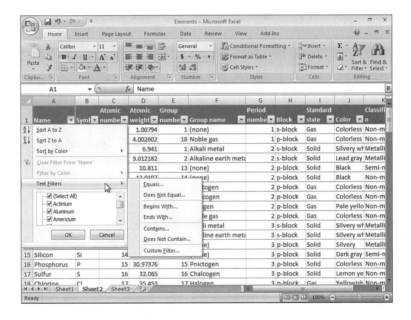

If your column contains numbers, clicking Number Filters reveals the submenu shown in Figure 15.14. Note the Top 10 command in this menu; the command is much more versatile than the name implies. When you choose this command, you see a dialog box that lets you select any number between 1 and 500; you can choose Bottom or Top, and you can specify percent as well. For example, you can ask to see only those records with values in the bottom 5 percent.

15

Figure 15.14
Number filters save
you the trouble of
performing calcula-
tions; you can quickly
filter to values above
or below average, for
example.

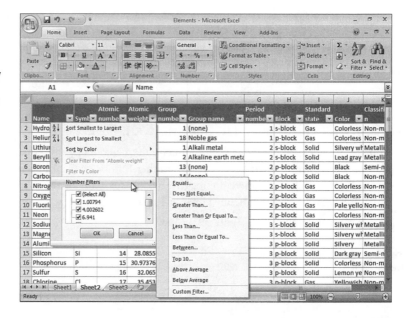

For date values, Excel offers an array of useful groupings, as Figure 15.15 shows. Note that
when you filter on a date column, the check boxes that appear themselves provide some
grouping of dates. In Figure 15.15, for example, there are check boxes for March and April,
with outline controls beside them. Clicking an outline control beside a month name reveals
individual dates within that month.

Figure 15.15
Date Filters enable
you to pluck out
records falling into
specific weeks,
months, quarters, or
years.

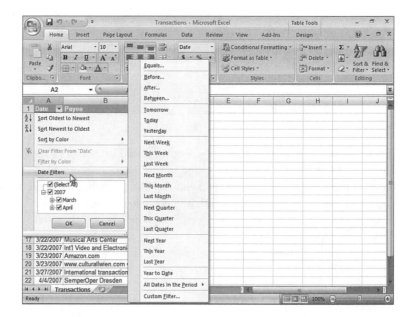

Filter criteria are cumulative. By combining criteria in different columns, you can successively filter a table or list to display an increasingly selective group of records. Although you can choose filter criteria in any order, it's best to start with columns that include the fewest options, because the table of choices for succeeding columns will be narrower and easier to navigate.

When you apply a filter to a column, Excel changes the drop-down arrow to include a funnel icon. That is one indication that a column has been filtered. Gaps in row numbers are another clue. When you filter, Excel hides rows that don't meet your criteria, but it leaves the remaining row numbers unchanged. If you see row 17 followed directly by row 31, chances are the intervening rows have been filtered. (They might also have been hidden explicitly, by means of the Hide and Unhide command on the Home tab's Format menu.)

To remove filter criteria for a column, open the filter drop-down again and choose the Clear Filter command. To remove all filtering criteria from a table or list, click Clear in the Sort and Filter group of the Data tab.

USING COMPARISON CRITERIA TO CREATE CUSTOM FILTERS

If the filtering options that appear when you click Text Filters, Number Filters, or Date Filters don't suffice for your needs, click Custom Filter at the bottom of the submenu. The Custom AutoFilter dialog box (see Figure 15.16) enables you to use any of the following *comparison operators* in combinations that are not possible using the regular filter menus:

- Equals/does not equal
- Is greater than/is less than
- Is greater than or equal to/is less than or equal to
- Begins with/does not begin with
- Ends with/does not end with
- Contains/does not contain

Figure 15.16
Use the Custom AutoFilter dialog box to combine criteria; if you need more than two criteria, use an Advanced Filter instead.

You can combine two criteria for a single column using the logical operator AND, or use the OR operator to tell Excel that you want to see records that match either of the criteria you specify for that column.

Select a comparison operator for the first criterion, and then click in the box to the right of the comparison operator and enter the value you want to use as a logical test. Or, use the drop-down list to select from all unique values in the column. If you add a second criterion for the same column, click And to select only rows in which both criteria are true; click Or to create a filter that shows rows in which either set of criteria is true.

TIP

> Although you're limited to only two criteria when you use AutoFilter's Custom option, you can easily work around this limitation by using Excel's capability to filter on criteria for two or more columns at once. Make a copy of the column you want to use in your filter, and specify a separate set of criteria in the AutoFilter box for that column.

FILTERING WITH ADVANCED CRITERIA

Compared with the one-click ease of AutoFilters, Excel's advanced filters are downright cumbersome. Still, they're the only way to accomplish some tasks, such as defining more than three criteria for a single column or finding only unique values within a list that contains duplicate entries. Advanced filters also let you specify more complex criteria than you can use with ordinary filters, including criteria based on formulas.

To use advanced filters, start by creating a *criteria range* on the same worksheet that contains the list. Although you can add this range anywhere on the list, we strongly recommend that you place it directly above the list, where it's unlikely to be affected by any changes you make to the sheet's design. Allow a minimum of three rows in the criteria range—one for the column labels, one for the criteria, and one to serve as a separator between the list and the criteria range.

TIP

> Add one extra row for each set of criteria you expect to use when filtering the list. In almost all circumstances, you can get by with a criteria range of five rows, which allows you to add up to three sets of criteria for each column while still maintaining a one-row separation between the criteria range and the list.

Copy the column labels from the list to the first row of the criteria range. The resulting range should look something like the example shown in Figure 15.17, which also includes three criteria and shows the results of the filter on the list.

Begin entering criteria in the row just below the column labels. You can enter text, numbers, dates, or logical values using comparison operators such as > and <. To find values that are greater than or equal to a specific value, use the >= operator. For example, >=1000 finds all values greater than or equal to 1000 in the specified column; in a text column, <C finds all entries that begin with A or B.

You can enter values in more than one column and in more than one row. When you do, Excel interprets your input as follows:

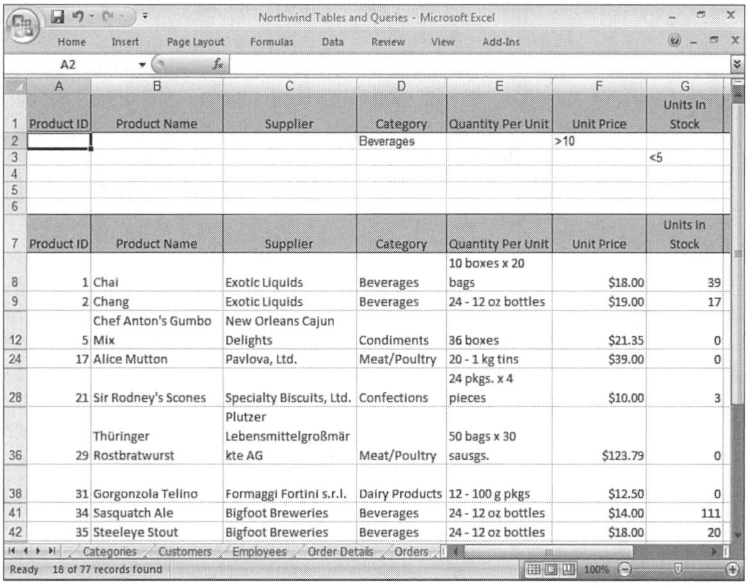

Figure 15.17
These criteria find all beverages with unit prices greater than 10, as well as any records with fewer than 5 units in stock.

			Northwind Tables and Queries - Microsoft Excel			
	Home	Insert	Page Layout	Formulas	Data	Review	View	Add-Ins

	A	B	C	D	E	F	G
1	Product ID	Product Name	Supplier	Category	Quantity Per Unit	Unit Price	Units In Stock
2				Beverages		>10	
3							<5
4							
5							
6							
7	Product ID	Product Name	Supplier	Category	Quantity Per Unit	Unit Price	Units In Stock
8	1	Chai	Exotic Liquids	Beverages	10 boxes x 20 bags	$18.00	39
9	2	Chang	Exotic Liquids	Beverages	24 - 12 oz bottles	$19.00	17
12	5	Chef Anton's Gumbo Mix	New Orleans Cajun Delights	Condiments	36 boxes	$21.35	0
24	17	Alice Mutton	Pavlova, Ltd.	Meat/Poultry	20 - 1 kg tins	$39.00	0
28	21	Sir Rodney's Scones	Specialty Biscuits, Ltd.	Confections	24 pkgs. x 4 pieces	$10.00	3
36	29	Thüringer Rostbratwurst	Plutzer Lebensmittelgroßmärkte AG	Meat/Poultry	50 bags x 30 sausgs.	$123.79	0
38	31	Gorgonzola Telino	Formaggi Fortini s.r.l.	Dairy Products	12 - 100 g pkgs	$12.50	0
41	34	Sasquatch Ale	Bigfoot Breweries	Beverages	24 - 12 oz bottles	$14.00	111
42	35	Steeleye Stout	Bigfoot Breweries	Beverages	24 - 12 oz bottles	$18.00	20

Categories / Customers / Employees / Order Details / Orders /

Ready   18 of 77 records found

- For values in more than one column within a single row, Excel looks for records that match all values that you specify in the row, the equivalent of a logical AND.

- For values in the same column in separate rows, Excel displays records that match any of the values, the equivalent of a logical OR.

In essence, each row in the criteria range equals a single *condition*. By mixing and matching conditions, you can filter a list in many ways, including the following:

- Multiple conditions for one column—Enter each condition in a separate cell under the column label in the criteria range. In the example shown in Figure 15.18, any row in which the group name is Noble gas, Pnictogen, or Chalcogen will match.

Group name
Noble gas
Pnictogen
Chalcogen

Figure 15.18

- One condition in each of several columns—Enter each condition under its respective column label in the same row. In Figure 15.19, for example, the criteria will find all halogens with atomic weight less than 90. Generally, this type of filter is much easier to apply using a simple filter.

Atomic weight	Group number	Group name
<90		Halogen

Figure 15.19

- Multiple conditions in multiple columns—Enter each set of conditions in its own row of the criteria range, and Excel will find rows in the list that match either set. Figure 15.20 finds halogens with atomic weights less than 90 and noble gases with atomic weights greater than 80.

Atomic weight	Group number	Group name
<90		Halogen
>80		Noble gas

Figure 15.20

15

TIP

To specify multiple criteria for the same column in the same row, add another column heading in the criteria range, using the same column label (extend the criteria range, if necessary, or replace the label for an existing column for which you're not defining conditions). For example, if you have a column called Amount, add a second column label, also called Amount, to your criteria range. Then, when you enter >3000 in one cell and <6000 in the other, both in the same row, Excel finds only records in which the Amount is between 3000 and 6000.

CAUTION

If you enter text in a criteria range, Excel finds all matching records that begin with that text. Thus, if you enter the letter *F* under the Category label, Excel finds all records whose category begins with *F*. To find only records that match the exact text you specify, you must enter the value using the following format: `="=text"` (where *text* is the value you want to use in your condition). Make sure to include both equals signs.

Finally, you can create conditions based on formulas. Although formulas can be a powerful way to filter a list, they are extremely challenging to enter, and the syntax is confusing. Unlike other conditions, which must appear under a label in the criteria range that matches the corresponding label in the list, you must not use a column label with a formula; enter the formulas in a cell beneath a blank label, or change the label above it so it does not match a label in the list. Individual references in the formula should come from the column label or the first record of the list, and the formulas must evaluate to TRUE or FALSE.

In the example in Figure 15.21, we started with a simple list of orders, in which each row contains a transaction number, a price per box, and a number of boxes. We want to identify the orders that represent the highest cost, which we've arbitrarily defined as a total of $300.

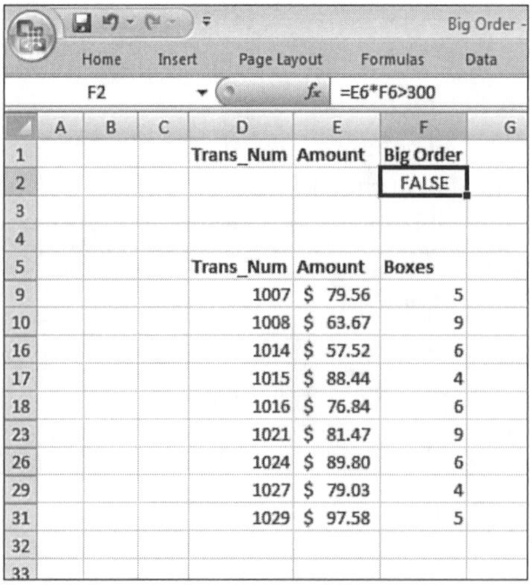

Figure 15.21
The formula in cell F2 contains relative references to values in the first row of the database (row 6); note that the label above it does not match a label in the list itself.

	A	B	C	D	E	F	G
1				Trans_Num	Amount	Big Order	
2						FALSE	
3							
4							
5				Trans_Num	Amount	Boxes	
9				1007	$ 79.56	5	
10				1008	$ 63.67	9	
16				1014	$ 57.52	6	
17				1015	$ 88.44	4	
18				1016	$ 76.84	6	
23				1021	$ 81.47	9	
26				1024	$ 89.80	6	
29				1027	$ 79.03	4	
31				1029	$ 97.58	5	
32							
33							

F2 = =E6*F6>300

Note that we've changed the label above the last column in the criteria range (cell F1) to read Big Order. As you can see from the formula bar, the formula in cell F2 multiplies the value in the Amount column by the value in the Boxes column for the first row of the list (E6*F6) to see whether it's greater than 300. The result of this filter finds 9 matching rows.

After you've created the criteria range and entered criteria, apply the filter to your list by following these steps:

1. Click Advanced, in the Sort and Filter group of the Data tab. The Advanced Filter dialog box appears (see Figure 15.22). Note that the values shown here correspond to values in Figure 15.20.

2. Click in the List Range box and then select the entire list, including the header row. (If you selected the list before opening the Advanced Filter dialog box, this range is already selected.)

3. Click in the Criteria Range box and select the portion of the criteria range that contains data. At a minimum, this must include one column label and one cell beneath that label. If your criteria include multiple rows, make sure you select each row. The portion of the criteria range you select must be a contiguous range.

Figure 15.22

4. Choose a destination for the Advanced Filter results, using the following options:

   • To filter the list in place, accept the default option under Action.

   • To extract records to another location, click the Copy to Another Location option; then click in the Copy To box and select the cell at the top-left corner of the range where you want the extracted records to appear (logically, this location is called the *extract range*). This location must be on the same worksheet as the list itself; if you want to extract specific fields, you must include column labels that correspond to the fields you want to extract. You do not need to extract every column from the list.

   • To filter out duplicate records, select the Unique Records Only check box. If you filter the list in place, this option excludes those rows in which the values in every column are identical. If you extract the results to a new location and specify a subset of columns, Excel defines duplicates based only on the columns in the extract range.

TIP

> By extracting unique records, you can quickly build a list of categories from a much larger list like the one in the examples shown here. Use no conditions in the criteria range. For the extract range, pick a cell below the list and enter the label of the column you want to extract (Category, in this case). When you run the Advanced Filter, Excel displays a list of all the unique values in your Category column, with no duplicates.

5. Click OK to apply the filter.

15

> **TIP**
>
> Use range names to skip some steps in this process. If you create named ranges called Database and Extract, Excel automatically selects them in the Advanced Filter dialog box each time you use it. Excel automatically creates a named criteria range each time you use the Advanced Filter dialog box.

Advanced filters don't update automatically when you enter new values in the criteria range. To apply the new criteria, you need to reopen the Advanced Criteria dialog box and click OK. To remove an in-place filter from a list, click Clear in the Sort and Filter group of the Data tab.

IMPORTING AND EXPORTING DATA

Using Excel, you can create a list from a text file; you can also save a list or table to a text file. You import and export text files when you want to share lists between programs, such as mailing-list management software and database programs that cannot read Excel worksheet files.

To import a text file as a list, first position the insertion point in the cell where you want the data to appear. Make sure no data appears below or to the right of the location you select, or it could be overwritten. Then follow these steps:

1. Choose From Text, in the Get External Data group of the Data tab.

2. In the Open dialog box, choose Text Files from the Files of Type list, select the file you want to import, and click Open. The Text Import Wizard appears.

3. Specify how Excel should separate fields in your import file. Pick Delimited if the list uses characters such as commas or tabs to identify each field; choose Fixed Width if each field starts at the same position in each row.

> **NOTE**
>
> If the settings look correct here and you're confident you don't need to adjust any other import options, click Finish to skip the remainder of the Import Text Wizard.

4. Click Next to display Step 2 of the wizard. If you're importing a *delimited* file, check that Excel has selected the correct options for your file. (In the example shown in Figure 15.23, we had to click the Comma check box before the wizard would correctly identify each field.) With a fixed-width file, click in the ruler to identify the beginning of each new column. Click Next again.

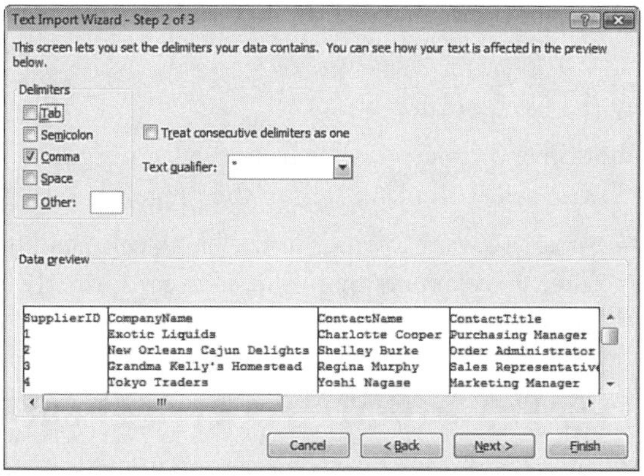

Figure 15.23
Be sure to specify the correct delimiters when importing a text file. Scroll through the Data Preview window, if necessary, to check a sufficient sample of records.

5. In the next step of the wizard, which is optional, choose formatting options for date/time and number fields, or specify any fields you don't want to import. Click Finish to move to the last step of the process. Excel displays the Import Data dialog box.

6. Ensure that the cell you want to use at the top-left corner of the list is selected. Adjust this location if necessary, or click New Worksheet to create the list without disturbing existing sheets.

7. Click OK to add the new list to your worksheet.

TIP

> By default, Excel creates an external query to the original file, so any changes you make to that text file can be reflected in your worksheet as well. If you want to permanently add the data to your worksheet and break the link to the external file, click Properties (in the Connections group of the Data tab), clear the Save Query Definition check box, and click OK to close the External Data Range Properties dialog box.

To save an existing list or table in a text file that you can import into another program, first make sure the data you want to save is on its own worksheet, with no other data on that sheet. (If necessary, copy the range to a new sheet before continuing.) Click to select the sheet that contains the table or list, click the Microsoft Office button, choose Save As, Other Formats, and choose one of Excel's compatible delimited formats: CSV (comma-delimited) or Text (tab-delimited).

After importing data into a worksheet, you might end up with some blank cells. In some situations, you might want to replace those blanks with a value, such as "NA" or zero. To do so, follow these steps:

15

1. Select the range that contains the blank cells that you want to change. Don't select any other cells.

2. Press F5 to display the Go To dialog box.

3. Click the Special button and choose Blanks from the list of options in the Go to Special dialog box. Click OK to select all blank cells in the range.

4. Type the number or text you want to enter in the blank cells, and then hold down the Ctrl key and press Enter. Excel enters that value in every formerly blank cell.

HOW PIVOTTABLE AND PIVOTCHART REPORTS WORK

PivotTables and PivotCharts are powerful tools for automatically summarizing and analyzing data without ever having to add a formula or function. As the name implies, you start with a list or table exactly like the ones we've discussed in the first half of this chapter; then you snap the rows and columns into position on a grid, and end up with a sorted, grouped, summarized, totaled, and subtotaled report. PivotTable reports are best for cross-tabulating lists—the more categories, the better. You can reduce a list of thousands of items to a single line, showing totals by category or department. Or you can create complex, multilevel groupings that show total expenses by department, grouped by budget category and by quarter. You can hide or show detail for each group by clicking outline controls. You can change the view or grouping in literally seconds, just by dragging items on or off the sheet and moving them between row, column, and page fields.

Start with a list that contains multiple fields, and then use Excel's PivotTable button to set up a blank PivotTable page with just a few clicks. Instead of sorting your list and entering formulas and functions, you drag fields around on the PivotTable Field List task pane to create a new view of your list—Excel groups the data and adds summary formulas automatically. PivotCharts (which we discuss in "Creating and Editing PivotCharts," later in this chapter) are the visual equivalent of PivotTables, letting you create killer charts just as quickly, by dragging fields on a chart layout page.

Unlike subtotals and outlines, which modify the structure of your list to display summaries, PivotTables and PivotCharts create new, independent elements in your workbook. When you add or edit data in a table, the changes show up in your PivotTables and PivotCharts as well; because they're separate elements, you can easily change the structure of a PivotTable or PivotChart, too, and your changes won't mess up the data in the underlying table or list.

Figure 15.24 shows the task pane that appears when you create a PivotTable. Initially, the PivotTable layout is blank. To populate the table, you drag fields from the Field List task pane to the table layout. Alternatively, you can drag fields to the four boxes—Report Filter, Row Labels, Column Labels, and Values—at the bottom of the task pane.

Figure 15.24
To populate the PivotTable, drag fields from the task pane to the layout—or to the boxes at the bottom of the task pane.

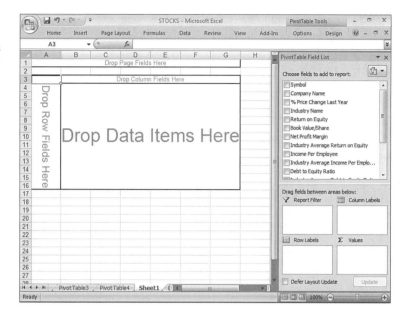

The Field List task pane includes every field in your source table or list. Use row fields and column fields to define how you want Excel to organize your PivotTable. The Data Items portion of the layout (and the Values box in the task pane) define which fields contain the information you want to summarize. Page fields on the layout (which correspond to the Report Filter box in the task pane) enable you to further refine your view by displaying a separate PivotTable for each item in a group, as though the table were on its own virtual page. You can use multiple row fields, column fields, or both, and you can specify which summary action you want Excel to perform on data items—the sum, average, or count of all related values, for instance.

What can you do with a PivotTable? The number of uses is limited only by your imagination. Despite their dramatically different structures, for example, each of the following four PivotTables started with the same list of information about publicly traded stocks, which we downloaded from an Internet-based online service. In its raw form, with its grand total of 106,224 separate data points, the list is a prescription for information overload. Each of the 6,639 rows contains 16 data fields for an individual publicly traded company, including its name, ticker symbol, and industry category, the exchange on which it trades, its high and low stock price for the past year, and financial measurements such as net profit margin and return on equity.

A decade ago, you had to be a professional financial analyst with access to a mainframe computer to crunch numbers this thoroughly; today, you can manage your own money with nothing more than a web browser and some Excel know-how.

15

Figure 15.25 shows a simple PivotTable that lets you see at a glance how many companies are in each industry category, along with the average increase or decrease in stock price from companies in that category over the past year. This PivotTable consists of a single row field and two data items.

Figure 15.25
With no column fields and only one row field, this PivotTable quickly counts the number of companies in each category and calculates the average price change for the year.

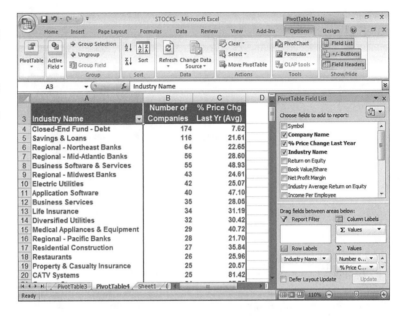

In Figure 15.26, more detail is added, displaying individual statistics for each company, and grouping the detail rows in alphabetical order by industry name. Note that this PivotTable includes four data items instead of two, and a slew of Excel formatting options are used to make the report more readable—changing fonts and font sizes, aligning type and adding background shading, and standardizing the number of decimal points in each column.

To slice the data even more finely and add an extra analytical dimension, you can drag more buttons from the Field List task pane to the layout (see Figure 15.27). Each row in the PivotTable is now grouped using unique values in two categories, and there are two column headings as well, one for each unique value in the Split in Last Year column field. (To make the PivotTable easier to read, the column headings were renamed from Yes and No to Split and No Split.) At the intersection of each row and column in the PivotTable, Excel counts the number of companies and calculates the average income per employee for all rows that match the row and column fields.

The resulting PivotTable, shown in Figure 15.27, is a concise and crystal-clear cross-tabulation, giving you a side-by-side analysis of the number of stocks that split in the past year versus those that didn't, broken down by industry category and exchange.

Figure 15.26
This PivotTable includes two row fields, Industry Name and Symbol.

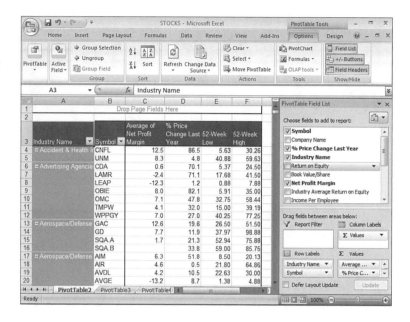

Figure 15.27
Add a column field to quickly compare related data points.

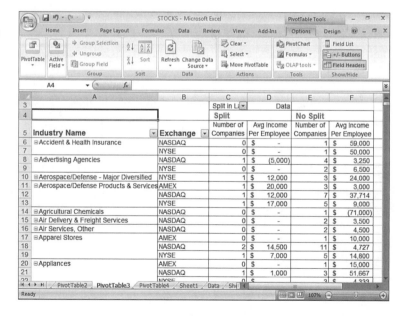

Literally hundreds of options are available in even a modestly complex PivotTable, but a PivotTable doesn't have to be large or complex to be effective. The PivotTable in Figure 15.28, for example, neatly summarizes more than 100,000 data points in just a few rows and columns.

Figure 15.28
Notice the grand totals under the rows in this PivotTable. Use the report filter, in cells A1:B1, to filter the entire table.

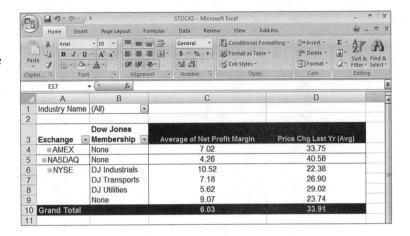

To produce this example, we used two column fields, two row fields, and one report filter (what Excel used to call a "page field")—a drop-down list that lets us filter the records in the entire table. Choosing (All) from the page field shows a summary of all data in the list; by selecting a different entry from the drop-down list, you can show the same breakdown for an individual industry name. Select one category at a time to flip through a series of otherwise identical PivotTables that focus on each category.

The layout Excel produced automatically included totals for each row and column; we kept only the grand total at the bottom of the PivotTable. We had to modify other default settings as well, including changing the default formula to calculate the average of our data items. To make the headings and totals easier to read, we did some rewording, and then changed fonts and alignment, added shading, and wrapped text.

WHEN SHOULD YOU USE A PIVOTTABLE?

PivotTables have several advantages over other worksheet models. Using the PivotTable Wizard, it's easy to create a PivotTable that summarizes all or part of a list in dozens of ways. Trying to accomplish the same task by entering formulas manually would take days. Also, because PivotTables and PivotCharts do not change your existing data or its arrangement on the worksheet, you can freely experiment with different PivotTable layouts. Use the Undo button to roll back any changes you make in a PivotTable layout. If you want to start over, you can delete the PivotTable page and run the wizard again.

PivotTables are the correct choice when all your data is in a table or list or in an external database you can query from Excel. PivotTables are not appropriate for structured worksheet models that include data-entry cells, subtotals, and summary rows. A PivotTable won't do much good on an annual budget worksheet, for example, because it already includes rows, columns, and subtotals. On the other hand, if you enter the raw data in a list (or import it from an external database), with each row containing a month, department, budget category, and amount, you can easily re-create that same layout in PivotTable form—and you'll have many more analytical options available to you later.

CREATING A PIVOTTABLE

To create a PivotTable from an existing table or list, select a cell in that table or list and click PivotTable, in the Tables group of the Insert tab. Excel prompts you for basic details about the PivotTable you want to create, including the location of the data source and where you want the PivotTable to appear (see Figure 15.29). Then it creates a blank layout and a Field List task pane for you (see Figure 15.24). To fill out the table, drag field headings to the layout or to the boxes at the bottom of the task pane.

Figure 15.29
Select a range or an external data source for your PivotTable.

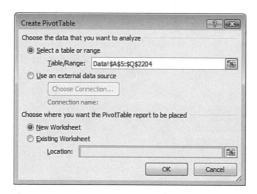

CAUTION

The PivotTable Wizard offers the option to place a PivotTable or PivotChart on an existing worksheet. In general, you should always choose to place a PivotTable on its own sheet. Adding a PivotTable to a sheet that contains data exposes you to the risk that changes you make to the list design will affect your PivotTable, or vice versa.

Don't be surprised if the PivotTable doesn't display properly at first. In particular, summary fields in the data area default to the SUM function. If you want to use COUNT, AVERAGE, or another summary function instead, see the following section.

EDITING AND UPDATING A PIVOTTABLE

You can add more fields to a PivotTable at any time. Simply drag from the Field List task pane, either to the layout or to one of the boxes at the bottom of the task pane. To remove a field, either drag its heading from the layout to a location outside the table. Or, more simply, clear the check box beside the field name in the Field List task pane.

To change the order of fields in rows, columns, or the data area, drag the field button and drop it in the correct location on the layout. Make sure you're pointing to the field button and not its label; you'll know you've aimed correctly when the mouse button turns to a four-headed pointer. Drag to another location and watch the mouse pointer and thick black lines for feedback on the correct "drop" location.

TIP

Using the mouse to rearrange the order of data items on a PivotTable can be frustrating. It's usually easier to right-click the field heading you want to move, choose Move, and then choose one of the options from the shortcut menu that appears.

To change the summary function used in the data area (from SUM to COUNT or AVERAGE, for example), right-click any data item (that is, any item in the body of the table) and choose Field Settings from the shortcut menu. That action opens the PivotTable Field dialog box, shown in Figure 15.30. Select a function from the Summarize By list; if you want to change the name from its default, do so in the Custom Name box, and then click OK to save the change.

Figure 15.30
You can change the summary function that Excel applies to values in your PivotTable.

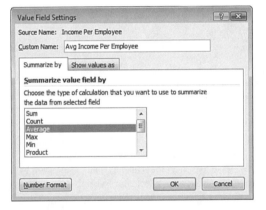

CHANGING SORT ORDER AND OTHER DISPLAY OPTIONS

The *default sort order* for rows and columns is usually alphanumeric. You can change the order of individual items by dragging them up or down (in the case of rows) or left or right (for columns). In other cases, you might want to adjust the default sort order. For example, if your PivotTable counts the number of items in each category, you might want to see categories with the highest number of items at the top of the list.

To change the order in which a field is sorted, click the drop-down arrow next to the field heading, and choose More Sort Options. Then fill out the Sort dialog box that appears. Use the More Options button in that dialog box to set additional options, such as whether you want to sort every time a report is updated. (If your data is massive you might want to uncheck this option.)

The drop-down arrow beside a field heading also gives you the ability to filter a field. If you only want to see certain items, or if you want to specify a range of items (for example, the top 10, or those falling within a specified range), click the drop-down arrow and make your wishes known. The filtering options work here the same way they do in ordinary tables and lists.

ADDING AND REMOVING SUBTOTALS

You can add subtotals to rows, columns, or both in a list. In some cases, Excel adds them automatically, even if they're not appropriate. Subtotals can add a useful way to see the impact of groupings in your PivotTable, or they can add clutter between rows and columns. Depending on the design of your PivotTable and what Excel did automatically, you might need to add or remove these subtotals.

The quickest way to specify subtotaling preferences is to select a cell within the PivotTable and then click Subtotals, in the Layout group of the Design tab. (The Design tab appears only when the selection lies within a PivotTable.) For finer control, follow these steps:

1. Right-click the heading for the field you're concerned with, and choose Field Settings from the shortcut menu. Excel displays the Field Settings dialog box, as shown in Figure 15.31.

Figure 15.31
Use the Subtotals options to add, edit, or hide subtotals for a row or column.

2. In the Subtotals section, choose Automatic to let Excel create subtotals for all items. Choose Custom and click a summary function to add one or more specific type of subtotals, such as COUNT and AVERAGE. Click None to remove all subtotals.

3. Click OK to exit the dialog box and make the changes you specified.

SWITCHING BETWEEN REPORT LAYOUTS

The Report Layout command in the Layout group of the Design tab gives you a choice of three layout options: Compact, Outline, and Tabular. Figure 15.26 shows an example of the tabular layout. Figures 15.32 and 15.33 show the same PivotTable in compact and outline layouts, respectively.

Figure 15.32
A PivotTable in compact layout.

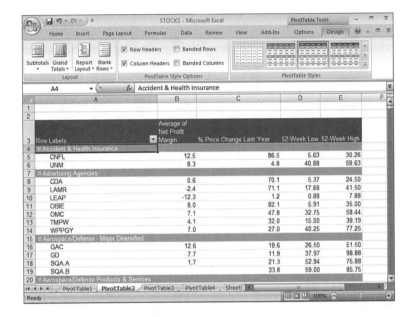

Figure 15.33
A PivotTable in outline layout.

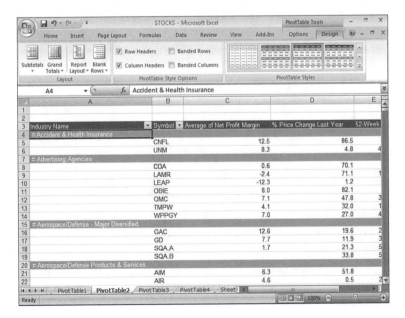

REMOVING BLANK CELLS AND ERROR MESSAGES

Because PivotTables automatically summarize all data, it's common to see blank cells and error messages in the data area. #DIV/0 errors, for example, are especially common when calculating averages because in a long list, it's almost certain that some items will have no matches in a particular row-and-column intersection. For example, if you're calculating average sales with regions in the column area and product categories in the row area, some regions will have no sales for a particular category. These aren't really errors; instead, you want the table to display a label such as NA, for Not Applicable.

Careful attention to blanks and error messages can make your PivotTable easier to read and make it look more professional. Here's how to adjust the appearance of blank cells and errors:

1. Right-click any part of the PivotTable and choose PivotTable Options from the context menu. Excel displays the PivotTable Options dialog box, as shown in Figure 15.34.

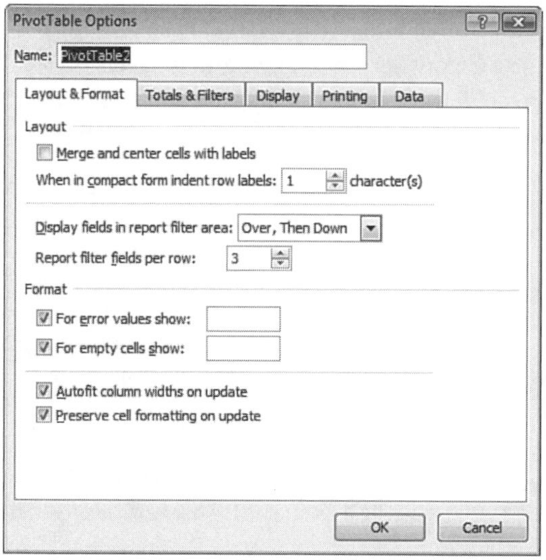

Figure 15.34
Use options in this dialog box to change the way a PivotTable displays blank cells and error messages.

2. On the Layout and Format tab of the PivotTable Options dialog box, select the For Error Values Show check box. Click in the box to the right and fill in the information you want to display instead of the error message, such as NA.

3. Select the For Empty Cells Show check box. If the field contains numeric data, enter 0 here; for a text field, enter the value you want Excel to display (NA, for instance) instead of leaving the cell blank.

4. Click OK to save your changes.

15

REFRESHING DATA IN A PIVOTTABLE

When you change the layout of a PivotTable, Excel automatically recalculates the resulting display of data. If you add or edit data in the underlying list, however, your changes do not appear immediately in the associated PivotTable. To be certain that the PivotTable reflects all recent changes, click the Update button on the Field List task pane.

> **TIP**
>
> If the Field List task pane isn't visible, first be sure your selection lies within the PivotTable. (The task pane disappears when you click outside the table.) If it's still not visible, click Field List, in the Show/Hide group of the Options tab. This command is a toggle; you can also use it to hide the task pane when it gets in your way. (But, more simply, you can suppress the task pane by clicking its Close button.)

CREATING AND EDITING PIVOTCHARTS

A PivotChart is a chart based on data in a PivotTable. Like its row-and-column–based counterpart, you can rearrange a PivotChart by dragging field labels on a chart sheet. When you change the layout of a PivotChart, Excel automatically rearranges the corresponding data in your PivotTable, and vice versa.

In general, any time you can use a PivotChart instead of a conventional chart, you should jump at the opportunity, because they're so much easier to create and edit.

PivotCharts follow almost exactly the same rules as charts you create from a conventional worksheet. The default chart type for a PivotChart is a stacked column chart, but you can change this to any chart type except X-Y (scatter) charts, bubble charts, and stock chart types. Chart options are identical to those found in regular charts.

> **NOTE**
>
> Every PivotChart requires a PivotTable, which it uses as its data source. You cannot create a PivotChart without adding a PivotTable to your worksheet as well.

The best way to create a PivotChart is to start by creating a relatively simple PivotTable—perhaps one with one field on the row axis and one field on the column axis. If you need additional fields, try setting them up as report filters (page fields).

Select any cell within your PivotTable and then click PivotChart in the Tools group of the Options tab. In the Insert Chart dialog gallery that appears, select a chart type and click OK. Excel draws the PivotChart, displays a new task pane (called the PivotChart Filter task pane) and adds some new tabs to the Ribbon (see Figure 15.35). (If you don't see the PivotChart Filter task pane, click PivotChart Filter in the Show/Hide group of the Analyze tab.)

Figure 15.35
PivotCharts are linked to PivotTables; changes to the layout of the chart affect the table immediately, and vice versa.

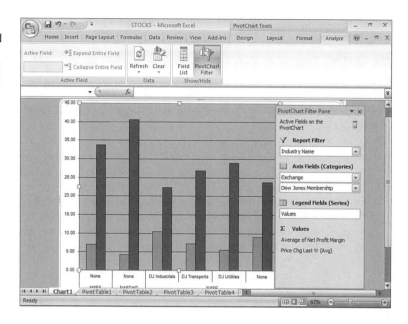

Of course, a chart doesn't include rows or columns, so the available drop zones on a blank PivotChart page are slightly different from their counterparts on a PivotTable. When you create a PivotChart from a PivotTable, row fields become category fields, and column fields become series fields.

Initially, the PivotChart appears on the same worksheet page as the PivotTable to which it is linked (we moved the example in Figure 15.35 to a separate chart sheet). That's usually a good thing, because the easiest way to rearrange the chart is by dragging field headings from one box to another within the PivotTable Field List, or by dragging them from one axis of the PivotTable to another (from the row axis to the column axis, for example). Any changes you make to the PivotTable are immediately reflected on the chart.

With PivotCharts, you can use the same formatting and editing options as with conventional charts. In particular, use right-click shortcut menus to choose a different chart type; format data series, axes, and the plot area; and add or edit colors and backgrounds to your chart.

→ For instructions on how to edit charts, **see** "Editing and Formatting Chart Elements," **p. 525.**

FORMATTING AND PRINTING PIVOTTABLES

When your selection lies within a PivotTable, Excel adds two tabs to the Ribbon, Options and Design. On the Design tab, you'll find a gallery of PivotTable styles. Like other types of styles in Excel 2007, these are well-designed combinations of colors and other formatting attributes, all linked to the current theme. You can change the appearance of your table dramatically by selecting a different style from the gallery.

→ For an overview of Excel's many formatting options, **see** Chapter 13, "Making Great-Looking Worksheets," **p. 401.**

15

You can format numbers and text in the data area of a PivotTable by selecting cells individually and choosing formatting options as you would in a normal worksheet. If you redefine your PivotTable later, however, you will lose this formatting. That can be exasperating if you're constantly losing, say, the number of decimal places you want to see in each data item. To apply number formatting that lasts, right-click any cell in the data area and choose Value Field Settings from the shortcut menu. Click the Number button and choose a format from the dialog box.

TIP

> When you create a PivotTable or PivotChart on a new worksheet, Excel assigns a generic name to the new sheet. To make your worksheets easier to understand, right-click the tab, choose Rename, and give the sheet a new name that helps identify it. (You can also double-click the existing tab name to make it available for editing.) To give the PivotTable itself a non-default name, click the Options tab. Then type a name into the PivotTable Name box, at the left edge of the Ribbon.

Sometimes you need to adjust other formatting options as well. For example, you might want to change the alignment of a column of numbers, change to a new font, or add a background shade behind the column. Here, too, you have two options: If you right-click the cells in question and choose Format Cells, you'll have access to all common cell formatting options—Number, Alignment, Font, and so on. But as soon as you rearrange your PivotTable, those custom formats vanish.

To lock cell formatting in place regardless of what you do with your PivotTable, right-click the heading for the field you want to format and choose Format Cells from the shortcut menu. Adjust desired formatting options and click OK.

EXTRA CREDIT: GROUPING ITEMS IN A PIVOTTABLE

Excel PivotTables are capable of splitting data into groups, even when you haven't organized your data in advance. This is a powerful feature that's useful in a variety of circumstances. When you choose to group data in a PivotTable, Excel analyzes the field you've chosen and displays a dialog box with choices that are appropriate for that type of data. For example, if you have a year's worth of scientific data that records daily weather details for a particular location, you might want to group average temperature, rainfall totals, and other details by week or by month. If you have a list of textbooks and other course material in which each row contains a product name, its category, and a price, you might want to group the list of products by category, and then by price within groups: $1.00–$10.00, $10.01–$20.00, and so on.

In the example shown here, a worksheet-based list contains data from an automated weather-monitoring station that continuously records temperature, rainfall, relative humidity, barometric pressure, and other details. Each row contains a date and time stamp plus details for that sampling period. In total, the sheet contains two years' worth of data, with 24 hourly data points for each day. Here's how to create a report that shows monthly trends for all three years:

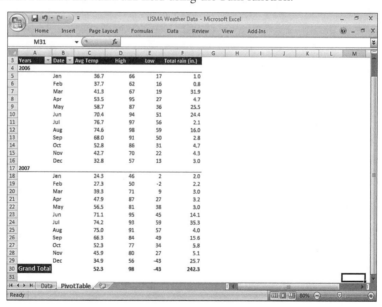

Figure 15.36

1. Create a PivotTable using the Date field in the Row area and the Temp and Rainfall fields in the Data area.

2. Right-click any entry in the Date column and choose Group from the shortcut menu. As Figure 15.36 shows, Excel correctly determines these are dates and offers to group by month. Because the sample extends over several years, choose Months and Years, and then click OK.

3. Drag two more copies of the Temp field into the Data area and format each one to show a different summary: Average, Max, and Min. Adjust the names of each summary as well. This step allows you to see the average temperature as well as the high and low marks for each month during the two-year period. Format the Rainfall field using the Sum function.

4. Adjust column formatting and number formats for each summary cell.

The results, shown in Figure 15.37, give a month-by-month snapshot of the weather, even though we started with a list that included only daily details.

Years	Date	Avg Temp	High	Low	Total rain (in.)
2006					
	Jan	36.7	66	17	1.0
	Feb	37.7	62	16	0.8
	Mar	41.3	67	19	31.9
	Apr	53.5	95	27	4.7
	May	58.7	87	36	25.5
	Jun	70.4	94	51	24.4
	Jul	76.7	97	56	2.1
	Aug	74.6	98	59	16.0
	Sep	68.0	91	50	2.8
	Oct	52.8	86	31	4.7
	Nov	42.7	70	22	4.3
	Dec	32.8	57	13	3.0
2007					
	Jan	24.3	46	2	2.0
	Feb	27.3	50	-2	2.2
	Mar	39.3	71	9	3.0
	Apr	47.9	87	27	3.2
	May	56.5	81	38	3.0
	Jun	71.1	95	45	14.1
	Jul	74.2	93	59	35.3
	Aug	75.0	91	57	4.0
	Sep	66.3	84	49	15.6
	Oct	52.3	77	34	5.8
	Nov	45.9	80	27	5.1
	Dec	34.9	56	-43	25.7
Grand Total		52.3	98	-43	242.3

Figure 15.37

CHAPTER 16

TURNING DATA INTO CHARTS

In this chapter

16

A REVAMPED CHARTING ENGINE

After 15 years, the charting engine in Office 2007 has been completely rewritten. Now you can create modern-looking charts with just a few mouse clicks. And you can tailor the appearance of those charts more easily than ever, because most of the formatting tools you need are available directly from the Ribbon.

The basic row-and-column worksheet grid is essential in helping you organize data and perform calculations, but it's difficult—and sometimes impossible—to analyze information and see patterns by staring at a sea of numbers.

Charts help you turn numeric data into visual displays in which you can identify trends and pick out patterns at a glance. By using lines, columns, bars, and pie slices to compare series of data over time and across categories, charts often provide clear answers to tough questions, such as these:

- How fast have geographic regions grown in the recent past?—A stacked column chart enables students of history and geography to compare annual rates of population growth for two or more countries in a single display. The same type of chart can be used to compare growth in industrial or agricultural output as well.

- Have school districts in your state seen improved test scores as a result of new educational initiatives?—You might not be able to tell from a table packed with hundreds of individual data points, but a line chart can help you clearly see the highs and lows and identify any trends.

- Just where does your family's money go?—If you've broken out a year's worth of expenditures by category, a pie chart helps you see which categories are taking more than their fair share—and devise strategies for reining in those expenses.

BUILDING AN EXCEL CHART

Building a chart in Excel 2007 is easier than in any previous version. Gone is the four-step Chart Wizard. To create a chart, you select a cell within your data range and choose a chart type on the Insert tab of the Ribbon. As shown in Figure 16.1, the Insert tab offers seven icons representing basic chart types: Column, Line, Pie, Bar, Area, Scatter, and Other Charts. Each icon opens a gallery of subtypes.

Click a chart type icon, choose a subtype from the gallery that appears, and Excel adds a chart to your worksheet. At the same time, it adds three new tabs—Design, Layout, and Format—to the right side of the Ribbon, under the heading Chart Tools. You can use these tabs to customize the appearance of your chart.

By default, all new Excel charts are embedded on the current worksheet. You can move the chart to its own chart sheet by means of the Move Chart button on the Design tab. Working with a chart on its own sheet gives you the maximum space for editing and formatting. Leaving the chart embedded on a worksheet lets you see the data and chart side by side.

Figure 16.1
Each of the seven chart type icons leads to a gallery of sub-types.

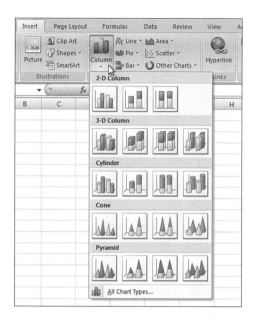

16

SELECTING DATA TO PLOT

When you create a chart, Excel automatically detects the data to be charted based on the current selection. If you select a single cell, Excel bases the chart on the current region—that is, the current block of contiguous cells. If you select a range of cells, Excel uses just that range.

NOTE

The number of points per series for a 2D chart is limited to 32,000. With 3D charts, the limit is 4,000 points per series. The total number of points per chart is limited to 256,000. The maximum number of series you can use in a chart is 255. If you have more series than this, you should seriously reconsider the point you're trying to make, because even Stephen Hawking would have trouble absorbing that much information at once.

Be sure the range you select includes all the data to be charted, as well as the labels you'll use for the categories. The range does not have to be contiguous. For example, to create a pie chart, you might want to select a row of column labels and a row of totals, ignoring the detail rows in between. Nor do you need to select all the data in a table, if all you want to chart is a subset of the data. For example, on a 12-month budget worksheet, you might want to show totals for only the months of October through December.

16

C A U T I O N

If the range you plan to plot ends with a row or column of totals, don't include those totals in your selection; otherwise, the totals will create one column or pie slice that overwhelms all the others.

When you select the data source, Excel attempts to identify category headings, value axis labels, and data series; it also chooses whether to plot data by rows or by columns. This choice is based on the number of items—if there are more columns than rows, Excel plots the data by column, placing the column headings along the category axis. If there are more rows than columns, or an equal number of rows and columns, Excel plots by rows.

Changing the way data is plotted can help emphasize different trends and patterns. For example, Figure 16.2 shows a worksheet that contains a small range of data. When plotted by columns (left), the data emphasizes the trends for each decade, and you can see at a glance that Arizona has grown faster than the other two southwestern states and faster than the United States as a whole. When plotted by rows, however (right), the chart encourages comparing how each state and the United States grew on a decade-by-decade basis and to draw conclusions on the consistency of each state's growth.

Figure 16.2
Changing the way that data is plotted—by columns or by rows—can change the story a chart tells.

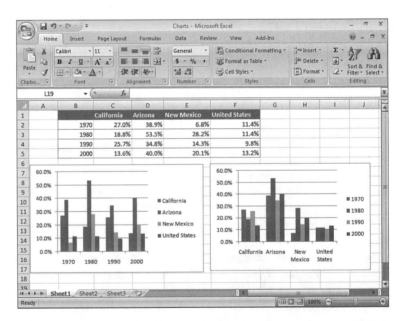

To reverse the order in which Excel plots the selected data, click Switch Rows/Columns, in the Data group of the Design tab. (If this tab is not visible, select a chart to display it.)

Normally, Excel plots data series from left to right and top to bottom. What do you do if your data source is arranged in alphabetical order, but you want to display the series in a different order—for instance, with the two most productive regions labeled first, or with dates in reverse order? If you don't want to change the arrangement of data on the worksheet, you can change the plotting order of the data series:

1. Click the chart border to select the entire chart and then click Data in the Data group of the Design tab.

2. Click any series name in the Legend Entries list. Use the Up or Down arrow icons to re-order the series in the list (see Figure 16.3).

Figure 16.3
You can change the order in which series are plotted by means of this dialog box.

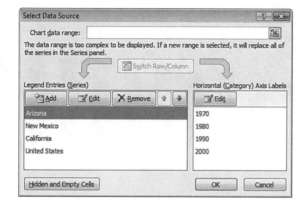

3. Repeat step 2 to resequence additional series.

4. Click OK to accept the changes.

SELECTING A CHART TYPE

When you create a new chart, Excel lets you select from 73 chart types in 14 categories (although a significant number of these choices are minor variations of others in the same category). Excel 2007 does away with the gallery of 20 built-in custom chart types. Instead, Excel 2007 offers 5 to 15 built-in custom layouts for each chart type. The type of data you're planning to plot usually dictates which type of chart you should use.

CHOOSING A STANDARD CHART TYPE

When you use the Insert tab to create a new chart, the first step is to specify what type of chart you want to create. After you create a chart, you can easily change it to a new type; right-click the chart area or plot area and choose Chart Type, or click the Chart Type button on the Design tab. The following sections discuss all the standard Excel chart types and describe how you can best use them.

COLUMN

This type of chart shows a comparison between values in one or more series, often over time as shown in Figure 16.4. Stacked column charts further divide the total for each column; in a chart depicting population growth, for example, you might divide the United States into East, West, Midwest, and South and measure how each geographic region grew as a component of the entire country's population growth. Select a column chart when you want to show comparisons between different data points, especially those that change over time. Avoid this chart type if each series includes so many data points that you'll be unable to distinguish individual columns.

Figure 16.4
Column charts are good for short series of time-oriented data.

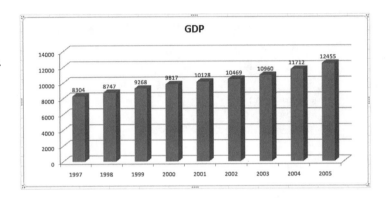

BAR

Think of a bar chart as a column chart turned on its side, with values along the horizontal axis and categories on the vertical axis. It de-emphasizes time comparisons and highlights winners and losers. Figure 16.5, for example, graphically illustrates how well each region has performed in a competition where the goal is to hit $1 million in donations.

Figure 16.5
Bar charts highlight winners and losers. In this example, it's easy to see which region is in the lead.

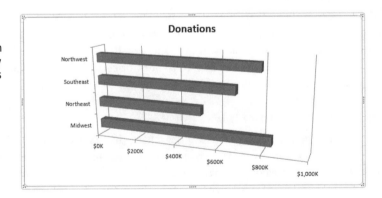

LINE

This chart type displays a trend, or the relationship between values over a time period. For example, Figure 16.6 plots a year's worth of monthly high temperatures for four U.S. cities. By placing temperatures on the value axis and using the category axis as the time scale, the dips and rises in the line show when the weather is getting cooler or warmer. Select a line chart when you have many data points to plot and want to show a trend over a period of time. Avoid this chart type when you're trying to show the relationship between numbers without respect to time, and when you have only a few data points to chart.

Figure 16.6
Line charts are most useful for showing trends over a period of time.

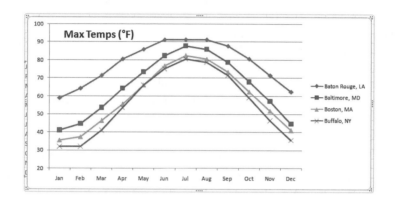

PIE

Pie charts show the relative size of all the parts in a whole—for example, the ethnic composition of a city. Pie charts have no x- or y-axis, and only one data series can be plotted.

Click Data Labels, in the Labels group of the Layout tab, to specify how each slice should be labeled. In Figure 16.7, each pie slice shows the category name and value. Other options include showing the percentage for each pie slice.

Figure 16.7
Pie charts are most useful for showing how each number contributes to the whole.

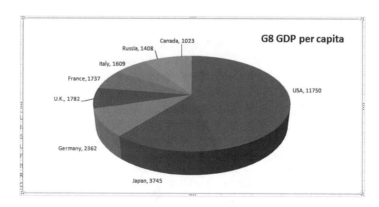

Use pie charts when you have only a few numbers to chart and want to show how each number contributes to the whole. Avoid this chart type when your data series includes many low numbers that contribute a very small percentage to the total. In this case, individual pie slices will be too small to compare.

XY (SCATTER)

Use a scatter chart to show correlations between different series of values when the element of time is unimportant—usually used for scientific analyses. For example, plotting daily high temperatures and ice cream sales over the course of a year will no doubt show clusters of high sales on hot days. Figure 16.8 shows a scatter chart that measures the correlation between employee absences and production errors for a fictitious firm (based on a template available at Microsoft Office Online). You can add various kinds of trendlines to scatter charts. Because the relationship of the x and y variables in this chart appears to be linear, we've added a linear trendline. To add a trendline to a scatter chart, select the chart, click Analysis on the Layout tab, and then click Trendline. To add the equation that defines the trendline, click More Trendline Options, at the bottom of the Trendline gallery.

Figure 16.8
Scatter charts help to illustrate correlations between two sets of data. We've added a linear trendline in this example to make the relationship even clearer.

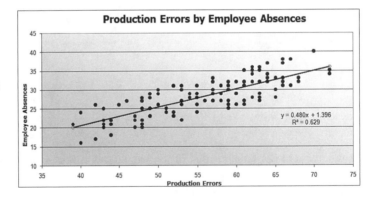

AREA

An area chart is a line chart in which the space between the series line and the category axis is filled in. This type of chart can be awkward to use with multiple series, unless you choose the cumulative subtype, which adds all the values together to illustrate cumulative change. Such a chart can be useful for showing the amount and magnitude of change. The cumulative area chart in Figure 16.9, for example, shows how much each division of a national organization contributes to total revenues over the course of a year.

DOUGHNUT

The doughnut chart is similar to a pie chart, except that it can contain more than one data series. Each ring of the doughnut chart represents a data series.

Figure 16.9
Area charts graphically illustrate cumulative changes—this example shows the year-long contribution of four regional divisions.

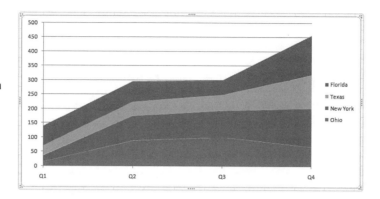

RADAR

Each category in a radar chart has its own value axis that extends from the center of the chart. Lines connect all the values in the same series.

> **TIP**
>
> Are you baffled by some of these chart types? You're not alone. According to Microsoft, both doughnut and radar chart types are popular among Excel users in the Far East but are rarely used in the United States and Europe.

SURFACE

Select this chart type to add a topographic layer over a column or area chart. Instead of assigning a color to each series, this chart type assigns different colors to similar values. The result resembles a topographic map, which can be used to show relationships among large amounts of data that might otherwise be hard to see.

BUBBLE

Bubble charts are similar to scatter charts, except they contain three series of data rather than two. Instead of placing a uniform-sized dot at the point where each pair of x- and y-values intersect, the data markers are bubbles whose size is determined by the values in a third series. Bubble charts often are used to present financial or market research information.

STOCK

Four built-in chart types make tracking open/high/low/close prices over time possible, as in the example in Figure 16.10. Combination chart types in this category enable you to plot volume traded as well. You also can adapt these chart types for scientific use, to show high-low values in experimental data. When choosing one of these chart types, your data columns must be in the exact order to match the chart type. The four possible stock chart types are

- High—Low—Close
- Open—High—Low—Close (see Figure 16.10)
- Volume—High—Low—Close
- Volume—Open—High—Low—Close

Figure 16.10
Each line in this stock chart shows the opening, high, low, and closing prices for a selected ticker symbol on a specific day.

USING COMBINATION CHARTS

It is possible in Excel to create charts that use a combination of chart types. The Line-Column chart type, for example, enables you to format one series of data along a line and another in columns. You can create this chart by starting with an ordinary column chart and then changing the chart type of one series to line.

The Pie-of-Pie and Pie-of-Bar combination charts, both available as subtypes in the Pie category, offer a clever solution when you have so many data points that your chart is difficult to read. As the example in Figure 16.11 shows, you can use a Pie-of-Bar chart to combine several smaller slices into a single large slice and then show the detail in a separate chart connected to the original.

Figure 16.11
Use a Pie-of-Bar chart to keep small slices of the pie from getting lost.

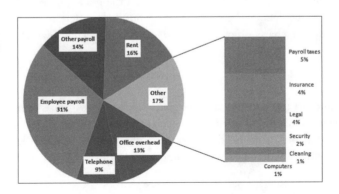

To create either of these combination chart types, open the Chart Type dialog box and select the Pie type; then select the appropriate chart subtype (Pie-of-Pie or Bar-of-Pie) from the list on the right and click OK. To adjust which slices of the pie will go in the secondary (pie or bar) chart, right-click either pie and select Format Data Series. Then click the Series Options tab and adjust the settings as shown in Figure 16.12.

Figure 16.12
Use this dialog box to shift slices of a pie from the primary chart to the secondary chart.

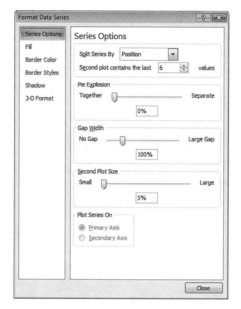

Using the Split Series By list, you can tell Excel to use a specific number of slices, or all slices below a certain value or percent. To move specific slices from the primary to the secondary chart, select the Custom option in the Split Series By list. Then, while the dialog box is still displayed, click a pie slice behind the dialog box. Use the Point Belongs To drop-down list to move the selected slice to the First Plot or Second Plot.

CREATING AND SAVING CUSTOM CHART TYPES

If you've extensively customized a chart, you can save its formatting settings and chart options as a chart template. All the custom chart types you save appear in the Templates category of the Insert Chart dialog box. When you choose a custom chart from this list, Excel applies all the saved options and format settings from the selected chart type to the current chart. This is an especially effective technique for managing a collection of formatted charts you use regularly. It's also an effective way to maintain a consistent style across charts within an organization.

To save a formatted chart as a template, follow these steps:

1. Select the chart.
2. Click Save as Template, in the Type group of the Design tab.
3. Choose a name that describes your customized chart.

To use the template subsequently when building a chart, follow these steps:

1. Select a data series from which you want to make a chart.
2. On the Insert tab, open any of the chart type icons.
3. At the bottom of the charting menu, select All Chart Types. The Insert Chart dialog box appears. A Templates folder appears at the top of the list of chart categories, as shown in Figure 16.13.

Figure 16.13
Your custom chart types are added to a Templates folder in the Insert Chart dialog box.

4. Click the Templates folder. Excel displays a thumbnail for each chart type. If you hover the mouse pointer over a thumbnail, you can see the name of the template.
5. Choose a custom template and click OK.

By default, all your custom chart templates are stored in the folder %appdata%\Microsoft\Templates\Charts. If you need to share templates with another computer, copy your template files from this folder. To browse to the Templates folder, click the Manage Templates button in the Insert Chart dialog box.

TIP

When you save a custom chart type, your entry in the user-defined gallery stores all formatting and chart options, but not the title text. You will be able to type a new title after creating the chart.

CREATING A DEFAULT CHART

The absolute quickest way to create an Excel chart is to select a data range and press Alt+F1. This creates a chart using all Excel's default chart options, embedded on the current work-sheet. (To create a default chart on a separate chart sheet, press F11 instead of Alt+F1.) On a clean installation of Office 2007, the default chart type is Column. If you prefer to use a different chart type as your default, open the Insert Chart dialog box, select the chart type you want to use, and click Set as Default Chart. The next time you press Alt+F1 or F11, Excel will create a chart using the current region or selected data with the chart options in your default chart type.

EDITING AND FORMATTING CHART ELEMENTS

Although the default settings for all the various chart types are often good enough to get you started, Excel offers a broad range of chart options that give you complete control over the look of the chart area, plot area, and other elements of your charts.

SELECTING A LAYOUT AND STYLE

Usually, a good place to begin tailoring a new chart is the Chart Layouts gallery. This visual menu, which appears on the Design tab when a chart is selected, presents a set of commonly used variants for the current chart type. Some of these have legends and titles, others have titles but no legends; some have axis titles, and others do not; some include gridlines, although others omit them. Some, such as the 11th item in the Chart Layouts gallery for a Line chart (see Figure 16.14) reduce the chart to a bare minimum of display elements. (Use this last option if you want to create a "sparkline" chart, as described in Edward Tufte's book *Beautiful Evidence*, http://www.edwardtufte.com/tufte/books_be.)

Figure 16.14
The Chart Layouts gallery offers commonly used combinations of titles, legends, and gridlines for the current chart type.

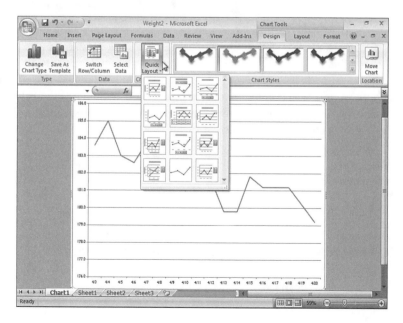

TIP

Creating a histogram in Excel 2003 required a bit of labor. You had to dive into a format-ting dialog box and find the control that removed the gaps between columns. In Excel 2007, you can turn an ordinary column chart into a histogram simply—by selecting Layout 8 in the Column Chart Layout gallery.

After you have selected the layout that comes closest to meeting your needs, move your mouse to the Chart Styles gallery, also on the Design tab. This gallery provides 48 thumbnails with various colors and effects, arranged into six rows and eight columns as shown in Figure 16.15.

Figure 16.15
Choose from various colors and effects in the Chart Styles gallery on the Design tab.

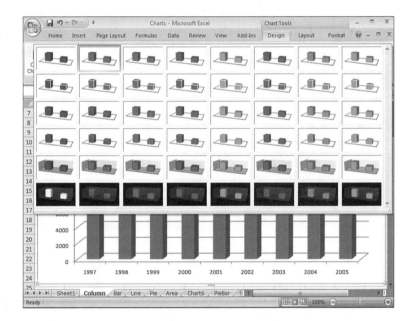

The six styles stacked in the first column, along the left edge of the gallery, are monochro-matic, suitable for output on a black and white printer. In the second column are styles that use a mix of colors from the current theme. Each of the remaining six columns uses one of the six accent colors in the current theme. The bottom row of the gallery contains color styles with dark backgrounds; these might be especially suitable when you plan to paste your chart into a PowerPoint presentation.

MOVING CHARTS

By default, all new charts are created as embedded objects in the current sheet. To move an embedded chart to a different sheet, or to move it to its own chart sheet, use the Move Chart button, in the Location group of the Design tab. (To move a chart to a new location on the current sheet, click the chart and drag.)

LABELING CHART ELEMENTS

Options for adding chart titles, axis titles, legends, and data labels are gathered together in the Labels group of the Layout tab. Each of these options opens a drop-down gallery, and at the bottom of each gallery is a More Options choice. Choosing More Options takes you to a Format dialog box with dozens of choices in several categories.

If you want to head directly to the Format dialog box, you can select the chart element you want to customize and then click Format Selection in the Current Selection group of the Layout tab. Alternatively, you can select a chart element and press Ctrl+1.

TIP

> Selecting a specific chart object by pointing to it can be difficult, especially on a small chart with many elements crowding one another for space. Try this simple shortcut: Use the Current Selection drop-down list in the Current Selection group of the Layout tab. Selecting any item from this list selects that item in the current chart. Then click the Format Selection button just under the drop-down list to display the Format dialog box for the selected object.

ADDING OR EDITING A TITLE

To add a title to a chart, use the Chart Title drop-down in the Labels group of the Layout tab, as shown in Figure 16.16. As the figure shows, you can choose between a centered title that lies over the chart and a centered title that sits above the chart (reducing the plot area). The decision is easily rescinded; in fact, after the title appears on your chart, you can move it anywhere you like, by selecting and dragging its bounding rectangle.

Figure 16.16
Excel offers two standard locations for the chart title.

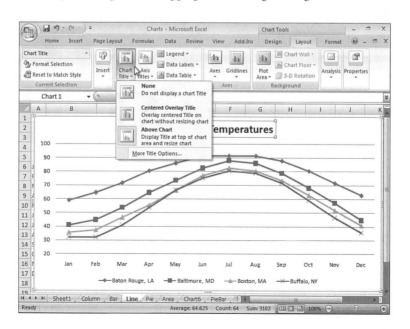

Initially, your chart title might read "Chart Title." To put something more useful in that place, select the title and type in the formula bar. To format individual words or characters in the title, select the title and drag your mouse across the characters you want to change. Then move the mouse upward slightly to make the mini-Toolbar appear. You should find all the formatting commands you need there. To format the entire title, right-click it. The mini-Toolbar appears, along with a context menu that includes a Format Chart Title command.

You can also apply some more exciting effects to your title by using commands in the Shape Styles and WordArt Styles groups of the Format tab.

ADDING AXIS TITLES

You can add a title to any available axis. The Axis Titles drop-down menu (in the Labels group of the Layout tab) includes separate submenus for each axis (see Figure 16.17). For the vertical axis, you can choose to display the title horizontally, vertically, or rotated. In all cases, adding an axis label reduces the size of the plot area. Formatting options for axis titles are the same as for chart titles.

Figure 16.17
Use this menu to add titles to the horizontal and vertical axes of the current chart.

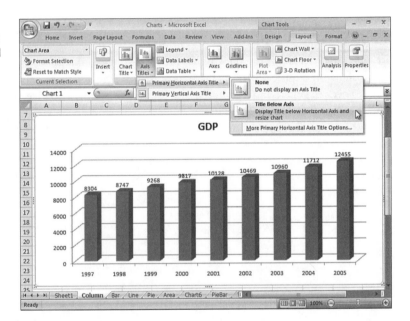

ADDING OR EDITING A LEGEND

To add a legend, click Legend in the Labels group of the Layout tab. The drop-down menu includes a variety of positioning options, some outside the chart, some overlaying it. After the legend appears, you can drag it for more precise positioning.

DISPLAYING DATA LABELS

Use data labels when you want to display data marker values, category labels, or percentages next to each point in a data series. The options in the Data Labels drop-down menu (in the Labels group of the Layout tab) control the placement and appearance of data labels for every data series. However, if you want to add labels for just one series, or even a single point, you can do so. Before clicking the Data Labels button on the Ribbon, click the series you want to label. To label a single point, click that point twice. The first click selects the whole series, and the second limits the selection to the point you clicked.

ADDING A DATA TABLE

Display a worksheet-style table directly in your chart to show the plotted worksheet data alongside the chart itself. If your chart includes a relatively small amount of data, a data table can make an effective addition, as the example in Figure 16.18 shows.

NOTE

> Data tables are available only in column, bar, line, area, and stock charts. You cannot
> add a data table to a pie, XY (scatter), doughnut, radar, surface, or bubble chart.

Figure 16.18
Data tables give your audience both views of the data—the visual display as well as the underlying numbers.

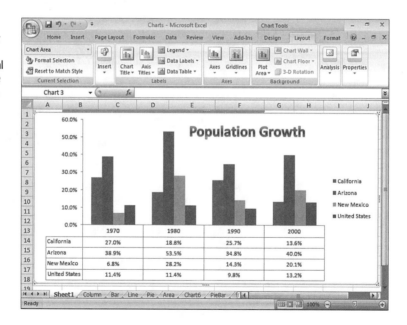

CUSTOMIZING AXES

Excel automatically chooses a scale for the horizontal and vertical axis. The default axis settings are not ideal in many situations. The defaults often lead to charts that are hard to interpret. Use the ideas in this section to customize the axes on your chart.

APPLYING A SCALING FACTOR TO THE VERTICAL AXIS

If the numbers along your vertical axis are multiples of a thousand or a million, you can make the axis a great deal easier to read by applying a scaling factor. Click Axes in the Axes group of the Layout tab and then choose Primary Vertical Axis. As Figure 16.19 shows, you have several scaling-factor options; the chart in that figure scales the national debt numbers by a billion. Note that Excel adds a label beside the axis to indicate the scaling factor.

Figure 16.19
Use the Axes options to eliminate zeros from your axis labels.

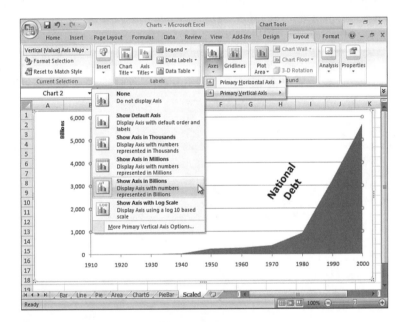

USING A TIME SERIES ALONG A HORIZONTAL AXIS

A quick glance at the chart on the left in Figure 16.20 might lead you to believe that population growth has been slowing in recent years. In the chart on the right, which uses the same data, it's clear that this is not the case.

Figure 16.20
Text years in the chart on the left cause Excel to plot data points at equal distance. The time scale in the chart on the right presents a more accurate view of the data.

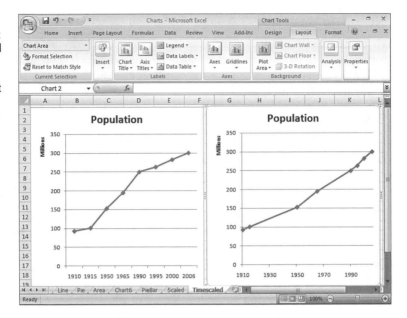

The difference is that in the chart on the left, the years have been entered on the worksheet as text. Excel treats them as categories, therefore, and spaces them equally along the horizontal axis. Because the source data is widely spaced in the early years (note the large gap between 1915 and 1960, for example) than in the later years, this category treatment generates an unrealistically high slope in the middle of the chart and an unrealistically low slope at the right.

In the chart on the right, the dates have been correctly entered as dates, and Excel has generated a time-scaled horizontal axis. Both charts plot the same data points, but in the second chart the position of the points along the horizontal axis reflects their true positions in time.

NOTE

> If your source data contains dates and you want to force the axis to be a text-based axis, you can do so by clicking Axes (in the Axes group of the Layout tab) and then selecting Primary Horizontal Axis. In the Primary Horizontal Axis menu, choose More Primary Horizontal Axis Options. In the Format Axis dialog box, under Axis Type, select Text Axis.

USING LOGARITHMIC SCALING

In some cases when a data series includes numbers of different orders of magnitude, it can be difficult to interpret the numbers using conventional scaling. In such cases, you might be able to make your point more effectively by switching to logarithmic scaling. To do so, click Axes in the Axes group of the Layout tab. Choose Primary Vertical Axis and then Show choose Axis with Log Scale.

PLOTTING A SERIES ON A SECONDARY AXIS

When your chart plots two or more series in entirely different numeric ranges, you will probably want to plot at least one of those series on a secondary vertical axis. Otherwise, some of your numbers will be too small to be read on the graph. To create a chart with two vertical axes, follow these steps:

1. Create the chart in the usual way, with a single vertical axis.
2. Select a data series you want to plot against a secondary axis.
3. Right-click and choose Format Data Series.
4. In the Format Data Series dialog box, select Secondary Axis.

After you have assigned one or more series to the secondary axis, you might need to adjust the scale of that axis, or of the primary axis. We discuss that procedure next.

CHANGING THE SCALE OF A VERTICAL AXIS

Excel normally sets the beginning and end points of a vertical axis to just below and just above the values in your data series. If you want to adjust the scale so it encompasses a larger or smaller numeric range, follow these steps:

1. Right-click the vertical axis and choose Format Axis.
2. In the Axis Options category of the Format Options dialog box, change the Minimum or Maximum setting (or both) from Auto to Fixed. Enter a new number in the text box, as shown in Figure 16.21.
3. Click Close to apply the changes to your chart.

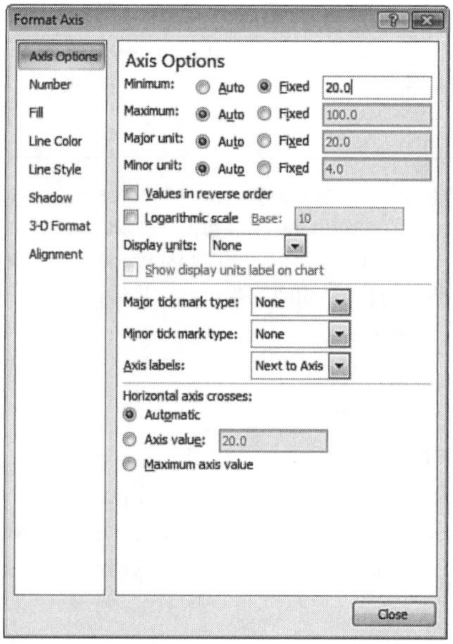

Figure 16.21
You can override the scale range for a chart. Note that the options shown here vary depending on the type of data.

SHOWING OR HIDING GRIDLINES

Gridlines are horizontal or vertical lines that extend through the plot area to help you visualize the connections between data points and values or categories. Use the Gridlines icon in the Axes group of the Layout tab to add or hide gridlines. For more control, use the More Gridlines Options selection to display the Format Gridlines dialog box. Here you can control the color, thickness, and style of the lines.

ADDING MOVING AVERAGES AND OTHER TRENDLINES

Excel's advanced charting options enable you to add details that help you spot trends more easily. For example, in a line chart that plots market data over time, you can add a moving average line that smoothes out some of the peaks and valleys in the data. Figure 16.22 shows an example of a moving average. The dark bumpy line is the raw data; the thinner, smoother line, is a 30-period moving average (that is, each point along that line plots the average of the most recent 30 points on the original line). To add a moving average to a chart, select the series you want to average and then click Trendline in the Analysis group of the Layout tab. The drop-down menu includes the item Two Period Moving Average. If you want some other period, click More Trendline Options. In the Format Trendline dialog box, select Moving Average and then specify the interval you want in the adjacent control.

Figure 16.22
A moving average line can smooth out the noise in your data.

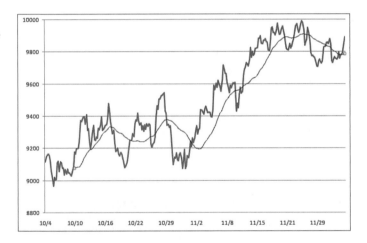

In addition to plotting moving averages, Excel can generate five kinds of "curve-fitting" trendlines: Exponential, Linear, Logarithmic, Polynomial, and Power. To see the full range of possibilities, click Trendline in the Analysis Group of the Layout tab and then click More Trendline Options. A linear trendline is the straight line that best describes a set of data; we saw an example earlier in this chapter (see Figure 16.8). The line is generated by a linear function in the form $y = mx + b$. The other options employ more complex functions to generate the trendline. Which trendline is appropriate depends on the nature of your data.

If you add a linear trendline to a chart, you also have the option of extrapolating the trend-line into the future or past. To extend a linear trendline into the future or past, follow these steps:

1. Select the series you want to analyze.

2. Click Trendline in the Analysis group of the Layout tab.

3. Click More Trendline Options.

4. In the Format Trendline dialog box (see Figure 16.23), select Linear. Then in the Forecast section of the same dialog box, specify the number of periods forward or back-ward you want to extrapolate.

Figure 16.23
Using the Forecast section of this dialog box, you can extend a linear trendline into the future or past.

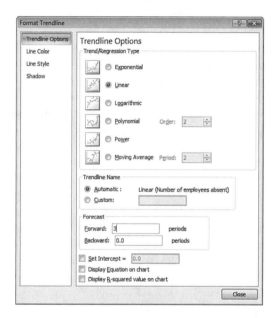

CUSTOMIZING A CHART'S APPEARANCE

As you progress from the Design tab to the Layout tab to the Format tab, you gain increas-ing control over the elements and appearance of your chart. The Design tab globally changes the chart type and colors on the chart. The Layout tab allows you to turn on or off certain elements of the chart. The Format tab offers complete control over fill, outline, shadow, reflection, glow, soft edges, bevel, and rotation of every chart element.

CHANGING FILL AND OUTLINE COLORS

Most default charts have a boring white or black background behind the data. Choose the plot area in a chart and use the Shape Fill drop-down list on the Format tab to add color to the chart. You can choose a theme color or standard color; build a color; or use a picture, gradient, or texture.

ADDING VISUAL EFFECTS

Office 2007's charting engine can add glow, shadow, reflection, soft edge, or bevel to most charting elements. To add pizzazz of this kind, click Shape Fill, Shape Outline, or Shape Effects, in the Shape Styles group of the Format tab. To add effects to the text in a chart, use the same three drop-down lists in the WordArt Styles group (also on the Format tab).

Excel also lets you add an enormous number of attention-getting elements in the drawing layer on top of a chart. For example, you can add text boxes to data markers to explain anomalies in your data or call attention to key numbers. Click Text Box in the Insert group of the Layout tab. Drag in the chart to add a blank text box. After you've added the desired text, you can then move it anywhere on the chart and reformat it to your liking.

TROUBLESHOOTING

FORMATTING COMBINATION CHARTS

I created a Pie-of-Pie or Pie-of-Bar chart, but I'm having trouble formatting it.

These combination chart types follow some fairly rigid rules. You cannot select either of the two charts individually. They are always side by side, and you cannot move them, although you can change their relative sizes. To show the link between the two charts, you can add or remove series lines; however, you cannot reformat these connecting lines.

ADDING NEW DATA TO A CHART

I've created a chart and now need to add new data. Can I do this without re-creating the chart?

When you select a data series on an embedded chart, the Range Finder displays a colored line around the corresponding range within the data source; the Range Finder also adds a border around the value axis labels and category labels, using different colors for each. Drag the selection by using the rectangular handle in the lower-right corner of each selection to extend or move the data range for each series. On a chart where the data source consists of a single contiguous range, selecting the chart area causes the Range Finder to highlight all the data series in one color, the value axis labels in another color, and category names in a third color.

Alternatively, you could simply generate your original chart from a table (as opposed to a mere list). When you add new rows to the table, your chart automatically picks up the new data. For more details about the what makes tables special, see "Lists Versus Tables," page 474.

EXTRA CREDIT: CREATE A MULTI-LEVEL CATEGORY AXIS

PivotCharts are a great way to create charts having multiple dimensions—for example, charts that show sales figures by product line for each of several company divisions. For an example of a PivotChart that has two dimensions along the category axis, see Figure 15.35, in the previous chapter.

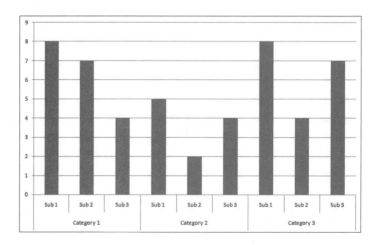

But PivotCharts are not the only way to do this. If you simply set up a range of data in the manner shown in Figure 16.24, Excel plots both the categories and the subcategories along the horizontal axis (see Figure 16.25).

All you need to do to create a chart of this kind is set up the data in a manner that Excel can recognize as a multi-level structure. Then create a chart in the usual way—select a cell in the data range and click a chart-type icon in the Charts group of the Insert tab. You can even extend this idea to additional levels of categorization, although your horizontal axis is likely to become harder to read if you do.

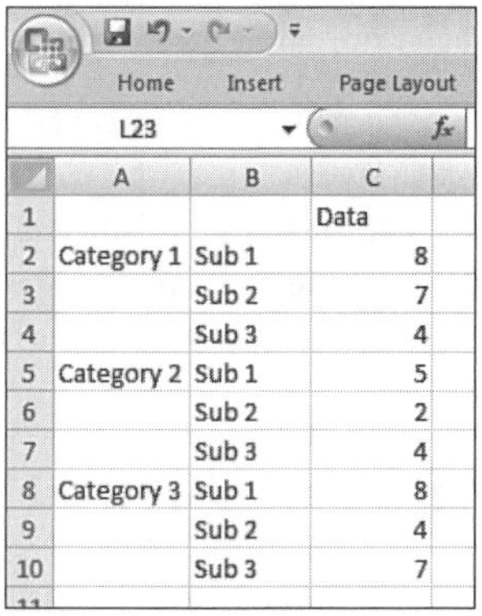

Figure 16.24

Figure 16.25
You don't need a PivotChart to plot subcategories within categories.

The biggest advantage of a PivotChart over an ordinary multi-level chart of this kind is that the PivotChart is easy to rearrange. When you're starting from a humongous database with many dimensions, PivotCharts give you invaluable flexibility. But sometimes you just need something quick and relatively unsophisticated. A multi-level chart can fit the bill nicely.

If you happen to create a chart like this and decide that you don't need the multi-level axis, right-click the axis and choose Format Axis. In the Format Axis dialog box (see Figure 16.26), remove the check from Multi-Level Category Labels.

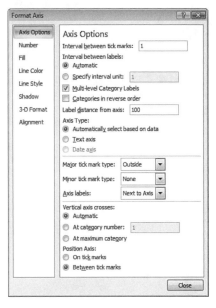

Figure 16.26

16

USING POWERPOINT

CHAPTER **17**

GETTING STARTED WITH POWERPOINT

In this chapter

WHAT IS POWERPOINT GOOD FOR?

Most people think of PowerPoint as the tool for delivering sales pitches and boring speeches at business meetings. It's even been parodied for its capability to boil big ideas down to trite summaries, most famously by Peter Norvig in a version of Abraham Lincoln's Gettysburg Address done, brilliantly, as a stack of banal PowerPoint slides. (See it for yourself at http://www.norvig.com/Gettysburg/.)

Thankfully, PowerPoint isn't just for business. You can use it for class reports, for meeting agendas and wrap-ups, and as a tool to spark ideas in a brainstorming session for your local nonprofit. You can create photo albums and multimedia slideshows, if you keep the text to a minimum and use creative transitions to show off digital pictures and movie clips. In fact, PowerPoint is a useful tool anytime you need to communicate ideas to an audience in a sequential manner using a simple outline, with a few graphics mixed in to keep it from becoming too dull. You can even publish your presentation to a website where anyone can read it in a browser window.

Of all the programs in Office, PowerPoint is probably the easiest to use. In fact, it's so easy to get started that you might be tempted to skip these chapters and just start typing. If you do that, you'll miss some wonderful time-saving tips and tricks buried in the program, not to mention some techniques you can use to make your presentations more interesting.

But before we get to all that, let's start with the nuts and bolts of a PowerPoint presentation.

ANATOMY OF A POWERPOINT PRESENTATION

The basic building block of a PowerPoint presentation is the *slide*—a block of content the size of a computer screen that typically contains a title, some text, and perhaps a picture or chart. A PowerPoint presentation typically contains many slides.

Figure 17.1 illustrates a PowerPoint presentation made up of 30 slides. The default (Normal) view includes notes attached to the current slide and a navigation panel on the left side that allows you to switch between a text outline and slide thumbnails.

A fully loaded slide (see Figure 17.2) includes at most six parts:

- The *title*, which usually sits at the top of the slide.
- *Body text*, the main part of the slide. More often than not, the text on a slide consists of a series of bulleted or numbered items. However, you can enter any kind of text in this part of a slide—bullets and numbers are not required.
- Some slides contain *content* in addition to text. You can add charts, tables, pictures, diagrams, and video clips to help illuminate your presentation.
- If you choose to display the *date and time*, these items appear at the lower-left corner in most themes.

Figure 17.1
PowerPoint's Normal view includes most of the information you need to assemble a presentation.

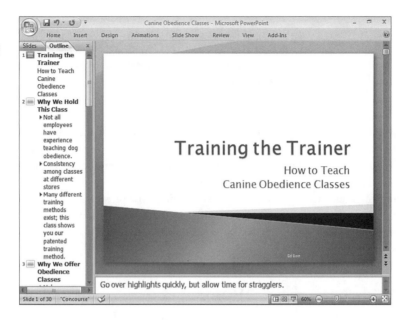

- The *footer*, another optional element, appears in most themes at the bottom of the slide, in the middle.
- Finally, you can choose to display a *slide number*. In most themes, its position is in the lower-right corner.

Figure 17.2
All the components of a PowerPoint slide are shown here, with slide thumbnails in place of a text outline.

Additional content   Slide title   Body text

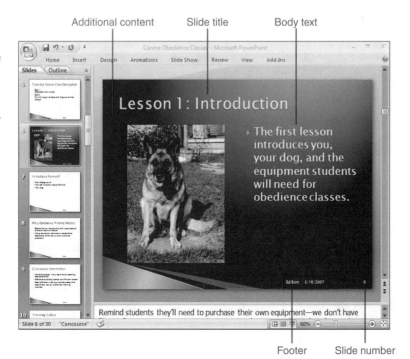

Footer   Slide number

NOTE

> Text and content sit inside resizable and movable containers called *placeholders,* which you can see if you click the text or graphic in the slide pane. PowerPoint Help screens sometimes refer to the placeholder and the text or content it contains as a "text object" or a "graphic object."

Most presentations begin with a *title slide*, which typically includes the title of the presentation, the speaker's name, and other introductory details. If you're planning a presentation as a class project, you might include the class name and number—Sociology 101, for instance; for a presentation to a business or civic group, you might include your name and the name of the organization you represent. Other slides in a presentation can also be title slides—you might use a title slide to introduce different portions of a long presentation, for example—but in most cases, you'll have just one title slide in a presentation, and it will serve as the first slide.

POWERPOINT FILE TYPES

PowerPoint uses three main file types: Presentation, Template, and Slide Show. For the most part, you can construct and deliver simple presentations without ever having to deal with the differences among these types of files. But before you can effectively use PowerPoint's advanced formatting options, you have to understand its file formats.

The Office 2007 Setup program registers a collection of PowerPoint file types. When you view the list of registered file types in Windows Explorer, you'll see the three major types listed in Table 17.1 (some variant HTML file types also work much the same as these).

TABLE 17.1   POWERPOINT FILE TYPES

File Type	File Extension	Default Action
PowerPoint Presentation	*.pptx	Open
PowerPoint Template	*.potx	New
PowerPoint Slide Show	*.ppsx	Show

Thus, from an Explorer window, if you double-click an icon whose file type is Presentation (.pptx), PowerPoint opens the file for editing. When you double-click an icon whose file type is Template (.potx), however, PowerPoint creates a new presentation, based on the template, and takes you to the first slide so you can begin editing. Finally, if you double-click an icon whose type is Slide Show (.ppsx), PowerPoint runs the show without ever showing you any of its slide-editing tools.

Here's the punch line: The internal structure of all three file formats is exactly the same. You can save any presentation as a Template or Slide Show file, and the contents of the file remain the same.

17

N O T E

> You might find inconsistent references to these three file types scattered throughout PowerPoint's Help files and dialog boxes. In this book, we use the three terms defined in this section—Presentation, Template, and Slide Show—to differentiate among the three file types.

When should you use each file type? Follow these general guidelines:

- Use the Presentation file type (.pptx) when you plan to edit the presentation and/or work with its design. To save a file as file type Presentation, choose Presentation from the Save as Type list in the Save As dialog box.

- Use the Template file type (.potx) when you create a presentation that you want to use as the basis for creating new presentations, or if you expect to "borrow" the presentation's design for use in other presentations. To save a file as a Template, choose PowerPoint Template from the Save as Type list in the Save As dialog box. When you select this file type, PowerPoint immediately changes the Save In location to the default Templates folder.

- Use the Slide Show file type (.ppsx) for presentations that you no longer need to edit or design. (Although it's possible to open this type of file from within PowerPoint, this is not the default action when you double-click its icon on the desktop or in an Explorer window.) Choose this file type if you want to start a slideshow directly from the desktop, or if you want someone else to be able to double-click a file icon and see the show. To save a file as a Slide Show, choose PowerPoint Show from the Save as Type list in the Save As dialog box.

T I P

> Because all three file types are internally identical, it's easy to change file types. Just open the file in PowerPoint, click the Microsoft Office button, choose Save As, and then choose Other Formats. In the Save As dialog box, choose a different format from the Save as Type list. If you're comfortable working with file extensions in an Explorer window or at a command prompt, you can change a file type by changing the three- or four-letter extension at the end of the filename; for example, changing the file extension from .pptx to .ppsx converts a Presentation into a Slide Show.

N O T E

> Like Excel 2007 and Word 2007, PowerPoint 2007 uses XML technology and file compression in its default file formats. As a result, PowerPoint 2007 files can be dramatically smaller than their counterparts in earlier versions. Microsoft also claims that the new XML architecture makes it easier to recover damaged files. The tradeoff? Users of earlier versions of PowerPoint can't open presentations stored in the new format unless they first install the Microsoft Office Compatibility Pack. To ensure that your presentations will be viewable by anyone using earlier versions, save them in the PowerPoint 97-2003 Presentation format.

CREATING A PRESENTATION

When you click the Microsoft Office button and choose New, PowerPoint presents the New Presentation dialog box, which includes a variety of options for creating or opening presentations (see Figure 17.3).

Figure 17.3
PowerPoint lets you choose whether you want to open an existing presentation, create a new presentation with or without content, or pull in a template.

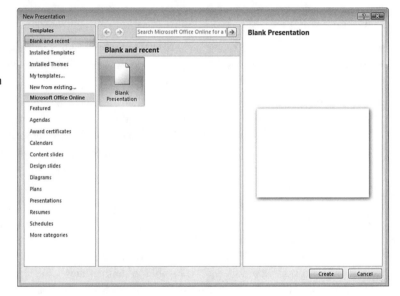

CREATING A BLANK PRESENTATION

If you choose Blank Presentation in the New Presentation dialog box and then click Create, PowerPoint generates a new presentation and displays a single title slide. Although it's a tedious way to work, you can build your presentation from this view, one slide at a time. Click the small arrow below New Slide, in the Slides group of the Home tab. When the gallery of layout options appears (see Figure 17.4), aim your mouse pointer at the layout that matches the kind of slide you want to add.

→ For tips on negotiating the layout maze, **see** "Picking the Best Slide Layout," **p. 564.**

In a blank PowerPoint presentation, each new slide you create is completely free of any design elements whatsoever. You get a white background, with text formatted in the default font (44-point for slide titles and 32-point for body text) and generic round bullets.

It is hard to imagine a layout duller than this default design. To replace it with one that contains coordinated colors, fonts, and graphics, click the Design tab, and then open the All Themes gallery (see Figure 17.5) by clicking the More arrow—near the lower-right corner of the Themes group.

Figure 17.4
Use the New Slide gallery to specify which placeholders will go on a slide and where they will sit.

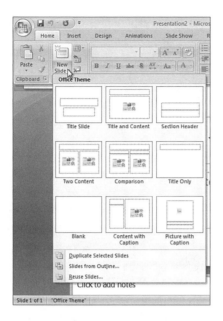

Figure 17.5
Options in the All Themes gallery use the same sets of colors as the comparably named themes in other Office applications.

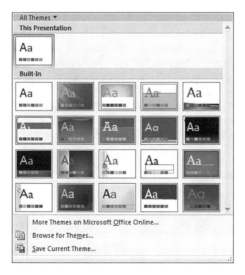

The themes provided in PowerPoint have the same names and the same designer-approved color combinations as their counterparts in Excel and Word. Choosing one of these themes can therefore help you create a consistent, eye-pleasing appearance for all your Office documents.

Like other Office 2007 galleries, the Themes gallery uses Live Preview, which means that if you hover your mouse over a theme, PowerPoint shows you what your slides will look like in that theme. When you click a theme, PowerPoint immediately applies it to the design of all slides in the current presentation. If you prefer to apply a theme only to the current slide (or to a selection of slides), right-click the theme and then click Apply to Selected Slides.

If you regularly prepare presentations for an organization or group that has certain standards for all presentations—logo in a specific location, identification of title slides, and so on—you might want to customize PowerPoint's "blank" presentation so it reflects those standards. That way, whenever you begin a new presentation, you'll have the basic requirements out of the way before you type your first bullet point.

To replace the PowerPoint default blank presentation with one of your own design, follow these steps:

1. Create the presentation you want to use as the "blank" presentation. Add slides, customize slide masters, and change designs until you're satisfied that the basic arrangement is a good starting point for any new presentations you create.

2. Click the Microsoft Office button, choose Save As, and then choose Other Formats. In the Save as Type list of the Save As dialog box, choose PowerPoint Template.

3. Type Blank in the File Name box and click Save.

TIP

By default, PowerPoint saves your new blank presentation in your personal Templates folder. To view the contents of this folder, open Windows Explorer, type `%appdata%\Microsoft\Templates` in the Windows Vista Search box, and press Enter. (You can also use the Run box to enter this address, by pressing the Windows logo key+R.) To change the blank template for all the users in your organization, you must copy the Blank Presentation design template file into the personal Templates folder for each user.

→ For more details on how and where Office programs organize files, **see** "Creating New Files," **p. 58.**

With a Blank Presentation file in the correct location, all "blank" presentations will be based on that file.

STARTING POWERPOINT WITH A TEMPLATE OR THEME

Don't like the idea of starting with a completely blank slate? PowerPoint gives you two ways to pick a design for the presentation before you roll up your sleeves and begin adding new slides:

NOTE

> A design, in this case, includes a background, font specifications for the title slide and other slides in the presentation, default bullets, and a handful of lesser settings—title locations, footers, slide numbering, and the like.

- Choose a presentation template, which gives you a presentation design as well as several ready-to-use slides. Click the Microsoft Office button, choose New, and then select Installed Templates. In the Installed Templates list, click a design template thumbnail to see more detail for the design (see Figure 17.6).

- Choose a presentation theme, which applies one of the PowerPoint themes as the default for your presentation. Click the Microsoft Office button, choose New, and then select Installed Themes. In the Installed Themes list, click a theme thumbnail to see more detail for the design.

When you have made your choice, click Create to start the new presentation.

Figure 17.6
In the Installed Templates gallery, click a thumbnail to get a closer look at the design.

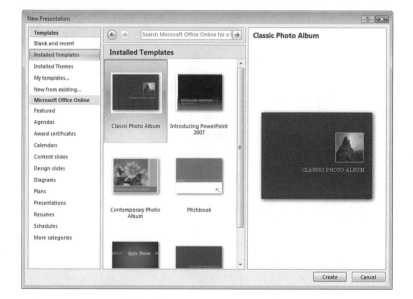

TIP

> Want more templates? Select the categories that appear under the Microsoft Office Online heading to see hundreds more. If you find one you like, click Download to install it on your system.

COPYING THE DESIGN OF AN EXISTING PRESENTATION

So, you've found a presentation with just the right design elements, even if the content is completely different from what you need.

PowerPoint makes it easy to recycle the design of an existing presentation. If you have the original presentation file, you can "borrow" its design without changing the content of your current presentation in any way.

Click the Design tab and then click the More button in the Themes group (the small arrow just to the right of the last-shown gallery item). In the gallery, click Browse for Themes. Then, in the Choose Theme or Themed Document dialog box, select the file whose design you want to copy. The chosen design is applied to your current presentation.

IMPORTING FROM A WORD OUTLINE

How many times have you written a report, a speech, or a set of talking points in Word and then realized that it would be more effective as a presentation? If you can import the document into Word and convert its headings to Word's default Heading 1 style, the rest is a snap.

TIP

> To convert a Word document into an outline that can be used in PowerPoint, you need to learn just a few simple Word shortcuts. In Word, click to select the paragraph you want to turn into a slide title and press Ctrl+Alt+1, which applies the Heading 1 style. For the text that will go into bullet points, press Ctrl+Alt+2 (Heading 2). Want bullet points beneath the bullet points? Press Ctrl+Alt+3 (Heading 3). Save the document and import it into PowerPoint for quick results.

To import a previously saved Word outline into PowerPoint, click the Microsoft Office button and choose Open. With the Files of Type list set to All Outlines, select the Word document, and then click Open.

When you import a Word document, Level 1 headings (formatted Heading 1 in Word) turn into the titles of new slides. Level 2 headings turn into top-level bullet points. Level 3 headings become second-level bullet points, and so on. In essence, the outline that you see in Word's Outline view is translated into a PowerPoint outline. Any body text beneath existing headings is discarded.

Each time PowerPoint encounters a Level 1 heading in Word, it starts a new slide and uses the Level 1 heading text for the slide's title. In other words, your presentation will include exactly one slide for each Level 1 heading in the Word document.

> **NOTE**
>
> You can also import files saved in HTML formats and turn them into a PowerPoint outline. (From the drop-down Files of Type list in the Open dialog box, choose All Web Pages.) During the import, PowerPoint turns each top-level heading into a new slide; all text underneath each heading is placed in a text box on the corresponding slide.

You can also insert an outline into the middle of an existing presentation. Select the slide you want the outline to follow and then choose Insert, Slides from Outline. PowerPoint converts the outline to new slides and inserts them after the selected slide.

DEVELOPING A PRESENTATION

PowerPoint starts in Normal view. You can return to that view at any time by clicking the View tab and then clicking Normal. In Normal view, you can see either a text outline of your presentation or thumbnails of all the slides. These two navigation options share a common pane at the left side of the window. In the main body of the window, the current slide appears, with the slide's notes just below it.

Normal view is customizable. To dismiss the left navigation pane and the notes pane temporarily, leaving only the current slide, click the X at the top left of the navigation pane. To restore both panes, click Normal on the View tab again. You can also drag the right edge of the navigation pane to resize that portion of the window.

EDITING THE PRESENTATION OUTLINE

If your logical left brain regularly overpowers your creative right brain, you might find that the simplest way to edit the text of a presentation is by working with the outline. This offers a simple presentation of your words, and working with them there is about like working with text in a word processor. Changes made in the outline are immediately reflected in the slides (the opposite is also true, of course).

To make the outline visible, if it's not already, click the View tab and then click Normal. Then, in the pane at the left side of the window, click the Outline tab.

You can use the Tab key to demote outline entries. When you press Tab, PowerPoint demotes the current line of text; that is, it moves the current line one level lower in the hierarchy. Alternatively, you can demote an item by right-clicking it in the outline and choosing Demote from the shortcut menu.

You can use similar techniques to promote items. Press Shift+Tab to elevate the current item, or right-click it and choose Promote from the shortcut menu.

You can create the text for an entire presentation this way, promoting and demoting as you go. When you type a line at the highest outline level, that line becomes the title of a new slide. Any line indented below that line becomes a bullet point, and you can nest bullet points to any level you desire.

In the outline, you can also change the order in which slides appear. To move an item to an earlier point in the presentation, right-click it and choose Move Up. Choose Move Down to make the selected item appear later in the presentation. This method is great for simple adjustments. If you need to move a slide to a more distant place in the presentation, you'll probably find it more effective to switch to Slide Sorter view.

USING SLIDE SORTER VIEW TO REARRANGE A PRESENTATION

Slide Sorter view (see Figure 17.7) gives you an opportunity to see the entire presentation all at once, making it easy to move slides around. In this view, you can also test out whatever transitions and animations you might have applied to your presentation. (*Transitions* control how a slide makes its initial appearance onscreen; *animations* control how components of the slide appear after the slide is onscreen. We discuss both in Chapter 19, "Adding Sizzle to a Presentation.")

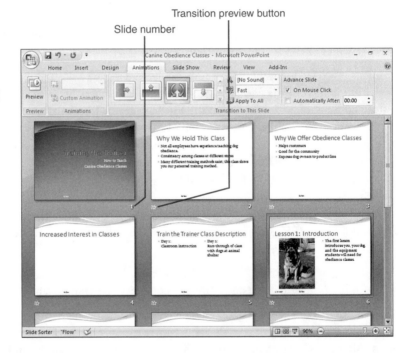

Figure 17.7
Slide Sorter view makes it easy to check transitions and animations.

To move to Slide Sorter view, click the View tab and then click Slide Sorter. Use the Zoom menu to configure the size of the thumbnails (and, by extension, the number of thumbnails visible on the screen).

To see the transition tools, click the Animations tab. Note, however, that to work with animations, you must return to Normal view.

Slide Sorter view is the easiest place to perform the following common tasks:

- Rearrange slides—Click and drag any slide to a different position.
- Add slides—Right-click the space between two slides and choose New Slide from the shortcut menu.
- Delete slides—Select one or more slides and then press the Delete key. (To select multiple slides, hold down Ctrl while clicking.)
- Preview transition effects—Click the Preview button below the slide, on the left.

PREVIEWING YOUR PRESENTATION IN SLIDE SHOW VIEW

At any point in the process of developing a presentation, you can preview the show itself. To see the presentation starting with the currently selected slide, just pick a slide (in any view), click the Slide Show tab, and then click From Current Slide, in the Start Slide Show group. (Alternatively, click the Slide Show button in the status bar.) This starts the show and allows you to use the same navigation techniques you would use if you were actually giving the presentation to an audience (for example, click to advance the slide, press Esc to exit). When the show is over, you return to the view you were using before starting the slideshow. If you want to see the entire presentation, starting with the first slide, click the Slide Show tab and then click From Beginning. (Alternatively, press F5.)

TIP

If you hold down the Control key as you click View Slide Show, the show appears in a small window that occupies the upper-left quadrant of the screen. Click elsewhere in the PowerPoint window to hide the show while you edit or create a slide; click the Resume Slide Show button to return and see your changes.

ADDING NOTES

The simplest way to add or modify notes is in Normal view, where you can expand the notes pane as needed to accommodate lengthy notes.

If the small notes pane isn't big enough to work with comfortably, click Notes Page, in the Presentation Views group of the View tab. This action hides the outline and shows you a full page as it will appear when you print out your notes for reference (see Figure 17.8).

If the notes for any particular slide extend beyond one page, Notes view expands the text area downward to accept what you type. If you print the notes for that particular slide, however, they'll be truncated at one page. Multi-page notes appear in Normal view.

VIEWING PRESENTATIONS IN A WEB BROWSER

If you save your presentation as a web page, the entire presentation can be viewed with a web browser (see Figure 17.9). The person looking at your presentation need not have PowerPoint installed to see all the details and navigate the presentation fully. (Note the navigation buttons along the bottom of the presentation, as well as the buttons that allow the viewer to show or hide the outline and notes pane.)

Figure 17.8
Notes Page view hides the outline and shows only the notes for one slide at a time.

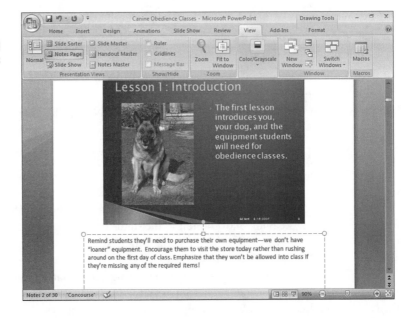

Figure 17.9
This PowerPoint presentation is being viewed through Internet Explorer.

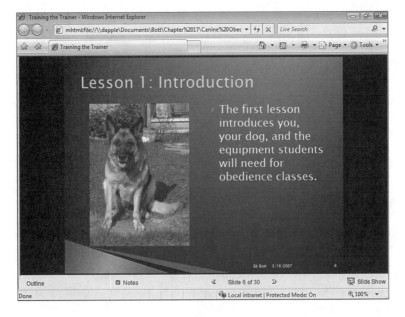

→ To learn how to save your presentation as a web page, **see** "Creating Presentations for the Web," **p. 619.**

To get the full effect of the browser-viewing option, the person viewing the presentation should be running a browser that was widely distributed in the twenty-first century: Internet

Explorer 5 or later, and any version of Firefox. Although you can create presentations that show up on older browsers (Internet Explorer 4 and earlier), there are extensive limitations on what they can do.

CAUTION

> This browser-viewing capability might not perform precisely the way you expect. In particular, you might be disappointed with the way diagonal lines (for example, in AutoShape callouts), WordArt, and organization charts appear when viewed in a browser window.
>
> Before you expend a lot of effort developing a presentation for the web, flesh out a few of the most complex graphics, stick them in a slide, and preview them in your browser. You can then save the slide as a web page and open it in a browser. If you do this regularly, you'll want to make a quick customization of the PowerPoint interface. The Web Page Preview command, previously available on the File menu, is not included in the PowerPoint Ribbon. To add it to the Quick Access Toolbar, click the Office button, click PowerPoint Options, and choose Customize. In the Choose Commands box, choose All Commands; select Web Page Preview from the list and click Add, then click OK to save the customization.
>
> Using the Web Page Preview option gives you a good indication of how the final presentation will appear, at least when using the browser installed on your PC. If you discover a display problem, consider saving the organization chart or AutoShape as a standard graphic and inserting it into a slide instead. Save the original as a hidden slide so you can edit it later.

17

MANAGING SLIDESHOWS

PowerPoint has several useful tools and techniques you can use to manage presentations. If you work in Slide Sorter view, it's easy to copy, move, insert, or delete slides, especially if you know the finer points. To paste a slide at the beginning of a presentation, go into Slide Sorter view, right-click to the left of the first slide, and then click Paste.

If you want to copy slides from one presentation and put them in another, select the slide after which you want the imported slides to appear (in Slide Sorter view, click between the slides). Then open the New Slide gallery, in the Slides group of the Home tab. Click Reuse Slides, at the bottom of the gallery, to display the Reuse Slides pane. Type the path of a PowerPoint file or use the Browse button to find one. PowerPoint displays thumbnails of the file's slides, as shown in Figure 17.10.

Hover the mouse over a thumbnail to see a magnified version. To add a slide, click it; to add all the slides, right-click any slide and choose Insert All Slides. PowerPoint adds the selected slides to the end of the current presentation and applies the current presentation's theme. If you don't want the current theme, select the Keep Source Formatting check box, at the bottom of the Reuse Slides pane.

Figure 17.10
The Reuse Slides pane enables you to pick and choose which slides to copy into the current presentation.

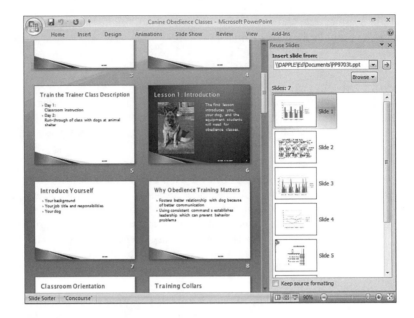

PowerPoint enables you to mark specific slides as *hidden*. Hidden slides appear in all views except Slide Show view, and they don't show up when the presentation is run. You can use hidden slides to prepare material that doesn't have to be in your presentation but might come up in a post-show Q&A period, for example.

To hide a slide, right-click the slide to be hidden (in the navigation pane in Normal view, or in Slide Sorter view) and choose Hide Slide from the shortcut menu. Repeat these steps to unhide a hidden slide.

If you deliver PowerPoint presentations regularly, you might have a main presentation that needs only a bit of tweaking for use with a variety of audiences. For example, you might have one version for teachers and a slightly different version for administrators. Or you might have short and long versions of a presentation, choosing one or the other depending on the time allotted for your talk. PowerPoint makes it easy to keep all your slides together in one file, but build separate, custom slideshows for specific situations.

To create a custom show, click Custom Slide Show in the Start Slide Show group of the Slide Show tab. Then click Custom Shows and click New. The Define Custom Show dialog box appears, as shown in Figure 17.11.

Select the slides you want to appear in the custom show and click Add. Note that you can move a slide—so it appears in a different sequence in the custom show—by clicking the up arrow or down arrow. Type in a name for the custom show and click OK. Repeat this process for other variations on the main show. You can now run any custom show any time you want; open the Custom Shows dialog box again, select the name of the show, and click Show.

Figure 17.11
Pick and arrange existing slides to be incorporated in a custom show.

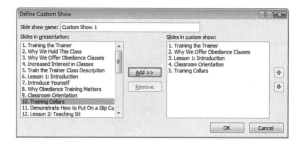

You can also use custom slideshows as a way to create alternate paths within a longer presentation. Move to the slide in your presentation where you want to branch out to one of these custom shows. Select a location for the link (perhaps in the body text, or in a drawing) and click Hyperlink on the Insert tab. In the Link To pane on the left side of the dialog box, pick Place in This Document. Scroll to the bottom of the list, as shown in Figure 17.12.

Figure 17.12
Hyperlink to one of the custom shows—in this example, Short Version.

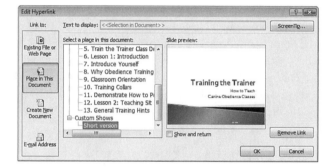

Choose the custom show to which you want to link and click OK. From that point on, whenever you encounter the slide with the hyperlink, click it to display the custom show.

To return to the main presentation after the custom show runs, select the Show and Return check box.

TIP

Alternatively, you can create a hyperlink on the last slide in the custom show to jump to whatever point in the main presentation you like.

→ For details about hyperlinking inside your presentation, **see** "Using Hyperlinks," **p. 559.**

You can tell PowerPoint that you want it to run a custom show, instead of the "normal" show, whenever you start a slideshow. To do so, click Set Up Show on the Slide Show tab. In the Set Up Show dialog box (see Figure 17.13), select a custom show from the Custom Show list in the Show Slides area.

Figure 17.13
Have PowerPoint run a custom show automatically by using the Custom Show setting.

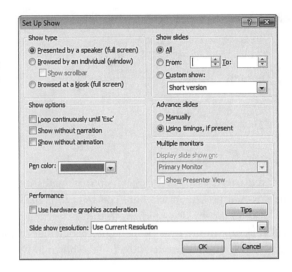

Custom shows can be a powerful feature. For example, you can put all your slides relating to a given topic inside one PowerPoint file and then pick and choose the slides you want to give for your main presentation. Set up a custom show called Main and then choose Main as the default show. That way, all your slides stay in one presentation file, the Main presentation runs whenever you start a slideshow, and you can easily and quickly add and remove slides from the Main presentation.

NAVIGATING THROUGH A PRESENTATION

PowerPoint presents a myriad of ways to navigate in a presentation. None of these techniques are right or wrong, better or worse than another; the trick is to use the technique that's most comfortable for you in the presentation environment.

MOUSE AND KEYBOARD SHORTCUTS

In addition to the navigation methods you've probably used (left mouse button to advance to the next slide, Backspace key to back up to the previous slide, Esc to end the current slideshow), PowerPoint also supports a wide variety of mouse and keyboard shortcuts:

- To advance from one slide to another, or perform the next animation on the current slide, you can click the left mouse button—but you can also press Enter, N (for Next), Page Down, right arrow, down arrow, or the spacebar. You can also right-click the screen during a presentation and choose Next.

- To move to the previous slide, or activate the preceding animation on the current slide, you can press Backspace—but you can also try P (for Previous), Page Up, left arrow, or the up arrow. Or you can right-click the screen and choose Previous.

- To end a presentation, in addition to the Esc key, you can right-click and choose End Show.

An almost-complete list of navigation controls is available by right-clicking the screen during a presentation and choosing Help, by pressing F1, or by referring to the Help topic "Slideshow Controls." Most of the controls are obscure, but a few might be worth memorizing:

- B (for Black) or pressing the period key toggles between displaying a black screen and showing the current slide.
- Similarly, W (for white) or pressing the comma key toggles a white screen.
- Tab cycles among all the hyperlinks on a slide.

The black- and white-screen options are useful when you're giving a slideshow and you come to a point where you want to talk without the help of slides. Clearing the contents of the screen allows your audience to focus on you without being distracted by the contents of the last slide.

> **TIP**
>
> This doesn't appear to be documented anywhere, but pressing the Home key during a presentation returns you to the first slide. Similarly, pressing the End key sends you to the final slide.

USING HYPERLINKS

Hyperlinks allow you to turn text, graphics, pictures, or almost anything else on a slide, into a "hot" link. Those hot links can point just about anywhere—a specific slide, the first or last slide in a presentation, the next or previous slides, files (whether on the local hard drive or the network), specific locations inside Word documents or Excel workbooks, and much more. As shown previously in Figure 17.12, you can even link to a custom show within the current presentation.

If the computer you're using for the presentation is connected to the web (or if the presentation itself is on the web), hyperlinks can also connect to web pages.

The easiest way to establish a hyperlink is to start by selecting whatever you want to hyperlink from (that is, the text, drawing, picture, and so on, that will be "hot" during the presentation) and then click Hyperlink on the Insert tab. (If you prefer, you can use the Office-wide shortcut Ctrl+K.)

The problem with hyperlinking to an object that requires another application, of course, is that there's no way to hyperlink to the next slide in your presentation. When you click a hyperlink that opens another program, you leave PowerPoint. When you then close the other application, you have to manually return to PowerPoint and move on to your next slide.

TIP

If you hyperlink to an entire PowerPoint presentation, you can run through that presentation, and when it's done, you are back where you started, at the "link from" slide.

ADVANCED NAVIGATION WITH ACTION SETTINGS

Action Settings are an older variation on hyperlinks that enable you to link to a few unusual locations in a presentation—in particular, the "last slide viewed." Action Settings also enable you to start a program, run a macro, and/or combine sounds with all the preceding.

If you want to be able to "jump back" to the previously viewed slide, your best bet is to set up an Action Button (see next section) with an Action Setting that moves to the previously viewed slide. This option allows you to link to a single slide from several locations and set up a "Return" button that always goes back to the right place. Action Settings allow you to navigate in powerful ways that aren't possible with hyperlinks.

To open the Action Settings dialog box (see Figure 17.14), select the text or graphic you want to make "hot" and then click Action on the Insert tab.

Figure 17.14
Action Settings provide the only (easy) way to return to the previously viewed slide.

Note that you can specify separate actions for a mouse over—where you move the mouse pointer over the "hot" area—and for a mouse click.

NAVIGATION SHORTHAND WITH ACTION BUTTONS

PowerPoint makes some kinds of hyperlinking easy by attaching predefined hyperlinking information to a group of AutoShapes called Action Buttons.

If you want to add a button that allows you to immediately move to the end of the presentation, use an Action Button. If you're creating a presentation for the web and want to create your own Next Slide and Previous Slide buttons, instead of relying on PowerPoint's built-in navigation bar, Action Buttons make it easy.

To place an Action Button on a slide, select the slide and click the Home tab. Then click the More arrow, in the lower-right corner of the Shapes gallery (in the Drawing group). The full Shapes gallery descends, at the bottom of which you'll find a set of Action Buttons (see Figure 17.15).

Figure 17.15
At the bottom of the Shapes gallery, the predefined Action Buttons cover many of the common hyperlinking bases.

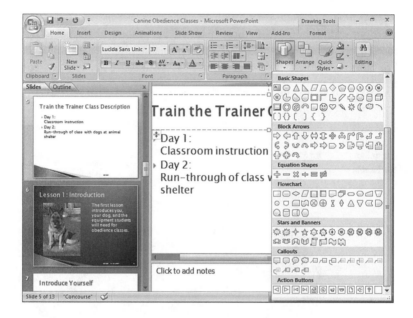

Several of the Action Buttons (for example, the question mark, information sign, and video camera) don't hyperlink to anything in particular; they just put the picture on the slide and bring up the Action Settings dialog box.

Most of the Action Buttons, however, have predefined actions associated with them. You can insert buttons on your slides to move to the first or last slide in the presentation, to go to the next or previous slide, or to return to the last viewed slide.

EXTRA CREDIT: USING POWERPOINT TO CREATE A PHOTO ALBUM

Got a folder full of digital pictures from your most recent vacation? PowerPoint can turn those into an impressive, stylish slideshow. Two of the installed templates, called Classic Photo Album and Contemporary Photo Album, are expressly designed for that purpose. To use either, click the Microsoft Office button, choose New, and then select Installed Templates in the pane at the left side of the New Presentation dialog box. You'll find the two photo-album templates, along with a handful of other useful items.

After you open a photo-album template, press F5 to play through it. The captions and photo layouts give you an idea of what you can do. Then delete the slides that come with the template, click the Home tab, and click New Slide. In the New Slide gallery, you find layouts for pictures in landscape and portrait orientations, with and without caption placeholders, for single pictures and multiples, and so on. There is plenty to work with, and you can tailor it all to your own needs and preferences. If you don't fancy the background colors that come with the template, for example, click the Design tab and apply a different theme.

After you have planted a picture on a slide, select that picture and click the Format tab (at the right end of the Ribbon, directly below the heading Picture Tools). Explore the options for editing and adorning your pictures. You can apply custom frames and other effects, adjust brightness and color, mold your picture to fit one of PowerPoint's shapes, and so on.

Figure 17.16 shows the Format tab atop a picture show that we threw together in minutes.

Figure 17.16
Use the Format tab to apply custom looks and effects to your pictures.

CHAPTER **18**

BUILDING YOUR PRESENTATION

In this chapter

PICKING THE BEST SLIDE LAYOUT

Although it's easy to add a new slide to a presentation, choosing the right slide layout isn't always so simple.

PowerPoint supports two broad categories of slides: *title slides* (typically the first slide in a presentation) and "regular" slides (which, confusingly, are usually just called slides). PowerPoint has one predefined layout for title slides and almost two dozen predefined layouts for regular slides.

Slide layouts aren't static: You can change a slide's layout by selecting the slide, choosing Format, Slide Layout, and clicking a layout in the Slide Layout task pane.

CHOOSING A SLIDE LAYOUT

Whether you're applying a layout to a brand-new slide (by clicking New Slide on the Home tab) or changing the layout of an existing slide (by clicking Layout on the Home tab), PowerPoint presents you with the Slide Layout choices shown in Figure 18.1.

Figure 18.1
The Slide Layout pane gives you nine ways to organize a slide.

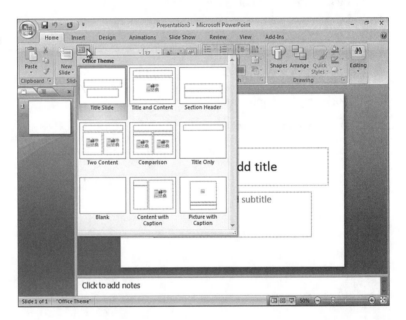

If you choose the first thumbnail in the Slide Layout pane, PowerPoint turns the new slide (or selected slide) into a title slide. Title slides are treated differently from other slides in a presentation—they're formatted independently of the rest of the slides, using the *Title Master*. They generally don't have bullet points and they generally do have a subtitle, so make sure you really want a title slide before making this choice.

→ For more information on editing title slides, **see** "Using the Slide Master," **p. 574.**

The distinction between a title slide and a "regular" slide comes into play because of the way master formatting changes ripple through a presentation. The only way you can manually turn a regular slide into a title slide is by applying the first layout, Title Slide, in the Slide Layout pane.

Other slide thumbnails in the Slide Layout dialog box (refer to Figure 18.1) contain one or more of the following:

- Text placeholders—Typically for bulleted and numbered lists.
- A general content placeholder—Ties into PowerPoint's Insert Object function. The standard content options include a simple grid (that is, a table), an Excel Chart, clip art, a picture (from a file), a SmartArt graphic, or a media clip.
- Combinations of content and text—The placeholders are arranged in various configurations.

TIP

Placeholders can be resized or dragged to fit your requirements. You need not settle for the size or placement established in the Slide Layout dialog pane.

18

The general content placeholder is a superset of the individual placeholders (tables, charts, and so on). In general, you do not limit your choices by using the Slide Layout pane's Content layouts, as opposed to the other layouts.

USING PLACEHOLDERS

With few exceptions, every slide layout has a title placeholder, which reserves space for the title of the slide; this text also appears at the highest hierarchical level in the presentation's outline.

Most slides also have at least one text placeholder. The contents of the text placeholder appear in the outline as points underneath the highest hierarchical level.

Slides that have two text placeholders generate separate outline sections for each placeholder. As you can see in Figure 18.2, PowerPoint gives each placeholder a number, which is used in the outline to keep track of what text belongs in which placeholder.

All the other kinds of slide layout placeholders are special kinds of graphic placeholders: table, chart, SmartArt Graphic, picture, clip art, media clip, and general content placeholders all contain graphics that don't appear in the outline. The only real difference among all these graphic placeholders, in fact, is the kind of link they provide to retrieve the graphic.

Figure 18.2
Multiple text place-holders receive separate numbers, as indicated in the outline pane.

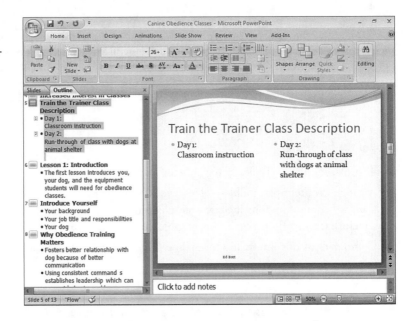

NOTE

You cannot manually insert a placeholder on a slide. Instead, you have to use the Slide Layout task pane. If you copy or paste a text placeholder, it appears as a text box on the slide, and any text you type is not available in the outline. As a result, you cannot add a third text placeholder to a slide.

GOING OUTSIDE THE PLACEHOLDERS

Not all slide activity takes place within placeholders. In fact, any of the items that can go in one of the many content placeholders can also be placed directly on the slide—no placeholder required.

Using the content placeholders to position graphics and other non-text items has two benefits: First, as the name implies, this technique holds a place open on the slide so PowerPoint can scale the inserted graphic or other object properly and move other placeholders out of the way as needed. Second, placeholders provide easy links to specific kinds of objects. If neither of these characteristics matters on a given slide, consider bypassing content placeholders entirely.

Graphics and drawings (for example, items that you insert via the Illustrations group of the Insert tab) placed directly on a slide go in the drawing layer.

→ To learn more about how the drawing layer stores graphics and drawings for your presentation, **see** "Working with the Drawing Layer," **p. 109.**

Note, in particular, that text entered in the drawing layer (say, inside a text box that you create using the Insert tab) does not appear in the outline.

EDITING SLIDES

Slides can contain text, bulleted and numbered lists, tables, and other content such as clip art and charts. In most cases, you can make changes to each of these elements directly on the slide itself, in Normal view.

ADDING AND EDITING TEXT

The highest-level points in a presentation's outline appear as slide titles. Everything else in the outline appears in text placeholders for slides within the presentation. The outline links to the slide strictly and exclusively via the title placeholder and the text placeholder.

If you try to enter more text than a placeholder can accommodate, PowerPoint automatically tries to shrink the text to fit within the confines of the placeholder. First, it tries to reduce the spacing between lines. If that doesn't work, it shrinks the size of the font. If you start to see your text shrinking, maybe it's time to take another look and see whether you need to trim some verbiage or split the slide into two.

→ To work from the outline, **see** "Editing the Presentation Outline," **p. 551.**

Whenever PowerPoint shrinks text to fit in a placeholder, an AutoFit Options action menu appears (it resembles the AutoCorrect action menu). If you don't want PowerPoint to squeeze the text into the placeholder, click the button and choose Stop Fitting Text to This Placeholder from the menu. When you choose this option, your text spills over onto the face of the slide. This action menu also gives you the options to split the text on the current slide into two slides, to continue on a new slide, or to change to a two-column layout (which only helps if your bulleted list consists of very short items).

> **TIP**
>
> On presentations that adhere to strict design guidelines, auto-fitting text damages the integrity of the design; it might also make the slide too hard to read. To turn off AutoFit, choose Control AutoCorrect Options on the AutoFit Options action menu. On the AutoFormat as You Type tab of the AutoCorrect dialog box, clear the check boxes labeled AutoFit Body Text to Placeholder and AutoFit Title Text to Placeholder.

> **TIP**
>
> In a bulleted list, use Ctrl+Tab to insert a tab character into the text. Pressing the Tab key by itself changes the bullet level.

You might also place text anywhere in the drawing layer—which is to say, on "top" of the slide—by inserting a text box or using one of the many different shapes available in the Shapes gallery (in the Illustrations group of the Insert tab).

In the case of shapes, PowerPoint allows you to type text that extends beyond the ends of the shape, but doesn't display that text. To make it visible, enlarge the shape. In text boxes,

PowerPoint expands the text box as necessary, while you type, to accommodate all the text you care to add. In neither case is the size of the text adjusted (as it is in text placeholders). In both cases, any text that extends beyond the edge of a slide when viewed in the slide pane does not show up on the slide when you view the slideshow or print that slide.

You can apply formatting to any text on a slide by selecting the text and then choosing the formatting. If you want to change the formatting on all slides, however—say, change all the titles on all the slides to a new font, or make all the first-level bullet points on all the slides green—you should use the Slide Master.

> **TIP**
>
> You can change all instances of a font (typeface) to another font by opening the Replace menu (in the Editing group of the Home tab) and choosing Replace Fonts.

→ For an explanation of how Slide Masters work, **see** "Using the Slide Master," **p. 574.**

PowerPoint applies AutoFormatting while you type, changing fractions (1/4 to ¼), ordinals (1st to 1ˢᵗ), "smart" curly quotes, dashes, and the like. It also changes a single quote in front of a number into a curly quote ('04 to '04), with the curl pointing in the correct direction, change (c) into a copyright symbol, and change several combinations of : and) into a smiley face.

→ For advice on making AutoCorrect work the way you want—and to turn the vexing changes off—**see** "Using AutoCorrect to Type Faster," **p. 90.**

WORKING WITH BULLETED AND NUMBERED LISTS

Most of the text you enter on slides appears as bulleted—or possibly numbered—items.

You can pick bullets or a numbering scheme when the insertion point is in any text, whether in the title placeholder, text placeholder, or even on the drawing layer.

If you've applied a theme to your presentation, PowerPoint has probably already selected a bullet character and formatted it with a color from the default palette for that theme. To change a bullet—say, to use a picture as a bullet—go through the Bullets and Numbering dialog box.

Click within the line you want to change, or select all the lines to change, and then click the Home tab and pull down the Bullets menu. Alternatively (and more simply), right-click the lines you want to change and choose Bullets from the shortcut menu. Then click Bullets and Numbering at the bottom of the gallery. The Bullets and Numbering dialog box, shown in Figure 18.3, appears.

> **TIP**
>
> Although you can change the bullet character for a single line, you will usually want to change all the bullets on a slide. To customize an entire presentation, perform these steps using the Slide Master rather than an individual slide.

Figure 18.3
PowerPoint enables
you to choose any
character or picture
as a bullet.

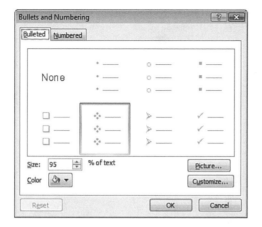

Choose a bullet character from the list of preset options, or click Customize to select a different character from any available font. You can also use a picture in any Office-compatible graphics format—GIF or JPEG, for example—as a bullet. To do so, click Picture (see Figure 18.4) and use one of the built-in bullets, or click Import to bring in a picture of your own.

TIP

PowerPoint stores the bullets just once, so you needn't be overly concerned about swelling file sizes if you stick to just one or two picture bullets. Your primary concern should be how legible the bullet will be in your presentation. Simple line art drawings— say, a pointing finger or a starburst—can help make your point. Washed-out photographs rendered in tiny sizes will only leave your audience squinting.

The Size **nn**% of Text box in the Bullets and Numbering dialog box (refer to Figure 18.3) adjusts the size of the bullet (whether picture or character), scaling it to the point size of the text. You can select any size between 25% and 400%.

NOTE

The Color drop-down list box in the Bullets and Numbering dialog box applies only to characters; it does not affect the color of a picture used as a bullet.

Numbered paragraphs renumber themselves as you add new items and delete or move existing ones. Follow these steps to number the lines in a slide:

1. Click within the line you want to number, or select a range of lines to be numbered. Auto numbering is supported only for the highest-level paragraphs; if you select lower-level paragraphs, they are ignored.

Figure 18.4
Choose a picture from among the ones offered, or import your own.

2. Click the Home tab, pull down the Numbering menu from the Paragraph group, and then choose Numbering. (Or right-click the text and choose Numbering from the shortcut menu.)

3. In the Bullets and Numbering dialog box, click the Numbered tab.

4. Pick the type of numbering you want—fairly simple Roman and Arabic numbers as well as alphabet sequences (a, b, c) are supported on the Numbered tab.

5. If you have a long numbered list that extends over multiple slides, specify a starting value other than 1.

The size and color formatting options mentioned for bullets earlier in this section apply to numbers, too.

If you want to construct multiple-level numbering schemes (for example, 1.1, 1.2, 1.3, 2.1, 2.2), you have to type and maintain the numbers manually.

WORKING WITH TABLES

PowerPoint supports several methods for constructing tables. To create a table on a slide with a content placeholder, for example, you can simply click the Table icon, the upper-left icon in the cluster of icons that appears in the content placeholder (the one that looks like a miniature spreadsheet). PowerPoint responds with a simple Insert Table dialog box, in which you indicate the number of rows and columns you want in your table. The table arrives as a drawing-layer object, which you can move, size, and format to suit. With the table selected, PowerPoint adds Design and Layout tabs to the Ribbon, under the new heading Table Tools. The Design tab is replete with formatting options, and the Layout tab enables you to do such things as insert and delete rows and columns, suppress gridlines, and merge and split cells.

If you're not starting from a slide with a content placeholder, you can get your table by clicking the Insert tab and pulling down the Table menu, at the left edge of the Ribbon. Choosing Insert Table from this menu produces the same simple dialog box that you would get by clicking the Table icon in a content placeholder. The resulting table exists in the drawing layer, and you can move it to a position appropriate for the surrounding text. Select the table and click the Format or Layout tabs to change the structure or appearance of the table.

As an alternative to using the Insert Table dialog box, you can click the Insert tab, open the Table menu, and then drag your mouse across the grid of cells that appears at the top of the menu. The effect is the same; you're just specifying your table's dimensions with a wave of the mouse instead of by filling out a form.

The methods just described generate tables in which all the rows initially have the same height and all the columns have the same width. (You can adjust column widths and row heights with the mouse, and PowerPoint will make height adjustments automatically if you type more text in a cell than will fit; but the tables start out evenly spaced.) If you want something more freeform, PowerPoint will accommodate you. Click the Insert tab, open the Table menu, and choose Draw Table. Your mouse pointer turns to a pencil. Drag out a rectangle to represent the outer borders of your table. Then click the Design tab (if it's not already active), and click Draw Table, in the Draw Borders group near the right end of the Ribbon. Your mouse cursor again takes on a pencil shape, and you can draw your table's row and column borders. When you work this way, you can put the cell boundaries anywhere you please. PowerPoint will draw perfectly straight vertical and horizontal lines, but they don't have to be evenly spaced and they don't have to extend the full height or width of the table. Thus, for example, you can have cells in one column that are twice as deep as the cells in neighboring columns. If at first you don't get exactly the layout you want, use the Eraser tool (directly to the right of Draw Table in the Design tab) to remove what you don't want; then try again.

Any of these approaches is fine for creating a new table from scratch in a PowerPoint slide. If you already have your tabular data set up in Excel or Word, of course, there's no need to re-create it in PowerPoint. Copy it from the source document and paste it into your presentation. Be sure to use Paste Special, though, not a simple Ctrl+V or Paste command. If you do the latter, you'll get the default HTML format, which will not please you. Click the Home tab, pull down the Paste menu, choose Paste Special, and then choose Microsoft Office Excel Worksheet Object or Microsoft Office Word Document Object. (These Paste Special options will appear somewhat differently if you're starting from nondefault file formats in Excel or Word; choose the format that includes the word *object*.)

The Table menu in PowerPoint also includes an Excel Spreadsheet command that enables you to create an Excel table object on a slide, starting from scratch. It works, but it's clumsy. If you need to whip up an Excel table object in a hurry, it's simpler to open Excel, create the table there, and then paste it into PowerPoint.

18

NOTE

Although tables created in PowerPoint look a lot like Word tables, there are fundamental differences, both in options and in implementation—the version in PowerPoint isn't nearly as powerful. If you need advanced cell formatting (for example, rotating text within cells), use the Draw Table feature in Word and then paste the resulting table into your presentation.

ADDING PICTURES, SMARTART, AND CLIP ART

Use the full array of Office drawing tools (available on the Home and Insert tabs as well as any Format tab that appears when you select an object) to insert pictures and text boxes; add shapes, SmartArt, or WordArt; set colors; connect shapes with lines; draw shadows; and so on.

→ For details about working in the drawing layer, **see** "Working with the Drawing Layer," **p. 109.**

Grids and guidelines help you line up drawing items; you can be a little imprecise as you add items and then, when you're finished, allow PowerPoint to line up things precisely. When working with pictures and other drawing tools, it's helpful to show gridlines on the screen. The simplest way to do this is to click the View tab, and then select the Gridlines check box in the Show/Hide group. For precise positioning of graphic objects, you might also find it useful to select the Ruler check box, in the same command group of the View tab.

To fine-tune the positions of PowerPoint's gridlines, select a graphic object, click the Format tab, open the Align menu, and choose Grid Settings. In the Grid and Guides dialog box (see Figure 18.5), you can adjust the grid spacing.

Figure 18.5
PowerPoint enables you to control the granularity of its grid, and whether drawings should be snapped to the grid.

Sometimes you want to know how far a picture lies from dead center. That's where drawing guides come in handy. If you choose to display drawing guides onscreen, you'll get horizontal and vertical lines that you can use to gauge how far any particular item on the slide sits, compared to dead center (see Figure 18.6). Click the guide, and its distance from center appears as a ScreenTip. You can drag the guides into any position you like, making even fine layout tasks easier. To add drawing guides, select Display Drawing Guides on Screen, in the Grid and Guides dialog box.

Figure 18.6
PowerPoint's drawing guides—one horizontal, one vertical—are shown here. Note that we've "parked" pictures in the unused region around the slide.

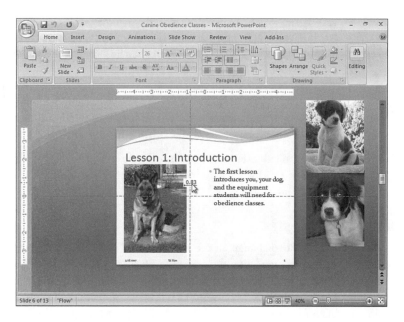

In the Grid and Guides dialog box, you can take your pick of two Snap To check boxes. You can choose to line up shapes so they snap to the grid, or use the Snap Objects to Other Objects setting to make them automatically abut each other or share a common axis.

PowerPoint also allows you to park pictures in the gray area outside a slide, but still in the slide pane. This option can come in handy if you have a few pictures you're considering for the slide, but can't make up your mind which one would be best: Parking them in the margin enables you to swap them in and out quickly. To get a picture into the margin, click and drag on the picture, moving it to the edge of the pane. It takes a little practice to get a picture positioned this way, but the picture remains handy without appearing on the slide itself. (This option is most useful in Normal view when you close the Outline/Slides pane on the left.)

Organizing Formats with Master Slides

Behind every great PowerPoint presentation lurk masters that control the presentation's appearance: the Slide Master, Notes Master, and Handouts Master. Each master stores detailed formatting information for a key part of the overall presentation: slides, speaker's notes, and hardcopy handouts, respectively.

These masters control many facets of the slides themselves—backgrounds, fonts (typeface, point sizes, colors, and the like), bullets, locations for all the main components, tabs, and indents. You can also use masters to specify pictures—a logo, for example—and boilerplate text that appears on all slides. As part of the Slide Master, PowerPoint also includes a separate master for every layout, which enables you to configure the appearance of each layout.

TIP

> If you want to put a graphic, a piece of text, or any other type of object on a bunch of slides, add it to the Slide Master. If you want the object to appear only on a specific layout, add it to the Layout Master instead.

Masters ensure a uniform appearance for your entire presentation. If you're preparing a presentation on behalf of an organization that already has a standard slideshow template, use it.

When you create a blank presentation, PowerPoint creates three generic masters—Slide, Notes, and Handouts. To work with master slides, click the View tab and then select Slide Master, Handout Master, or Notes Master.

USING THE SLIDE MASTER

Whenever you want to change all the slides in your presentation (except the title slides) in exactly the same way, you should change the *Slide Master*. If you want to put a logo on all your slides, for example, add the graphic to the Slide Master instead of editing each individual slide. The same is true if you want to put identical text on all the slides—or change a color, modify a font, or use a different kind of bullet. Making changes to the Slide Master automatically changes all the slides in your presentation. For example, if you change the Slide Master's first-level bullet text to 20-point Arial bold, all the slides in your presentation will have their first-level bullets in that font.

When you click the View tab and then click Slide Master, PowerPoint switches to Slide Master view, adds a Slide Master tab to the left end of the Ribbon (bumping the Home tab from its accustomed position), and displays a set of thumbnails in the left pane (see Figure 18.7). The top thumbnail represents the Slide Master; changes you make here affect all layouts. The remaining thumbnails represent your various layouts; changes you make in one of these affect only a particular layout.

NOTE

> When you hover the mouse pointer over a layout thumbnail, a Screen Tip tells you both the name of the layout and the number of slides in the current presentation that use that layout.

The Slide Master includes placeholders for the title (Master title style) and bullet text (Master text style), as well as a background design (usually assigned by the theme you apply from the Design tab). The Slide Master also has placeholders for a date, footer, and slide number.

To change the formatting of the title or bullets, click inside the placeholder, switch to the Home tab, and apply font or paragraph formatting. Similarly, you can click inside the date, footer, or slide number placeholders and adjust their formatting.

Figure 18.7
Use the Slide Master to manage the design of all slides in a presentation.

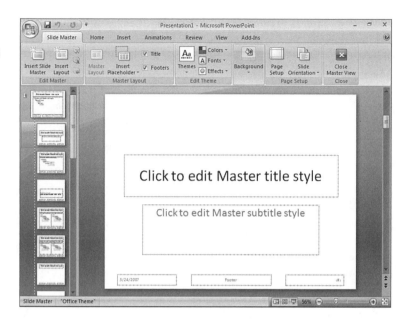

For example, if you want the title on all slides to be left aligned (instead of centered), click once inside the title placeholder, select the text, and then click the Home tab and use the Align Text Left command (in the Paragraph group).

In a Slide Master, you can set formatting and bullets for each level of bulleted text in the body of your presentation. The easiest way to accomplish this task is by applying a theme. To change the formatting of the bullet points in your presentation manually, switch into Slide Master view and then click the Slide Master thumbnail for editing. To change the formatting of text in the highest-level bullet points, click the line that reads "Click to edit Master text styles" and apply the formatting as follows:

- You can change the font, font size, font color, and indent level.
- You can change the bullet character used on all slides based on this Master Slide. To do this, display the Home tab, pull down the Bullets list, and choose the bullet you like.

Repeat this process for the second-, third-, fourth-, and fifth-level bullet items by clicking the appropriate line and applying the formatting.

Similarly, you can resize or move any of the placeholders on the Slide Master. If you move the title placeholder down a half inch on the Slide Master, the titles on all slides will move down half an inch.

TIP

> To "tighten up" the distance between the bullet and text, choose View, Ruler, and adjust the tab stops. PowerPoint aligns each level's bullet and text with the stops shown on the ruler.

PowerPoint ignores any text you type into the title or subtitle placeholders. But if you type text into the date, footer, or slide number placeholders, PowerPoint repeats the text on all slides.

NOTE

> If you override a Slide Master setting by applying formatting to a particular slide, you break the link between the setting and the master; subsequent changes to the master won't affect that particular slide. To restore the link, right-click the slide in the Slide pane and then click Reset Slide. Alternatively, click Reset in the Slides group of the Home tab.

USING THE LAYOUT MASTERS

The various layout masters (all the masters in Slide Master view, *except* the one at the top of the slide pane) control the formatting and placeholder positions of individual layouts in your presentation. The placeholders you see depend on the layout. Some have content placeholders; others have only title and text placeholders.

In the same way that PowerPoint maintains a link between the Slide Master and the slides in a presentation, the program also maintains links between the Slide Master (the one at the top of the slide pane) and individual layout masters. For example, if you change the title formatting in the Slide Master, that change is propagated to each of the layout masters. However, if you change the formatting in a layout master, that link is broken and subsequent changes to the Slide Master do not affect that particular layout.

Unfortunately, PowerPoint doesn't offer a straightforward reset command to patch up such a broken link. You can fix the link by hand, as follows:

1. In the layout master, click the placeholder that is no longer linked to the Slide Master, and press Delete to remove it.
2. Select the Slide Master.
3. Click the placeholder you want to restore on the layout master and then press Ctrl+C.
4. Return to the layout master and press Ctrl+V to paste the placeholder.

CHANGING THE BACKGROUND OF EVERY SLIDE

If you want a logo, a graphic, or a drawing item to appear on all slides, place it on the Slide Master. Any object in the Slide Master's drawing layer appears in the drawing layer of all slides in the same location it occupies on the Slide Master.

Text you place on the Slide Master behaves the same way. For example, in a presentation that contains sensitive data, you might want to add the word *Confidential* to every slide; for a presentation that's under construction, you could add the word *Draft*; and so on. To put identical text on every slide, follow these steps:

1. Switch into Slide Master view and select the Slide Master.

2. Click the Insert tab and then click Text Box. Draw a text box on the Slide Master and adjust its size and position as needed.

3. Click in the text box and enter the text you want to repeat on all slides. This text will not show up in the outline.

4. To format the text box, right-click the edge of the box and choose Format Shape. You might want to add a thick line around the box, for example, or change its background color.

Similarly, if you want a logo, fixed text, or other drawing item to appear within a particular layout, put it on the corresponding layout master.

You'll find by far the richest vein of background customizing options when you learn how to develop, modify, and apply themes. Use these techniques to customize the Master Slides included with PowerPoint's ready-made designs, or devise your own masters and store them for future use.

→ To work with themes, **see** "Applying and Modifying Themes" **p. 582.**

WORKING WITH HEADERS AND FOOTERS

If you're used to working with headers and footers in Word or Excel, PowerPoint's Header and Footer dialog box might be confusing initially. On a slide, you'll search in vain for a header. Paradoxically, though, you can move the Footer Area placeholder, which normally appears centered at the bottom of the slide, to any location—including the top. The Notes Master and Handout Master contain both a Header Area and a Footer Area, positioned by default at the top left and bottom left of printed pages; you can move these placeholders anywhere on the page as well.

In addition, all masters include placeholders for the date and slide number, which normally appear at the bottom of the slide but can be moved anywhere on the slide. When working with any of these elements on the Title Master or Slide Master, follow these guidelines:

- The Date Area placeholder can show the current date—that is, the date the slideshow is being presented. To add a date field of this sort, select the Date Area placeholder. Then click Header and Footer in the Text group of the Insert tab. In the Header and Footer dialog box (see Figure 18.8), select the Date and Time check box, select the Update Automatically option, and then use the drop-down list to select a date format. If you want to track different versions of a presentation as you change it, select the Fixed option instead of the Update Automatically option, and then enter a descriptive text label (it doesn't have to include the date); remember to enter a new description when you save an updated version of the presentation.

- The Footer Area placeholder can carry any text you want, and you can drag it to any location on the slide. You can use this element to label each slide with the name of a school or civic organization, the class for which you're preparing it, or even with the title of the presentation itself.

- The Number Area placeholder can be confusing if it appears near other numbers on a slide. Slide numbers are rarely useful (you might rely on them as a visual reminder of how many slides are left), and they're frequently distracting. If you decide to use slide numbers, keep them subtle, and remember that you can always make the font smaller than the default provided by PowerPoint.

If you look closely at a Slide Master, you'll see that these three placeholders all have dummy values:

- The Date Area placeholder includes the current date.
- The Footer placeholder includes a dummy value called Footer.
- The Number Area placeholder includes a dummy value called <#>.

To show (or hide) the date/time, footer, or slide number placeholders and their contents, do the following:

1. Click Header and Footer, in the Text group of the Insert tab, to display the Header and Footer dialog box (see Figure 18.8). If necessary, click the Slide tab.

2. Select the appropriate check boxes to display any or all of the three placeholders on all slides; clear the check mark to hide the selected placeholder.

3. Use the entries under the check boxes to define what, if anything, replaces the dummy entries—the current date or a footnote, for example.

4. Click Apply to All to make the change to all slides in your presentation. To avoid applying the same change to the title slide, select the Don't Show on Title Slide check box.

Figure 18.8
Use this dialog box to specify which placeholders appear and replacements for the three Slide Master dummy values.

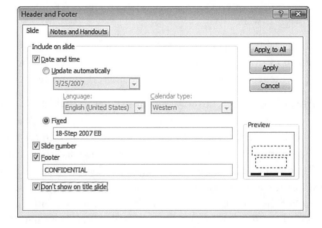

> **NOTE**
>
> If you open the Header and Footer dialog box from Normal view, you can change the display of dates, slide numbers, and footers on an individual slide (click Apply) or on the Slide Master (click Apply to All). If you're certain you don't want to use one of these placeholders, you can safely delete it.

TIP

> If you are likely to use the same headers or footers or other master elements in additional presentations, save a copy of the presentation as a template. (Click the Microsoft Office button, choose Save As, choose Other Formats, and then select PowerPoint Template in the Save as Type list.)

REMOVING SLIDE MASTER ELEMENTS FROM A SINGLE SLIDE

You can have the slide number appear on every slide except one. You might need to do this if one slide includes a big chart, for example, and you need every square inch of slide space to hold it. You might think that you could select the slide number placeholder on a single slide and press the Delete key to remove it. If you try it, however, you'll see that this approach doesn't work.

In fact, removing elements of the Slide Master from an individual slide is an all-or-nothing proposition: You get all of them, or you get none of them. This can be particularly vexing when the design you've chosen includes a graphic object—and most of the designs included with PowerPoint include graphics—or when you have a graphic element, such as a logo, that's supposed to appear on all slides.

To remove *all* the Slide Master elements (except the Title Area placeholder and Object Area placeholder) from a single slide layout:

1. Select the layout master.
2. Select Hide Background Graphics, in the Background group of the Slide Master tab.

If this method is too drastic—you want to remove only one element, for example, on just one slide—you can cover the element up, instead of removing it:

1. Create a small rectangle by clicking Shapes on the Insert tab and choosing the rectangle shape.
2. Make the rectangle just slightly larger than the element you want to eliminate. If you need to adjust the size in finer increments than the tool normally allows, press the Alt key while making the adjustments.
3. Drag the rectangle over the element.
4. On the Format tab, click the down arrow next to the Shape Fill icon. There should be a color very close to the background color available at the beginning of the first or second line of color swatches. Choose the color closest to the background color.
5. On the Format tab, click the down arrow next to the Shape Outline icon. Click the down arrow next to the Line Color icon. Choose the same color you just chose for the fill color, or choose No Line.

If you match the colors carefully, your audience will never know.

18

To accomplish the same trick on multiple slides, even those with fancy multi-colored backgrounds, make a copy of the master slide, remove the element from the copy, and then use this master for the slides where you want the one element removed.

CREATING SPEAKER NOTES AND AUDIENCE HANDOUTS

The *Notes Master* and *Handout Master* behave differently from the Slide Master; their only function is to provide extremely rudimentary instructions for printing speaker notes and audience handouts.

Speaker notes and *handouts*, in PowerPoint, are designed to be printed on letter-size paper. Each page typically holds one slide. On speaker notes, the slide appears at the top of the page, with the notes for that slide at the bottom. Handouts, by contrast, consist solely of printed copies of the slides.

To set PowerPoint printing options for speaker notes, follow these steps:

1. Go into Notes Master view (see Figure 18.9) by clicking Notes Master on the View tab. You will almost always want to adjust the Zoom factor by using the Zoom button or slider in the status bar.

Figure 18.9
Use the Notes Master view to change the layout and formatting of your notes pages.

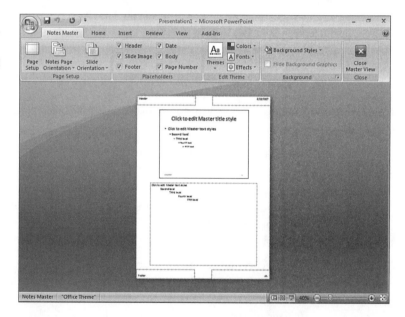

2. Apply formatting to the Notes Body Area just as you would to the Slide Master's text placeholder—click the desired bullet level and apply text formatting.
3. Resize and/or move the slide placeholder and the Notes Body Area.

4. Move the header placeholder, footer placeholder, date/time placeholder, and page number placeholder (marked "Number Area"). Note that you can type text into any of these placeholders and the text will appear on the notes.

5. Control the appearance and contents of those four placeholders by clicking Header and Footer on the Insert tab and setting the check boxes as needed.

When you're satisfied with the formatting, print the speaker notes—click the Microsoft Office button, choose Print, choose Notes Pages in the Print What box, and click OK.

TIP

> Color slides—particularly those with dark backgrounds—invariably print better on a black-and-white printer if you select the Grayscale check box in the Print dialog box.

Click Handout Master on the View tab to see the layout for your handouts. As Figure 18.10 illustrates, you can use the Slides Per Page drop-down to change the page layout so that each page includes two, three, four, six, or nine slides. If you choose the three-slides-per-page layout, PowerPoint adds blank lines next to the slides so the audience can take notes. You can also move or format the Header Area, Footer Area, Date Area, and Number Area (which contains a page number rather than slide numbers, as in the presentation itself). Here, too, you can type text into any of these placeholders and the text will appear on the handouts.

Figure 18.10
The three-slides-per-page handout layout saves paper and gives your audience space to add their own notes on the right.

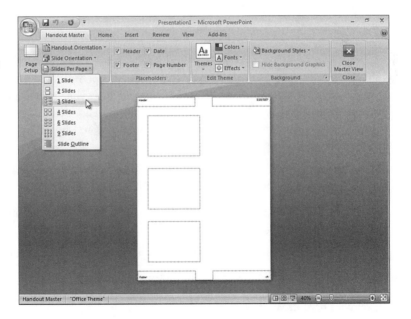

TIP

> The only reason to use the Handout Master view is if you want to add text or graphics to your handouts. You can adjust headers and footers using the Header and Footer dialog box, and you can choose a layout for printing handout sheets from the Print dialog box. (Click the Microsoft Office button, choose Print, select Handouts from the Print What box, and choose a number from the Slides Per Page list.)

APPLYING AND MODIFYING THEMES

PowerPoint themes control the appearance of a presentation. By allowing you to save, modify, and reuse designs—including dozens of Microsoft-supplied samples—PowerPoint makes it easy to create presentations that are visually appealing and consistent. Consistency is especially important when you want a group of presentations from the same organization to share a common look.

Don't be intimidated by the themes included with PowerPoint. These are only a starting point. Feel free to adapt, combine, customize, and tweak to your heart's content. If you come up with a theme that really gets your point across, save the presentation as a template and use it to design new presentations.

A *theme* is a set of colors, fonts, effects, and background styles. In some themes, these elements are consistent in every slide layout, while in other themes, you see different elements in some layouts. In any case, between them, these elements completely control the look of a presentation.

→ To change every slide in a presentation, **see** "Organizing Formats with Master Slides," **p. 573**.

CHOOSING THE BEST THEME FOR YOUR PRESENTATION

Nothing detracts more from a good presentation than a poor design. To choose the best possible design for a presentation, consider your audience, your image, and your message. For a serious, low-key presentation, stick with a no-nonsense design. If you're trying to impress your audience with your energy and ability to project bold ideas, go with bold graphics and vivid colors.

After you have a clear vision of the image you want to project, you're ready to choose a theme. To pick a theme for your presentation, follow these steps:

1. Start with an existing presentation or create a new blank presentation.
2. Display the Themes group by clicking the Design tab on the Ribbon.
3. In the Themes group, click the More button to open the Themes gallery.
4. If you don't see a theme you like, click More Themes on Microsoft Office Online to look for updated themes on the Web. Or click Browse for Themes to look for themes on your hard drive or network.
5. When you've found a suitable design, click it. PowerPoint applies the theme's colors, fonts, effects, and background styles to every slide in your presentation.

MODIFYING THEME COLORS

The *theme colors* are a set of 12 colors that represent presentation text, background, accents (such as chart data markers), and hyperlinks. PowerPoint comes with more than 20 ready-made color schemes, each of which includes foreground and background colors that work well together.

The problem is that sometimes you don't want the colors to blend together so harmoniously. From time to time, a little bit of dash can be a good thing. For example, the color schemes that ship with PowerPoint can be very soothing when applied to text and backgrounds. But when you have a chart on the screen, you want the bars to stand apart from each other.

You can create your own color schemes by using any colors that your video settings will support. Table 18.1 lists the components of a set of theme colors with which you can work.

TABLE 18.1 THEME COLOR COMPONENTS

Component	Description
Text/Background - Dark 1	The default text color and one of the four possible background colors.
Text/Background - Light 1	The default background color and the secondary text color that PowerPoint uses if you switch to a background color that's incompatible with the color specified as Text/Background - Dark 1.
Text/Background - Dark 2	One of the four possible background colors.
Text/Background - Light 2	One of the four possible background colors.
Accent 1 through Accent 6	PowerPoint uses these six colors for chart data markers.
Hyperlink	The color of the text of hyperlinks that haven't been "followed" (that is, clicked and activated).
Followed Hyperlink	The color of hyperlinked text that has been "followed."

18

Just as you can change any detail on a Master Slide, you can change the colors in the current presentation by changing the theme colors of any master. PowerPoint saves colors along with the theme; if you apply a new theme, PowerPoint discards any previous color changes and applies the colors from the new theme to your presentation.

PowerPoint uses theme colors in many places. For example, the Background Styles gallery (discussed later in this chapter in "Choosing the Best Background") offers colors from the current theme, and the colors used to create graphics in many standard designs change when you change themes.

CHOOSING NEW THEME COLORS

To apply theme colors to your presentation, first apply the theme you want to use. Then follow these steps:

1. Click the Design tab.
2. In the Themes group, click the Colors button to display the Theme Colors gallery, as shown in Figure 18.11.

Figure 18.11
Use the Theme Colors gallery to select or create theme colors for your presentation.

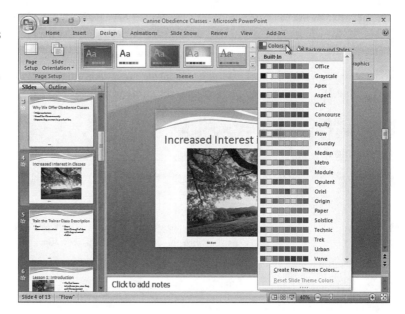

3. Hover the mouse over any gallery item to see a preview of its effect. When you see the one you want to apply, click it. Or click Create New Theme Colors at the bottom of the gallery and use the Create New Theme Colors dialog box (see Figure 18.12) to create your own scheme.

NOTE

In the Create New Theme Colors dialog box, select your colors for each element, type a name for the theme colors, and then click Save. Your custom theme colors will now appear in the Theme Colors gallery, so you can reuse them any time you like.

CHANGING COLORS ON SELECTED SLIDES

If you decide you need to change one color on a slide—perhaps it clashes with a picture or doesn't contrast enough with a chart—you might want to consider changing the entire color scheme for that slide.

Figure 18.12
Use the Create New Theme Colors dialog box to create custom theme colors.

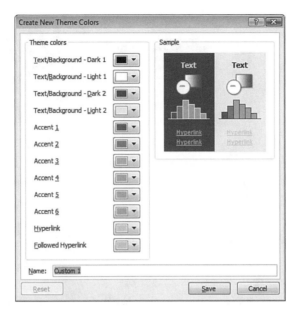

The procedure for changing the color scheme for a single slide (or a selection of slides) is nearly identical to the procedure outlined in the preceding section. First, select the slides you want to modify; then, in step 3, right-click the theme colors you want to use and choose Apply to Selected Slides instead of Apply to All Slides.

USING THEME FONTS

Each presentation theme also applies a set of theme fonts to your presentation. These fonts consist solely of typefaces (other font characteristics, such as size and weight, aren't part of the theme fonts), and each theme fonts collection specifies two fonts—one for headings and one for body text.

To apply theme fonts to your presentation, follow these steps:

1. Click the Design tab.

2. In the Themes group, click the Fonts button to display the Theme Fonts gallery (see Figure 18.13).

3. Hover the mouse pointer over any gallery item to see a preview of its effect. When you see the one you want to apply, click it. Or click Create New Theme Fonts and use the Create New Theme Fonts dialog box (see Figure 18.14) to specify custom fonts.

Figure 18.13
Use the Theme Fonts gallery to select or create theme fonts for your presentation.

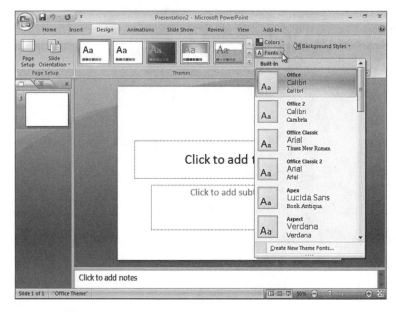

Figure 18.14
Use the Create New Theme Fonts dialog box to assign custom theme fonts.

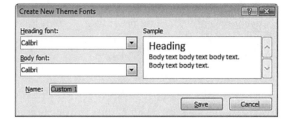

NOTE

In the Create New Theme Fonts dialog box, select a Heading Font and a Body Font, type a name for the theme fonts, and then click Save. Your custom theme fonts will now appear in the Theme Fonts gallery for reuse in other presentations.

Note that when you change fonts as part of a theme, your changes apply to all slides using that theme. PowerPoint 2007 does not allow you to apply the theme fonts to some slides and not to others.

USING THEME EFFECTS

In PowerPoint 2007, a theme also includes a set of theme effects. These control a number of formatting elements, including shadows, glowing, bevels, soft edges, 3D, and line styles. The effects apply mostly to shapes and SmartArt diagrams.

To apply theme effects to your presentation, follow these steps:

1. Click the Design tab.

2. In the Themes group, click the Effects button to display the Theme Effects gallery (see Figure 18.15).

Figure 18.15
Use the Theme Effects gallery to select theme effects for your presentation.

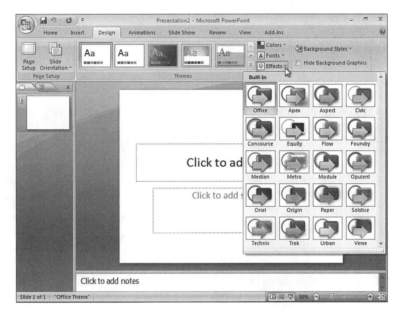

3. Hover the mouse over any gallery item to see a preview of its effect. When you see the one you want to apply, click it.

Note that, unlike theme colors and fonts, theme effects can't be applied only to selected slides. There's also no way to create your own custom theme effects.

CHOOSING THE BEST BACKGROUND

The background of your presentation—the canvas that sits behind all elements on your slides—offers a wide range of possibilities. The background might include solid colors, gradient fills of one or two colors, textures, or patterns; you can also import a graphic file (in GIF, JPEG, Windows Metafile, or any other compatible graphics format) to use as the background.

In addition to the fundamental design principles discussed earlier in this chapter, your selection of a background should be influenced by the medium you'll use for the presentation. If you're going to make the presentation in a darkened room on a large, high-contrast screen, you can get away with just about any combination of colors. But if you're presenting in a low-contrast situation (in a room where ambient light will fall on the screen, for example), make sure you use light letters on a dark background or vice versa. Those who have trouble discerning colors in low-contrast situations will thank you.

To change the background, do the following:

1. Apply the theme or theme colors you want.

2. Select the Design tab.

3. Select the Background Styles list to display a gallery of backgrounds, as shown in Figure 18.16. Note that the four colors you see along the top row are the four Text/Background colors specified in the current theme.

Figure 18.16
Use the Background Styles gallery to select or create a background for your presentation.

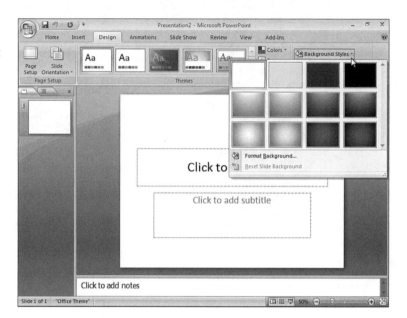

4. Hover the mouse pointer over any gallery item to see a preview of its effect. If you see the one you want to apply, click it; otherwise, click Format Background to open the Format Background dialog box (see Figure 18.17).

Build your background using any of the following techniques:

- To select a solid background color, click Solid Fill and choose a new color from the Color drop-down list. (For a more extensive selection, click More Colors.)

- To create a one- or two-color gradient, click Gradient Fill to display a new set of controls (see Figure 18.18) and use those controls to set up the gradient.

Figure 18.17
The Format
Background dialog
box shows
PowerPoint's exten-
sive set of tools for
changing back-
grounds.

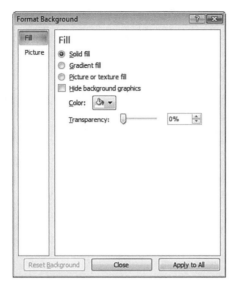

Figure 18.18
Click Gradient Fill to
see the gradient-
related controls.

18

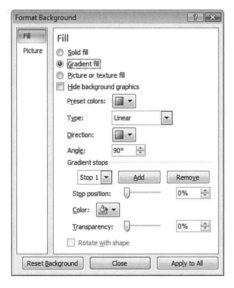

■ To use an image or texture as the background, click Picture or Texture Fill to display a
new set of controls (see Figure 18.19) and use those controls to select and configure the
picture or texture (you can use the samples included with PowerPoint or import your
own). You can also import a picture to use as the background; the picture will be
stretched to fit the slide.

Figure 18.19
Click Picture or
Texture Fill to see the
picture and texture-
related controls.

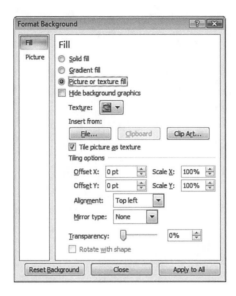

- When you've constructed the background you want, click Apply to All to have the
  changes take effect throughout your presentation.

If you want to apply the background to selected slides only, select the slides you want to use
and then, in step 4, right-click the background you want to use and choose Apply to Selected
Slides.

SAVING A CUSTOM THEME

When you make changes to some or all of a theme's components—the colors, fonts, effects,
and background—it can take a long time to get things just right. If you think you'll be using
this modified theme in other presentations, the last thing you want to do is repeat the customizing procedures every time.

You can avoid this drudgery by saving your theme modifications as a custom theme. This
theme will then appear in the Themes gallery, so you can apply it to another presentation
with just a few mouse clicks. Follow these steps:

1. Make your changes to the theme colors, fonts, effects, and background.
2. In the Design tab, display the Themes gallery and click Save Current Theme.
   PowerPoint displays the Save Current Theme dialog box and selects the Document
   Themes folder.
3. Type a filename for your theme and click Save.

CHANGING PARAGRAPH AND TEXT FORMATTING

Not all presentation text is created equal, and not all text falls into PowerPoint's relentless and presumed point-by-point-by-point format. Sometimes you might want to center a line of text to make it stand out. In other presentations, you might want to ensure that each top-level bullet point has an extra bit of space after it, to make the presentation more readable from the back of the room. Then there's the inevitable bold text, italic text, and even the typographer's nightmare, bold italic text. All these treatments have a place in your repertoire of presentation tricks.

In general, PowerPoint paragraph and text formatting options mirror those available in Word. Select whatever you want to change—paragraphs, words, characters—and then use the Home tab's Font and Paragraph groups to apply the changes.

> **NOTE**
>
> To change paragraph or text formatting for all the slides in your presentation, change the Slide Master. To change paragraph or text formatting for a particular layout, if your presentation uses the layout multiple times, change the master for that layout; otherwise, change the slide directly.

USING PARAGRAPH FORMATTING

All the standard paragraph formatting settings found in Word are at your disposal, including alignment (right, center, and left), spacing (double and triple), and so on. These options are available in the Home tab's Paragraph group.

> **NOTE**
>
> To remove bullets from a paragraph, click inside the paragraph, select the Home tab, and then either pull down the Bullets list and click None, or click the Bullets button.

To change tab stops and adjust the behavior of tab characters, you must use the ruler (select Ruler in the Show/Hide group of the View tab).

Some tab formatting options you might use in other Office applications do not exist in PowerPoint. For example, there is no easy way to put a tab stop in every cell of a table; you have to enter them all manually.

USING FONTS

Professional designers recommend you stick with one font for titles and another for text. Using too many fonts detracts from a presentation.

To adjust any font effects, select some text and use the Home tab's Font group. You can also right-click the selected text and choose Font from the shortcut menu. All standard effects are available in the Font dialog box: color, bold, italic, bold italic, underline, shadow,

18

emboss, and superscript/subscript. You can also adjust the elevation of superscripts and subscripts in the Offset box.

If you're planning to deliver your presentation on a large screen, avoid italicized fonts, which often end up looking like wavy blobs. You can use underline to emphasize a word or phrase instead, or consider using bold.

REPLACING FONTS THROUGHOUT A PRESENTATION

If you're trying to change all the Times New Roman in a presentation to Garamond, you might be tempted to change the Title Master and Slide Master and call it a day.

Unfortunately, if you've applied any manual formatting to individual slides, the link between the slide and its master might be broken. In that case, even if the master is updated, the slide might not make the switch.

→ To change every slide in your presentation, **see** "Using the Slide Master," **p. 574.**

To truly change all occurrences of Times New Roman to Garamond, select the Home tab, pull down the Replace list, and then choose Replace Fonts. Choose Times New Roman from the Replace drop-down list; choose Garamond from the With list. Click OK to apply the change throughout the presentation—even in the masters. This solution is especially useful when you inherit a presentation created by someone who used a font you don't have.

NOTE

This technique changes only the font; you can't use the dialog box to change point size.

TROUBLESHOOTING

SLIDE MASTER LINK DAMAGE

I changed the Slide Master, but some of the slides in my presentation haven't been updated with the changes.

If you do something odd (for example, delete one of the placeholders in a slide), it's possible to break the link between a slide and the Slide Master. After the link has been broken, changes to the Slide Master are no longer propagated to the slide. To reset the link, select the slide and then click Reset on the Home tab. (Or right-click the slide in the Slides pane and choose Reset Slide from the shortcut menu.)

EXTRA CREDIT: CREATING TOP-NOTCH NOTES AND HANDOUTS

PowerPoint's canned layouts for speaker notes and handouts have the singular advantage of being easy to use. If you just want your audience to have a place to scribble notes about your talk, these basic templates will do the trick.

But for truly professional-looking leave-behinds, consider sending the presentation to Word, which offers much better formatting and printing options than the basic notes and handout layouts in PowerPoint. After polishing your presentation to perfection, click the Microsoft Office button, click Publish, and then choose Create Handouts in Microsoft Office Word. Using the choices in the Send to Microsoft Office Word dialog box, Word creates a new document with blank lines next to the thumbnails, in a format suitable for handouts (see Figure 18.20).

Figure 18.20
Use the layout options in Microsoft Word to export your presentation in a variety of ways.

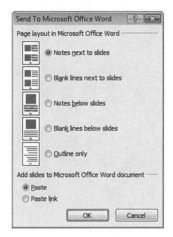

You can use all of Word's editing tools to add content and sizzle to the resulting document, or insert the presentation into an existing document, such as a corporate backgrounder or product datasheets.

After you've finished creating your handouts, consider how your audience will use them before you begin your presentation! When audience members can look at your handout and jump ahead to a topic that specifically concerns them, you might find it difficult to keep their attention focused on what you're saying. The solution? Hand out a one- or two-page summary of your presentation before the talk begins, with room for your audience to jot down comments and questions, but pass out the unabridged handouts *after* your presentation is complete.

CHAPTER 19

ADDING SIZZLE TO A PRESENTATION

BANISHING BORING SLIDE SHOWS

If you're in a hurry, you can whip out a PowerPoint slideshow in minutes. Type in an outline, pick a theme, save your file, and—voilà—instant presentation. Alas, that quick and dirty technique also results in a boring presentation, and if your audience has any experience with PowerPoint they'll know instantly that you didn't put much effort into your slideshow.

It takes only a little time and energy to liven up a presentation. In this chapter, we focus on the tricks that add instant visual interest without requiring a design degree or hours of careful tweaking. By adding animations, you can turn a static, 2D slideshow into one that sizzles. Add sound and multimedia and you move into a completely new dimension.

USING TRANSITIONS TO CONTROL PACING

PowerPoint makes it easy to control what your audience sees on the screen when you move from one slide to another. You can arrange things so one slide replaces another onscreen, just as it would if you clicked through a carousel of 35mm slides. Or you can add wipes, dissolves, and other varieties of eye-catching (and frequently distracting) transitions. Properly done, transitions (sometimes also called *transition effects* or *slide transitions*) provide a breathing space between slides. Improperly done, your presentation will look amateurish and detract from helping you make your point—which, after all, is the purpose of PowerPoint.

The nature of that breathing space lies totally at your control—a subtle, quick fade to black; a pixelated dissolve that leaves the old slide in view for quite some time; shutters and checkerboards; and dozens more. Transitions can help add an ambience to your presentation. You might want a more abrupt transition if you're trying to project a snappy, rapid-fire image, and a more relaxed transition when the situation calls for a less formal approach.

Mixing and matching transitions jars the audience every bit as badly as ransom-note mixed fonts. For that reason, we recommend that you select one transition and use it exclusively throughout your presentation, with perhaps a few slides here and there getting "special treatment"—just to keep the audience awake.

When dealing with transitions, it's always easiest to work in Normal view, because Live Preview enables you to preview transitions before selecting the one you want.

NOTE

> Although you might think that a transition is defined between slides—showing how to *fade out* on the first slide and *fade in* on the next—PowerPoint doesn't work that way. Instead, you assign a transition to a slide, and that particular transition takes place when the slide is shown—it's a fade-in effect.

TIP

> By creatively using transitions, you can simulate some slide animation effects that simply aren't possible with PowerPoint's built-in animation tools. For example, in a presentation that shows the geographic changes in Eastern Europe over time you might want to put together a map with each country fading into position, but you want some countries to disappear after two or more mouse clicks, so you can emphasize the changes in the map. PowerPoint doesn't offer a "hide after *N* mouse clicks" animation option, so you can't animate that slide directly. In these cases, use a transition to fake animation: Build two slides—one to show the "before" image and the other for the "after" image—and then run a quick transition between the two. Your audience will be impressed.

APPLYING A TRANSITION TO ONE SLIDE

To set a transition for a single slide, select that slide (by displaying it in Normal view). Then click the Animations tab and click the More button in the Transitions to This Slide group. This opens the Transitions gallery (see Figure 19.1).

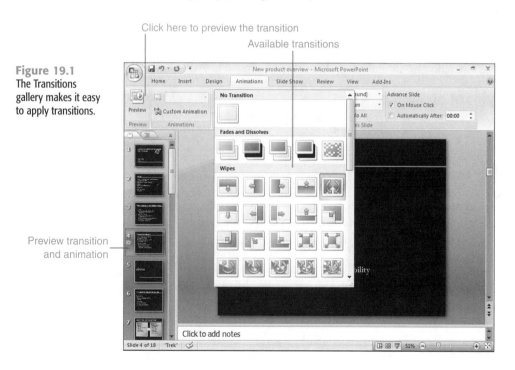

Figure 19.1
The Transitions gallery makes it easy to apply transitions.

If you're in Normal view, when you hover the mouse pointer over a transition, PowerPoint's Live Preview shows the effect for you. When you see an effect you like, click it to apply it. PowerPoint shows a preview of the transition you selected, and it also adds a small icon to indicate that a transition effect has been applied (see Figure 19.1). To see the transition again, click this icon, or click Preview in the Animations tab.

> **TIP**
>
> If you want your transitions and animations to appear when your presentation is viewed from a web browser, you must click the Microsoft Office button, click PowerPoint Options, click the Advanced tab (in the left pane), click Web Options (at the bottom of the dialog box), and then select Show Slide Animation While Browsing.

APPLYING A TRANSITION TO A GROUP OF SLIDES

To assign the same transition to a group of slides, switch to Slide Sorter view and select the slides with which you want to use the same transition. Hold down the Ctrl key as you click to select single slides, or hold down the Shift key and click to select a contiguously numbered group. Then select the transition you want from the Animation tab's Transitions gallery

> **TIP**
>
> To select all the slides in the presentation, click one slide and then press Ctrl+A.

PowerPoint goes through a preview of the transitions and animations on the thumbnails for all the selected slides. (To interrupt this mass preview, press Escape.) To see the transition and animation on an individual slide, click the Preview Transition icon below the slide.

> **CAUTION**
>
> When you apply a transition to a slide, PowerPoint replaces any transitions you previously applied to that slide.

CONTROLLING SLIDE TRANSITION SPEED

The options in the Transition to This Slide group on the Animations tab give you additional control over the transition between slides. You can

- Set the speed to slow, medium, or fast.
- Tell PowerPoint how you want to advance to the next slide during a presentation: manually, by clicking the mouse, or automatically, after a preset interval. Note that this setting controls how the slide exits and is thus unrelated to the transition effect you set for the current slide.
- Make PowerPoint play a sound during the transition.

> **TIP**
>
> In general, resist the temptation to select the Loop Until Next Sound check box, which is certain to distract almost any audience, unless you have a specific impression in mind: a suspenseful tick-tick-tick leading up to the next slide, for example, might be appropriate. But consider the reaction if a question from the audience takes you 10 minutes to answer—with the tick-tick-tick going all the time.

The two Advance settings—On Mouse Click and Automatically After—operate independently. If you activate both options, PowerPoint shows the next slide when the timer expires, or when you click the slide, whichever comes first. If you leave both boxes unchecked, the slide advances only when you press the spacebar, the Enter key, or one of PowerPoint's other keyboard presentation *control keys*.

→ For a definitive list of presentation control keys, **see** "Mouse and Keyboard Shortcuts," **p. 558.**

ANIMATING TEXT AND OBJECTS ON A SLIDE

Just as you use transition effects to control how a slide fades in, you use *animations* to control how the individual elements of a slide make their appearance. By showing one bullet point at a time, for example, you can make sure your audience concentrates on what you're saying now rather than reading the rest of the bullets on your slide and mentally calculating how much longer you're going to speak.

The most rudimentary form of slide animation displays each bullet point on a slide one at a time: You click the mouse (or tap the spacebar) and the slide's title appears. Click again, and the first bullet point appears onscreen. Keep clicking to display each bullet point on the list. Other animations enable you to specify that bullet points fly in or zoom from any direction. You can also choose fades, dissolves, wipes, and other visual effects.

T I P

> PowerPoint's selection of ready-made animation schemes is conveniently divided into four groups: Basic, Subtle, Moderate, and Exciting. We recommend you stick with Basic and Subtle for the most part. Reserve the Moderate and Exciting effects for the special slide that really deserves to stand out from the pack.

19

You can apply animations to almost any part of a slide—not just to bullet-list items, but to titles and graphics as well—and then activate the animations by clicking the mouse or using PowerPoint's built-in timers. Used sparingly, these animations can add punch to your presentation, augmenting your spoken words with powerful visuals. Say you have a graph that illustrates the growth in the number of websites created each year since the birth of the World Wide Web in 1993. You could show the whole graph, all at one time, and emphasize the spike in the final number verbally. Much more effectively, however, you could have the bars fly onto the graph one at a time—building up, in your narration, to the spike in the most recent year.

You can use animations to coordinate sounds, so they play as predetermined parts of the slide appear. You can also place text on a slide one character, word, or paragraph at a time. For example, use animations to start movies and other types of video clips at predetermined intervals after the slide first appears. Or use them to dim or change the color of items on the slide, in conjunction with the appearance of a new item.

TIP

> For sophisticated animation effects, break the clip-art objects apart, and then animate each element separately. Duplicating elements and using flying effects can also create the illusion of motion.

ANIMATING BULLET POINTS

Animating the arrival of bullet points on a slide gives you control over how much information your audience sees, and when. Moving one bullet point at a time onto the slide enables you to keep your audience running at your pace, particularly if you know that people in the audience have a tendency to read ahead. Also consider using bullet animation if you want to save some surprising or emphatic points for the end of the slide.

CAUTION

> If you remove the capability to advance a slide based on mouse clicks (by clearing the On Mouse Click check box in the Transition to This Slide group), you also remove the capability to animate bullet points with a mouse click. Instead, if you've provided an automatic advance time (in the Automatically After *nn:nn* box), PowerPoint divides that time equally among the bullet points and presents each in turn, automatically.
>
> If you select the Automatically After *nn:nn* check box in the Transition to This Slide group, PowerPoint shows each of the bullet points automatically if you don't click soon enough. Here, too, each bullet point is given an equal amount of time.

TIP

> If you have animated bullet points, don't forget to show them as you're making the presentation! You would be amazed how many presenters show the first point, talk about multiple animated bullet points on a slide, and then forget to click to put the other bullet points on the screen so their audience can follow along.

The easiest way to animate a set of bullet points is as follows:

1. Select the placeholder containing the bullet items you want to animate.
2. Click the Animations tab.
3. Pull down the Animate menu in the Animations tab. (Initially the text box beside the drop-down arrow will say No Animation.) Allow the mouse pointer to hover over an option to preview an effect, and click to select an animation.

Figure 19.2 shows the drop-down menu for a placeholder containing a two-level bullet list. If you started by selecting a different element—the title text for a slide, for example—the menu will be different. In Figure 19.2, a typical case, the menu offers three types of ready-made animations—Fade, Wipe, and Fly In—as well as a Custom Animation command. Each of the ready-made animations can be selected to appear All at Once or By 1st Level Paragraphs. If you choose All at Once, the entire text block fades, wipes, or flies in as a unit.

If you select By 1st Level Paragraphs, the top-level bullet items—**Seasonal blooms** and **Garden architecture**, in our example—are animated separately.

Figure 19.2
The Animations menu offers a short list of ready-made animations, plus a Custom Animation command.

Options in the Transition to This Slide group, near the right end of the Ribbon, control the behavior of these animations (and any others you create via the Custom Animation command). As set in Figure 19.2, these options cause the selected animation to take place silently, at medium speed. If you choose By 1st Level Paragraphs, the animation advances (that is, the next bullet item appears) when the presenter clicks the mouse. By selecting the Automatically After check box and specifying a time value, you can have the animation proceed on mouse click or after a set interval, whichever comes first. And by clearing the On Mouse Click check box and selecting the Automatically After check box, you can have the animation governed only by time interval.

CREATING A CUSTOM ANIMATION

The options that appear in the Animations drop-down menu are fine but very limited. PowerPoint offers a huge collection of jazzier animation effects in the Custom Animation pane. To get there, click Custom Animation, at the bottom of the Animation menu. Or, more simply, click Custom Animation in the Animations group of the Animations tab (without opening the Animations menu). Figure 19.3 shows the Custom Animation pane, with the same two-level bullet list selected.

Figure 19.3
The Custom Animation pane provides hundreds of animation options, ranging from sedate to well over the top.

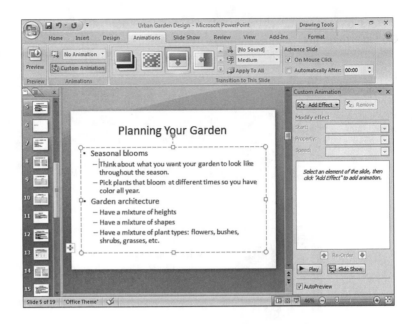

To create a custom animation, select the placeholder you want to animate and then click Add Effect. (If the Add Effect button is not available, you haven't yet selected anything that can be animated.) As Figure 19.4 shows, clicking Add Effect opens a drop-down menu with four items, each of which generates a cascading submenu (the figure shows the submenu options for Entrance animations). The submenu initially presents the animation effects that Microsoft thinks you're most likely to want. If you select one of the many additional effects available via the More Effects item at the bottom of the submenu, that item will acquire its own spot on the menu. So, for example, if you fancy Boomerang, Swish, or Swivel in all your slides, you won't have to dive into the More Effects dialog box every time you want one of those effects.

Using custom animations, you can animate each item in a bullet list separately. In a two-level list such as the one shown in Figures 19.2 through 19.4, you can animate just the primary bullets (bringing their subordinate entries along with them), or you can animate each primary and secondary bullet item separately. In the following example, we'll create a fly-in-from-bottom animation, on mouse click, for each primary and secondary bullet item:

1. With the entire text placeholder selected and the Custom Animation pane displayed, click Add Effect and then open the Entrance submenu (see Figure 19.4).

2. Select Fly In. PowerPoint displays the number 1 to the left of the first primary bullet item and each of its subordinates, and the number 2 beside the second primary bullet item and each of that item's subordinates (see Figure 19.5). That means that, as the animation stands now, the first mouse click will bring in the first primary item and its subordinates; the second click will bring in the remaining items.

Figure 19.4
To reach any of PowerPoint's hundreds of animation effects, click Add Effect.

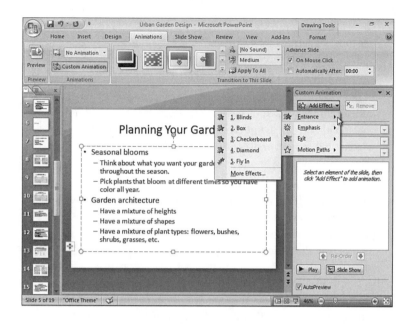

Figure 19.5
The numbers 1 and 2 to the left of the bullet items indicate which items will fly in on the first and second mouse clicks.

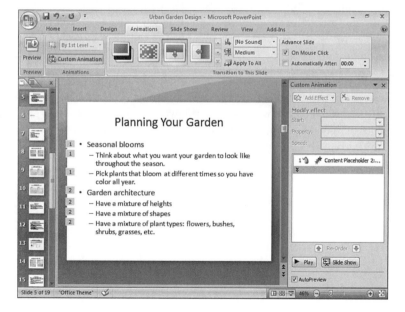

3. Click the downward chevron in the main window of the Custom Animation pane. PowerPoint responds by displaying each primary and secondary bullet item in that part of the Custom Animation pane (see Figure 19.6).

4. In the Custom Animation pane, select the first secondary bullet item ("Think about what you…"). The Start field now reads With Previous, indicating that, as things stand, the selected bullet item arrives when its predecessor arrives—in other words, it's not animated separately (see Figure 19.7).

5. Continue in this manner until all primary and secondary bullet items have been animated. At that point, you should see mouse icons next to each item in the Custom Animation pane, and separate numbers should appear to the left of each item on the slide itself (see Figure 19.8).

In this simple example, we haven't made any changes in the Direction and Speed boxes. All items will fly in at top speed from the bottom of the screen. By manipulating direction and speed, you can individualize the animations, if you want. By clicking one of the Re-Order buttons, you can even arrange to have the bullet items arrive out of sequence—assuming you can think of a good reason for doing that.

The Play and Slide Show buttons, near the bottom of the Custom Animation pane, provide ways to check your work. Play displays the animations without requiring you to click the mouse (hence, it's good for a quick test). Slide Show begins a slideshow at the current slide, so you can practice bringing in bullet points with your mouse.

If you're frustrated because you can't copy custom animation effects from slide to slide, see "Custom Animation Tricks" in the "Troubleshooting" section at the end of this chapter.

Figure 19.6

Figure 19.7

19

Figure 19.8
The mouse icons in the Custom Animation pane and numbers to the left of the bullet items on the slide confirm that each bullet item will appear with a separate mouse click.

TIP

To add a custom animation to every slide, animate the Slide Master. You can apply any animation effect to any item on the Slide Master—title, text, background pictures, date/time, footer, and slide number. You can also animate the layout masters.

ANIMATING THE DRAWING LAYER

PowerPoint allows you to animate any items in the drawing layer—text boxes, drawings, shapes, clip art, charts, embedded Excel or Word objects, org charts, and more. Before you try, however, it's important that you understand how the drawing layer works, and how to use it in conjunction with the Custom Animation dialog box.

→ For an explanation of how Office programs use the drawing layer, **see** "Working with the Drawing Layer," **p. 109.**

Say you've created a dramatic slide that features your organization's new president. You've added a scanned photo to the slide, and you want the photo to "dissolve" onto the screen with applause—and you hope the audience will join in. Here's how:

1. Display the slide in Normal view and click to select the picture.

2. Click Custom Animation on the Animations tab.

3. In the Custom Animation task pane, click Add Effect, Entrance, More Effects. Choose Fade and click OK.

4. Click the down arrow in the timing review list next to the picture. Choose Effect Options. In the Sound box, pick Applause and click OK.

Now when the slide appears on the screen, the picture will "fade in," accompanied by the sounds of applause. Use similar techniques to animate any object on the drawing layer.

HIDING AND UNCOVERING SLIDE CONTENTS

There's a trick to using items in the drawing layer that all too frequently escapes PowerPoint users. If you carefully match the color of a shape in the drawing layer to the color of the background, you can use animation on these shapes to *hide* parts of your presentation.

Say you have a slide that includes an image and you want to unveil only parts of that image, one at a time. PowerPoint has no built-in option for animating parts of images. Here's how to use animations to show one piece of the image at a time:

1. Create the slide and insert the image. For best results, make sure the slide's background is a solid color.

2. Click Shapes on the Insert tab, and then click the Rectangle tool. Draw a rectangle around the part of the image you want to hide. If you have trouble covering the image precisely and need more control, hold down the Alt key as you drag.

3. Click Shape Fill, in the Shape Styles group of the Format tab. Select the color that most nearly matches the background color. (If you're using defined color schemes, you should be able to select an exact match.)

4. Click Shape Outline, in the Shape Styles group of the Format tab. Select the same color you selected in the preceding step.

5. Repeat steps 2, 3, and 4 to draw rectangles around each box, including appropriate sections of the connecting lines.

6. Click Custom Animation on the Animations tab. Select the Rectangles AutoShapes you added to the slide, and choose whatever Exit Effect suits your fancy. In the timing review sequence list, arrange the order so the first rectangle is the last in order. Apply additional effects (applause, for example) if desired.

The presentation will now reveal each piece of the image when you click the mouse.

ANIMATING CHART COMPONENTS

You can animate every piece of a chart separately. For example, to dramatically demonstrate five years of steady growth, try sliding each bar in the chart up from the bottom of the slide, one after the other. To focus on the differences between economic growth in the economies of Europe and Asia over the past 30 years, show the bars for Europe first, and then reveal the corresponding bars for the Asian economy.

Before you undertake this advanced animation, make sure you understand how to create a chart in Excel, how to insert a chart into a slide, and how to use the Custom Animation dialog box.

→ To learn how to create a chart in Excel, **see** Chapter 16, "Turning Data into Charts," **p. 513.**

To animate an Excel chart, you must put the chart in a slide's object placeholder. To put an existing Excel chart into a chart placeholder, first create the chart in Excel and copy it to the Clipboard. Then display the slide in PowerPoint and use the Slide Layout pane to apply a layout of the suitable size and shape. The ideal choice, of course, is a Content or Text and Content layout, but you can actually use any layout. PowerPoint is smart enough to paste the chart into the correct location and replace a text placeholder with an object placeholder if necessary.

Paste the chart into the new slide. PowerPoint places your chart in the slide as an embedded Excel object. You can double-click the chart to edit it using Excel. At this point, you can animate the chart.

To make each bar of a bar chart appear independently on the screen, follow these steps:

1. Open the slide that contains the chart. Select the chart and choose Custom Animation, on the Animations tab.

2. In the Custom Animation task pane, choose Add Effect and pick an Entrance effect such as Diamond.

3. Click the down arrow next to the chart object in the timing review list and choose Effect Options. On the Chart Animation tab, choose the method you want to use to introduce chart elements. The chart can come in all at once; by Series (that is, all similarly colored columns appear, followed by all columns with the next color, and so on); by Category (each group of columns that falls into one group on the y-axis appears, and then the next group); or by individual columns within each Series or Category (see Figure 19.9).

4. Test your animation by clicking the Play button.

Because PowerPoint gives you the capability to present data by Series or Category, the animation sequence for chart effects can be complex. Use the Play button as you work to make sure the order is correct.

19

Figure 19.9
Individual chart elements appear in the sequence defined on the Chart Animation tab.

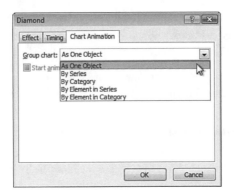

ADDING MUSIC, SOUNDS, AND VIDEO TO YOUR PRESENTATION

PowerPoint puts you in the director's chair when it comes to adding sounds, clip art (including pictures with movement such as animated GIFs), extended musical accompaniment, and even movie clips. But just because it *can* be done doesn't necessarily mean it *should* be done. Multimedia components in a presentation tend to overwhelm the audience. Be sure you really want to draw your audience's attention away from what you're saying before you insert a multimedia clip.

ADDING MUSIC, SOUNDS, AND VIDEO CLIPS

The easiest way to add multimedia to a presentation is to use the Media Clips group of the Insert tab. Select the slide on which you want the media to appear and then use the following techniques:

- Inserting a sound file—Click Sound in the Media Clips group of the Insert tab. (Alternatively, pull down the Sound menu and choose Sound from File.) Use the Insert Sound dialog box to select a sound file and click OK.

- Inserting a sound clip—Pull down the Sound menu in the Media Clips group of the Insert tab and choose Sound from Clip Organizer. PowerPoint opens the Clip Art pane and displays the clips from the Sounds collection. Click the sound clip you want to use.

- Inserting CD audio—Pull down the Sound menu in the Media Clips group of the Insert tab and choose Play CD Audio Track. PowerPoint displays the Insert CD Audio dialog box (see Figure 19.10). Choose the track(s) you want to play and click OK.

TIP

> If you see the AutoPlay dialog box when you insert the CD, close it to avoid starting the CD. If you have enabled CD AutoPlay on your system, Windows will begin playing an audio CD as soon as you insert it into the drive. When this happens, PowerPoint won't be able to take control of the CD to let you select a track. To give control back to PowerPoint, open Windows Media Player (or whatever program is configured as the default for playing CDs) and stop the CD. Close the player to let PowerPoint use the CD.

PowerPoint doesn't identify the actual CD in the drive; it knows only to play the tracks you've specified, no matter which CD might be in there. If you forget to put a CD in the drive when running a presentation, PowerPoint continues as if there were no track(s) to be played.

Figure 19.10
As long as you have the CD in your PC's drive, PowerPoint automatically calculates how much time it will take to play the tracks you select.

- Inserting recorded audio—Pull down the Sound menu in the Media Clips group of the Insert tab and choose Record Sound. PowerPoint displays the Record Sound dialog box (see Figure 19.11). Type a name for the recording and then click the Record button. This technique is useful if your PC has a functioning microphone because it means you can record a sound to be played with slides—you can even prerecord narration for every slide and, using timed advancing on the slides, deliver an entire presentation without being physically present.

19

CAUTION

Using audio clips in presentations viewed over the Web can cause annoying delays in playback, unless the viewer has a high-speed connection.

Figure 19.11
If you have a microphone, you can use the Record Sound dialog box to record narration for your presentation.

- Inserting a movie file—Click Movie, Movie from File, in the Media Clips group of the Insert tab. Use the Insert Movie dialog box to select the movie file and click OK.

- Inserting a movie clip (animated GIF)—Click Movie, Movie from Clip Organizer in the Media Clips group of the Insert tab. PowerPoint opens the Clip Art pane and displays the clips from the Movies collection. Click the movie clip you want to use.

NOTE

> You'll find animated GIFs in the Clip Organizer. Office 2007 does not include any tools that allow you to edit an animated GIF; to change one of these images, you must use a program specifically designed to handle this graphic format, such as MagicViewer from Crayon Software (http://www.crayonsoft.com).

In each case (except inserting a movie clip), PowerPoint displays a dialog box asking you how you want the media to start in the slideshow. Choose Automatically if you want the movie or sound to begin as soon as the slide appears. If you choose When Clicked, you'll have to click the picture (or the speaker icon) to play the sound or show the video during the presentation.

CONTROLLING A VIDEO OR SOUND CLIP

To change the behavior of a video or sound clip after you place it on a slide—whether it's in a placeholder or in the drawing layer—select the clip (or the speaker icon representing a sound object), click the Animations tab, and click Custom Animation. On the Add Effects menu (or the Change menu, if an effect is already applied), you'll notice a new Sound Actions or Movie Actions menu that allows you to define Play, Pause, or Stop effects. After applying an effect, right-click the trigger, choose Effect Options, and use the Movie Settings or Sound Settings tab to see options that apply only to the type of media clip you've inserted.

Use these options to create a video introduction to a slide with bullet points. The slide should appear first, with the title and background. Then, as quickly as PowerPoint can manage, the video clip should play. Finally, after the clip is over, the video should disappear and your bullet points should slide onto the screen.

Here's how to do it:

1. Select the slide you plan to use, and enter its title and bullet points.

2. To place the video clip in the drawing layer, click Movie, Movie from File on the Insert tab. Select the file and click OK.

3. When PowerPoint asks, "How do you want the movie (or sound) to start in the slideshow?" click Automatically.

4. Resize the movie clip window and position it where you want the movie to appear. Ignore the bullet points for the time being—they won't be there when the video runs—and concentrate on getting the movie clip positioned properly.

5. Click the movie clip window and click Custom Animation on the Animations tab. You'll see the movie file appear at the top of the timing review list, with a 0 next to it (indicating that the movie will run as soon as the slide appears).

6. Select the Text placeholder and the title, click Add Effect in the Custom Animation task pane, and select an effect to assign to all the text on the slide. In Figure 19.12, we've used the Fly In effect. The bullet points appear in the timing review list directly below the animation.

Figure 19.12
The timing review list indicates that the Butterfly.wmv animation will run before the bullet points appear.

7. Click the down arrow next to the media clip at the top of the timing review list. Choose Effect Options. In the Effect Options dialog box (see Figure 19.13), click the Movie Settings tab and select the Hide While Not Playing check box. Then click the Effect tab and choose Hide After Animation from the After Animation drop-down list. This combination of settings ensures that the movie clip will play and then disappear before the bullet points arrive. Click OK to close the Play Movie dialog box.

8. Click the down arrow next to the entry for the bullet points in the timing review list and select Start After Previous. This setting ensures that the first bullet point will appear immediately after the movie clip finishes.

Click Play on the Custom Animation pane and you'll see how all this ties together.

19

Figure 19.13
Tell the movie clip to disappear when it's finished playing.

TIP

Loop and rewind options vary depending on the type of multimedia clip you select. To work with these settings, click the Effect and Timing tabs in the Play Movie dialog box.

COMBINING TRANSITION EFFECTS

You can tie each animated element on a slide to a hyperlink or action setting. When you click a hyperlinked element or an item that includes an action setting, the animation takes place before the hyperlink or action setting kicks in.

→ For hyperlink information specific to PowerPoint, **see** "Using Hyperlinks," **p. 559.**

Combining custom animation and action settings needn't be overly confusing because they typically operate on different slide components. For example, you can apply a sound "animation" to the appearance of bullet points on a slide, but you can apply the sound "action setting" only to the words (and characters) in the bullet point.

Surprisingly, however, there's one action that you can implement only through hyperlinks and action settings: the mouseover. All the fancy animation techniques discussed in this chapter are tied to mouse clicks, or internal timers.

For example, if you want to make a video clip start by passing the mouse over the clip, you *must* use action settings. Select the clip, click Action on the Insert tab, select the Mouse Over tab in the Action Settings dialog box, and then adjust options to suit.

→ For details, **see** "Advanced Navigation with Action Settings," **p. 560.**

TROUBLESHOOTING

CUSTOM ANIMATION TRICKS

I created a slick custom animation for one slide, but I can't figure out how to copy the animation effects to other slides in my presentation.

Although PowerPoint has no built-in way to copy a custom animation from one slide to another, here's an undocumented trick that enables you to reuse custom animations: Make a copy of a slide, and then change the title and bullets on the copy. The copy includes all the custom animation settings of the original.

For example, if you've created a nifty custom animation on slide 20, how do you move it to slides 17, 18, and 19? You could edit the animation settings for each of the other three slides, but that's a cumbersome process. Instead, make three copies of slide 20, and then move the existing text from the old slides to the copies. Delete the old slides when you've finished.

Hiding a Clip with a Click

I have a movie clip on one of my slides, and I'd like that clip to play and then disappear, but I want to control when the clip disappears. Is this possible?

Yes, you can configure the clip to disappear when you click the mouse. Navigate to the slide. Then, in the list of triggers, open the drop-down list associated with the clip trigger and click Effect Options. In the Effect tab, use the After Animation list to select Hide on Next Mouse Click. Click OK to put the setting into effect. When you run the slideshow and when you're ready to hide the clip, click anywhere on the slide.

Extra Credit: Preparing a Presentation for Email

PowerPoint's E-mail command (click the Microsoft Office button, Send, E-mail) makes it easy to send the current presentation to an email recipient, either as a slideshow or an editable PowerPoint document. PowerPoint opens your default mail program, displays a message form, and supplies the current document as an attachment. You fill out the To, CC, and Subject lines, add a message if you choose, and click the Send button.

Before you use this command, consider the following:

- **Do you want your recipient to be able to edit your presentation, or do you just want him or her to see the slides?** To send a show, as opposed to a full PowerPoint document, first save your presentation in that format. (Click the Microsoft Office button, Save As, and then choose PowerPoint Show.) When your recipient opens the attachment, it plays as a slideshow. (You can still open and edit it in PowerPoint, of course.) If you aren't looking for editing collaboration, it's better just to send the show.

- **If you are sending the document to a collaborator, does that person have Office 2007 or a converter that will allow the file to open in Office 2003 or earlier?** If you're not sure, save the file in the PowerPoint 97–2003 Presentation format before emailing it.

- **Can you streamline (or abridge) the presentation to avoid taxing your recipient's patience?** Your recipient is essentially a captive, and your presentation may very well be seen as an intrusion. Short and snappy will win more points than long and clever. Avoid on-click bullet animations. Your recipient won't know they're there, and they'll just slow down the show.

- **Will your attachment overwhelm your recipient's email system?** The email form that PowerPoint presents shows the size of the attachment you're about to send (rounded up in some cases). Check this number before you click the Send button. (Alternatively, you can check the size of the presentation file in Windows Explorer, before you use the Send Email command.) Some mail systems handle large attachments without complaint; others reject them. If you're not sure how large a file your recipient can handle, ask first.

19

CHAPTER 20

DELIVERING A PRESENTATION WITH STYLE

In this chapter

PLANNING YOUR PRESENTATION

You've finished preparing all your slides. You've created a visually interesting presentation with transitions that help move the narrative along. Now all you have to do is stand and deliver.

Far too many presentations fail because the presenter doesn't anticipate what could reasonably go wrong, or doesn't prepare for questions that can be answered with a few facts, figures, or slides.

On the other hand, some less-than-flashy presenters with solid but uninspired slides regularly draw raves from appreciative audiences. Why? Because they step through points logically and in sequence, and when questions arise, they have solid answers, ready and waiting—and right at hand in their speaker notes.

THE IMPORTANCE OF PREPARATION

It's no secret, and no coincidence, that the best presenters rehearse their presentations over and over, in front of different groups that closely parallel the target audience. Before they stand up on stage, they take apart their presentation, slide by slide, and then edit, reorganize, put it back together, and test it again.

You might be tempted to practice in front of a mirror, and if your primary concern is the mechanics of the presentation, that's a reasonable approach. But if you want to get a point across, nothing beats jumping into the lion's den. Practice delivering the presentation to people who are willing to stop you when they don't understand and make suggestions when your points miss their mark. If you're working on a pitch to a nonprofit, invite some members of the organization to listen to a preview. If you're preparing a classroom presentation, see if your study group will act as a trial audience.

PowerPoint includes a number of tools that will help you prepare, refine, and ultimately deliver the presentation. But in the final analysis, they won't help a bit unless you have the content down pat. The best presentations practically deliver themselves.

ORGANIZING YOUR REMARKS WITH SPEAKER NOTES

Some people are capable of delivering a perfect presentation without notes. But what if you don't have a photographic memory or weeks to rehearse? For those of us who are chronically short on spare time and brain cells, there's no substitute for PowerPoint's *speaker notes*.

→ For an overview of notes, **see** "Adding Notes," **p. 553.**

The easiest way to construct and maintain notes is in PowerPoint's Normal view, where the Notes pane appears below the slide. Normally, this window displays only a few lines; to look at all the notes for a given slide, go to Notes view by choosing Notes Page on the View tab.

You can do little to change the appearance of the Notes page, except for adjusting tab stops. Because default tab stops start at one inch, you might find yourself running out of room if you indent text on a note page that contains lots of text; follow these steps to adjust the tabs and give the indented text a little extra room:

1. In Normal or Slide Sorter view, select the slide with the notes you want to change.

2. Click the View tab and then Notes Page. Then select the Ruler check box (in the Show/Hide group).

3. Click once to position the insertion point in the notes placeholder below the slide. Then click and drag on the bottom of the ruler to adjust the tab stops.

To change the tab spacing on all your Notes pages, bring up the Notes Master (click Notes Master, on the View tab), adjust the tab stops on the ruler, and save your changes to the master.

> **TIP**
>
> If you can anticipate any questions your audience might ask when a particular slide is on the screen, consider typing the question (and a possible answer, of course) at the bottom of the Notes page for that slide. To make it easier to identify the questions while you're flipping through your notes, set them off in bold or italic.

USING POWERPOINT'S TIMER TO REHEARSE A PRESENTATION

When you practice a presentation, PowerPoint can start a timer to keep track of the amount of time you spend on each slide and on the presentation as a whole. These timings can be useful in several situations:

- Timing your presentation helps you identify slides that are too complex or contain too much detail. If you find yourself spending five minutes explaining a single slide, consider simplifying the slide or splitting it into two or more. Likewise, if you discover you're racing through one part of your presentation, taking only a few seconds on each slide, that might be a clue that those slides are too elementary.

- PowerPoint timers help you set up the presentation so that slides advance automatically. This capability might be useful if, for example, you need to have both hands free to work with a physical prop. In this case, you can use the timings from your rehearsals to specify how long PowerPoint should display each slide before advancing.

- With the help of a special timer on the Rehearsal dialog box, you can plan your presentation so you don't overrun a tight time slot. The Rehearsal timer appears onscreen to tell you how long you've spent on each slide. Although few people use the Rehearsal timer during a final presentation, it can help you keep on top of timing during the preparation phase.

To rehearse a presentation using the timer, follow these steps:

1. Gather all the notes you'll need and then open the presentation in PowerPoint, preferably using the same computer you'll use when you actually deliver the presentation.

2. Click Rehearse Timings on the Slide Show tab. As your presentation begins, the Rehearsal dialog box appears onscreen (see Figure 20.1).

20

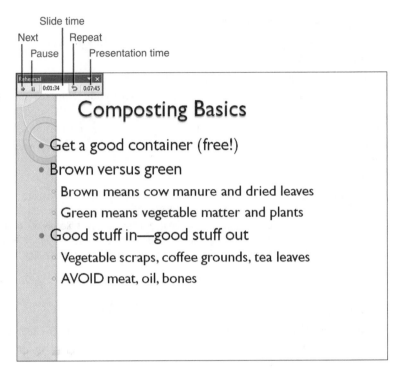

Figure 20.1
Keep track of the time spent on each slide by using the Slide Meter.

3. Run through your presentation normally. Try to speak at a natural pace, using your notes if necessary, and click your way through slides and animations.

   • Watch the Slide Time box to see how much time you've spent on the current slide. If you bump into an unexpected snag—you lose your place in your notes, for example—click the Pause button to stop the clock. Click Next to proceed.

   • If you get flustered, click Repeat to turn back the clock—that is, reset the time on the current slide to zero and subtract the appropriate amount of time from the Presentation Time counter. Resume your presentation at that slide.

NOTE

Clicking the Repeat button causes animations to repeat, starting with the first animation on the slide, but you must click once on the screen before the first repeat animation appears.

4. When you finish the presentation, PowerPoint tells you how long the entire presentation took and asks whether you want to update the times associated with each slide to reflect the latest numbers. If you click Yes, the timing numbers appear in Slide Sorter view, to the lower left of each slide (see Figure 20.2).

Figure 20.2
The results of the last (accepted) timing run appear to the lower left of each slide.

Unfortunately, there is no way to keep a history of timing runs, or to selectively re-record timings on a slide-by-slide basis. You must either accept all the new times, or reject them all. You can manually adjust the timing of a single slide by entering a time in the Automatically After box, on the Animations tab.

NOTE

If you show the same slide more than once (such as if you back up or use it in a custom show), the timer keeps statistics only for the final time it appears.

To set an individual slide so it advances automatically after a specific amount of time, you must use the Slide Transition dialog box.

→ For details on timing, **see** "Using Transitions to Control Pacing," **p. 596.**

RUNNING A SLIDESHOW

PowerPoint offers an enormous—even overwhelming—variety of options to help you run a slideshow. One piece of advice rises above all others: If you're not sure what to do next during a presentation, right-click the screen. Don't press Escape. Right-click.

The right-click context menu available from the presentation screen gives you instant access to nearly every option you'll ever need to run a slideshow. For example, you can jump to any slide if you know the title, move backward, blank the screen, or perform a dozen other important gyrations—even if you don't remember the shortcut key for a particular obscure option. Unless you need to create a new slide in the middle of your presentation (it happens), right-click to steer your way out of trouble.

CREATING PRESENTATIONS FOR THE WEB

The fact that web browsers are practically ubiquitous might tempt you to save your PowerPoint presentation as a web page and hit the road with only a browser to make the presentation.

In many situations, saving your presentation as a web page is a good idea:

■ Internet Explorer is available just about anywhere you go, so you needn't worry whether PowerPoint is installed on the PC you'll use for your presentation.

20

- Running in a browser in full screen mode—with toolbars and menus hidden—your presentation will look almost exactly the same as if you were using PowerPoint for the show.

- It's a great "Road Warrior" fallback. If your notebook dies a few minutes before you have to give the presentation, you can easily connect to the Internet from another PC and be right back in business.

- The outline shown in the browser can actually make presenting easier—although viewers might find it distracting. For example, if you forget which slide contains a specific bullet point, you can expand and collapse the outline dynamically to find the point and then jump to the slide in question with one click.

But there are also potential problems when you rely on a web server and a browser for your presentation:

- Unless there's a wide communications pipeline straight from your presentation PC to the web server, a browser-based presentation always runs slower than a presentation run in PowerPoint—in some cases, much, much slower. You can reduce this performance penalty by saving the web page to portable media (CD, DVD, or USB flash drive) and running it from a local drive.

- When you're running in a browser, some of the PowerPoint presentation navigation techniques don't work. Pressing the Enter key and the spacebar doesn't advance slides. Pressing B doesn't blank the screen. And, if you right-click a slide, you get the browser's context menu, not PowerPoint's.

If you decide to use a browser to make your presentation, always practice with the browser you're going to use.

 If you're having problems getting your transition and/or animation effects to display in a web browser, see "Viewing Transition and Animation Effects in a Browser" in the "Troubleshooting" section at the end of this chapter.

Another excellent reason to save a presentation as a web page is to allow your audience to view the presentation at its leisure, without the benefit of your commentary. By posting the results on your website, you can provide ready access to your slideshow without having to worry about whether your audience has PowerPoint installed. If you regularly save presentations as web pages, consider adjusting some of the settings available for this format. Click the Microsoft Office button, click PowerPoint Options, click the Advanced tab, and then click the Web Options button (it's at the bottom of the dialog box).

In the Web Options dialog box, the options available on the General tab, shown in Figure 20.3, are unique to PowerPoint. (Settings on the other five tabs affect all Office programs.) To eliminate the annoyance of forcing your audience to click several times to see all parts of a slide, for instance, you might want to turn off slide animations by clearing the Show Slide Animation While Browsing box.

Figure 20.3
These options are unique to PowerPoint presentations saved as web pages.

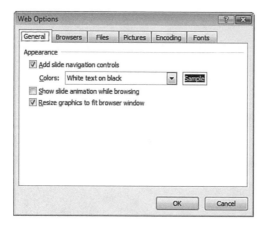

To save a presentation for use on the Web, click the Microsoft Office button, choose Save As, click Other Formats, and then select Single File Web Page in the Save as Type list. The resulting file can be opened in Internet Explorer 5.0 or later. (The presentation will generally not be viewable in non-Microsoft browsers.)

SETTING UP A SLIDESHOW

When creating a presentation, you can add a variety of features, including narration, animations, and preset timings. When you deliver the presentation, however, you might be using a different computer than the one you created. In addition, you might want to tweak the settings of the slideshow to match its intended use, especially if someone other than you will be the presenter.

TUNING YOUR PRESENTATION FOR YOUR HARDWARE

When you take your slideshow on the road, you might be asked to use a different computer than you're used to. This can cause two problems:

- Performance might suffer if you use demanding transitions and animations. Effects that work well on your top-of-the-line desktop computer may poke along on a computer with a less robust video card, a slower CPU, and insufficient RAM.

- Your carefully drafted design might turn into a crowded, unreadable mess if the video resolution of the presentation machine is significantly less than the computer you used to create the show.

To deal with either of these problems, you need to make some adjustments. Click Set Up Slide Show on the Slide Show tab. The resulting dialog box (see Figure 20.4) includes several useful options.

20

Figure 20.4
To avoid problems when showing a presentation at a lower resolution, use the options in the Performance box.

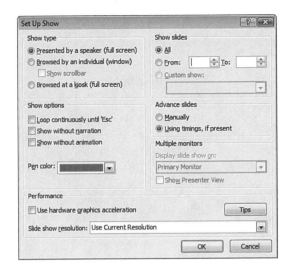

Two areas in particular are worth noting here. Consider selecting the Show Without Narration and Show Without Animation check boxes if you notice that the presentation is dragging unacceptably on the presenting machine. If you know that your target machine is going to use a specific resolution—say, 800×600—adjust the Slide Show Resolution setting in the Performance box and preview your show *before* you hit the road. If any slides look odd or distorted, you can edit them in advance.

USING TWO MONITORS

If you have dual monitors set up and recognized by the operating system (including a setup in which you connect your notebook or desktop PC to a TV in addition to a standard monitor or LCD screen), you can tell PowerPoint to show the presentation on one monitor, while you control the presentation in a Normal-like view on the other monitor.

The primary monitor, which you use to control the presentation, displays the presentation in Normal view. Alternatively, you can have PowerPoint display "presenter tools," which give you slide thumbnails, buttons for showing the next and previous slide, a timer, speaker notes, and a black screen button. The secondary monitor shows the usual presentation full-screen.

To set up a presentation for dual monitors, click Set Up Show on the Slide Show tab, and in the Multiple Monitors box, point PowerPoint to the secondary monitor. If you want presenter tools to appear on the primary screen, select the Show Presenter View check box.

USING HIDDEN SLIDES TO ANTICIPATE QUESTIONS

If you anticipate a question and have the answers handy in your presentation notes, your audience will be impressed. If you can cut immediately to a new slide that answers that question, your audience will sit up and take notice.

Hidden slides offer a clever way to prepare for topics that you want to bring up only if someone asks. If you anticipate that someone in your audience might ask a question about slide 4, for example, here's how to be ready with a slide that answers the question:

1. Switch to Slide Sorter view and click after the final slide in the presentation. Click New Slide on the Home tab, and create the slide that will answer the expected question.

2. Double-click to open your new slide in Normal view and add whatever content you need. Then, in an inconspicuous location, add a text box (saying, perhaps, "Back to presentation") or a picture to use as a button to return to the originating slide.

> **TIP**
>
> If you choose Shapes on the Insert tab and then select the Return action button from the Action Buttons section of the gallery, you will achieve the same results as step 2 and 3 here. The only difference is that you'll end up with the default "return" icon image.

3. Select the picture or text box. Then select Action on the Insert tab. On the Mouse Click tab of the Action Settings dialog box, click Hyperlink To, and choose Last Slide Viewed from the drop-down list. Click OK to save this setting. During the presentation, you'll be able to click this hyperlink and return to the originating slide.

→ For details on action settings, **see** "Advanced Navigation with Action Settings," **p. 560**.

4. On the Slide Show tab, choose Hide Slide. Because the slide is hidden, it never appears in the normal course of a presentation.

5. Return to slide 4 and create a hyperlink to this new, hidden slide. Attach the hyperlink to a small picture or piece of text—anything that will jog your memory without alerting your audience that you've prepared a "hidden" answer to a specific question.

→ For more about hyperlinks inside PowerPoint, **see** "Using Hyperlinks," **p. 559.**

When you deliver the presentation and a member of the audience asks the question, click the hyperlink, discuss the issues on the hidden slide, and then click the Back to Presentation button at the bottom of the hidden slide to return to the main presentation.

> **TIP**
>
> You can use the same technique if the answer to a question requires more than one slide. Instead of creating a hyperlink that jumps to a specific slide, however, create one that jumps to a custom presentation. You can branch back from the end of the custom presentation with yet another hyperlink that's specifically tied to the originating slide—just remember to use it during the presentation!

Hidden slides are marked in Slide Sorter view and in the Slides navigation pane with a slash through the slide number. In the Hyperlink dialog box, you can spot hidden slides by looking for those that have the slide number in parentheses.

→ For more on custom shows, **see** "Managing Slideshows," **p. 555.**

WRITING OR DRAWING ON SLIDES

Sometimes in the course of delivering a presentation, you might want to "draw" on a slide: Like a commentator on a TV football broadcast, you can use circles and arrows to drive home a point. You can use a fine-line ballpoint option, a thicker (virtual) felt tip instrument, or a broad highlighter, and in all these pen options you choose the color.

To begin marking up a slide while your slideshow is running, right-click the screen, choose Pointer Options, and then choose one of the three pen types. Then drag with the mouse to draw in the screen. If you want to remove your annotation, right-click again, choose Pointer Options, and then choose Eraser. With the eraser active, a single click on an annotation is all it takes to remove it. (You don't have to remove your annotations during the slideshow, however; when you finish the show, PowerPoint will ask if you want to preserve your "ink" or get rid of it.)

If you use the pen regularly, you'll appreciate the following shortcuts:

- To change pen colors, right-click the screen, choose Pointer Options, Ink Color, and choose among the colors offered.

- When you finish marking up the slide, you can restore the pointer to an arrow by pressing Escape. (Don't press Escape a second time, however, or you'll suddenly exit your presentation!)

- To quickly switch between the currently selected pen type and the arrow pointer, press Ctrl+P (pen) and Ctrl+A (arrow).

- To erase all that you have drawn on a slide, press E on the keyboard.

- When using the mouse pointer to draw, press Enter or the spacebar to advance to the next animation or slide.

PACKAGING A PRESENTATION FOR USE ON OTHER COMPUTERS

A presentation doesn't always require stand-up delivery. Sometimes, in fact, a carefully crafted slideshow can literally present itself. If you've created a PowerPoint presentation that you want to allow other people to view even when you're not around, you can tie the pieces of the presentation into a tidy package and copy it to a CD using the Package for CD feature.

Packaging a presentation involves three steps:

1. Select the files you want to include on the CD. You can include multiple presentations and add supporting files, such as embedded TrueType fonts and music or video clips.

2. Adjust any or all of the following options:

    - Specify whether you want the presentation to play automatically (AutoRun) when inserted into a Windows computer.

- Decide whether you want to include the PowerPoint Viewer.
- Password-protect confidential presentation files so that only authorized users can open or edit the files. The PowerPoint Viewer will prompt for an Open or Modify password based on the options you select.

3. Save the package. Using Windows XP or Windows Vista, you can save directly to a compatible CD burner.

TIP

> Using the Package for CD feature is an effective way to archive presentations for safe-keeping. A single CD can easily contain more than 100 typical presentations. If you use CDs as an archive medium, you needn't include the PowerPoint Viewer, and you can turn off AutoRun as well.

A saved presentation delivered through the PowerPoint Viewer looks exactly as it would if you were to present the slideshow from PowerPoint. Transitions, animations, navigation techniques, and other features are unchanged. You can't add annotations, of course, and making any changes requires that you open the presentation in PowerPoint and save the changed file to a new CD.

SAVING A PRESENTATION ON A CD

After you've polished your presentation to a high gloss and you're satisfied with its content and design, you can copy it to a CD using the following steps:

1. With the presentation open in PowerPoint, click the Microsoft Office button and choose Publish, Package for CD. The Package for CD dialog box appears, as shown in Figure 20.5.
2. Change the default name in the Name the CD box. Although this step is optional, we recommend that you do so to make it easier to identify the CD when you open it using Windows Explorer. The name you enter must be 16 characters or fewer.

Figure 20.5
Use this dialog box to package your presentation on a CD.

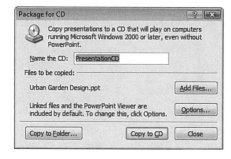

3. The current presentation is included by default and cannot be removed. To include other files on the CD (such as additional presentations or supporting media clips), click the Add Files button and use the Browse dialog box to select the files.

4. Click the Options button and adjust any of the options shown in Figure 20.6. By default, the PowerPoint Viewer is included, all presentations are played automatically, and passwords are left blank. This is your opportunity to add, open, or modify passwords. Click OK.

5. After inserting a blank CD into your CD or DVD burner, click Copy to CD to begin recording. If your computer does not include a drive that supports CD writing, click Copy to Folder instead, choose a name and location for the saved folder, and click OK. You can burn the saved folder to a CD later.

Figure 20.6
Choose options for your packaged presentation.

USING THE POWERPOINT VIEWER

When you use the AutoRun option on a CD-based presentation, it should require no effort from the intended audience beyond inserting the CD into the appropriate drive. If the person who created a CD chose not to use the AutoRun option, or if AutoRun is disabled on the target computer, open the CD in Windows Explorer, double-click the Pptview icon, and choose the saved presentation from the Open dialog box, which appears automatically when the Viewer opens.

PRINTING YOUR PRESENTATION

Eventually, you'll want to print out a presentation. Print options enable you to generate speaker notes for yourself, handouts for your audience, and copies of the slides for you to study and revise whenever you have some free time, even if you're not at your PC.

20

CHOOSING WHICH ELEMENTS TO PRINT

When you choose File, Print, PowerPoint opens the Print dialog box, shown in Figure 20.7. Several of the options shown here are unique to PowerPoint and allow you to exercise excellent control over printed pages.

CAUTION

> Avoid the Quick Print command unless you're absolutely certain you want to send your entire presentation to the default printer using current settings. If you have any doubts, press Ctrl+P instead, or click the Microsoft Office button and choose Print.

The Print What box offers four choices, as shown in Table 20.1.

Figure 20.7
Although many Print options are common to all Office programs, those at the bottom of this dialog box are unique to PowerPoint.

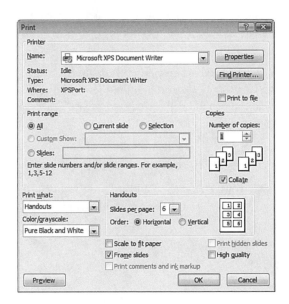

TABLE 20.1 PRINTING OPTIONS

Print What	Means
Slides	One slide per page in portrait orientation; the slide fills up the whole page.
Handouts	Multiple slides per page, based on the number in the Slides Per Page box, formatted according to the Handout Master that has the same number of slides per page.
Notes Pages	One slide per page, formatted according to the Notes Master.
Outline View	No slides, only outline text, formatted according to the Outline setting on the Handout Master.

→ For details on notes and handouts formatting, **see** "Creating Speaker Notes and Audience Handouts," **p. 580.**

TIP

Before sending a long presentation to a color printer, click the Preview button in the Print dialog box. This gives you one last opportunity to look over the proposed printed output and make sure that your color copies will turn out as you expect.

PREPARING A COLOR PRESENTATION FOR A BLACK-AND-WHITE PRINTER

When you print PowerPoint slides on a black-and-white printer, you might be disappointed at the way Windows translates color to black-and-white pages. Shadowing in graphs loses much of its definition. All but the lightest backgrounds completely obliterate any nuances in the foreground—to the point of obscuring text, in many cases.

For the best-quality printed output, use PowerPoint's built-in grayscale converter, which is optimized for the colors in presentation designs. By taking liberties with your slides—converting dark backgrounds to light when needed, for example—it produces extremely readable black-and-white output.

To preview what your slides look like when viewed through this special grayscale converter, click Grayscale, in the Colors/Grayscale group of the View tab. You'll be sent into Color/Grayscale View, and the Ribbon will include a new Grayscale tab that enables you to tweak the grayscale settings.

You can also see how your slides will look by using PowerPoint's Print Preview: Just click the Microsoft Office button, choose Print, and then choose Print Preview.

To print using the grayscale converter, click the Print button while in Print Preview, or choose the Office button, Print, and select the Grayscale option at the bottom of the Print dialog box.

TROUBLESHOOTING

VIEWING TRANSITION AND ANIMATION EFFECTS IN A BROWSER

I've added transitions and animation effects to my slides, but they don't appear when I view my presentation in a web browser.

If none of your transition or animation effects appear in the browser, open the presentation, click the Microsoft Office button, and click PowerPoint Options. Click the Web Options button at the bottom of the Advanced section of the Options dialog box. On the General tab of the Options dialog box, click the Web Options button. Then, on the General tab of the Web Options dialog box, select the Show Slide Animation While Browsing check box. Click OK to close each dialog box and save your presentation.

Extra Credit: A Preflight Checklist for Presenters

In the course of this chapter, as well as in preceding chapters, we've mentioned a few of the basic principles of presenting effectively: maintain a clean, consistent design that doesn't distract your audience from what you're going to say; keep the text lean, so that your audience doesn't spend all its time reading instead of listening; rehearse and then rehearse some more, so that you can deliver the goods smoothly and on time; anticipate questions and prepare answers for them—including, if appropriate, additional hidden slides that address particular questions. Here's an additional checklist of things to do on show day:

- **Make sure the equipment works—and that you know how to work it.** Arrive early so you can test your presentation in the room where you will deliver it, on the equipment you will use.

- **Test the readability of your text in the room where you will present.** If it can't be read from the back of the room, someone is going to give you a lousy review. Find those inscrutable slides while there's still time to edit.

- **Turn off the screensaver.** You don't need bubbles or ribbons wafting across the screen while you pause to take questions.

- **If you deliver your presentation from a mobile computer running Windows Vista, turn on Presentation Settings.** Open the Mobility Center in Windows Vista and then click Turn On in the Presentation Settings tile. Presentation Settings automatically turn off the screensaver and any other system notifications. You can also adjust the speaker volume, and Windows will remember your settings whenever you turn Presentation Settings on again.

- **Check the spelling and grammar of your slide text one more time**. The only thing worse than having a typo (or "thinko") on your computer screen is having it projected to a room full of critical readers. If possible, find a friendly extra set of eyes to look over your slides before you step up to the podium.

20

PART

V

USING ONENOTE

CHAPTER **21**

ONENOTE ESSENTIALS

In this chapter

ANATOMY OF A ONENOTE NOTEBOOK

The basic design and function of OneNote sets it far apart from its siblings in the Office family. Word, Excel, and PowerPoint are all about creating documents containing similar data, each saved as a single file. OneNote allows you to collect data in a dizzying variety of types and organize all that data within a marvelously expandable program window that resembles a paper notebook. The notebook format is ideally suited for students, of course, but chances are you'll find uses for it even if you never set foot in a classroom. And its organizational tools adapt to your personal style, whether you're the throw-it-in-a-shoebox type or a neat freak who sorts and labels everything.

You'll rarely if ever have to deal directly with OneNote data files. Instead, you create sections and add pages within the OneNote window, and it does the dirty work of creating files and indexing each notebook's contents so you can find stuff when you need it. You never have to save a notebook—OneNote does that in the background, even creating backup copies at regular intervals to ensure that you never lose a scrap of information, a scribbled note, a screen clipping, or a snippet from a web page.

The first time you open OneNote, the program creates a pair of generic databases called Work and Personal, plus a OneNote 2007 Guide saved as a separate notebook. Figure 21.1 shows the OneNote window after we've customized this initial setup and gives us a chance to introduce the pieces that make up each OneNote notebook.

Figure 21.1
OneNote doesn't use the Ribbon interface found in other Office programs; instead, you use old-style menus and toolbars.

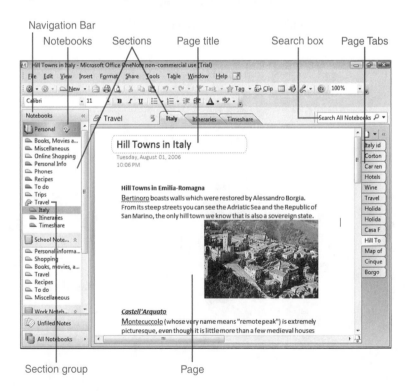

Navigation Bar
Notebooks Sections Page title Search box Page Tabs
Section group Page

You can use these generic notebooks if you find the head start useful—replacing the introductory text on each sample page with your own notes and adding new pages as needed. Or you can get rid of the sample notebooks in favor of your own, built from scratch.

In this section, we explain how to create and manage the individual elements that you'll use in OneNote.

CREATING, OPENING, AND MANAGING NOTEBOOKS

Each *notebook* corresponds to a folder and is stored by default in the OneNote Notebooks folder in your Documents folder. Each notebook gets its own entry in the Navigation Bar along the left side of the OneNote window.

To create a new notebook, follow these steps:

1. Choose File, New, Notebook.

2. In the Name box, enter the name you want to assign to the notebook. The text you enter here appears in the Navigation Bar and is used as the name of the corresponding folder.

> **TIP**
>
> In the Color box, OneNote automatically cycles through available colors, assigning a unique color to each notebook. The assigned color is used on the notebook icon in the Navigation Bar and also serves as the background color for the Page Tabs bar. Instead of accepting the random color selection, you might want to select a specific color for each notebook—red for school, green for personal, and so on. To change a notebook's name or color after creating it, choose Notebook Properties from the File menu.

3. Choose a template on which to base your new notebook and then click Next:
   - Use the default settings to create a new notebook based on the Blank template, with a single section (New Section 1) containing a single white page; or
   - Choose an entry in the From Template box if you'd prefer to use a saved template containing additional sections. In Figure 21.2, for instance, we've selected the Student Semester Notebook template, which contains a to-do list, sections for three classes and two projects (to add a new class or project, copy one of these sections), and a few other useful pages.

4. On the Who Will Use This Notebook? page, choose the default option: I Will Use It on This Computer. Click Next.

5. On the Confirm Notebook Location page, verify that the new notebook is going to be included in the proper folder. The location in the Path box should point to the folder that contains your other notebooks.

Figure 21.2
Use one of these templates to create a new notebook with a handful of ready-made sections.

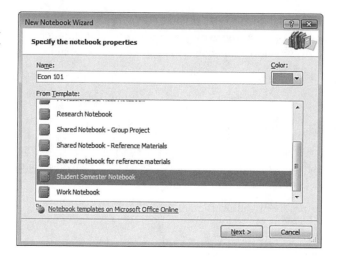

CAUTION

Do not enter the name of your new notebook in the Path box! OneNote adds this value automatically using the name you entered earlier in the wizard. Look at the Full Path value (displayed in gray text, just below the Path box) to confirm that your folder name is correct.

6. Click Create to save the new notebook and open it in OneNote.

→ For details about how you can use a OneNote notebook on multiple computers or share it with other people, **see** "Sharing a OneNote Notebook," **p. 678.**

OneNote remembers which notebooks are open and reopens those that were open previously each time you start the program. To open a notebook you previously closed, choose File, Open, Notebook. Browse to the folder containing your notebook files, click to add its name to the Folder Name box, and then click Open.

To rename a notebook, right-click its color-coded heading in the Navigation Bar, click Rename (or Properties—both menu choices lead to the same dialog box), and change the text in the Display Name box in the Notebook Properties dialog box, as shown in Figure 21.3.

21

Figure 21.3
Changing the text in this box changes the name you see in OneNote's Navigation Bar, but it doesn't change the name of the folder containing your files.

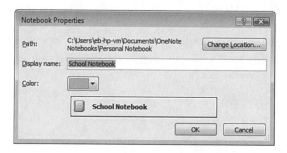

To close an open notebook, right-click its heading and choose Close This Notebook.

To move the files that make up a notebook, click Change Location and browse to the folder where you want your notebook to be stored. One good reason to use this feature is for retaining notebooks you no longer use on a regular basis; create a OneNote Archives folder and move notebooks from the default OneNote Notebooks folder when they're ready to go into cold storage.

TIP

> If you're even mildly obsessive about file management, or if you occasionally prune data files from within Windows Explorer, you'll need to pay a little attention to make sure the names of each notebook and its associated folder stay in sync. The easiest way to do this is to close the notebook, rename the folder in Windows Explorer, and then open the renamed folder in OneNote. Use the Notebook Properties dialog box to change the display name to match the folder name.

CREATING AND MANAGING SECTIONS

Sections are the basic building blocks of OneNote. Each section can contain multiple pages and subpages and is stored in a single file that uses the .one filename extension. When you click a section name in the Navigation Bar, its contents appear in the main OneNote window and you can begin working with pages in that section. You can also switch to a new section in the current notebook by clicking the section tab above the main OneNote window.

TIP

> Moving a OneNote notebook to a different computer can be a challenge. Copying a folder full of .one files leaves open the chance that one or more sections will be lost. For ease of travel, use OneNote's Single File Package format, which packs the entire notebook and all its sections into one file with the .onepkg extension. Double-click the file on the other end to unpack it into a folder containing all its accompanying section files.

 Are one or more sections missing from a notebook? See "Dealing with Orphaned Sections," in the "Troubleshooting" section at the end of this chapter.

You can freely drag sections up and down in a notebook to change their order. You can also drag sections to move them from one notebook to another. For more fine-grained section management tasks, right-click a section and choose Move. The Move Section To dialog box (see Figure 21.4) allows you to move the selected section before or after another section; you can even create a new section group on the fly.

The folder icon that appears next to each section name in the Navigation Bar is color-coded. If you have a preferred color scheme, you can change these colors; right-click the section name and choose one of the 16 available colors from the Section Color menu.

21

Figure 21.4
Use the Move command to choose a new location for the selected section.

From this same menu, you can also tighten security on an individual section by assigning a password to the section file. No one (yourself included) will be able to open the section file until they first enter the password.

FILING SECTIONS INTO GROUPS

What happens if you create so many sections you can't scan them easily? That's the idea behind *section groups*—when you choose File, New, Section Group, you create a subfolder within the current folder. Any sections you drag into the new section group appear in the navigation bar together, indented beneath the section group heading. (For an example, see the Travel section group, in Figure 21.1, earlier in this chapter.)

CREATING PAGES AND SUBPAGES

The final (and most important) building block of any OneNote notebook is the *page*. Pages are stored in sections, and you can create an essentially infinite number of pages in any section—moving them up or down the Pages Bar, dragging them to other sections in the same notebook or in a completely different notebook. If you create a new notebook from a OneNote template, each section normally contains at least one page. To create a new blank page, click the New Page icon at the top of the Page Tabs bar.

If you'd prefer to have some design and organization work done for you, click the arrow to the right of the New Page tab and choose More Template Choices and Options from the drop-down list. As Figure 21.5 shows, OneNote includes a decent selection of templates for pages, all neatly categorized in the task pane.

21

Figure 21.5
Page templates include background images, colors, and predefined areas for entering particular types of notes.

Two additional options in the Templates task pane are worth noting:

- The drop-down list in the Choose Default Template region allows you to pick one of the saved templates and use it as the base page when you click the New Page button in the current section.

- If none of the ready-made templates is exactly right, create your own (starting with the most useful template you can find). Then click Save Current Page as a Template. OneNote creates a new My Templates section at the top of the Templates task pane and saves the new template there.

In the following section, we explain what you can do with pages.

WHAT CAN YOU PUT ON A NOTEBOOK PAGE?

So far, with all these notebooks, sections, section groups, and pages, we've yet to add a single word or picture. That all changes as soon as we click on a page and begin typing. That page is a blank slate that can hold a broad range of data types. Regardless of its type, though, each individual chunk of data lives in a *container*. If the data consists of text, the container resembles the one shown in Figure 21.6.

21

Move handle

Figure 21.6
You can resize or
move any text con-
tainer. If you use the
Sizing handle to
change its size or
shape, the text mar-
gins change to fit
your container.

Hill Towns in Emilia-Romagna
Bertinoro boasts walls which were
restored by Alessandro Borgia.
From its steep streets you can see
the Adriatic Sea and the Republic
of San Marino, the only hill town
we know that is also a sovereign
state.

— Sizing handle

Normally, all containers are hidden and you see only the data they contain. When you hover the mouse pointer over a container, it becomes visible. When you click within a container, it becomes active and you can see borders. Use the Move handle at the top of the container (the mouse pointer turns to a four-headed arrow to indicate its function) to move the container elsewhere on the page. Use the Sizing handle on the right border to change the width of the container. You can also use the common Cut, Copy, and Paste operations to move containers between pages, in the same notebook or in a different notebook.

Inside of a container, you can find any of the following data types:

- Text—You can add text by clicking and typing, by pasting from the Clipboard, or by sending a snippet of a web page from Internet Explorer.

- Handwritten text—If you have a Tablet PC, you can use the stylus as a pen to jot down notes or write an entire novel. OneNote saves your jottings as ink and adds the underlying text to its index so you can find notes.

→ For more details about pens, ink, and other Tablet PC features, **see** Chapter 25, "Using Office on a Tablet PC," **p. 711.**

→ For more on how to search for information in OneNote, **see** "Finding Information in a Notebook," **p. 648.**

- Drawing or picture—You can paste any type of graphic into a OneNote notebook, including pictures from web pages, digital photographs, and art you create using Office SmartArt and drawing tools.

TIP

OneNote's Snipping Tool allows you to grab a portion of any screen, save it to the Clipboard, and paste it into a OneNote page. The snipped section is pasted as a picture, even if it includes only text. To snip part of a screen, right-click the OneNote icon in the notification area on the right of the Windows taskbar and then choose Create Screen Clipping (or, with OneNote open but minimized, press the Windows logo key+S). Click and drag the mouse pointer to highlight the portion of the screen you want to snip. When you release the mouse button, your snippet is pasted into OneNote.

■ Bullet/number list—Like Word, OneNote allows you to create lists and automatically adds bullets or numbering when you reorder items in the list. If you click a list and enter a number followed by a period or closing parenthesis, OneNote converts it to a numbered list automatically. If you enter an asterisk or a "greater than" sign (>), OneNote converts your character to a symbol and begins a bullet list.

> **TIP**
>
> To disable automatic creation of numbered or bulleted lists, choose Tools, Options, click the Editing tab, and clear the Apply Numbering to Lists Automatically and Apply Bulleting to Lists Automatically check boxes.

→ You can also create to-do lists in OneNote, with check boxes at the beginning of each item; **see** "Tagging Notes for Follow-up," **p. 663.**

■ Table—You can insert a table, with or without borders, into any OneNote page. Choose Table, Insert Table to create a generic table using a predetermined number of rows and columns. Use the same menu (or right-click any portion of an existing table and use the Table shortcut menu) to add or remove rows and columns or change the formatting of text in a table.

> **TIP**
>
> Want to create a table in a hurry? Click anywhere on a page and type a word, phrase, or a numeric value, and then press Tab. OneNote automatically creates a table with the text you typed in the first cell of the first row and the insertion point positioned in a new second column. Press Tab to create another column, and press Enter to create a new row. Press Enter twice to stop creating new rows and begin entering plain text in the container.

■ Audio/video—If your computer has a microphone, you can record an audio clip and save it directly in a OneNote page. This is especially useful for class notes, because OneNote synchronizes the clip with your typed notes. If you have a video camera (such as a webcam), you can add a video recording.

→ For more details on using audio and video recordings in OneNote, **see** "Saving Audio and Video Notes," **p. 673.**

■ Web page (or portion of one)—When you copy a portion of a web page and paste it into OneNote, the entire selection appears in its own container, including any graphics and hyperlinks from the original page. In addition, OneNote adds a hyperlink at the bottom of the container that you can click to return to the source directly. (See the "Extra Credit: Sending Web Pages to OneNote" section at the end of this chapter for more details on how your web browser and OneNote work together.)

■ Files—From the Insert menu, you can choose File to add a link to an existing file. Choose Files as Printouts to send the printed output from a file into the current page. The printout option inserts a picture of the file you select, exactly as it would look if you had sent it to a printed page.

21

If the Save as Printouts menu option is grayed out, see "Restoring the Capability to Save Printouts," in the "Troubleshooting" section at the end of this chapter.

NOTE

> When should you copy and paste a document's content, and when should you use the Insert, Files as Printouts option? The chief difference is the document's appearance. As you'll quickly discover when you try to paste formatted text into a OneNote page, the appearance can radically change. In particular, line spacing often disappears, fonts can change sizes, and graphics can shift position. On the plus side, you can select, edit, reformat, and delete the pasted text and graphics. Using the printout option preserves the exact appearance of the original document, but you lose the option to work with the text and other elements that make up the document.

TIP

> OneNote has basic calculating capabilities built into it. Enter a mathematical formula—2+2, for instance—followed by an equal sign. As soon as you press Enter, OneNote calculates the result of the equation. OneNote knows addition and subtraction (using a plus or minus sign, respectively), multiplication (asterisk), and division (forward slash). It can also calculate percentages if you enter a percent sign and perform exponentiation (2^16 calculates 2 to the 16th power). Finally, you can use any of 15 supported functions, including SQRT, which returns the square root of a number, and PMT, which calculates loan payments. For a full list of supported functions, type the search term **equations** in OneNote Help.

Each time you paste a new piece of text or click outside an existing container to begin typing, you create a new container. Each container is completely independent and can be moved, sized, and edited separately from others. If you want to merge the contents of two note containers, follow these steps:

1. Aim the mouse pointer at the Move handle on top of the first container.

2. Hold down the Shift key, click the mouse button, and drag to position the container over the second container into which you want to move it.

3. Release the mouse button to complete the merge.

Each paragraph within a text container (and each item in a list) is a separate object. When you hover the mouse pointer over a paragraph, a small selection box appears to its left. Click that box to select the entire paragraph; drag the selection box up or down to move the paragraph or list item to a new order in the container.

The container for a picture or other graphic object works differently from a text container. To move a picture, aim the mouse pointer at any of the dashed lines that make up the container; when the pointer turns to a four-headed arrow, drag the picture to its correct location. To resize a picture, click any of the container's borders to reveal sizing handles, as shown in Figure 21.7. Use the sizing handles on the right side or the bottom to change the width or height; use the sizing handle in the lower-right corner to change the picture size while maintaining the correct aspect ratio.

Figure 21.7
When you select a OneNote container that holds a photo, these sizing handles appear.

CUSTOMIZING THE ONENOTE INTERFACE

You can adjust the OneNote interface to suit your preferences. If you have a large monitor and you want every tool one click away, you can turn on every feature. For a notebook or Tablet PC, you might prefer a less cluttered, even Spartan approach.

The following list contains a sampling of ways you can tweak the main OneNote window to make it suit your preferences:

- Navigation Bar—Adjust the width of this pane, which shows all open notebooks, by dragging its right border. Click the chevron to the right of the Notebooks heading to collapse the bar to a thin pane, in which each notebook heading is turned on its side. Figure 21.8 shows the before and after views. To collapse the sections within a given notebook, click the up/down chevron to the right of the notebook's name.

Figure 21.8
With a single click, you can collapse the contents of a note-book or shrink the Navigation Bar (shown in full at left) to a narrow strip (right).

- Page tabs—You can make the page tabs list wider (and thus make it easier to see the titles of each page) by dragging the edge of the page tabs bar left or right. Click the chevron to the right of the New Page button to collapse the column of tabs to its bare minimum; click again to restore it to normal width.

TIP

Normally, the Navigation Bar appears on the left side of the main OneNote window and the page tabs and vertical scroll bar appear on the right. You can move any of these elements to the other side of the screen if you prefer that arrangement. Choose Tools, Options, and click the Display tab. Select the Page Tabs Appear on the Left box or the Vertical Scroll Bar Appears on the Left box to move either of these elements. Clear the Navigation Bar Appears on the Left box to move it to the right.

- Task pane—Choose View, Task Pane (or use the keyboard shortcut Ctrl+F1) to show or hide this element, which appears by default on the right side of the OneNote window. Click the handle to the left of the task pane's title to move it to any other edge of the window (on a Tablet PC, it works better at the bottom of the screen). Click the arrow to the right of the task pane title to display a drop-down list of all available task panes, or click the Left and Right buttons to cycle among all options.
- Toolbars—Right-click any visible toolbar (or choose View, Toolbars) to display a list of all available toolbars. Click to make a toolbar visible, as indicated by the check mark to its left, as shown in Figure 21.9. Click again to clear the check mark and hide the toolbar. To add or remove buttons from OneNote's toolbars, click the Customize option at the bottom of the Toolbars menu.

Figure 21.9
Click any toolbar on this list to make it visible. Click again to hide it.

21

PRINTING, PUBLISHING, AND EXPORTING INFORMATION FROM ONENOTE

OneNote is designed first and foremost as a personal productivity application. But occasionally you'll want to share information from OneNote with other people. You can do that in a variety of ways, including printing all or part of a notebook, sending one or more pages as an email attachment, or saving OneNote pages in a different file format.

PRINTING ONENOTE PAGES

The simplest option for getting notebook pages out of OneNote is to make printed copies. You'll find two useful options (Print and Print Preview) on the File menu, but don't click either one until you decide exactly what you want to print. You can print a single page, a group of pages, or all pages in the current section. If a page in your notebook requires more than one printed page, OneNote takes care of splitting it up for you.

NOTE

> Want to print part of a single page? Sorry, you can't. The only way to accomplish this task is to select the parts you want to print, paste them into a new page, and then print that page.

To print a single page or all pages in the current section, don't bother making any selection first. To print two or more pages in the current section, hold down the Shift key and click to select the tab for each page.

Choose File, Print to display the Print dialog box, shown in Figure 21.10.

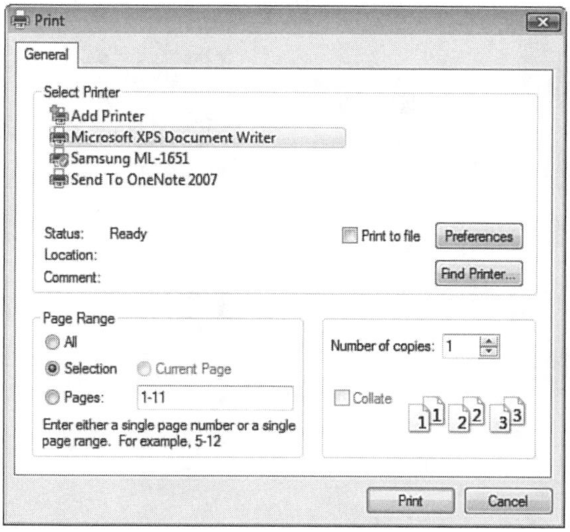

Figure 21.10
The options in the Print dialog box can be confusing at first, so pay attention.

21

This dialog box should be familiar. You select a printer and choose the number of copies to print, just as in any other Office program. The Page Range section, however, is potentially confusing. Let's break down what happens with each of the options in the Page Range section:

- Click All to print the entire contents of the current notebook. This option is available regardless of whether you made a selection before displaying the Print dialog box.

- Click Selection to print the full contents of the current page or of all selected pages if you selected multiple pages before opening the Print dialog box.

- The Pages option is available only if you have not selected an entire page (or multiple pages). If this option is available, you can enter a single page number or a single page range and print just those pages from the current section. In the example in Figure 21.10, the current section contains 11 pages. The default range includes all pages in the current section, numbered starting at the top of the page tabs list. To skip the first page and print the next three pages, for example, enter 2–4 in the Pages box.

What's most confusing about this dialog box is that the Selection option doesn't have the same meaning it does in other Office programs (or in most Windows programs, for that matter). Regardless of what text or objects you select on a page, the Selection option prints the full current page.

To avoid confusion, consider using the Print Preview option on the File menu instead. As you can see in Figure 21.11, the Print Preview dialog box gives you confirmation of exactly what you're about to print and allows some additional options, including footer and page numbering options.

Figure 21.11
Use the Print Preview dialog box for finer control over printed OneNote notebooks.

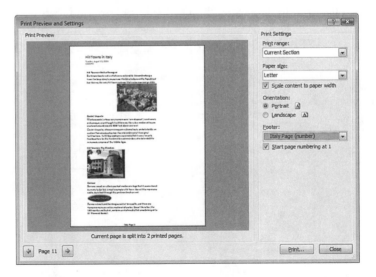

The Print Range box includes three options by default. The effect of the Current Page or Current Section option should be self-explanatory. Choose Page Group if you want to include all subpages of the current page. If you select multiple pages before opening the Print Preview dialog box (by holding down the Ctrl key as you click), a fourth option, Selected Pages, appears. This option prints all the pages you selected.

Use the Footer box to add a descriptive footer along the bottom of each printed page, with or without a page number, or to eliminate the footer completely. The footer format uses the notebook title only and cannot be customized.

SAVING NOTEBOOK PAGES IN ANOTHER FORMAT

How do you share a notebook page with someone else when they don't have OneNote installed on their computer? How do you make all or part of a OneNote notebook available on the web? Try saving a page, multiple pages, or even an entire notebook section in another format.

You can accomplish this task from either of two similar dialog boxes. Choose File, Save As to open the dialog box shown in Figure 21.12. The default selection is OneNote Sections, but you can change the Save as Type option to other formats if you want, including Single File Web Page, Microsoft Office Word Document, or Microsoft Office Word XML Document.

Figure 21.12
To save the current section as a Word document, choose these options from the Save As dialog box.

NOTE

Although the Current Notebook option is available in the Save As and Publish dialog boxes, it works only with the OneNote Single Package format. If you try to save a complete notebook as a Word document or web page, you'll get an error message.

Choose File, Publish Pages and you'll end up at a very similar dialog box. Instead of a Save button, this dialog box has a Publish button. Also, it defaults to Selected Pages in the Page Range section, and the default format is Single File Web Page. Use this option if you want to save a group of pages in a format that can be opened in a web browser.

FINDING INFORMATION IN A NOTEBOOK

As explained in Chapter 3, "Organizing and Finding Your Files," you can find just about anything within an Office document by using Windows Desktop Search. In OneNote, additional search tools are neatly integrated into the program itself, making it possible for you to quickly find pages containing a particular word or phrase.

The starting point for all OneNote searches is the Search box, which appears just to the right of the section tabs. Enter a word or phrase in this box, and then click the arrow to the right of the magnifying glass icon. Figure 21.13 shows the choices available on this menu.

Figure 21.13
When you search for a word or phrase, you can restrict the search by section or notebook.

If you know that the page you're looking for is in a particular notebook or section, you can increase the odds of finding it fast by narrowing the scope of the search to This Notebook or This Section. OneNote remembers the choice you make here and uses that same setting the next time you launch a search.

 If you're having trouble finding a word or phrase that you know is in a saved notebook, see "What to Do When Searches Don't Work," in the Troubleshooting section at the end of this chapter.

If your search is successful, the Search box expands as shown in Figure 21.14. The color changes to a bright yellow, and the tabs for any sections or pages that contain the search term change to the same color, giving you instant visual feedback of the search results.

The text immediately after the search term shows the number of pages that contain that term. Use the Previous Match and Next Match buttons to move quickly from page to page, or click View List to open the Search Results Task Pane, as shown in Figure 21.15.

Figure 21.14
The Search box provides instant access to results when your search is complete.

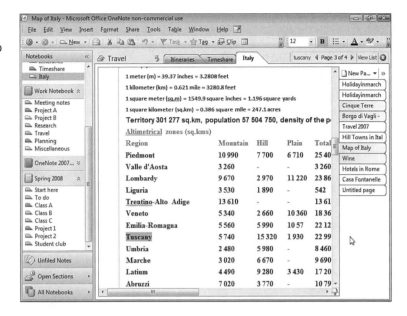

Figure 21.15
This task pane view provides a sortable list of matching results, with page titles and a snippet of context for each one.

Click any page title in the list to jump to that page immediately, even if it's in another notebook.

TROUBLESHOOTING

DEALING WITH ORPHANED SECTIONS

I tried to reorganize a notebook by shifting around some section files (with the .one *extension) in Windows Explorer. Now none of the* .one *files I moved show up when I open the notebook folder to which I moved them.*

You can't move section files between notebooks by dragging them around in Windows Explorer. A OneNote notebook contains sections only if you create them in that notebook or drag them from another notebook. The next time you want to shuffle sections between notebooks, do it in OneNote and allow the program to manage files behind the scenes.

To rearrange the orphaned sections, press Ctrl+O (or choose File, Open, Section), select the missing sections from the list of .one files, and click Open. All sections you open in this fashion appear in a normally hidden Open Sections group at the bottom of the Navigation Bar. You can now drag sections from here into the open notebooks where you want them to reside permanently. OneNote makes a copy of the section in the folder for the notebook you choose, leaving the original section file untouched.

After you've successfully found a home for all your disconnected sections, you can delete the original section files.

RESTORING THE CAPABILITY TO SAVE PRINTOUTS

I want to add a document to a OneNote page and have it appear exactly as it would when printed, but the Files As Printouts options is grayed out on the File menu. What's wrong?

OneNote does its printout magic by creating a virtual printer called Send to OneNote 2007 in your Printers folder. If this printer is missing, you'll experience the symptoms you describe here. One possible explanation is that you're using a 64-bit Windows version; in that case, OneNote is unable to create the virtual printer. If you're using a 32-bit Windows version, try reinstalling or repairing OneNote to see if this fixes the problem.

WHAT TO DO WHEN SEARCHES DON'T WORK

I entered a search term and clicked the Search button, but OneNote says my term doesn't exist. What's wrong?

Check your spelling first. It's possible the term you entered is misspelled or, worse, that the term in your notebook is misspelled. Next, check the search scope to make sure you're looking in the correct location. If you've restricted the search to the current section, you might need to choose All Notebooks. Is the term in a password-protected notebook? If so, you'll need to unlock that notebook to search its contents. If all else fails, try some other searches with terms that you know are in the current section or notebook. If those fail, too, it might be necessary to rebuild the Windows Desktop Search index.

EXTRA CREDIT: SENDING WEB PAGES TO ONENOTE

One of the best uses for OneNote is as a tool for web research. If you're tracking down facts, figures, and sources for a term paper, it's tiring to constantly shift back and forth between your browser and your preferred note-taking application. With OneNote, you don't ever have to leave your browser window.

The secret is a small button that OneNote adds to Internet Explorer 7 when you install it. By default, it's hidden at the end of the Internet Explorer Command Bar, so your first task is to give it a position with more visibility: Here's how:

1. In Internet Explorer 7, click Tools, Toolbars, Customize.
2. In the Customize Toolbar dialog box, select the Send to OneNote button in the Current Toolbar Buttons list on the right, as shown in Figure 21.16, and click Move Up.

Figure 21.16

3. Keep clicking until the button is at the top of the list, and then click Close.

After making this change, the Send to OneNote button appears at the left of the Command Bar, as shown in Figure 21.17.

When you click this button, Internet Explorer sends the current web page to OneNote and pastes it into OneNote. If you make a selection first, only the selected text and graphics are copied. If you make no selection, OneNote copies the entire page. In either case, OneNote adds a link to the source page at the bottom of each note.

Figure 21.17
The Send to OneNote as it appears in Internet Explorer.

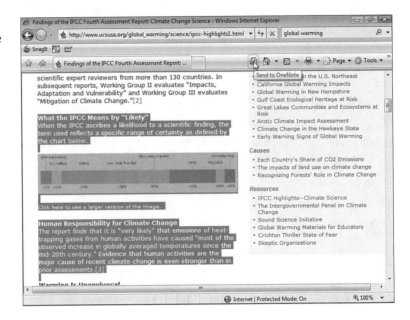

By default, each web note goes on a new page in the Unfiled Notes section. You can change this setting so that web notes go on the current page or on a new page in the current section. To make this change, choose Tools, Options, click the Send to OneNote tab, and choose the appropriate option.

After you learn how useful OneNote is for web research, you'll wonder how you ever did without it.

ORGANIZING AND ARRANGING INFORMATION IN ONENOTE

In this chapter

22

FORMATTING TEXT AND LISTS

As we noted in the previous chapter, OneNote is designed for freeform note-taking. That doesn't mean its contents have to be a jumble, however. You can alter the look of text that you type on a OneNote page by changing fonts and font sizes or adjusting attributes. You can add bullets or automatically number items in a list. Outlining tools allow you to organize ideas into a hierarchy. You can even alter the format of the page itself by adding lines, rules, and background images.

FORMATTING TEXT

As with every other program in the Office family, before you can change the formatting of text, you have to select it. Here are some of the many ways you can select text:

- Drag the mouse pointer to select a character, a sentence, or part of a paragraph.
- Double-click to select a word, and triple-click to select a paragraph.
- Click the handle at the top of a container to select all text in that container.
- Click Edit, Select, All (or press Ctrl+A) to select all text in the current paragraph. Do it again to select all text in the current container, and do it once more to select all text in all containers on the current page.
- If the pointer is in a table, click Edit, Select and use the Table, Column, Row, and Cell menus to select the text in those locations.

→ For details on how to enter text and work with containers, **see** "What Can You Put on a Notebook Page," **p. 639.**

> **TIP**
>
> As with Word, OneNote applies character formatting to the entire word if you position the insertion point in a word without making a selection. That's handy when you're working with one-word headings or you're italicizing or bold-facing a word for emphasis.

After making a selection, you can change text formatting by opening the Fonts task pane. Choose Format, Font or press Ctrl+F1 to display this task pane, shown in Figure 22.1.

You can change the font, font size, or font color, or apply any of the six attributes shown here. Any selections you make in this pane take effect on the current selection immediately.

ORGANIZING TEXT AS AN OUTLINE

Every time you press Enter in a block of text, OneNote marks the end of a paragraph. Initially, any text you type in a container is formatted as a Level 1 heading. Click at the beginning of a new or existing paragraph and press Tab to demote that paragraph to a Level 2 heading, or press Shift+Tab to promote a subheading one level. A OneNote outline can contain as many levels of headings as will fit on the width of the page.

Figure 22.1
Use this task pane to apply fonts and text attributes to any text selection.

You can rearrange any sequence of paragraphs into outline form. Using the selection handle at the left of every paragraph (shown in Figure 22.2), you can select a heading and everything beneath it and then drag the handle up or down in the outline.

Figure 22.2
Click this handle to select this heading and all its subheadings and then move it up or down or apply formatting to the selection.

You can also expand or collapse an outline to show more or less detail. To collapse the outline for a single heading, right-click the selection handle for that heading and choose an option from the Hide Levels Below menu, as shown in Figure 22.3. To collapse the entire outline, select all text in the outline (or all text at Level 1) and then choose the appropriate menu option. Double-click the selection handle to expand a section.

Figure 22.3
Use this menu to hide outline text below a level you select.

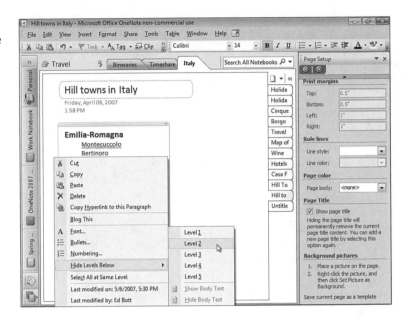

Although you can't save formatting and apply it automatically as you can using Word styles, you can select all text at a specific outline level and reformat everything at that level. Choose Edit, Select, All at Level 1 (or any level through Level 5) or right-click the selection handle for a specific level and choose Select All at Same Level. After making the selection, use the Fonts task pane to apply text formatting to the selection.

TIP

> By default, OneNote uses 11-point Calibri for all new text you type. If you prefer a different font, choose Tools, Options, click Editing, and choose a font, size, and color from the Default Font section.

CUSTOMIZING BULLETS AND NUMBERED LISTS

Just as in Word, you can add bullets or automatic numbering to any list of items in a OneNote text container. Bullets are applied to the current selection in any of the following four ways:

- Begin a new line with an asterisk or a greater than (>) sign and then press the spacebar; OneNote immediately turns the character into a matching bullet.

- Click the Bullets button on the Formatting toolbar to apply a plain black bullet to the selection.

- Click the drop-down arrow to the right of the Bullets button on the Formatting toolbar to choose one of five predefined bullet formats.

■ Choose Format, Bullets (or click More from the bottom of the drop-down menu on the Bullets toolbar button) to open the Bullets task pane shown in Figure 22.4. Choose the button character you prefer and, optionally, adjust the spacing between the chosen character and the beginning of the list item.

22

Figure 22.4
Use any of these bullet characters to set off items in a list.

When you press Enter at the end of a bulleted list item, OneNote creates a new list item that begins with the same bullet character. To stop automatically adding bullets before new list items, press Enter twice.

TIP

If you don't like the spacing of items in a list, bulleted or not, you can adjust it. Choose Format, List (or click the List shortcut at the bottom of the Bullets task pane) to open the List task pane, where you can adjust both horizontal and vertical spacing for the current list. Note that any settings you make here apply only to the current list; new lists use the default settings. To save a set of default list formats, create a formatted list on a blank page and then save that page as a template. You can then use that template to create a new page and copy the formatted container from the new page to the current one.

OneNote can also automatically number items in a list, a feature that comes in handy if you're putting together a prioritized to-do list, for example. As with bullets, you can use the Numbering button to apply a default format (1., 2., 3....) or use that button's drop-down list to choose from a list of five predefined formats. For more advanced numbering formats, especially for use with outlines, choose Format, Numbering to open the task pane shown in Figure 22.5. The list includes 19 predefined formats.

Figure 22.5
To apply automatic numbering to an outline, select all or part of the outline first, and then use this task pane.

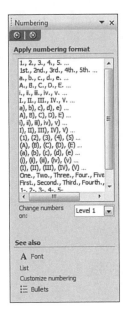

If you can't find the exact combination you prefer, click Customize Numbering from the bottom of the Numbering task pane. That opens a separate task pane where you can mix and match number formats and punctuation, as shown in Figure 22.6.

Figure 22.6
Want to build your own numbering format? Mix and match numbers and punctuation here.

As with bulleted lists, OneNote continues numbering until you click the Numbering button or press Enter twice to turn off the feature. If you drag items up or down in the list, the numbering shifts to accommodate the new order you create. As with bulleted lists, the choices you make here apply only to the current list; if you want to save a custom list format, do so on a blank page and then save that page as a template.

→ For more details on reusing pages, **see** "Saving Page Templates," **p. 662.**

CHANGING THE LOOK OF ONENOTE PAGES

Any new page you create in OneNote picks up the formatting assigned to it by the default page template. In a clean install of OneNote, this template is blank, and so new pages have a plain white background, with a page title and no lines or rules.

You can adjust any of the settings for the current page by choosing File, Page Setup, which opens the Page Setup task pane shown in Figure 22.7.

Figure 22.7
You can change the overall look and feel of any OneNote page using settings in this task pane.

In the remainder of this section, we'll explain how to use each of the settings in this task pane.

CHANGING PAPER SIZE

The default paper size for a OneNote page is Auto. With this setting selected, the width and height of the page can expand freely to accommodate whatever you type. If you choose a predefined paper size and orientation, OneNote adjusts the width, height, and margins to

22

match your selections. You can adjust any of those settings to override the defaults. In Figure 22.8, for instance, we've set up the current page to match the size and dimensions of a standard index card but changed the left margin from its default 1" to 0.5".

Figure 22.8
If you define a specific page size, the page boundaries don't expand when you reach the edge.

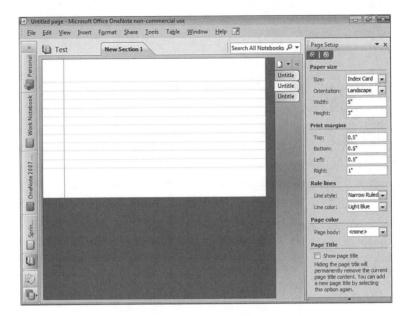

Defining a specific paper size is important when you know your notes will ultimately be printed out on paper of that size. Although you can drag a container so it goes off the defined page and into the OneNote margins, doing so gives you clear visual feedback that the printout will have problems.

ADDING RULES AND GRID LINES

Using the Page Setup task pane also allows you to add lines or grids to a page. The Rule Lines menu allows you to choose from a set of line styles that range from narrow to very wide, with a choice of 16 colors. These lines aren't just for visual effect, either. When you add rules or a grid to a page, OneNote uses those indicators to determine where the insertion point should be positioned. In Figure 22.9, for instance, we've turned the current page into a neat facsimile of the grid paper you're likely to use in a science lab.

When rules or grids are enabled, all containers "snap" to the selected lines, making it easier to arrange different blocks of notes neatly. (You can turn off this feature by choosing Edit, Snap to Grid and clearing the highlight on this menu option.) Changing the line style does not move existing containers.

Figure 22.9
With this grid turned on, OneNote positions the pointer in the square nearest to where you click, so all your notes line up neatly.

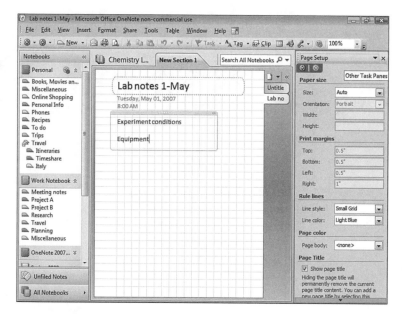

TIP

> Want a neat page without the distraction of visible lines? Choose the Small Grid option from the Line Style list and then choose <none> from the Line Color list. All your typed text will line up neatly, and containers you move will magically snap into position, even though the page appears to be completely free of lines.

CHANGING THE PAGE BACKGROUND

If you leave the Page Color setting blank, the current page has a white background. You can choose any of 16 colors from the Page Body list. Although the names are the same as those in the Line Color list, the colors themselves are different shades. As a result, you can choose Red Chalk from both the Line Color and Page Body lists and count on having the proper contrast, as shown in the example in Figure 22.10. Some color combinations don't work at all, of course. For example, Apple lines disappear completely on a Purple Mist background.

Finally, you can use a picture as a background for a page. To do so, add a picture to a page using Insert, Pictures, From Files. Crop or move the picture to the location where you want to see it permanently and then right-click the picture and choose Set Picture as Background. With this option selected, the picture no longer lives in a movable, resizable container but instead serves as part of the background. You can add a text container directly on top of it, if the background is light enough, or add notes around the image. This technique is useful for adding logos or a personal picture to personalize notebook pages.

Figure 22.10
It's OK to choose the same color for lines and the page body—in fact, colors of the same name are designed to work together.

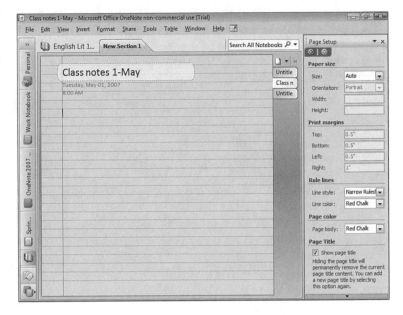

TIP

The only other obvious change you can make to a section within a notebook is to change its color. For sections and section groups, right-click the section heading in the Navigation bar or along the row of section tabs at the top of the contents window and then choose from one of the 16 available colors. The color you select fills the border around the current page, the Page Tabs list, and the section tab.

→ For details about how to change the color or name of a notebook, **see** "Creating, Opening, and Managing Notebooks," **p. 635.**

SAVING PAGE TEMPLATES

After you create a custom page, one of the most useful things you can do with it is save it as a template for later use. For example, if you've created a page using small grid lines and a Red Chalk background color on which you keep lab notes from a chemistry class, you can save that page as a template by clicking Save Current Page as a Template from the bottom of the Page Setup task pane (choose File, Page Setup). You can also add containers with boilerplate text and headings (a to-do list of assignments, space for a summary, reminders on items to include in pages based on that template, and so forth).

After you've saved the template, create a new Chemistry Notes section and choose Format, Templates. In the Templates task pane, choose your newly saved template from the list under the Choose Default Template heading (look under the My Templates category). From now on, any new pages you create in this section will use that template's formatting and text.

NOTE

> Changing a saved template has no effect on pages you've already created using the earlier version of that template. Templates are a starting point for new pages, not a live set of formatting instructions.

TIP

> Although you can create a template from scratch, you should always explore the collection of ready-made templates in OneNote and at Office Online to see whether anyone else has done a good job of building a template for the same purpose. Modifying a well-made template by changing a few colors and editing boilerplate text is much easier than doing it all yourself.

TAGGING NOTES FOR FOLLOW-UP

The trouble with freeform notes is that they're so, well, freeform. If you've filled a collection of notebooks with hundreds of pages on all sorts of topics, how do you make sure that really important items don't get lost? That's where *tags* come in.

A OneNote *tag* is essentially a bookmark that you can apply to any of the content on a page. Every tag has a label; an icon is optional. You can attach a tag to a page title, a snippet of text, a heading, a picture, or any other object on a OneNote page.

NOTE

> OneNote's Insert menu also includes an Outlook Task option, which allows you to attach flags to text, pages, or containers in OneNote. These flags have follow-up dates attached and are linked to tasks in Microsoft Outlook. In Office Home and Student 2007, this capability is unavailable, because Outlook isn't included with this package. As a result, we don't cover it here.

Figure 22.11 shows a page containing four types of tags. The item at the top is tagged as a Definition; the formatting for that tag includes green highlighting and no icon. The exclamation point and question mark icons indicate Critical and Question tags, respectively. The check boxes in front of the two items under the Homework heading mean that those items are tagged as To Do items.

22

To Do items are special. When you click the check box that identifies this type of item, it changes to a check mark, indicating the item is completed.

OneNote includes a list of 29 default tags. To apply a tag, first make a selection, and then click the drop-down arrow to the right of the Tag button on the Standard toolbar or choose Insert, Tag. (To remove a tag, right-click the item or the icon that identifies the tag and choose Remove Tag from the context menu.)

Figure 22.11
Aim the mouse pointer at any tag's icon to see the label for that tag.

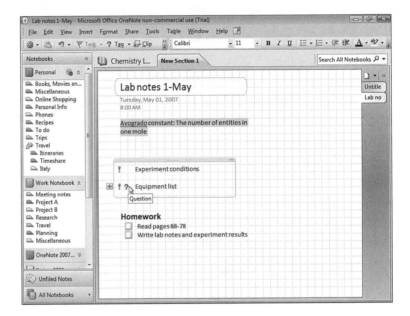

The top 9 tags on this menu have keyboard shortcuts (Ctrl+1 through Ctrl+9). The menu itself accommodates 18 tags, and the remainder are available by clicking More at the bottom of the Tag menu.

Does that long list include everything you might want to use to jog your memory? Does it include some tags you'll never use? No, and yes. The obvious solution to this cluttered list is to customize it, removing tags you don't need, adding those that are personal to you, and changing the order or design of your personal tags to make them easier to apply and find.

You can do all of these tasks from the Customize My Tags task pane, shown in Figure 22.12. To open this pane, choose Insert, Tag, Customize My Tags.

Figure 22.12
Use this task pane to change the list of tags available to you and to modify their appearance and shortcut keys.

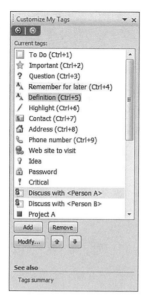

In this dialog box, you can do any of the following tasks:

- Click Add to insert a new task. This opens the Modify Tag dialog box shown in Figure 22.13. Replace the generic name (Undefined) with a more descriptive label (Homework, for example).

    By default, the new tag has no icon associated with it. (The default selection on the Symbol list, represented by the repeated letter *A*, is None.) Click the Symbol menu to choose an icon, as shown in Figure 22.14, and adjust the font color and highlight color if you want to really make the new tag stand out.

- To remove an existing tag, click to select its entry in the Current Tags list and then click Remove.

- By default, new tags are added at the bottom of the list. To change the position of a new or existing tag, select it and click the Up or Down buttons.

- Any tag you move into the top nine slots on the Current Tags list automatically gets a matching keyboard shortcut attached to it. To assign Ctrl+3 to a tag, move it to the third position on the list.

Figure 22.13

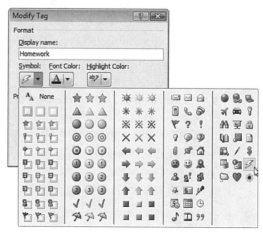

Figure 22.14

22

- To change the label, symbol, or formatting of a defined tag, select it and click Modify. You'll want to do this with the Discuss with <Person A> and <Person B> tags, replacing the generic text with names of real people.

The real power of tags becomes apparent when you open the Tags Summary task pane (Insert, Tag, Show All Tagged Notes). As you can see in Figure 22.15, this pane includes a sortable list of links to everything you've tagged.

Figure 22.15
Use the Group Tags By menu to change the arrangement of items on this list.

Several options in this section deserve additional discussion:

- Use the Group By list to sort the results by date, tag name, section, page title, or the tagged text. Using Tag Name as the grouping criterion, for example, enables you to easily find all your items flagged as Critical or Important.

- Select the Show Only Unchecked Items box to hide any completed To Do items.

- Select an entry from the Search list to restrict the display of tagged items by section, by notebook, or by date.

- The results listed here represent the results of the search you performed when you first opened this task pane. If you add, change, or remove tags from a notebook, the list isn't updated until you click Refresh Results and rerun the search.

- Click Create Summary Page to make a copy of all items in the search results and add them to a new page. Note that the items on the new summary page include only the tagged text and are not linked in any way to the original item.

An additional option on the Standard toolbar is labeled Task (on the Insert menu, it's more fully labeled Outlook Task). This option is similar to the Tag function, except it creates a task in Microsoft Outlook and offers the option to assign a date to the task. Because Outlook is not included in Office 2007 Home and Student, this option is grayed out and unavailable unless you install Outlook separately.

EXTRA CREDIT: SHARE ONENOTE PAGES VIA EMAIL

OneNote is well suited for typing notes and random text you plan to consult for your own personal use later, but it's also easy to share notebook pages with other people.

To send a OneNote page as email, choose File, Email (or use the Ctrl+Shift+E shortcut). This opens a new message in your default email program. In Windows Mail, which is included with Windows Vista, the result includes at least two file attachments, as shown in Figure 22.16. One is the page saved in OneNote format, the other is the same page saved as a self-contained HTML file suitable for opening in a web browser or email program.

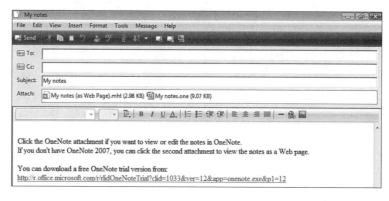

Figure 22.16

Address the message, add or edit any text to explain what's included, and click Send. If you know for certain that your recipient does not have OneNote, you can delete the .one attachment before sending.

If your recipient uses an HTML-compatible email program such as Outlook, Outlook Express, Windows Mail, or Mozilla Thunderbird, the HTML-formatted attachment appears in the message body. Icons and highlighting for tags appear as well.

At the bottom of the message body, OneNote adds a tagline that encourages the recipient to get her own copy of OneNote. If you'd prefer to replace this text with something more personal and less commercial, choose Tools, Options, click the Sending Email tab, and change the text in the signature box. To forgo the automatic signature completely, clear the Add the Following Signature check box.

CHAPTER 23

ONENOTE FOR EXPERTS

In this chapter

TWEAKING ONENOTE FOR MAXIMUM EFFICIENCY

For a seemingly simple program, OneNote has a surprising number of options. With some judicious tweaking, you can substantially increase your productivity with OneNote.

For starters, learn how to use the OneNote Quick Launcher. This icon resides in the notification area at the right side of the Windows taskbar. Right-click this icon to display the menu shown in Figure 23.1.

Figure 23.1
The OneNote Quick Launcher sits in the Windows taskbar and offers quick access to useful functions.

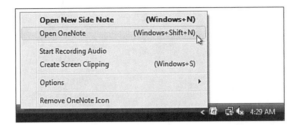

If you just want to jot down a quick note, the last thing you want is to be slowed down by the logistics of opening OneNote, finding the right notebook and section, and creating a new page. By the time you accomplish all that, it's understandable if you forget what you meant to write down.

So skip all that and create a *Side Note* instead. The Side Note window is a stripped-down, streamlined version of a OneNote page. It includes no page title and no menus or other navigation elements. To open a Side Note window, press the Windows logo key + N, or right-click the OneNote Quick Launcher icon in the notification area on the right side of the taskbar. You get a single toolbar along the top, as shown in Figure 23.2. Type your note, close the window, and continue doing whatever you were doing before inspiration struck.

> **TIP**
>
> Normally, double-clicking the OneNote Quick Launcher icon opens a new Side Note. If you'd prefer to open the full OneNote program window, choose Options, OneNote Icon Defaults, and select Open OneNote. For fast access to both options, learn the keyboard shortcuts: press the Windows logo key + N to open a Side Note; use the same combination with the Shift key to open the full OneNote program.

Side Notes are saved in the Unfiled Notes section. By default, this section is not part of any other notebook; the Unfiled Notes.one file is created automatically and saved in your OneNote Notebooks folder.

Click the Unfiled Notes shortcut at the bottom of the Navigation Bar to view Side Notes and other items that have landed here. You'll want to review the contents of this folder from time to time and consolidate those Side Notes to other pages in other notebooks.

Figure 23.2
Use a Side Note window to jot down quick notes without the fuss of opening OneNote.

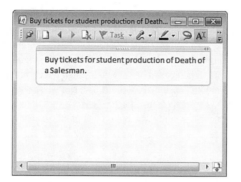

Two other types of notes end up in the Unfiled Notes section as well. If you send all or part of a web page to OneNote using the Send to OneNote button in Internet Explorer, it lands here. The same is true if you use the Send to OneNote printer to capture output from another program.

If you'd prefer either of these types of notes to be filed elsewhere, click Tools, Options, and choose the Send to OneNote tab, shown in Figure 23.3.

Figure 23.3
Use this dialog box to customize the location where your web notes and printouts are filed.

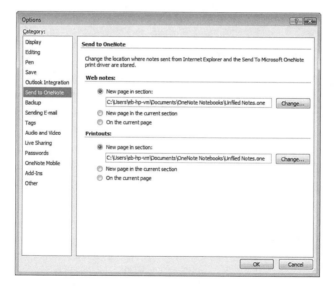

Click Change to choose a section in an existing notebook (or create a new section) as the destination for new web notes or printouts. Want to see all your web notes filed in a Web Research section? Go ahead.

TIP

Should you select New Page in the Current Section or On the Current Page as the destination for web notes or printouts? The default setting assumes that you start with your web browser or another program and add notes on the fly, depositing this research in a holding area. Every so often, you'll need to go through the collection of notes and printouts, filing them in more appropriate sections. The two alternative options work well if you always start in OneNote, create a page or select a section to accommodate your research, and then begin sending web notes or printouts to OneNote.

23

If you'd prefer that Side Notes and other on-the-fly content go to a section in an existing notebook rather than to the catch-all Unfiled Notes notebook, click Save in the Options dialog box. In this dialog box, shown in Figure 23.4, click Unfiled Notes Section in the Paths box, click Modify, and then select a section from an existing notebook.

Figure 23.4
Options in the Save dialog box let you tweak the location where OneNote saves unfiled notes.

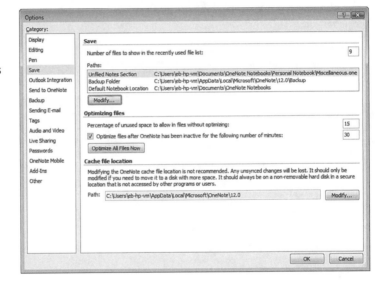

CAUTION

Before you change the location of the Unfiled Notes section, do yourself a favor and move all existing pages out of that section and into the section you want to use. After emptying the Unfiled Notes section, change the default location, close OneNote, and delete the Unfiled Notes.one file in OneNote Notebooks folder. When you reopen OneNote, you'll find that clicking the Unfiled Notes shortcut at the bottom of the Navigation Bar displays the contents of the new location.

SAVING AUDIO AND VIDEO NOTES

In previous chapters, we discussed the most common forms of input for OneNote: text, entered via the keyboard or from the Clipboard, and pictures, which can be pasted or sent from a web page or printout. But OneNote pages can also hold audio and video notes, and the results can be extremely useful.

If you use OneNote to take lecture notes in a classroom, why not use your notebook computer's built-in microphone to record the instructor's remarks as you type? The recording is saved within your notebook, and OneNote is even smart enough to synchronize the recording with your typed notes. So if you're baffled by something you typed, you can click the Play button, listen to the original remarks, and solve the mystery.

If you have a video camera, you can add a visual dimension in addition to the audio content.

To get started, make sure your microphone (and camera, if you're planning to use video notes as well) are properly configured in Windows. Then open OneNote, choose Tools, Options, and click the Audio and Video tab, shown in Figure 23.5.

Figure 23.5
The Tuning Wizard is available only if you have both an audio and video device attached to your computer.

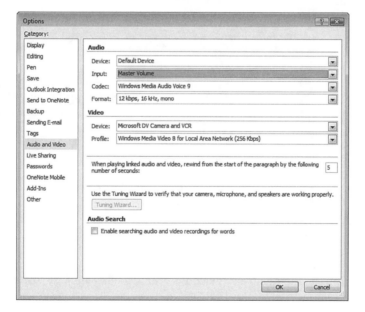

If you're recording a conversation and rich sonic quality isn't important, use the default settings. For both audio and video, you can choose different codecs and formats with a corresponding increase in both quality and the amount of disk space consumed by recordings.

23

For technical details about what each codec does and why you might choose one over the other, visit http://www.microsoft.com/windows/windowsmedia/forpros/codecs/codecs.aspx.

After verifying that your equipment is set up correctly, you can begin adding audio or video content to a OneNote page. To start, click anywhere in the page where you want your recording to be created and then click the Record Audio Only button on the Standard toolbar or choose Insert, Audio Recording (or Video Recording, if you're using a video camera with a microphone). Your recording begins immediately. On the current page, OneNote inserts an icon that links to the embedded recording, adds a date and time stamp, and displays the Audio and Video Recording toolbar. Figure 23.6 shows the page as the recording is in progress.

Figure 23.6
Use the Pause button on the toolbar to suspend a recording. If you click Stop, you have no way to resume and must start a new recording.

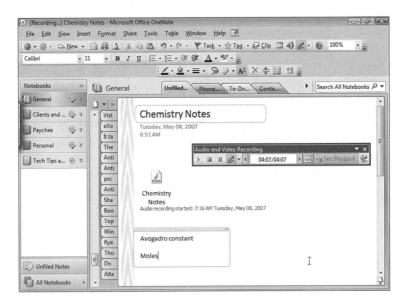

The controls on the Audio and Video Recording toolbar are fairly standard. Use the Stop button to end a recording, or click Pause to keep the file open without recording. Click Pause again to resume recording. The Play, Pause, and Stop buttons work exactly as you expect during playback. The Audio gauge keeps track of the current recording's length as you record; during playback, it shows the running time and the total time.

TIP

While a recording is under way, the Record button on the Standard toolbar is highlighted in orange. Clicking this button has the same effect as clicking the Stop button on the Audio and Video Recording toolbar.

When you click the Stop button, your file is saved, and you can't add any more to it. If you remain on the same page and click the Record button again, OneNote adds an icon for a second file, with its own time stamp. You can continue this way, adding as many recordings as you like. The bad news is that your page will be cluttered with icons. The good news? OneNote keeps track of the order of each recording and accumulates the elapsed time. During playback, when you reach the end of the first file, it jumps to the beginning of the second file and continues playing, and then jumps to the third file at the end of that segment.

As you record, you can type in the same page that holds the sound file icon. OneNote synchronizes the recording with your notes. To play back the recording, you have two choices:

- Double-click the icon for the file that contains the recording. Drag the split bar in the middle of the Audio gauge to move forward or backward in the timeline. As you play back the recording, OneNote highlights the section of your notes based on the synchronization markers it made originally.

- Click in your notes and look for a Play icon to the left of the current paragraph, as shown in Figure 23.7. When you click that icon, OneNote begins playing back the recording you made, beginning with the section that's synchronized with that portion of your notes.

Figure 23.7
Click the icon to the left of any paragraph to begin playing the audio or video recorded as you typed that portion of your notes.

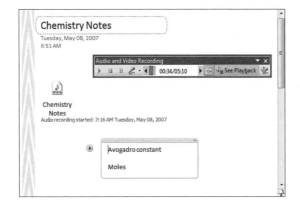

NOTE

> OneNote stores the audio files saved with each page in its Audio Cache folder, which is located in %localappdata%\Microsoft\OneNote\12.0\. The files themselves are stored in a format that cannot be played directly.

Thanks to built-in speech recognition, you can search your audio notes as well. This feature takes some processing power and time (two or three hours for every hour of audio), so enable it only if you need the capability to search for specific words or phrases in audio recordings. To enable this feature, open the OneNote Options dialog box, click Audio and Video, and select the Enable Searching Audio and Video Recordings for Words check box.

USING HYPERLINKS IN ONENOTE

You're accustomed to using hyperlinks to web pages (beginning with the http: prefix) and email addresses (using the mailto: prefix). But you might not realize that you can create live links in OneNote pages that lead to other Office documents or to specific locations on other OneNote pages, including pages in other sections and notebook.

Let's start with the easy stuff. When you send a web page to OneNote or paste a snippet of text or a graphic from a web page, OneNote adds a tagline at the bottom of the container that includes a clickable link to the source page.

So what happens if you copy a range from an Excel workbook or a sentence from a Word document and paste it into OneNote? You get the same tagline at the end of the pasted item, with a clickable link to the source file, using the file:/// prefix followed by the full path to the file.

You can also create hyperlinks to paragraphs in OneNote and use those links elsewhere in OneNote or in another Office program. These links use the prefix onenote: and are tied directly to a specific page in a specific section in a specific notebook, using unique identifiers that remain constant even if you rename a page or section.

TIP

> You can create hyperlinks to a paragraph, a page, a section, or an entire notebook. Just right-click on the object and use the context menu. If you right-click on a page tab, for instance, choose Copy Hyperlink to This Page. After you copy a hyperlink from any OneNote object, you can use that link to create a shortcut on the Windows desktop, in a folder, or on the Start menu. If you've created a separate section for your Chemistry lab notes, for example, right-click the section tab, choose Copy Hyperlink to This Section, and then use the New, Shortcut menu to create a shortcut on the Windows desktop that opens that section directly.

Say, for example, that you've been collecting research for a paper on which you're working and saving your notes to OneNote pages. You want to pull together bits and pieces from your notes to use as the framework for the paper. Here's how:

1. Create a new blank page for the report outline.

2. Switch to your first note page, click in a paragraph you want to use in the report, right-click, and choose Copy Hyperlink to This Paragraph from the context menu. (If you prefer to use page titles for the hyperlinks, click the page tab and choose Copy Hyperlink to This Page.)

3. Switch back to the report outline page, right-click at the spot where you want the link to appear, and choose Paste.

4. Repeat steps 1–3 for every additional note page.

You can now flesh out your outline. When you want more information from your notes, use the hyperlinks to jump directly to the linked page containing your full notes on that subject. When the outline is complete and you're ready to turn it into a polished paper, choose File, Send To, Microsoft Office Word.

An alternate use of hyperlinks is to create linked pages. This technique is useful when you have an outline that contains topics you want to research or write about and one or more of the topics in the outline deserves its own page.

So, for example, you might have a OneNote page containing a list of names of historical figures about whom you're planning to write. Select the name Ludwig van Beethoven from the list, right-click, and choose Create Linked page. OneNote creates a new page at the end of the current section, using the composer's name as its title, and turns the text you selected into a link to that page.

As long as each name in the list is a paragraph of its own, you can select the entire list, right-click, and choose Create Linked Page from the context menu. If the list contains five names, you'll end up with five new pages, each with a link on the original page, as shown in Figure 23.8.

Figure 23.8
When you create a linked page, the text in your selection is the hyperlink text and also serves as the title for the new page.

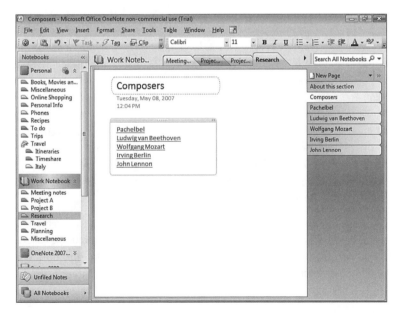

If you're having trouble keeping links in sync, see "Dealing with Broken Hyperlinks," in the Troubleshooting section at the end of this chapter.

SHARING A ONENOTE NOTEBOOK

Most of the time, you'll probably be content to work with OneNote on your own personal computer. But OneNote was made for sharing. In fact, it has some dazzling smarts when it comes to keeping notebooks in sync on two computers. In this section, we'll explain the two circumstances where this capability comes in handy.

If you're creating a notebook from scratch, you can create a shared notebook easily. Use the new Notebook Wizard (File, New, Notebook) to set up sharing, as shown in Figure 23.9. This wizard walks you through the process and is ideal for making sure you don't miss a step.

Figure 23.9
When creating a new notebook, decide up front whether you want to make it available for sharing.

USING A NOTEBOOK ON TWO COMPUTERS

Do you have a portable computer you carry to school and a desktop computer you work with at home? As long as the computers can connect across a network, you can open the same notebook on both machines and keep the contents perfectly in sync. OneNote can reconcile changes even when both documents have changed since the last time they were synced with one another.

Say you've been working with OneNote primarily on your portable PC, where you've been using it to take classroom notes, which you stored in a notebook called Class Notes. To work with the notebook on your desktop computer, make sure both computers are on the same network and can access shared files on the other computer; then follow these steps:

1. On your notebook computer, open Windows Explorer and find the Class Notes folder. (Unless you've changed the default location, this should be in the OneNote Notebooks subfolder in your Documents folder.) Make this folder available for sharing, with full read/write access.

TIP

> If you have access to a file server or another computer that already has shared access for both computers, close the notebook in OneNote, move the folder to the shared location, and then reopen it. If you're using Windows Vista, you can move the notebook to the Public folder and make it available for sharing there.

23

2. On your desktop computer, open OneNote, choose File, Open, Notebook, and navigate to the shared folder you set up in Step 1. Click Open.

3. Look at the heading in the Navigation Bar for the Notebook you just opened. Aim the mouse pointer to the Sync icon—the green circle, with or without a check mark, to the right of the notebook name. You should see a ScreenTip like the one shown in Figure 23.10.

4. Click the Sync icon to display the Shared Notebook Synchronization dialog box shown in Figure 23.11.

Figure 23.10

Figure 23.11
Any notebook you open from a shared folder on another computer becomes eligible for synchronization using the settings shown here.

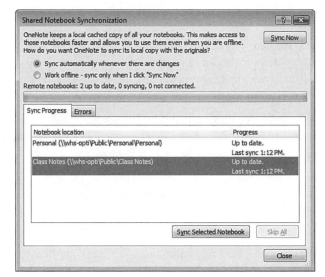

5. Make sure the notebook is synchronized; if it's not yet synchronized, click Sync Selected Notebook.

During this initial setup, OneNote creates a local copy of the remote notebook in its cache folder. If you disconnect from the network, you can continue to work with the notebook. Any changes you make while online are reflected on the other copy immediately, even if the notebook is open on the other computer. If you make changes while disconnected from the network, those changes are synced as soon as you reconnect, unless you choose to work offline and allow only manual synchronization.

After you finish setting up synchronization on the shared file, any changes you make are reflected in the other copy as soon as it syncs again.

OneNote's synchronization is smart, working on a container basis so you can comfortably make changes to either copy of a notebook and be certain that all those changes will be reflected in the other copy next time you sync. If you make changes on both locations, OneNote includes all changes and additions.

SHARING A NOTEBOOK WITH OTHER PEOPLE

The second form of sharing allows you to collaborate with another person (or persons) with all of you working in OneNote on the same notebook section at the same time. This feature is called Live Sharing, and it allows you to set up a Live Sharing Session with anyone over the network or over the Internet. (All parties in the session must have OneNote 2007 running to join in.)

To get started, open the section you want to share and choose Share, Live Sharing Session, Start Sharing Current Session. This opens the Start Live Session task pane, shown in Figure 23.12.

If you're planning to share the session with another computer on your same small network and you're certain nothing confidential is at stake, you can skip the password. Otherwise, enter a temporary password that anyone joining the session will have to type. Click Start Live Sharing Session to continue.

If this is the first time you've set up a Live Sharing Session, you'll be warned that all pages in the current section will be visible to other participants. Click OK to continue. You're now in the Current Live Session task pane, as shown in Figure 23.13.

As the originator of the session, you see an icon alongside the section you're sharing. If you're joining a session set up by someone else, you'll see a Live Shared Sections group at the bottom of the Navigation Bar.

Figure 23.12
Entering a temporary password here prevents anyone from joining the session who hasn't been invited.

23

Figure 23.13
Any participant in the live shared session can invite other participants.

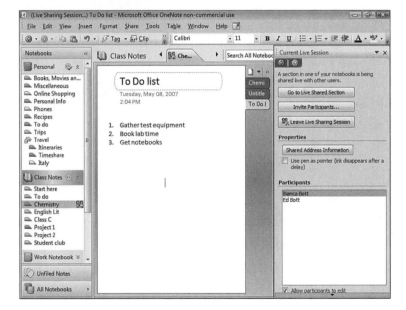

As the originator, you can invite other participants, who need an IP address and port number to successfully connect. If you're comfortable with networking, you can click Share, Live Sharing Session, Join Live Session and enter the address directly. To make it easier on participants, click Invite Participants, which opens an email message, creates a OneNote invitation shortcut, and fills in the message body with connection instructions and IP addresses.

When a remote participant joins the session, he sees the same task pane you see, and his name is added to the Participants list. At any time, any participant can leave by clicking the Leave Live Sharing Session button.

While the shared session is active, anyone can add text and pictures, draw with a pen, insert graphics, add new pages or change existing ones—and the changes are reflected practically in real time. If you want to allow other participants to view your work but not change it, clear the Allow Participants to Edit check box at the bottom of the Current Live Session task pane.

When the originator of a session leaves or you're otherwise disconnected from a shared session, participants are still able to view the contents of the shared section, but no changes are possible. At the top of the editing window, you'll see a message like the one shown in Figure 23.14. To make changes, reconnect or drag the section into a different notebook.

Figure 23.14
If you're disconnected from a shared section, you see the message at the top of this page.

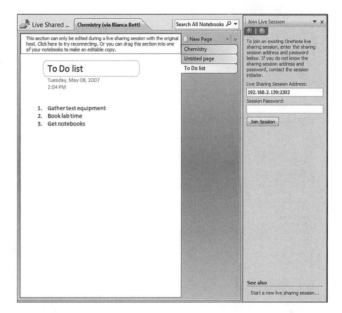

TROUBLESHOOTING

DEALING WITH BROKEN HYPERLINKS

I created a group of linked pages and then moved the pages to new locations. Now some of the links work, but others fail, with OneNote complaining that it can't find the page when I click a link.

Linked pages have some intelligence behind them, but it doesn't extend to different notebooks. If you rename the page or move it to another section within the same notebook, the link will continue to work. However, if you move the page to another notebook, the link breaks instantly. You'll need to edit the link manually to make it work again. Use the Search box to find the page in the new notebook, right-click the page tab, and choose Copy Hyperlink to This Page. Now right-click the broken link, choose Edit Hyperlink, and paste the copied link into the Address box. When you click OK, the link should work again.

EXTRA CREDIT: BACKING UP ONENOTE

Over the course of a year or two, your collection of OneNote notebooks can grow large and incredibly valuable. If you shudder to even think of the possibility of losing all that work, make sure you have an excellent backup plan. OneNote includes a selection of settings to help you.

By default, OneNote automatically backs up all pages in all notebooks, keeping the two most recent copies. These backups are stored in %localappdata%\Microsoft\OneNote\12.0\Backup. If you inadvertently delete a notebook, a section, or a page, you can recover it quickly by opening this folder and opening the backed-up notebook.

You don't have to remember that location, either. To open the Backup folder, choose Tools, Options, click the Save tab, and double-click the Backup Folder entry in the paths list. To change the location where backups are saved (to a shared network folder, for example), click Backup Folder and click Modify.

To set a different backup schedule, open Tools, Options and click Backup. Choose a value from the Automatically Back Up My Notebook at the Following Time Interval list, as shown in Figure 23.15.

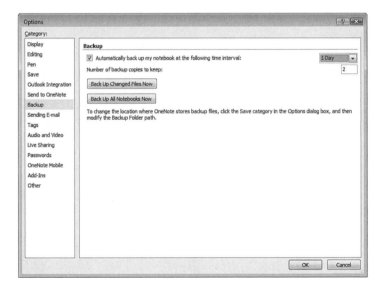

Figure 23.15

The default is one day, but you can choose to perform automatic backups every minute if you want. Pick a schedule that's comfortable for you and choose how many backups you want to save. If you do backups daily and save 5 copies, you'll always have at least a week's worth of backups from which to choose.

PART

VI

ADVANCED TASKS AND FEATURES

CHAPTER **24**

EXTENDING OFFICE WITH TEMPLATES, MACROS, AND ADD-INS

In this chapter

Office 2007 is unquestionably a powerful suite of software. But no software package can be all things to all users. Microsoft designed its Office applications to support extensions you can use to augment a program's features in ways that serve your own specific needs. The principal vehicles for doing this are via macros and add-ins. You can also kick-start the document creation process by using templates created by other people.

Macros, which can be used for anything from automating simple routine tasks to creating elaborate applications, are based on a programming language called Visual Basic for Applications (VBA), which is built in to all Office applications. You don't have to be schooled in the programming arts to use macros, however. As we'll see in this chapter (and as Chapter 26, "Using Macros to Automate Routine Tasks," will explain in further detail), even if you know nothing at all about VBA, you can enhance your productivity in Office by running macros created by others. Or you can let your Office programs create simple macros for you by recording steps that you take and translating them into VBA.

You can think of an *add-in* as a more elaborate sort of macro—a program that runs in the context of one or more Office applications and alters or extends the basic functionality of its host application. These are typically third-party products that you download, license, and install, just as you might a game or some other piece of standalone software. Not all add-ins are extra-cost items, however (and many of those that are can be installed free in time-limited trial versions). Your Office suite includes a handful of Excel add-ins that are available but not installed by default (because the add-ins would be a waste of disk space and memory if you didn't need them). We'll show you how to use those add-ins and look at some of the many third-party add-ins in this chapter.

EXTENDING YOUR OFFICE EXPERTISE WITH THIRD-PARTY TEMPLATES

Sometimes what you need most to get a particular job done is not a tool that extends the capabilities of an Office application (as a macro or add-in might), but simply a well-made model showing how someone else has accomplished the task. To meet that need, you'll want to explore the hundreds of free templates available at Microsoft Office Online. You can get to these in either of the following ways:

- Click the Microsoft Office button in Word, Excel, or PowerPoint. Click New and then select one of the categories under Microsoft Office Online. Then select one of the templates that appears.

- Use your Web browser to go to http://office.microsoft.com/en-us/templates. Choose a category under the heading Browse Templates and then follow the instructions to download a template.

The first method enables you to choose from templates for a specific application—Word, Excel, or PowerPoint. At times, you might not be sure which application is appropriate to use, however, and in those cases it's better to start at Microsoft's website.

The Office Online template library is extensive, having been built up from many sources over a period of many years. You'll find templates designed for all versions of Office from Office 97 onward. (The version of Office for which a template was designed is indicated on the website but is not apparent when you download templates via the New command.) If you want a template to show you how to use the latest Office features—some of the new conditional formatting capabilities in Excel, for example—you need to restrict your search to Office 2007. On the other hand, if you're just looking to accomplish a certain task quickly (creating a nicely styled expense report, for example), the older templates are often as good as the newer ones.

Many of the Office Online templates are quite general in purpose—budgets, expense reports, brochures, diagrams, and so on. Others are startlingly specific (see, for example, the Word template "Complaint to Principal About Teacher" or the Excel template "6 Step Sermon Planning Workbook for Pastors"). In any case, a good browse will be worth your while. The remainder of this section includes a few examples of useful and practical items you might find.

CREATE A BROCHURE IN WORD

Word can generate stylish two-fold and three-fold brochures, but setting up the layout can be time-consuming if you've never done it before. Try starting from a template instead of starting from scratch. The Brochure template shown in Figure 24.1 provides layout, attractive gradients, and instructions. All you have to do is print the template unchanged (so you have instructions to refer to as you work) and then replace the instructional text with your own.

Figure 24.1
To create a preformatted brochure, replace the instructional text with your own words and pictures.

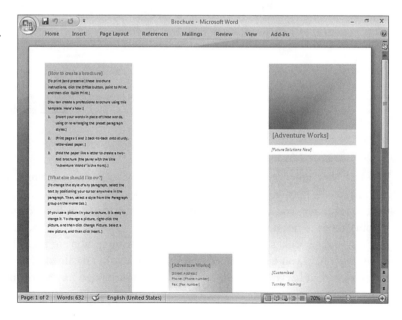

CREATE A FAMILY BUDGET IN EXCEL

The budget template shown in Figure 24.2 exemplifies several of the new data-management features in Excel 2007. The arrow icons at the left edge of column D and in cell G17, for example, are supplied via conditional formatting. If the actual cost for a line item rises above the projected cost, that item's arrow turns south and changes from yellow to red. The formulas in row 4 make effective use of structured referencing. The formula shown in the formula bar in Figure 24.2, for example, adds the Actual Cost item in the Total line of the Housing table to the Actual Cost in the Total line of the Transportation table—and so on. Meanwhile, the filter arrows for the various table headers make it easy for you to sort line items by projected or actual cost (or the difference between projected and actual) or to focus a table on items that meet some criterion—for example, the top five items in terms of actual cost.

Figure 24.2
This budget template makes effective use of structured referencing and conditional formats.

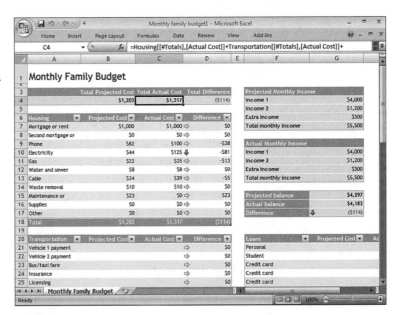

PLAN YOUR WEDDING IN ONENOTE

The OneNote notebook depicted in Figure 24.3 has sections covering many of the organizational details for a moderately elaborate wedding. In the Budget and Coordination section, for example, you can enter estimated and actual expenses for everything from the groom's shoes to lighting and balloons. The Photographer section includes both a scheduling page and a checklist to help you remember what questions to ask. The Guest and Gift List section help you track invitations sent, accepted, and declined; shower and wedding gifts received and acknowledged; accommodations arranged for out-of-town attendees, and so on.

OneNote doesn't have a simple mechanism for connecting to Microsoft Office Online. To download the Wedding Planner notebook (or any of several other planning notebooks), direct your browser to http://office.microsoft.com/en-us/templates/CT101423511033.aspx.

Figure 24.3
You can plan everything from rings to roses in this OneNote template.

EXPANDING OFFICE WITH MACROS

If you're brand new to the Office macro language, VBA, probably the best way to get started is to use the macro recorder in Word, Excel, or PowerPoint (see Chapter 26 for details). Pick any task you do repeatedly—formatting worksheet cells or adjusting column widths in Excel, for example—and let the recorder translate your keystrokes and mouse actions into lines of VBA code. Then take a look at the code in the Visual Basic Editor and see if you can figure out what's going on. (Whether you can or not, you'll have a macro you can reuse any time you need to perform the same tedious task.)

If in recording macros you develop an appetite to learn more, and to learn how to code your own macros (which can be far more versatile than macros you record), you can turn to numerous books on the subject. If you already have intermediate to advanced VBA skills and want to learn more from an accomplished Excel developer, we recommend John Walkenbach's Power Utility Pak (PUP) version 7. PUP (see Figure 24.4) is an extensive set of utilities that expands the native Excel feature set in almost every direction. Its 70 add-in tools and 53 worksheet functions either enable you to do things that Excel itself cannot (such as create perpetual calendars, set reminder alarms, or search for text within comments) or simplify tasks that are awkward to accomplish in Excel (such as formatting superscripts and subscripts).

Figure 24.4
Power Utility Pak (PUP) version 7 uses VBA to add 70 new tools and 53 new worksheet functions to Excel.

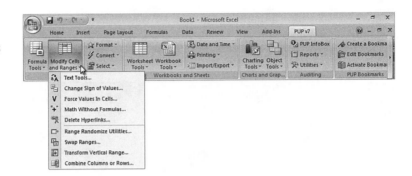

As a Swiss Army knife for Excel users, PUP is worth its $40 price tag (a 30-day free trial is available). By studying the VBA source code (available for an additional $20), you can learn advanced programming techniques by example, or customize the utilities to suit your own needs. For more information, see http://j-walk.com/ss/pup/pup7/.

INSTALLING AND RUNNING ADD-INS

Add-ins come in many shapes and forms. Some are based on Microsoft's Component Object Model (COM) and implemented as executable (.EXE) files, even though they have no stand-alone function. (Typically an add-in of this kind launches its host Office application and installs itself when you run the executable.) Others are written in VBA, Microsoft's macro language, and might need to be opened by some action you take within the host application. Usually, if you purchase a third-party add-in or download a trial version, the publisher provides instructions about how to activate it, and you won't have to do anything further.

Add-ins typically make their functionality accessible by modifying the Ribbon in some way. Some simply add a tab called Add-ins. For example, the screen-capture utility SnagIt (the program used to capture screens for this book) is essentially a standalone program. But it also includes add-in modules for Excel, Word, and PowerPoint. You can use these add-ins to capture an image (a window or a screen region, for example) and paste it into the current Office document, in a single step. In the context of these Office applications, SnagIt sets up an Add-ins tab with a single custom toolbar (see Figure 24.5). (For more information about SnagIt, see http://www.techsmith.com/snagit.asp.)

Figure 24.5
As an add-in for Word, PowerPoint, or Excel, the screen-capture utility SnagIt adds an Add-in tab, with a single custom toolbar, to the Ribbon.

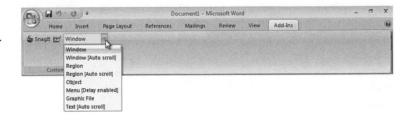

The Add-ins tab's Custom Toolbars group can accommodate multiple add-ins. Figure 24.6, for example, shows Word with two add-ins attached to this part of the user interface—the aforementioned SnagIt and the bibliographic utility EndNote. (EndNoteX supports Word 2007 and is an invaluable tool for managing research citations and bibliographies. For information, see http://www.endnote.com/. If you run Office 2007 in Windows Vista, be sure to read the compatibility notes at http://www.endnote.com/enword2k7.asp.)

Figure 24.6
The Custom Toolbars group in Word appears when you install compatible third-party programs like the two shown here.

Other add-ins amend the Ribbon in more elaborate ways by adding their own tabs and groups. Figure 24.4, for example, shows the custom tab created by PUP7. Figure 24.7 shows the user interface of Palisade's @Risk, an add-in that performs Monte Carlo simulations and risk analysis in Excel. (For information about @Risk, see http://www.palisade.com/risk/. For information about a comparable risk-analysis add-in, Decisioneering's Crystal Ball, visit http://www.crystalball.com/.)

Figure 24.7
Add-ins like this one can create new tabs on the Ribbon dedicated exclusively to their features.

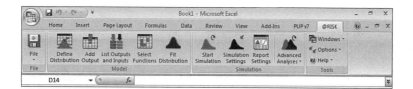

USING ADD-INS TO CREATE YOUR OWN RIBBON CUSTOMIZATIONS

If an add-in can modify the Ribbon for its own purposes, why not an add-in that simply enables you to tailor the Ribbon yourself? Although the native Office 2007 user interface does not provide you with a way to modify the Ribbon (a shortcoming that early adopters of Office 2007, who were used to customizing menu bars and toolbars in Office 2003, were quick to point out), add-ins for this purpose are available.

RECREATING THE OFFICE 2003 USER INTERFACE

Do you miss the old menus and toolbars? Or are you simply ambivalent about the new Ribbon-based interface? Microsoft decided not to include a "classic mode" option in Office 2007, but you can install one yourself, with the help of Classic Menu for Office 2007.

Classic Menu doesn't replace the Ribbon; it simply adds a Menus tab and some familiar-looking toolbars (see Figure 24.8). The Menus tab essentially recreates the old menu system (with modifications necessary to accommodate changes in the new Office applications' feature sets). You can install it for Word, Excel, and PowerPoint, or only for a certain one of those applications. If you really hate the Ribbon, you can minimize it and rely exclusively on the Menus tab. Or you can simply use the Menus tab as a useful fallback for those times when you just can't find what you're looking for in the new interface. A free trial of Classic Menu for Office 2007 is available at http://www.addintools.com/english/menuoffice/.

Figure 24.8
With Classic Menu for Office 2007, you can add the Office 2003 menus and toolbars to the Office 2007 Ribbon.

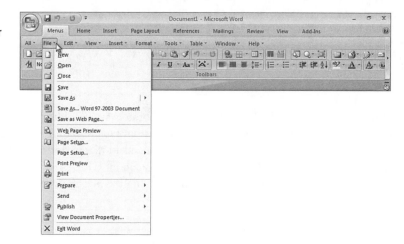

Reorganizing the Ribbon

Microsoft not only declined to include a classic user interface option in Office 2007; it also decided not to give you any convenient way to rearrange the Ribbon. So if you like the Ribbon but want it arrayed differently, you need to turn to a third-party tool. Patrick Schmid's RibbonCustomizer fits the bill.

RibbonCustomizer, shown in Figure 24.9 in the context of PowerPoint (it also works in Word and Excel), lets you add new tabs or remove existing ones, populate new tabs with whatever groups you want to use, create your own groups with any commands you want, and change the order in which tabs and groups appear. You can even toggle between the default Ribbon and your own customized version. No programming is required. The add-in comes with a feature tour, and demos are available at http://pschmid.net/office2007/ribboncustomizer. You can download a 30-day trial at that site, or simply use a free "starter" version for as long as you like.

Figure 24.9
RibbonCustomizer addresses a major shortcoming of the Office 2007 Ribbon interface, allowing you to rearrange the Ribbon to suit your needs and preferences.

USING THE ADD-INS THAT COME WITH EXCEL 2007

As we mentioned near the beginning of this chapter, Excel 2007 comes with a handful of add-ins that, because they are relatively specialized, are not installed by default. It's possible that you'll find one or two of these useful. To see what's available and to install selected add-ins, follow these steps:

1. Click the Microsoft Office button.
2. Click Excel Options.
3. In the left pane of the Excel Options dialog box, click Add-ins.
4. In the Manage drop-down menu (at the bottom of the dialog box), select Excel Add-ins.
5. Click Go.

The available add-ins appear as a set of items with check boxes (see Figure 24.10). Select any add-ins you want to install and click OK. Depending on whether the selected items have ever been installed on your computer, you might need to confirm the installation and wait while the Office setup routine does its thing.

NOTE

Figure 24.10 presents the list of add-ins supplied by Microsoft. If you (or someone else) has made VBA-based add-ins available, you might see additional items on the list.

Figure 24.10
Microsoft ships these add-ins with Excel 2007, but does not install them by default.

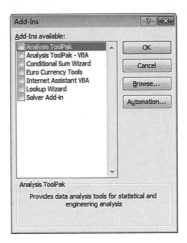

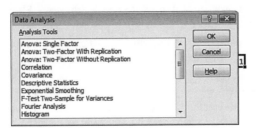

24

Two of the seven Microsoft add-ins provide additional functions for use in VBA code. The remaining five are of potential use to non-programming Excel users.

DOING STATISTICS WITH THE ANALYSIS TOOLPAK

If you're a veteran of earlier Excel versions, you might have already installed the Analysis Toolpak to make its 80+ analytical functions available to your worksheet formulas. These functions, ranging from the simple but useful (RANDBETWEEN, for example, which takes some of the grunt work out of generating random integers in a specified numeric range) to the highly specialized (the set of functions that deal with bond values, for example), are no longer tucked away in the add-in. They're now a core part of Excel.

The rest of the Analysis Toolpak consists of a set of statistical utilities (see Figure 24.11). These should not be considered the equivalent of a dedicated statistics package, but they might very well help you get through a basic statistics class. To use the utilities, install the add-in, and then click Data Analysis, in the Analysis group of the Data tab. Select a utility, click OK, and then supply the necessary parameters in the ensuing dialog box. Figure 24.12 shows a sample of the output from the Descriptive Statistics utility.

Figure 24.11
The Analysis Toolpak allows you to choose from a selection of standard data analysis tools.

Figure 24.12
The Descriptive Statistics utility generates a table of statistical measures from a specified input range.

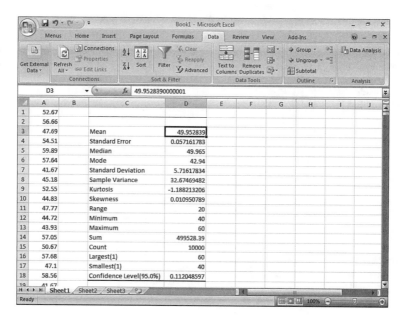

USING WIZARDS TO SIMPLIFY LOOKUPS AND CONDITIONAL SUMS

The Conditional Sum Wizard and Lookup Wizard add-ins don't accomplish anything that you couldn't do with worksheet formulas, but they can save you the trouble of looking up function syntax. Assume, for example, that in Figure 24.13 you want to total the values in column B by the divisions listed in column A. You could do this with the SUMIF function, the DSUM function, or an array formula based on the SUM and IF functions. Or you could put the Conditional Sum Wizard to work. As all good wizards do, this one presents a series of dialog boxes that ask what values you want to total, for what condition you're testing, and where you want to place the result. At the end of the interview, you get an array formula, as shown in Figure 24.14.

The Lookup Wizard performs a similar kind of service, relieving you of the need to understand the VLOOKUP, HLOOKUP, and MATCH functions. If you need to pluck values from lookup tables—for example, to find the tax due for a given income level and filing status by searching through an IRS table—the Lookup Wizard can do the job.

After they are installed, the Conditional Sum Wizard and Lookup Wizard are both accessible in the Solutions group of the Formulas tab.

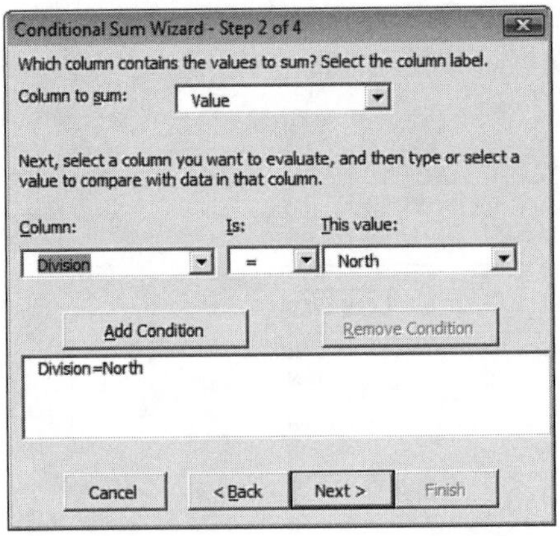

Figure 24.13
Use the Conditional Sum Wizard to make short work of complex formulas that would be mind-numbingly difficult to create manually.

	A	B	C	D	E	F
1	Division	Value				
2	North	8				
3	West	10		North	198	
4	North	14		South		
5	North	30		East		
6	South	16		West		
7	North	48				
8	North	65				
9	West	48				
10	East	100				
11	West	3				
12	West	34				
13	East	55				
14	South	38				
15	South	67				
16	West	56				
17	North	33				
18	East	74				
19	South	87				
20	West	5				
21	West	26				
22						
23						

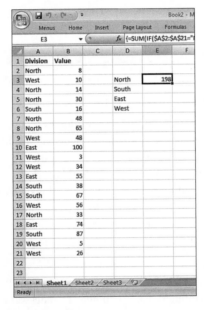

Figure 24.14
The Conditional Sum Wizard generated the array formula in E3.

Converting Currencies with the Euro Currency Tools

The Euro Currency Tools add-in, which, when installed, appears as a command in the Solutions group of the Formulas tab, performs conversions between the European Currency

Unit (Euro) and the currencies of individual European Union countries that have adopted the Euro. If you need to know how many Austrian Schillings a particular number of Euros represents, for example, this add-in does the job.

TIP

> To perform conversions between U.S. dollars and various currencies around the world (including the Euro), don't turn to the Euro Currency Wizard. Instead, download Microsoft's Currency Rate Calculator template. This template, which sets up a Web query to Microsoft's MSN MoneyCentral site, is deeply buried in the New Workbook dialog box. Click the Microsoft Office button and choose New. At the bottom of the Templates pane on the left side of the new Workbook dialog box, choose More Categories. When the More Categories list appears, click Calculators. Then browse through the gallery of calculator templates and double-click Currency Rate Calculator.

In addition to installing a couple of interactive commands, the Euro Currency Tools add-in adds a EUROCONVERT worksheet function to Excel. (To find it, click the Formulas tab, click Insert Function, select All from the category list, and scroll through the alphabetical list until you reach the newly added function.)

SOLVING OPTIMIZATION PROBLEMS WITH THE SOLVER ADD-IN

The most ambitious of the Microsoft-supplied add-ins for Excel, Solver is a program that solves linear and nonlinear optimization problems. Such problems seek to find a maximum or minimum value of a cell (for example, to maximize profit or minimize cost), given variable inputs and one or more constraints.

Figure 24.15, for example, illustrates a linear programming problem of the sort you might encounter in a basic algebra class. A farmer has 180 acres to divide between two crops, alfalfa and soy beans. The crops yield different amounts of revenue per acre and incur different costs for seed and labor. The farmer wants to maximize his income, given the constraints that total seed expenditure must not exceed $1,200 and total labor expenditure must not exceed $4,000.

After installing Solver, you could tackle this problem by clicking the Solver button, in the Analysis group of the Data tab, and filling out the Solver Parameters dialog box as shown in Figure 24.16. Note that the dialog box specifies the cell whose value you want to optimize (called the target cell), the fact that you want to optimize it by maximizing it (in a different kind of problem, you might be seeking to minimize some target cell), the cells that you can adjust to achieve your solution, and the constraints that must be met.

Figure 24.15
Solver makes quick work of a linear optimization problem like this one.

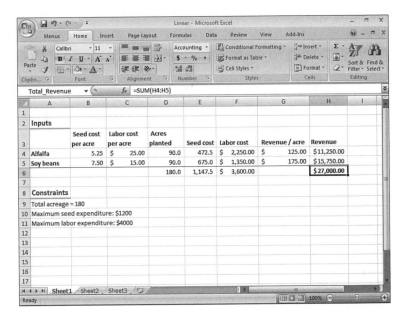

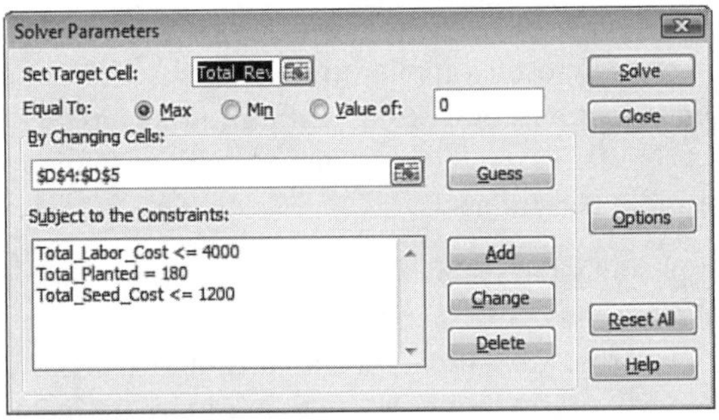

Figure 24.16
Setting up Solver parameters entails specifying a target cell (and whether to maximize or minimize it), the cells whose values can be changed, and the constraints that must be met.

Clicking Solve in Figure 24.16 generates the solution shown in Figure 24.17. Note that the Solver Results dialog box lets you revert to your original values or keep the ones that Solver found.

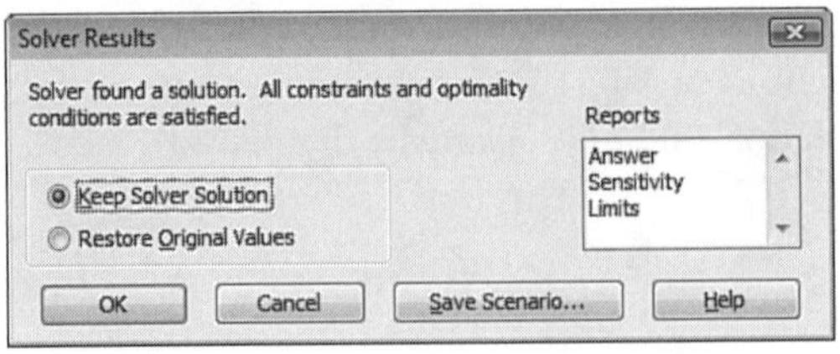

Figure 24.17
If Solver finds a solution, you can keep its results or restore the ones with which you started.

Solver is capable of dealing with much more complex problems than this, of course, including problems in which the relationship between the target cell and one or more inputs is nonlinear.

MANAGING SECURITY FOR ADD-INS, MACROS, AND OTHER EXTERNAL CONTENT

Add-ins, macros, ActiveX controls, and other forms of active external content have the potential to make your Office applications far more useful than they were in their out-of-the-box state. But as you might have noticed, they also have the potential to trigger security warnings. If you've ever encountered a message bar comparable to the one shown in Figure 24.18, you know what we mean.

Figure 24.18
Ever alert, Office 2007 wards off all potential security threats by default.

Security warnings like the one in Figure 24.18 often appear below the Ribbon whenever you open or download a file that the host application perceives as a potential threat—which essentially means anything that contains executable code. Macros embody code, so Office disables them (by default). When opening a file or downloading something from the Internet triggers a security warning, you can click the adjacent Options button to bypass the security measures for the current item. You might then see a dialog box similar to the one shown in Figure 24.19.

Figure 24.19
Clicking the Options button on a security warning message bar gives you the opportunity to enable the current content.

There's nothing wrong with tranquilizing the watchdogs on a case-by-case basis by selecting Enable This Content in dialog boxes like the one shown in Figure 24.19. But you can save yourself time and frustration by training the dogs to bark only when you want them to. The next section shows you how.

NOTE

If you never see a message bar like the one shown in Figure 24.18, but macros, add-ins, or ActiveX controls fail to run, it's possible that the message bars themselves have been turned off. Click the Microsoft Office button in Word, Excel, or PowerPoint and then click Word Options, Excel Options, or PowerPoint Options. In the left pane of the Options dialog box, select Trust Center. Then click Trust Center Settings. In the left pane of the Trust Center, click Message Bar. Be sure the Show the Message Bar in All Applications When Content Has Been Blocked option is selected.

TIP

When a security warning appears in a message bar, you don't have to make an immediate decision about whether to allow the blocked content. You can begin working with the document in question and decide later. The message bar is a docked, modeless dialog box—one that remains on screen until you send it away. (You can do that by clicking Options or the Cancel button at the right side of the bar.) This represents a design improvement over the security dialog boxes in earlier versions, which, because they were modal, were often thoughtlessly dismissed.

SETTING SECURITY OPTIONS IN THE TRUST CENTER

The Trust Center provides a central location for security settings in Office applications. With seven categories—Trusted Publishers, Trusted Locations, Add-ins, ActiveX Settings, Macro Settings, Message Bar, and Privacy Options—the Trust Center provides a much more granular approach to security settings than the High-Medium-Low mechanism used by previous Office iterations. (In Excel, an additional Trust Center category is called External Content.) You can make your system hyper-alert for potentially harmful ActiveX controls, for example, while giving macros *carte blanche*.

To get to the Trust Center, click the Microsoft Office button and then click Word Options, Excel Options, or PowerPoint options (depending on which program you're using). In the left pane of the Options dialog box, click Trust Center, and then click the Trust Center Settings dialog box.

TIP

If you think that opening the Trust Center requires an impressive number of mouse clicks, you're not alone. Fortunately, there's often a quicker way. If you're presented with a Security Options dialog box, such as the one shown in Figure 24.19, look for a link labeled Open the Trust Center, in the lower-left corner of the dialog box. This takes you there directly; no need to pass Go.

Be aware that some of the options you configure in the Trust Center (macro settings, for example) apply only to the current application, not to the whole suite. Others, such as Trusted Publishers, are global. We will point out which is which.

USING THE TRUSTED PUBLISHERS LIST

A *trustworthy publisher* is a supplier of content whose goods have a valid, current (not expired) digital signature backed by a reputable certification authority. (A *digital signature* is a cryptographic means of ensuring the authenticity of something, such as an email message, contract, or software component. The presence of a valid digital signature provides assurance that the item in question comes from whom it purports to come from and has not been altered on route to you.) If you configure either add-in security or macro security to require digital signatures, you might see a dialog box similar to one of the boxes shown in Figure 24.20 when you attempt to run or install an active item.

Figure 24.20
If you have configured Office to look for valid digital signatures, you can use links or options in these dialog boxes to white-list particular publishers.

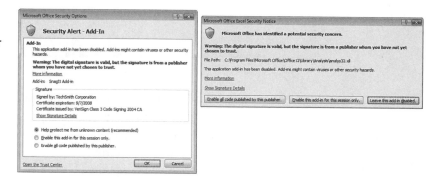

If you see a dialog box like either of these, look for an option or a button labeled Enable All Code Published by This Publisher. By selecting the option (or clicking the button), you can elevate the publisher in question from trustworthy status to trusted status, and Office will give the green flag to all subsequent downloads or installs. You can inspect the list of trusted publishers in the Trust Center (see Figure 24.21).

Note that there is no way to add a vendor to the Trusted Publishers list from within the Trust Center. Instead, you populate the list on a vendor-by-vendor basis when an Office application presents a dialog box of the form shown in Figure 24.20. What you can do in the Trust Center is view a publisher's certificate and, if necessary, remove vendors from the list.

NOTE

A single Trusted Publishers list is maintained by all Office applications, and this list is also shared with Internet Explorer. It's possible that you will see entries in the Trust Center that arrived by way of an Internet Explorer dialog box, as opposed to an Office dialog box. If you upgraded an earlier version of Office to Office 2007, you might also see a Prior Trusted Sources list enumerating publishers that you trusted in that earlier version.

Figure 24.21
Vendors in the Trusted Publishers list are assumed to be benign.

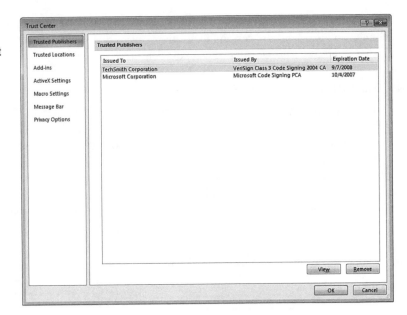

BYPASSING SECURITY MEASURES BY STORING DOCUMENTS IN TRUSTED LOCATIONS

One of the most convenient features of the Office 2007 security apparatus is the Trusted Locations list. Any document you load from a trusted location is waved through security, regardless of whether it includes macros, ActiveX controls, links to external data sources, or links to external Excel workbooks. There is one exception. (There always is.) An ActiveX control that has a "kill bit" set in the registry is terminated on sight, even if it dwells within a document stored in a trusted location. This drastic treatment is accorded only to ActiveX controls that are known (by Microsoft) to be malevolent.

The Trusted Locations list is intended to serve as an inducement not to turn off the standard security measures. If you're frustrated by message bars and security warnings for documents that you know are benign, resist the temptation to blow away the whole security service. Instead, simply move the documents in question to a trusted location. Or add their current folder to the Trusted Locations list.

Word, Excel, and PowerPoint each maintain its own Trusted Locations list, and each application provides certain trusted folders by default—such as the folders for templates and startup documents. Figure 24.22 shows the default list for Excel. You can add locations or remove or edit existing ones by means of the three buttons below the list.

Figure 24.22
Documents opened from a trusted location are assumed to present no security threat.

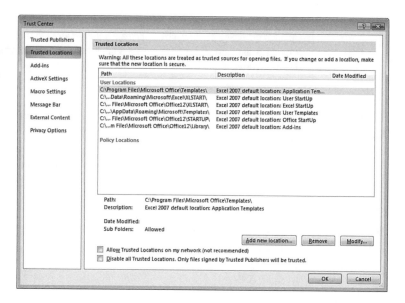

NOTE

The Policy Locations section of the Trusted Locations list holds locations established by a system administrator. Unless you work in an environment managed by an IT staff, this area will presumably be empty.

When you add a trusted location (see Figure 24.23), the dialog box that appears gives you the opportunity to add a description of the location—a few words about the folder's purpose and the kinds of documents you plan to store there, for example. The check box in the middle of the dialog box gives you the option of extending trust to subfolders of the specified folder. To see whether an item in the current list includes subfolders, highlight it and read the text beside the words *Sub Folders*, near the bottom of the dialog box (see Figure 24.22).

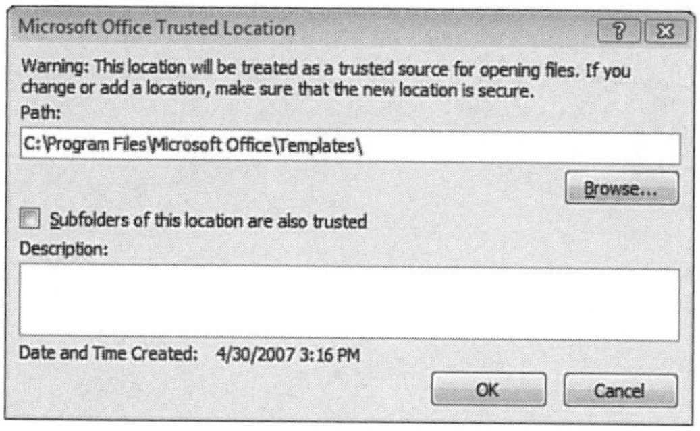

Figure 24.23
When you add a trusted location, you can write a short description of its purpose; you can also extend trust to the location's subfolders.

TIP

> Although the dialog box in which you create a trusted location is titled Microsoft Office Trusted Location, the location you create is application-specific. To make a folder available as a trusted location to all of your Office applications, repeat the process in each.

Although you can easily make your entire document store a trusted location, by adding the Documents folder (or My Documents, if you're running Windows XP) to the list and enabling its subfolders, doing so is nearly tantamount to turning off security altogether. If you are the least bit concerned about protecting yourself from malicious active content, you should adhere to the following guidelines:

- Trust specific folders, not vast trees of folders and subfolders.
- Do not trust folders to which other users have write access.
- Do not trust folders on network servers (doing so is disallowed by default). If you must, select the Allow Trusted Locations on My Network (Not Recommended) check box.

CAUTION

> Do not add any folder to your list of trusted locations that can be used for temporary storage of email attachments. Do not, for example, trust the folder pointed to by the system variable %LocalAppData%\Temp.

CONFIGURING ADD-IN SECURITY

Add-ins, accessory programs that augment the built-in functionality of one or more Office applications, are, by default, allowed to run without notification or warning. (They are, in fact, the only form of external code that Office doesn't ward off in some manner by default.) Because add-ins can conceivably be designed to do harm, you have the option of applying more restrictive settings. The Add-ins section of the Trust Center presents three check boxes (see Figure 24.24).

Figure 24.24
Add-ins are permitted to run by default, but you can use these check boxes to raise the security bar.

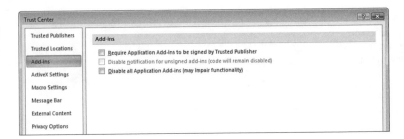

NOTE

Add-in security settings apply only to the current application. Thus, for example, if you want to allow add-ins in Word and Excel but disallow them completely in PowerPoint, you can leave the default settings for Excel and Word in place, open the Trust Center in PowerPoint, and select Disable All Application Add-ins. Your setting in PowerPoint does not override your settings in Word and Excel.

If you're really concerned that someone might install a malicious add-in on your system, you can select the Disable All Application Add-ins check box. A more moderate approach, however, and one that would likely be as effective, would be to select the Require Application Add-ins to Be Signed by Trusted Publisher check box. Having done that, you can use the Trusted Publishers list to separate the add-ins you trust from those you do not.

With the Require Application Add-ins to Be Signed by Trusted Publisher check box selected, the option to disable unsigned add-ins without notification becomes available (that's the second check box, the one grayed out in Figure 24.24). Selecting both of those check boxes will ensure that only signed add-ins from trusted publishers will be allowed to run. Add-ins lacking a digital signature will be rejected without notification to you.

CONFIGURING ACTIVEX SECURITY

An ActiveX control is a snippet of code that uses the Component Object Model (COM) to perform some presumably useful task, such as adding a toolbar, input control, or small application to the program that hosts it. ActiveX controls have a greater potential for causing mayhem than the other forms of active content discussed in this chapter, because they have access to such things as your file system and registry. On the other hand, precisely because they are powerful and responsive, and because many websites rely on them, it would be difficult to live entirely without them.

Figure 24.25 shows the default security settings and available options for ActiveX controls. Note that these settings are global; that is, changes made in one Office application apply to the others as well.

Figure 24.25
These default ActiveX security settings make for a reasonable tradeoff between functionality and safety.

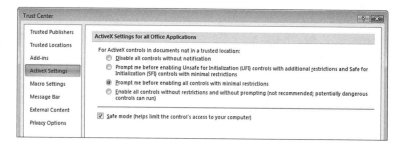

The first and fourth option buttons for ActiveX security are probably self-explanatory. The first disables all controls, no questions asked, no prompts presented. Choose this if you're completely averse to risk. The fourth enables all controls, no prompts, no message bars. This one is for thrill-seekers only; Microsoft doesn't recommend it, and neither do we.

The remaining two options are more opaque than anything else in the Trust Center. The differences between the two options are minimal. With either setting, if an ActiveX control arrives in the context of a document that also includes a VBA project (that is, one or more macros written in Visual Basic for Applications), the control is blocked and you are presented with a message bar. If you use the message bar to enable the control, the control functions—but only in the current document and the current session.

> **TIP**
>
> If you're bothered by security warnings when you use a document that has a known-to-be-trustworthy ActiveX control, move that document to one of the folders listed in your Trusted Locations. The only scrutiny Office gives to ActiveX controls that come from trusted locations is to look for the kill bit. Otherwise, the control is assumed to be benign.

With both the second and the third options, if you open a document containing ActiveX controls, and all of those controls have been marked by their developers as Safe for Initialization (SFI), the controls run, and you are not prompted for approval. If you open a document containing one or more ActiveX controls that have not been signed as Safe for Initialization, you are presented with a message bar. With either option, if you use the message bar to approve the control, it runs, but the second option imposes more restrictions on the control than does the third.

CONFIGURING MACRO SECURITY

The four macro-security options, shown in Figure 24.26, are "per-application" settings. If you never use macros in Word or PowerPoint, for example, but use them all the time in Excel, you can apply a more restrictive setting in the two programs where you don't need them.

Figure 24.26
The settings for macro security are application-specific.

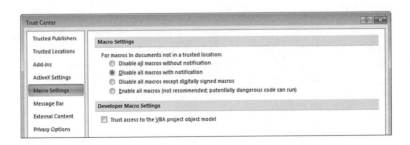

If you write or record your own macros, you might be tempted, despite Microsoft's disapproval, to select the fourth option in this dialog box, Enable All Macros. That's because the default setting, Disable All Macros with Notification, will block your own work along with any other macros that come along. (You can enable the blocked content by going through a Security Options dialog box similar to Figure 24.19, but those extra mouse clicks will get to be a major annoyance before long.) But, as we have said before, it's more prudent to keep some level of security in place but move your macro-laden files to a trusted location.

If you don't write your own macros and want nothing to do with macros written by anyone else, you can select the first option, Disable All Macros Without Notification. Be aware, though, that this option really precludes a potential source of pleasure and productivity enhancement. You don't have to be a programmer to make effective use of macros; you can use your programs' macro-recording features to simplify tedious, repetitive tasks, without having to learn a line of VBA code.

→ For more details about creating and editing macros, **see** Chapter 26, "Using Macros to Automate Routine Tasks." **p. 721.**

If you opt for the middle ground, note that the third option is slightly more permissive than the second. The second option, Disable All Macros with Notification, blocks macros even if they come with a valid digital signature from a trusted publisher. The third option gives free passage to digitally signed macros, provided you have added their developers to your Trusted Publishers list.

SETTING SECURITY OPTIONS FOR EXTERNAL CONTENT IN EXCEL

In Excel only, the Trust Center includes an additional category called External Connections. This category is concerned with two types of hazards: connections to external data (such as queries to or PivotTables based on a corporate database) and formulas that link cells in one workbook to cells in another. In both cases, the default settings (see Figure 24.27) prompt for approval. You can disable either form of external content altogether, but you'll be turning off extremely useful Excel functionality if you do so. You can also turn off the security dogs for either content type and live with the risks—as you have always done in the past if you've used earlier versions of Excel. Our own take on this one is that the risks are minimal and don't merit the hassle of warning prompts.

Figure 24.27
Excel, by default, prompts for approval when you connect to external data or link one workbook to another.

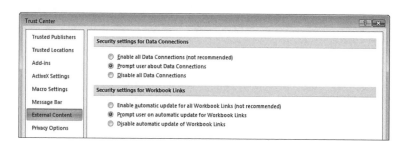

CHAPTER 25

USING OFFICE ON A TABLET PC

In this chapter

OFFICE 2007 AND THE TABLET PC

On most desktop and notebook computers, you enter text with a keyboard and manipulate onscreen objects with a mouse. But those traditional input devices take a backseat when you use a Tablet PC with a compatible version of Windows and Office 2007.

In design, a Tablet PC is a notebook computer with a few hardware twists. When you use a Tablet PC, you typically hold it so the screen appears in portrait orientation rather than the landscape mode you're used to on conventional hardware. Instead of using a keyboard and mouse, you control Windows and Office using a pen-shaped stylus—oh, let's just call it a pen—that takes the place of a mouse and allows you to select and manipulate text and objects, make menu selections, and click buttons by tapping the touch-sensitive screen. The pen also serves as a way to draw lines, sketch diagrams, and tap out text using an onscreen keyboard. Most importantly, you can use the pen to scribble your own notes, just as if you were jotting them down on a piece of paper. In all these cases, your data appears on the screen as *ink*, a special type of data we'll discuss in much more detail shortly.

You can't turn just any old notebook into a Tablet PC; the screen has to be capable of accepting digitized input from the pen. Along with the input hardware, you need an operating system that supports these alternative input methods. Tablet PCs built before early 2007 came with Windows XP Tablet PC Edition, a customized version of Windows XP Professional sold only with Tablet PC hardware. Tablet PCs sold after the beginning of 2007 with Windows Vista preinstalled already support Tablet PC features. In broad terms, the Tablet-centric features available in Office 2007 are similar in Windows XP Tablet PC Edition and Windows Vista, although Vista is much more polished, accurate, and usable. In this chapter, we assume you're running Office 2007 on Windows Vista Home Premium, Business, or Ultimate edition, all of which support Tablet features.

NOTE

> Do you have an older Tablet PC? If it's running Windows XP Tablet PC Edition, make sure you install Windows XP Service Pack 2, which includes a significant upgrade to all Tablet-specific features. Better yet, consider upgrading that older Tablet PC to Windows Vista. For an online evaluation of your hardware and to determine whether it's suitable for the upgrade, see Microsoft's website or check with your PC's manufacturer.

Office 2007 recognizes when it has been installed on a computer running a Tablet-compatible version of Windows and automatically enables features that take advantage of the hardware.

Most Tablet PCs are convertible models, where you can choose between Tablet mode and conventional mode, with a keyboard and pointing device. When creating Word documents, Excel workbooks, and PowerPoint presentations, you'll probably use the PC in that mode most often, to quickly enter text and numbers using the keyboard and perform basic formatting and organization tasks. Tablet mode is more comfortable and effective when you're reading and reviewing documents that have already been created. The pen makes it easier to mark up the page with circles, underlines, and handwritten comments or changes. (If you're a teacher and your students create their assignments in Word format, you can strike fear into your students' hearts by grading their papers with a virtual red felt pen.)

What if you want to use the pen to jot down notes of phone conversations, meeting minutes, shopping lists, and other sorts of random, free-form text? Don't even think about pressing Word into service for an occasional handwritten document of this sort—it's ill-suited to this task on a day-to-day basis. Word's drawing layer greatly limits your ability to enter and edit text, and you're still faced with the dilemma of how to save, organize, and search multiple documents containing ink-based text that isn't typically included in Windows searches.

Use OneNote instead. Although you can use OneNote on a desktop PC and type notes onto pages, it's especially effective on a Tablet PC, thanks to its capability to store ink and its versatile selection of pens and other writing and drawing tools. You don't need to convert your notes into text; OneNote automatically recognizes ink-based content and adds it to its searchable index, making it possible for you to quickly locate handwritten words and phrases anywhere within a notebook. And it's easy to send Word documents to OneNote and OneNote pages back to Word.

A Tablet PC isn't for everyone, but if you're attracted to the idea of taking handwritten notes and adding annotations to documents, you should take a close look at a Tablet PC running Office. And if you like OneNote, we predict you'll love it on a Tablet PC, where you can freely mash up just about any type of data with hand-drawn annotations and sketches.

USING THE PEN AS A POINTING DEVICE

In Word, Excel, and PowerPoint, the Tablet pen normally acts as a pointer, which you can use to point and click or—with the help of the onscreen keyboard—to enter text.

In this, its most basic mode, the pen functions as a substitute for the mouse. As you move the pen tip just above the screen, the pointer moves along the same path. Instead of clicking, you tap the pressure-sensitive pen tip using any of the following techniques:

- Tap once—This has the same effect as clicking the left mouse button to select an object.
- Tap twice in quick succession—This works the same as double-clicking the left mouse button.
- Press and hold—This displays shortcut menus and other actions normally triggered by clicking the right mouse button.
- Press, hold, and drag—This is equivalent to holding down the left mouse button; drag the pen tip to select a group of objects or block of text, lifting it off the screen at the end of the selection.

25

On a Tablet PC running Windows Vista, you have an additional option called Pen Flicks. These are mouse gestures that allow you to perform common navigation or editing tasks by flicking the pen tip in any of eight directions. Using the default settings, for example, flicking the pen tip up and to the right (NE on the compass) copies the current selection to the Clipboard. A flick toward the upper left deletes the current selection. You can change actions assigned to each of the eight Pen Flicks actions: Open the Customize Flicks dialog box (Control Panel, Pen and Input Devices, Flicks tab), choose (add) from the top of the menu for the direction you want to change, and then type a name and a key combination to assign to that pen flick. In Figure 25.1, for instance, we've assigned the Add Hyperlink (Ctrl+K) shortcut to the leftward flick (due west on the compass). Now, in any Office document, we can call up the Add Hyperlink dialog box with alacrity.

Figure 25.1
Remember that pen flicks are used in all Windows programs, not just in Office, so customize carefully.

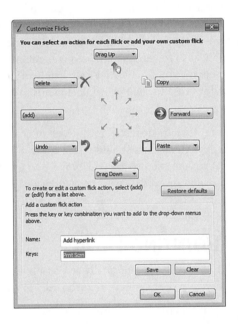

Using the Ribbon in Word, Excel, or PowerPoint is particularly easy on a Tablet PC. Tap any heading to display the choices on that tab, and then tap commands, menus, or gallery items just as if you were pointing and clicking with a mouse. For basic reading and formatting, where no text entry is required, this option is extremely effective. You can also use the pen to create SmartArt graphics and drag the pieces around, using the onscreen keyboard to add small amounts of text.

ALL ABOUT INK

When you use the Tablet PC's pen to draw, sketch, or write in an Office document editing window, the data you create is called *ink*. In Office, ink is a full-fledged object type with its own properties and behaviors, just like AutoShapes and pictures.

In OneNote, ink can be used almost anywhere in the program, alongside text, graphics, screen clippings, hyperlinks, and even synchronized with recorded voice or video recordings. In Word, Excel, and PowerPoint, ink sits in the drawing layer, and you can use the Format Ink dialog box and options on the Ink Tools tab (see Figure 25.2) to change the color and width of the ink. (The Ink Tools tab is visible only when you select an existing ink object or click Start Inking on the Review tab.) You can select an ink annotation, copy it to the Clipboard, and then paste it into another Office program—or into any application that supports ink.

Figure 25.2
These Ink Tools are visible only when you're working with ink.

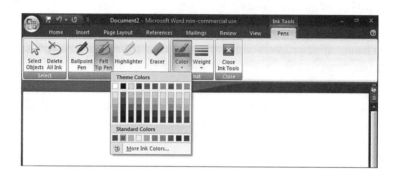

→ For more details on how to work with items on the drawing layer, **see** "Working with the Drawing Layer," **p. 109.**

25

What makes ink different from the kind of scribbling you might do with the Windows Paint program? One huge difference is handwriting recognition. Although ink sits in the drawing layer, it actually contains some attributes normally associated with text. You can use the surprisingly accurate handwriting recognition capabilities in any Tablet-compatible Windows version to convert your scribbled notes into text, which can then be pasted into a document.

When you write something that Windows recognizes as text, it stores the recognized text in the background, without changing the ink version displayed on the screen. This stored text is searchable, which means you can find notes fast in OneNote even if you wrote them by hand. In the three Ribbon-based programs, you can convert the recognized ink to its text equivalent by selecting the inked text, right-clicking (press the pen tip and hold it down briefly), and choosing Copy as Text from the shortcut menu, at which point you can paste the copied text into the text portion of the document. (You have to manually delete the ink from the drawing layer.) With OneNote, you can select inked text, right-click, choose Convert Handwriting to Text from the shortcut menu, and complete the transformation in one step.

TIP

You need a Tablet PC to create ink in an Office document. (The one exception is in Slide Show view in PowerPoint, where you can create ink annotations using any computer.) However, you don't need any special hardware to work with ink that has been saved in a document. The ink is treated as an object, the same as a drawing object. If Windows XP Tablet PC Edition or a Tablet-aware version of Windows Vista is running, you can work with the ink as ink; on all other Windows versions, the ink behaves as if it were a drawing.

ADDING INK TO AN OFFICE DOCUMENT

To begin adding ink in Word, Excel, or PowerPoint, click the Start Inking button on the Review tab. This action reveals the Ink Tools add-in with the Pens tab shown earlier in Figure 25.2. When you ink using these tools, your scribbles appear as annotations over or under typed text and graphics—essentially, freeform objects in the drawing layer. When you press the pen tip against the screen and begin drawing, that marks the beginning of a new stroke, which ends when you lift the pen off the screen. A drawing typically contains many strokes, and so can text: depending on your penmanship, a word or even a single letter might be made up of multiple strokes.

You can mark up a Word document, an Excel worksheet, or a PowerPoint slide using your own handwriting or freehand illustration. While delivering a PowerPoint presentation, you can take notes directly on the slides and then save the results.

In Word, but not in PowerPoint or Excel, you can add handwritten comments to a document in addition to adding annotations directly on the document. Click the Ink Comment command on the Review tab to open the Comment pane. These notes appear in comment balloons and can be tracked on a per-user basis. Figure 25.3 shows a marked-up Word document that contains an ink comment.

Figure 25.3
Ink comments use the same format as typed comments in Word's Review pane.

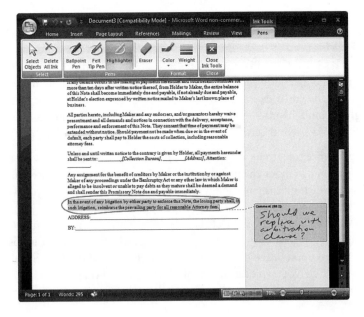

CHANGING THE LOOK OF INK

On the Ink Tools tab, the Pens group allows you to select from four virtual pens. The Ballpoint and Felt Tip options produce similar results, with a slightly thicker stroke for the latter. The Highlighter adds a color marking over any portion of the screen, similar to the results you use to mark up a magazine or book with a yellow highlighter. With any of these three virtual pens, you can change the color and line width at any time.

TIP

> If you use the Highlighter pen to mark a word, phrase, or value, or if you use one of the other pens to underline a similar block of typed text, Office is smart enough to link the ink with the beginning of the text. If you insert or delete text (in Word or PowerPoint) or cells (in Excel) above the highlighted/underlined portion, your ink travels with the text to which it's attached. This technique is less effective with circles, however, or with drawn arrows and lines that point to typed text or numbers.

The final option in the Pens section is the Eraser. This one doesn't work quite the same way as its Ribbon-mates to the left. When you click the Eraser option, the pen pointer changes shape and immediately deletes any ink stroke it touches. No rubbing required. (In OneNote, the Stroke Eraser works exactly like the single Eraser in the Ribbon-based Office programs, or you can shave smaller pieces off of strokes using the Small, Medium, and Large Eraser tools.)

ENTERING AND EDITING TEXT ON A TABLET PC

On a Tablet PC, the standard way to enter text into dialog boxes and programs that don't recognize ink (such as Notepad) is to use the Tablet PC Input Panel. To make the Input Panel appear, use one of the following techniques:

- In Windows XP Tablet PC Edition, you can summon this box by using a pen *gesture*, which consists of holding the pen tip over the bottom of the screen and moving it quickly back and forth.

- In Windows Vista, the Input Panel tucks into the left side of the screen with only a small stub sticking out. Click that stub to reveal the Input Panel, or drag it to slide up and down the screen.

- When you hover the pen point just above any point on the screen where you can enter text, a small icon appears, as shown in Figure 25.4.

Figure 25.4

The Input Panel floats over the current window (you can dock it to the top or bottom of the screen if you prefer, or click the Close button to slide it back into its hiding place along the left side of the screen). The three icons on the left allow you to select one of its three text entry options: Writing Pad, Character Pad, and Onscreen Keyboard. When you use the Writing Pad (shown in Figure 25.5), you write just as if you were using a piece of paper. The ink recognizer interprets your letters at the bottom of the panel, and if you reach the end of the input box it helpfully adds another line. You can click the recognized word to correct a single character or to choose a different word from the recognizer's dictionary. If the results are acceptable, click Insert to add the text at the current insertion point, just as if you had typed it.

Figure 25.5
When you use the Writing Pad, the Tablet PC Input Panel turns handwriting into text and sends it to the current insertion point.

For some tasks, the handwriting recognition offered by the Input Panel actually gets in the way. This might be the case if you're entering scientific terms that aren't in the dictionary. In that case, you can click the Keyboard icon in the Input Panel and use the onscreen keyboard to fill in precise values (see Figure 25.6). In this mode, the Input Panel enters the "typed" text one character at a time and responds to function keys and keyboard shortcuts just as if you had used a real keyboard.

Figure 25.6
Using the Onscreen Keyboard is a more accurate way to enter text that isn't included in a standard dictionary.

The third variation of the Input Panel is the Character Pad, shown in Figure 25.7, which allows you to enter or change one character at a time using a fill-in-the-blank text form. In this mode, you enter characters one at a time, and each character is recognized independently; the ink recognizer doesn't try to match your input with its dictionary. This tool is most useful when filling in dialog boxes and password prompts.

In Office 2007, you'll typically use the Input Panel to make minor edits to a document or to fill in a dialog box. (We can't imagine using the Input Panel to enter more than a paragraph of text.) For long blocks of text, use a keyboard or the Ink tools.

Figure 25.7
Use the Character Pad to enter text one letter of number at a time.

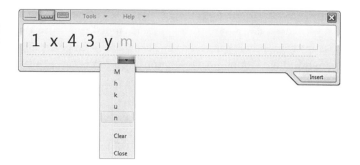

As we noted in the previous section, you begin entering ink by clicking the Start Inking button on the Review tab. In Word, you can begin writing anywhere on the current page. When you add ink writing to an Excel worksheet or PowerPoint slide, the ink appears in the drawing layer, directly on top of the current work surface. As with any drawing object, you can select, move, copy, delete, resize, or format the ink.

ADDING, VIEWING, AND PRINTING INK ANNOTATIONS

You can use annotations to make editing marks (drawing a line through text you want deleted, for instance), scribble short questions, highlight words and phrases, or add drawings. By default, annotations appear in a red felt-tip pen. As with ink writing, you can change the pen style to a ball point or a highlighter, and you can change the color as well.

Figure 25.8 shows a marked-up PowerPoint slide.

25

Figure 25.8
Use ink annotations to suggest changes in an Office document without affecting the document's content.

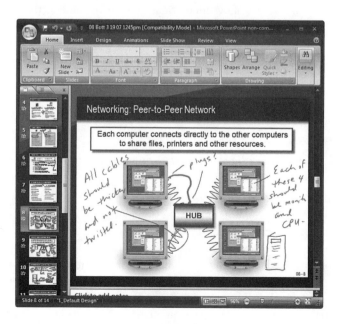

One big advantage of ink annotations is that anyone—with or without a Tablet PC—can remove them with just a few mouse clicks. If users embed comments directly with a document, you risk inadvertently leaving a comment behind, with potentially embarrassing effects. But after dealing with all ink annotations, you can remove them using the following techniques:

- In Word, display the Review tab, click Start Inking, and click Delete All Ink. All ink in the drawing layer of the current document is deleted instantly, with no confirmation. You can undo this action. (Note that ink in text boxes or in comments is untouched by this command.)

- In Excel, display the Review tab, click Start Inking, and click Delete All Ink. You are prompted to confirm that you want to delete all ink annotations on all worksheets in the current workbook. You can undo this action until you save and close the workbook.

- In PowerPoint, you can remove markup from a single slide or the entire presentation. Click Delete in the Comments group on the Review tab and choose Delete All Markup on the Current Slide or Delete All Markup in This Presentation.

 If ink annotations won't stay put within a Word document, see "Locking Documents When Using Annotations" in the "Troubleshooting" section at the end of this chapter.

Anyone who can read an Office document—with or without a Tablet PC—can view and manage ink annotations with just a few mouse clicks. To show or hide ink, click the Review tab and select or clear the Ink option on the Show Markup list.

To show or hide ink annotations when printing a copy of a document, worksheet, or presentation, choose Print from the Office menu. In Word, choose Document Showing Markup from the Print What box to show annotations; choose Document (the default) to hide annotations. In PowerPoint, select or clear the Print Comments and Ink Markup option on the Print dialog box. In Excel, ink annotations appear on printed pages if the annotations are visible on the screen; you can't control print options separately.

TROUBLESHOOTING

LOCKING DOCUMENTS WHEN USING ANNOTATIONS

 I added some annotations to a Word document and then made some edits. Now some, but not all, of the annotations are in the wrong place. How can I keep this from happening?

When you insert annotations, they appear in the drawing layer and "float" on the page. When possible, Office programs anchor the annotations to the adjacent text, but this doesn't work consistently. If you draw a circle around an object on the page and then add a new sentence before the portion you circled, the text shifts down the page, but the ink might stay where you originally added it. To ensure that your annotations stay in sync with your document's content, you need to lock the document's layout. Click Protect Document on the Review tab and then click Restrict Editing and Formatting. Select the check box under Editing Restrictions, and select either Comments or No Changes (Read-Only). Click Yes, Start Enforcing Protection to make your changes effective.

CHAPTER **26**

USING MACROS TO AUTOMATE ROUTINE TASKS

In this chapter

GETTING STARTED WITH MACROS

Office *macros* are small computer programs that perform tasks on your behalf. And when we say small, we mean very small. A skilled programmer can create a macro that does something meaningful with just a few lines of program code, written in the underlying programming language of Office, Visual Basic for Applications (VBA).

Anyone can create powerful macros using tools built into Word, Excel, and PowerPoint (OneNote does not support the use of macros). But most people never use Office macros. Why? The two most common reasons are

- They have no idea what macros can do.
- They have no desire to become a programmer.

After you learn what macros can do, you'll probably think of dozens of ways you can use them to automate simple tasks. But there's no getting around the fact that you have to invest some time and effort before you can use macros successfully. For instance, in Word, Excel, or PowerPoint, you can turn on a macro recorder that captures the results of your clicks and keystrokes as you perform a task. The recorder generates program code that you can save as a macro you can play back later to perform the same task. As we note in this chapter, however, most recorded macros require some tweaking of the generated code before they will work as you expect. As a result, you need to understand basic programming principles to make the most of these tools.

If you learned how to create and use macros in a previous Office version, your skills are directly transferable to Office 2007. First, though, you have to find all those familiar tools. In Office 2007 programs that use the new Ribbon-based interface, you'll find a tiny Macros group at the far right of the View tab (see Figure 26.1); it contains basic tools for viewing existing macros and recording a new one.

26

Figure 26.1
The default Macros group contains this limited set of tools for creating and managing macros.

You'll find a more complete set of macro-related tools on the Developer tab, which is normally hidden. To unhide it so you can begin using macros in Word, Excel, or PowerPoint, click the Office button, click Word (or Excel or PowerPoint) Options, and click to select the check box next to Show Developer tab in the Ribbon. As Figure 26.2 shows, the Code group contains commands to open the Visual Basic Editor, the Macros dialog box, the macro recorder, and the Macro Security dialog box.

Figure 26.2
You'll find a more complete set of macro tools on the Developer tab, which is hidden by default.

TIP

> When you make the Developer tab visible in one Office program, it becomes visible in all other Ribbon-based programs as well.

The more you know about macros and VBA, the more you're able to use them effectively. In this chapter, we explain how macros work, how to troubleshoot recorded macros, and how to manage a collection of macros.

WHAT CAN YOU DO WITH A MACRO?

Most of the time, you use the individual programs that make up Microsoft Office interactively—typing text, inserting graphics, formatting, saving, and printing. That's fine when you're creating new content, but it's no fun at all when you have to perform the same task regularly. Even a procedure that requires only three or four mouse clicks can become unbearable if you have to repeat it several times a day. The problem is even more acute if you perform any weekly tasks using Word or Excel where the step-by-step instructions are so complicated you have to print out a cheat sheet. If you have any such complicated task on your daily or weekly to-do list, you're a prime candidate to create a macro that automates that task using a single command.

Macros can be surprisingly short—even a one-line macro can perform helpful tasks—or they can run for hundreds of lines, with loops and variables and input boxes, and other elements you normally associate with a full-fledged programming language.

26

NOTE

> In this chapter, we focus on the core elements of understanding, creating, fine-tuning, and using macros. For more detailed instructions, you'll need to find other sources of information. One surprisingly useful source is just a click away. The Help file for each program in the Office family includes a Developer Reference section that explains basic concepts. This resource defines the purpose and syntax of each available programming object, often with code samples that you can cut and paste directly into your own projects. To see the local copy of the Developer Reference, open the Help window for the program for which you're planning to write a macro, click the drop-down arrow to the right of the Search box, and choose Developer Reference under the Content from This Computer section.

With rare exceptions, you can create a macro to automate any task you can do manually in Word, Excel, or PowerPoint.

Macros are ideal for automating routine drudge work—those everyday tasks that normally require multiple menu selections and mouse clicks. For example, you can use macros to do any of the following tasks:

- Print letters and companion envelopes for a mailing by selecting the correct paper trays for letterhead, additional pages, and envelopes.

- Apply complex formatting rules—everything from scanning reports to ensuring that all Level 1 headings start with a number, to validating the searchable keywords in a memo, to correcting common typographical mistakes such as two spaces following a period.

- Collate and aggregate worksheets, complete with charts and custom pivot tables, based on Excel spreadsheets submitted by individuals working on separate parts of the project. When changes come, roll the new numbers into the master report in minutes.

- Retrieve data from an Excel membership list and generate letters in Word for all members who haven't signed up for an upcoming event or who haven't paid their annual dues.

You can use macros for simple tasks, such as toggling a group of Word or Excel settings for a specific task, or for complex document assembly processes. You can assign a macro to a toolbar button, a keyboard shortcut, or a menu command.

What shouldn't you do with macros? Each individual Office program includes features that help you automate tasks without having to use macros. When there's a good alternative to writing a custom macro, the alternative is almost always preferable:

- For inserting boilerplate text into documents, workbooks, or slides, it's usually more efficient to use AutoCorrect or AutoText entries.

- Before you write a custom macro to find and replace characters, try Word's extremely capable Find feature.

- Excel's automatic data-entry and list-management features can help you accomplish many complex tasks without having to work with VBA code.

→ For hints on how to bring in boilerplate text, **see** "Using AutoCorrect to Type Faster," **p. 90.**
→ To tailor a Find in Word, **see** "Finding and Replacing Text and Other Parts of a Document," **p. 182.**

26

USING THE VISUAL BASIC EDITOR

The *Visual Basic Editor* (see Figure 26.3) is the tool you use to view and edit Office macros.

To open the Visual Basic Editor in Word, Excel, or PowerPoint, press Alt+F11. The Visual Basic Editor sits in its own window, separate from the Office application that opened it. For the simple tasks that we describe in this chapter, you'll use only the code window, where you can see the code created by the macro recorder and directly edit it. If you're interested in exploring the editor in more detail, use its excellent Help files.

Figure 26.3
The Visual Basic Editor usually contains two dockable, resizable panes, plus a large open area for writing programs and creating custom dialog boxes.

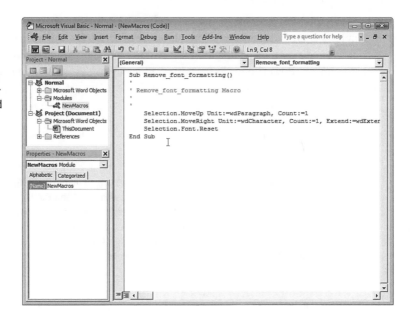

HOW OFFICE APPLICATIONS STORE MACROS

Each Office program handles macros in a slightly different way. Although the precise details are complex, here's a quick summary of how each Office application stores macros:

- Word—For security reasons, Word does not allow you to store macros in default document (.docx) and template (.dotx) formats. To save a macro, you must use a macro-enabled document (with the .docm extension), a macro-enabled template (.dotm), or the global macro-enabled template known as Normal.dotm. When you open a document that is associated with a macro-enabled template, macros in that template become available. If you store macro-enabled templates in the %ProgramFiles%\Microsoft Office\Office12\Startup folder, Word gives you access to macros stored in those templates whenever you start Word.

→ For details on template locations, **see** "Where Does Word Store Templates?" **p. 306.**

- Excel—Like Word, Excel prohibits saving macros in standard workbook and template formats; instead, you must use macro-enabled workbooks (`.xlsm`) or templates (`.xltm`). Unlike Word, Excel does *not* maintain a link between a workbook and the template you use to create it; if you add or edit a macro in a template, that macro is available only in new workbooks you create with that template. Excel automatically opens all workbooks in the %appdata%\Microsoft\Excel\XLSTART folder when it starts, including the hidden workbook Personal.xlsm. Thus, all macros in Personal.xlsm are available all the time.

→ For details on templates, **see** "Customizing Excel," **p. 393.**

- PowerPoint—PowerPoint stores macros in macro-enabled presentations (`.pptm`) and templates (`.potm`). Like Excel, PowerPoint uses templates only to create new files, so adding or editing macros in a template will not affect existing presentations based on that template. PowerPoint does *not* have a Startup folder or anything resembling a global template. Macros written or recorded in earlier versions of PowerPoint should work in PowerPoint 2007.

→ To understand the role of templates in PowerPoint, **see** "PowerPoint File Types," **p. 544.**

CAUTION

> Unless you're a skilled programmer, avoid trying to automate anything but the most routine PowerPoint tasks with VBA. Compared with Word and Excel, its capability to help you with everyday tasks is incomplete. There's no easy way to copy macros from one presentation to another short of copying and pasting code in the Visual Basic Editor. The lack of a global template makes it difficult to manage macros, and there is precious little documentation unless you dive into the Visual Basic Editor.

RECORDING SIMPLE MACROS

Word and Excel allow you to kick off the Macro Recorder by choosing Macros on the View tab and then clicking the Record Macros menu. The Macro Recorder exists in PowerPoint 2007 as well, but the command to start and stop the recorder has been inexplicably left off the View and Developer tabs. To record a PowerPoint macro, use the legacy keyboard commands Alt+T, M, R to start, and use the same keyboard combination to stop recording.

In theory, when you turn on the macro recorder, VBA "watches" as you perform some action or series of actions. When you turn off the recorder, you can replay the resulting recorded macro to replicate that series of actions.

In practice, you'll more often use the macro recorder to eliminate the tedious steps of creating a macro. Unfortunately, a recorded macro rarely solves a real-world problem by itself. After recording a macro, you'll typically need to make some modifications.

You can also use the recorder to capture the steps of a particular task and then copy all or part of the recorded macro into a larger macro.

HOW THE MACRO RECORDER CAPTURES ACTIONS

As anyone who's used the Office macro recorder for more than a few minutes can tell you, the macro recorder can't record every single action you take. There are two fundamental reasons why the recorder can fail:

- The action you take might not have an exact translation in the application's object model. For example, if you record a macro in PowerPoint to change first-level bullet points in a presentation to 18-point bold, the macro won't work because PowerPoint's object model doesn't include commands for working with first-level bullet points.

CAUTION

This type of failure, generally completely undocumented, happens without any warning to you. The recorder doesn't stop and there's no other feedback. You know the failure occurred only because the macro fails to work when you play it back.

- The action you take might be ambiguous; in other words, the recorder might not be able to tell exactly what you want to do. For example, if you type this paragraph into a new, blank Word document and use the mouse to select it, the VBA/Word macro recorder has no way of knowing what you're trying to do. Are you selecting the current paragraph? Or are you selecting the first paragraph that starts with the word "The"? Maybe you really want to select the tenth paragraph in the document. Or the first one with more than a hundred words. That's why the recorder usually won't record mouse actions—there's just too much ambiguity, most of the time, when you use the mouse.

After you turn on the macro recorder, it records the effect of your actions, not the actions themselves. The full effect of your actions goes into the recorded macro, not the means you used to apply them. For example:

- If you choose File, Open, switch to a subfolder in your Documents folder, and double-click a file called Mydoc.docx, the recorder notes that you opened Mydoc.docx—not that you went through all the pointing and clicking.

- If you choose Format, Font, and change the font to Wingdings, the recorder records the fact that you changed the font to Wingdings—but it also picks up all the other formatting settings that happened to be set by default in the Font dialog box, including font size, bold, italic, underline, and so on.

- If you open a dialog box, navigate to a specific tab, and then stop recording the macro, the recorder ignores your actions because you didn't actually do anything. You can't use this technique to automate the process of opening a specific dialog box to make a selection.

- If your insertion point is inside a paragraph in a Word document, and you want to tell the recorder to select the first word in that paragraph, double-clicking the first word in the paragraph will not work. If you try to double-click the first word in the paragraph,

26

the recorder won't let you do it. The recorder can't record your double-click action because it's ambiguous. You know that you want to select the first word in the current paragraph, but there's no way to specify that precisely by clicking with the mouse. For all the recorder knows, you might want to select the fiftieth word on the page, or the first word on the tenth line, or the last capitalized word in the paragraph.

When recording, instead of using the mouse, you'll frequently have to resort to obscure keyboard navigation keys. To move to the beginning of the current paragraph in Word (or the previous paragraph, if the insertion point is already at the beginning of a paragraph), press Ctrl+↑. To select the word to the right of the insertion point (the first word in the paragraph, if you previously moved to the beginning of the paragraph), press Ctrl+Shift+ →. To italicize the word, press Ctrl+I.

> **TIP**
>
> Nobody, but nobody, memorizes all of Word's obscure key combinations. To create a lengthy document listing them all, open the Macros dialog box, click in the Macro Name box, type **listcommands**, and then click OK. Unfortunately, there's no easy equivalent for PowerPoint or Excel.

RECORDING A MACRO

Word, Excel, and PowerPoint include simple macro recorders that all work in essentially the same way. To record a macro in Word, for example, follow these steps:

1. Create a new document or open an existing document.

2. Click the View tab, click Macros, and choose Record Macro. In the Record Macro dialog box (see Figure 26.4), click in the Macro Name box and type a name (**ItalicizeFirstWord**, in this example).

Figure 26.4
Replace the generic Macro1 name with a descriptive macro name, but don't use spaces or punctuation marks.

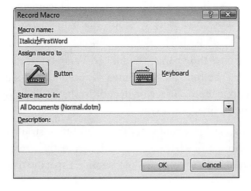

NOTE

> Macro names can contain up to 255 letters and numbers. They can contain underlines but no spaces or other punctuation marks. Names must start with a letter and cannot duplicate certain reserved names (for example, cell addresses in Excel).

3. Choose a location for the macro (the current document or a template, for example). If you want to assign the macro to a keyboard shortcut or toolbar button, click the respective button. (You can change either shortcut assignment after the macro has been recorded. See the "Troubleshooting" section at the end of this chapter.) The Description box is blank by default; if you want, you can enter additional explanatory text about the macro. Click OK to begin recording.

4. You'll see the Recording pointer, which includes a picture of a cassette tape beneath the familiar arrow. In addition, the Stop Recording toolbar appears in the status bar (the Excel and PowerPoint versions of this toolbar are slightly different, but both include a Stop Recording button). Perform any actions you want to record in your macro.

5. Click the Stop Recording button on the status bar or choose Stop Recording from the Macros menu on the View tab. Or press Alt+T, M, R.

TESTING THE MACRO

After recording a macro, it's essential that you test it to see whether it works the way you expect. To quickly run a Word macro, follow these steps:

1. Open a document or create a new document. If necessary, click to position the insertion point at an appropriate location in the document.

CAUTION

> Don't use a "live" document when testing. Always work with a backup copy or a dummy document you create just for testing.

26

2. To run the macro, click Macros on the View tab. You'll see the Macros dialog box shown in Figure 26.5.

3. Click the name of the macro you want to run and press Enter or click Run. If all goes well, the macro performs the task you intended.

4. For more complete troubleshooting, click in another location within the document, and repeat steps 1–3.

Using the Macro dialog box enables you to run all currently available macros, regardless of which program you're using. If you're going to use the macro regularly, it's easier to assign the macro to the Quick Access toolbar, or to a keyboard shortcut, as we explain in the Troubleshooting section at the end of this chapter.

Figure 26.5
All available macros appear in the Macros dialog box.

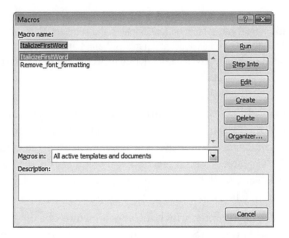

TROUBLESHOOTING RECORDED MACROS

Macros rarely work right the first time. Recorded macros, in particular, frequently require some tweaking before they work as intended. If the macro you recorded doesn't work, re-record it and see whether you can use a different method for accomplishing the same result. Edit a recorded macro only when it works most of the time, but occasionally fails to work the way you expect, or triggers an error message.

STEPPING THROUGH AND EDITING RECORDED MACROS

Fortunately, Office makes it relatively easy to edit a recorded macro. It even supports you in your bug-extermination efforts by allowing you to run the macro program one line at a time, and see what the effect of each command might be. Here's how to use the Visual Basic Editor to step through a macro recorded in Word (the steps in Excel and PowerPoint are virtually identical):

1. Create a new document or open an existing document and position the insertion point as necessary. For example, to test a macro that italicizes the first word in a paragraph, be sure to click inside a paragraph in the current document.

2. On the View tab, click Macros. In the Macros dialog box, select the name of the macro you want to troubleshoot and click Step Into. The Visual Basic Editor opens, with your macro visible in the right pane (see Figure 26.6). You'll see a large yellow arrow appear to the left of the Sub line, and the Sub line will be highlighted.

3. Arrange the windows on your desktop so you can see both the program (in this case, Word) and the Visual Basic Editor at the same time. Click the window holding the Visual Basic Editor.

4. To begin executing the VBA code one step at a time, press F8, or choose Debug, Step Into. The first line of the macro—the Sub line—executes.

Figure 26.6
When you step into a macro for troubleshooting, the line that's about to be run appears highlighted.

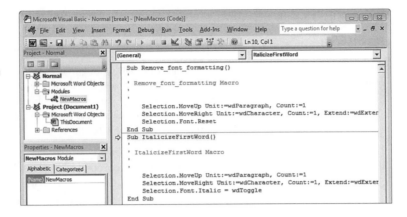

5. Press F8 again, and watch carefully as the macro performs the next actions; repeat this process, one command at a time.

6. When you reach the End Sub line, the Visual Basic Editor stops. You can start all over again, if you like, beginning with step 4.

Frequently, you'll be able to identify the location of the problem (or problems) in a macro by stepping through it in this way. Although the solution might not be at all clear—there are lots of VBA commands, and each one behaves in a different way—being able to narrow the problem down to a line or two can make a huge difference.

After you isolate the line that you suspect is causing the problem, position the insertion point within that line and press F1. That action brings up context-sensitive VBA Help, which might present a possible solution.

Follow the same procedures to step through Excel and PowerPoint macros; you'll find recorded macros in the current workbook or presentation, in a module called Module1. Press F8 to step through the macro.

COMMON RECORDED MACRO MISTAKES

When a recorded macro doesn't work as you expect, chances are the problem is one of several common errors. Table 26.1 lists common mistakes and suggested troubleshooting steps.

TABLE 26.1 COMMON MACRO PROBLEMS

Macro Error	Troubleshooting Suggestion
A key combination doesn't work the way you thought it would.	Many navigation keys have easy-to-understand descriptions (select next word, or move down one paragraph), but they behave oddly in unusual circumstances—inside a Word table, cell, or at the end of a document, for example. Find a different key combination that accomplishes the same task in a slightly different way.

continues

TABLE 26.1   CONTINUED

Macro Error	Troubleshooting Suggestion
Formatting commands overwrite existing formatting.	When you apply formatting using the Format menu, the application might replace all formatting with the new format. If you want to add the new formatting—for example, boldfacing a word while leaving intact other attributes, such as italic—use shortcut keys to apply formatting (Ctrl+B to apply bold).
A repeating macro doesn't do the entire job.	Recorded macros rarely incorporate the kind of repetition you anticipate. To create a macro that loops properly, you almost always have to edit it manually. (One exception—Replace All will loop through an entire document, worksheet, or presentation.)

In addition, any number of unusual circumstances can trigger errors in recorded macros. For example, if you search for the word *widget* in a document where that word is in a footer and not in the body of the document, the search will succeed. When you record that action in a VBA/Word macro, everything appears to work just fine. But when you play back the recorded macro in the same document, Word won't find the word you're looking for no matter how many times you run it—in fact, it will trigger a run time error. The recorded version of the Find operation works differently from the interactive version when it comes to footers.

TESTING AND BULLET-PROOFING MACROS

Just because a macro appears to work in a handful of simple tests doesn't mean that the macro will work correctly all the time. Word macros are notorious for working properly inside simple documents, but failing—without any warning whatsoever—when run on a table, in text boxes, on pictures, in a document with Track Changes enabled, in headers and footers, in comments, in footnotes, and on and on. It can be devilishly difficult to find the problems and, after they are found, to figure out how to fix them.

Will your recorded macro work properly every time you run it? Frankly, there's no way to know for sure—VBA macros hardly fall into the category of "probably correct" computer programs—but you can improve the odds of a macro working correctly by employing two time-honored testing techniques:

- Trace through the logic. In most cases, that means stepping through the macro, as explained earlier in this section. Watch for behavior or settings that you don't understand.

- Test it in a wide variety of circumstances. Try to think of odd situations that might make the macro fail, and then see whether it does. Ask a friend to test a macro, if possible, because testers will think of situations that just don't occur to you.

For example, the ItalicizeFirstWord macro example (in the "Recording a Macro" section earlier in this chapter) should italicize the first word in the current paragraph, but in one particular case it won't. When the insertion point is at the beginning of a paragraph, this macro italicizes the first word of the *preceding* paragraph. Running through the macro a step at a time reveals that the culprit is the MoveUp command; when you point to that command and press F1, the context-sensitive help suggests several examples. The solution? You have to MoveRight once before performing a MoveUp, to stay in the original paragraph.

The recorded ItalicizeFirstWord macro contains a second problem as well. When you run the macro and then leave the insertion point in the same paragraph and run the macro again, it *removes* the italic formatting from the first word. Stepping through the macro again lets us see the problem: The Selection.Font.Italic line toggles the italic attribute on and off. According to the Help file, the Italic property "can be set to `True`, `False`, or `wdToggle`." Changing the value from `wdToggle` to `True` causes it to work properly.

RUNNING MACROS

Although each of the Office programs offers myriad ways to run macros, three simple methods in Word, Excel, or PowerPoint will get you going:

- On the View tab, click Macros to open the Macros dialog box, which contains a list of all currently available macros. Use this technique for macros you run occasionally.
- Before you start recording a macro, you can choose to assign the macro to a menu (Word only) or a specific key combination (Word or Excel).
- After recording a macro, you can create or change its assignment to a Quick Access toolbar button or to a key combination.

→ For details on setting up macros as buttons, **see** "Customizing the Quick Access Toolbar," **p. 33.**

DIGITALLY SIGNING MACROS YOU CREATE

Office 2007 includes a number of security measures to help protect you from macro-based malware. *Digital signatures* lie at the heart of the approach most frequently encountered by Office users.

A digital signature identifies the source of a macro. Developers must apply for digital signatures from *certifying authorities*, which verify the identity of developers before issuing them a signature. Certifying authorities can revoke a certificate after issuing it if they discover evidence that a developer is distributing viruses or unsafe software.

The default settings for Office 2007 disable all macros except those included as part of files stored in trusted locations (typically the Templates and startup folders).

→ For more details on trusted locations, **see** "Setting Security Options in the Trust Center," **p. 702.**

Those are excellent security precautions, but they get in the way if you create a document, workbook, presentation, or template that contains macros you want to reuse or share with other people.

26

If you are writing VBA programs that you want to share with other people without requiring them to lower their security settings to unacceptable levels, you must:

- Acquire a digital certificate.
- "Sign" your VBA project.
- Tell the people who will be using your macros what your signature looks like, and what they need to do to get your macros working.

NOTE

> If your users have their security set to disable macros without notification, they won't be able to use your macros, and they won't be told why unless you sign your macros.

→ For more details on setting up security levels to manage macros, **see** "Managing Security for Add-ins, Macros, and Other External Content," **p. 701.**

You have three options for obtaining a digital certificate:

- You can create an *unauthenticated certificate* by running Selfcert.exe, the Digital Certificate for VBA Projects application. This utility is normally found in the Microsoft Office Tools folder on the Programs menu. If it isn't installed on your computer, rerun Office Setup and click Add or Remove Features. Click the plus sign (+) next to Office Shared Features, click Digital Signature for VBA Projects, and then click Run from My Computer. Click Update. This certificate is stored in the Registry and is required to run macros in Office applications that prohibit the use of any unsigned macros. It can be used to sign macros only on the computer on which it was created. An unauthenticated certificate represents no security at all: Anybody can create an unauthenticated certificate claiming to be anyone, even Bill Gates. When a user opens a VBA project that's signed with an unauthenticated certificate, he or she will always be asked to verify that he trusts the source of the project.

- If you work for a large organization, you might be able to get a certificate from your group's certification authority (your network administrator will use Microsoft Certificate Server to generate the file for you).

- You can buy an authenticated certificate from VeriSign (http://www.verisign.com) or thawte (http://www.thawte.com)—look for "developer certs" or "code signing digital IDs." Avoid Class 2 IDs, which certify the existence of a particular email address—Selfcert.exe works just as well. Class 3 IDs, for organizations, cost hundreds of dollars for the first year (subsequent years are at a reduced price) and are best-suited for commercial software developers.

To sign a VBA project, follow these steps:

1. Open the project (template, document, workbook, or presentation) using the associated application.
2. Press Alt+F11 to start the VBA Editor.
3. In Project Explorer, highlight the project you want to sign.
4. Choose Tools, Digital Signature. Click the Choose button and select either a new certificate or change an existing one. Click OK to save your changes.

After using your self-generated digital certificate to sign a project, you can examine its contents by clicking the Detail button. A self-signed certificate is marked with a red X that indicates it is not trusted because it can't be traced back to a trusted certifying authority.

If you copy a document, template, or workbook containing a macro project that has been digitally signed with a self-generated certificate, you'll be unable to open any of those macros on another computer. Windows protests that it can't authenticate the certificate and thus gives you only the option to disable the macros and open the document.

Are you stymied? Not at all. If you're absolutely, positively confident of the identity of the party who created the macros—for instance, if you created and signed them yourself on one computer and you want to use them on another computer in the same office—you can tell Windows that you want your self-generated certificate to be fully trusted. To do this, you need to install the certificate as a Trusted Root Certification Authority. Follow these steps:

1. On the computer containing the original signed project, click Start and and click in the Search box (Windows Vista) or click Run (Windows XP) and click in the Open box. Enter `certmgr.msc` and click OK. The Windows Certificates console opens.
2. Select your self-generated certificate from the Personal store, right-click, and choose Export from the All Tasks menu.
3. Save the exported certificate to a removable drive or a network share so you can transfer it to the other computer.
4. On the computer where you want to use the signed project, open the Windows Certificates console (certmgr.msc).
5. Select the Trusted Root Certification Authorities store, right-click, and choose Import from the All Tasks menu. Navigate to the file you saved and click OK.

Now when you inspect the properties of the certificate, you'll see that the red X has been replaced with an official seal of approval. You'll also discover that your macros work flawlessly on the new computer.

TROUBLESHOOTING

CHANGING THE KEY COMBINATION FOR A MACRO

I recorded a macro and told Word to run it whenever I press Shift+F5. I changed my mind after discovering that Word has a built-in command already assigned to Shift+F5. How do I change the macro so it runs when I push Shift+F6, and restore Word's built-in command to Shift+F5?

In Word, click the arrow at the right of the Quick Access Toolbar and choose More Commands from the menu. This opens the Customize tab of the Word Options dialog box; click the Customize button at the bottom of the dialog box, to the right of the Keyboard Shortcuts heading. In the Categories list on the left, click Macros; then, in the Macros list on the right, select the name of the macro that you recorded. In the Current Keys box at the lower left, click the unwanted keyboard shortcut (in this case, Shift+F5), and then click Remove. That removes the Shift+F5 key assignment for your recorded macro and restores the assignment to Word's default command. Click in the Press New Shortcut Key box, and press Shift+F6. Click Assign; then click Close twice. Shift+F5 will revert to the old GoBack function. Shift+F6 will run your recorded macro.

In Excel, the procedure is much simpler: Open the Macros dialog box, click the name of the macro and click the Options button. Your keyboard shortcut can consist of Ctrl+ any letter or number. Clear the box to remove the shortcut, or type a new letter to change it.

EXTRA CREDIT: GETTING READY TO TACKLE VBA

Ready to start working with VBA? Good. Take a few moments to organize your screen and customize the Visual Basic Editor. That way, you won't have to hunt and click so much to get going. (To start the Visual Basic Editor, just start your favorite Office program and press Alt+F11.)

The behavior of the Visual Basic Editor is controlled by choosing Tools, Options and clicking the Editor tab. In particular, consider selecting the Require Variable Declaration check box. That will protect you from the single most common source of programming errors—misspellings.

If you do a lot of VBA programming, do yourself a favor and take advantage of the Windows support for multiple monitors. That way, you can keep the Visual Basic Editor window open on one monitor and view the current Office application on the other monitor. If you have only a single screen to work with, arrange your windows so that the application is in the top half of the screen and the Visual Basic Editor is in the bottom half. In either of these configurations, you can step through your program, keeping track of the active command in the Visual Basic Editor window, while watching the effects of your program in the top window.

As you become more proficient, you might want to add the Immediate Window (choose View, Immediate Window) so you can change variable values as the program runs and test unfamiliar VBA commands. You might also want to get rid of the Properties window (in the lower-left corner; View, Properties Window) if you won't be working with custom-built dialog boxes.

Even if you're new to programming and have only just begun writing your first VBA programs, you should always keep several tips in mind:

- Use lots of comments. To add a comment, place a single quotation mark at the beginning of the line and then type the comment text. Yes, you can remember precisely what each line of code in your program does, and what each variable's duty in life might be. But when you look at your program a year from now, it will all be gibberish unless you add a lot of comments now, while it's still fresh in your mind.

- Don't be afraid to experiment. You aren't going to break anything. The real beauty of VBA is that you can try something, see how (or whether) it works, and then try something else. Amazing things have been discovered by trial and error.

- Remember that nothing is perfect, and VBA certainly follows that rule. Although VBA itself is reasonably stable and predictable, the underlying object models in all the Office applications have lots and lots (and lots and lots) of rough edges. Go slowly, step through all your programs, and be observant.

- Test. Then test some more. Then give your program to 10 friends, and have them all test it even more. Everyone has a slightly different configuration, and odd settings can throw off even the most well-conceived program.

- Keep your sense of humor. Programming is fun. But it's also hard work. The machine isn't out to get you—even though there will certainly be days when you think it is.

- Ask questions. Nobody knows it all. And even if they did, by the time they figured out the last nuance of the last feature, they would've forgotten what they knew in the first place.

- No matter what happens, there's always another revision. VBA is a dynamic language and every new version brings some exciting new capabilities. Stay on top of the wave, and you'll be able to solve problems that would curl the hair of mere mortals.

26

INDEX

THIS BOOK IS SAFARI ENABLED

INCLUDES FREE 45-DAY ACCESS TO THE ONLINE EDITION

The Safari® Enabled icon on the cover of your favorite technology book means the book is available through Safari Bookshelf. When you buy this book, you get free access to the online edition for 45 days.

Safari Bookshelf is an electronic reference library that lets you easily search thousands of technical books, find code samples, download chapters, and access technical information whenever and wherever you need it.

TO GAIN 45-DAY SAFARI ENABLED ACCESS TO THIS BOOK:

- Go to **http://www.quepublishing.com/safarienabled**

- Complete the brief registration form

- Enter the coupon code found in the front of this book on the "Copyright" page

If you have difficulty registering on Safari Bookshelf or accessing the online edition, please e-mail customer-service@safaribooksonline.com.

  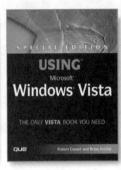